GW00675084

THE BOOK OF
COMMON PRAYER

THE BOOK OF COMMON PRAYER

AND ADMINISTRATION OF THE SACRAMENTS
AND OTHER RITES AND CEREMONIES OF THE CHURCH
ACCORDING TO THE USE OF THE CHURCH OF IRELAND
TOGETHER WITH THE PSALTER OR PSALMS OF DAVID
POINTED AS THEY ARE TO BE SUNG OR SAID IN CHURCHES
AND THE FORM AND MANNER OF MAKING, ORDAINING
AND CONSECRATING OF BISHOPS PRIESTS AND DEACONS

DUBLIN
THE COLUMBA PRESS
BY AUTHORITY OF THE GENERAL SYNOD OF THE CHURCH OF IRELAND
2004

Published by
the columba press
55A Spruce Avenue, Stillorgan Industrial Park, Blackrock, Co Dublin

Designed by Bill Bolger
Origination by The Columba Press
Typeset in FF Scala
Printed and bound in Belgium by Splichal nv, Turnhout

Pew edition ISBN 1-85607-429-3
Presentation edition ISBN 1-85607-432-3
Large print edition ISBN 1-85607-433-1
Desk edition ISBN 1-85607-434-x
Presentation Desk edition ISBN 1-85607-435-8

Table of Contents

THE PREFACE
PREFIXED AT THE REVISION OF 2004

In 1997 the General Synod of the Church of Ireland, after careful consideration, requested the Church's Liturgical Advisory Committee to prepare a new edition of the Book of Common Prayer. Since disestablishment, two previous editions of the Book of Common Prayer had been produced (in 1878 and in 1926), but this new Book of Common Prayer was to include not only services of the Church handed down through the centuries but also services in contemporary language. In the three decades prior to 1997 the General Synod had authorised a large number of services in modern language as alternatives to those contained in the Book of Common Prayer; and thus this book, now given to the Church, represents the cumulative labours of committee and of synod over many generations.

In undertaking our task, we embraced a time-honoured vision of Common Prayer which informs the contents and presentation of this book. We sought to unify the worship of God's people, while allowing reasonable scope for diversity within the essential unity of the Church's prayer. We were determined to produce a book which would have equal capacity to enrich private as well as corporate devotion. We desired that this book, like previous editions of it, should properly articulate and embody the Church's faith. We hoped that the book would strengthen our bonds of unity with sister churches who share our approach to Common Prayer, and we were therefore fully attentive to the reports of successive meetings of the International Anglican Liturgical Consultation.

We trust that this book will be used and treasured by many congregations and individuals in the years to come, and that its contents will permeate and shape their experience of prayer. Nevertheless, we must always remind ourselves that words, however memorable, beautiful or useful, are never to be confused with worship itself. The words set out on these pages are but the beginning of worship. They need to be appropriated with care and devotion by the People of God so that, with the aid of the Holy Spirit, men and women may bring glory to the Father and grow in the knowledge and likeness of Jesus Christ.

This book therefore leaves its compilers' hands with the hope and prayer that it will prove to be a worthy instrument by which to proclaim the Church's praise of God in the generation to come. It is of course only by God's gift that his faithful people 'do him true and laudable service', but we pray also that this book will have the capacity to draw God's people in our time to a fresh experience of the beauty of holiness.

THE PREFACE
PREFIXED AT THE REVISION OF 1926

At the Session of the General Synod of the Church of Ireland in 1909, the Bishops were requested to take counsel with a committee formed from among the Representative Members of the General Synod, and to report upon the best manner in which, without making any modification in doctrine or in the ritual Canons, the Rubrics and Services of the Church might be adapted to the requirements of the present time.

During a period of sixteen years, the General Synod considered a large number of proposals which gave promise of enriching the Book of 1878, or of adapting it more fully to the needs of a new day. The Book now put forth by authority is the result of the labour of those years.

THE PREFACE
PREFIXED AT THE REVISION OF 1878

When this Church of Ireland ceased to be established by law, and thereupon some alteration in our Publick Liturgy became needful, it was earnestly desired by many that occasion should be taken for a new and full review thereof (such as had already more than once been made in former times), and for considering what other changes the lapse of years or exigency of our present times and circumstances might have rendered expedient. And though we were not unaware of many dangers attending on such an attempt, yet we were the more willing to make it, because we perceived to our comfort that all men, on all sides, professed their love and reverence for the Book of Common Prayer in its main substance and chief parts, and confessed that it contained the true doctrine of Christ, and a pure manner and order of Divine Service, according to the holy Scriptures and the practice of the Primitive Church; and that what was sought by those who desired such a review was not any change of the whole tenor or structure of the Book, but the more clear declaration of what they took to be its true meaning, and the removing of certain expressions here and there, which they judged open to mistake or perversion. And as this Church has already, in its Convention of 1870, received and approved the Book as it then stood and was in use, so we now declare that, in such changes as we have made on this review, we imply no censure upon the former Book, as containing anything contrary to the Scriptures, when it is rightly understood and equitably construed. The true reasons of such changes will, for the most part, appear on a comparison of the two Books; but it has been thought good to add some further explanation why certain things have been altered and others retained.

As concerning the Holy Communion, some of our brethren were at first earnest that we should remove from the Prayer Book certain expressions, which they thought might seem to lend some pretext for the teaching of doctrine concerning the presence of Christ in that Sacrament repugnant to that set forth in the Articles of Religion, wherein it is expressly declared that the Body of Christ is given, taken, and eaten in the Supper only after an heavenly and spiritual manner, and that the mean whereby it is therein received and eaten is faith; but, upon a full and impartial review, we have not found in the Formularies any just warrant for such teaching, and therefore, in this behalf, we have made no other change than to add to the Catechism one question, with an answer taken out of the Twenty-eighth of the said Articles.

As for the error of those who have taught that Christ has given Himself or His Body and Blood in this Sacrament, to be reserved, lifted up, carried about, or worshipped, under the veils of Bread and Wine, we have already in the Canons prohibited such acts and gestures as might be grounded on it, or lead thereto; and it is sufficiently implied in the Note at the end of the Communion Office (and we now afresh declare) that the posture of kneeling prescribed to all communicants is not appointed for any purpose of such adoration; but only for a signification of our humble and grateful acknowledgement of the benefits of Christ, which are in the Lord's Supper given to all worthy receivers, and for the avoiding of such profanation and disorder as might ensue if some such reverent and uniform posture were not enjoined.

In the Formularies relating to Baptism we have made no substantial change, though some have desired to alter or omit certain expressions touching which diversities of opinion have prevailed among faithful members of our Church. At the same time, we desire fully to recognize the liberty of expounding these Formularies hitherto allowed by the general practice of the Church.

And as concerning those points whereupon such liberty has been allowed, we hereby further declare that no Minister of this Church is required to hold or teach any doctrine which has not been clearly determined by the Articles of Religion.

The Special Absolution in the Office for the Visitation of the Sick has been the cause of offence to many; and as it is a form unknown to the Church in ancient times, and as we saw no adequate reason for its retention, and no ground for asserting that its removal would make any change in the doctrine of the Church, we have deemed it fitting that, in the special cases contemplated in this Office, and in that for the Visitation of Prisoners, absolution should be pronounced to penitents in the form appointed in the Office for the Holy Communion.

No change has been made in the formula of Ordination of Priests, though desired by some; for, upon a full review of our Formularies, we deem it plain, and here declare that, save in the matter of Ecclesiastical censures, no power or authority is by them ascribed to the Church or to any of its Ministers in respect of forgiveness of sins after Baptism, other than that of declaring and pronouncing, on God's part, remission of sins to all that are truly penitent, to the quieting of their conscience, and the removal of all doubt or scruple; nor is it anywhere in our Formularies taught or implied that confession to, and absolution by, a Priest are any conditions of God's pardon but, on the contrary, it is fully taught that all Christians who sincerely repent, and unfeignedly believe the Gospel, may draw nigh, as worthy Communicants, to the Lord's Table without any such confession or absolution; which comfortable doctrine of God's free forgiveness of sins is also more largely set forth in the Homily of Repentance and in that of the Salvation of Mankind.

With reference to the Athanasian Creed (commonly so called), we have removed the Rubric directing its use on certain days; but, in so doing, this Church has not withdrawn its witness as expressed in the Articles of Religion, and here again renewed, to the truth of the Articles of the Christian Faith therein contained.

In revising the Table of Lessons, we have judged it convenient to follow generally the new Table which the Church of England has lately adopted, with these principal exceptions, that whereas in that Table some Lessons are still taken out of the Books called Apocryphal, we have so arranged ours as that all the Lessons shall be taken out of the Canonical Scriptures; and we have included in our Lectionary the whole of the Revelation of St John.

And now, if some shall complain that these changes are not enough, and that we should have taken this opportunity of making this Book as perfect in all respects as they think it might be made, or if others shall say that these changes have been unnecessary or excessive, and that what was already excellent has been impaired by doing that which, in their opinion, might well have been left undone, let them, on the one side and the other, consider that men's judgements of perfection are very various, and that what is imperfect, with peace, is often better than what is otherwise more excellent, without it.

THE PREFACE
PREFIXED AT THE REVISION OF 1662

It hath been the wisdom of the Church of England, ever since the first compiling of her publick Liturgy, to keep the mean between the two extremes, of too much stiffness in refusing, and of too much easiness in admitting any variation from it. For, as on the one side common experience sheweth, that where a change hath been made of things advisedly established, no evident necessity so requiring, sundry inconveniences have thereupon ensued; and those many times more and greater than the evils, that were intended to be remedied by such change: So on the other side, the particular Forms of divine worship, and the Rites and Ceremonies appointed to be used therein, being things in their own nature indifferent, and alterable, and so acknowledged; it is but reasonable that upon weighty and important considerations, according to the various exigency of times and occasions, such changes and alterations should be made therein, as to those that are in place of Authority should from time to time seem either necessary or expedient. Accordingly we find, that in the Reigns of several Princes of blessed memory since the Reformation, the Church upon just and weighty considerations her thereunto moving, hath yielded to make such alterations in some particulars, as in their respective times were thought convenient: Yet so, as that the main body and essentials of it (as well in the chiefest materials, as in the frame and order thereof) have still continued the same unto this day, and do yet stand firm and unshaken, notwithstanding all the vain attempts and impetuous assaults made against it by such men as are given to change, and have always discovered a greater regard to their own private fancies and interests, than to that duty they owe to the publick.

By what undue means, and for what mischievous purposes the use of the Liturgy (though enjoined by the laws of the land, and those laws never yet repealed) came, during the late unhappy confusions, to be discontinued, is too well known to the world, and we are not willing here to remember. But when, upon his Majesty's happy restoration, it seemed probable, that, amongst other things, the use of the Liturgy also would return of course (the same having never been legally abolished) unless some timely means were used to prevent it; those men who under the late usurped powers had made it a great part of their business to render the people disaffected thereunto, saw themselves in point of reputation and interest concerned (unless they would freely acknowledge themselves to have erred, which such men are very hardly brought to do) with their utmost endeavours to hinder the restitution thereof. In order whereunto divers pamphlets were published against the Book of Common Prayer, the old objections mustered up, with the addition of some new ones, more than formerly had been made, to make the number swell. In fine, great importunities were used to his sacred Majesty, that the said Book might be revised, and such alterations therein, and additions thereunto made, as should be thought requisite for the ease of tender consciences: whereunto his Majesty, out of his pious inclination to give satisfaction (so far as could be reasonably expected) to all his subjects of what persuasion soever, did graciously condescend.

In which review we have endeavoured to observe the like moderation, as we find to have been used in the like case in former times. And therefore of the sundry alterations proposed unto us, we have rejected all such as were either of dangerous consequence (as secretly striking at some established doctrine, or laudable practice of the Church of England, or indeed of the whole Catholick Church of Christ) or else of no consequence at all, but utterly frivolous and vain. But such alterations as were tendered to us (by what persons, under what pretences, or to what purpose soever tendered) as seemed to us in any degree requisite or expedient, we have willingly, and of our own accord assented unto: Not enforced so to do by any strength of Argument, convincing us of the necessity of making the said alterations: for we are fully persuaded in our judgements (and we here profess it to the world) that the Book, as it stood before established by Law, doth not contain in it any thing contrary to the Word of God, or to sound doctrine, or which a godly man may not with a good conscience use and submit unto, or which is not fairly defensible against any that shall oppose the same; if it shall be allowed such just and favourable construction as in common equity ought to be allowed to all human writings, especially such as are set forth by Authority, and even to the very best translations of the holy Scripture itself.

Our general aim therefore in this undertaking was, not to gratify this or that party in any their unreasonable demands; but to do that, which to our best understandings we conceived might most tend to the preservation of peace and unity in the Church; the procuring of reverence, and exciting of piety, and devotion in the publick worship of God; and the cutting off occasion from them that seek occasion of cavil or quarrel against the Liturgy of the Church. And as to the several variations from the former Book, whether by alteration, addition, or otherwise, it shall suffice to give this general account, That most of the alterations were made, either first, for the better direction of them that are to officiate in any part of Divine Service; which is chiefly done in the Kalendars and Rubricks: or secondly, for the more proper expressing of some words or phrases of ancient usage in terms more suitable to the language of the present times, and the clearer explanation of some other words and phrases, that were either of doubtful signification, or otherwise liable to misconstruction: or thirdly, for a more perfect rendering of such portions of holy

Scripture, as are inserted into the Liturgy; which, in the Epistles and Gospels especially, and in sundry other places, are now ordered to be read according to the last Translation: and that it was thought convenient, that some Prayers and Thanksgivings, fitted to special occasions, should be added in their due places; particularly for those at Sea, together with an Office for the Baptism of such as are of riper years: which, although not so necessary when the former Book was compiled, yet by the growth of Anabaptism, through the licentiousness of the late times crept in amongst us, is now become necessary, and may be always useful for the baptizing of natives in our plantations, and others converted to the Faith.

If any man, who shall desire a more particular account of the several alterations in any part of the Liturgy, shall take the pains to compare the present Book with the former; we doubt not but the reason of the change may easily appear.

And having thus endeavoured to discharge our duties in this weighty affair, as in the sight of God, and to approve our sincerity therein (so far as lay in us) to the consciences of all men; although we know it impossible (in such variety of apprehensions, humours and interests, as are in the world) to please all; nor can expect that men of factious, peevish, and perverse spirits should be satisfied with any thing that can be done in this kind by any other than themselves: Yet we have good hope, that what is here presented, and hath been by the Convocations of both Provinces with great diligence examined and approved, will be also well accepted and approved by all sober, peaceable, and truly conscientious sons of the Church of England.

THE ORIGINAL PREFACE (1549)

ALTERED IN 1552 AND 1662

CONCERNING THE SERVICE OF THE CHURCH

There was never any thing by the wit of man so well devised, or so sure established, which in continuance of time hath not been corrupted: as, among other things, it may plainly appear by the Common Prayers in the Church, commonly called Divine Service. The first original and ground whereof if a man would search out by the ancient Fathers he shall find that the same was not ordained but of a good purpose, and for a great advancement of godliness. For they so ordered the matter, that all the whole Bible (or the greatest part thereof) should be read over once every year; intending thereby, that the Clergy, and especially such as were Ministers in the congregation, should (by often reading and meditation in God's Word) be stirred up to godliness themselves, and be more able to exhort others by wholesome doctrine, and to confute them that were adversaries to the Truth; and further, that the people (by daily hearing of holy Scripture read in the Church) might continually profit more and more in the knowledge of God, and be the more inflamed with the love of his true Religion.

But these many years passed, this godly and decent order of the ancient Fathers hath been so altered, broken, and neglected, by planting in uncertain Stories, and Legends, with multitude of Responds, Verses, vain Repetitions, Commemorations, and Synodals; that commonly when any book of the Bible was begun, after three or four chapters were read out, all the rest were unread. And in this sort the book of Isaiah was begun in Advent, and the book of Genesis in Septuagesima; but they were only begun, and never read through: after like sort were other books of holy Scripture used. And moreover, whereas St Paul would have such language spoken to the people in the Church, as they might understand, and have profit by hearing the same; the service in this Church of England these many years hath been read in Latin to the people, which they understand not; so that they have heard with their ears only, and their heart, spirit, and mind, have not been edified thereby.

And furthermore, notwithstanding that the ancient Fathers have divided the Psalms into seven portions, whereof every one was called a Nocturn: now of late time a few of them have been daily said, and the rest utterly omitted. Moreover, the number and hardness of the rules called the *Pie*, and the manifold changings of the service, was the cause, that to turn the Book only was so hard and intricate a matter, that many times there was more business to find out what should be read, than to read it when it was found out.

These inconveniences therefore considered, here is set forth such an order, whereby the same shall be redressed. And for a readiness in this matter, here is drawn out a kalendar for that purpose, which is plain and easy to be understood; wherein (so much as may be) the reading of holy Scripture is so set forth that all things shall be done in order, without breaking one piece from another. For this cause be cut off Anthems, Responds, Invitatories, and such like things as did break the continual course of the reading of the Scripture.

Yet because there is no remedy, but that of necessity there must be some Rules; therefore certain Rules are here set forth; which, as they are few in number, so they are plain and easy to be understood. So that here you have an order for prayer, and for the reading of the holy Scripture, much agreeable to the mind and purpose of the old Fathers, and a great deal more profitable and commodious, than that which of late was used. It is more profitable because here are left out many things, whereof some are untrue, some uncertain, some vain and superstitious; and nothing is ordained to be read, but the very pure Word of God, the holy Scriptures, or that which is agreeable to the same; and that in such a language and order as is most easy and plain for the understanding both of the readers and hearers. It is also more commodious, both for the shortness thereof, and for the plainness of the order, and for that the rules be few and easy.

And whereas heretofore there hath been great diversity in saying and singing in Churches within this Realm; some following Salisbury Use, some Hereford Use, and some the Use of Bangor, some of York, some of Lincoln; now from henceforth all the whole Realm shall have but one Use.

And forasmuch as nothing can be so plainly set forth, but doubts may arise in the use and practice of the same; to appease all such diversity (if any arise) and for the resolution of all doubts concerning the manner how to understand, do, and execute, the things contained in this Book; the parties that so doubt, or diversely take any thing, shall alway resort to the Bishop of the Diocese, who by his discretion shall take order for the quieting and appeasing of the same; so that the same order be not contrary to any thing contained in this Book. And if the Bishop of the Diocese be in doubt, then he may send for the resolution thereof to the Archbishop.

CONCERNING CEREMONIES (1549)

Of such Ceremonies as be used in the Church, and have had their beginning by the institution of man, some at the first were of godly intent and purpose devised, and yet at length turned to vanity and superstition: some entered into the Church by undiscreet devotion, and such a zeal as was without knowledge; and for because they were winked at in the beginning, they grew daily to more and more abuses, which not only for their unprofitableness, but also because they have much blinded the people, and obscured the glory of God, are worthy to be cut away, and clean rejected: other there be, which although they have been devised by man, yet it is thought good to reserve them still, as well for a decent order in the Church (for the which they were first devised) as because they pertain to edification, whereunto all things done in the Church (as the Apostle teacheth) ought to be referred.

And although the keeping or omitting of a Ceremony, in itself considered, is but a small thing; yet the wilful and contemptuous transgression and breaking of a common order and discipline is no small offence before God. 'Let all things be done among you,' saith Saint Paul, 'in a seemly and due order;' The appointment of the which order pertaineth not to private men; therefore no man ought to take in hand, nor presume to appoint or alter any publick or common order in Christ's Church, except he be lawfully called and authorized thereunto.

And whereas in this our time, the minds of men are so diverse, that some think it a great matter of conscience to depart from a piece of the least of their Ceremonies, they be so addicted to their old customs; and again on the other side, some be so new-fangled, that they would innovate all things, and so despise the old, that nothing can like them, but that is new: It was thought expedient, not so much to have respect how to please and satisfy either of these parties, as how to please God, and profit them both. And yet lest any man should be offended, whom good reason might satisfy, here be certain causes rendered, why some of the accustomed Ceremonies be put away, and some retained and kept still.

Some are put away, because the great excess and multitude of them hath so increased in these latter days, that the burthen of them was intolerable; whereof Saint Augustine in his time complained, that they were grown to such a number, that the estate of Christian people was in worse case concerning that matter, than were the Jews. And he counselled that such yoke and burthen should be taken away, as time would serve quietly to do it. But what would Saint Augustine have said, if he had seen the Ceremonies of late days used among us; whereunto the multitude used in his time was not to be compared? This our excessive multitude of Ceremonies was so great, and many of them so dark, that they did more confound and darken, than declare and set forth Christ's benefits unto us. And besides this, Christ's Gospel is not a ceremonial law (as much of Moses' law was) but it is a Religion to serve God, not in bondage of the figure or shadow, but in the freedom of the spirit; being content only with those Ceremonies which do serve to a decent order and godly discipline, and such as be apt to stir up the dull mind of man to the remembrance of his duty to God, by some notable and special signification, whereby he might be edified. Furthermore, the most weighty cause of the abolishment of certain Ceremonies was, that they were so far abused, partly by the superstitious blindness of the rude and unlearned, and partly by the unsatiable avarice of such as sought more their own lucre, than the glory of God; that the abuses could not well be taken away, the thing remaining still.

But now as concerning those persons, which peradventure will be offended, for that some of the old Ceremonies are retained still: if they consider that without some Ceremonies it is not possible to keep any order or quiet discipline in the Church, they shall easily perceive just cause to reform their judgements. And if they think much that any of the old do remain, and would rather have all devised anew: then such men granting some Ceremonies convenient to be had, surely where the old may be well used, there they cannot reasonably reprove the old, only for their age, without bewraying of their own folly. For in such a case they ought rather to have reverence unto them for their antiquity, if they will declare themselves to be more studious of unity and concord, than of innovations and new-fangleness, which (as much as may be with the true setting forth of Christ's Religion) is always to be eschewed. Furthermore, such shall have no just cause with the Ceremonies reserved to be offended. For as those be taken away which were most abused, and did burden men's consciences without any cause; so the other that remain, are retained for a discipline and order, which (upon just causes) may be altered and changed, and therefore are not to be esteemed equal with God's Law. And moreover, they be neither dark nor dumb Ceremonies, but are so set forth, that every man may understand what they do mean, and to what use they do serve. So that it is not like that they in time to come should be abused, as other have been. And in these our doings we condemn no other Nations, nor prescribe any thing but to our own people only: For we think it convenient that every country should use such Ceremonies as they shall think best to the setting forth of God's honour and glory, and to the reducing of the people to a most perfect and godly living, without error or superstition; and that they should put away other things, which from time to time they perceive to be most abused, as in men's ordinances it often chanceth diversely in divers countries.

THE CALENDAR
THE CHRISTIAN YEAR

SUNDAYS

All Sundays celebrate the paschal mystery of the death and resurrection of Christ. Nevertheless, they also reflect the character of the seasons in which they are set.

PRINCIPAL HOLY DAYS

The principal holy days which are to be observed are:

Christmas Day 25 December

Easter Day

The Day of Pentecost (Whitsunday)

On these days the Holy Communion is celebrated in every cathedral and parish church unless the ordinary shall otherwise direct.

The Epiphany 6 January

In any year where there is a Second Sunday of Christmas The Epiphany may be observed on that Sunday.

The Presentation of Christ 2 February

The Presentation of Christ may be observed on the Sunday falling between 28 January and 3 February.

Maundy Thursday

The Ascension Day

Trinity Sunday

All Saints' Day 1 November

All Saints' Day may be observed on the Sunday falling between 30 October and 5 November.

On these days it is fitting that the Holy Communion be celebrated in every cathedral and in each parish church or in a church within a parochial union or group of parishes.

Good Friday is also a principal holy day.

The liturgical provision for the above days may not be displaced by any other observance.

The Seasons

Advent

The four Sundays and weekdays preceding Christmas Day

Christmas

Christmas Day to the eve of The Epiphany

Epiphany

From The Epiphany to the Presentation of Christ

When 6 January is a Sunday the Festival of the Baptism of our Lord is observed on 13 January.

Lent

From Ash Wednesday to Easter Eve

Within Lent the last two weeks are commonly called Passiontide.

Easter

The Fifty Days from Easter Day to the Day of Pentecost

Within Eastertide no festival listed below may displace the celebration of Sunday as a memorial of the Resurrection.

Rogation Days are the three days before the Ascension Day, when prayer is offered for God's blessing on the fruits of the earth and human labour.

The nine days following the Ascension Day until Pentecost are days of prayer and preparation to celebrate the outpouring of the Spirit.

Ordinary Time

There are two parts of the year which are not included in seasons. In the first, from the day after the Presentation of Christ to Shrove Tuesday, the day before Ash Wednesday, Sundays are designated as Sundays before Lent, the number depending on the date of Easter. In the second, from the Monday after the Day of Pentecost to the Eve of Advent Sunday, Sundays are designated in relation to Trinity Sunday, the last five as Sundays before Advent.

On the very rare occasions when there are twenty-three Sundays between Trinity Sunday and the Fifth Sunday before Advent, the Collect and Postcommunion of the Third Sunday before Lent are used on the Twenty-third Sunday after Trinity.

Ash Wednesday, the First Day of Lent

The Monday, Tuesday and Wednesday of Holy Week

Easter Eve

No celebration of a festival takes place during Holy Week.

Days of Discipline and Self-Denial

Ash Wednesday

The other weekdays of Lent

All Fridays in the year except Christmas Day, The Epiphany, the Fridays following Christmas Day and Easter, and festivals outside the season of Lent

Festivals

The Naming and Circumcision of Jesus	1 January
The Baptism of our Lord	*The First Sunday after The Epiphany*
The Conversion of Saint Paul	25 January
Saint Brigid	1 February
Saint Patrick	17 March
Saint Joseph of Nazareth	19 March
The Annunciation of our Lord	25 March
Saint Mark the Evangelist	25 April
Saint Philip and Saint James, Apostles	1 May
Saint Matthias	14 May
The Visitation of the Blessed Virgin Mary	31 May
Saint Columba	9 June
Saint Barnabas	11 June
The Birth of Saint John the Baptist	24 June
Saint Peter	29 June
Saint Thomas	3 July
Saint Mary Magdalene	22 July
Saint James the Apostle	25 July
The Transfiguration of our Lord	6 August
Saint Bartholomew	24 August
The Birth of the Blessed Virgin Mary	8 September
Saint Matthew	21 September
Saint Michael and all Angels	29 September
Saint Philip the Deacon	11 October
Saint Luke	18 October
Saint James, the Brother of our Lord	23 October
Saint Simon and Saint Jude	28 October
The Kingship of Christ	*The Sunday before Advent*

Saint Andrew	30 November
Saint Stephen	26 December
Saint John the Evangelist	27 December
The Holy Innocents	28 December

Liturgical provision is made for the above days in this book.

EMBER DAYS

Days of prayer for those ordained or preparing for ordination: the Wednesday, Friday and Saturday after the first Sunday in Lent, the Day of Pentecost, 14 September and 13 December.

These may be varied by the ordinary to relate to times of ordination in the diocese.

RULES TO ORDER OBSERVANCE OF FESTIVALS

Festivals falling on a Sunday may be transferred to the following Monday or at the discretion of the minister to the next suitable weekday.

Festivals falling on the first Sunday of Christmas may be observed on that day or transferred to the next available weekday.

When Saint Patrick's Day falls on the Sixth Sunday in Lent or the Monday or Tuesday of Holy Week it is observed on the previous Saturday. When Saint Patrick's Day falls on another Sunday of Lent it may be observed on the Sunday or on the previous Saturday or the following Monday.

When Saint Joseph's Day or the Annunciation of our Lord falls on a Sunday in Lent or in Holy Week they are observed on the Monday following the Second Sunday of Easter or at the discretion of the minister on another suitable weekday in the same week.

When the Annunciation of our Lord or Saint Mark's Day falls in the first week of Easter they are observed on the Monday following the Second Sunday of Easter or at the discretion of the minister on another suitable weekday in the same week.

Festivals falling on a Sunday of Eastertide are observed on the Monday following or at the discretion of the minister on another suitable weekday in the same week.

When Saint Columba's Day or Saint Barnabas' Day falls on Trinity Sunday they are observed on the Monday following or at the discretion of the minister on another suitable weekday in the same week.

Festivals not covered by the above rules may be observed on the Sunday or on a suitable weekday in the same week.

A list of persons associated with dioceses of the Church in Ireland.

Some are church founders, some are reformers and re-builders, some went as missionaries to carry the Gospel to other lands. Dates are those linked with their names; some are those of the anniversary of their deaths. These are included for reference and to remind us of the continuing work of the Holy Spirit in the Church in all ages. The post-Reformation 'worthies' included reflect the Church of Ireland's relationship with other parts of the Anglican Communion.

Munchin, abbot. Limerick diocese. 7th century	2 January
Edan, bishop. Ferns diocese. 632	31 January
BRIGID or Bríd, Abbess of Kildare. circa 525	1 February
Kieran of Seirkeiran. Ossory diocese. circa 545	5 March
PATRICK. 461	17 March
Macartan, bishop. Clogher diocese. circa 505	24 March
Laserian, abbot. Leighlin diocese. 639	18 April
Assicus (or Tassach), bishop. Elphin diocese. 470	27 April
Comgall of Bangor, abbot. Down diocese. 602	10 May
Carthagh, bishop. Lismore diocese. 637	14 May
Brendan, the Navigator. Ardfert & Clonfert dioceses. 577	16 May
Kevin. Glendalough diocese. 618	3 June
Jarlath. Tuam diocese. circa 550	6 June
Colman. Dromore diocese. 6th century	7 June
COLUMBA. Abbot of Iona. 597	9 June
Richard FitzRalph, archbishop. Armagh. 1360	27 June
Moninne of Killeavy. Armagh diocese. 518	6 July
Kilian, bishop and martyr. Kilmore diocese. 689	8 July
Declan of Ardmore, bishop. Cloyne diocese. 5th century	24 July
Felim. Kilmore diocese. circa 560	9 August
Crumnathy (or Nathi). Achonry diocese. circa 610	9 August
Muredach (or Murtagh). Killala diocese. circa 480	12 August
Jeremy Taylor, bishop. Down and Connor and Dromore. 1667	13 August
Fachtna (or Fachanan), bishop. Ross diocese. 6th century	14 August
Charles Inglis, bishop in N. America from Raphoe. 1816	16 August
Oengus Mac Nisse of Dalriada. Connor diocese. 514	3 September
Ciarán of Clonmacnoise. circa 545	9 September

Finnian of Movilla in the Ards. Down diocese. 579	10 September
Ailbhe, bishop. Emly diocese. circa 526	12 September
Eunan, abbot. Raphoe diocese. 7th century	23 September
Fin Barre. Cork diocese. 623	25 September
Canice, bishop. Ossory diocese. 6th century	11 October
Móibhí, teacher. 545	12 October
Gall, missionary. Down diocese. 630	16 October
Otteran, abbot. Waterford diocese. 563	27 October
Malachy, bishop. Armagh and Down dioceses. 1148	3 November
Laurence O'Toole. Dublin and Glendalough dioceses. 1180	14 November
Columbanus, abbot. Down diocese. 615	23 November
Colman. Cloyne diocese. 601	24 November
Finnian of Clonard, abbot. Meath diocese. circa 549	12 December
Flannan. Killaloe diocese. 640	18 December

THE TABLE OF READINGS

The Revised Common Lectionary
adapted for use in the Church of Ireland

Introduction to the Lectionary

1 The Lectionary for the Principal Service on Sundays and Holy Days
This is the Revised Common Lectionary with minor adaptations. In each of the three years one of the synoptic gospels is read through as the Gospel reading, Matthew in Year A (beginning Advent Sunday 2004, 2007 et seq.), Mark in Year B (beginning Advent Sunday 2005, 2008 et seq.), Luke in Year C (beginning Advent Sunday 2006, 2009, et seq.). John is read on festivals and in seasons of all three years and in Year B where the shorter Gospel of Mark does not provide material for the whole year.

Epistle readings are drawn from the New Testament letters and are read semi-continuously: not every verse of every epistle, but so as to convey in a representative way the teaching of the apostles. While there is no attempt to link this reading with the Gospel reading except at festivals, there is a general significance in the relating of the choice of readings. For example, readings from Romans, the high point of Saint Paul's theology, are appointed in the year in which Matthew, which contains more of Jesus' teaching than the other synoptic gospels, is featured.

For seasons and festivals the Old Testament reading points to either the Gospel or the Epistle reading. Between the First Sunday after Trinity and the Sunday before Advent a choice is offered, which should be made and then adhered to for the whole year. Option 1 (indicated as CONTINUOUS) is for semi-continuous reading, giving over three years a salvation-history view of the Old Testament presenting in particular the narrative material. Option 2 (indicated as PAIRED) follows the pattern in the Roman Catholic and American Episcopal Church lectionaries where the Old Testament reading has a somewhat thematic linking relationship with the New Testament readings that follow, usually the Gospel reading. The Psalm is a reflection and response to the Old Testament reading.

It is recommended that all three readings be read.

Alternative Old Testament lessons in Eastertide have been provided in this table from the lectionary of the Episcopal Church of the USA.

2 A Lectionary for a Second Service

This has been prepared by the Church of England Liturgical Commission to supplement the Revised Common Lectionary. In this table some passages are included which differ from its provisions.

It also follows a three-year cycle and has been designed to complement the Revised Common Lectionary without conflicting with it.

It may be used at an Evening Service whether Evening Prayer, A Service of The Word, or Holy Communion. A Gospel reading for use when the service is Holy Communion is always provided when the New Testament reading is not from one of the gospels. (This is always indicated by the ‡ symbol.)

3 A Lectionary for a Third Service

This has also been prepared by the Church of England Liturgical Commission. It is designed for use by those who require a lectionary when Morning Prayer is said before the principal service of Holy Communion or where there is a tradition of two principal morning services for which separate lectionaries are desired. On Sundays after Trinity the readings (but not the psalms) are the same in all three years.

4 Festivals and Other Occasions

The table of readings provided for Festivals, and that for Other Occasions, were prepared by the Liturgical Advisory Committee in co-operation with the Church of England Liturgical Commission.

5 Readings from the Books called 'Apocrypha'

On a few Sundays, and on certain Festivals, first readings are provided from the non-canonical books mentioned in Article 6 'which the Church doth read for example of life and instruction in manners, but yet doth not apply to them to establish any doctrine'. These are drawn from the books of Wisdom, Ecclesiasticus (the Wisdom of Jesus ben Sirach), 1 Maccabees and Tobit. The passages chosen have a thematic relationship to either the Gospel or Epistle readings which follow. For each of such readings an alternative reading from the canonical books is provided. The words which may be said after a reading from the Apocrypha are usually, 'Here ends the reading'.

Any version of the Bible from the versions approved by the House of Bishops may be used for the readings. Readings are 'cited' from the *New Revised Standard Version (1989)*. Those using other versions will need to check and, if necessary, adjust. The citation of psalms has been adjusted to the versification of the Psalter in this book.

EXTENSIONS AND OPTIONS

In this cycle of readings some passages have necessarily been abbreviated. When appropriate any reading may be lengthened. In some cases lengthening is suggested by the inclusion of verse numbers in brackets, in others readings may be lengthened at discretion.

On Sundays between The Epiphany and Ash Wednesday and between Trinity Sunday and Advent Sunday, while the authorised lectionary provision remains the norm, the minister may occasionally depart from the lectionary provision for sufficient pastoral reasons or for preaching and teaching purposes.

A TABLE OF EPISTLES AND GOSPELS

A table of epistles and gospels from the 1926 edition of the prayer book is given on pages 71-73. This may be used with Holy Communion One.

A PROPER

This is a set of readings appointed for any particular Sunday or Holy Day. Those for Sundays in Ordinary Time are numbered from 0 to 29.

SUNDAYS AND PRINCIPAL HOLY DAYS

The First Sunday of Advent
Between 27 November and 3 December   *Violet*

Principal Service

Year A	Year B	Year C
Isaiah 2: 1-5	Isaiah 64: 1-9	Jeremiah 33: 14-16
Psalm 122	Psalm 80: 1-8, 18-20	Psalm 25: 1-9
Romans 13: 11-14	1 Corinthians 1: 3-9	1 Thessalonians 3: 9-13
Matthew 24: 36-44	Mark 13: 24-37	Luke 21: 25-36

Second Service

Psalm 9 *or* 9: 1-8	Psalm 25 *or* 25: 1-9	Psalm 9 *or* 9: 1-8
Isaiah 52: 1-12	Isaiah 1: 1-20	Joel 3: 9-21
Matthew 24: 15-28 (*or* 1-28)	Matthew 21: 1-13	Revelation 14:13 - 15:4
		‡ John 3: 1-17

Third Service

Psalm 44	Psalm 44	Psalm 44
Micah 4: 1-7	Isaiah 2: 1-5	Isaiah 51: 4-11
1 Thessalonians 5: 1-11	Luke 12: 35-48	Romans 13: 11-14

The Second Sunday of Advent
Between 4 and 10 December   *Violet*

Principal Service

Year A	Year B	Year C
Isaiah 11: 1-10	Isaiah 40: 1-11	Baruch 5: 1-9
Psalm 72: 1-7, 18-19	Psalm 85: 1-2, 8-13	*or* Malachi 3: 1-4
Romans 15: 4-13	2 Peter 3: 8-15a	Canticle: *Benedictus*
Matthew 3: 1-12	Mark 1: 1-8	Philippians 1: 3-11
		Luke 3: 1-6

Second Service

Psalms 11, (28)	Psalm 40	Psalms 75, (76)
1 Kings 18: 17-39	(*or* 40: 12-19)	Isaiah 40: 1-11
John 1: 19-28	1 Kings 22: 1-28	Luke 1: 1-25
	Romans 15: 4-13	
	‡ Matthew 11: 2-11	

Third Service

Psalm 80	Psalm 80	Psalm 80
Amos 7	Baruch 5: 1-9	Isaiah 64: 1-7
Luke 1: 5-20	*or* Zephaniah 3: 14-20	Matthew 11: 2-11
	Luke 1: 5-20	

The Third Sunday of Advent
Between 11 and 17 December   *Violet*

Principal Service

Year A	Year B	Year C
Isaiah 35: 1-10	Isaiah 61: 1-4, 8-11	Zephaniah 3: 14-20
Psalm 146: 4-10	Psalm 126	Canticle: *Song of Isaiah*
or Canticle: *Magnificat*	*or* Canticle: *Magnificat*	*or* Psalm 146: 4-10
James 5: 7-10	1 Thessalonians 5: 16-24	Philippians 4: 4-7
Matthew 11: 2-11	John 1: 6-8, 19-28	Luke 3: 7-18

Psalms 12, (14)	**Second Service**	Psalms 50: 1-6; 62
Isaiah 5: 8-30	Psalm 68: 1-19	(*or* 50: 1-6)
Acts 13: 13-41	(*or* 68: 1-8)	Isaiah 35: 1-10
‡ John 5: 31-40	Malachi 3: 1-4; 4	Luke 1: 57-66
	Philippians 4: 4-7	(*or* 1: 57-80)
	‡ Matthew 14: 1-12	

	Third Service	
Psalm 68: 1-19	Psalms 50: 1-6; 62	Psalms 12; 14
Zephaniah 3: 14-20	Isaiah 12	Isaiah 25: 1-9
Philippians 4: 4-7	Luke 1: 57-66	1 Corinthians 4: 1-5

The Fourth Sunday of Advent

Between 18 and 24 December

Violet

Principal Service

Year A	Year B	Year C
Isaiah 7: 10-16	2 Samuel 7: 1-11, 16	Micah 5: 2-5a
Psalm 80: 1-8, 18-20	Canticle: *Magnificat*	Canticle: *Magnificat*
Romans 1: 1-7	*or* Psalm 89: 1-4, 19-26	*or* Psalm 80: 1-8
Matthew 1: 18-25	Romans 16: 25-27	Hebrews 10: 5-10
	Luke 1: 26-38	Luke 1: 39-45 (46-55)

	Second Service	
Psalms 113,(126)	Psalms 113, (131)	Psalms 123, (131)
1 Samuel 1: 1-20	Zechariah 2: 10-13	Isaiah 10:33 - 11:10
Revelation 22: 6-21	Luke 1: 39-55	Matthew 1: 18-25
‡ Luke 1: 39-45		

	Third Service	
Psalm 144	Psalm 144	Psalm 144
Micah 5: 2-5a	Isaiah 7: 10-16	Isaiah 32: 1-8
Luke 1: 26-38	Romans 1: 1-7	Revelation 22: 6-21

Christmas Day

25 December

White or Gold

Principal Service

Set I : Years A, B, C	Set II : Years A, B, C	Set III : Years A, B, C
Isaiah 9: 2-7	Isaiah 62: 6-12	Isaiah 52: 7-10
Psalm 96	Psalm 97	Psalm 98
Titus 2: 11-14	Titus 3: 4-7	Hebrews 1: 1-4, (5-12)
Luke 2: 1-14, (15-20)	Luke 2: (1-7), 8-20	John 1: 1-14, (15-18)

Any of the sets above may be used on the evening of Christmas Eve and on Christmas Day in any year. Set III should be used at some service during the season of Christmas.

Second Service	**Third Service**
Years A,B,C	Years A,B,C
Psalm 8 *or* 110	Psalm 8 *or* 110
Isaiah 65: 17-25	Isaiah 62: 1-5
Philippians 2: 5-11 *or* Acts 13: 16-17, 22-25 *or* Matthew 1: 18-25	Matthew 1: 18-25
or Luke 2: 1-20 *if it has not been used at the principal service of the day*	

The First Sunday of Christmas
Between 26 December and 1 January

White or Gold

Principal Service

Year A	Year B	Year C
Isaiah 63: 7-9	Isaiah 61:10 - 62: 3	1 Samuel 2: 18-20, 26
Psalm 148	Psalm 148	Psalm 148
Hebrews 2: 10-18	Galatians 4: 4-7	Colossians 3: 12-17
Matthew 2: 13-23	Luke 2: 15-21	Luke 2: 41-52

The Readings for The Epiphany may be preferred. Readings for Saint Stephen, Saint John the Evangelist, Holy Innocents, and The Circumcision and Naming of Jesus may be used when one of those festivals falls on this Sunday.

Second Service

Psalm 132	Psalm 132	Psalm 132
Isaiah 49: 7-13	Isaiah 35: 1-10	Isaiah 61: 1-11
Philippians 2: 1-11	Colossians 1: 9-20	Galatians 3:27 - 4:7
‡ Luke 2: 41-52	or Luke 2: 41-52	‡ Luke 2: 15-21

Third Service

Psalm 105: 1-11	Psalm 105: 1-11	Psalm 105: 1-11
Isaiah 35: 1-6	Isaiah 63: 7-9	Isaiah 41:21 - 42:1
Galatians 3: 23-25	Ephesians 3: 5-12	1 John 1: 1-7

The Second Sunday of Christmas
Between 2 and 5 January

White or Gold

Principal Service
Year A, B, C
Jeremiah 31: 7-14
or Ecclesiasticus 24: 1-12
Psalm 147: 13-21
or Wisdom 10: 15-21
Ephesians 1: 3-14
John 1: (1-9), 10-18

The Readings for The Epiphany may be preferred.

Second Service

Psalm 135	Psalm 135	Psalm 135
Isaiah 41: 21 - 42: 4	Isaiah 46: 3-13	1 Samuel 1: 20-28
Colossians 1: 1-14	Romans 12: 1-8	1 John 4: 7-16
‡ Matthew 2: 13-23	‡ Matthew 2: 13-23	‡ Matthew 2: 13-23

Third Service

Psalm 87	Psalm 87	Psalm 87
Jeremiah 31: 15-17	Zechariah 8: 1-8	Isaiah 12
2 Corinthians 1: 3-12	Luke 2: 41-52	1 Thessalonians 2: 1-8

The Epiphany
6 January   *White*

Principal Service
Years A, B, C
Isaiah 60: 1-6
Psalm 72: 1-7, 10-15
Ephesians 3: 1-12
Matthew 2: 1-12

Second Service
Years A, B, C
Psalms 98; 100
Baruch 4:36 - 5:9
or Isaiah 60: 1-9
John 2: 1-11

Third Service
Years A, B, C
Psalm 138
Jeremiah 31: 7-14
John 1: 29-34

The First Sunday after The Epiphany: The Baptism of Christ   *White*
Between 7 and 13 January

Principal Service

Year A	Year B	Year C
Isaiah 42: 1-9	Genesis 1: 1-5	Isaiah 43: 1-7
Psalm 29	Psalm 29	Psalm 29
Acts 10: 34-43	Acts 19: 1-7	Acts 8: 14-17
Matthew 3: 13-17	Mark 1: 4-11	Luke 3: 15-17, 21-22

Second Service

Psalms 46, 47	Psalms 46, 47	Psalms 46, 47
Joshua 3: 1-8, 14-17	Isaiah 42: 1-9	Isaiah 55: 1-11
Hebrews 1: 1-12	Ephesians 2: 1-10	Romans 6: 1-11
‡ Luke 3: 15-22	‡ Matthew 3: 13-17	‡ Mark 1: 4-11

Third Service

Psalm 89: 19-29	Psalm 89: 19-29	Psalm 89: 19-29
Exodus 14: 15-22	1 Samuel 16: 1-3, 13	Isaiah 42: 1-9
1 John 5: 6-9	John 1: 29-34	Acts 19: 1-7

The Second Sunday after The Epiphany   *White*
Between 14 and 20 January

Principal Service

Year A	Year B	Year C
Isaiah 49: 1-7	1 Samuel 3: 1-10, (11-20)	Isaiah 62: 1-5
Psalm 40: 1-12	Psalm 139: 1-5, 12-18	Psalm 36: 5-10
1 Corinthians 1: 1-9	Revelation 5: 1-10	1 Corinthians 12: 1-11
John 1: 29-42	*or* 1 Corinthians 6: 12-20	John 2: 1-11
	John 1: 43-51	

Second Service

Psalm 96	Psalm 96	Psalm 96
Ezekiel 2: 1 - 3: 4	Isaiah 60: 9-22	1 Samuel 3: 1-20
Galatians 1: 11-24	Hebrews 6:17 - 7:10	Ephesians 4: 1-16
‡ John 1: 43-51	‡ Matthew 8: 5-13	‡ John 1: 29-42

Psalm 145: 1-12
Jeremiah 1: 4-10
Mark 1: 14-20

Psalm 145: 1-12
Isaiah 62: 1-5
1 Corinthians 6: 12-20

Psalm 145: 1-12
Isaiah 49: 1-7
Acts 16: 11-15

The Third Sunday after The Epiphany

Between 21 and 27 January

White

Principal Service

Year A	Year B	Year C
Isaiah 9: 1-4	Jonah 3: 1-5, 10	Nehemiah 8: 1-3, 5-6, 8-10
Psalm 27: 1, 4-12	Psalm 62: 5-12	Psalm 19
1 Corinthians 1: 10-18	1 Corinthians 7: 29-31	1 Corinthians 12: 12-31a
Matthew 4: 12-23	Mark 1: 14-20	Luke 4: 14-21 (22-30)

Second Service

Psalm 33 *or* 33: 1-12	Psalm 33 *or* 33: 1-12	Psalm 33 *or* 33: 1-12
Ecclesiastes 3: 1- 11	Jeremiah 3:21 - 4: 22	Numbers 9: 15-23
1 Peter 1: 3-12	Titus 2: 1-8, 11-14	1 Corinthians 7: 17-24
‡ Luke 4: 14-21	‡ Matthew 4: 12-23	‡ Mark 1: 21-28

Third Service

Psalm 113	Psalm 113	Psalm 113
Amos 3: 1-8	Jonah 3: 1-5, 10	Deuteronomy 30: 11-15
1 John 1: 1-4	John 3: 16-21	3 John 1, 5-8

The Fourth Sunday after The Epiphany

Between 28 January and 3 February

White

Principal Service

Year A	Year B	Year C
Micah 6: 1-8	Deuteronomy 18: 15-20	Ezekiel 43: 27 - 44: 4
Psalm 15	Psalm 111	*or* Jeremiah 1: 4-10
1 Corinthians 1: 18-31	1 Corinthians 8: 1-13	Psalm 48
Matthew 5: 1-12	Mark 1: 21-28	1 Corinthians 13: 1-13
		Luke 2: 22-40
		or 4: 21-30

The Readings of the Presentation of Christ may be used if this is the nearest Sunday to 2 February.

Second Service

Psalm 34 *or* 34: 1-10	Psalm 34 *or* 34: 1-10	Psalm 34 *or* 34: 1-10
Genesis 28: 10-22	1 Samuel 3: 1-20	1 Chronicles 29: 6-19
Philemon 1-16	1 Corinthians 14: 12-20	Acts 7: 44-50
‡ Mark 1: 21-28	‡ Matthew 13: 10-17	‡ John 4: 19-29a

Third Service

Psalm 71: 1-6, 15-17	Psalm 71: 1-6, 15-17	Psalm 71: 1-6, 15-17
Haggai 2: 1-9	Jeremiah 1: 4-10	Micah 6: 1-8
1 Corinthians 3: 10-17	Mark 1: 40-45	1 Corinthians 6: 12-20

The Sunday between 4 and 10 February
if before the Second Sunday before Lent

Principal Service

Year A	Year B	Year C
Isaiah 58: 1-9a, (9b-12)	Isaiah 40: 21-31	Isaiah 6: 1-8, (9-13)
Psalm 112: 1-9 (10)	Psalm 147: 1-12, 21c	Psalm 138
1 Corinthians 2: 1-12, (13-16)	1 Corinthians 9: 16-23	1 Corinthians 15: 1-11
Matthew 5: 13-20	Mark 1: 29-39	Luke 5: 1-11

Second Service

Psalms (1), 2	Psalms (1, 3), 4	Psalm 5
Judges 5	Judges 5	Judges 5
James 5	James 5	James 5
‡ Mark 1: 29-39	‡ Luke 5: 1-11	‡ Matthew 5: 13-20

Third Service

Psalms 5, 6	Psalms 2, 3	Psalms 3, 4
Jeremiah 26: 1-16	Jeremiah 26: 1-16	Jeremiah 26: 1-16
Acts 3: 1-10	Acts 3: 1-10	Acts 3: 1-10

The Sunday between 11 and 17 February
if before the Second Sunday before Lent

Principal Service

Year A	Year B	Year C
Deuteronomy 30: 15-20	2 Kings 5: 1-14	Jeremiah 17: 5-10
or Ecclesiasticus 15: 15-20	Psalm 30	Psalm 1
Psalm 119: 1-8	1 Corinthians 9: 24-27	1 Corinthians 15: 12-20
1 Corinthians 3: 1-9	Mark 1: 40-45	Luke 6: 17-26
Matthew 5: 21-37		

Second Service

Psalms (7), 13	Psalm 6	Psalms (5), 6
Amos 2: 4-16	Numbers 13: 1-2, 27-33	Wisdom 6: 1-21
Ephesians 4: 17-32	Philippians 2: 12-28	*or* Hosea 1: 1-11
‡ Mark 1: 40-45	‡ Luke 6: 17-26	Colossians 3: 1-22
		‡ Matthew 5: 21-37

Third Service

Psalm 10	Psalm 7	Psalm 7
Jeremiah 30: 1-3, 10-22	Jeremiah 30: 1-3, 10-22	Jeremiah 30: 1-3, 10-22
Acts 6	Acts 6	Acts 6

The Sunday between 18 and 21 February
if before the Second Sunday before Lent

Principal Service

Year A	Year B	Year C
Leviticus 19: 1-2, 9-18	Isaiah 43: 18-25	Genesis 45: 3-11, 15
Psalm 119: 33-40	Psalm 41	Psalm 37: 1-11, 40-41
1 Corinthians 3: 10-11, 16-23	2 Corinthians 1: 18-22	1 Corinthians 15: 35-38, 42-50
Matthew 5: 38-48	Mark 2: 1-12	Luke 6: 27-38

Psalm 18: 1-20
or 18: 21-30
Amos 3: 1-8
Ephesians 5: 1-17
‡ Mark 2: 1-12

Second Service
Psalm 10
Numbers 20: 2-13
Philippians 3: 7-21
‡ Luke 6: 27-38

Psalms (11), 13
Wisdom 11:21 - 12: 11
or Hosea 10: 1-8, 12
Galatians 4: 8-20
‡ Matthew 5: 38-48

Third Service
Psalms 21, 23
Jeremiah 33: 1-11
Acts 8: 4-25

Psalm 9
Jeremiah 33: 1-11
Acts 8: 4-25

Psalm 10
Jeremiah 33: 1-11
Acts 8: 4-25

The Second Sunday before Lent   *Green*
Occurrence of this Sunday depends on the dates of Easter Day and of Ash Wednesday.

Principal Service
| | | Option A: Creation |
| Year A | Year B | Year C |

Genesis 1: 1 - 2: 3
Psalm 136
or Psalm 136: 1-9,(23-26)
Romans 8: 18-25
Matthew 6: 25-34

Proverbs 8: 1, 22-31
Psalm 104: 26-37
Colossians 1: 15-20
John 1: 1-14

Genesis 2: 4b-9, 15-25
Psalm 65
Revelation 4
Luke 8: 22-35

Option B: PROPER 3

Isaiah 49: 8-16a
Psalm 131
1 Corinthians 4: 1-5
Matthew 6: 24-34

Hosea 2: 14-20
Psalm 103: 1-13, 22
2 Corinthians 3: 1-6
Mark 2: 13-22

Ecclesiasticus 27: 4-7
or Isaiah 55: 10-13
Psalm 92: 1-4, 12-15
1 Corinthians 15: 51-58
Luke 6: 39-49

Second Service
Psalm 148
Proverbs 8: 1, 22-31
Revelation 4
‡ Luke 12: 16-31

Psalm 65
Genesis 2: 4b-25
Luke 8: 22-35

Option A: Creation
Psalm 147 *or* 147: 13-21
Genesis 1:1 - 2:3
Matthew 6: 25-34

Option B: PROPER 3
Psalm 31: 1-16 *or* 31: 1-8
Amos 9: 5-15
Ephesians 6: 1-20
‡ Mark 2: 23 - 3:6

Psalms 20, (26)
Numbers 22:21 - 23:12
Philippians 4: 10-20
‡ Luke 6: 39-49

Psalms (11), 13
Hosea 14
Galatians 5: 2-10
‡ Matthew 6: 1-8

Third Service
Psalms 100, 150
Job 38: 1-21
Colossians 1: 15-20

Psalms 29, 67
Deuteronomy 8: 1-10
Matthew 6: 25-34

Option A: Creation
Psalm 104: 1-25
Job 28: 1-11
Acts 14: 8-17

Option B: PROPER 3
Psalm 25
Lamentations 1: 7-20a
Acts 8: 26-40

Psalm 16
Lamentations 1: 7-20a
Acts 8: 26-40

Psalm 21
Lamentations 1: 7-20a
Acts 8: 26-40

The Sunday before Lent (Transfiguration Sunday)   *White or Green*

Ash Wednesday   *Violet*

The First Sunday in Lent   *Violet*

Principal Service

Year A	Year B	Year C
Genesis 2: 15-17; 3: 1-7	Genesis 9: 8-17	Deuteronomy 26: 1-11
Psalm 32	Psalm 25: 1-9	Psalm 91: 1-2, 9-16
Romans 5: 12-19	1 Peter 3: 18-22	Romans 10: 8b-13
Matthew 4: 1-11	Mark 1: 9-15	Luke 4: 1-13

Second Service

Psalm 50: 1-15	Psalm 119: 17-32	Psalm 119: 73-88
Deuteronomy 6: 4-9, 16-25	Genesis 2: 15-17; 3: 1-7	Jonah 3
Luke 15: 1-10	Romans 5: 12-19	Luke 18: 9-14
	or Luke 13: 31-35	

Third Service

Psalm 119: 1-16	Psalm 77	Psalm 50: 1-15
Jeremiah 18: 1-11	Exodus 34: 1-10	Micah 6: 1-8
Luke 18: 9-14	Romans 10: 8b-13	Luke 5: 27-39

The Second Sunday in Lent   *Violet*

Principal Service

Year A	Year B	Year C
Genesis 12: 1-4a	Genesis 17: 1-7, 15-16	Genesis 15: 1-12, 17-18
Psalm 121	Psalm 22: 23-31	Psalm 27
Romans 4: 1-5, 13-17	Romans 4: 13-25	Philippians 3: 17 - 4: 1
John 3: 1-17	Mark 8: 31-38	Luke 13: 31-35
* or Matthew 17: 1-9	* or Mark 9: 2-9	* or Luke 9: 28-36

Second Service

Psalm 135 *or* 135: 1-14	Psalm 135 *or* 135: 1-14	Psalm 135 *or* 135: 1-14
Numbers 21: 4-9	Genesis 12: 1-9	Jeremiah 22: 1-9, 13-17
Luke 14: 27-33	Hebrews 11: 1-3, 8-16	Luke 14: 27-33
	‡John 8: 51-59	

Third Service

Psalm 74	Psalm 105: 1-6, 37-45	Psalm 119: 161-176
Jeremiah 22: 1-9	Isaiah 51: 1-11	Genesis 17: 1-7, 15-16
Matthew 8: 1-13	Galatians 3: 1-9, 23-29	Romans 11: 13-24

* The selections in italics are used when Option B has been taken on the Sunday before Lent. As these are accounts of the Transfiguration they are not used when the Sunday before Lent has been observed as Transfiguration Sunday.

The Third Sunday in Lent   *Violet*

Principal Service

Year A	Year B	Year C
Exodus 17: 1-7	Exodus 20: 1-17	Isaiah 55: 1-9
Psalm 95	Psalm 19	Psalm 63: 1-9
Romans 5: 1-11	1 Corinthians 1: 18-25	1 Corinthians 10: 1-13
John 4: 5-42	John 2: 13-22	Luke 13: 1-9

Psalm 40	Psalms 11, 12	Psalms 12, 13
Joshua 1: 1-9	Exodus 5:1 - 6:1	Genesis 28: 10-19a
Ephesians 6: 10-20	Philippians 3: 4b-14	John 1: 35-51
‡ John 2: 13-22	*or* Matthew 10: 16-22	

Third Service

Psalm 46	Psalm 18: 1-25	Psalms 26, 28
Amos 7: 10-17	Jeremiah 38	Deuteronomy 6: 4-9
2 Corinthians 1: 1-11	Philippians 1: 1-26	John 17: 1a, 11b-19

The Fourth Sunday in Lent   *Violet*

Principal Service

Year A	Year B	Year C
1 Samuel 16: 1-13	Numbers 21: 4-9	Joshua 5: 9-12
Psalm 23	Psalm 107: 1-3, 17-22	Psalm 32
Ephesians 5: 8-14	Ephesians 2: 1-10	2 Corinthians 5: 16-21
John 9: 1-41	John 3: 14-21	Luke 15: 1-3, 11b-32

Second Service

Psalm 31: 1-16 *or* 1-8	Psalms 13, 14	Psalm 30
Micah 7	Exodus 6: 2-13	Prayer of Manasseh
or Prayer of Manasseh	Romans 5: 1-11	*or* Isaiah 40: 27 - 41:13
James 5	‡ John 12: 1-8	2 Timothy 4: 1-18
‡ John 3: 14-21		‡ John 11: 17-44

If the Principal Service readings have been displaced by Mothering Sunday provisions, they may be used at the Second Service.

Third Service

Psalm 19	Psalm 27	Psalms 84, 85
Isaiah 43: 1-7	1 Samuel 16: 1-13	Genesis 37: 3-4, 12-36
Ephesians 2: 8-14	John 9: 1-25	1 Peter 2: 16-25

Mothering Sunday

Exodus 2: 1-10 *or* 1 Samuel 1: 20-28
Psalm 34: 11-20 *or* 127: 1-4
2 Corinthians 1: 3-7 *or* Colossians 3: 12-17
Luke 2: 33-35 *or* John 19: 25-27

The Fifth Sunday in Lent   *Violet*

Principal Service

Year A	Year B	Year C
Ezekiel: 37: 1-14	Jeremiah 31: 31-34	Isaiah 43: 16-21
Psalm 130	Psalm 51: 1-13	Psalm 126
Romans 8: 6-11	*or* 119: 9-16	Philippians 3: 4b-14
John 11: 1-45	Hebrews 5: 5-10	John 12: 1-8
	John 12: 20-33	

Psalm 30	Second Service	
Lamentations 3: 19-33	Psalm 34 *or* 34: 1-10	Psalm 35 *or* 35: 1-9
Matthew 20: 17-34	Exodus 7: 8-24	2 Chronicles 35: 1-6, 10-16
	Romans 5: 12-21	Luke 22: 1-13
	‡ Luke 22: 1-13	

Psalm 86	Psalm 107: 1-22	Psalms 111, 112
Jeremiah 31: 27-37	Exodus 24: 3-8	Isaiah 35: 1-10
John 12: 20-33	Hebrews 12: 18-29	Romans 7:21 - 8:4

The Sixth Sunday in Lent (Palm Sunday)   *Red or Violet*

Principal Service

Year A	Year B	Year C
Liturgy of the Palms	*Liturgy of the Palms*	*Liturgy of the Palms*
Matthew 21: 1-11	Mark 11: 1-11	Luke 19: 28-40
Psalm 118: 1-2, 19-29	*or* John 12: 12-16	Psalm 118: 1-2, 19-29
	Psalm 118: 1-2, 19-29	
Liturgy of the Passion	*Liturgy of the Passion*	*Liturgy of the Passion*
Isaiah 50: 4-9a	Isaiah 50: 4-9a	Isaiah 50: 4-9a
Psalm 31: 9-16	Psalm 31: 9-16	Psalm 31: 9-16
Philippians 2: 5-11	Philippians 2: 5-11	Philippians 2: 5-11
Matthew 26: 14 - 27: 66	Mark 14: 1 - 15: 47	Luke 22: 14 - 23: 56
or Matthew 27: 11-54	*or* Mark 15: 1-39, (40-47)	*or* Luke 23: 1-49

Psalm 80	Psalm 69: 1-20	Psalm 69: 1-20
Isaiah 5: 1-7	Isaiah 5: 1-7	Isaiah 5: 1-7
Matthew 21: 33-46	Mark 12: 1-12	Luke 20: 9-19

Psalms 61, 62	Psalms 61, 62	Psalms 61, 62
Zechariah 9: 9-12	Zechariah 9: 9-12	Zechariah 9: 9-12
Luke 16: 19-31	1 Corinthians 2: 1-12	1 Corinthians 2: 1-12

Monday in Holy Week   *Red or Violet*

Principal Service
Years A, B, C
Isaiah 42: 1-9
Psalm 36: 5-11
Hebrews 9: 11-15
John 12: 1-11

Psalm 41	Third Service
Lamentations 1: 1-12a	Psalm 25
Luke 22: 1-23	Lamentations 2: 8-19
	Colossians 1: 18-23

Tuesday in Holy Week   *Red or Violet*

Principal Service
Years A, B, C
Isaiah 49: 1-7
Psalm 71: 1-14
1 Corinthians 1: 18-31
John 12: 20-36

Second Service
Psalm 27
Lamentations 3: 1-18
Luke 22: 24-53 *or* 39-53

Third Service
Psalm 55: 13-24
Lamentations 3: 40-51
Galatians 6: 11-18

Wednesday in Holy Week   *Red or Violet*

Principal Service
Years A, B, C
Isaiah 50: 4-9a
Psalm 70
Hebrews 12: 1-3
John 13: 21-32

Second Service
Psalm 102 *or* 102: 1-15
Wisdom 1:16 - 2:1; 2: 12-22
or Jeremiah 11: 18-20
Luke 22: 54-71

Third Service
Psalm 88
Isaiah 63: 1-9
Revelation 14:18 - 15:4

Maundy Thursday   *Red or Violet*
                                              White at Holy Communion

Principal Service
Years A, B, C
Exodus 12: 1-4, (5-10),
11-14
Psalm 116: 1, 10-17
1 Corinthians 11: 23-26
John 13: 1-17, 31b-35

Second Service
Psalm 39
Leviticus 16: 2-24
Luke 23: 1-25

Third Service
Psalms 42, 43
Exodus 11
Ephesians 2: 11-18

Good Friday

Years A, B, C
Isaiah 52: 13 - 53: 12
Psalm 22
Hebrews 10: 16-25
or 4: 14-16; 5: 7-9
John 18:1 - 19:42

Second Service
Psalms 130, 143
Genesis 22: 1-18

A part of John 18 *and* 19 *if
not used at Principal Service*

In the evening: John 19: 38-42
or Colossians 1: 18-23

Third Service
Psalm 69
Lamentations 5: 15-22

A part of John 18 and 19 *if
not used at Principal Service
or* Hebrews 10: 1-10

Easter Eve

Principal Service
Years A, B, C
Job 14: 1-14
or Lamentations 3: 1-9,
19-24
Psalm 31: 1-4, 15-16
1 Peter 4: 1-8
Matthew 27: 57-66
or John 19: 38-42

Second Service
Psalm 142
Hosea 6: 1-6
John 2: 18-22

Third Service
Psalm 116
Job 19: 21-27
1 John 5: 5-12

Easter Vigil Readings

A minimum of three Old Testament readings should be chosen. The readings from Exodus 14 and from Romans 6 should always be used. The Gospel reading varies each year.

Reading	*Response*
Genesis 1: 1 - 2: 4a	Psalm 136: 1-9,23-26
Genesis 7: 1-5,11-18; 8: 6-18; 9: 8-13	Psalm 46
Genesis 22: 1-18	Psalm 16
Exodus 14: 10-31; 15: 20-21	Canticle: Exodus 15: 1b-13,17-18
Isaiah 55: 1-11	Canticle: *Song of Isaiah*
Baruch 3: 9-15, 32 - 4: 4	
or Proverbs 8: 1-8,19-21; 9: 4b-6	Psalm 19
Ezekiel 36: 24-28	Psalms 42 and 43
Ezekiel 37: 1-14	Psalm 143
Zephaniah 3: 14-20	Psalm 98
Romans 6: 3-11	Psalm 114

Year A: Matthew 28: 1-10
Year B: Mark 16: 1-8
Year C: Luke 24: 1-12

Easter Day – The First Sunday of Easter   *White or Gold*

Principal Service

Year A	Year B	Year C
Acts 10: 34-43	Acts 10: 34-43	Acts 10: 34-43
or Jeremiah 31: 1-6	*or* Isaiah 25: 6-9	*or* Isaiah 65: 17-25
Psalm 118: 1-2, 14-24	Psalm 118: 1-2, 14-24	Psalm 118: 1-2, 14-24
or Easter Anthems	*or* Easter Anthems	*or* Easter Anthems
Colossians 3: 1-4	1 Corinthians 15: 1-11	1 Corinthians 15: 19-26
or Acts 10: 34-43	*or* Acts 10: 34-43	*or* Acts 10: 34-43
John 20: 1-18	John 20: 1-18	John 20: 1-18
or Matthew 28: 1-10	*or* Mark 16: 1-8	*or* Luke 24: 1-12

When the Old Testament selection is chosen, the Acts reading is used as the second reading at Holy Communion.

Second Service

Psalms 114, 117	Psalms 114, 117	Psalm 66 *or* 66: 1-11
Song of Solomon 3: 2-5; 8: 6-7	Ezekiel 37: 1-14	Isaiah 43: 1-21
John 20: 11-18	Luke 24: 13-35	1 Corinthians 15: 1-11
if not read at Principal Service		*or* John 20: 19-23
or Revelation 1: 12-18		

Third Service

Psalm 105: 37-43	Psalm 66: 1-11	Psalms 114, 117
Exodus 14: 10-18, 26 - 15: 2	Genesis 1: 1-5, 26-31	Ezekiel 47: 1-12
Revelation 15: 2-4	2 Corinthians 5: 14 - 6: 2	John 2: 13-22

The Second Sunday of Easter

Principal Service

Year A	Year B	Year C
Acts 2: 14a, 22-32	Acts 4: 32-35	Acts 5: 27-32
or Genesis 8: 6-16; 9: 8-16	*or* Isaiah 26: 2-9, 19	*or* Job 42: 1-6
Psalm 16	Psalm 133	Psalm 118: 14-29 *or* 150
1 Peter 1: 3-9	1 John 1: 1 - 2: 2	Revelation 1: 4-8
John 20: 19-31	John 20: 19-31	John 20: 19-31

On the Sundays of Easter either the Acts reading is used as a first reading or the alternative from the Old Testament.

Second Service

Psalm 30: 1-5	Psalm 143: 1-11	Psalm 16
Daniel 6: 1-23 *or* 6: 6-23	Isaiah 26: 1-9, 19	Isaiah 52:13 - 53: 12
Mark 15:46 - 16:8	Luke 24: 1-12	*or* 53: 1-6, 9-12
		Luke 24: 13-35

Third Service

Psalm 81: 1-10 *or* 81: 1-16	Psalm 22: 20-31	Psalm 136: 1-16
Exodus 12: 1-17	Isaiah 53: 6-12	Exodus 12: 1-13
1 Corinthians 5: 6b-8	Romans 4: 13-25	1 Peter 1: 3-12

The Third Sunday of Easter

Principal Service

Year A	Year B	Year C
Acts 2: 14a, 36-41	Acts 3: 12-19	Acts 9: 1-6, (7-20)
or Isaiah 43: 1-12	*or* Micah 4: 1-5	*or* Jeremiah 32: 36-41
Psalm 116: 1-3, 10-17	Psalm 4	Psalm 30
1 Peter 1: 17-23	1 John 3: 1-7	Revelation 5: 11-14
Luke 24: 13-35	Luke 24: 36b-48	John 21: 1-19

Second Service

Psalm 48	Psalm 142	Psalm 86
Haggai 1: 13 - 2: 9	Deuteronomy 7: 7-13	Isaiah 38: 9-20
1 Corinthians 3: 10-17	Revelation 2: 1-11	John 11: (17-26), 27-44
‡ John 2: 13-22	‡ Luke 16: 19-31	

Third Service

Psalm 23	Psalm 77: 11-20	Psalm 80: 1-8
Isaiah 40: 1-11	Isaiah 63: 7-15	Exodus 15: 1-2, 9-18
1 Peter 5: 1-11	1 Corinthians 10: 1-13	John 10: 1-19

Principal Service

Year A	Year B	Year C
Acts 2: 42-47	Acts 4: 5-12	Acts 9: 36-43
or Nehemiah 9: 6-15	*or* Ezekiel 34: 1-10	*or* Numbers 27: 12-23
Psalm 23	Psalm 23	Psalm 23
1 Peter 2: 19-25	1 John 3: 16-24	Revelation 7: 9-17
John 10: 1-10	John 10: 11-18	John 10: 22-30

Second Service

Psalm 29: 1-10	Psalm 81: 8-16	Psalms 113, 114
Ezra 3: 1-13	Exodus 16: 4-15	Isaiah 63: 7-14
Ephesians 2: 11-22	Revelation 2: 12-17	Luke 24: 36-49
‡ Luke 19: 37-48	‡ John 6: 30-40	

Third Service

Psalm 106: 6-24	Psalm 119: 89-96	Psalm 146
Nehemiah 9: 6-15	Nehemiah 8: 1-12	1 Kings 17: 17-24
1 Corinthians 10: 1-13	Luke 24: 25-32	Luke 7: 11-23

Principal Service

Year A	Year B	Year C
Acts 7: 55-60	Acts 8: 26-40	Acts 11: 1-18
or Deuteronomy 6: 20-25	*or* Deuteronomy 4: 32-40	*or* Leviticus 19: 1-2, 9-18
Psalm 31: 1-5, 15-16	Psalm 22: 25-31	Psalm 148
1 Peter 2: 2-10	1 John 4: 7-21	Revelation 21: 1-6
John 14: 1-14	John 15: 1-8	John 13: 31-35

Second Service

Psalm 147: 1-12	Psalm 96	Psalm 98
Zechariah 4: 1-10	Isaiah 60: 1-14	Daniel 6: (1-5), 6-23
Revelation 21: 1-14	Revelation 3: 1-13	Mark 15: 46 – 16: 8
‡ Luke 2: 25-32, (33-38)	‡ Mark 16: 9-16	

Third Service

Psalm 30	Psalm 44: 16-27	Psalm 16
Ezekiel 37: 1-12	2 Maccabees 7: 7-14	2 Samuel 7: 4-13
John 5: 19-29	*or* Daniel 3: 16-28	Acts 2: 14a, 22-32, (33-36)
	Hebrews 11:32 - 12:2	

Principal Service

Year A	Year B	Year C
Acts 17: 22-31	Acts 10: 44-48	Acts 16: 9-15
or Isaiah 41: 17-20	*or* Isaiah 45: 11-13, 18-19	*or* Joel 2: 21-27
Psalm 66: 7-18	Psalm 98	Psalm 67
1 Peter 3: 13-22	1 John 5: 1-6	Revelation 21: 10, 22 - 22: 5
John 14: 15-21	John 15: 9-17	John 14: 23-29
		or John 5: 1-9

Second Service		
Psalms 87, 36: 5-10	Psalm 45	Psalms 126, 127
Zechariah 8: 1-13	Song of Solomon 4: 16 - 5: 2;	Zephaniah 3: 14-20
Revelation 21:22 - 22:5	8: 6-7	Matthew 28: 1-10, 16-20
‡ John 21: 1-14	Revelation 3: 14-22	
	‡ Luke 22: 24-30	

Third Service		
Psalm 73: 21-28	Psalm 104: 28-34	Psalm 40: 1-9
Job 14: 1-2, 7-15; 19: 23-27a	Ezekiel 47: 1-12	Genesis 1: 26-28 *or* 1: 26-31
1 Thessalonians 4: 13-18	John 21: 1-19	Colossians 3: 1-11

The Ascension Day   *White or Gold*

Principal Service

Years A, B, C

Acts 1: 1-11

or Daniel 7: 9-14

Psalm 47 *or* 93

Ephesians 1: 15-23

or Acts 1: 1-11

Luke 24: 44-53

Acts 1: 1-11 is read either as First or Second Reading. It must not be omitted.

Second Service

Psalm 8
Song of the Three 29-37
or 2 Kings 2: 1-15
Revelation 5
‡ Matthew 28: 16-20

Third Service

Psalm 110
Isaiah 52: 7-15
Hebrews 7: 11-28 *or* 7: 26-28

Principal Service

Year A	Year B	Year C
Acts 1: 6-14	Acts 1: 15-17, 21-26	Acts 16: 16-34
or Ezekiel 39: 21-29	*or* Exodus 28: 1-4, 9-10,	*or* 1 Samuel 12: 19-24
Psalm 68: 1-10, 32-35	29-30	Psalm 97
1 Peter 4: 12-14; 5: 6-11	Psalm 1	Revelation 22: 12-14,
John 17: 1-11	1 John 5: 9-13	16-17, 20-21
	John 17: 6-19	John 17: 20-26

Second Service

Psalm 47	Psalm 147: 1-12	Psalm 68: 1-19, 32-35
2 Samuel 23: 1-5	Isaiah 61: 1-11	Isaiah 44: 1-8
Ephesians 1: 15-23	Luke 4: 14-21	Ephesians 4: 7-16
‡ Mark 16: 14-20		‡ Luke 24: 44-53

Third Service

Psalm 104: 26-35	Psalm 76	Psalm 99
Isaiah 65: 17-25	Isaiah 14: 3-15	Deuteronomy 34: 1-12
Revelation 21: 1-8	Revelation 14: 1-13	Luke 24: 44-53
		or Acts 1: 1-8

The Day of Pentecost (Whit Sunday)   *Red, Green weekdays*

Principal Service

Year A	Year B	Year C
Acts 2: 1-21	Acts 2: 1-21	Acts 2: 1-21
or Numbers 11: 24-30	*or* Ezekiel 37: 1-14	*or* Genesis 11: 1-9
Psalm 104: 26-36, 37b	Psalm 104: 26-36, 37b	Psalm 104: 26-36, 37b
1 Corinthians 12: 3b-13	Romans 8: 22-27	Romans 8: 14-17
or Acts 2: 1-21	*or* Acts 2: 1-21	*or* Acts 2: 1-21
John 20: 19-23	John 15: 26-27; 16: 4b-15	John 14: 8-17, (25-27)
or 7: 37-39		

Acts 2: 1-21 is read either as First or Second Reading. It must not be omitted.

Second Service

Psalms 67, 133	Psalm 139: 1-11	Psalms 36: 5-10; 150
Joel 2: 21-32	*or* 139: 1-18, 23-24	Exodus 33: 7-20
Acts 2: 14-21 (22-38)	Ezekiel 36: 22-28	2 Corinthians 3: 4-18
‡ Luke 24: 44-53	Acts 2: 22-38	‡ John 16: 4b-15
	‡ John 20: 19-23	

Third Service

Psalm 87	Psalm 145	Psalm 33: 1-12
Genesis 11: 1-9	Isaiah 11: 1-9	Isaiah 40: 12-23
Acts 10: 34-48	*or* Wisdom 7: 15-23, (24-27)	*or* Wisdom 9: 9-17
	1 Corinthians 12: 4-13	1 Corinthians 2: 6-16

White, Green weekdays and until Advent

Principal Service

Year A	Year B	Year C
Genesis 1: 1 - 2: 4a	Isaiah 6: 1-8	Proverbs 8: 1-4, 22-31
or Isaiah 40: 12 - 17, 27- 31	Psalm 29	Psalm 8
Psalm 8	Romans 8: 12-17	Romans: 5: 1-5
2 Corinthians 13: 11-13	John 3: 1-17	John 16: 12-15
Matthew 28: 16-20		

Second Service

Psalms 93, 150	Psalm 104: 1-10	Psalm 73: 1-3, 16-28
Isaiah 6: 1-8	Ezekiel 1: 4-10, 22-28a	Exodus 3: 1-15
John 16: 5-15	Revelation 4: 1-11	John 3: 1-17
	‡ Mark 1: 1-13	

Third Service

Psalm 86: 8-13	Psalm 33: 1-12	Psalm 29
Exodus 3: 1-6, 13-15	Proverbs 8: 1-4, 22-31	Isaiah 6: 1-8
John 17: 1-11	2 Corinthians 13: (5-10), 11-13	Revelation 4: 1-11

The Sunday between 29 May and 4 June
if after Trinity Sunday

PROPER 4
Green

Principal Service

Year A	Year B	Year C
CONTINUOUS		
Genesis 6: 9-22; 7: 24;	1 Samuel 3: 1-10, (11-20)	1 Kings 18: 20-21,
8: 14-19	Psalm 139: 1-5, 12-18	(22-29), 30-39
Psalm 46		Psalm 96
PAIRED		
Deuteronomy 11: 18-21,	Deuteronomy 5: 12-15	1 Kings 8: 22-23, 41-43
26-28	Psalm 81: 1-10	Psalm 96: 1-9
Psalm 31: 1-5, 19-24		
Romans 1: 16-17; 3: 22b-	2 Corinthians 4: 5-12	Galatians 1: 1-12
28, (29-31)	Mark 2: 23 - 3: 6	Luke 7: 1-10
Matthew 7: 21-29		

A consistent choice for the year should be made of either the continuous set or the paired set of Old Testament Readings and Psalms in Propers 4 to 29. In the paired set there is a semi-thematic link with the Epistle or Gospel reading.

Second Service

Psalm 33 *or* 33: 13-22	Psalm 35 *or* 35: 1-10	Psalm 39
Ruth 2: 1-20a	Jeremiah 5: 1-19	Genesis 4: 1-16
Luke 8: 4-15	Romans 7: 7-25	Mark 3: 7-19
	‡ Luke 7: 1-10	

Third Service

Psalm 37: 1-18	Psalms 28, 32	Psalm 41
Deuteronomy 5: 1-21	Deuteronomy 5: 1-21	Deuteronomy 5: 1-21
Acts 21: 17-39a	Acts 21: 17-39a	Acts 21: 17-39a

The Sunday between 5 and 11 June
if after Trinity Sunday

Principal Service

Year A	Year B	Year C
CONTINUOUS		
Genesis 12: 1-9	1 Samuel 8: 4-11, (12-15),	1 Kings 17: 8-16, (17-24)
Psalm 33: 1-12	16-20; (11: 14-15)	Psalm 146
	Psalm 138	
PAIRED		
Hosea 5: 15 - 6: 6	Genesis 3: 8-15	1 Kings 17: 17-24
Psalm 50: 7-15	Psalm 130	Psalm 30
Romans 4: 13-25	2 Corinthians 4: 13 - 5: 1	Galatians 1: 11-24
Matthew 9: 9-13, 18-26	Mark 3: 20-35	Luke 7: 11-17

Second Service

Psalms (39), 41	Psalm 37: 1-11 *or* 37: 1-17	Psalm 44 *or* 44: 1-9
1 Samuel 18: 1-16	Jeremiah 6: 16-21	Genesis 8: 15 - 9: 17
Luke 8: 41-56	Romans 9: 1-13	Mark 4: 1-20
	‡ Luke 7: 11-17	

Third Service

Psalm 38	Psalm 36	Psalm 45
Deuteronomy 6: 10-25	Deuteronomy 6: 10-25	Deuteronomy 6: 10-25
Acts 22: 22 - 23: 11	Acts 22: 22 - 23: 11	Acts 22: 22 - 23: 11

The Sunday between 12 and 18 June
if after Trinity Sunday

Principal Service

Year A	Year B	Year C
CONTINUOUS		
Genesis 18: 1-15, (21: 1-7)	1 Samuel 15: 34 - 16: 13	1 Kings 21: 1-10, (11-14),
Psalm 116: 1, 10-17	Psalm 20	15-21a
		Psalm 5: 1-8
PAIRED		
Exodus 19: 2-8a	Ezekiel 17: 22-24	2 Samuel 11: 26 - 12: 10,
Psalm 100	Psalm 92: 1-4, 12-15	13-15
		Psalm 32
Romans 5: 1-8	2 Corinthians 5: 6-10,	Galatians 2: 15-21
Matthew 9: 35 - 10: 8,	(11-13), 14-17	Luke 7: 36 - 8: 3
(9-23)	Mark 4: 26-34	

Psalms (42), 43
1 Samuel 21: 1-15
Luke 11: 14-28

Psalm 39
Jeremiah 7: 1-16
Romans 9: 14-26
‡ Luke 7:36 - 8:3

Psalms 52, (53)
Genesis 13
Mark 4: 21-41

Psalm 45
Deuteronomy 10: 12 - 11: 1
Acts 23: 12-35

Psalms 42, 43
Deuteronomy 10: 12 - 11: 1
Acts 23: 12-35

Psalm 49
Deuteronomy 10: 12 - 11: 1
Acts 23: 12-35

The Sunday between 19 and 25 June
if after Trinity Sunday

PROPER 7
Green

Year A	Year B	Year C
CONTINUOUS		
Genesis 21: 8-21	1 Samuel 17: (1a, 4-11, 19-23) 32-49	1 Kings 19: 1-4, (5-7), 8-15a
Psalm 86: 1-10, 16-17	Psalm 9: 9-20	Psalms 42, 43
	or 1 Samuel 17: 57 - 18: 5, 10-16	
	Psalm 133	
PAIRED		
Jeremiah 20: 7-13	Job 38: 1-11	Isaiah 65: 1-9
Psalm 69: 8-11,(12-17), 18-20	Psalm 107: 1-3, 23-32	Psalm 22: 19-28
Romans 6: 1b-11	2 Corinthians 6: 1-13	Galatians 3: 23-29
Matthew 10: 24-39	Mark 4: 35-41	Luke 8: 26-39

Psalms 46, (48)	Psalm 49	Psalms (50), 57
1 Samuel 24: 1-17	Jeremiah 10: 1-16	Genesis 24: 1-27
Luke 14: 12-24	Romans 11: 25-36	Mark 5: 21-43
	‡ Luke 8: 26-39	

Psalm 49	Psalm 48	Psalm 55: 1-16, 18-21
Deuteronomy 11: 1-15	Deuteronomy 11: 1-15	Deuteronomy 11: 1-15
Acts 27: 1-12	Acts 27: 1-12	Acts 27: 1-12

Principal Service

Year A	Year B	Year C
CONTINUOUS		
Genesis 22: 1-14	2 Samuel 1: 1, 17-27	2 Kings 2: 1-2, 6-14
Psalm 13	Psalm 130	Psalm 77: 1-2, 11-20
PAIRED		
Jeremiah 28: 5-9	Wisdom 1: 13-15; 2:23-24	1 Kings 19: 15-16, 19-21
Psalm 89: 1-4, 15-18	Psalm 30	Psalm 16
Romans 6: 12-23	2 Corinthians 8: 7-15	Galatians 5: 1, 13-25
Matthew 10: 40-42	Mark 5: 21-43	Luke 9: 51-62

Second Service

Psalm 50 *or* 50: 1-15	Psalms (52), 53	Psalms (59: 1-6, 18-20), 60
1 Samuel 28: 3-19	Jeremiah 11: 1-14	Genesis 27: 1-40
Luke 17: 20-37	Romans 13: 1-10	Mark 6: 1-6
	‡ Luke 9: 51-62	

Third Service

Psalms 52, 53	Psalm 56	Psalm 64
Deuteronomy 15: 1-11	Deuteronomy 15: 1-11	Deuteronomy 15: 1-11
Acts 27: 13-44 *or* 27: 33-44	Acts 27: 13-44 *or* 27: 33-44	Acts 27: 13-44 *or* 27: 33-44

Principal Service

Year A	Year B	Year C
CONTINUOUS		
Genesis 24: 34-38, 42-49, 58-67	2 Samuel 5: 1-5, 9-10	2 Kings 5. 1-14
Psalm 45: 10-17	Psalm 48	Psalm 30
PAIRED		
Zechariah 9: 9-12	Ezekiel 2: 1-5	Isaiah 66: 10-14
Psalm 145: 8-15	Psalm 123	Psalm 66: 1-8
Romans 7: 15-25a	2 Corinthians 12: 2-10	Galatians 6: (1-6), 7-16
Matthew 11: 16-19, 25-30	Mark 6: 1-13	Luke 10: 1-11, 16-20

Psalms 56, (57)	Psalms 63, (64)	Psalms 65, (70)
2 Samuel 2: 1-11; 3: 1	Jeremiah 20: 1-11a	Genesis 29: 1-20
Luke 18:31 - 19:10	Romans 14: 1-17	Mark 6: 7-29
	‡ Luke 10: 1-11, 16-20	

Third Service

Psalm 55: 1-15, 18-22	Psalm 57	Psalm 74
Deuteronomy 24: 10-22	Deuteronomy 24: 10-22	Deuteronomy 24: 10-22
Acts 28: 1-16	Acts 28: 1-16	Acts 28: 1-16

The Sunday between 10 and 16 July

PROPER 10
Green

Principal Service

Year A	Year B	Year C
CONTINUOUS		
Genesis 25: 19-34	2 Samuel 6: 1-5, 12b-19	Amos 7: 7-17
Psalm 119: 105-112	Psalm 24	Psalm 82
PAIRED		
Isaiah 55: 10-13	Amos 7: 7-15	Deuteronomy 30: 9-14
Psalm 65: (1-7), 8-13	Psalm 85: 8-13	Psalm 25: 1-9
Romans 8: 1-11	Ephesians 1: 3-14	Colossians 1: 1-14
Matthew 13: 1-9, 18-23	Mark 6: 14-29	Luke 10: 25-37

Second Service

Psalms 60, (63)	Psalm 66 or 66: 1-9	Psalm 77 or 77: 1-12
2 Samuel 7: 18-29	Job 4: 1; 5: 6-27	Genesis 32: 9-30
Luke 19:41 - 20:8	or Ecclesiasticus 4: 11-31	Mark 7: 1-23
	Romans 15: 14-29	
	‡ Luke 10: 25-37	

Third Service

Psalms 64, 65	Psalm 65	Psalm 76
Deuteronomy 28: 1-14	Deuteronomy 28: 1-14	Deuteronomy 28: 1-14
Acts 28: 17-31	Acts 28: 17-31	Acts 28: 17-31

The Sunday between 17 and 23 July

Green

Principal Service

Year A	Year B	Year C
CONTINUOUS		
Genesis 28: 10-19a	2 Samuel 7: 1-14a	Amos 8: 1-12
Psalm 139: 1-11, 23-24	Psalm 89: 20-37	Psalm 52
PAIRED		
Wisdom 12: 13, 16-19	Jeremiah 23: 1-6	Genesis 18: 1-10a
or Isaiah 44: 6-8	Psalm 23	Psalm 15
Psalm 86: 11-17		
Romans 8: 12-25	Ephesians 2: 11-22	Colossians 1: 15-28
Matthew 13: 24-30, 36-43	Mark 6: 30-34, 53-56	Luke 10: 38-42

Second Service

Psalms 67, (70)	Psalm 73 *or* 73: 23-28	Psalm 81
1 Kings 2: 10-12; 3: 16-28	Job 13:13 - 14:6	Genesis 41: 1-16, 25-37
Acts 4: 1-22	*or* Ecclesiasticus 18: 1-14	1 Corinthians 4: 8-13
‡ Mark 6: 30-34, 53-56	Hebrews 2: 5-18	‡ John 4: 31-35
	‡ Luke 10: 38-42	

Third Service

Psalm 71	Psalms 67; 70	Psalms 82; 100
Deuteronomy 30: 1-10	Deuteronomy 30: 1-10	Deuteronomy 30: 1-10
1 Peter 3: 8-18	1 Peter 3: 8-18	1 Peter 3: 8-18

The Sunday between 24 and 30 July

PROPER 12
Green

Principal Service

Year A	Year B	Year C
CONTINUOUS		
Genesis 29: 15-28	2 Samuel 11: 1-15	Hosea 1: 2-10
Psalm 105: 1-11, 45b	Psalm 14	Psalm 85
or 128		
PAIRED		
1 Kings 3: 5-12	2 Kings 4: 42-44	Genesis 18: 20-32
Psalm 119: 129-136	Psalm 145: 10-19	Psalm 138
Romans 8: 26-39	Ephesians 3: 14-21	Colossians 2: 6-15, (16-19)
Matthew 13: 31-33, 44-52	John 6: 1-21	Luke 11: 1-13

	Second Service	
Psalms 75, (76)	Psalm 74 *or* 74: 11-16	Psalm 88 *or* 88: 1-10
1 Kings 6: 11-14; 23-38	Job 19: 1-27a	Genesis 42: 1-25
Acts 12: 1-17	*or* Ecclesiasticus 38: 24-34	1 Corinthians 10: 1-24
‡ John 6: 1-21	Hebrews 8	‡ Matthew 13: 24-30 (31- 43)
	‡ Luke 11: 1-13	

	Third Service	
Psalm 77	Psalm 75	Psalm 95
Song of Solomon 2	Song of Solomon 2	Song of Solomon 2
or 1 Maccabees 2: (1-14), 15-22	*or* 1 Maccabees 2: (1-14), 15-22	*or* 1 Maccabees 2: (1-14), 15-22
1 Peter 4: 7-14	1 Peter 4: 7-14	1 Peter 4: 7-14

The Sunday between 31 July and 6 August

PROPER 13
Green

	Principal Service	
Year A	Year B	Year C
CONTINUOUS		
Genesis 32: 22-31	2 Samuel 11:26 - 12:13a	Hosea 11: 1-11
Psalm 17: 1-7, 16	Psalm 51: 1-13	Psalm 107: 1-9, 43
PAIRED		
Isaiah 55: 1-5	Exodus 16: 2-4, 9-15	Ecclesiastes 1: 2, 12-14;
Psalm 145: 8-9, 15-22	Psalm 78: 23-29	2: 18-23
		Psalm 49: 1-12
Romans 9: 1-5	Ephesians 4: 1-16	Colossians 3: 1-11
Matthew 14: 13-21	John 6: 24-35	Luke 12: 13-21

	Second Service	
Psalm 80 *or* 80: 1-8	Psalm 88 *or* 88: 1-10	Psalm 107: 1-32 *or* 107: 1-16
1 Kings 10: 1-13	Job 28	Genesis 50: 4-26
Acts 13: 1-13	*or* Ecclesiasticus 42: 15-25	1 Corinthians 14: 1-19
‡ John 6: 24-35	Hebrews 11: 17-31	‡ Mark 6: 45-52
	‡ Luke 12: 13-21	

	Third Service	
Psalm 85	Psalm 86	Psalm 106: 1-10
Song of Solomon 5: 2-16	Song of Solomon 5: 2-16	Song of Solomon 5: 2-16
or 1 Maccabees 3: 1-12	*or* 1 Maccabees 3: 1-12	*or* 1 Maccabees 3: 1-12
2 Peter 1: 1-15	2 Peter 1: 1-15	2 Peter 1: 1-15

Principal Service

Year A	Year B	Year C
CONTINUOUS		
Genesis 37: 1-4, 12-28	2 Samuel 18: 5-9, 15, 31-33	Isaiah 1: 1, 10-20
Psalm 105: 1-6, 16-22, 45b	Psalm 130	Psalm 50: 1-8, 23-24
PAIRED		
1 Kings 19: 9-18	1 Kings 19: 4-8	Genesis 15: 1-6
Psalm 85: 8-13	Psalm 34: 1-8	Psalm 33: 12-22
Romans 10: 5-15	Ephesians 4: 25 - 5: 2	Hebrews 11: 1-3,8-16
Matthew 14: 22-33	John 6: 35, 41-51	Luke 12: 32-40

Second Service

Psalm 86	Psalm 91 *or* 91: 1-12	Psalms 108, (116)
1 Kings 11:41 - 12:20	Job 39:1 - 40:4	Isaiah 11: 10 - 12: 6
Acts 14: 8-20	*or* Ecclesiasticus 43: 13-33	2 Corinthians 1: 1-22
‡ John 6: 35, 41-51	Hebrews 12: 1-17	‡ Mark 7: 24-30
	‡ Luke 12: 32-40	

Third Service

Psalm 88	Psalm 90	Psalm 115
Song of Solomon 8: 5-7	Song of Solomon 8: 5-7	Song of Solomon 8: 5-7
or 1 Maccabees 14: 4-15	*or* 1 Maccabees 14: 4-15	*or* 1 Maccabees 14: 4-15
2 Peter 3: 8-13	2 Peter 3: 8-13	2 Peter 3: 8-13

Principal Service

Year A	Year B	Year C
CONTINUOUS		
Genesis 45: 1-15	1 Kings 2: 10-12; 3: 3-14	Isaiah 5: 1-7
Psalm 133	Psalm 111	Psalm 80: 1-2, 9-20
PAIRED		
Isaiah 56: 1, 6-8	Proverbs 9: 1-6	Jeremiah 23: 23-29
Psalm 67	Psalm 34: 9-14	Psalm 82
Romans 11: 1-2a, 29-32	Ephesians 5: 15-20	Hebrews 11: 29 - 12: 2
Matthew 15: (10-20), 21-28	John 6: 51-58	Luke 12: 49-56

	Second Service	
Psalm 90 *or* 90: 1-12	Psalms (92), 100	Psalm 119: 17-32
2 Kings 4: 1-37	Exodus 2:23 - 3:10	*or* 119: 17-24
Acts 16: 1-15	Hebrews 13: 1-15	Isaiah 28: 9-22
‡ John 6: 51-58	‡ Luke 12: 49-56	2 Corinthians 8: 1-9
		‡ Matthew 20: 1-16

	Third Service	
Psalm 92	Psalm 106: 1-10	Psalm 119: 33-48
Jonah 1	Jonah 1	Jonah 1
or Ecclesiasticus 3: 1-15	*or* Ecclesiasticus 3: 1-15	*or* Ecclesiasticus 3: 1-15
2 Peter 3: 14-18	2 Peter 3: 14-18	2 Peter 3: 14-18

The Sunday between 21 and 27 August

PROPER 16
Green

Principal Service

Year A	Year B	Year C
CONTINUOUS		
Exodus 1: 8 - 2: 10	1 Kings 8: (1, 6, 10-11),	Jeremiah 1: 4-10
Psalm 124	22-30, 41-43	Psalm 71: 1-6
	Psalm 84	
PAIRED		
Isaiah 51: 1-6	Joshua 24: 1-2a, 14-18	Isaiah 58: 9b-14
Psalm 138	Psalm 34: 15-22	Psalm 103: 1-8
Romans 12: 1-8	Ephesians 6: 10-20	Hebrews 12: 18-29
Matthew 16: 13-20	John 6: 56-69	Luke 13: 10-17

	Second Service	
Psalm 95	Psalm 116 *or* 116: 11-17	Psalm 119: 49-72
2 Kings 6: 8-23	Exodus 4:27 - 5:1	*or* 119: 49-56
Acts 17: 15-34	Hebrews 13: 16-21	Isaiah 30: 8-21
‡ John 6: 56-69	‡ Luke 13: 10-17	2 Corinthians 9
		‡ Matthew 21: 28-32

	Third Service	
Psalm 104: 1-25	Psalm 115	Psalm 119: 73-88
Jonah 2	Jonah 2	Jonah 2
or Ecclesiasticus 3: 17-29	*or* Ecclesiasticus 3: 17-29	*or* Ecclesiasticus 3: 17-29
Revelation 1	Revelation 1	Revelation 1

The Sunday between 28 August and 3 September

Principal Service

Year A	Year B	Year C
CONTINUOUS		
Exodus 3: 1-15	Song of Solomon 2: 8-13	Jeremiah 2: 4-13
Psalm 105: 1-6, 23-26, 45c	Psalm 45: 1-2, 6-9	Psalm 81: 1, 10-16
or 115		
PAIRED		
Jeremiah 15: 15-21	Deuteronomy 4: 1-2, 6-9	Ecclesiasticus 10: 12-18
Psalm 26: 1-8	Psalm 15	*or* Proverbs 25: 6-7
		Psalm 112
Romans 12: 9-21	James 1: 17-27	Hebrews 13: 1-8, 15-16
Matthew 16: 21-28	Mark 7: 1-8, 14-15, 21-23	Luke 14: 1, 7-14

Second Service

Psalm 105: 1-15	Psalm 119: 1-16	Psalm 119: 81-96
2 Kings 6: 24-25; 7: 3-20	*or* 119: 9-16	*or* 119: 81-88
Acts 18: 1-16	Exodus 12: 21-27	Isaiah 33: 13-22
‡ Mark 7: 1-8, 14-15, 21-23	Matthew 4:23 - 5:20	John 3: 22-36

Third Service

Psalm 107: 1-32 *or* 107: 1-22	Psalm 119: 17-40	Psalm 119: 161-176
Jonah 3: 1-9	Jonah 3: 1-9	Jonah 3: 1-9
Revelation 3: 14-22	Revelation 3: 14-22	Revelation 3: 14-22

The Sunday between 4 and 10 September

Principal Service

Year A	Year B	Year C
CONTINUOUS		
Exodus 12: 1-14	Proverbs 22: 1-2, 8-9,	Jeremiah 18: 1-11
Psalm 149	22-23	Psalm 139: 1-5, 12-18
	Psalm 125	
PAIRED		
Ezekiel 33: 7-11	Isaiah 35: 4-7a	Deuteronomy 30: 15-20
Psalm 119: 33-40	Psalm 146	Psalm 1
Romans 13: 8-14	James 2: 1-10, (11-13),	Philemon 1-21
Matthew 18: 15-20	14-17	Luke 14: 25-33
	Mark 7: 24-37	

Psalms 108, (115) Psalm 119: 41-56 Psalms (120), 121
Ezekiel 12: 21 - 13: 16 *or* 119: 49-56 Isaiah 43: 14 - 44: 5
Acts 19: 1-20 Exodus 14: 5-31 John 5: 30-47
‡ Mark 7: 24-37 Matthew 6: 1-18

Third Service

Psalm 119: 17-32 Psalm 119: 57-72 Psalms 122, 123
Jonah 3:10 - 4:11 Jonah 3:10 - 4:11 Jonah 3:10 - 4:11
or Ecclesiasticus 27: 30 - 28: 9 *or* Ecclesiasticus 27: 30 - 28: 9 *or* Ecclesiasticus 27: 30 - 28: 9
Revelation 8: 1-5 Revelation 8: 1-5 Revelation 8: 1-5

The Sunday between 11 and 17 September

PROPER 19
Green

Principal Service

Year A	Year B	Year C
CONTINUOUS		
Exodus 14: 19-31	Proverbs 1: 20-33	Jeremiah 4: 11-12, 22-28
Psalm 114	Psalm 19	Psalm 14
	or Canticle: *Song of Wisdom*	
PAIRED		
Genesis: 50: 15-21	Isaiah 50: 4-9a	Exodus 32: 7-14
Psalm 103: (1-7), 8-13	Psalm 116: 1-8	Psalm 51: 1-11
Romans 14: 1-12	James 3: 1-12	1 Timothy 1: 12-17
Matthew 18: 21-35	Mark 8: 27-38	Luke 15: 1-10

Second Service

Psalm 119: 41-48, (49-64) Psalm 119: 73-88 Psalms 124, 125
Ezekiel 20: 1-8; 33-44 *or* 119: 73-80 Isaiah 60
Acts 20: 17-38 Exodus 18: 13-26 John 6: 51-69
‡ Mark 8: 27-38 Matthew 7: 1-14

Third Service

Psalm 119: 65-88 Psalm 119: 105-120 Psalms 126, 127
Isaiah 44: 24 - 45: 8 Isaiah 44: 24 - 45: 8 Isaiah 44: 24 - 45: 8
Revelation 12: 1-12 Revelation 12: 1-12 Revelation 12: 1-12

The Sunday between 18 and 24 September

Principal Service

Year A	Year B	Year C
CONTINUOUS		
Exodus 16: 2-15	Proverbs 31: 10-31	Jeremiah 8: 18 - 9: 1
Psalm 105: 1-6, 37-45	Psalm 1	Psalm 79: 1-9
PAIRED		
Jonah 3: 10 - 4: 11	Wisdom 1: 16 - 2: 1, 12-22	Amos 8: 4-7
Psalm 145: 1-8	*or* Jeremiah 11: 18-20	Psalm 113
	Psalm 54	
Philippians 1: 21-30	James 3: 13 - 4: 3, 7-8a	1 Timothy 2: 1-7
Matthew 20: 1-16	Mark 9: 30-37	Luke 16: 1-13

Second Service

Psalm 119: 113-136	Psalm 119: 137-152	Psalms (128), 129
or 119: 121-128	*or* 119: 137-144	Ezra 1
Ezekiel 33: 23, 30 - 34:10	Exodus 19: 10-25	John 7: 14-36
Acts 26: 1, 9-25	Matthew 8: 23-34	
‡ Mark 9: 30-37		

Third Service

Psalm 119: 153-176	Psalm 119: 153-176	Psalms 130; 131
Isaiah 45: 9-22	Isaiah 45: 9-22	Isaiah 45: 9-22
Revelation 14: 1-5	Revelation 14: 1-5	Revelation 14: 1-5

The Sunday between 25 September and 1 October

Principal Service

Year A	Year B	Year C
CONTINUOUS		
Exodus 17: 1-7	Esther 7: 1-6, 9-10;	Jeremiah 32: 1-3a, 6-15
Psalm 78: 1-4, 12-16	9: 20-22	Psalm 91: 1-6, 14-16
	Psalm 124	
PAIRED		
Ezekiel 18: 1-4, 25-32	Numbers 11: 4-6, 10-16,	Amos 6: 1a, 4-7
Psalm 25: 1-8	24-29	Psalm 146
	Psalm 19: 7-14	
Philippians 2: 1-13	James 5: 13-20	1 Timothy 6: 6-19
Matthew 21: 23-32	Mark 9: 38-50	Luke 16: 19-31

Psalms (120, 123), 124	Psalms 120, 121	Psalms 134, 135 *or* 135: 1-13
Ezekiel 37: 15-28	Exodus 24	Nehemiah 2
1 John 2: 22-29	Romans 1: 18-32	John 8: 31-33, 48-59
‡ Mark 9: 38-50	‡ Matthew 9: 1-8	

Psalms 125, 126, 127	Psalm 122	Psalm 132
Isaiah 48: 12-22	Isaiah 48: 12-22	Isaiah 48: 12-22
Luke 11: 37-54	Luke 11: 37-54	Luke 11: 37-54

The Sunday between 2 and 8 October

PROPER 22
Green

Principal Service

Year A	Year B	Year C
CONTINUOUS		
Exodus 20: 1-4, 7-9, 12-20	Job 1: 1; 2: 1-10	Lamentations 1: 1-6
Psalm 19	Psalm 26	Psalm 137: 1-6
PAIRED		
Isaiah 5: 1-7	Genesis 2: 18-24	Habakkuk 1: 1-4; 2: 1-4
Psalm 80: 8-16	Psalm 8	Psalm 37: 1-9
Philippians 3: 4b-14	Hebrews 1: 1-4; 2: 5-12	2 Timothy 1: 1-14
Matthew 21: 33-46	Mark 10: 2-16	Luke 17: 5-10

Psalm 136 *or* 136: 1-9	Psalms 125, 126	Psalm 142
Proverbs 2: 1-11	Joshua 3: 7-17	Nehemiah 5: 1-13
1 John 2: 1-17	Romans 2: 1-16	John 9
‡ Mark 10: 2-16	‡ Matthew 10: 1-22	

Psalms 128, 129, 134	Psalms 123, 124	Psalm 141
Isaiah 49: 13-23	Isaiah 49: 13-23	Isaiah 49: 13-23
Luke 12: 1-12	Luke 12: 1-12	Luke 12: 1-12

The Sunday between 9 and 15 October

Principal Service

Year A	Year B	Year C
CONTINUOUS		
Exodus 32: 1-14	Job 23: 1-9, 16-17	Jeremiah 29: 1, 4-7
Psalm 106: 1-6, 19-23	Psalm 22: 1-15	Psalm 66: 1-11
PAIRED		
Isaiah 25: 1-9	Amos 5: 6-7, 10-15	2 Kings 5: 1-3, 7-15c
Psalm 23	Psalm 90: 12-17	Psalm 111
Philippians 4: 1-9	Hebrews 4: 12-16	2 Timothy 2: 8-15
Matthew 22: 1-14	Mark 10: 17-31	Luke 17: 11-19

Second Service

Psalm 139: 1-18	Psalms 127, (128)	Psalm 144
or 139: 1-11	Joshua 5:13 - 6:20	Nehemiah 6: 1-16
Proverbs 3: 1-18	Romans 2: 17-29	John 15: 12-27
1 John 3: 1-15	‡ Matthew 11: 20-30	
‡ Mark 10: 17-31		

Third Service

Psalms 138, 141	Psalms 129, 130	Psalm 143
Isaiah 50: 4-10	Isaiah 50: 4-10	Isaiah 50: 4-10
Luke 13: 22-30	Luke 13: 22-30	Luke 13: 22-30

The Sunday between 16 and 22 October

Principal Service

Year A	Year B	Year C
CONTINUOUS		
Exodus 33: 12-23	Job 38: 1-7, (34-41)	Jeremiah 31: 27-34
Psalm 99	Psalm 104: 1-10, 26, 37c	Psalm 119: 97-104
PAIRED		
Isaiah 45: 1-7	Isaiah 53: 4-12	Genesis 32: 22-31
Psalm 96: 1-9, (10-13)	Psalm 91: 9-16	Psalm 121
1 Thessalonians 1: 1-10	Hebrews 5: 1-10	2 Timothy 3: 14 - 4: 5
Matthew 22: 15-22	Mark 10: 35-45	Luke 18: 1-8

Psalms 142, (143: 1-11)
Proverbs 4: 1-18
1 John 3:16 - 4:6
‡ Mark 10: 35-45

Psalm 141
Joshua 14: 6-14
Romans 3: 1-20
‡ Matthew 12: 1-21

Psalms (146), 149
Nehemiah 8: 9-18
John 16: 1-11

Third Service

Psalms 145, 149
Isaiah 54: 1-14
Luke 13: 31-35

Psalms 133, 134, 137: 1-6
Isaiah 54: 1-14
Luke 13: 31-35

Psalm 147
Isaiah 54: 1-14
Luke 13: 31-35

The Sunday between 23 and 29 October

PROPER 25
Green

Principal Service

Year A	Year B	Year C
CONTINUOUS		
Deuteronomy 34: 1-12	Job 42: 1-6, 10-17	Joel 2: 23-32
Psalm 90: 1-6, 13-17	Psalm 34: 1-8, (19-22)	Psalm 65
PAIRED		
Leviticus 19: 1-2, 15-18	Jeremiah 31: 7-9	Ecclesiasticus 35: 12-17
Psalm 1	Psalm 126	*or* Jeremiah 14: 7-10, 19-22
		Psalm 84: 1-7
1 Thessalonians 2: 1-8	Hebrews 7: 23-28	2 Timothy 4: 6-8, 16-18
Matthew 22: 34-46	Mark 10: 46-52	Luke 18: 9-14

Second Service

Psalm 119: 89-104
Ecclesiastes 11 & 12
2 Timothy 2: 1-7
‡ Mark 12: 28-34

Psalm 119: 121-136
Ecclesiastes 11 & 12
2 Timothy 2: 1-7
‡ Luke 18: 9-14

Psalm 119: 1-16
Ecclesiastes 11 & 12
2 Timothy 2: 1-7
‡ Matthew 22: 34-46

Third Service

Psalm 119: 137-152
Isaiah 59: 9-20
Luke 14: 1-14

Psalm 119: 89-104
Isaiah 59: 9-20
Luke 14: 1-14

Psalm 119: 105-128
Isaiah 59: 9-20
Luke 14: 1-14

The Sunday between 30 October and 5 November PROPER 26
Green

Principal Service

Year A	Year B	Year C
CONTINUOUS		
Joshua 3: 7-17	Ruth 1: 1-18	Habakkuk 1: 1-4; 2: 1-4
Psalm 107: 1-7, 33-37	Psalm 146	Psalm 119: 137-144
PAIRED		
Micah 3: 5-12	Deuteronomy 6: 1-9	Isaiah 1: 10-18
Psalm 43	Psalm 119: 1-8	Psalm 32: 1-8
1 Thessalonians 2: 9-13	Hebrews 9: 11-14	2 Thessalonians 1: 1-4, 11-12
Matthew 23: 1-12	Mark 12: 28-34	Luke 19: 1-10

Second Service

Psalms 111, 117	Psalm 145 *or* 145: 1-9	Psalm 145 *or* 145: 1-9
Daniel 7: 1-18	Daniel 2: 1-48 *or* 1-11, 25-48	Lamentations 3: 22-33
Luke 6: 17-31	Revelation 7: 9-17	John 11: 1-44 *or* 32-44
	‡ Matthew 5: 1-12	

Third Service

Psalm 33	Psalms 112, 149	Psalm 87
Isaiah 66: 20-23	Jeremiah 31: 31-34	Job 19: 21-27a
Ephesians 1: 11-23	1 John 3: 1-3	Colossians 1: 9-14

The Sunday between 6 and 12 November PROPER 27
Green

Principal Service

Year A	Year B	Year C
CONTINUOUS		
Joshua 24: 1-3a, 14-25	Ruth 3: 1-5; 4: 13-17	Haggai 1: 15b - 2: 9
Psalm 78: 1-7	Psalm 127	Psalm 145: 1-5, 18-22 *or* 98
PAIRED		
Wisdom 6: 12-16	1 Kings 17: 8-16	Job 19: 23-27a
or Amos 5: 18-24	Psalm 146	Psalm 17: 1-9
Psalm 70		
1 Thessalonians 4: 13-18	Hebrews 9: 24-28	2 Thessalonians 2: 1-5, 13-17
Matthew 25: 1-13	Mark 12: 38-44	Luke 20: 27-38

Psalms (20), 82
Judges 7: 2-22
John 15: 9-17

Psalms 46, (82)
Isaiah 10:33 - 11:9
John 14: 1-29 (or 23-29)

Psalm 40
1 Kings 3: 1-15
Romans 8: 31-39
‡ Matthew 22: 15-22

Third Service

Psalm 91
Deuteronomy 17: 14-20
1 Timothy 2: 1-7

Psalm 136
Micah 4: 1-5
Philippians 4: 6-9

Psalms 20, 90
Isaiah 2: 1-5
James 3: 13-18

The Sunday between 13 and 19 November

PROPER 28
Green

Principal Service

Year A	Year B	Year C
CONTINUOUS		
Judges 4: 1-7	1 Samuel 1: 4-20	Isaiah 65: 17-25
Psalm 123	Psalm 16	Canticle: *Song of Isaiah*
PAIRED		
Zephaniah 1: 7, 12-18	Daniel 12: 1-3	Malachi 4: 1-2a
Psalm 90: 1-8, (9-11), 12	Psalm 16	Psalm 98
1 Thessalonians 5: 1-11	Hebrews 10: 11-14,	2 Thessalonians 3: 6-13
Matthew 25: 14-30	(15-18), 19-25	Luke 21: 5-19
	Mark 13: 1-8	

Second Service

Psalm 89: 19-37 or 89: 19-29	Psalm 95	Psalms (93), 97
1 Kings 1: 15-40 or 1-40	Daniel 3 or 3: 13-30	Daniel 6
Revelation 1: 4-18	Matthew 13: 24-30, 36-43	Matthew 13: 1-9, 18-23
‡ Luke 9: 1-6		

Third Service

Psalm 98	Psalm 96	Psalm 132
Daniel 10: 19-21	1 Samuel 9:27 - 10:2a;	1 Samuel 16: 1-13
Revelation 4	10: 17-26	Matthew 13: 44-52
	Matthew 13: 31-35	

Principal Service

Year A	Year B	Year C
CONTINUOUS		
Ezekiel 34: 11-16, 20-24	2 Samuel 23: 1-7	Jeremiah 23: 1-6
Psalm 100	Psalm 132: 1-12, (13-18)	Canticle: *Benedictus*
PAIRED		
Ezekiel 34: 11-16, 20-24	Daniel 7: 9-10, 13-14	Jeremiah 23: 1-6
Psalm 95: 1-7	Psalm 93	Psalm 46
Ephesians 1: 15-23	Revelation 1: 4b-8	Colossians 1: 11-20
Matthew 25: 31-46	John 18: 33-37	Luke 23: 33-43

Second Service

Psalms 93, (97)	Psalm 72 *or* 72: 1-7	Psalm 72 *or* 72: 1-7
2 Samuel 23: 1-7	Daniel 5	1 Samuel 8: 4-20
or 1 Maccabees 2: 15-29	John 6: 1-15	John 18: 33-37
Matthew 28: 16-20		

Third Service

Psalms 29, 110	Psalms 29, 110	Psalms 29, 110
Isaiah 4:2 - 5:7	Isaiah 32: 1-8	Zechariah 6: 9-15
Luke 19: 29-38	Revelation 3: 7-22	Revelation 11: 15-18

FESTIVALS

The Naming and Circumcision of Jesus — *White*
1 January

Holy Communion	Morning Prayer	Evening Prayer
Numbers 6: 22-27	Psalm 103	Psalm 115
Psalm 8	Deuteronomy 30: 11-20	Genesis 17: 1-12a,
Galatians 4: 4-7	Romans 2: 17-29	(12b-16)
Luke 2: 15-21		Acts 3: 1-16

The Conversion of Saint Paul — *White*
25 January

Holy Communion	Morning Prayer	Evening Prayer
Jeremiah 1: 4-10	Psalm 66	Psalm 119: 41-56
Psalm 67	Ezekiel 3: 22-27	Ecclesiasticus 39: 1-10
Acts 9: 1-22	Philippians 3: 1-14	*or* Isaiah 56: 1-8
Matthew 19: 27-30		Colossians 1: 24 - 2: 7

Saint Brigid — *White*
1 February

Holy Communion	Morning Prayer	Evening Prayer
Hosea 6: 1-4	Psalm 138	Psalms 123; 131
Psalm 134	Isaiah 40: 1-5	Isaiah 61: 10 - 62: 5
1 John 1: 1-4	1 Corinthians 1: 26-31	3 John 2-8
John 10: 7-16		

The Presentation of Christ in the Temple — *White*
2 February (May be observed on the Sunday nearest to 2 February)

Holy Communion	Morning Prayer	Evening Prayer
Malachi 3: 1-5	Psalms 48, 146	Psalms 122, 132
Psalm 24: 1-10 *or* 24: 7-10	Haggai 2: 1-9	Exodus 13: 1-16
or 84	John 2: 18-22	Romans 12: 1-5
Hebrews 2: 14-18		
Luke 2: 22-40		

Saint Patrick — *White*
17 March

Holy Communion	Morning Prayer	Evening Prayer
Tobit 13: 1b-7	Psalm 106: 1-5	Psalm 96
or Deuteronomy 32: 1-9	Isaiah 51: 1-8	Isaiah 8: 19 - 9: 2
Psalm 145: 1-13	Acts 16: 6-10	Luke 6: 20-31
2 Corinthians 4: 1-12		
John 4: 31-38		

Saint Joseph of Nazareth

White

19 March

Holy Communion	Morning Prayer	Evening Prayer
2 Samuel 7: 4-16	Psalms 25, 147: 1-12	Psalms 1, 112
Psalm 89: 26-36	Isaiah 11: 1-10	Genesis 50: 22-26
Romans 4: 13-18	Matthew 13: 54-58	Matthew 2: 13-23
Matthew 1: 18-25		

The Annunciation of our Lord to the Blessed Virgin Mary

White

25 March

Holy Communion	Morning Prayer	Evening Prayer
Isaiah 7: 10-14	Psalms 111, 113	Psalms 131, 146
Psalm 40: 5-10	1 Samuel 2: 1-10	Isaiah 52: 1-12
Hebrews 10: 4-10	Romans 5: 12-21	Hebrews 2: 5-18
Luke 1: 26-38		

Saint Mark

Red

25 April

Holy Communion	Morning Prayer	Evening Prayer
Proverbs 15: 28-33	Psalm 37: 23-41	Psalm 45
or Acts 15: 35-41	Isaiah 62: 6-10	Ezekiel 1: 4-14
Psalm 119: 9-16	*or* Ecclesiasticus 51: 13-30	2 Timothy 4: 1-11
Ephesians 4: 7-16	Acts 12:25 - 13:13	
Mark 13: 5-13		

Saint Philip and Saint James

Red

1 May

Holy Communion	Morning Prayer	Evening Prayer
Isaiah 30: 15-21	Psalm 139: 1-18, 23-24	Psalm 149
Psalm 119: 1-8	Proverbs 4: 10-18	Job 23: 1-12
Ephesians 1: 3-10	James 1: 1-12	John 1: 43-51
John 14: 1-14		

Saint Matthias

Red

14 May

Holy Communion	Morning Prayer	Evening Prayer
Isaiah 22: 15-25	Psalm 16; 147: 1-12	Psalm 80
Psalm 15	1 Samuel 2: 27-35	1 Samuel 16: 1-13a
Acts 1: 15-26	Acts 2: 37-47	Matthew 7: 15-27
John 15: 9-17		

The Visitation of the Blessed Virgin Mary
31 May

Holy Communion	Morning Prayer	Evening Prayer
Zephaniah 3: 14 -18	Psalms 85, 150	Psalms 122, 127, 128
Psalm 113	1 Samuel 2: 1-10	Zechariah 2: 10-13
Romans 12: 9-16	Mark 3: 31-35	John 3: 25-30
Luke 1: 39-49 (50-56)		

Saint Columba
9 June

White

Holy Communion	Morning Prayer	Evening Prayer
Micah 4: 1-5	Psalm 34: 1-8	Psalm 96
Psalm 34: 9-15	Isaiah 42: 5-12	Micah 7: 14-20
Romans 15: 1-6	2 Corinthians 4: 5-10	Matthew 28: 16-20
John 12: 20-26		

Saint Barnabas
11 June

Red

Holy Communion	Morning Prayer	Evening Prayer
Job 29: 11-16	Psalms 101, 117	Psalm 147
Psalm 112: 1-9	Jeremiah 9: 23-24	Ecclesiastes 12: 9-14
Acts 11: 19-30	Acts 4: 32-37	*or* Tobit 4: 5-11
John 15: 12-17		Acts 9: 26-31

The Birth of Saint John the Baptist
24 June

White

Holy Communion	Morning Prayer	Evening Prayer
Isaiah 40: 1-11	Psalms 50, 149	Psalms 80, 82
Psalm 85: 7-13	Ecclesiasticus 48: 1-10	Malachi 4
Acts 13: 14b-26	*or* Malachi 3: 1-6	Matthew 11: 2-19
or Galatians 3: 23-29	Luke 3: 1-17	
Luke 1: 57-66, 80		

Saint Peter
29 June

Red

Holy Communion	Morning Prayer	Evening Prayer
Ezekiel 3: 22-27	Psalms 71, 113	Psalms 124, 138
Psalm 125	Isaiah 49: 1-6	Ezekiel 34: 11-16
Acts 12: 1-11	Acts 11: 1-18	John 21: 15-22
Matthew 16: 13-19		

Saint Thomas
3 July

Holy Communion	Morning Prayer	Evening Prayer
Habakkuk 2: 1-4	Psalm 92	Psalms 139: 1-18, 23-24
Psalm 31: 1-6	2 Samuel 15: 17-21	Job 42: 1-6
Ephesians 2: 19-22	*or* Ecclesiasticus 2	1 Peter 1: 3-12
John 20: 24-29	John 11: 1-16	

Saint Mary Magdalene
22 July

White

Holy Communion	Morning Prayer	Evening Prayer
Song of Solomon 3: 1-4	Psalms 30, 32	Psalm 63
Psalm 42: 1-10	1 Samuel 16: 14-23	Zephaniah 3: 14-20
2 Corinthians 5: 14-17	Luke 8: 1-3	Mark 15: 40 - 16: 8
John 20: 1-2, 11-18		

Saint James
25 July

Red

Holy Communion	Morning Prayer	Evening Prayer
Jeremiah 45: 1-5	Psalms 7, 29	Psalm 94
Psalm 126	2 Kings 1: 9-15	Jeremiah 26: 1-16
Acts 11: 27 - 12: 2	Luke 9: 46-56	Mark 1: 14-20
Matthew 20: 20-28		

The Transfiguration of our Lord
6 August

White

Holy Communion	Morning Prayer	Evening Prayer
Daniel 7: 9-10, 13-14	Psalms 27, 150	Psalm 72
Psalm 97	Ecclesiasticus 48: 1-10	Exodus 24: 12-18
2 Peter 1: 16-19	*or* 1 Kings 19: 1-16	2 Corinthians 3
Luke 9: 28-36	1 John 3: 1-3	

Saint Bartholomew
24 August

Red

Holy Communion	Morning Prayer	Evening Prayer
Isaiah 43: 8-13	Psalms 86, 117	Psalms 91, 116
Psalm 145: 1-7	Genesis 28: 10-17	Ecclesiasticus 39: 1-10
Acts 5: 12-16	John 1: 43-51	*or* Deuteronomy 18: 15-19
Luke 22: 24-30		Matthew 10: 1-22

The Birth of the Blessed Virgin Mary
8 September

White

Holy Communion	Morning Prayer	Evening Prayer
Isaiah 61: 10-11	Psalms 98, 138	Psalm 132
Psalm 45: 10-17	Isaiah 7: 10-15	Song of Solomon 2: 1-7
Galatians 4: 4-7	Acts 1: 6-14	Luke 11: 27-28
Luke 1: 46-55		

Saint Matthew
21 September

Red

Holy Communion	Morning Prayer	Evening Prayer
Proverbs 3: 13-18	Psalms 49, 117	Psalm 119: 33-40,89-96
Psalm 119: 65-72	1 Kings 19: 15-21	Ecclesiastes 5: 4-12
2 Corinthians 4: 1-6	2 Timothy 3: 14-17	Matthew 19: 16-30
Matthew 9: 9-13		

Saint Michael and all Angels
29 September

White

Holy Communion	Morning Prayer	Evening Prayer
Genesis 28: 10-17	Psalms 34, 150	Psalm 91 *or* 148
Psalm 103: 19-22	Tobit 12: 6-22	Daniel 10: 4-21
Revelation 12: 7-12	*or* Daniel 12; 1-4	Revelation 5
John 1: 47-51	Acts 12: 1-11	

Saint Philip the Deacon
11 October

Red

Holy Communion	Morning Prayer	Evening Prayer
Acts 8: 26-40	Psalm 87	Psalm 125
or Isaiah 40:27 - 41:1	Isaiah 49: 1-6	Deuteronomy 32: 1-3
Psalm 119: 105-112	Acts 8: 4-13	Acts 21: 7-16
Colossians 1: 9-13		
or Acts 8: 26-40		
Luke 10: 1-12		

Saint Luke
18 October

Red

Holy Communion	Morning Prayer	Evening Prayer
Isaiah 35: 3-6	Psalms 145, 146	Psalm 103
or Acts 16: 6-12a	Isaiah 55: 1-13	Ecclesiasticus 38: 1-14
Psalm 147: 1-7	Luke 1: 1-4	*or* Isaiah 61: 1-6
2 Timothy 4: 5-17		Colossians 4: 7-18
Luke 10: 1-9		

Saint James, the Brother of our Lord

23 October

Holy Communion	Morning Prayer	Evening Prayer
Isaiah 49: 1-6	Psalm 119: 145-168	Psalms 122, 125
Psalm 1	Jeremiah 11: 18-23	Isaiah 65: 17-25
Acts 15: 12-22	Matthew 10: 16-22	Galatians 1: 18-24
Mark 3: 31-35		

Saint Simon and Saint Jude

Red

28 October

Holy Communion	Morning Prayer	Evening Prayer
Isaiah 28: 14-16	Psalms 116, 117	Psalm 119: 1-16
Psalm 119: 89-96	Wisdom 5: 1-16	1 Maccabees 2: 42-66
Ephesians 2: 19-22	*or* Isaiah 45: 18-25	*or* Jeremiah 3: 11-18
John 15: 17-27	Luke 6: 12-16	Jude 1-4, 17-25

All Saints

White

1 November (*May be observed on the Sunday nearest to 1 November*)

Holy Communion

Year A	Year B	Year C
Jeremiah 31: 31-34	Wisdom 3: 1-9	Daniel 7: 1-3, 15-18
Psalm 34: 1-10	*or* Isaiah 25: 6-9	Psalm 149
Revelation 7: 9-17	Psalm 24	Ephesians 1: 11-23
or 1 John 3: 1-3	Revelation 21: 1-6a	Luke 6: 20-31
Matthew 5: 1-12	John 11: 32-44	

Morning Prayer	Evening Prayer
Psalms 15, 84, 149	Psalms 148, 150
Isaiah 65: 17-25	Ecclesiasticus 44: 1-15
Luke 9: 18-27	*or* Isaiah 40: 27-31
	Hebrews 11: 32 - 12:2

Saint Andrew

Red

30 November

Holy Communion	Morning Prayer	Evening Prayer
Isaiah 52: 7-10	Psalms 47; 48	Psalms 87, 96
Psalm 19: 1-6	Ezekiel 47: 1-12	Zechariah 8: 20-23
Romans 10: 12-18	*or* Ecclesiasticus 14: 20-27	John 1: 35-42
Matthew 4: 18-22	John 12: 20-32	

Saint Stephen
26 December   *Red or White*

Holy Communion
2 Chronicles 24: 20-22
Psalm 119: 161-168
Acts 7: 51-60
Matthew 10: 17-22

Morning Prayer
Psalms 13, 31: 1-8
Jeremiah 26: 12-15
Acts 6

Evening Prayer
Psalms 57, 86
Genesis 4: 1-10
Matthew 23: 34-39

Saint John
27 December   *White*

Holy Communion
Exodus 33: 7-11a
Psalm 117
1 John 1: 1-9
John 21: 19b-25

Morning Prayer
Psalm 21
Exodus 33: 12-23
1 John 2: 1-11

Evening Prayer
Psalm 97
Isaiah 6: 1-8
1 John 5: 1-12

The Holy Innocents
28 December   *White*

Holy Communion
Jeremiah 31: 15-17
Psalm 124
1 Corinthians 1: 26-29
Matthew 2: 13-18

Morning Prayer
Psalms 36, 146
Baruch 4: 21-27
or Genesis 37: 13-20
Matthew 18: 1-10

Evening Prayer
Psalms 123, 128
Isaiah 49: 14-25
Mark 10: 13-16

OTHER OCCASIONS

Dedication Festival

Year A
Haggai 2: 6-9
Psalm 84: 1-3
1 Peter 2: 4-10
John 2: 13-22

Year B
1 Kings 8: 22-30
Psalm 122
Hebrews 12: 18-24
John 10: 22-29

Year C
Genesis 28: 11-18
or 1 Chronicles 29: 6-19
Psalm 122 *or* 84: 1-3
Ephesians 2: 19-22
Matthew 21: 12-16

Harvest Thanksgiving

Year A
Deuteronomy 8: 7-18
Psalm 65
2 Corinthians 9: 6-15
Luke 17: 11-19

Year B
Joel 2: 21-27
Psalm 126
1 Timothy 2: 1-7
Matthew 6: 25-33

Year C
Deuteronomy 26: 1-11
Psalm 100
Philippians 4: 4-9
John 6: 25-35

Bible Sunday
May be observed on the last Sunday of October or other convenient Sunday

Year A	Year B	Year C
Nehemiah 8: 1-4, (5-6), 8-12	Isaiah 55: 1-11	Isaiah 45: 22-25
Psalm 119: 97-104	Psalm 19: 7-14	Psalm 119: 129-136
or 119: 105-112	2 Timothy 3: 14 - 4: 5	Romans 15: 1-6
Colossians 3: 12-17	John 5: 36b-47	Luke 4: 16-24
Matthew 24: 30-35		

Ember Days

Jeremiah 1: 4-9 *or* Numbers 11: 16-17, 24-29 *or* Numbers 27: 15-23
Psalm 84: 7-12 *or* Psalm 122 *or* Psalm 134
Acts 20: 28-35 *or* 1 Corinthians 3: 5-11 *or* 1 Peter 4: 7-11
Matthew 9: 35-38 *or* Luke 12: 35-43 *or* Luke 4: 16-21 *or* John 4: 31-38
Any combination of the above may be used.

Rogation Days

Deuteronomy 8: 1-10 *or* 1 Kings 8: 35-40 *or* Job 28: 1-11
Psalm 104: 23-32 *or* Psalm 107: 1-9 *or* Psalm 121
Philippians 4: 4-7 *or* 2 Thessalonians 3: 6-13 *or* 1 John 5: 12-15
Matthew 6: 1-15 *or* Mark 11: 22 -24 *or* Luke 11: 5-13
Any combination of the above may be used.

The Guidance of the Holy Spirit

Isaiah 61: 1-3
Psalm 86: 9-12, 16-17
1 Corinthians 12: 4-13
John 14: 15-26

Peace

Micah 4: 3-5
Psalm 29: 1-4, 9, 10
1 Timothy 2: 1-5
Matthew 5: 43 - 48

Mission

Isaiah 49: 1-6
Psalm 96: 1-4, 11
Ephesians 2: 13-18
Matthew 9: 35-38

Unity

Ezekiel 37: 15-22
Psalm 133
Ephesians 4: 1-6
John 17: 11-23

A TABLE OF EPISTLES AND GOSPELS

Drawn from those appointed in the Book of Common Prayer 1926
which may be used at Holy Communion with Collects One

Advent 1	Romans 13: 8-14	Matthew 21: 1-13
Advent 2	Romans 15: 4-13	Luke 21: 25-33
Advent 3	1 Corinthians 4: 1-5	Matthew 11: 2-10
Advent 4	Philippians 4: 4-7	John 1: 19-28
		CHRISTMAS
Nativity (night)	Titus 2: 11-14	Matthew 1: 18-25
Nativity (day)	Hebrews 1: 1-12	John 1: 1-14
Christmas 1	Galatians 4: 1-7	Matthew 1: 18-25
Christmas 2	1 John 4: 9-16	John 1: 14-18
		EPIPHANY
Epiphany	Ephesians 3: 1-12	Matthew 2: 1-12
Epiphany 1	Romans 12: 1-5	Luke 2: 41-52
Epiphany 2	Romans 12: 6-16a	John 2: 1-11
Epiphany 3	Romans 12: 16b-21	Matthew 8: 1-13
Epiphany 4	Romans 13: 1-7	Matthew 8: 23-34
		BEFORE LENT
5 before Lent	Colossians 3: 12-17	Matthew 13: 24-30
4 before Lent	1 Corinthians 9: 24-27	Matthew 20: 1-16
3 before Lent	1 John 4: 1-6	John 3: 16-21
2 before Lent	2 Corinthians 11: 19-31	Luke 8: 4-15
1 before Lent	1 Corinthians 13: 1-13	Luke 18: 31-43
		LENT
Ash Wednesday	Joel 2: 12-17	Matthew 6: 16-21
Lent 1	2 Corinthians 6: 1-10	Matthew 4: 1-11
Lent 2	1 Thessalonians 4: 1-8	Matthew 15: 21-28
Lent 3	Ephesians 5: 1-14	Luke 11: 14-28
Lent 4	Galatians 4: 21-31	John 6: 1-14
Lent 5	Hebrews 9: 11-15	John 8: 46-59a
Lent 6	Philippians 2: 5-11	Matthew 27: 1-54
Monday in Holy Week	Isaiah 63: 1-19	Mark 14: 1-72
Tuesday in Holy Week	Isaiah 50: 5-11	Mark 15: 1-39
Wednes. in Holy Week	Hebrews 9: 16-28	Luke 22: 1-71
Maundy Thursday	1 Corinthians 11: 23-34	Luke 23: 1-49

| Good Friday | Hebrews 10: 1-25 | John 19: 1-37 |
| Easter Eve | 1 Peter 3: 17-22 | Matthew 27: 57-66 |

EASTER

Easter Day	Colossians 3: 1-7	John 20: 1-10
(A first service)	Hebrews 13: 20-21	Mark 16: 1-8
Monday	Acts 10: 34-43	Luke 24: 13-35
Tuesday	Acts 13: 26-41	Luke 24: 36-48
Easter 2	1 Corinthians 5: 6-8	John 20: 19-23
Easter 3	1 Peter 2: 19-25	John 10: 11-16
Easter 4	1 Peter 2: 11-17	John 16: 16-22
Easter 5	James 1: 17-21	John 16: 5-14
Easter 6	James 1: 22-27	John 16: 23-33
Ascension Day	Acts 1: 1-11	Mark 16: 14-20
Easter 7	1 Peter 4: 7-11	John 15: 26 - 16: 4b
Pentecost	Acts 2: 1-11	John 14: 15-31b

AFTER PENTECOST AND BEFORE ADVENT

| Monday | Acts 10: 34-48 | John 3: 16-21 |
| or Tuesday | Acts 8: 14-17 | John 10: 1-10 |

Trinity Sunday	Revelation 4: 1-11	John 3: 1-15
Trinity 1	1 John 4: 7-21	Luke 16: 19-31
Trinity 2	1 John 3: 13-24	Luke 14: 16b-24
Trinity 3	1 Peter 5: 5-14	Luke 15: 1-10
Trinity 4	Romans 8: 18-23	Luke 6: 36-42
Trinity 5	1 Peter 3: 8-15a	Luke 5: 1-11
Trinity 6	Romans 6: 3-11	Matthew 5: 20-26
Trinity 7	Romans 6: 19-23	Mark 8: 1-9
Trinity 8	Romans 8: 12-17	Matthew 7: 15-21
Trinity 9	1 Corinthians 10: 1-13	Luke 16: 1-9
Trinity 10	1 Corinthians 12: 1-11	Luke 19: 41-47a
Trinity 11	1 Corinthians 15: 1-11	Luke 18: 9-14
Trinity 12	2 Corinthians 3: 4-9	Mark 7: 31-37
Trinity 13	Galatians 3: 16-22	Luke 10: 23-37
Trinity 14	Galatians 5: 16-24	Luke 17: 11-19
Trinity 15	Galatians 6: 11-18	Matthew 6: 24-34
Trinity 16	Ephesians 3: 13-21	Luke 7: 11-17
Trinity 17	Ephesians 4: 1-6	Luke 14: 1-11
Trinity 18	1 Corinthians 1: 4-8	Matthew 22: 34-46
Trinity 19	Ephesians 4: 17-32	Matthew 9: 1-8
Trinity 20	Ephesians 5: 15-21	Matthew 22: 1-14

Trinity 21	Ephesians 6: 10-20	John 4: 46-54
5 before Advent	Philippians 1: 3-11	Matthew 18: 21-35
4 before Advent	Philippians 3: 17-21	Matthew 22: 15-22
3 before Advent	Colossians 1: 3-12	Matthew 9: 18-26
2 before Advent	1 John 3: 1-8	Matthew 24: 23-31
1 before Advent	Jeremiah 23: 5-8	John 6: 5-14

FESTIVALS

Naming & Circumcision	Ephesians 2: 11-18	Luke 2: 15-21
Conversion of St Paul	Acts 9: 1-22	Matthew 19: 27-30
St Brigid	1 John 1: 1-4	John 10: 7-16
Presentation	Malachi 3: 1-5	Luke 2: 22-40
St Patrick	Revelation 22: 1-5	Matthew 10: 16-23
St Joseph	2 Samuel 7: 4, 8-16	Luke 2: 41-52
Annunciation	Isaiah 7: 10-15	Luke 1: 26-38
St Mark	Ephesians 4: 7-16	John 15: 1-11
St Philip & St James	James 1: 1-12	John 14: 1-14
St Matthias	Acts 1: 15-26	Matthew 11: 25-30
Visitation	Romans 12: 9-16b	Luke 1: 39-47
St Columba	2 Corinthians 4: 5-11	Matthew 28: 16-20
St Barnabas	Acts 11: 22-30	John 15: 12-16
Birth of John Baptist	Isaiah 40: 1-11	Luke 1: 57-80
St Peter	Acts 12: 1-11	Matthew 16: 13-19
St Thomas	Ephesians 2: 19-22	John 20: 19-29
St Mary Magdalene	2 Corinthians 5: 14-18	John 20: 1-3, 11-18
St James	Acts 11: 27 - 12: 3a	Matthew 20: 20-28
Transfiguration	2 Peter 1: 12-18	Luke 9: 28-36
St Bartholomew	Acts 5: 12-16	Luke 22: 24-30
Birth of BVM	Isaiah 7: 10-15	Luke 1: 46-55 *or* Luke 2: 1-7
St Matthew	2 Corinthians 4: 1-6	Matthew 9: 9-13
St Michael & All Angels	Revelation 12: 7-12	Matthew 18: 1-10
St Philip the Deacon	Acts 8: 26-40	Matthew 13: 47-52
St Luke	2 Timothy 4: 5-15	Luke 10: 1-7a
St James of Jerusalem	Acts 15: 12-22a	Matthew 13: 54-58
St Simon & St Jude	Jude 1-8	John 15: 17-27
All Saints' Day	Revelation 7: 2-12	Matthew 5: 1-12
St Andrew	Romans 10: 9-21	Matthew 4: 18-22
St Stephen	Acts 7: 55-60	Matthew 23: 34-39
St John	1 John 1: 1-10	John 21: 19-25
Holy Innocents	Revelation 14: 1-5	Matthew 2: 13-18

A Table of Epistles and Gospels 73

DATES OF EASTER 2004 - 2030

The Date of Easter and Other Variable Dates

Year	Ash Wednesday	Easter Day	Ascension Day	Pentecost	Advent 1
2004	25 Feb	11 April	20 May	30 May	28 Nov
2005	9 Feb	27 March	5 May	15 May	27 Nov
2006	1 March	16 April	25 May	4 June	3 Dec
2007	21 Feb	8 April	17 May	27 May	2 Dec
2008	6 Feb	23 March	1 May	11 May	30 Nov
2009	25 Feb	12 April	21 May	31 May	29 Nov
2010	17 Feb	4 April	13 May	23 May	28 Nov
2011	9 March	24 April	2 June	12 June	27 Nov
2012	22 Feb	8 April	17 May	27 May	2 Dec
2013	13 Feb	31 March	9 May	19 May	1 Dec
2014	5 March	20 April	29 May	8 June	30 Nov
2015	18 Feb	5 April	14 May	24 May	29 Nov
2016	10 Feb	27 March	5 May	15 May	27 Nov
2017	1 March	16 April	25 May	4 June	3 Dec
2018	14 Feb	1 April	10 May	20 May	2 Dec
2019	6 March	21 April	30 May	9 June	1 Dec
2020	26 Feb	12 April	21 May	31 May	29 Nov
2021	17 Feb	4 April	13 May	23 May	28 Nov
2022	2 March	17 April	26 May	5 June	27 Nov
2023	22 Feb	9 April	18 May	28 May	3 Dec
2024	14 Feb	31 March	9 May	19 May	1 Dec
2025	5 March	20 April	29 May	8 June	30 Nov
2026	18 Feb	5 April	14 May	24 May	29 Nov
2027	10 Feb	28 March	6 May	16 May	28 Nov
2028	1 March	16 April	25 May	4 June	3 Dec
2029	14 Feb	1 April	10 May	20 May	2 Dec
2030	6 March	21 April	30 May	9 June	1 Dec

GENERAL DIRECTIONS FOR PUBLIC WORSHIP

1 The Holy Communion is the central act of worship of the Church. Morning and Evening Prayer are other regular services of public worship. One of the forms of Service of the Word may replace Morning or Evening Prayer at the discretion of the Minister. It is the privilege and duty of members of the Church to join in public worship on the Lord's Day as the weekly commemoration of Christ's Resurrection, and on the principal holy days. Holy Communion is to be celebrated on the principal holy days as set out in the Calendar and regularly on Sundays and festivals for which provision is made in this book.

2 Services in Irish. Worship in the Church of Ireland may be conducted in the Irish language, or in other languages understood by those present.

3 Notes and Rubrics. The notes incorporated into the services in this book give guidance and directions as to how a service is to be ordered and have deliberately been kept to a minimum and simplified to facilitate an acceptable flexibility. When a certain posture is particularly appropriate, it is indicated thus: *Stand* or *Kneel*. Where a rubric states that a section is to be 'said', this is to be understood to include 'or sung' and vice versa.

4 Bible Versions. Any translation of the scriptures sanctioned by the House of Bishops for use in public worship may be used. References in tables of readings are to the versification of the *New Revised Standard Version* 1989. Those to psalms are to the psalter in this book.

5 Readings. The passages to be read on Sundays, principal holy days and festivals are set out in the Table of Readings (pages 24ff). Readings for weekdays may be found in the table of weekday readings as approved by the House of Bishops. Readings are announced in the following way: 'A reading from (*Book*), chapter..., beginning at verse....'

6 Hymns may be sung at appropriate points in any service, either as directed or at the discretion of the presiding minister. In the selection of

hymns careful attention should be given to ensure that they are appropriate to the Bible readings and sermon.

7 Musical Settings. Where parts of the service are sung to a musical setting, the words for which the setting were composed may be used.

8 Sermon. A sermon or homily should be preached on Sundays and on principal holy days.

9 Silence. The Great Silence is prescribed in Holy Communion Two. Periods of silence may be kept as indicated and at any other point in services at the discretion of the presiding minister.

10 Holy Baptism is normally administered at the principal service on a Sunday or holy day. Baptism should be preceded by appropriate preparation.

11 Weekday Services. Shorter forms of Morning and Evening Prayer are provided for weekdays, as are Compline, a Late Evening Office and an order for daily prayer. Holy Communion Two may be shortened as specified in the notes of that service. The readings at the Holy Communion may be those from the table of weekday readings approved by the House of Bishops, the Gospel reading always being included.

12 State Prayers. Wherever words in any service are enclosed in square brackets to which N.I. is prefixed, such words are to be used in Northern Ireland only; and wherever words are enclosed in square brackets to which R.I. is prefixed, such words are to be used in the Republic of Ireland only.
For churches and chapels in Northern Ireland, the archbishop of Armagh may direct any alterations that may be required from time to time in prayers which relate to the sovereign or members of the Royal Family.

13 Absolution. At Morning and Evening Prayer One and elsewhere in this book when the presiding minister is a deacon or a reader and where no provision is made, instead of the absolution, the collect of the Twenty-first Sunday after Trinity may be used, or a short period of silence may be kept.

14 At the Holy Communion.

(a) Members of the Church should partake of the Lord's Supper regularly and frequently after careful preparation.

(b) The priest who presides at the Holy Communion must be episcopally ordained. The Gospel should be read, where possible, by a deacon. The bishop of the diocese may permit lay persons approved by him to assist the priest in the administration of the bread and wine.

(c) Holy Communion shall not be celebrated unless there is at least one person present to communicate together with the priest.

(d) At the time of the celebration of the Holy Communion the communion table is to be covered by a white cloth.

(e) The bread to be used shall be the best and purest bread that can be obtained. Care is to be taken that the wine is fit for use.

Any of the consecrated bread and wine remaining after the administration of the communion is to be reverently consumed.

(f) After the communion the vessels shall be carefully and thoroughly cleansed with water.

15 Giving. Members of the Church should give generously, regularly and proportionately, towards the ministry and mission of the Church, and to works of charity.

SENTENCES OF SCRIPTURE

These may be used at Morning Prayer or Evening Prayer or at Holy Communion Two as indicated in those services.

Seek the Lord while he may be found, call upon him while he is near. *Isaiah 55: 6*

God is spirit, and those who worship him must worship in spirit and in truth. *John 4: 24*

In everything by prayer and supplication with thanksgiving let your requests be made known to God. *Philippians 4: 6*

Through Christ let us continually offer a sacrifice of praise to God, that is, the fruit of lips that acknowledge his name. *Hebrews 13: 15*

To the only God our Saviour, through Jesus Christ our Lord, be glory, majesty, dominion, and authority, before all time and now and for ever. Amen. *Jude 25*

Worship the Lord in the beauty of holiness: let the whole earth stand in awe of him. *Psalm 96: 9*

Those who wait for the Lord shall renew their strength, they shall mount up with wings like eagles, they shall run and not be weary, they shall walk and not faint. *Isaiah 40: 31*

SEASONAL

First Sunday of Advent to December 24

The glory of the Lord shall be revealed, and all people shall see it together. *Isaiah 40: 5*

Repent, for the kingdom of heaven is at hand. *Matthew 3: 2*

Christmas

To us a child is born, to us a son is given, and the government will be on his shoulders. And he will be called Wonderful Counsellor, Mighty God, Everlasting Father, Prince of Peace. *Isaiah 9: 6*

I bring you good news of great joy that will be for all the people. Today in the town of David a Saviour has been born to you; he is Christ the Lord. *Luke 2: 10,11*

God's love was revealed among us in this way: God sent his only Son into the world so that we might live through him. *1 John 4: 9*

Epiphany

From the rising of the sun to its setting my name is great among the nations, and in every place incense is offered to my name, and a pure offering; for my name is great among the nations, says the Lord. *Malachi 1: 11*

God who said, 'out of darkness light shall shine', has caused his light to shine in our hearts, the light which is knowledge of the glory of God in the face of Jesus Christ. *2 Corinthians 4: 6 (REB)*

The grace of God has appeared, bringing salvation to all. *Titus 2: 11*

Ordinary Time – Before Lent

Jesus said: 'Come to me, all who are weary and burdened, and I will give you rest.' *Matthew 11: 28*

Ash Wednesday to Fourth Sunday in Lent

The sacrifice acceptable to God is a broken spirit; a broken and contrite heart, O God, you will not despise. *Psalm 51: 17*

To the Lord our God belong mercy and forgiveness, for we have rebelled against him, and have not obeyed the voice of the Lord our God by following his laws, which he set before us. *Daniel 9: 9,10*

Fifth Sunday of Lent to Good Friday

Jesus said: 'For their sake I consecrate myself, that they too may be consecrated by the truth.' *John 17: 19*

God proves his love for us in that while we still were sinners Christ died for us. *Romans 5: 8*

Christ himself bore our sins in his body on the tree, so that we might die to sin and live for righteousness. By his wounds you have been healed. *1 Peter 2: 24*

We have been buried with Christ by baptism into death, so that, just as Christ was raised from the dead by the glory of the Father, so we too might walk in newness of life. *Romans 6: 4*

Blessed be the God and Father of our Lord Jesus Christ! By his great mercy he has given us a new birth into a living hope through the resurrection of Jesus Christ from the dead. *1 Peter 1: 3*

Since we have a great high priest who has passed through the heavens, Jesus, the Son of God, let us hold fast to the faith we profess. *Hebrews 4: 14,16*

God's love has been poured into our hearts through the Holy Spirit that has been given to us. *Romans 5: 5*

Round the throne of God, day and night they never cease to sing, 'Holy, holy, holy is the Lord God Almighty, who was and is and is to come.' *Revelation 4: 8*

Jesus said: 'You will receive power when the Holy Spirit has come upon you; and you will be my witnesses.' *Acts 1: 8*

If anyone is in Christ, there is a new creation: everything old has passed away; see, everything has become new. *2 Corinthians 5: 17*

In Christ God was reconciling the world to himself. *2 Corinthians 5: 19*

Jesus said: 'Remember, I am with you always, to the end of the age.' *Matthew 28: 20*

Our help is in the name of the Lord, who made heaven and earth. *Psalm 124: 7*

Since we are surrounded by so great a cloud of witnesses, let us also lay aside every weight, and the sin which clings so closely, and let us run with perseverance the race that is set before us, looking to Jesus the pioneer and perfecter of our faith. *Hebrews 12: 1,2*

The righteous will be remembered for ever; the memory of the righteous is a blessing. *Psalm 112: 6, Proverbs 10: 7*

Rogation and Harvest

The earth is the Lord's and all that is in it. *Psalm 24: 1*

Times of thanksgiving

Let the nations be glad and sing for joy, for you judge the peoples with equity and guide the nations upon earth. *Psalm 67: 4*

O give thanks to the Lord, call on his name; make known his deeds among the peoples. Sing to him, sing praises to him: tell of all his marvellous works. *Psalm 105: 1,2*

Times of trouble

God is our refuge and strength, a very present help in trouble. *Psalm 46: 1*

PENITENTIAL

When the wicked turn away from the wickedness they have committed and do what is lawful and right, they shall save their life. *Ezekiel 18: 27*

I know my transgressions, and my sin is ever before me. *Psalm 51: 3*

Hide your face from my sins, and blot out all my iniquities. *Psalm 51: 9*

The sacrifice acceptable to God is a broken spirit: a broken and a contrite heart, O God, you will not despise. *Psalm 51: 17*

Rend your hearts and not your clothing. Return to the Lord, your God: for he is gracious and merciful, slow to anger, and abounding in steadfast love, and relents from punishing. *Joel 2: 13*

To the Lord our God belong mercy and forgiveness, for we have rebelled against him, and have not obeyed the voice of the Lord our God by following his laws, which he set before us. *Daniel 9: 9,10*

Correct me, Lord, but in just measure; not in your anger, or you will bring me to nothing. *Jeremiah 10: 24*

Repent, for the kingdom of heaven is at hand. *Matthew 3: 2*

I will arise and go to my father, and I will say unto him, Father, I have sinned against heaven, and before you; I am no longer worthy to be called your son. *Luke 15: 18,19*

Do not enter not into judgement with your servant, O Lord; for no one living is righteous before you. *Psalm 143: 2*

If we say that we have no sin, we deceive ourselves, and the truth is not in us. If we confess our sins, he who is faithful and just will forgive us our sins, and cleanse us from all unrighteousness. *1 John 1: 8,9*

Morning and Evening Prayer

MORNING AND EVENING PRAYER

SENTENCES OF SCRIPTURE

Minister

When the wicked man turneth away from his wickedness that he hath committed, and doeth that which is lawful and right, he shall save his soul alive.

Ezekiel 18: 27

I acknowledge my transgressions: and my sin is ever before me.

Psalm 51: 3

Hide thy face from my sins, and blot out all mine iniquities. *Psalm 51: 9*

The sacrifices of God are a broken spirit: a broken and a contrite heart, O God, thou wilt not despise. *Psalm 51: 17*

Rend your heart, and not your garments, and turn unto the Lord your God: for he is gracious and merciful, slow to anger, and of great kindness, and repenteth him of the evil. *Joel 2: 13*

To the Lord our God belong mercies and forgivenesses, though we have rebelled against him: neither have we obeyed the voice of the Lord our God, to walk in his laws which he set before us. *Daniel 9: 9,10*

O Lord, correct me, but with judgement; not in thine anger, lest thou bring me to nothing. *Jeremiah 10: 24; Psalm 6: 1*

Repent ye; for the kingdom of heaven is at hand. *Matthew 3: 2*

I will arise and go to my father, and will say unto him, Father, I have sinned against heaven, and before thee, and am no more worthy to be called thy son. *Luke 15: 18,19*

Enter not into judgment with thy servant, O Lord; for in thy sight shall no man living be justified. *Psalm 143: 2*

If we say that we have no sin, we deceive ourselves, and the truth is not in us; but if we confess our sins, he is faithful and just to forgive us our sins, and to cleanse us from all unrighteousness. *1 John 1: 8,9*

Behold, I bring you good tidings of great joy, which shall be to all people: for unto you is born this day, in the city of David, a Saviour, which is Christ the Lord.
Luke 2: 10,11

(*For* EASTER)
Christ is risen from the dead, and become the first-fruits of them that slept.
1 Corinthians 15: 20

(*For* ASCENSION)
Him hath God exalted with his right hand to be a Prince and a Saviour, for to give repentance to Israel, and forgiveness of sins.
Acts 5: 31

(*For* WHITSUNTIDE)
If ye then, being evil, know how to give good gifts unto your children, how much more shall your heavenly Father give the Holy Spirit to them, that ask him?
Luke 11: 13

The minister says this Exhortation, or a portion of it:
Dearly beloved brethren, the Scripture moveth us in sundry places to acknowledge and confess our manifold sins and wickedness; and that we should not dissemble nor cloke them before the face of almighty God our heavenly Father; but confess them with an humble, lowly, penitent and obedient heart; to the end that we may obtain forgiveness of the same, by his infinite goodness and mercy. And although we ought at all times humbly to acknowledge our sins before God; yet ought we most chiefly so to do, when we assemble and meet together to render thanks for the great benefits that we have received at his hands, to set forth his most worthy praise, to hear his most holy Word, and to ask those things which are requisite and necessary, as well for the body as the soul. Wherefore I pray and beseech you, as many as are here present, to accompany me with a pure heart, and humble voice, unto the throne of the heavenly grace, saying after me:

Instead of the Exhortation the minister may say
Let us humbly confess our sins unto almighty God.

Kneel

Almighty and most merciful Father; We have erred and strayed from thy ways like lost sheep. We have followed too much the devices and desires of our own hearts. We have offended against thy holy laws. We have left undone those things which we ought to have done; And we have done those things which we ought not to have done; And there is no health in us. But thou, O Lord, have mercy upon us, miserable offenders. Spare thou them, O God, which confess their faults. Restore thou them that are penitent; According to thy promises declared unto mankind in Christ Jesus our Lord. And grant, O most merciful Father, for his sake; That we may hereafter live a godly, righteous, and sober life, To the glory of thy holy Name. Amen.

The Absolution

or Remission of sins is pronounced by the priest alone.

Almighty God, the Father of our Lord Jesus Christ, who desireth not the death of a sinner, but rather that he may turn from his wickedness, and live; and hath given power, and commandment, to his Ministers, to declare and pronounce to his people, being penitent, the Absolution and Remission of their sins: He pardoneth and absolveth all them that truly repent, and unfeignedly believe his holy Gospel. Wherefore let us beseech him to grant us true repentance, and his Holy Spirit, that those things may please him which we do at this present; and that the rest of our life hereafter may be pure and holy; so that at the last we may come to his eternal joy; through Jesus Christ our Lord. **Amen.**

The Lord's Prayer

Our Father, who art in heaven, Hallowed be thy Name, Thy kingdom come, Thy will be done, On earth as it is in heaven. Give us this day our daily bread. And forgive us our trespasses, As we forgive those who trespass against us. And lead us not into temptation, But deliver us from evil. For thine is the kingdom, The power, And the glory, For ever and ever. Amen.

O Lord, open thou our lips
and our mouth shall show forth thy praise.

O God, make speed to save us.
O Lord, make haste to help us.

Stand

Glory be to the Father, and to the Son, and to the Holy Spirit;
as it was in the beginning, is now, and ever shall be, world without end.
Amen.

Praise ye the Lord.
The Lord's name be praised.

At Evening Prayer turn to page 93

AT MORNING PRAYER

VENITE *is said or sung.*
Psalm 95

1   O come let us | sing un·to the | Lord; ▪
    let us heartily rejoice in the | strength of | our sal|vation.

2   Let us come before his | presence · with | thanksgiving ▪
    and show ourselves | glad in | him with | psalms.

3   For the Lord is a | great | God ▪
    and a great | King a·bove | all | gods.

4   In his hand are all the | corners · of the | earth ▪
    and the strength of the | hills is | his | also.

5† The sea is his and | he | made it, ▪
    and his | hands pre|pared the · dry | land.

6   O come let us worship and | fall | down ▪
    and kneel be|fore the | Lord our | Maker.

7   For he is the | Lord our | God; ▪
    and we are the people of his pasture, | and the | sheep of · his | hand.

8   Today if ye will | hear his | voice: ▪
    harden not your hearts, as in the provocation
        and as in the day of temp|tation | in the | wilderness;

9   When your | fathers | tempted me, ▪
     provèd | me and | saw my | works.

10   Forty years long was I grieved with this gener|ation · and | said, ▪
     It is a people that do err in their hearts,
        for they | have not | known my | ways.

11   Unto whom I sware | in my | wrath, ▪
     that they should not | enter | into · my | rest.

        Glory | be · to the | Father, ▪
        and to the Son, | and · to the | Holy | Spirit;
        as it | was in · the be|ginning, ▪
        is now and ever shall be, | world with·out | end. A|men.

On Ash Wednesday and Good Friday Venite *may be omitted.*

On Easter Day and seven days after

THE EASTER ANTHEMS

1 Corinthians 5: 7,8   Romans 6: 9-11   1 Corinthians 15: 20-22

1   Christ our passover is | sacri·ficed | for us, ▪
     therefore | let us | keep the | feast,

2   Not with the old leaven
        nor with the leaven of | malice · and | wickedness: ▪
     but with the unleavened bread | of sin|cerity · and | truth.

3   Christ being raised from the dead | dieth · no | more; ▪
     death hath no | more do|minion | over him.

4   For in that he died, he died unto | sin | once; ▪
     but in that he liveth, he | liveth | unto | God.

5   Likewise reckon ye also yourselves to be dead indeed | unto | sin; ▪
     but alive unto God through | Jesus | Christ our | Lord.

6   Christ is | risen · from the | dead: ▪
     and become the | first-fruits of | them that | slept.

7   For since by | man came | death, ▪
     by man came also the resur|rection | of the | dead.

8   For as in Adam | all | die, ▪
     even so in Christ shall | all be | made a|live.

        Glory | be · to the | Father, ▪
        and to the Son, | and · to the | Holy | Spirit;
        as it | was in · the be|ginning, ▪
        is now and ever shall be, | world with·out | end. A|men.

THE PSALM OR PSALMS

Glory I be · to the I Father, ■
and to the Son, I and · to the I Holy I Spirit;
as it I was in · the be|ginning, ■
is now and ever shall be, I world with·out I end. A|men.
is repeated at the end of every Psalm.

A Lesson

from the Old Testament is read.
If three lessons are used the Lesson is from the New Testament.

TE DEUM

1   We praise I thee O I God, ■
    we acknowledge I thee to I be the I Lord.
2   All the earth doth I worship I thee, ■
    the I Father I ever|lasting.
3   To thee all angels cry aloud
        the heavens and all the I powers there|in, ■
    to thee Cherubim and Seraphim con|tin·ual|ly do I cry,
4   Holy,| Holy,| Holy,| Lord I God · of Sa|baoth: ■
    heaven and earth are full of the I majes·ty I of thy I glory.
5   The glorious company of the apostles I praise I thee; ■
    the goodly fellowship of the I prophets I praise I thee.
6   The I noble I army ■ _of I martyrs I praise I thee.
7   The I holy I Church ■
    throughout all the world I doth ac|knowledge I thee;
8   The Father of an I infin·ite I majesty, ■
    thine honourable, true, and only Son
        also the I Holy I Spirit · the I Comforter.

9   Thou art the King of I glory · O I Christ. ■
    Thou art the ever|lasting I Son of · the I Father.
10 When thou tookest upon thee to de|liver I man, ■
    thou didst not ab|hor the I Virgin's I womb.

11† When thou hadst overcome the | sharpness · of | death, ▪
   thou didst open the kingdom of | heaven · to | all be|lievers.

12 Thou sittest at the right | hand of | God: ▪
   in the | glory | of the | Father.

13 We be|lieve that | thou ▪＿shalt | come to | be our | judge.

14 We therefore pray thee | help thy | servants, ▪
   whom thou hast re|deemed · with thy | precious | blood.

15 Make them to be numbered | with thy | saints ▪
   in | glory | ever|lasting.

16 O Lord, save thy people and | bless thine | heritage:▪
   govern them and | lift them | up for | ever.

17 Day by day we | magni·fy | thee: ▪
   and we worship thy Name ever, | world with|out | end.

18 Vouch|safe, O | Lord, ▪
   to | keep us · this | day with·out | sin.

19 O Lord, have | mercy · up|on us, ▪
   have | mercy · up|on | us.

20 O Lord, let thy mercy | lighten · up|on us, ▪
   as our | trust | is in | thee.

21 O Lord, in | thee · have I | trusted: ▪
   let me | never | be con|founded.

or BENEDICITE *(page 124)*

or URBS FORTITUDINIS *Isaiah 26: 1-4,7,8*

1 We have a | strong | city: ▪
   salvation will God ap|point for | walls and | bulwarks.

2 Open | ye the | gates: ▪
   that the righteous nation which keepeth the | truth may | enter | in.

3 Thou wilt keep him in perfect peace whose mind is | stayed on | thee ▪
   be|cause he | trusteth · in | thee.

4 Trust ye in the | Lord for | ever: ▪
   for our rock of | ages | is the | Lord.

5 The way of the | just is | uprightness; ▪
   thou that art upright dost di|rect the | path · of the | just.

6   Yea in the way of thy judgements O Lord have we | waited · for | thee; ▪
     the desire of our soul is to thy Name, |
         and · to the re|membrance · of | thee.
         Glory | be · to the | Father, ▪
         and to the Son, | and · to the | Holy | Spirit;
         as it | was in · the be|ginning, ▪
         is now and ever shall be, | world with·out | end. A|men.

or LAUDATE DOMINUM *Psalm 148*

A LESSON
from the New Testament is read.
If three lessons are used this is always a Gospel reading.

BENEDICTUS
The Song of Zechariah   Luke 1: 68-79

1   Blessèd be the Lord | God of | Israel, ▪
     for he hath visited | and re|deemed his | people,

2   And hath raised up a mighty sal|vation | for us ▪
     in the | house of · his | servant | David;

3   As he spake by the mouth of his | holy | Prophets ▪
     which have been | since the | world be|gan;

4   That we should be | saved · from our | enemies, ▪
     and from the | hands of | all that | hate us,

5   To perform the mercy | promised · to our | forefathers, ▪
     and to re|member · his | holy | covenant;

6   To perform the oath which he sware to our | fore·father | Abraham: ▪
     that | he would | give | us,

7   That we being delivered out of the | hand of · our | enemies ▪
     might serve | him with|out | fear,

8   In holiness and | righteous·ness be|fore him ▪
     all the | days | of our | life.

9   And thou, child, shalt be called the | Prophet · of the | Highest, ▪
     for thou shalt go before the face of the | Lord · to pre|pare his | ways;

10   To give knowledge of salvation | unto · his | people, ▪
     for the re|mission | of their | sins,

11 Through the tender mercy | of our | God ▪
   whereby the day-spring from on | high hath | visit·ed | us,

12 To give light to them that sit in darkness
   and in the | shadow · of | death, ▪
   and to guide our feet | into · the | way of | peace.

   Glory | be · to the | Father, ▪
   and to the Son, | and · to the | Holy | Spirit;
   as it | was in · the be|ginning, ▪
   is now and ever shall be, | world with·out | end. A|men.

or JUBILATE *Psalm 100*

1 O be joyful in the Lord | all ye | lands; ▪
   serve the Lord with gladness
   and come before his | presence | with a | song.

2 Be ye sure that the Lord | he is | God; ▪
   it is he that hath made us and not we ourselves
   we are his people | and the | sheep of · his | pasture.

3 O go your way into his gates with thanksgiving
   and into his | courts with | praise; ▪
   be thankful unto him and speak | good of | his | name.

4 For the Lord is gracious, his mercy is | ever|lasting, ▪
   and his truth endureth from gener|ation · to | gener|ation.

   Glory | be · to the | Father, ▪
   and to the Son, | and · to the | Holy | Spirit;
   as it | was in · the be|ginning, ▪
   is now and ever shall be, | world with·out | end. A|men.

Continue on page 95 with the Apostles' Creed

THE PSALM OR PSALMS

A LESSON
from the Old Testament is read.

MAGNIFICAT *The Song of the Blessed Virgin Mary Luke 1: 46-55*

1   My soul doth | magni·fy the | Lord, ▪
    and my spirit hath re|joiced in | God my | Saviour.

2   For | he · hath re|garded ▪‿
    the lowliness | of his | hand|maiden.

3   For be|hold from | henceforth ▪
    all gener|ations · shall | call me | blessèd.

4   For he that is mighty hath | magni·fied | me, ▪
    and | holy | is his | Name.

5† And his mercy is on | them that | fear him ▪
    through|out all | gener|ations.

6   He hath showèd | strength · with his | arm, ▪
    he hath scattered the proud, in the imagin|ation | of their | hearts.

7   He hath put down the mighty | from their | seat ▪
    and hath ex|alted · the | humble · and | meek.

8   He hath filled the hungry with | good | things ▪
    and the rich | he hath · sent | empty · a|way.

9   He remembering his mercy hath holpen his | servant | Israel, ▪
    as he promised to our forefathers, Abraham | and his | seed for | ever.

        Glory | be · to the | Father, ▪
        and to the Son, | and · to the | Holy | Spirit;
        as it | was in · the be|ginning, ▪
        is now and ever shall be, | world with·out | end. A|men.

or CANTATE DOMINO *Psalm 98 (page 133)*

A LESSON
from the New Testament is read.

NUNC DIMITTIS *The Song of Simeon Luke 2: 29-32*

1   Lord, now lettest thou thy servant de|part in | peace: ▪
    ac|cording | to thy | word.

2   For mine eyes have seen | thy sal|vation ▪
    which thou hast prepared be|fore the | face of · all | people;

3   To be a light to | lighten · the | Gentiles ▪
    and to be the glory of thy | people | Isra|el.

        Glory | be · to the | Father, ▪
        and to the Son, | and · to the | Holy | Spirit;
        as it | was in · the be|ginning, ▪
        is now and ever shall be, | world with·out | end. A|men.

or DEUS MISEREATUR *Psalm 67 (page 134)*

I believe in God, the Father almighty,
maker of heaven and earth;
And in Jesus Christ his only Son our Lord;
who was conceived by the Holy Spirit,
born of the Virgin Mary,
suffered under Pontius Pilate,
was crucified, dead, and buried.
He descended into hell.
The third day he rose again from the dead.
He ascended into heaven,
and sitteth on the right hand of God the Father almighty.
From thence he shall come to judge the quick and the dead.
I believe in the Holy Spirit,
the holy catholic Church,
the communion of saints,
the forgiveness of sins,
the resurrection of the body,
and the life everlasting. Amen.

The Lord be with you
and with thy Spirit.

Kneel
Let us pray.
Lord, have mercy upon us.
Christ, have mercy upon us.
Lord, have mercy upon us.

Our Father, who art in heaven, Hallowed be thy Name, Thy kingdom come, Thy will be done, On earth as it is in heaven. Give us this day our daily bread. And forgive us our trespasses, As we forgive those who trespass against us. And lead us not into temptation, But deliver us from evil. Amen.

The minister stands and says
O Lord, show thy mercy upon us
and grant us thy salvation.

N.I. [O Lord, save the Queen]
R.I. [O Lord, guide and defend our rulers]
and mercifully hear us when we call upon thee.

Endue thy ministers with righteousness
and make thy chosen people joyful.

O Lord, save thy people
and bless thine inheritance.

Give peace in our time, O Lord,
because there is none other that fighteth for us, but only thou, O God.

O God, make clean our hearts within us
and take not thy Holy Spirit from us.

THE COLLECTS
The Collect of the day is said and the following collects:

AT MORNING PRAYER

THE SECOND COLLECT *For Peace*

O God, who art the author of peace and lover of concord, in knowledge of whom standeth our eternal life, whose service is perfect freedom; Defend us thy humble servants in all assaults of our enemies; that we, surely trusting in thy defence, may not fear the power of any adversaries; through the might of Jesus Christ our Lord. **Amen.**

THE THIRD COLLECT *For Grace*

O Lord, our heavenly Father, almighty and everlasting God, who hast safely brought us to the beginning of this day: Defend us in the same with thy mighty power; and grant that this day we fall into no sin, neither run into any kind of danger; but that all our doings may be ordered by thy governance, to do always that is righteous in thy sight; through Jesus Christ our Lord. **Amen.**

AT EVENING PRAYER

THE SECOND COLLECT *For Peace*

O God, from whom all holy desires, all good counsels and all just works do proceed; Give unto thy servants that peace which the world cannot give; that both, our hearts may be set to obey thy commandments, and also that by thee we being defended from the fear of our enemies may pass our time in rest and quietness; through the merits of Jesus Christ our Saviour. **Amen.**

THE THIRD COLLECT *For Aid against all Perils*

Lighten our darkness, we beseech thee, O Lord: and by thy great mercy defend us from all perils and dangers of this night; for the love of thy only Son, our Saviour Jesus Christ. **Amen.**

or For Grace and Protection

O Almighty Lord, and everlasting God, vouchsafe, we beseech thee, to direct, sanctify and govern both our hearts and bodies, in the ways of thy laws, and in the works of thy commandments; that through thy most mighty protection, both here and ever, we may be preserved in body and soul; through our Lord and Saviour Jesus Christ. **Amen.**

AN ANTHEM OR HYMN *may be sung.*

A SERMON *may be preached here*
or after the following prayers.

PRAYERS
The prayers always conclude with A Prayer of Saint Chrysostom
and THE GRACE.

N.I. [A Prayer for the Queen's *Majesty*

O Lord, our heavenly Father, high and mighty, King of kings, Lord of lords, the only Ruler of princes, who dost from thy throne behold all dwellers upon earth: Most heartily we beseech thee with thy favour to behold our most gracious Sovereign *Lady, Queen ELIZABETH*; and so replenish *her* with the grace of thy Holy Spirit, that *she* may alway incline to thy will, and walk in thy way: Endue *her* plenteously with heavenly gifts; grant *her* in health and wealth long to live; strengthen *her* that *she* may vanquish and overcome all *her* enemies; and finally, after this life, *she* may attain everlasting joy and felicity; through Jesus Christ our Lord. **Amen.**]

N.I. [A Prayer for the Royal Family

Almighty God, the fountain of all goodness, we humbly beseech thee to bless *   and all the Royal Family: Endue them with thy Holy Spirit; enrich them with thy heavenly grace; prosper them with all happiness; and bring them to thine everlasting kingdom; through Jesus Christ our Lord. **Amen.**]

Here shall be inserted the names and titles of members of the Royal Family as directed.

N.I. [A Prayer for the High Court of Parliament

Most gracious God, we humbly beseech thee, as for this kingdom in general, so especially for the High Court of Parliament, at this time assembled, that thou wouldest be pleased to direct and prosper all their consultations to the advancement of thy glory, the good of thy Church, the safety, honour, and welfare of our Sovereign, and *her* Dominions; that all things may be so ordered and settled by their endeavours upon the best and surest foundations, that peace and happiness, truth and justice, religion and piety, may be established among us for all generations. These and all other necessaries, for them, for us, and thy whole Church, we humbly beg in the Name and Mediation of Jesus Christ our most blessed Lord and Saviour. **Amen.**]

R.I. [A prayer for the President and all in authority

Almighty God, who rulest over the kingdoms of the world; We commend to thy merciful care the people of this land, that being guarded by thy providence, they may dwell secure in thy peace. Grant to the President of this State and to all in authority, wisdom and strength to know and to do thy will. Fill them with the love of truth and righteousness, that they may serve thy people faithfully to thy honour and glory; through Jesus Christ our Lord. **Amen.**]

R.I. [A prayer for the Houses of the Oireachtas

Almighty God, source of all authority and wisdom: guide by your Spirit those who represent us in Dáil and Seanad. As representatives of the people keep them humble, as legislators make them compassionate, and as politicians defend their integrity. So may the proceedings of the Oireachtas serve the truth and promote the common good. We pray in the name of Jesus Christ, the servant Lord. **Amen.**]

A Prayer for the Clergy and People

Almighty and everlasting God, who alone workest great marvels: Send down upon our Bishops and Clergy, and all People committed to their charge, the healthful Spirit of thy grace; and that they may truly please thee, pour upon them the continual dew of thy blessing. Grant this, O Lord, for the honour of our Advocate and Mediator, Jesus Christ. **Amen.**

O God, the Creator and Preserver of all mankind, we humbly beseech thee for all sorts and conditions of men; that thou wouldest be pleased to make thy ways known unto them, thy saving health unto all nations. More especially, we pray for the good estate of the Catholic Church; that it may be so guided and governed by thy good Spirit, that all who profess and call themselves Christians may be led into the way of truth, and hold the faith in unity of spirit, in the bond of peace, and in righteousness of life. Finally, we commend to thy fatherly goodness all those who are any ways afflicted or distressed, in mind, body, or estate; [*especially those for whom our prayers are desired*]; that it may please thee to comfort and relieve them according to their several necessities, giving them patience under their sufferings, and a happy issue out of all their afflictions. And this we beg for Jesus Christ his sake. **Amen.**

A General Thanksgiving

Almighty God, Father of all mercies, We thine unworthy servants Do give thee most humble and hearty thanks For all thy goodness and loving-kindness to us, and to all men. We bless thee for our creation, preservation and all the blessings of this life: But above all, for thine inestimable love In the redemption of the world by our Lord Jesus Christ; For the means of grace, and for the hope of glory.

And, we beseech thee, give us that due sense of all thy mercies, That our hearts may be unfeignedly thankful, And that we show forth thy praise, Not only with our lips but in our lives; By giving up ourselves to thy service, And by walking before thee in holiness and righteousness all our days; Through Jesus Christ our Lord, To whom with thee and the Holy Spirit Be all honour and glory, World without end. Amen.

A Prayer of Saint Chrysostom

Almighty God, who hast given us grace at this time with one accord to make our common supplications unto thee; and dost promise that when two or three are gathered together in thy Name thou wilt grant their requests: Fulfil now, O Lord, the desires and petitions of thy servants as may be most expedient for them; granting us in this world knowledge of thy truth, and in the world to come life everlasting. **Amen.**

The grace of our Lord Jesus Christ, and the love of God, and the fellowship of the Holy Spirit, be with us all evermore. **Amen.** *2 Corinthians 13: 14*

AN ORDER FOR
MORANING AND EVENING PRAYER
DAILY THROUGHOUT THE YEAR

The Gathering of God's People

Stand
The Greeting is said.
The Lord be with you
and also with you.

On Easter Day
Christ is risen.
The Lord is risen indeed. Alleluia! *Luke 24: 34*

SENTENCES OF SCRIPTURE

A sentence of scripture may be read from those provided on pages 78-82.

A hymn may be sung.

The minister may introduce the service in these or other suitable words:
Beloved in Christ,
we come together to offer to Almighty God
our worship and praise and thanksgiving,
to confess our sins and to receive God's forgiveness,
to hear his holy word proclaimed,
to bring before him our needs and the needs of the world,
and to pray that in the power of his Spirit
we may serve him and know the greatness of his love.

The minister says
Let us confess our sins to God our Father.

Kneel. Silence is kept.

Heavenly Father,
we have sinned against you and against our neighbour
in thought and word and deed,
through negligence, through weakness,
through our own deliberate fault;
by what we have done
and by what we have failed to do.
We are truly sorry and repent of all our sins.
For the sake of your Son Jesus Christ who died for us,
forgive us all that is past;
and grant that we may serve you in newness of life
to the glory of your name. Amen.

The priest pronounces the absolution.
Almighty God, who forgives all who truly repent,
have mercy on you,
pardon and deliver you from all your sins,
confirm and strengthen you in all goodness,
and keep you in eternal life;
through Jesus Christ our Lord. **Amen.**

*If no priest is present the absolution is omitted and the following prayer may
be said:*
Merciful Lord,
grant to your faithful people pardon and peace,
that we may be cleansed from all our sins,
and serve you with a quiet mind;
through Jesus Christ our Lord. **Amen.**

Proclaiming and Receiving the Word

At Evening Prayer turn to page 109

AT MORNING PRAYER

Stand

O Lord, open our lips
and our mouth will proclaim your praise.

O God, make speed to save us.
O Lord, make haste to help us.

Glory to the Father, and to the Son, and to the Holy Spirit;
as it was in the beginning, is now, and shall be for ever. Amen.

Praise the Lord.
The Lord's name be praised.

FIRST CANTICLE

VENITE *Psalm 95: 1-7 or 1-11*

1   O come let us sing ǀ out · to the ǀ Lord; ▪
    let us shout in triumph to the ǀ rock of ǀ our salǀvation.

2   Let us come before his ǀ face with ǀ thanksgiving ▪
    and cry ǀ out · to him ǀ joyfully · in ǀ psalms.

3   For the Lord is a ǀ great ǀ God ▪
    and a great ǀ king aˑbove ǀ all ǀ gods.

4   In his hand are the ǀ depths · of the ǀ earth ▪
    and the peaks of the ǀ mountains · are ǀ his ǀ also.

5† The sea is his and ǀ he ǀ made it, ▪
    his hands ǀ moulded ǀ dry ǀ land.

6   Come let us worship and ǀ bow ǀ down ▪
    and kneel beǀfore the ǀ Lord our ǀ maker.

7   For he is the ǀ Lord our ǀ God; ▪
    we are his ǀ people · and the ǀ sheep of · his ǀ pasture.

8   Today if only you would | hear his | voice, ▪
do not harden your | hearts · as you | did · in the | wilderness;

9   When your | forebears | tested me, ▪
put me to the proof though | they had | seen my | works.

10   Forty years long I loathed that gene|ration · and | said, ▪
It is a people who err in their hearts,
    for they | do not | know my | ways;

11   Of whom I | swore · in my | wrath, ▪
They | shall not | enter · my | rest.
    Glory to the Father, and | to the | Son, ▪
    and | to the | Holy | Spirit;
    as it was in the be|ginning, is | now, ▪
    and shall be for | ever. | A|men.

or

JUBILATE *Psalm 100*

1   O shout to the Lord in triumph | all the | earth; ▪
serve the Lord with gladness
    and come before his | face with | songs of | joy.

2   Know that the Lord | he is | God; ▪
it is he who has made us and we are his
    we are his | people · and the | sheep of · his | pasture.

3   Come into his gates with thanksgiving
    and into his | courts with | praise; ▪
give thanks to him and | bless his | holy | name.

4   For the Lord is good
    his loving mercy | is for | ever, ▪
his faithfulness through|out all | gener|ations.
    Glory to the Father, and | to the | Son, ▪
    and | to the | Holy | Spirit;
    as it was in the be|ginning, is | now, ▪
    and shall be for | ever. | A|men.

or

In Eastertide

THE EASTER ANTHEMS
1 Corinthians 5: 7,8 Romans 6: 9-11 1 Corinthians 15: 20-22

1   Christ our passover has been | sacri·ficed | for us, ▪
therefore let us | cele|brate the | feast,

2   Not with the old leaven of cor|ruption · and | wickedness, ∎
    but with the unleavened | bread of · sin|cerity · and | truth.

3   Christ, once raised from the dead | dies no | more; ∎
    death has no | more do|minion | over him.

4   In dying, he died to sin | once for | all; ∎
    in | living, · he | lives to | God.

5   See yourselves therefore as | dead to | sin; ∎
    and alive to God in | Jesus | Christ our | Lord.

6   Christ has been | raised · from the | dead: ∎
    the | firstfruits · of | those who | sleep.

7   For as by | man came | death, ∎
    by man has come also the resur|rection | of the | dead.

8   For as in | Adam · all | die, ∎
    even so in Christ shall | all be | made a|live.

        Glory to the Father, and | to the | Son, ∎
        and | to the | Holy | Spirit;
        as it was in the be|ginning, is | now, ∎
        and shall be for | ever. | A|men.

These and other canticles may be used in other versions and forms e.g. from the Church Hymnal.

FIRST READING

The reader may say
A reading from ... chapter ... beginning at verse ...
After the reading silence may be kept.

PSALM

One or more of the appointed Psalms is sung, ending with
Glory to the Father, and | to the | Son, ∎
and | to the | Holy | Spirit;
as it was in the be|ginning, is | now, ∎
and shall be for | ever. | A|men.

The reader may say

A reading from ... chapter ... beginning at verse ...

After the reading silence may be kept.

If the service is not the Principal Service of the day only two readings are used.

TE DEUM *in full, or part 1, or part 2, or both these parts*

Part 1

1   We praise you, O God,
        we acclaim you | as the | Lord; ▪
   all creation worships you,
        the | Father | ever|lasting.

2   To you all angels, all the | powers of | heaven, ▪
   the cherubim and seraphim, | sing in | endless | praise:

3   Holy, holy, holy Lord| God of | power and | might, ▪
   heaven and | earth are | full of · your | glory.

4   The glorious company of a|postles | praise you; ▪
   the noble | fellowship · of | prophets | praise you.

5   The white-robed army of | martyrs | praise you; ▪
   throughout the world, the | holy | Church ac|claims you:

6   Father, of majesty unbounded,
        your true and only Son, worthy | of all | praise, ▪
   the Holy Spirit| advo|cate and | guide.

Part 2

7   You, Christ, are the | King of | glory, ▪
   the e|ternal | Son of · the | Father.

8   When you took our flesh to | set us | free, ▪
   you humbly | chose the | Virgin's | womb.

9   You overcame the | sting of | death ▪
   and opened the kingdom of | heaven · to | all be|lievers.

10   You are seated at God's right | hand in | glory: ▪
   we believe that you will | come to | be our | judge.

11   Come then, Lord, and | help your | people, ▪
   bought with the | price of | your own | blood,

12   and bring us | with your | saints ▪
   to | glory | ever|lasting.

Part 3

13 Save your people, Lord, and I bless your · inIheritance: ∎
    goverń and upIhold them I now and I always.

14 Day by I day we I bless you: ∎
    we I praise your I name for I ever.

15 Keep us today, Lord, I from all I sin: ∎
    have I mercy · on us, I Lord, have I mercy.

16 Lord, show us your I love and I mercy, ∎
    for we I put our I trust in I you.

17† In you, Lord, I is our I hope, ∎
    let us I never · be I put to I shame.

or

any of the Canticles (pages 117-135) except BENEDICTUS

The reader may say

A reading from the Gospel according to ... chapter ... beginning at verse ...
After the reading silence may be kept.

BENEDICTUS *The Song of Zechariah Luke 1: 68-79*

1 Blessèd be the Lord the I God of I Israel, ∎
    who has come to his I people · and I set them I free.

2 The Lord has raised up for us a I mighty I saviour, ∎
    born of the I house of · his I servant I David.

3 Through the holy prophets God I promised · of I old ∎
    to save us from our enemies,
        from the I hands of I those who I hate us,

4 to show I mercy · to our I forebears, ∎
    and to reImember · his I holy I covenant.

5 This was the oath God swore to our I father I Abraham: ∎
    to set us I free · from the I hand of · our I enemies.

6 Free to worship him withIout I fear, ∎
    holy and righteous before him I all the I days of · our I life.

7   And you, child, shall be called the prophet of the ǀ Most ǀ High, ▪
for you will go before the ǀ Lord · to preǀpare his ǀ way,

8   To give his people knowledge ǀ of salǀvation ▪
by the forǀgiveness · of ǀ all their ǀ sins.

9   In the tender compassion ǀ of our ǀ God ▪
the dawn from on ǀ high shall ǀ break upǀon us.

10   To shine on those who dwell in darkness‿
    and the ǀ shadow · of ǀ death, ▪
and to guide our feet ǀ into · the ǀ way of ǀ peace.
    Glory to the Father, and ǀ to the ǀ Son, ▪
    and ǀ to the ǀ Holy ǀ Spirit;
    as it was in the beǀginning, is ǀ now, ▪
    and shall be for ǀ ever. ǀ Aǀmen.

or any of the New Testament Canticles on pages 117-135

or any of the New Testament Canticles on pages 117-135

THE SERMON
may be preached here or at some other place in the service.

A hymn may be sung.

Continue on page 112 with the Apostles' Creed

AT EVENING PRAYER

Stand

O Lord, open our lips
and our mouth will proclaim your praise.

O God, make speed to save us.
O Lord, make haste to help us.

Glory to the Father, and to the Son, and to the Holy Spirit;
as it was in the beginning, is now, and shall be for ever. Amen.

Praise the Lord.
The Lord's name be praised.

First Canticle

A SONG OF THE LIGHT

1   Hail, gladdening light, of his pure glory poured,
Who is the immortal Father, heavenly, blest,
Holiest of holies, Jesus Christ our Lord.

2   Now we are come to the sun's hour of rest.
The lights of evening round us shine:
We hymn the Father, Son, and Holy Spirit divine.

3   Worthiest art thou at all times to be sung
With undefiled tongue.
Son of our God, giver of life, alone:
Therefore in all the world thy glories, Lord, they own.

or

DEUS MISEREATUR *Psalm 67 (page 664)*

or

ECCE NUNC *Psalm 134*

1   Come bless the Lord, all you | servants · of the | Lord: ∎
you that by night | stand · in the | house of · the | Lord.

2   Lift up your hands toward the holy place and | bless the | Lord: ∎
may the Lord bless you from Zion
       the | Lord who · made | heaven · and | earth.

Glory to the Father, and | to the | Son, ▪
and | to the | Holy | Spirit;
as it was in the be|ginning, is | now, ▪
and shall be for | ever. | A|men.

or in Eastertide
THE EASTER ANTHEMS *(page 120)*
These and other canticles may be used in other versions and forms e.g. from Church Hymnal.

PSALM

One or more of the appointed Psalms is sung, ending with
Glory to the Father, and | to the | Son, ▪
and | to the | Holy | Spirit;
as it was in the be|ginning, is | now, ▪
and shall be for | ever. | A|men.

FIRST READING

The reader may say
A reading from ... chapter ... beginning at verse ...
After the reading silence may be kept.

SECOND CANTICLE

MAGNIFICAT   *The Song of the Blessed Virgin Mary   Luke 1 :46-55*

1   My soul proclaims the | greatness · of the | Lord, ▪
    my spirit re|joices · in | God my | Saviour,

2   who has looked with favour on his | lowly | servant; ▪
    from this day all gene|rations · will | call me | blessèd;

3† the Almighty has done | great things | for me ▪
    and | holy | is his | name.

4   God has mercy on | those who | fear him, ▪
    from gene|ration · to | gene|ration.

5   The Lord has shown | strength · with his | arm ▪
    and scattered the | proud in | their con|ceit,

6   casting down the mighty | from their | thrones ▪
    and | lifting | up the | lowly.

7   God has filled the hungry with | good | things ▪
    and sent the | rich a|way | empty.

8   He has come to the aid of his | servant | Israel ■
    to re|member · the | promise of | mercy,

9   The promise | made to · our | forebears, ■
    to Abraham | and his | children · for | ever.
        Glory to the Father, and | to the | Son, ■
        and | to the | Holy | Spirit;
        as it was in the be|ginning, is | now, ■
        and shall be for | ever. | A|men.

or any of the New Testament canticles in The Canticles (pages 117-135)

SECOND READING

The reader may say
A reading from ... chapter ... beginning at verse ...
After the reading silence may be kept.

If the service is the Principal Service of the day the order of readings and canticles at Morning Prayer is followed with canticles appropriate to the evening.

THIRD CANTICLE

NUNC DIMITTIS   *The Song of Simeon   Luke 2: 29-32*

1   Now, Lord, you let your servant | go in | peace: ■
    your | word has | been ful|filled.

2   My own eyes have | seen the · sal|vation ■
    which you have prepared in the | sight of | every | people.

3   A light to re|veal you · to the | nations ■
    and the | glory · of your | people | Israel.
        Glory to the Father, and | to the | Son, ■
        and | to the | Holy | Spirit;
        as it was in the be|ginning, is | now, ■
        and shall be for | ever. | A|men.

or any of the New Testament canticles in The Canticles (pages 117-135)

THE SERMON
may be preached here or at some other place in the service.

A hymn may be sung.

I believe in God, the Father almighty,
  creator of heaven and earth.
I believe in Jesus Christ, God's only Son, our Lord.
  who was conceived by the Holy Spirit,
  born of the Virgin Mary,
  suffered under Pontius Pilate,
  was crucified, died and was buried;
  he descended to the dead.
  On the third day he rose again;
  he ascended into heaven,
  he is seated at the right hand of the Father,
  and he will come again to judge the living and the dead.
I believe in the Holy Spirit,
  the holy catholic Church,
  the communion of saints,
  the forgiveness of sins,
  the resurrection of the body,
  and the life everlasting. Amen.

The Prayers of the People

The Lord be with you
and also with you.

Kneel
Let us pray.

Lord, have mercy.
Christ, have mercy.
Lord, have mercy.

**Our Father in heaven,
  hallowed be your name,
  your kingdom come,
  your will be done,
    on earth as in heaven.
Give us today our daily bread.**

Forgive us our sins
  as we forgive those who sin against us.
Lead us not into temptation
  but deliver us from evil.
For the kingdom, the power, and the glory are yours
  now and for ever. Amen.

or

Our Father, who art in heaven,
  hallowed be thy name,
  thy kingdom come,
  thy will be done,
    on earth as it is in heaven.
Give us this day our daily bread.
  And forgive us our trespasses
  as we forgive those who trespass against us.
And lead us not into temptation,
  but deliver us from evil.
For thine is the kingdom, the power, and the glory,
  for ever and ever. Amen.

The versicles and responses may be said.
Show us your mercy, O Lord,
and grant us your salvation.

N.I. [O Lord, save the Queen
and grant her government wisdom.]

R.I. [O Lord, guide and defend our rulers
and grant our government wisdom.]

Let your ministers be clothed with righteousness
and let your servants shout for joy.

O Lord, save your people
and bless those whom you have chosen.

Give peace in our time, O Lord,
and let your glory be over all the earth.

O God, make clean our hearts within us
and renew us by your Holy Spirit.

The Collect of the day is said and one or more of these collects:

AT MORNING PRAYER

O God, the author of peace and lover of concord,
to know you is eternal life, and to serve you is perfect freedom:
Defend us in all assaults of our enemies,
that we, surely trusting in your protection,
may not fear the power of any adversaries;
through Jesus Christ our Lord. **Amen.**

O Lord, our heavenly Father, almighty and everliving God,
we give you thanks for bringing us safely to this day:
Keep us from falling into sin or running into danger,
and in all things guide us to know and do your will;
through Jesus Christ our Lord. **Amen.**

Go before us, Lord, in all our doings, with your most gracious favour,
and further us with your continual help;
that in all our works begun, continued and ended in you,
we may glorify your holy name,
and finally by your mercy attain everlasting life;
through Jesus Christ our Lord. **Amen.**

Heavenly Father,
in whom we live and move and have our being:
We humbly pray that your Holy Spirit may so guide and govern us
that in all the cares and occupations of our daily life,
we may never forget your presence
but may remember that we are always walking in your sight,
through Jesus Christ our Lord. **Amen.**

AT EVENING PRAYER

O God
from whom all holy desires
all good judgements
and all just works proceed:
Give to your servants
that peace which the world cannot give,
that our hearts may be set to obey your commandments,
and that we, being defended from the fear of our enemies,
may pass our time in rest and quietness;
through Jesus Christ your Son our Lord. **Amen.**

Lighten our darkness, O Lord, we pray
and in your great mercy defend us
from all perils and dangers of this night;
for the love of your only Son, our Saviour Jesus Christ. **Amen.**

Grant, O Lord,
that the word which we hear this day
may so take root in our hearts,
that we, living in accordance with your holy will,
may ever praise and magnify your glorious name;
through Jesus Christ our Lord. **Amen.**

A hymn or anthem may be sung.
Prayers and thanksgivings, or a litany, may be said.
A hymn may be sung.

Going Out as God's People

The prayers may end with one of the following or an appropriate blessing:

The Lord be with you
and also with you.

Let us bless the Lord.
Thanks be to God.

The grace of our Lord Jesus Christ,
and the love of God,
and the fellowship of the Holy Spirit,
be with us all evermore. **Amen.**   *2 Corinthians 13: 14*

To God, who by the power at work within us,
is able to do far more abundantly
than all we ask or think,
to him be glory in the Church and in Christ Jesus
to all generations for ever and ever. **Amen.**   *Ephesians 3: 20*

To the King of Ages, immortal, invisible, the only God,
be honour and glory for ever and ever. **Amen.**   *1 Timothy 1: 17*

May the God of hope
fill you with all joy and peace in believing,
so that by the Holy Spirit
you may abound in hope. **Amen.**   *Romans 15: 13*

THE CANTICLES

* indicates that this is a traditional language canticle

POINTING OF THE GLORIA PATRI

Glory | be · to the | Father, ▪
and to the Son, | and · to the | Holy | Spirit;
as it | was in · the be|ginning, ▪
is now and ever shall be, | world with·out | end. A|men.

or

Glory to the Father, and | to the | Son, ▪
and | to the | Holy | Spirit;
as it was in the be|ginning, is | now, ▪
and shall be for | ever. | A|men.

In the pointed canticles † indicates that the verse should be sung to the second part of an Anglican double chant.

1   VENITE   *Psalm 95*

1   O come let us sing | out · to the | Lord; ▪
     let us shout in triumph to the | rock of | our sal|vation.

2   Let us come before his | face with | thanksgiving ▪
     and cry | out · to him | joyfully · in | psalms.

3   For the Lord is a | great | God ▪
     and a great | king a·bove | all | gods.

4   In his hand are the | depths · of the | earth ▪
     and the peaks of the | mountains · are | his | also.

5†   The sea is his and | he | made it, ▪
     his hands | moulded | dry | land.

6   Come let us worship and | bow | down ▪
     and kneel be|fore the | Lord our | maker.

7   For he is the | Lord our | God; ▪
     we are his | people · and the | sheep of · his | pasture.

8   Today if only you would | hear his | voice, ▪
     do not harden your | hearts · as you | did · in the | wilderness;

9   When your | forebears | tested me, ▪
     put me to the proof though | they had | seen my | works.

10   Forty years long I loathed that gene|ration · and | said, ▪
     It is a people who err in their hearts,
          for they | do not | know my | ways;

11   Of whom I | swore · in my | wrath, ▪
     They | shall not | enter · my | rest.
     Glory ...

2   VENITE   *Psalm 95*   *Traditional*

1   O come let us | sing un·to the | Lord; ▪
     let us heartily rejoice in the | strength of | our sal|vation.

2   Let us come before his | presence · with | thanksgiving ▪
     and show ourselves | glad in | him with | psalms.

3   For the Lord is a | great | God ▪
     and a great | King a·bove | all | gods.

4　In his hand are all the | corners · of the | earth ▪
　　and the strength of the | hills is | his | also.

5†　The sea is his and | he | made it, ▪
　　and his | hands pre|pared the · dry | land.

6　O come let us worship and | fall | down ▪
　　and kneel be|fore the | Lord our | Maker.

7　For he is the | Lord our | God; ▪
　　and we are the people of his pasture, | and the | sheep of · his | hand.

8　Today if ye will | hear his | voice: ▪
　　harden not your hearts, as in the provocation
　　　　and as in the day of temp|tation | in the | wilderness;

9　When your | fathers | tempted me, ▪
　　provèd | me and | saw my | works.

10　Forty years long was I grieved with this gene|ration · and | said, ▪
　　It is a people that do err in their hearts,
　　　　for they | have not | known my | ways;

11　Unto whom I sware | in my | wrath, ▪
　　that they should not | enter | into · my | rest.
　　Glory ...

3　JUBILATE　*Psalm 100*

1　O shout to the Lord in triumph | all the | earth; ▪
　　serve the Lord with gladness
　　　　and come before his | face with | songs of | joy.

2　Know that the Lord | he is | God; ▪
　　it is he who has made us and we are his
　　　　we are his | people · and the | sheep of · his | pasture.

3　Come into his gates with thanksgiving
　　　　and into his | courts with | praise; ▪
　　give thanks to him and | bless his | holy | name.

4　For the Lord is good
　　　　his loving mercy | is for | ever, ▪
　　his faithfulness through|out all | gene|rations.
　　Glory ...

4   JUBILATE   *Psalm 100*   *Traditional*

1   O be joyful in the Lord | all ye | lands; ▪
     serve the Lord with gladness
          and come before his | presence | with a | song.

2   Be ye sure that the Lord | he is | God; ▪
     it is he that hath made us and not we ourselves
          we are his people | and the | sheep of · his | pasture.

3   O go your way into his gates with thanksgiving
          and into his | courts with | praise; ▪
     be thankful unto him and speak | good of | his | name.

4   For the Lord is gracious, his mercy is | ever|lasting, ▪
     and his truth endureth from gene|ration · to | gene|ration.
     Glory .....

5   THE EASTER ANTHEMS
     1 Corinthians 5: 7,8   Romans 6: 9-11   1 Corinthians 15: 20-22

1   Christ our passover has been | sacri·ficed | for us, ▪
     therefore let us | cele|brate the | feast,

2   Not with the old leaven of cor|ruption · and | wickedness, ▪
     but with the unleavened | bread of · sinc|erity · and | truth.

3   Christ, once raised from the dead | dies no | more; ▪
     death has no | more do|minion | over him.

4   In dying, he died to sin | once for | all; ▪
     in | living, · he | lives to | God.

5   See yourselves therefore as | dead to | sin; ▪
     and alive to God in | Jesus | Christ our | Lord.

6   Christ has been | raised · from the | dead: ▪
     the | firstfruits · of | those who | sleep.

7   For as by | man came | death, ▪
     by man has come also the resur|rection | of the | dead.

8   For as in | Adam · all | die, ▪
     even so in Christ shall | all be | made a|live.
     Glory ...

6   THE EASTER ANTHEMS   *Traditional*

1   Christ our passover is | sacri·ficed | for us, ▪
    therefore | let us | keep the | feast,

2   Not with the old leaven
            nor with the leaven of | malice · and | wickedness: ▪
    but with the unleavened bread | of sin|cerity · and | truth.

3   Christ being raised from the dead | dieth · no | more; ▪
    death hath no | more do|minion | over him.

4   For in that he died, he died unto | sin | once; ▪
    but in that he liveth, he | liveth | unto | God.

5   Likewise reckon ye also yourselves to be dead indeed | unto | sin; ▪
    but alive unto God through | Jesus | Christ our | Lord.

6   Christ is | risen · from the | dead: ▪
    and become the | first-fruits · of | them that | slept.

7   For since by | man came | death, ▪
    by man came also the resur|rection | of the | dead.

8   For as in Adam | all | die, ▪
    even so in Christ shall | all be | made a|live.
    Glory ...

7   BENEDICTUS   *The Song of Zechariah   Luke 1: 68-79   ELLC*

1   Blessèd be the Lord the | God of | Israel, ▪
    who has come to his | people · and | set them | free.

2   The Lord has raised up for us a | mighty | saviour, ▪
    born of the | house of · his | servant | David.

3   Through the holy prophets God | promised · of | old ▪
    to save us from our enemies,
            from the | hands of | those who | hate us,

4   to show | mercy · to our | forebears, ▪
    and to re|member · his | holy | covenant.

5   This was the oath God swore to our | father | Abraham: ▪
    to set us | free · from the | hand of · our | enemies.

6   Free to worship him with|out | fear, ▪
    holy and righteous before him | all the | days of · our | life.

7   And you, child, shall be called the prophet of the | Most | High, ▪
    for you will go before the | Lord · to pre|pare his | way,

8　To give his people knowledge | of sal|vation ▪
　　by the for|giveness · of | all their | sins.

9　In the tender compassion | of our | God ▪
　　the dawn from on | high shall | break up|on us.

10　To shine on those who dwell in darkness⌣
　　　　and the | shadow · of | death, ▪
　　and to guide our feet | into · the | way of | peace.
　　Glory ...

8　BENEDICTUS　*The Song of Zechariah　Luke 1: 68-79　Traditional*

1　Blessèd be the Lord | God of | Israel, ▪
　　for he hath visited | and re|deemed his | people,

2　And hath raised up a mighty sal|vation | for us ▪
　　in the | house of · his | servant | David;

3　As he spake by the mouth of his | holy | Prophets ▪
　　which have been | since the | world be|gan;

4　That we should be | saved · from our | enemies, ▪
　　and from the | hands of | all that | hate us,

5　To perform the mercy | promised · to our | forefathers, ▪
　　and to re|member · his | holy | covenant;

6　To perform the oath which he sware to our | fore·father | Abraham: ▪
　　that | he would | give | us,

7　That we being delivered out of the | hand of · our | enemies ▪
　　might serve | him with|out | fear,

8　In holiness and | righteous·ness be|fore him ▪
　　all the | days | of our | life.

9　And thou, child, shalt be called the | Prophet · of the | Highest, ▪
　　for thou shalt go before the face of the | Lord · to pre|pare his | ways;

10　To give knowledge of salvation | unto · his | people, ▪
　　for the re|mission | of their | sins,

11　Through the tender mercy | of our | God ▪
　　whereby the day-spring from on | high hath | visit·ed | us,

12　To give light to them that sit in darkness
　　　　and in the | shadow · of | death, ▪
　　and to guide our feet | into · the | way of | peace.
　　Glory ...

9 BENEDICITE *The Song of the Three 35-65*

1 Bless the Lord ǀ all creǀated things: ▪
sing his ǀ praise · and exǀalt him · for ǀ ever.

2 Bless the ǀ Lord you ǀ heavens: ▪
sing his ǀ praise · and exǀalt him · for ǀ ever.

3 Bless the Lord you ǀ angels · of the ǀ Lord: ▪
bless the ǀ Lord all ǀ you his ǀ hosts.

4 Bless the Lord you waters aǀbove the ǀ heavens: ▪
sing his ǀ praise · and exǀalt him · for ǀ ever.

5 Bless the Lord ǀ sun and ǀ moon: ▪
bless the ǀ Lord you ǀ stars of ǀ heaven.

6 Bless the Lord all ǀ rain and ǀ dew: ▪
sing his ǀ praise · and exǀalt him · for ǀ ever.

7 Bless the Lord all ǀ winds that ǀ blow: ▪
bless the ǀ Lord you ǀ fire and ǀ heat.

8 Bless the Lord scorching wind and ǀ bitter ǀ cold: ▪
sing his ǀ praise · and exǀalt him · for ǀ ever.

9 Bless the Lord dews and ǀ falling ǀ snows: ▪
bless the ǀ Lord you ǀ nights and ǀ days.

10 Bless the Lord ǀ light and ǀ darkness: ▪
sing his ǀ praise · and exǀalt him · for ǀ ever.

11 Bless the Lord ǀ frost and ǀ cold: ▪
bless the ǀ Lord you ǀ ice and ǀ snow.

12 Bless the Lord ǀ lightnings · and ǀ clouds: ▪
sing his ǀ praise · and exǀalt him · for ǀ ever.

13 O let the earth ǀ bless the ǀ Lord; ▪
bless the ǀ Lord you ǀ mountains · and ǀ hills.

14 Bless the Lord all that ǀ grows · in the ǀ ground: ▪
sing his ǀ praise · and exǀalt him · for ǀ ever.

15 Bless the ǀ Lord you ǀ springs: ▪
bless the ǀ Lord you ǀ seas and ǀ rivers.

16 Bless the Lord you whales and all that ǀ swim · in the ǀ waters: ▪
sing his ǀ praise · and exǀalt him · for ǀ ever.

17 Bless the Lord all ǀ birds · of the ǀ air: ▪
bless the ǀ Lord you ǀ beasts and ǀ cattle.

18 Bless the Lord all | men · on the | earth: ▪
   sing his | praise · and ex|alt him · for | ever.

19 O people of God | bless the | Lord: ▪
   bless the | Lord you | priests · of the | Lord.

20 Bless the Lord you | servants · of the | Lord: ▪
   sing his | praise · and ex|alt him · for | ever.

21 Bless the Lord all men of | upright | spirit: ▪
   bless the Lord you that are | holy · and | humble · in | heart.

22 Bless the Father the Son and the | Holy | Spirit: ▪
   sing his | praise · and ex|alt him · for | ever.

10 BENEDICITE *The Song of the Three 35-65* *Traditional*

1 O all ye works of the Lord | bless · ye the | Lord: ▪
   praise him and | magni·fy | him for | ever.

2 O ye Angels of the Lord | bless · ye the | Lord: ▪
   O ye | Heavens | bless · ye the | Lord.

3 O ye Waters that be above the Firmament | bless · ye the | Lord. ▪
   O all ye Powers of the | Lord | bless · ye the | Lord.

4 O ye Sun and Moon | bless · ye the | Lord: ▪
   O ye Stars of | Heaven | bless · ye the | Lord.

5 O ye Showers and Dew | bless · ye the | Lord: ▪
   O ye Winds of | God | bless · ye the | Lord.

6 O ye Fire and Heat | bless · ye the | Lord: ▪
   O ye Winter and | Summer | bless · ye the | Lord.

7 O ye Dews and Frosts | bless · ye the | Lord: ▪
   O ye Frost and | Cold | bless · ye the | Lord.

8 O ye Ice and Snow | bless · ye the | Lord: ▪
   O ye Nights and | Days | bless · ye the | Lord.

9† O ye Light and Darkness | bless · ye the | Lord: ▪
   O ye Lightnings and | Clouds | bless · ye the | Lord.

10 O let the Earth | bless the | Lord: ▪
   yea let it praise him and | magni·fy | him for | ever.

11 O ye Mountains and Hills | bless · ye the | Lord: ▪
   O all ye Green Things upon the | Earth | bless · ye the | Lord.

12 O ye Wells | bless · ye the | Lord: ▪
    O ye Seas and | Floods | bless · ye the | Lord.
13 O ye Whales and all that move in the Waters | bless · ye the | Lord: ▪
    O all ye Fowls of the | Air | bless · ye the | Lord.
14† O all ye Beasts and Cattle | bless · ye the | Lord: ▪
    O ye Children of | Men | bless · ye the | Lord.

15 O let Israel | bless the | Lord: ▪
    praise him and | magni·fy | him for | ever.
16 O ye Priests of the Lord | bless · ye the | Lord: ▪
    O ye Servants of the | Lord | bless · ye the | Lord.
17 O ye Spirits and Souls of the Righteous | bless · ye the | Lord: ▪
    O ye holy and humble Men of | heart | bless · ye the | Lord.
18 O Ananias, Azarias, and Misael | bless · ye the | Lord: ▪
    praise him and | magni·fy | him for | ever.
    Glory ...

11 TE DEUM   *ELLC*

Part 1

1   We praise you, O God,
        we acclaim you | as the | Lord; ▪
    all creation worships you,
        the | Father | ever|lasting.
2   To you all angels, all the | powers of | heaven, ▪
    the cherubim and seraphim, | sing in | endless | praise:
3   Holy, holy, holy Lord, God of | power and | might, ▪
    heaven and | earth are | full of · your | glory.
4   The glorious company of a|postles | praise you; ▪
    the noble | fellowship · of | prophets | praise you.
5   The white-robed army of | martyrs | praise you; ▪
    throughout the world, the | holy | Church ac|claims you:
6   Father, of majesty unbounded,
        your true and only Son, worthy | of all | praise, ▪
    the Holy Spirit, | advo|cate and | guide.

Part 2

7   You, Christ, are the ˈ King of ˈ glory, ▪
    the eˈternal ˈ Son of · the ˈ Father.

8   When you took our flesh to ˈ set us ˈ free, ▪
    you humbly ˈ chose the ˈ Virgin's ˈ womb.

9   You overcame the ˈ sting of ˈ death ▪
    and opened the kingdom of ˈ heaven · to ˈ all beˈlievers.

10 You are seated at God's right ˈ hand in ˈ glory: ▪
    we believe that you will ˈ come to ˈ be our ˈ judge.

11 Come then, Lord, and ˈ help your ˈ people, ▪
    bought with the ˈ price of ˈ your own ˈ blood,

12 and bring us ˈ with your ˈ saints ▪
    to ˈ glory ˈ everˈlasting.

Part 3

13 Save your people, Lord, and ˈ bless your · inˈheritance: ▪
    govern and upˈhold them ˈ now and ˈ always.

14 Day by ˈ day we ˈ bless you: ▪
    we ˈ praise your ˈ name for ˈ ever.

15 Keep us today, Lord, ˈ from all ˈ sin: ▪
    have ˈ mercy · on us, ˈ Lord, have ˈ mercy.

16 Lord, show us your ˈ love and ˈ mercy, ▪
    for we ˈ put our ˈ trust in ˈ you.

17† In you, Lord, ˈ is our ˈ hope, ▪
     let us ˈ never · be ˈ put to ˈ shame.

12 TE DEUM *Traditional*

Part 1

1   We praise ˈ thee O ˈ God, ▪
    we acknowledge ˈ thee to ˈ be the ˈ Lord.

2   All the earth doth ˈ worship ˈ thee, ▪
    the ˈ Father ˈ everˈlasting.

3   To thee all angels cry aloud
    the heavens and all the ˈ powers thereˈin, ▪
    to thee Cherubim and Seraphim conˈtin·ualˈly do ˈ cry,

4   Holy, Holy, Holy, Lord ˈ God · of Saˈbaoth: ▪
    heaven and earth are full of the ˈ majes·ty ˈ of thy ˈ glory.

5 The glorious company of the apostles | praise | thee; ▪
the goodly fellowship of the | prophets | praise | thee.

6 The | noble | army ▪‿of | martyrs | praise | thee.

7 The | holy | Church ▪
throughout all the world | doth ac|knowledge | thee;

8 The Father of an | infin·ite | majesty, ▪
thine honourable, true, and only Son,
also the | Holy | Spirit · the | Comforter.

Part 2

9 Thou art the King of | glory · O | Christ. ▪
Thou art the ever|lasting | Son of · the | Father.

10 When thou tookest upon thee to de|liver | man, ▪
thou didst not ab|hor the | Virgin's | womb.

11† When thou hadst overcome the | sharpness · of | death, ▪
thou didst open the kingdom of | heaven · to | all be|lievers.

12 Thou sittest at the right | hand of | God, ▪
in the | glory | of the | Father.

13 We be|lieve that | thou ▪‿shalt | come to | be our | judge.

14 We therefore pray thee | help thy | servants, ▪
whom thou hast re|deemed · with thy | precious | blood.

15 Make them to be numbered | with thy | saints ▪
in | glory | ever|lasting.

Part 3

16 O Lord, save thy people and | bless thine | heritage:▪
govern them and | lift them | up for | ever.

17 Day by day we | magni·fy | thee: ▪
and we worship thy Name ever, | world with|out | end.

18 Vouch|safe, O | Lord, ▪
to | keep us · this | day with·out | sin.

19 O Lord, have | mercy · up|on us, ▪
have | mercy · up|on | us.

20 O Lord, let thy mercy | lighten · up|on us, ▪
as our | trust | is in | thee.

21 O Lord, in | thee · have I | trusted: ▪
let me | never | be con|founded.

13 MAGNIFICAT *The Song of the Virgin Mary* *Luke 1: 46-55* ELLC

1   My soul proclaims the | greatness · of the | Lord, ▪
     my spirit re|joices · in | God my | Saviour,

2   who has looked with favour on his | lowly | servant; ▪
     from this day all gene|rations · will | call me | blessèd;

3†   the Almighty has done | great things | for me ▪
     and | holy | is his | name.

4   God has mercy on | those who | fear him, ▪
     from gene|ration · to | gene|ration.

5   The Lord has shown | strength · with his | arm ▪
     and scattered the | proud in | their con|ceit,

6   casting down the mighty | from their | thrones ▪
     and | lifting | up the | lowly.

7   God has filled the hungry with | good | things ▪
     and sent the | rich a|way | empty.

8   He has come to the aid of his | servant | Israel ▪
     to re|member · the | promise of | mercy,

9   The promise | made to · our | forebears, ▪
     to Abraham | and his | children · for | ever.
     Glory ...

14 MAGNIFICAT *The Song of the Virgin Mary* *Luke 1: 46-55*
Traditional

1   My soul doth | magni·fy the | Lord, ▪
     and my spirit hath re|joiced in | God my | Saviour.

2   For | he · hath re|garded ▪‿
     the lowliness | of his | hand|maiden.

3   For be|hold from | henceforth ▪
     all gener|ations · shall | call me | blessèd.

4   For he that is mighty hath | magni·fied | me, ▪
     and | holy | is his | Name.

5†   And his mercy is on | them that | fear him ▪
     through|out all | gene|rations.

6   He hath showèd | strength · with his | arm, ▪
     he hath scattered the proud, in the imagin|ation | of their | hearts.

7 He hath put down the mighty | from their | seat ∎
   and hath ex|alted · the | humble · and | meek.
8 He hath filled the hungry with | good | things ∎
   and the rich | he hath · sent | empty · a|way.
9 He remembering his mercy hath holpen his | servant | Israel, ∎
   as he promised to our forefathers, Abraham | and his | seed for | ever.
   Glory ...

15 NUNC DIMITTIS *The Song of Simeon* *Luke 2: 29-32* *ELLC*
1 Now, Lord, you let your servant | go in | peace: ∎
   your | word has | been ful|filled.
2 My own eyes have | seen the · sal|vation ∎
   which you have prepared in the | sight of | every | people.
3 A light to re|veal you · to the | nations ∎
   and the | glory · of your | people | Israel.
   Glory ...

16 NUNC DIMITTIS *The Song of Simeon* *Luke 2: 29-32*
Traditional
1 Lord, now lettest thou thy servant de|part in | peace: ∎
   ac|cording | to thy | word.
2 For mine eyes have seen | thy sal|vation ∎
   which thou hast prepared be|fore the | face of · all | people;
3 To be a light to | lighten · the | Gentiles ∎
   and to be the glory of thy | people | Isra|el.
   Glory ...

17 GREAT AND WONDERFUL *Revelation 15: 3,4 and 5: 13b*
1 Great and wonderful are your deeds Lord | God, · the All|mighty: ∎
   just and true are your | ways O | King · of the | nations.
2 Who shall not revere and praise your | name O | Lord? ∎
   for | you a|lone are | holy.
3 All nations shall come and worship | in your | presence: ∎
   for your just | dealings · have | been re|vealed.
4 To him who sits on the throne and | to the | Lamb ∎
   be praise and honour, glory and might,
        for ever and | ever. | A|men.

18 URBS FORTITUDINIS *Isaiah 26: 1-4,7,8*

1   We have a | strong | city: ◾
salvation will God ap|point for | walls and | bulwarks.

2   Open | ye the | gates: ◾
that the righteous nation which keepeth the | truth may | enter | in.

3   Thou wilt keep him in perfect peace whose mind is | stayed on | thee ◾
be|cause he | trusteth · in | thee.

4   Trust ye in the | Lord for | ever: ◾
for our rock of | ages | is the | Lord.

5   The way of the | just is | uprightness; ◾
thou that art upright dost di|rect the | path · of the | just.

6   Yea in the way of thy judgements O Lord have we | waited · for | thee; ◾
the desire of our soul is to thy Name, |
    and · to the re|membrance · of | thee.
Glory ...

19 SAVIOUR OF THE WORLD
Suitable for use in penitential seasons

1   Jesus, Saviour of the world,
    come to us | in your | mercy: ◾
we look to | you to | save and | help us.

2   By your cross and your life laid down
    you set your | people | free: ◾
we look to | you to | save and | help us.

3   When they were ready to perish you | saved · your dis|ciples: ◾
we look to | you to | come to · our | help.

4   In the greatness of your mercy, loose us | from our | chains, ◾
forgive the | sins of | all your | people.

5†   Make yourself known as our Saviour and | mighty · De|liverer; ◾
save and | help us · that | we may | praise you.

6   Come now and dwell with us | Lord Christ | Jesus:◾
hear our | prayer · and be | with us | always.

7   And when you | come in · your | glory:◾
make us to be one with you
    and to share the life of your | kingdom. | A|men.

20 BLESS THE LORD *The Song of the Three 29-34*

1 Bless the Lord the | God of · our | forebears, ▪
   sing his | praise · and ex|alt him · for | ever.

2 Bless his holy and | glori·ous | name, ▪
   sing his | praise · and ex|alt him · for | ever.

3 Bless him in his holy and | glori·ous | temple, ▪
   sing his | praise · and ex|alt him · for | ever.

4 Bless him who be|holds the | depths, ▪
   sing his | praise · and ex|alt him · for | ever.

5 Bless him seated be|tween the | cherubim, ▪
   sing his | praise · and ex|alt him · for | ever.

6 Bless him on the | throne of · his | kingdom, ▪
   sing his | praise · and ex|alt him · for | ever.

7 Bless him in the | heights of | heaven, ▪
   sing his | praise · and ex|alt him · for | ever.

8 Bless the Father the Son and the | Holy | Spirit, ▪
   sing his | praise · and ex|alt him · for | ever.

21 GLORY AND HONOUR *Revelation 4: 11 and 5: 9, 10, 13b*

1 Glory and | honour · and | power ▪
   are yours by | right O | Lord our | God.

2 For you cre|ated | all things ▪
   and by your | will they | have their | being.

3 Glory and | honour · and | power ▪
   are yours by | right O | Lamb · for us | slain;

4 For by your blood you ransomed | us for | God ▪
   from every race and language
   from | every | people · and | nation.

5 To make us a | kingdom of | priests, ▪
   to stand and | serve be|fore our | God.

6 To him who sits on the throne and | to the | Lamb ▪
   be praise and honour, glory and might,
   for ever and | ever. | A|men.

22 THE SONG OF CHRIST'S GLORY *Philippians 2: 6-11*

1 Christ Jesus was in the | form of | God, ▪
   but he did not | cling · to e|quality · with | God.

2 He emptied himself, taking the | form · of a | servant, ▪
   and was | born · in our | human | likeness.

3 And being found in human form he | humbled · him|self, ▪
   and became obedient unto death, | even | death · on a | cross.

4 Therefore God has | highly · ex|alted him, ▪
   and bestowed on him the | name a·bove | every | name.

5 That at the name of Jesus every | knee should | bow, ▪
   in heaven and on | earth and | under · the | earth;

6 and every tongue confess that Jesus | Christ is | Lord, ▪
   to the glory of God the | Father. | A|men.

23 THE SONG OF ISAIAH *Isaiah 12: 2-6*

1 Surely God is | my sal|vation; ▪
   I will | trust, · and will | not · be a|fraid.

2 for the Lord God is my | strength · and my | might; ▪
   he has be|come | my sal|vation.

3 With joy you will draw water from the | wells of · sal|vation. ▪
   And you will say in that day:
       Give thanks to the | Lord, | call on · his | name;

4 Make known his deeds a|mong the | nations; ▪
   pro|claim · that his | name is · ex|alted.

5 Sing praises to the Lord, for | he has · done | gloriously; ▪
   let this be | known in | all the | earth.

6 Shout aloud and sing for joy, O | royal | Zion, ▪
   for great in your midst is the | Holy | One of | Israel.
   Glory ...

24 THE SONG OF WISDOM *Wisdom 7: 26 - 8: 1*

1 Wisdom is the brightness of eternal light,
       the spotless mirror of God's | power at | work, ▪
   the | image | of God's | goodness.

2 Wisdom is but one, yet | she can · do | all things; ▪
   herself un|changing, · she makes | all things | new.

3   Age after age, she enters holy souls
        and makes them friends of | God, and | prophets, ▪
    beloved of | God as | her com|panions.

4   Wisdom is more beautiful | than the | sun, ▪
    surpassing every constel|lation | of the | stars.

5   Her radiance is greater than the | light of | day; ▪
    for day's light is | followed | by the | night.

6   Against wisdom no | evil · can pre|vail; ▪
    she reaches mightily from one end of the earth to the other,
        and | orders | all things | well.
    Glory ...

25 ECCE NUNC *Psalm 134*

1   Come bless the Lord, all you | servants · of the | Lord: ▪
    you that by night | stand · in the | house of · the | Lord.

2   Lift up your hands toward the holy place and | bless the | Lord: ▪
    may the Lord bless you from Zion,
        the | Lord who · made | heaven · and | earth.
    Glory ...

26 CANTATE DOMINO *Psalm 98*

1   O sing unto the Lord a | new | song; ▪
    for | he hath · done | marvel·lous | things.

2   With his own right hand, and with his | holy | arm ▪
    hath he | gotten · him|self the | victory.

3   The Lord declared | his sal|vation; ▪
    his righteousness
        hath he openly | showed · in the | sight of · the | heathen.

4   He hath remembered his mercy and truth
        towards the | house of | Israel, ▪
    and all the ends of the world have seen the sal|vation | of our | God.

5   Show yourselves joyful unto the Lord, | all ye | lands: ▪
    sing, re|joice and | give | thanks.

6   Praise the Lord up|on the | harp: ▪
    sing to the | harp · with a | psalm of | thanksgiving.

7   With trumpets | also · and | shawms, ▪
    O show yourselves joyful be|fore the | Lord the | King.

8   Let the sea make a noise, and all that I therein I is; ∎
    the round world, and I they that I dwell there\|in.

9   Let the floods clap their hands,
        and let the hills be joyful together be\|fore the I Lord; ∎
    for he I cometh to I judge the I earth.

10 With righteousness shall he I judge the I world, ∎
    and the I people I with I equity.
    Glory ...

27 DEUS MISEREATUR   *Psalm 67*

1   God be merciful unto I us and I bless us; ∎
    and shew us the light of his countenance, and be I merci·ful I unto I us

2   That thy way may be I known up·on I earth, ∎
    thy saving I health a·mong I all I nations.

3   Let the people I praise thee · O I God, ∎
    yea let I all the I people I praise thee.

4   O let the nations re\|joice · and be I glad; ∎
    for thou shalt judge the folk righteously,
    and govern the I nations · up\|on I earth.

5   Let the people I praise thee · O I God, ∎
    yea, let I all the I people I praise thee.

6   Then shall the earth bring I forth her I increase, ∎
    and God, even our own God, shall I give us I his I blessing.

7   God I shall I bless us; ∎
    and all the I ends · of the I world shall I fear him.
    Glory ...

28 A SONG OF THE LIGHT

1   Hail, gladdening light, of his pure glory poured,
    Who is the immortal Father, heavenly, blest,
    Holiest of holies, Jesus Christ our Lord.

2   Now we are come to the sun's hour of rest.
    The lights of evening round us shine:
    We hymn the Father, Son, and Holy Spirit divine.

3   Worthiest art thou at all times to be sung
    With undefiled tongue.
    Son of our God, giver of life, alone:
    Therefore in all the world thy glories, Lord, they own.

DAILY PRAYER: WEEKDAYS

MORNING PRAYER

PREPARATION

A Sentence of Scripture *(pages 78-82)*

Versicles and Responses *(page 87 or 103)*

THE WORD OF GOD

A Psalm *as appointed*

A Canticle *which may be said here or between the readings*

Monday	Te Deum *(page 125)*
Tuesday	Benedicite *(page 123)*
Wednesday	The Song of Isaiah *(page 132)*
Thursday	Urbs Fortitudinis *(page 130)*
Friday	Saviour of the World *(page 130)*
Saturday	The Song of Wisdom *(page 132)*

One or two readings, *the second from the New Testament*

The Gospel Canticle: Benedictus *(page 121)*

The Apostles' Creed *may be said*

PRAYER

Lesser Litany

Weekday Intercessions and Thanksgivings
Those on pages 139-144 may be used

The Collect of the day *may be said or one of the collects on page 114*

The Lord's Prayer

The Ending

EVENING PRAYER

Penitence *(page 102)*

Versicles and Responses *(page 87 or 103)*

THE WORD OF GOD

A Psalm *as appointed*

A Canticle

Monday	Great and Wonderful *(page 129)*
Tuesday	Bless the Lord *(page 131)*
Wednesday	Nunc Dimittis *(page 129)*†
Thursday	The Song of Christ's Glory *(page 132)*
Friday	Glory and Honour *(page 131)*
Saturday	The Easter Anthems *(page 120)*

† *When Nunc Dimittis is used it may be the Gospel Canticle and Magnificat may be used at this place.*

One or more readings

The Gospel Canticle: Magnificat *(page 128)*

PRAYER

Lesser Litany

Intercessions and Thanksgivings
Those on pages 139-144 may be used if not used in the morning

The Collect of the day *may be said or another collect*

The Lord's Prayer

The Ending

DAILY PRAYER: A SIMPLE STRUCTURE

This reflects the way the Church structures its common prayer and may be a basis for personal or family devotions.

PREPARATION

A Sentence of Scripture *(pages 78-82)*

A Prayer of Penitence
That on page 102 may be used or one of the Penitential Kyries on pages 224-236

Praise
'Glory to God in the highest ...' *on page 203*
or 'Holy, holy, holy ...' *on page 209 may be used*

THE WORD OF GOD

A Psalm
The canticles Venite on page 118 or Jubilate on page 120 may be used instead

A Bible Reading

A Canticle *Any of those on pages 117-135 may be used*

PRAYER

Intercessions and Thanksgivings *Those on page 139-144 may be used*

The Collect of the Day *or another collect*

The Lord's Prayer

An Ending *(page 116)*

The choice of psalm and reading may be from the appointed weekday lectionary or from some other system of regular bible reading.

MONDAY
Creation in Christ: Creation and Providence

Almighty God,
maker of all good things:
Father, Lord of all creation,
in Christ you have shown us the purpose of your providence,
and call us to be responsible in the world.

INTERCESSION

We pray for THE WORLD
  all the nations ...
  our own country ...
  those in authority ...
  the peace of the world ...
  racial harmony ...
  those who maintain order ...

THANKSGIVING

Almighty God, we give you thanks
  for the order of created things, the resources of the earth,
  and the gift of human life ...

  for the continuing work of creation,
  our share in it,
  and for creative vision and inventive skill ...

  for your faithfulness to us in patience and in love,
  and for every human response of obedience
  and humble achievement ...

CONCLUDING PRAYER

**May we delight in your purpose
and work to bring all things to their true end;
through Jesus Christ our Lord. Amen.**

The Incarnate Life of Christ: Revelation and Human Knowledge

God our Father,
you gave us your Son, Jesus Christ,
to share our life on earth,
to grow in wisdom,
to toil with his hands,
and to make known the ways of your kingdom.

We pray for THE COMMUNITY
       those who work ...
       the unemployed ...
       those in education ...
       those in research ...
       those in communications ...
       those who maintain the life of the community ...

God our Father, we give you thanks
       for Christ's revelation of yourself,
       his care for people,
       and his joy in obedience ...

       for the value he gave to human labour,
       the strength he promised us for service,
       the call to follow in his way ...

       for all opportunities of work and of leisure,
       all truth that we have learned,
       and all discoveries we have made ...

**Give us deeper reverence for the truth,
and such wisdom in the use of knowledge
that your kingdom may be advanced
and your name glorified;
through Jesus Christ our Lord. Amen.**

The Cross of Christ: Reconciliation and Human Relationships

Loving Father,
you have reconciled us to yourself in Christ;
by your Spirit you enable us to live as your sons and daughters.

We pray for PERSONAL RELATIONSHIPS
       the home, and family life ...
       children deprived of home ...
       friends, relations and neighbours ...
       relationships in daily life and work ...
       those who are estranged ...
       those who feel unloved ...
       all ministries of care ...

Loving Father, we give you thanks
       for the obedience of Christ fulfilled in the cross,
       his bearing of the sin of the world,
       his mercy for the world, which never fails ...

       for the joy of loving and being loved,
       for friendship,
       the lives to which our own are bound,
       the gift of peace with you and with one another ...

       for the communities in whose life we share
       and all relationships in which reconciliation may be known ...

**Help us to share in Christ's ministry
of love and service to one another;
through the same Jesus Christ our Lord,
who in the unity of the Holy Spirit
is one with you for ever. Amen.**

The Resurrection of Christ: The Household of Faith, the Church

Eternal God,
you have raised Jesus Christ from the dead
and exalted him to your right hand in glory;
through him you have called your Church into being,
that your people might know you
and make your name known.

INTERCESSION

We pray for THE CHURCH
       the Church universal, and local ...
       the unity of the Church ...
       the ministries of the Church ...
       the mission of the Church ...
       the renewal of the Church ...
       all Christians in this place ...

THANKSGIVING

Eternal God, we give you thanks
       for the apostolic gospel committed to your Church,
       the continuing presence and power of your Spirit,
       the ministry of Word, Sacrament and Prayer ...

       for the mission in which you have called us to share,
       the will to unity, and its fruit in common action,
       the faithful witness of those who are true to Christ ...

       for all works of compassion
       and every service that proclaims your love.

CONCLUDING PRAYER

In peace and unity
may your people offer the unfailing sacrifice of praise,
and make your glory known;
through Jesus Christ our Lord. Amen.

The Priestly Ministry of Christ: All that meets Human Need

Gracious God and Father,
you have given your Son for us all,
that his death might be our life
and his affliction our peace.

INTERCESSION

We pray for THE SUFFERING
     the hungry ...
     the refugees ...
     the prisoners ...
     the persecuted ...
     all who bring sin and suffering to others ...
     all who seek to bring care and relief ...

THANKSGIVING

Gracious God and Father, we give you thanks
     for the cross of Christ at the heart of creation,
     the presence of Christ in our weakness and strength,
     the grace of Christ to transform our suffering ...

     for all ministries of healing,
     all agencies of relief,
     all that sets us free from pain, fear and distress ...

     for the assurance that your mercy knows no limit,
     and for the privilege of sharing Christ's ministry in prayer.

CONCLUDING PRAYER

**In darkness and in light,
in trouble and in joy,
help us to trust your love,
to serve your purpose
and to praise your name;
through Jesus Christ our Lord. Amen.**

Consummation in Christ: The Fulfilment of the Divine Purpose

Eternal God,
you have declared in Christ
the completion of all your purpose of love.

We pray for PEOPLE IN NEED
those who are tempted ...
those in despair ...
those who are sick ...
those with disabilities or who have special needs ...
those who are enslaved by addictions ...
the elderly and the dying ...
those who mourn ...
all ministries of care and healing ...

Eternal God, we give thanks
for the triumphs of the gospel that herald your salvation,
the signs of renewal that declare the coming of your kingdom,
the examples of human lives that reveal your work of grace ...

for all those who have died in the faith of Christ ...

for the unceasing praise of the company of heaven,
the promise to those who mourn that all tears shall be wiped away,
the pledge of death destroyed and victory won ...

for our foretaste of eternal life
through baptism and eucharist,
our hope in the Spirit,
the communion of saints ...

**May we live by faith,
walk in hope and be renewed in love,
until the world reflects your glory
and you are all in all.
Even so, come Lord Jesus. Amen.**

SOME PRAYERS AND THANKSGIVINGS

FROM EARLIER EDITIONS OF *The Book of Common Prayer*
AND FROM *Alternative Prayer Book*

The World

FOR CHRISTIAN CITIZENSHIP

Look, we beseech thee, O Lord, upon the people of this land who are called after thy holy Name; and grant that they may ever walk worthy of their Christian profession. Grant unto us all that, laying aside our divisions, we may be united in heart and mind to bear the burdens which are laid upon us. Help us to respond to the call of our country according to our several powers; put far from us selfish indifference to the needs of others; and give us grace to fulfil our daily duties with sober diligence. Keep us from all uncharitableness in word or deed; and enable us by patient continuance in well-doing to glorify thy Name; through Jesus Christ our Lord.

FOR THE PEACE OF THE WORLD

Almighty God, from whom all thoughts of truth and peace proceed; Kindle, we pray thee, in every heart the true love of peace; and guide with thy pure and peaceable wisdom those who take counsel for the nations of the earth; that in tranquillity thy kingdom may go forward, till the earth is filled with the knowledge of thy love; through Jesus Christ our Lord.

THE EUROPEAN UNION

O Lord our heavenly Father, we pray you to guide and direct the member states of the European Union. Draw us closer to one another, and help us to attain justice and freedom, and to use our resources for the good of people everywhere; through Jesus Christ our Lord.

FOR IRELAND

Almighty and merciful God, who in days of old didst give to this land the benediction of thy holy Church; Withdraw not, we pray thee, thy favour from us, but so correct what is amiss, and supply what is lacking, that we may more and more bring forth fruit to thy glory; through Jesus Christ our Lord.

N.I. [A Prayer for Queen Elizabeth the Second

Almighty God, the fountain of all goodness, we humbly beseech thee to behold thy servant, *Queen Elizabeth.* Endue *her* with thy Holy Spirit; enrich *her* with thy heavenly grace; prosper *her* with all happiness; and bring *her* to thine everlasting kingdom; through Jesus Christ our Lord.]

Pastoral

For Candidates for Confirmation

O God, who through the teaching of thy Son Jesus Christ didst prepare the disciples for the coming of the Comforter; Make ready, we beseech thee, the hearts and minds of thy servants who at this time are seeking the gifts of the Holy Spirit through the laying on of hands, that, drawing near with penitent and faithful hearts, they may be filled with the power of his divine presence; through the same Jesus Christ our Lord.

For Hospitals and Infirmaries

Almighty God, whose blessed Son went about doing good, and healing all manner of sickness; Continue, we beseech thee, this his gracious work among us, especially in the hospitals and infirmaries of our land; cheer, heal, and sanctify the sick; grant to the physicians, surgeons, and nurses wisdom and skill, sympathy and patience; and send down thy blessing on all who labour to relieve suffering and to forward thy purposes of love; through Jesus Christ our Lord.

For Those in Affliction or Distress

Almighty Father, be present, we beseech thee, with those who are in sorrow, in suffering, in sickness, or in distress; and be thou their abiding stay and succour; for the sake of Jesus Christ our Lord.

The Sick and Suffering

Heavenly Father, we pray for the sick and suffering. Help them to know your love that they may seek strength from you, and find peace and healing in your presence; through Jesus Christ our Lord.

Grant, O Lord, to all who are bereaved, the spirit of faith and courage, that they may have strength to meet the days to come with steadfastness and patience, not sorrowing as those without hope, but in thankful remembrance of thy great goodness in past years, and in the sure expectation of a joyful reunion in the heavenly places; and this we ask in the Name of Jesus Christ our Lord.

O God, who art present in every place; Mercifully hear our prayers for those whom we love, now absent from us; watch over them, we beseech thee, and protect them in all anxiety, danger, and temptation; teach us and them to know that thou art always near, and that we are one in thee for ever; through Jesus Christ our Lord.

O almighty God, whose way is in the sea and whose paths are in the great waters: Be present, we beseech thee, with all seafarers in the manifold dangers of the deep; protect them from all perils, prosper them in their course, and bring them in safety to the haven where they would be, with a grateful sense of thy mercies; through Jesus Christ our Lord.

Seasonal

O almighty God, who alone art without variableness or shadow of turning, and hast safely brought us, through the changes of time, to the beginning of another year; We beseech thee to pardon the sins we have committed in the year which is past, and give us grace that we may spend the remainder of our days to thy honour and glory; through Jesus Christ our Lord.

Almighty God, Lord of heaven and earth, in whom we live, and move, and have our being; who dost cause thy sun to rise on the evil and on the good, and sendest rain both upon the just and the unjust; We beseech thee at this time favourably to behold thy people who call upon thee, and send thy blessing down from heaven to give us a fruitful season; that, our hearts being continually filled with thy goodness, we may evermore give thanks unto thee in thy holy Church; through Jesus Christ our Lord.

The Church's Ministry

Almighty God, our heavenly Father, who hast purchased to thyself an universal Church by the precious blood of thy dear Son; Mercifully look upon the same, and at this time so guide and govern the minds of thy servants the bishops and pastors of thy flock, that they may lay hands suddenly on no one, but faithfully and wisely make choice of fit persons to serve in the sacred ministry of thy Church. And to those which shall be ordained to any holy function give thy grace and heavenly benediction; that both by their life and doctrine they may set forth thy glory, and set forward the salvation of all people; through Jesus Christ our Lord.

ON THE DAY ON WHICH DEACONS OR PRIESTS ARE ORDERED

Almighty God, the giver of all good gifts, who of thy divine providence hast appointed divers orders in thy Church; Give thy grace, we humbly beseech thee, to all those who are this day called to any office and administration in the same; and so replenish them with the truth of thy doctrine, and endue them with innocency of life, that they may faithfully serve before thee, to the glory of thy great name, and the benefit of thy holy Church; through Jesus Christ our Lord.

FOR THE INCREASE OF THE MINISTRY

O almighty God, look mercifully upon the world, redeemed by the blood of thy dear Son, and send forth many more to do the work of the ministry, that perishing souls may be rescued, and thy glorious triumph may be hastened by the perfecting of thine elect; through the same thy Son, Jesus Christ our Lord.

DURING THE VACANCY OF A SEE

O almighty God, who by thy Holy Spirit dost move the hearts of thy people; May it please thee so to direct the counsels of those who are appointed to choose a bishop for this Church and diocese, that we may be given a pastor who in faithfulness and wisdom shall lead thy flock in the way of holiness; through Jesus Christ our Lord.

Almighty God, the giver of every good gift, look graciously, we beseech thee, on thy Church, and so guide with thy heavenly wisdom the minds of those to whom is committed the choice of a minister for this parish, that we may receive a faithful pastor, who shall feed thy flock according to thy will, and make ready a people acceptable unto thee; through Jesus Christ, thine only Son our Lord.

The Church

FOR CHRISTIAN UNITY

O God, the Father of our Lord Jesus Christ, our only Saviour, the Prince of Peace; Give us grace seriously to lay to heart the great dangers we are in by our unhappy divisions. Take away all hatred and prejudice, and whatsoever else may hinder us from godly union and concord: that, as there is but one Body, and one Spirit, and one hope of our calling, one Lord, one Faith, one Baptism, one God and Father of us all, so we may henceforth be all of one heart, and of one soul, united in one holy bond of truth and peace, of faith and charity, and may with one mind and one mouth glorify thee; through Jesus Christ our Lord.

FOR CHRISTIAN UNITY

O Lord Jesus Christ, who didst say to thine Apostles, Peace I leave with you, my peace I give unto you; Regard not our sins, but the faith of thy Church, and grant it that peace and unity which is agreeable to thy will; who livest and reignest with the Father and the Holy Spirit, one God, world without end.

FOR THE RENEWAL OF THE CHURCH

God the Holy Spirit, come in power and bring new life to the Church; renew us in love and service, and enable us to be faithful to our Lord and Saviour Jesus Christ.

FOR THE CHURCH OF THIS LAND

Hear us, most merciful God, for that part of the Church which thou hast planted in our land, that it may hold fast the faith which thou gavest unto the Saints, and in the end bear much fruit to eternal life; through Jesus Christ our Lord.

Lord God, the Father of lights and the Fountain of all wisdom, who hast promised, through thy Son Jesus Christ, to be with thy universal Church to the end of the world; We humbly beseech thee with thy favour to behold the Bishops, Clergy, and People, who are about to assemble and take counsel together [*or*, who are now assembled and taking counsel together] in thy Name, for this Church. Mercifully grant that thy Holy Spirit may rest upon them, enlighten, and guide them; and that all their consultations may be prospered to the advancement of thy honour and glory, and the welfare of thy Church. Lead them and us into all truth; that so this Church may evermore hold fast and abide in the Apostolic and true Catholic faith, and serve thee without fear in pureness of worship and life, according to thy holy will; through Jesus Christ our Lord and Saviour.

Almighty God, we beseech thee to bless this our parish. Forgive us our many and grievous sins. Draw us nearer to thyself, and cause true religion to increase and abound amongst us. Prosper the reading and preaching of thy Word, and bless all the ministrations of thy Church. Give patience to the sick and afflicted, and make their sufferings a blessing to them. Visit with thy favour the schools and all who teach or learn therein; and make us to grow in grace and in the knowledge of thee and of thy dear Son, whom to know is life eternal. Hear us for the sake of him who died for us, Jesus Christ our Lord.

Almighty God, who by thy Son Jesus Christ didst give commandment to the apostles, that they should go into all the world, and preach the gospel to every creature; Grant to us, whom thou hast called into thy Church, a ready will to obey thy Word, and fill us with a hearty desire to make thy way known upon earth, thy saving health among all nations. Look with compassion on all that have not known thee, and upon the multitudes that are scattered abroad as sheep having no shepherd. O heavenly Father, Lord of the harvest, have respect, we beseech thee, to our prayers, and send forth labourers into thine harvest. Fit and prepare them by thy grace for the work of their ministry; give them the spirit of power, and of love, and of a sound mind; strengthen them to endure hardness; and grant that thy Holy Spirit may prosper their work, and that by their life and doctrine they may set forth thy glory, and set forward the salvation of all people; through Jesus Christ our Lord.

O God, our heavenly Father, we humbly pray thee to bless abundantly the efforts that are now being made [or, about to be made] to turn thy people in this parish [and diocese] to more sincere repentance and more living faith. Prepare all hearts to receive the seed of thy Word. Grant that it may take deep root, and bring forth fruit to thy glory. Arouse the careless amongst us, humble the self-righteous, soften the hardened, encourage the fearful, relieve the doubting, bring many souls in loving faith and self-surrender to thyself, and visit us with thy salvation; through Jesus Christ our Lord.

General and Concluding Prayers

A PRAYER OF THE EASTERN CHURCH

Be mindful, O Lord, of thy people present here before thee, and of those who are absent through age, sickness, or infirmity. Care for the infants, guide the young, support the aged, encourage the faint-hearted, collect the scattered, and bring back the wandering to thy fold. Travel with the voyagers, defend the widows, shield the orphans, deliver the captives, heal the sick. Succour all who are in tribulation, necessity, or distress. Remember for good all those that love us, and those that hate us, and those that have desired us, unworthy as we are, to pray for them. And those whom we have forgotten, do thou, O Lord, remember. For thou art the helper of the helpless, the saviour of the lost, the refuge of the wanderer, the healer of the sick. Thou, who knowest the need of each one, and hast heard their prayer, grant unto each according to thy merciful loving-kindness, and thy eternal love; through Jesus Christ our Lord.

FOR A RIGHT USE OF THE LORD'S DAY

O Lord Jesus Christ, who as on this day didst rise from the dead; Teach us to reverence this thy holy day, and give us grace so to use it, that we may rise to newness of life, to thy honour and glory, who livest and reignest with the Father and the Holy Spirit, one God, world without end.

O heavenly Father, in whom we live and move and have our being; We humbly pray thee so to guide and govern us by thy Holy Spirit, that in all the cares and occupations of our daily life we may never forget thee, but remember that we are ever walking in thy sight; through Jesus Christ our Lord.

FOR PARDON

O God, whose nature and property is ever to have mercy and to forgive; Receive our humble petitions; and, though we be tied and bound with the chain of our sins, yet let the pitifulness of thy great mercy loose us; for the honour of Jesus Christ, our Mediator and Advocate.

FOR FAITHFULNESS

Remember, O Lord, that which thou hast wrought in us, and not what we deserve; and as thou hast called us to thy service, make us worthy of our calling; through Jesus Christ our Lord.

FOR PROTECTION

Almighty and eternal God, sanctify our hearts and bodies in the ways of your laws and in the works of your commandments; that under your protection we may be preserved in body and soul; through Jesus Christ our Lord.

FOR GUIDANCE

Go before us, Lord, in all our doings with your most gracious favour, and further us with your continual help; that in all our works begun, continued and ended in you, we may glorify your holy name, and finally by your mercy attain everlasting life; through Jesus Christ our Lord.

A CONCLUDING PRAYER

Heavenly Father, you have promised through your Son, Jesus Christ, that when we meet in his name, and pray according to his mind, he will be among us and hear our prayer. In love and wisdom fulfil our desires, and give us your greatest gift, which is to know you, the only true God, and Jesus Christ our Lord, who lives and reigns with you and the Holy Spirit, one God, now and for ever.

or

Almighty God, the fountain of all wisdom, you know our needs before we ask, and our ignorance in asking; have compassion on our weakness, and give us those things which for our unworthiness we dare not, and in our blindness we cannot ask; for the sake of your Son, Jesus Christ our Lord.

Thanksgivings

For the Church

Almighty God, whose mercy is over all thy works; We praise thee for the blessings which have been brought to mankind by thy holy Church throughout all the world. We bless thee for the grace of thy sacraments; for our fellowship in Christ with thee, and with one another; for the teaching of the Scriptures and for the preaching of thy Word. We thank thee for the holy example of thy saints in all ages; for thy servants departed this life in thy faith and fear, and for the memory and example of all that has been true and good in their lives. And we humbly beseech thee that we may be numbered with them in the great company of the redeemed in heaven; through Jesus Christ our Lord.

or

Almighty God, we praise you for the blessings brought to the world through your Church. We bless you for the grace of the sacraments, for our fellowship in Christ with you and with each other, for the teaching of the Scriptures, and for the preaching of your word. We thank you for the holy example of your saints, for your faithful servants departed this life, and for the memory and example of all that has been true and good in their lives. Number us with them in the company of the redeemed in heaven; through Jesus Christ our Lord.

For the holy scriptures

Almighty God, we thank you for the gift of your holy Word. May it be a lantern to our feet, a light to our paths, and a strength in our lives. In the name of your Son, Jesus Christ our Lord.

COMPLINE

Stand

The Lord Almighty grant us a quiet night and a perfect end. **Amen.**

Brethren, be sober, be vigilant; because your adversary the devil, as a roaring lion, walketh about, seeking whom he may devour: whom resist, steadfast in the faith. *1 Peter 5: 8, 9.*

But thou, O Lord, have mercy upon us.
Thanks be to God.

O God, make speed to save us.
O Lord, make haste to help us.

Glory be to the Father, and to the Son, and to the Holy Spirit;
as it was in the beginning, is now, and ever shall be, world without end. Amen.

Praise ye the Lord.
The Lord's Name be praised.

PSALM

One or more of the following, or any other suitable psalm:

Psalm 4   *Cum invocarem.*

1   Hear me when I call, O God of my righteousness: ▪
    thou hast set me at liberty when I was in trouble;
        have mercy upon me, and hearken unto my prayer.

2   O ye sons of men, how long will ye blaspheme mine honour, ▪
    and have such pleasure in vanity, and seek after lying?

3   Know this also, that the Lord hath chosen to himself
        the man that is godly: ▪
    when I call upon the Lord, he will hear me.

4   Stand in awe, and sin not: ▪
    commune with your own heart, and in your chamber, and be still.

5 Offer the sacrifice of righteousness ∎
   and put your trust in the Lord.

6 There be many that say: ∎
   Who will show us any good?

7 Lord, lift thou up ∎
   the light of thy countenance upon us.

8 Thou hast put gladness in my heart, ∎
   more than men have, when corn and wine increase.

9 I will lay me down in peace, and take my rest: ∎
   for it is thou, Lord, only, that makest me dwell in safety.

      Glory be to the Father, ∎
      and to the Son, and to the Holy Spirit;
      as it was in the beginning, ∎
      is now and ever shall be, world without end. Amen.

Psalm 31: 1-6   *In te, Domine, speravi.*

1 In thee, O Lord, have I put my trust: ∎
   let me never be put to confusion, deliver me in thy righteousness.

2 Bow down thine ear to me: ∎
   make haste to deliver me.

3 And be thou my strong rock, and house of defence, ∎
   that thou mayest save me.

4 For thou art my strong rock, and my castle: ∎
   be thou also my guide, and lead me for thy Name's sake.

5 Draw me out of the net, that they have laid privily for me, ∎
   for thou art my strength.

6 Into thy hands I commend my spirit, ∎
   for thou hast redeemed me, O Lord, thou God of truth.

      Glory be to the Father, ∎
      and to the Son, and to the Holy Spirit;
      as it was in the beginning, ∎
      is now and ever shall be, world without end. Amen.

Psalm 91   *Qui habitat.*

1 Whoso dwelleth under the defence of the Most High ∎
   shall abide under the shadow of the Almighty.

2   I will say unto the Lord, Thou art my hope, and my strong hold: ▪
    my God, in him will I trust.

3   For he shall deliver thee from the snare of the hunter ▪
    and from the noisome pestilence.

4   He shall defend thee under his wings,
        and thou shalt be safe under his feathers: ▪
    his faithfulness and truth shall be thy shield and buckler.

5   Thou shalt not be afraid for any terror by night, ▪
    nor for the arrow that flieth by day;

6   For the pestilence that walketh in darkness, ▪
    nor for the sickness that destroyeth in the noon-day.

7   A thousand shall fall beside thee, and ten thousand at thy right hand, ▪
    but it shall not come nigh thee.

8   Yea, with thine eyes shalt thou behold ▪
    and see the reward of the ungodly.

9   For thou, Lord, art my hope: ▪
    thou hast set thine house of defence very high.

10 There shall no evil happen unto thee, ▪
    neither shall any plague come nigh thy dwelling.

11 For he shall give his angels charge over thee ▪
    to keep thee in all thy ways.

12 They shall bear thee in their hands ▪
    that thou hurt not thy foot against a stone.

13 Thou shalt go upon the lion and adder: ▪
    the young lion and the dragon shalt thou tread under thy feet.

14 Because he hath set his love upon me, therefore will I deliver him: ▪
    I will set him up, because he hath known my Name.

15 He shall call upon me, and I will hear him: ▪
    yea, I am with him in trouble; I will deliver him,
        and bring him to honour.

16 With long life will I satisfy him ▪
    and show him my salvation.

        Glory be to the Father, ▪
        and to the Son, and to the Holy Spirit;
        as it was in the beginning, ▪
        is now and ever shall be, world without end. Amen.

Psalm 134   *Ecce nunc.*

1   Behold now, praise the Lord, ▪
      all ye servants of the Lord;

2   Ye that by night stand in the house of the Lord, ▪
      even in the courts of the house of our God.

3   Lift up your hands in the sanctuary ▪
      and praise the Lord.

4   The Lord that made heaven and earth ▪
      give thee blessing out of Sion.

         Glory be to the Father, ▪
         and to the Son, and to the Holy Spirit;
         as it was in the beginning, ▪
         is now and ever shall be, world without end. Amen.

READING

One of the following, or some other appropriate passage of Scripture:

Thou, O Lord, art in the midst of us, and we are called by thy Name; leave us not, O Lord our God. *Jeremiah 14: 9*

or

Come unto me, all ye that labour and are heavy laden, and I will give you rest. Take my yoke upon you, and learn of me; for I am meek and lowly in heart: and ye shall find rest unto your souls. For my yoke is easy, and my burden is light. *Matthew 11: 28-30*

or

Now the God of peace, that brought again from the dead our Lord Jesus, that great Shepherd of the sheep, through the blood of the everlasting covenant, make you perfect in every good work to do his will, working in you that which is well-pleasing in his sight, through Jesus Christ; to whom be glory for ever and ever. Amen. *Hebrews 18: 20,21*

An address may follow.

Stand

Into thy hands, O Lord, I commend my spirit.
For thou hast redeemed me, O Lord, thou God of truth.

Before the ending of the day,
Creator of the world, we pray
That thou with wonted love wouldst keep
Thy watch around us while we sleep.

O let no evil dreams be near,
Or phantoms of the night appear;
Our ghostly enemy restrain,
Lest aught of sin our bodies stain.

Almighty Father, hear our cry
Through Jesus Christ our Lord most high,
Who with the Holy Ghost and thee
Doth live and reign eternally. Amen.

The seasonal variations of verse 3 from the Church Hymnal may be used at the appropriate times of the year.

Keep me as the apple of an eye.
Hide me under the shadow of thy wings.

**Preserve us, O Lord, while waking, and guard us while sleeping,
that awake we may watch with Christ, and asleep we may rest in peace.**

NUNC DIMITTIS   *Luke 2: 29-32*

1   Lord, now lettest thou thy servant depart in peace, ▪
     according to thy word.
2   For mine eyes have seen thy salvation, ▪
     which thou hast prepared before the face of all people;
3   To be a light to lighten the Gentiles ▪
     and to be the glory of thy people Israel.
          Glory be to the Father, ▪
          and to the Son, and to the Holy Spirit;
          as it was in the beginning, ▪
          is now and ever shall be, world without end. Amen.

**Preserve us, O Lord, while waking, and guard us while sleeping,
that awake we may watch with Christ, and asleep we may rest in peace.**

I believe in God, the Father almighty,
maker of heaven and earth;
And in Jesus Christ his only Son our Lord;
who was conceived by the Holy Spirit,
born of the Virgin Mary,
suffered under Pontius Pilate,
was crucified, dead, and buried.
He descended into hell.
The third day he rose again from the dead.
He ascended into heaven,
and sitteth on the right hand of God the Father almighty.
From thence he shall come to judge the quick and the dead.
I believe in the Holy Spirit,
the holy catholic Church,
the communion of saints,
the forgiveness of sins,
the resurrection of the body,
and the life everlasting. Amen.

Kneel
Let us pray.

Lord, have mercy upon us.
Christ, have mercy upon us.
Lord, have mercy upon us.

Our Father, who art in heaven, Hallowed be thy Name, Thy kingdom come, Thy will be done, On earth as it is in heaven. Give us this day our daily bread. And forgive us our trespasses, As we forgive those who trespass against us. And lead us not into temptation, But deliver us from evil. Amen.

Blessed art thou, Lord God of our fathers,
to be praised and glorified above all for ever;

Let us bless the Father, the Son, and the Holy Spirit.
Let us praise him and magnify him for ever.

Blessed art thou, O Lord, in the firmament of heaven
to be praised and glorified above all for ever.

The Almighty and most merciful Lord guard us and give us his blessing.
Amen.

We confess to God Almighty, the Father, the Son, and the Holy Spirit, That we have sinned in thought, word, and deed, Through our own grievous fault. Wherefore we pray God to have mercy upon us.
Almighty God, have mercy upon us, Forgive us all our sins, Deliver us from all evil, Confirm and strengthen us in all goodness, And bring us to life everlasting; Through Jesus Christ our Lord. Amen.

The priest, when present, pronounces the absolution.
May the Almighty and merciful Lord grant unto you pardon and remission of all your sins, time for amendment of life, and the grace and comfort of the Holy Spirit. **Amen.**

Wilt thou not turn again and quicken us
that thy people may rejoice in thee?

O Lord, shew thy mercy upon us
and grant us thy salvation.

Vouchsafe, O Lord, to keep us this night without sin.
O Lord, have mercy upon us, have mercy upon us.

O Lord, hear our prayer
and let our cry come unto thee.

Let us pray.

One or more of the following:

Lighten our darkness, we beseech thee, O Lord; and by thy great mercy defend us from all perils and dangers of this night; for the love of thy only Son, our Saviour, Jesus Christ. **Amen.**

Be present, O merciful God, and protect us through the silent hours of this night, so that we, who are wearied by the changes and chances of this fleeting world, may repose upon thy eternal changelessness; through Jesus Christ our Lord. **Amen.**

Look down, O Lord, from thy heavenly throne, illuminate the darkness of this night with thy celestial brightness, and from the children of light banish the deeds of darkness; through Jesus Christ our Lord. **Amen.**

O Lord Jesus Christ, Son of the Living God, who at this evening hour didst rest in the sepulchre, and didst thereby sanctify the grave to be a bed of hope to thy people: Make us so to abound in sorrow for our sins, which were the cause of thy passion, that when our bodies lie in the dust, our souls may live with thee: who livest and reignest with the Father and the Holy Spirit, one God world without end. **Amen.**

Visit, we beseech thee, O Lord, this place (*or,* our homes), and drive away all the snares of the enemy; Let thy holy angels dwell herein (*or,* therein) to preserve us in peace; and may thy blessing be upon us evermore; through Jesus Christ our Lord. **Amen.**

We will lay us down in peace and take our rest.
For it is thou, Lord, only, that makest us dwell in safety.

The Lord be with you
and with thy spirit.

Let us bless the Lord.
Thanks be to God.

The Almighty and merciful Lord, the Father, the Son, and the Holy Spirit, bless and preserve us this night and for evermore. **Amen.**

This Office, or the part which follows the Apostles' Creed, is suitable for use at evening devotions at home.

A LATE EVENING OFFICE

Blessed be our God for all time, now and for evermore. **Amen.**

Glory to you, our God, glory be to you,
Holy Spirit, Comforter,
treasure of all goodness and giver of life,
come and dwell in us,
cleanse us from all sin,
and in your love bring us to salvation.

Holy God, holy and strong,
holy and immortal,
have mercy on us.

Psalm 134

1   Come bless the Lord, all you servants of the Lord, ▪
    you that by night stand in the house of the Lord.

2   Lift up your hands towards the holy place ▪
    and bless the Lord.

3   May the Lord bless you from Zion, ▪
    the Lord who made heaven and earth.

        Glory to the Father, and to the Son, ▪
        and to the Holy Spirit;
        as it was in the beginning, is now, ▪
        and shall be for ever. Amen.

or another suitable psalm

A READING
from the New Testament

MEDITATION
on the Reading

NUNC DIMITTIS   *The Song of Simeon*

1   Lord, now you let your servant go in peace, ▪
    your word has been fulfilled.

2   My own eyes have seen the salvation ▪
    which you have prepared in the sight of every people.

3   A light to reveal you to the nations ▪
      and the glory of your people Israel.
            Glory to the Father, and to the Son, ▪
            and to the Holy Spirit;
            as it was in the beginning, is now, ▪
            and shall be for ever. Amen.

and/or a hymn

PRAYER

Let us pray to the Lord with all our heart and with all our soul.
Lord, have mercy.

Let us pray for all Christian people, that they may live in love and truth.
Lord, have mercy.

Let us pray for all ministers of the Church, and for our brothers and sisters in Christ.
Lord, have mercy.

Let us pray for peace throughout the world, and for all governments.
Lord, have mercy.

Let us pray for our neighbours and for all our friends.
Lord, have mercy.

Let us pray for those who hate us as we pray for those who love us.
Lord, have mercy.

Let us pray for refugees and prisoners, and for all who are exposed to the dangers of travel.
Lord, have mercy.

Let us pray for all sick people, for the sorrowful and the dying.
Lord, have mercy.

Let us pray for the abundance of the fruits of the earth, and that the poor and hungry may receive a just share.
Lord, have mercy.

Let us remember our brothers and sisters who have entered into eternal rest.
Blessed are the dead who die in the Lord.

Let us continue praying in silence
Silence is kept.
or
Let us continue praying in a time of open prayer.
A period of open prayer follows.

The leader brings either of these to an end saying
Lord, in your mercy
hear our prayer.

Our Father in heaven ...
or
Our Father, who art in heaven ...

Lord Almighty,
come and scatter the darkness of our hearts
by the light of your presence;
that we may know you
the Light of the world
and the one true God,
blessed this night and for evermore. Amen.

Let us bless the Lord.
Thanks be to God.

May the Almighty and merciful God,
the Father, the Son, and the Holy Spirit,
bless us and keep us. **Amen.**

SERVICE OF THE WORD

THE STRUCTURE OF THE SERVICE

Preparation

* A liturgical Greeting

  An invitation to worship

  A hymn *may be sung.*

* Penitence *may be at this part of the service or in* Response.

* An Acclamation *and/or* a Song of praise

  Metrical forms of canticles may be used, or a hymn may be sung.

* The Collect of the day

Ministry of the Word

* Readings *from the Bible*

* A Psalm *and/or* a Scripture Song *may precede or follow readings.*

  A Bible Responsory *may follow a reading.*

* The Sermon

  A hymn *may be sung.*

Response

* An Affirmation of Faith

  The Apostles' Creed, the Nicene Creed, the Affirmation of Faith from the Renewal of Baptismal Vows (page 400) or a scriptural affirmation of Faith.

* The Prayers

     Intercessions and Thanksgiving

     Penitence *(if not used above)*

     A general collect

  The whole section is concluded with The Lord's Prayer *in one of its approved forms.*

  A hymn *may be sung.*

Dismissal

* A dismissal prayer

  The Blessing

  A salutation

*Sections marked with * are mandatory in any service based on this structure.*

Service of the Word is for use on occasions when the prescribed services of Morning and Evening Prayer or Holy Communion may not meet the needs of a particular congregation.

A basic structure for all such services is provided.

Examples of working out that structure approved by the House of Bishops have been published. Resource material authorised by the House of Bishops such as *Patterns for Worship* (Church House Publishing 2002) or *Common Worship: Times and Seasons* (Church of England 2004) may be used to work out other forms based on the Structure.

GUIDELINES

1 The Structure has four sections:

Preparation: A Greeting, an invitation to worship, a hymn of praise to God, an act of penitence (but this may on occasion be more appropriate in the section called the *Response*) and an Acclamation.

The Collect of the day is the climax of the *Preparation* and leads in to the *Ministry of the Word*.

Ministry of the Word: The Reading and exposition of Holy Scripture is the central part of the service. The use of the Psalms whether sung in metrical versions, or chanted or recited from the Psalter in this book, enables the congregation to interact with the Readings. Periods of silence also help this interaction. The use of Scripture Songs ('canticles') is recommended.

Response: Normally an Affirmation of Faith is followed by prayers for the Church and for the World. Sometimes penitence is also appropriate if not used in the *Preparation*. After a General Collect the climax of this section comes as the congregation says together the Lord's Prayer. In this section the Offering may come before or after the Prayers.

The service ends with *The Dismissal*. Either a Dismissal Prayer or a Blessing may be followed by a final salutation.

2 The keynote of *Service of the Word* is simplicity. It should not have a complicated opening. The service begins with a *Greeting* and *Invitation* to worship. This governs the choice of any hymn to be sung at this point.

3 *Penitence* will normally be expressed in the *Preparation*.

4 The *Acclamation* is a proclamation of God's majesty and love that derives from the *Greeting* and *Invitation*. Traditional elements like the *Sursum Corda* and *Sanctus*, as well as Canticles such as *Gloria in Excelsis* may have a place here.

5 The *Collect of the day* is given a special position, similar to its use in the Communion Service: the climax of the *Preparation*. It is the 'link' with all the other worship of the Church on the day. It may be introduced with a 'one-line' bidding, deriving from the central thrust of the prayer. For example: the minister may say, 'As we prepare to use the Collect of this Sunday, let us in silence pray for God's guidance.' (Or for spiritual strength or whatever is the central point of the particular collect.) After twenty seconds or so of silent prayer the Collect is then recited.

6 *Psalms* and what are entitled *Scripture Songs* are vital components of the Service. Metrical versions of some Psalms are to be found in *Church Hymnal*. Other sources of psalmody and different ways of using it can be explored.

7 There should be at least two *Readings* from the Bible. Normally the Sunday lectionary will determine the selection. On occasion readings may be presented in dramatised form.

8 The use of the terminology, *The Sermon*, the legally recognized word in the Church of Ireland, does not rule out a variety of ways of proclaiming the message of the Gospel; these may include drama, interviews and other techniques.

9 When appropriate the *Sermon* may be followed by a hymn. An *Affirmation of Faith* is regarded as essential. On some occasions it might be deemed suitable for an act of penitence to precede the *Affirmation of Faith* in the *Response*.

10 The section containing the *Prayers* should conclude with a *General Collect*. The climax of the *Prayers*, indeed of the whole *Response*, is the *Lord's Prayer*, with an appropriate introduction.

11 The service ends with the *Dismissal*. If a concluding hymn is customary it is better for this to precede the *Blessing* and final salutation.

12 Periods of silence are important. Some indications of where these are most suitable have been given. Care and instruction are needed so that worshippers can learn how to use silence in worship.

Construction is by one of two methods:

1 A verse of scripture is read by the minister.
     This is repeated by the congregation.
   The minister says some complementary words of scripture.
     The congregation repeats the first verse again.
   There is a trinitarian ascription
     Finally the congregation repeats the scripture verse a third time.

2 A verse of scripture is read by the minister.
     A different but complementary verse is spoken by the congregation.
   Another verse is spoken by the minister.
     The congregation repeats its response.
   The Gloria is spoken by the minister.
     The congregation again repeats its response.

Similar responsories will be found in the Canadian *Book of Alternative Services* (1985), in the New Zealand *Prayer Book* (1988), in *Promise of his Glory* (1990) and in *Celebrating Common Prayer* (1992).

The Litany

THE LITANY

O God the Father, of heaven:
have mercy upon us miserable sinners.
O God the Father, of heaven:
have mercy upon us miserable sinners.

O God the Son, Redeemer of the world:
have mercy upon us miserable sinners.
O God the Son, Redeemer of the world:
have mercy upon us miserable sinners.

O God the Holy Spirit, proceeding from the Father and the Son: have
mercy upon us miserable sinners.
O God the Holy Spirit, proceeding from the Father and the Son: have
mercy upon us miserable sinners.

O holy, blessed, and glorious Trinity, three Persons and one God: have
mercy upon us miserable sinners.
O holy, blessed, and glorious Trinity, three Persons and one God: have
mercy upon us miserable sinners.

Remember not, Lord, our offences, nor the offences of our forefathers;
neither take thou vengeance of our sins: spare us, good Lord, spare thy
people, whom thou hast redeemed with thy most precious blood, and be
not angry with us for ever.
Spare us, good Lord.

From all evil and mischief; from sin, from the craft and assaults of the
devil; from thy wrath, and from everlasting damnation,
Good Lord, deliver us.

From all blindness of heart; from pride, vain-glory, and hypocrisy; from
envy, hatred, and malice, and all uncharitableness,
Good Lord, deliver us.

From fornication, and all other deadly sin; and from all the deceits of the
world, the flesh, and the devil,
Good Lord, deliver us.

From lightning and tempest; from plague, pestilence, and famine; from battle and murder, and from sudden death,
Good Lord, deliver us.

From all sedition, privy conspiracy, and rebellion; from all false doctrine, heresy, and schism; from hardness of heart, and contempt of thy Word and Commandment,
Good Lord, deliver us.

By the mystery of thy holy Incarnation; by thy holy Nativity and Circumcision; by thy Baptism, Fasting, and Temptation,
Good Lord, deliver us.

By thine Agony and bloody Sweat; by thy Cross and Passion; by thy precious Death and Burial; by thy glorious Resurrection and Ascension; and by the coming of the Holy Spirit,
Good Lord, deliver us.

In all time of our tribulation; in all time of our wealth; in the hour of death, and in the day of judgement,
Good Lord, deliver us.

We sinners do beseech thee to hear us, O Lord God; and that it may please thee to rule and govern thy holy Church universal in the right way;
We beseech thee to hear us, good Lord.

N.I. [That it may please thee to guard and bless thy servant *Elizabeth*, our most gracious *Queen* and Governor, and to rule *her* heart in thy faith, fear, and love; that *she* may evermore have affiance in thee, and ever seek thy honour and glory;
We beseech thee to hear us, good Lord.]

N.I. [That it may please thee to bless and preserve *... and all the Royal Family;
We beseech thee to hear us, good Lord.]
* Here shall be said the names and titles of members of the Royal Family, as directed.

R.I. [That it may please thee to protect and guide thy servant the President;
We beseech thee to hear us, good Lord.]

That it may please thee to illuminate all Bishops, Priests, and Deacons, with true knowledge and understanding of thy Word; and that both by their preaching and living they may set it forth, and shew it accordingly;
We beseech thee to hear us, good Lord.

That it may please thee to further the work of the Church in all the world, and to send forth labourers into thy harvest;
We beseech thee to hear us, good Lord.

N.I. [That it may please thee to endue the Ministers of the Crown, and all in authority, with grace, wisdom, and understanding;
We beseech thee to hear us, good Lord.]

R.I. [That it may please thee to endue the Ministers of this State, and all in authority, with grace, wisdom, and understanding;
We beseech thee to hear us, good Lord.]

N.I. [That it may please thee to bless and keep the Magistrates, giving them grace to execute justice and to maintain truth;
We beseech thee to hear us, good Lord.]

N.I. [That it may please thee to bless and keep the forces of the *Queen* and to shield them in all dangers and adversities;
We beseech thee to hear us, good Lord.]

R.I. [That it may please thee to bless and keep all who guard our shores, and to shield them in all dangers and adversities ;
We beseech thee to hear us, good Lord.]

That it may please thee to bless and keep all thy people;
We beseech thee to hear us, good Lord.

That it may please thee to give to all nations unity, peace, and concord;
We beseech thee to hear us, good Lord.

That it may please thee to give us an heart to love and fear thee, and diligently to live after thy commandments;
We beseech thee to hear us, good Lord.

That it may please thee to give to all thy people increase of grace to hear meekly thy Word, and to receive it with pure affection, and to bring forth the fruits of the Spirit;
We beseech thee to hear us, good Lord.

That it may please thee to bring into the way of truth all such as have erred, and are deceived;
We beseech thee to hear us, good Lord.

That it may please thee to strengthen such as do stand; and to comfort and help the weak-hearted; and to raise up them that fall; and finally to beat down Satan under our feet;
We beseech thee to hear us, good Lord.

That it may please thee to succour, help, and comfort, all that are in danger, necessity, and tribulation;
We beseech thee to hear us, good Lord.

That it may please thee to preserve all that travel by land, by water, or by air, all women labouring of child, all sick persons, and young children; and to shew thy pity upon all prisoners and captives;
We beseech thee to hear us, good Lord.

That it may please thee to defend, and provide for, the fatherless children, and widows, and all that are desolate and oppressed;
We beseech thee to hear us, good Lord.

That it may please thee to have mercy upon all men;
We beseech thee to hear us, good Lord.

That it may please thee to forgive our enemies, persecutors, and slanderers, and to turn their hearts;
We beseech thee to hear us, good Lord.

That it may please thee to give and preserve to our use the kindly fruits of the earth, so as in due time we may enjoy them;
We beseech thee to hear us, good Lord.

That it may please thee to give us true repentance; to forgive us all our sins, negligences, and ignorances; and to endue us with the grace of thy Holy Spirit to amend our lives according to thy holy Word;
We beseech thee to hear us, good Lord.

Son of God : we beseech thee to hear us.
Son of God : we beseech thee to hear us.

O Lamb of God: that takest away the sins of the world;
Grant us thy peace.

O Lamb of God: that takest away the sins of the world;
Have mercy upon us.

O Christ, hear us.
O Christ, hear us.

Lord, have mercy upon us.
Lord, have mercy upon us.

Christ, have mercy upon us.
Christ, have mercy upon us.

Lord, have mercy upon us.
Lord, have mercy upon us.

Our Father, who art in heaven, Hallowed be thy Name, Thy kingdom come, Thy will be done, On earth as it is in heaven. Give us this day our daily bread. And forgive us our trespasses, As we forgive those who trespass against us. And lead us not into temptation, But deliver us from evil. Amen.

A Prayer of Saint Chrysostom

Almighty God, who hast given us grace at this time with one accord to make our common supplications unto thee; and dost promise that when two or three are gathered together in thy Name thou wilt grant their requests; Fulfil now, O Lord, the desires and petitions of thy servants, as may be most expedient for them; granting us in this world knowledge of thy truth, and in the world to come life everlasting. **Amen.**

The grace of our Lord Jesus Christ, and the love of God, and the fellowship of the Holy Spirit, be with us all evermore. **Amen.** *2 Corinthians 13: 14*

THE LITANY
IN CONTEMPORARY LANGUAGE

The Litany is recommended for use on Sundays, Wednesdays and Fridays, particularly in the seasons of Advent and Lent and on Rogation Days.

When it is used as a separate service it may be preceded by a psalm, canticle or hymn and one of the readings of the day.

The Litany may be used in Morning Prayer or Evening Prayer after the Apostles' Creed as The Prayers of the People when it should conclude with the Collect of the Day and the Lord's Prayer.

The Litany may be said in whole or in part. Sections 1 and 5 should always be said.

I

God the Father, creator of heaven and earth,
have mercy on us.

God the Son, Redeemer of the world,
have mercy on us.

God the Holy Spirit, giver of life,
have mercy on us.

Holy, blessed and glorious Trinity, three Persons in one God,
have mercy on us.

2

Save us, good Lord, from all sin and wickedness, from pride, hypocrisy and conceit, from envy, hatred and malice, and all uncharitableness,
save us, good Lord.

From sins of thought, word and deed, from the lusts of the flesh, from the deceits of the world and the snares of the devil,
save us, good Lord.

From fire, storm and flood, from disease, pestilence and want, from war and murder, and from dying unprepared,
save us, good Lord.

From all false doctrine, from hardness of heart, from contempt of your word and commandment, and from the evil of schism.
save us, good Lord.

In times of sorrow and in times of joy, in the hour of death, and in the day of judgement,
save us, good Lord.

3

Save us, Lord Christ, by the mystery of your holy incarnation, by your birth, childhood and obedience, by your baptism, fasting and temptation,
save us, Lord Christ.

By your ministry in word and work, by your mighty acts of power, and by your preaching of the kingdom,
save us, Lord Christ.

By your agony and trial, by your cross and passion, and by your precious death and burial,
save us, Lord Christ.

By your mighty resurrection, by your glorious ascension, and by your sending of the Holy Spirit,
save us, Lord Christ.

4

FOR THE CHURCH

Hear us, good Lord: govern and direct your holy Church, fill it with love and truth, and grant it that unity which is your will,
hear us, good Lord.

Give your Church courage to preach the gospel and to make disciples of all the nations,
hear us, good Lord.

Give knowledge and understanding to bishops, priests and deacons, that by their life and teaching they may proclaim your word,
hear us, good Lord.

Give all people grace to receive your word and to bring forth the fruit of the Spirit,
hear us, good Lord.

Bring all who have erred and are deceived into the way of truth,
hear us, good Lord.

Guard and bless our rulers, especially ...
and grant that they may trust in you, and seek your honour and glory,
hear us, good Lord.

Bless our country, and give grace, wisdom and understanding to all in authority,
hear us, good Lord.

Bless the European Union,
and draw us closer to one another in justice and freedom,
hear us, good Lord.

Bless those who administer the law, that they may uphold justice in honesty and truth,
hear us, good Lord.

Bless and keep all who maintain peace and safety,
hear us, good Lord.

Give to all nations unity, peace and concord,
hear us, good Lord.

FOR ALL PEOPLE ACCORDING TO THEIR NEEDS
Strengthen the faithful, comfort and help the faint-hearted, raise up those who fall, and drive out all evil,
hear us, good Lord.

Support and encourage all who are in poverty, unemployment or distress, protect those whose work is dangerous, and keep in safety all who travel,
hear us, good Lord.

Keep fathers, mothers and children united in their family life, and give them wisdom and strength in times of stress,
hear us, good Lord.

Heal the sick, care for the old and lonely, and comfort the bereaved,
hear us, good Lord.

Remember the poor who long to hear good news: give us the will to strengthen them through acts of generous love,
hear us, good Lord.

Show your pity on victims of strife, on the homeless and the hungry, on prisoners, and on all who live in fear,
hear us, good Lord.

Forgive our enemies, persecutors and slanderers, and turn their hearts,
hear us, good Lord.

Guide and direct all who influence others through the written or the spoken word, and inspire all who serve mankind in science, industry and art,
hear us, good Lord.

Bless and keep all your people,
hear us, good Lord.

Teach us to use the resources of the earth to your glory, that all may share in your goodness and praise you for your loving kindness,
hear us, good Lord.

5

Saviour of the world, forgive our sins, known and unknown, things done, and left undone; grant us the grace of your Holy Spirit that we may amend our lives according to your holy word, and share with all your people the joys of your eternal kingdom.

Jesus, Lamb of God,
have mercy on us.

Jesus, bearer of our sins,
have mercy on us.

Jesus, Redeemer of the world,
give us your peace.

The end of the Litany

When the Litany is used as a separate service it is followed by the Lord's Prayer.

Holy Communion

THE ORDER FOR THE
ADMINISTRATION OF THE LORD'S SUPPER,
OR
HOLY COMMUNION

The priest stands at the Lord's Table. The people kneel.

Our Father, who art in heaven, Hallowed be thy name, Thy kingdom come, Thy will be done, On earth as it is in heaven. Give us this day our daily bread. And forgive us our trespasses, As we forgive those who trespass against us. And lead us not into temptation, But deliver us from evil. Amen.

THE COLLECT FOR PURITY

Almighty God, unto whom all hearts be open, all desires known, and from whom no secrets are hid; Cleanse the thoughts of our hearts by the inspiration of thy Holy Spirit, that we may perfectly love thee, and worthily magnify thy holy Name; through Christ our Lord. **Amen.**

THE COMMANDMENTS

Minister

God spake these words, and said; I am the Lord thy God: Thou shalt have none other gods but me.

Lord, have mercy upon us, and incline our hearts to keep this law.

Thou shalt not make to thyself any graven image, nor the likeness of any thing that is in heaven above, or in the earth beneath, or in the water under the earth: thou shalt not bow down to them, nor worship them: for I the Lord thy God am a jealous God, and visit the sins of the fathers upon the children unto the third and fourth generation of them that hate me, and shew mercy unto thousands in them that love me and keep my commandments.

Lord, have mercy upon us, and incline our hearts to keep this law.

Thou shalt not take the Name of the Lord thy God in vain; for the Lord will not hold him guiltless that taketh his Name in vain.

Lord, have mercy upon us, and incline our hearts to keep this law.

Remember that thou keep holy the Sabbath day. Six days shalt thou labour, and do all that thou hast to do; but the seventh day is the Sabbath of the Lord thy God. In it thou shalt do no manner of work, thou, and thy son, and thy daughter, thy man-servant, and thy maid-servant, thy cattle, and the stranger that is within thy gates. For in six days the Lord made heaven and earth, the sea, and all that in them is, and rested the seventh day: wherefore the Lord blessed the seventh day, and hallowed it.

Lord, have mercy upon us, and incline our hearts to keep this law.

Honour thy father and thy mother: that thy days may be long in the land which the Lord thy God giveth thee.

Lord, have mercy upon us, and incline our hearts to keep this law.

Thou shalt do no murder.

Lord, have mercy upon us, and incline our hearts to keep this law.

Thou shalt not commit adultery.

Lord, have mercy upon us, and incline our hearts to keep this law.

Thou shalt not steal.

Lord, have mercy upon us, and incline our hearts to keep this law.

Thou shalt not bear false witness against thy neighbour.

Lord, have mercy upon us, and incline our hearts to keep this law.

Thou shalt not covet thy neighbour's house, thou shalt not covet thy neighbour's wife, nor his servant, nor his maid, nor his ox, nor his ass, nor any thing that is his.

Lord, have mercy upon us, and write all these thy laws in our hearts, we beseech thee.

Or

Hear what our Lord Jesus Christ saith:

Thou shalt love the Lord thy God with all thy heart, and with all thy soul, and with all thy mind. This is the first and great Commandment. And the second is like unto it, Thou shalt love thy neighbour as thyself. On these two Commandments hang all the Law and the Prophets.

Lord, have mercy upon us, and write these thy laws in our hearts, we beseech thee.

Priest
Let us pray.

THE COLLECT OF THE DAY

THE LESSON

Reader
The Lesson is written in the ... chapter of ... beginning at the ... verse.
At the end of the Lesson,
Here endeth the Lesson.

THE PSALM

THE EPISTLE

Reader
The Epistle is written in the ... chapter of ... beginning at the ... verse.
At the end of the Epistle,
Here endeth the Epistle.

Stand

THE GOSPEL

Minister
The holy Gospel is written in the ... chapter of the Gospel according to ...
beginning at the ... verse.
Glory be to thee, O Lord.
After the Gospel,
Thanks be to thee, O Lord, *or* **Hallelujah.**

THE NICENE CREED

I believe in one God the Father Almighty,
Maker of heaven and earth,
and of all things visible and invisible:
And in one Lord Jesus Christ,
the only-begotten Son of God,
Begotten of his Father before all worlds,
God of God, Light of Light,
Very God of very God,
Begotten, not made,
Being of one substance with the Father;

By whom all things were made:
Who for us men, and for our salvation, came down from heaven,
And was incarnate by the Holy Spirit of the Virgin Mary,
And was made man,
And was crucified also for us under Pontius Pilate.
He suffered and was buried,
And the third day he rose again according to the Scriptures,
And ascended into heaven,
And sitteth on the right hand of the Father.
And he shall come again with glory
to judge both the quick and the dead:
Whose kingdom shall have no end.
And I believe in the Holy Spirit,
The Lord, and Giver of life,
Who proceedeth from the Father and the Son,
Who with the Father and the Son together
is worshipped and glorified,
Who spake by the Prophets.
And I believe one Catholic and Apostolic Church.
I acknowledge one Baptism for the remission of sins.
And I look for the Resurrection of the dead,
And the life of the world to come. Amen.

THE SERMON

The priest begins THE OFFERTORY, *saying one or more of the Sentences on page*
192-194.
The alms for the poor are received.
Bread and wine for communion are placed upon the table.

Minister
Let us pray for the whole state of Christ's Church militant here in earth.

Almighty and everliving God, who by thy holy Apostle hast taught us to
make prayers, and supplications, and to give thanks, for all men; We
humbly beseech thee most mercifully [*to accept our alms and oblations,*
and] to receive these our prayers, which we offer unto thy Divine Majesty;

beseeching thee to inspire continually the universal Church with the spirit of truth, unity and concord: And grant, that all they that do confess thy holy Name may agree in the truth of thy holy Word, and live in unity and godly love.

N.I. [We beseech thee also to save and defend all Christian Kings, Princes, and Governors; and especially thy servant *ELIZABETH* our *Queen*; that under *her* we may be godly and quietly governed: And grant unto *her* whole Council, and to all that are put in authority under *her*, that they may truly and impartially minister justice, to the punishment of wickedness and vice, and to the maintenance of thy true religion, and virtue.]

R.I. [We beseech thee also so to direct and dispose the hearts of all Christian Rulers, that they may truly and impartially minister justice, to the punishment of wickedness and vice, and to the maintenance of thy true religion, and virtue.]

Give grace, O heavenly Father, to all Bishops and Curates, that they may both by their life and doctrine set forth thy true and lively Word, and rightly and duly administer thy holy Sacraments: And to all thy People give thy heavenly grace; and especially to this Congregation here present; that, with meek heart and due reverence, they may hear and receive thy holy Word; truly serving thee in holiness and righteousness all the days of their life.

And we most humbly beseech thee of thy goodness, O Lord, to comfort and succour all them, who in this transitory life are in trouble, sorrow, need, sickness, or any other adversity.

And we also bless thy holy Name for all thy servants departed this life in thy faith and fear; beseeching thee to give us grace so to follow their good examples, that with them we may be partakers of thy heavenly kingdom: Grant this, O Father, for Jesus Christ's sake, our only Mediator and Advocate. **Amen.**

One of the Exhortations on pages 197-200 or part of one may be read.

Ye that do truly and earnestly repent you of your sins, and are in love and charity with your neighbours, and intend to lead a new life, following the commandments of God, and walking from henceforth in his holy ways; Draw near with faith, and take this holy Sacrament to your comfort; and make your humble confession to Almighty God, meekly kneeling upon your knees.

Almighty God, Father of our Lord Jesus Christ, Maker of all things, Judge of all men; We acknowledge and bewail our manifold sins and wickedness, Which we, from time to time, most grievously have committed, By thought, word, and deed, Against thy Divine Majesty, Provoking most justly thy wrath and indignation against us. We do earnestly repent, And are heartily sorry for these our misdoings; The remembrance of them is grievous unto us; The burden of them is intolerable. Have mercy upon us, Have mercy upon us, most merciful Father; For thy Son our Lord Jesus Christ's sake, Forgive us all that is past; And grant that we may ever hereafter Serve and please thee In newness of life, To the honour and glory of thy Name; Through Jesus Christ our Lord. Amen.

The priest or the bishop when present stands and pronounces this absolution:
Almighty God, our heavenly Father, who of his great mercy hath promised forgiveness of sins to all them that with hearty repentance and true faith turn unto him; Have mercy upon you; pardon and deliver you from all your sins; confirm and strengthen you in all goodness; and bring you to everlasting life; through Jesus Christ our Lord. **Amen.**

Hear what comfortable words our Saviour Christ saith unto all that truly turn to him.
Come unto me all that travail and are heavy laden, and I will refresh you.
Matthew 11: 28
So God loved the world, that he gave his only-begotten Son, to the end that all that believe in him should not perish, but have everlasting life.
John 3: 16
Hear also what Saint Paul saith.
This is a true saying, and worthy of all men to be received, That Christ Jesus came into the world to save sinners. *1 Timothy 1: 15*

Hear also what Saint John saith.

If any man sin, we have an Advocate with the Father, Jesus Christ the righteous: and he is the propitiation for our sins. *1 John 2: 1, 2*

Priest

Lift up your hearts.
We lift them up unto the Lord.

Let us give thanks unto our Lord God.
It is meet and right so to do.

It is very meet, right, and our bounden duty, that we should at all times, and in all places, give thanks unto thee, O Lord, Holy Father, Almighty Everlasting God:

The Proper Preface, if any, follows.

Therefore with Angels and Archangels and with all the company of heaven, we laud and magnify thy glorious Name; evermore praising thee, and saying,
Holy, Holy, Holy, Lord God of hosts,
heaven and earth are full of thy glory:
Glory be to thee, O Lord most high. Amen.

PROPER PREFACES

CHRISTMAS DAY, and seven days after.
Because thou didst give Jesus Christ thine only Son to be born as at this time for us; who, by the operation of the Holy Spirit, was made very man of the substance of the Virgin Mary his mother; and that without spot of sin, to make us clean from all sin. Therefore with Angels, etc.

EASTER DAY, and seven days after.
But chiefly are we bound to praise thee for the glorious Resurrection of thy Son Jesus Christ our Lord: for he is the very Paschal Lamb, which was offered for us, and hath taken away the sin of the world; who by his death hath destroyed death, and by his rising to life again hath restored to us everlasting life. Therefore with Angels, etc.

Through thy most dearly beloved Son Jesus Christ our Lord; who after his most glorious Resurrection manifestly appeared to all his Apostles, and in their sight ascended up into heaven to prepare a place for us; that where he is, thither we might also ascend, and reign with him in glory. Therefore with Angels, etc.

WHITSUNDAY

Through Jesus Christ our Lord; who, after that he had ascended up far above all the heavens and was set down at thy right hand, did as at this time pour forth upon the children of adoption thy holy and life-giving Spirit; that through his glorious power the joy of the everlasting Gospel might come abroad into all the world; whereby we have been brought out of darkness and error into the clear light and true knowledge of thee, and of thy Son Jesus Christ. Therefore with Angels, etc.

The Feast of TRINITY only.

Who with thine only-begotten Son and the Holy Spirit art one God, one Lord; in Trinity of Persons, and in Unity of Substance: for that which we believe of thy glory, O Father, the same we believe of the Son, and of the Holy Spirit, without any difference or inequality. Therefore with Angels, etc.

After each of which Prefaces shall immediately be sung or said,

Therefore with Angels and Archangels, and with all the company of heaven, we laud and magnify thy glorious Name; evermore praising thee, and saying,

Holy, Holy, Holy, Lord God of hosts,
heaven and earth are full of thy glory:
Glory be to thee, O Lord most high. Amen.

PRAYER OF HUMBLE ACCESS

We do not presume to come to this thy Table, O merciful Lord, trusting in our own righteousness, but in thy manifold and great mercies. We are not worthy so much as to gather up the crumbs under thy Table. But thou art the same Lord, whose property is always to have mercy: Grant us therefore, gracious Lord, so to eat the flesh of thy dear Son Jesus Christ, and to drink his blood, that our sinful bodies may be made clean by his body, and our souls washed through his most precious blood, and that we may evermore dwell in him, and he in us. Amen.

Priest

Almighty God, our heavenly Father, who of thy tender mercy didst give thine only Son Jesus Christ to suffer death upon the Cross for our redemption; who made there (by his one oblation of himself once offered) a full, perfect, and sufficient sacrifice, oblation, and satisfaction, for the sins of the whole world; and did institute, and in his holy Gospel command us to continue, a perpetual memory of that his precious death, until his coming again:

Hear us, O merciful Father, we most humbly beseech thee; and grant that we receiving these thy creatures of bread and wine, according to thy Son our Saviour Jesus Christ's holy institution, in remembrance of his death and passion, may be partakers of his most blessed Body and Blood: Who, in the same night that he was betrayed, * took Bread; and, when he had given thanks, † he brake it, and gave it to his disciples saying, Take, eat; ‡ this is my Body which is given for you: Do this in remembrance of me. Likewise after supper he § took the Cup; and, when he had given thanks, he gave it to them, saying, Drink ye all of this: ¡ for this is my Blood of the New Testament which is shed for you and for many for the remission of sins: Do this, as oft as ye shall drink it, in remembrance of me. **Amen.**

* Here the priest is to take the paten.
† And here to break the bread. ‡ And here to lay a hand upon all the bread.
§ Here the priest is to take the cup. ¡ And here to lay a hand upon every vessel (be it chalice or flagon) in which there is any wine to be consecrated.

The ministers receive Communion.

Communicants are given the bread with the words

The Body of our Lord Jesus Christ, which was given for thee, preserve thy body and soul unto everlasting life. Take and eat this in remembrance that Christ died for thee, and feed on him in thy heart by faith with thanksgiving.

Communicants are given the cup with the words

The Blood of our Lord Jesus Christ, which was shed for thee, preserve thy body and soul unto everlasting life. Drink this in remembrance that Christ's Blood was shed for thee, and be thankful.

If the consecrated bread or wine be all spent before all have communicated, the priest is to consecrate more, according to the Form prescribed above: beginning at Our Saviour Christ in the same night *etc., for the blessing of the bread: and at* Likewise after supper, *etc., for the blessing of the cup.*

Our Father, who art in heaven,
 hallowed be thy name,
 thy kingdom come,
 thy will be done,
  on earth as it is in heaven.
Give us this day our daily bread.
 And forgive us our trespasses,
 as we forgive those who trespass against us.
And lead us not into temptation,
 but deliver us from evil.
For thine is the kingdom, the power, and the glory;
 for ever and ever. Amen.

Either or both of the following prayers:

O Lord and heavenly Father, we thy humble servants entirely desire thy fatherly goodness mercifully to accept this our sacrifice of praise and thanksgiving; most humbly beseeching thee to grant that, by the merits and death of thy Son Jesus Christ, and through faith in his blood, we and all thy whole Church may obtain remission of our sins, and all other benefits of his passion.

And here we offer and present unto thee, O Lord, ourselves, our souls and bodies, to be a reasonable, holy, and lively sacrifice unto thee; humbly beseeching thee, that all we, who are partakers of this Holy Communion, may be fulfilled with thy grace and heavenly benediction.

And although we be unworthy, through our manifold sins, to offer unto thee any sacrifice, yet we beseech thee to accept this our bounden duty and service; not weighing our merits, but pardoning our offences, through Jesus Christ our Lord; By whom, and with whom, in the unity of the Holy Spirit, all honour and glory be unto thee, O Father Almighty, world without end. **Amen.**

Holy Communion One **189**

Almighty and everliving God, we most heartily thank thee, for that thou dost vouchsafe to feed us who have duly received these holy mysteries, with the spiritual food of the most precious Body and Blood of thy Son our Saviour Jesus Christ; and dost assure us thereby of thy favour and goodness towards us; and that we are very members incorporate in the mystical body of thy Son, which is the blessed company of all faithful people; and are also heirs, through hope, of thy everlasting kingdom, by the merits of the most precious death and passion of thy dear Son.

And we most humbly beseech thee, O heavenly Father, so to assist us with thy grace, that we may continue in that holy fellowship, and do all such good works as thou hast prepared for us to walk in; through Jesus Christ our Lord, to whom, with thee and the Holy Spirit, be all honour and glory, world without end. **Amen.**

GLORIA IN EXCELSIS

Glory be to God on high,
and in earth peace, good will towards men.
We praise thee, we bless thee, we worship thee, we glorify thee,
we give thanks to thee for thy great glory,
O Lord God, heavenly King, God the Father Almighty.

O Lord, the only-begotten Son Jesu Christ;
O Lord God, Lamb of God, Son of the Father,
that takest away the sins of the world, have mercy upon us.
Thou that takest away the sins of the world, have mercy upon us.
Thou that takest away the sins of the world, receive our prayer.
Thou that sittest at the right hand of God the Father,
have mercy upon us.

For thou only art holy; thou only art the Lord;
thou only, O Christ, with the Holy Spirit,
art most high in the glory of God the Father. Amen.

A POSTCOMMUNION PRAYER
may be said.

Priest (or the bishop, when present)

The peace of God, which passeth all understanding, keep your hearts and minds in the knowledge and love of God, and of his Son Jesus Christ our Lord: And the blessing of God Almighty, the Father, the Son, and the Holy Spirit, be amongst you and remain with you always. **Amen.**

Lay not up for yourselves treasure upon the earth; where the rust and moth doth corrupt, and where thieves break through and steal: but lay up for yourselves treasures in heaven; where neither rust nor moth doth corrupt, and where thieves do not break through and steal.

Matthew 6: 19,20

Whatsoever ye would that men should do unto you, even so do unto them; for this is the Law and the Prophets. *Matthew 7: 12*

Remember the words of the Lord Jesus, how he said, It is more blessed to give than to receive. *Acts 20: 35*

Not every one that saith unto me, Lord, Lord, shall enter into the kingdom of heaven; but he that doeth the will of my Father which is in heaven.

Matthew 7: 21

Let your light so shine before men, that they may see your good works, and glorify your Father which is in heaven. *Matthew 5: 16*

He that soweth little shall reap little; and he that soweth plenteously shall reap plenteously. Let every man do according as he is disposed in his heart, not grudgingly, or of necessity; for God loveth a cheerful giver.

2 Corinthians 9: 6,7

Godliness is great riches, if a man be content with that he hath: for we brought nothing into the world, neither may we carry any thing out.

1 Timothy 6: 6,7

Charge them who are rich in this world, that they be ready to give, and glad to distribute; laying up in store for themselves a good foundation against the time to come, that they may attain eternal life.

1 Timothy 6: 17,18,19

To do good, and to distribute, forget not; for with such sacrifices God is well pleased. *Hebrews 13: 16*

Ye shall not appear before the Lord empty. Every man shall give as he is able, according to the blessing of the Lord thy God which he hath given thee. *Deuteronomy 16: 16,17*

Do ye not know, that they who minister about holy things live of the sacrifice; and they who wait at the altar are partakers with the altar? Even so hath the Lord also ordained, that they who preach the Gospel should live of the Gospel.

1 Corinthians 9: 13,14

If we have sown unto you spiritual things, is it a great matter if we shall reap your worldly things?

1 Corinthians 9: 11

Let him that is taught in the Word minister unto him that teacheth, in all good things. Be not deceived, God is not mocked: for whatsoever a man soweth that shall he reap.

Galatians 6: 6,7

God is not unrighteous, that he will forget your works, and labour that proceedeth of love; which love ye have shewed for his Name's sake, who have ministered unto the saints, and yet do minister.

Hebrews 6: 10

While we have time, let us do good unto all men; and specially unto them that are of the household of faith.

Galatians 6: 10

Whoso hath this world's good, and seeth his brother have need, and shutteth up his compassion from him, how dwelleth the love of God in him?

1 John 3: 17

He that hath pity upon the poor lendeth unto the Lord: and look, what he layeth out, it shall be paid him again.

Proverbs 19: 17

Blessed be the man that provideth for the sick and needy: the Lord shall deliver him in the time of trouble.

Psalm 41: 1

Lift up your eyes, and look on the fields, for they are white already to harvest: and he that reapeth receiveth wages, and gathereth fruit unto life eternal; that both he that soweth and he that reapeth may rejoice together.

John 4: 35,36

After which may be said one or these following:

CHRISTMAS

Ye know the grace of our Lord Jesus Christ, that, though he was rich, yet for your sakes he became poor, that ye through his poverty might be rich.

1 Corinthians 8: 9

EASTER

Christ our passover is sacrificed for us: therefore let us keep the feast.

1 Corinthians 5: 7,8

ASCENSION

When he ascended up on high, he led captivity captive, and gave gifts unto men.
Ephesians 4: 8

WHITSUNTIDE

God hath sealed us, and given the earnest of the Spirit in our hearts.
2 Corinthians 1: 22

TRINITY SUNDAY

Now unto the King eternal, immortal, invisible, the only wise God, be honour and glory for ever and ever. Amen.
1 Timothy 1: 17

Thine, O Lord, is the greatness, and the power, and the glory, and the victory, and the majesty: for all that is in the heaven and in the earth is thine; thine is the kingdom, O Lord, and thou art exalted as head above all. Now therefore, our God, we thank thee, and praise thy glorious Name: for all things come of thee, and of thine own have we given thee.
1 Chronicles 29: 11,13,14

POSTCOMMUNION COLLECTS
which may be said before the Blessing

Assist us mercifully, O Lord, in these our supplications and prayers, and dispose the way of thy servants towards the attainment of everlasting salvation; that, among all the changes and chances of this mortal life they may ever be defended by thy most gracious and ready help; through Jesus Christ our Lord. **Amen.**

Almighty God, with whom do live the spirits of them that depart hence in the Lord; We humbly beseech thee that it may please thee, of thy gracious goodness, shortly to accomplish the number of thine elect, and to hasten thy kingdom; that we, with all those that are departed in the true faith of thy holy Name, may have our perfect consummation and bliss, both in body and soul, in thy eternal and everlasting glory; through Jesus Christ our Lord. **Amen.**

O Almighty Lord, and everlasting God, vouchsafe, we beseech thee, to direct, sanctify, and govern both our hearts and bodies, in the ways of thy laws, and in the works of thy commandments; that through thy most mighty protection, both here and ever, we may be preserved in body and soul; through our Lord and Saviour Jesus Christ. **Amen.**

Grant, we beseech thee, almighty God, that the words, which we have heard this day with our outward ears, may through thy grace be so grafted inwardly in our hearts, that they may bring forth in us the fruit of good living, to the honour and praise of thy Name; through Jesus Christ our Lord. **Amen.**

Prevent us, O Lord, in all our doings with thy most gracious favour, and further us with thy continual help; that in all our works begun, continued, and ended in thee, we may glorify thy holy Name, and finally by thy mercy obtain everlasting life; through Jesus Christ our Lord. **Amen.**

Most merciful Father, we beseech thee to send upon the ministers of thy Word and Sacraments thy heavenly blessing; that they may be clothed with righteousness, and that thy Word spoken by their mouths may have such success, that it may never be spoken in vain. Grant also, we humbly pray thee, that thy people may have grace to hear and receive what they shall deliver out of thy most holy Word, or agreeable to the same; to the honour and glory of thy Name, and the increase of thy kingdom; through Jesus Christ our Lord. **Amen.**

O God, who hast made of one blood all nations of men for to dwell on the face of the whole earth, and didst send thy blessed Son to preach peace to them that are afar off, and to them that are nigh; Grant that the peoples of the world may feel after thee and find thee; and hasten, O Lord, the fulfilment of thy promise to pour out thy Spirit upon all flesh; through Jesus Christ our Lord. **Amen.**

In the Ember Weeks
Almighty God, our heavenly Father, who hast purchased to thyself an universal Church by the precious blood of thy dear Son; Mercifully look upon the same, and at this time so guide and govern the minds of thy servants the Bishops and Pastors of thy flock, that they may lay hands suddenly on no one, but faithfully and wisely make choice of fit persons to serve in the sacred Ministry of thy Church. And to those which shall be ordained to any holy function give thy grace and heavenly benediction; that both by their life and doctrine they may set forth thy glory, and set forward the salvation of all men; through Jesus Christ our Lord. **Amen.**

Almighty God, the giver of all good gifts, who of thy Divine Providence hast appointed divers Orders in thy Church; Give thy grace, we humbly beseech thee, to all those who are to be * called to any office and administration in the same; and so replenish them with the truth of thy doctrine, and endue them with innocency of life, that they may faithfully serve before thee, to the glory of thy great Name, and the benefit of thy holy Church; through Jesus Christ our Lord. **Amen.**

* *On the day of the ordering the words* this day *may be substituted for the words* to be.

Almighty God, the fountain of all wisdom, who knowest our necessities before we ask, and our ignorance in asking; We beseech thee to have compassion upon our infirmities; and those things, which for our unworthiness we dare not, and for our blindness we cannot, ask, vouchsafe to give us, for the worthiness of thy Son Jesus Christ our Lord. **Amen.**

Almighty God, who hast promised to hear the petitions of them that ask in thy Son's Name; We beseech thee mercifully to incline thine ears to us that have made now our prayers and supplications unto thee; and grant that those things which we have faithfully asked according to thy will, may effectually be obtained, to the relief of our necessity, and to the setting forth of thy glory; through Jesus Christ our Lord. **Amen.**

Whereas it is ordained in this Office for the Administration of the Lord's Supper, that the Communicants should receive the same kneeling; (which order is well meant, for a signification of our humble and grateful acknowledgement of the benefits of Christ therein given to all worthy receivers, and for the avoiding of such profanation and disorder in the Holy Communion, as might otherwise ensue;) yet, lest the same kneeling should by any persons, either out of ignorance and infirmity, or out of malice and obstinacy, be misconstrued and depraved; It is here declared, That thereby no adoration is intended, or ought to be done, either unto the Sacramental Bread or Wine there bodily received, or unto any Corporal Presence of Christ's natural Flesh and Blood. For the Sacramental Bread and Wine remain still in their very natural substances, and therefore may not be adored; (for that were Idolatry, to be abhorred of all faithful Christians;) and the natural Body and Blood of our Saviour Christ are in Heaven, and not here; it being against the truth of Christ's natural body to be at one time in more places than one.

Dearly beloved, on ... day next I purpose, through God's assistance, to administer to all such as shall be religiously and devoutly disposed the most comfortable Sacrament of the Body and Blood of Christ; to be by them received in remembrance of his meritorious Cross and Passion; whereby alone we obtain remission of our sins, and are made partakers of the kingdom of heaven. Wherefore it is our duty to render most humble and hearty thanks to Almighty God our heavenly Father, for that he hath given his Son our Saviour Jesus Christ, not only to die for us, but also to be our spiritual food and sustenance in that holy Sacrament. Which being so divine and comfortable a thing to them who receive it worthily, and so dangerous to them that will presume to receive it unworthily; my duty is to exhort you in the mean season to consider the dignity of that holy mystery, and the great peril of the unworthy receiving thereof; and so to search and examine your own consciences, (and that not lightly, and after the manner of dissemblers with God; but so) that ye may come holy and clean to such a heavenly Feast, in the marriage-garment required by God in holy Scripture, and be received as worthy partakers of that holy Table.

The way and means thereto is; First, to examine your life and conduct by the rule of God's commandments; and whereinsoever ye shall perceive yourselves to have offended, either by will, word, or deed, there to bewail your own sinfulness, and to confess yourselves to Almighty God, with full purpose of amendment of life. And if ye shall perceive your offences to be such as are not only against God, but also against your neighbours; then ye shall reconcile yourselves unto them; being ready to make restitution and satisfaction, according to the uttermost of your powers, for all injuries and wrongs done by you to any other; and being likewise ready to forgive others that have offended you, as ye would have forgiveness of your offences at God's hand: for otherwise the receiving of the Holy Communion doth nothing else but increase your condemnation. Therefore if any of you be a blasphemer of God, an hinderer or slanderer of his Word, an adulterer, or be in malice, or envy, or in any other grievous crime, repent you of your sins, or else come not to that holy Table; lest, after the taking of that holy Sacrament, the devil enter into you, as he entered into Judas, and fill you full of all iniquities, and bring you to destruction both of body and soul.

And because it is requisite, that no man should come to the Holy Communion, but with a full trust in God's mercy, and with a quiet conscience; therefore if there be any of you, who by this means cannot quiet his own conscience herein, but requireth further comfort or counsel, let him come to me, or to some other discreet and learned Minister of God's Word, and open his grief; that by the ministry of God's holy Word, he may receive the benefit of absolution, together with spiritual counsel and advice, to the quieting of his conscience, and avoiding of all scruple and doubtfulness.

Or, in case the priest shall see the people negligent to come to the Holy Communion, instead of the former, this Exhortation shall be used:

TWO

Dearly beloved brethren, on ... I intend, by God's grace, to celebrate the Lord's Supper: unto which, in God's behalf, I bid you all that are here present; and beseech you, for the Lord Jesus Christ's sake, that ye will not refuse to come thereto, being so lovingly called and bidden by God himself. Ye know how grievous and unkind a thing it is, when a man hath prepared a rich feast, decked his table with all kind of provision, so that there lacketh nothing but the guests to sit down; and yet they who are called (without any cause) most unthankfully refuse to come. Which of you in such a case would not be moved? Who would not think a great injury and wrong done unto him? Wherefore, most dearly beloved in Christ, take ye good heed, lest ye, withdrawing yourselves from this holy Supper, provoke God's indignation against you. It is an easy matter for a man to say, I will not communicate, because I am otherwise hindered with worldly business. But such excuses are not so easily accepted and allowed before God. If any man say, I am a grievous sinner, and therefore am afraid to come: wherefore then do ye not repent and amend? When God calleth you, are ye not ashamed to say ye will not come? When ye should return to God, will ye excuse yourselves, and say ye are not ready? Consider earnestly with yourselves how little such feigned excuses will avail before God. They that refused the feast in the Gospel, because they had bought a farm, or would try their yokes of oxen, or because they were married, were not so excused, but counted unworthy of the heavenly Feast. I, for my part, shall be ready; and, according to mine office, I bid you in the Name of God, I call you in Christ's behalf, I exhort you, as ye love your own salvation, that ye will be partakers of this Holy Communion. And as the Son of God did vouchsafe to yield up his soul by death upon the Cross for your salvation; so it is your duty to receive the Communion in remembrance of the sacrifice of his death, as he himself hath commanded: which if ye shall neglect to do, consider with your-selves how great injury ye do unto God, and how sore punishment hangeth over your heads for the same; when ye wilfully abstain from the Lord's Table, and separate from your brethren, who come to feed on the banquet of that most heavenly food. These things if ye earnestly consider, ye will by God's grace return to a better mind: for the obtaining whereof we shall not cease to make our humble petitions unto Almighty God our heavenly Father.

At the time of the celebration of the Communion (those who do not intend to communicate having had opportunity to withdraw), the communicants being conveniently placed for the receiving of the holy Sacrament, the priest may say this Exhortation.
Note, that if this Exhortation be not read at the time of the Celebration of the Communion, it shall, nevertheless, be read to the people by the curate at such times as he shall think fit, and at the least three times in the year.

THREE

Dearly beloved in the Lord, ye that mind to come to the Holy Communion of the Body and Blood of our Saviour Christ, must consider how Saint Paul exhorteth all persons diligently to prove and examine themselves, before they presume to eat of that Bread, and drink of that Cup. For as the benefit is great, if with a true penitent heart and lively faith we receive that holy Sacrament; (for then we spiritually eat the flesh of Christ, and drink his blood; then we dwell in Christ, and Christ in us; we are one with Christ, and Christ with us;) so is the danger great, if we receive the same unworthily. For then we are guilty of the Body and Blood of Christ our Saviour; we eat and drink judgement to ourselves, not considering the Lord's Body. Judge therefore yourselves, brethren, that ye be not judged of the Lord; repent you truly for your sins past; have a lively and steadfast faith in Christ our Saviour; amend your lives, and be in perfect charity with all men; so shall ye be meet partakers of those holy mysteries. And above all things ye must give most humble and hearty thanks to God, the Father, the Son, and the Holy Spirit, for the redemption of the world by the death and passion of our Saviour Christ, both God and man; who did humble himself, even to the death upon the Cross, for us miserable sinners, who lay in darkness and the shadow of death; that he might make us the children of God, and exalt us to everlasting life. And to the end that we should alway remember the exceeding great love of our Master, and only Saviour, Jesus Christ, thus dying for us, and the innumerable benefits which by his precious blood-shedding he hath obtained to us; he hath instituted and ordained holy mysteries, as pledges of his love, and for a continual remembrance of his death, to our great and endless comfort. To him therefore, with the Father and the Holy Spirit, let us give (as we are most bounden) continual thanks; submitting ourselves wholly to his holy will and pleasure, and studying to serve him in true holiness and righteousness all the days of our life. Amen.

The Celebration of
THE HOLY COMMUNION
ALSO CALLED THE LORD'S SUPPER OR THE EUCHARIST

The Gathering of God's People

*The bishop or priest who presides greets the congregation
with the following words:*
The Lord be with you
and also with you.

or

Grace, mercy and peace
from God our Father and the Lord Jesus Christ
be with you all
and also with you.

or, from Easter Day until Pentecost:
Christ is risen!
The Lord is risen indeed. Alleluia!

*A sentence of scripture may be read (see pages 78-82), and the presiding
minister may introduce the liturgy of the day.*

THE COLLECT FOR PURITY

Almighty God,
to whom all hearts are open,
all desires known,
and from whom no secrets are hidden;
Cleanse the thoughts of our hearts
by the inspiration of your Holy Spirit,
that we may perfectly love you,
and worthily magnify your holy name;
through Christ our Lord. Amen.

or another suitable opening prayer

The prayers of penitence may take place at this point or before or after the Intercessions.

The Commandments may be read (and should be read during Advent and Lent), or The Beatitudes (pages 223-224), or The Summary of the Law:

Hear what our Lord Jesus Christ says:
You shall love the Lord your God with all your heart
and with all your soul and with all your mind.
This is the first and great commandment.
And the second is like it.
You shall love your neighbour as yourself.
On these two commandments depend all the law
and the prophets.   *Matthew 22: 37-39*
Lord, have mercy on us,
and write these your laws in our hearts.

The Confession is introduced with appropriate words, such as:
God so loved the world that he gave his only Son Jesus Christ, to save us from our sins, to intercede for us in heaven, and to bring us to eternal life.

Let us then confess our sins in penitence and faith,
firmly resolved to keep God's commandments
and to live in love and peace:

Silence

Almighty God, our heavenly Father,
we have sinned in thought and word and deed,
and in what we have left undone.
We are truly sorry and we humbly repent.
For the sake of your Son, Jesus Christ,
have mercy on us and forgive us,
that we may walk in newness of life
to the glory of your name. Amen.

The presiding minister pronounces the absolution:

Almighty God,
who forgives all who truly repent,
have mercy on you,
pardon and deliver you from all your sins,
confirm and strengthen you in all goodness,
and keep you in eternal life;
through Jesus Christ our Lord. **Amen.**

Suitable penitential sentences may be used instead of the confession and absolution (pages 224-236) with these responses:

Lord, have mercy.
Lord, have mercy.

Christ, have mercy.
Christ, have mercy.

Lord, have mercy.
Lord, have mercy.

GLORIA IN EXCELSIS

This canticle may be omitted in Advent and Lent and on weekdays which are not holy days. Other versions of this canticle may be used, or when appropriate another suitable hymn of praise.

**Glory to God in the highest,
and peace to God's people on earth.
Lord God, heavenly King,
almighty God and Father,
we worship you, we give you thanks,
we praise you for your glory.
Lord Jesus Christ, only Son of the Father,
Lord God, Lamb of God,
you take away the sin of the world:
have mercy on us;
you are seated at the right hand of the Father,
receive our prayer.
For you alone are the Holy One,
you alone are the Lord,
you alone are the Most High,
Jesus Christ, with the Holy Spirit,
in the glory of God the Father. Amen.**

*The presiding minister introduces the Collect, allowing a short space for silence,
and the people respond to the Collect with their* **Amen.**

Proclaiming and Receiving the Word

THE FIRST READING
is normally from the Old Testament.

At the end the reader may say
This is the Word of the Lord.
Thanks be to God.

THE PSALM
'Glory to the Father...' may be omitted.

THE SECOND READING
is from the New Testament.

At the end the reader may say
This is the Word of the Lord.
Thanks be to God.

THE GRADUAL
A canticle, psalm, hymn, anthem or acclamation may be sung.

Stand

THE GOSPEL READING
The Gospel Reading is introduced by the following words:
Hear the Gospel of our Saviour Christ,
according to ... chapter ... beginning at verse ...
Glory to you, Lord Jesus Christ.
and concludes with:
This is the Gospel of the Lord.
Praise to you, Lord Jesus Christ.

THE SERMON
is preached here or after the Creed.

The Nicene Creed is said on Sundays and principal holy days. The Creed may be omitted on ordinary weekdays or on festivals which are not principal holy days.

We believe in one God,
the Father, the Almighty,
maker of heaven and earth,
of all that is,
seen and unseen.

We believe in one Lord, Jesus Christ,
the only Son of God,
eternally begotten of the Father,
God from God, Light from Light,
true God from true God,
begotten, not made,
of one Being with the Father.
Through him all things were made.
For us and for our salvation
he came down from heaven,
was incarnate by the Holy Spirit of the Virgin Mary,
and was made man.
For our sake he was crucified under Pontius Pilate;
he suffered death and was buried.
On the third day he rose again
in accordance with the Scriptures;
he ascended into heaven
and is seated at the right hand of the Father.
He will come again in glory to judge the living and the dead,
and his kingdom will have no end.

We believe in the Holy Spirit,
the Lord, the giver of life,
who proceeds from the Father and the Son,
who with the Father and the Son is worshipped and glorified,
who has spoken through the prophets.
We believe in one holy catholic and apostolic Church.
We acknowledge one baptism for the forgiveness of sins.
We look for the resurrection of the dead,
and the life of the world to come. Amen.

The Prayers of the People

The Intercessions will normally include prayer for:
>   *the universal Church of God*
>   *the nations of the world*
>   *the local community*
>   *those in need*
> *and remembrance of, and thanksgiving for, the faithful departed.*

When appropriate, the prayers may be more focussed on one or two themes.

Prayers may be read by a deacon or lay person, or may be in silence with biddings, or may be in the form of open prayer, where members of the congregation contribute.

If a versicle and response are required after each section, one of the following may be said or sung:

Lord, in your mercy:
hear our prayer.
or
Lord, hear us:
Lord, graciously hear us.
or
Kyrie eleison.

At the end of the Intercessions the following may be used when appropriate:
Merciful Father,
accept these our prayers
for the sake of your Son,
our Saviour Jesus Christ. Amen.

or other suitable words

or

Accept our prayers through Jesus Christ our Lord, who taught us to pray:
Our Father ...

If the Lord's Prayer is used at this point in the service, it is not used after the Great Thanksgiving.

If the Penitence comes at this point of the service it may be followed by:

We do not presume to come to this your table,
merciful Lord,
trusting in our own righteousness
but in your manifold and great mercies.
We are not worthy so much as to gather up the crumbs under your table.
But you are the same Lord,
whose nature is always to have mercy.
Grant us, therefore, gracious Lord,
so to eat the flesh of your dear Son Jesus Christ,
and to drink his blood,
that our sinful bodies may be made clean by his body,
and our souls washed through his most precious blood,
and that we may evermore dwell in him and he in us. Amen.

THE PEACE

The presiding minister introduces the Peace with these or other suitable words:
Christ is our peace.
He has reconciled us to God in one body by the cross.
We meet in his name and share his peace.
or
Jesus said, A new commandment I give to you,
that you love one another:
even as I have loved you, that you also love one another.   *John 13: 34*
or
If you forgive others their sins,
your heavenly Father will also forgive you;
but if you do not forgive others,
neither will your Father forgive your sins.   *Matthew 6: 14-15*

followed by:
The peace of the Lord be always with you
and also with you.

It is appropriate that the congregation share with one another a sign of peace.
This may be introduced with the words:
Let us offer one another a sign of peace.

Celebrating at the Lord's Table

The table may be prepared by a deacon or lay people.
The gifts of money may be brought forward and presented.

AT THE PREPARATION OF THE TABLE

The bread and wine shall be placed on the table for the communion if this has not already been done, and one of the following may be said:

Be present, be present,
Lord Jesus Christ
our risen high priest;
make yourself known in the breaking of bread. **Amen.**

Wise and gracious God,
you spread a table before us;
nourish your people with the word of life,
and the bread of heaven. **Amen.**

How can I repay the Lord
for all the benefits he has given to me?
I will lift up the cup of salvation
and call upon the name of the Lord.
I will fulfil my vows to the Lord
in the presence of all his people.

Psalm 116: 12-14

Lord, yours is the greatness
and the power and the glory
and the victory and the majesty;
for all things come from you
and of your own we give you.

1 Chronicles 29: 11,14

THE TAKING OF THE BREAD AND WINE

Stand
The bishop or priest who presides takes the bread and wine and may say

Christ our passover has been sacrificed for us
therefore let us celebrate the feast.

One of the following Eucharistic Prayers is said by the presiding minister:

Prayer 1

The Lord is here.
His Spirit is with us.
or
The Lord be with you
and also with you.

Lift up your hearts.
We lift them to the Lord.

Let us give thanks to the Lord our God.
It is right to give our thanks and praise.

Father, almighty and everliving God,
at all times and in all places
it is right to give you thanks and praise:

When there is a Proper Preface it follows here (pages 224-235)

And so with all your people,
with angels and archangels,
and with all the company of heaven,
we proclaim your great and glorious name,
for ever praising you and saying:

Holy, holy, holy Lord,
God of power and might,
heaven and earth are full of your glory.
Hosanna in the highest!

Blessed is he who comes in the name of the Lord.
Hosanna in the highest!

Blessed are you, Father,
the creator and sustainer of all things;
you made us in your own image,
male and female you created us;
even when we turned away from you,
you never ceased to care for us,
but in your love and mercy you freed us from the slavery of sin,
giving your only begotten Son to become man
and suffer death on the cross to redeem us:
he made there the one complete and all-sufficient sacrifice
for the sins of the whole world:
he instituted,
and in his holy Gospel commanded us to continue,
a perpetual memory of his precious death
until he comes again.

On the night that he was betrayed he took bread;
and when he had given thanks to you, he broke it,
and gave it to his disciples, saying, Take, eat,
this is my body which is given for you.
Do this in remembrance of me.

In the same way, after supper he took the cup;
and when he had given thanks to you,
he gave it to them, saying, Drink this, all of you,
for this is my blood of the new covenant
which is shed for you and for many
for the forgiveness of sins.
Do this, as often as you drink it,
in remembrance of me.

Therefore, Father, with this bread and this cup
we do as Christ your Son commanded:
we remember his passion and death,
we celebrate his resurrection and ascension,
and we look for the coming of his kingdom.

Accept through him, our great high priest,
this our sacrifice of praise and thanksgiving;
and as we eat and drink these holy gifts,
grant by the power of the life-giving Spirit
that we may be made one in your holy Church
and partakers of the body and blood of your Son,
that he may dwell in us and we in him:

Through the same Jesus Christ our Lord,
by whom, and with whom, and in whom,
in the unity of the Holy Spirit,
**all honour and glory are yours, Almighty Father,
for ever and ever. Amen.**

Continue on page 218 at The Lord's Prayer

Prayer 2

The indented paragraphs may be added to the prayer at the appropriate season or day.

The Lord is here.
His Spirit is with us.
or
The Lord be with you
and also with you.

Lift up your hearts.
We lift them to the Lord.

Let us give thanks to the Lord our God.
It is right to give our thanks and praise.

All glory and honour, thanks and praise
be given to you at all times and in all places,
Lord, holy Father, true and living God,
through Jesus Christ our Lord.

For he is your eternal Word
through whom you have created all things
from the beginning
and formed us in your own image.

In Advent

> In him the day of our deliverance has dawned.
> We rejoice that through him you make all things new
> and we look for his coming in power and majesty to judge
> the world.

In your great love you gave him
to be made man for us and to share our common life.

At Christmas, Presentation, Annunciation

> By the power of the Holy Spirit
> he was born of the Virgin Mary his mother,
> and we have seen his glory,
> glory as of the only Son from the Father.

You have revealed in him your eternal plan of salvation
and showed him to be the light of all the nations.
His glory has shone among us,
glory as of the only Son from the Father.

In Lent

He was tempted in every way as we are,
yet he did not sin;
and he gives us strength to control our desires,
and to walk in his way of love.

In obedience to your will
your Son our Saviour offered himself as a perfect sacrifice,
and died on the cross for our redemption.
Through him you have freed us from the slavery of sin
and reconciled us to yourself, our God and Father.

In Passiontide and Holy Week

For he is the true passover Lamb
who was offered for us
and has taken away the sin of the world.

In Eastertide

For he is the true passover Lamb
who was offered for us
and has taken away the sin of the world.
By his death he has destroyed death
and by his rising to life
he has restored to us eternal life.

He is our great high priest
whom you raised from death
and exalted to your right hand on high
where he ever lives to intercede for us.

In Ascensiontide

He has passed beyond our sight,
not to abandon us but to be our hope,

that where he is we might also be
and reign with him in glory.

Through him you have sent upon us
your holy and life-giving Spirit
and made us a royal priesthood
called to serve you for ever.

On the Day of Pentecost

By the same Spirit
we are led into all truth
and given power to proclaim with boldness
the glorious gospel to all the world.

On Trinity Sunday

You have revealed to us your glory and love
in the glory and love of the Son and of the Holy Spirit;
three persons, one God,
ever to be worshipped and adored.

On Saints' Days

You have called us into the fellowship of (... and) all your
saints, and set before us the example of their witness
and of the fruit of your Spirit in their lives.

Therefore with angels and archangels
and with all the company of heaven
we proclaim your great and glorious name,
for ever praising you and saying:
Holy, holy, holy Lord,
God of power and might,
heaven and earth are full of your glory.
Hosanna in the highest.

Merciful Father, we thank you
for these gifts of your creation, this bread and this wine,
and we pray that we who eat and drink them
in the fellowship of the Holy Spirit
in obedience to our Saviour Christ
in remembrance of his death and passion
may be partakers of his body and his blood,

who on the night he was betrayed took bread;
and when he had given you thanks
he broke it, and gave it to his disciples, saying,
Take, eat. This is my body which is given for you;
Do this in remembrance of me.
After supper, he took the cup,
and again giving you thanks
he gave it to his disciples, saying,
Drink from this, all of you.
This is my blood of the new covenant
which is shed for you and for many
for the forgiveness of sins.
Do this, as often as you drink it, in remembrance of me.

Father, with this bread and this cup,
we do as our Saviour has commanded:
we celebrate the redemption he has won for us;
we proclaim his perfect sacrifice,
made once for all upon the cross,
his mighty resurrection and glorious ascension;
and we look for his coming
to fulfil all things according to your will.
Christ has died;
Christ is risen;
Christ will come again.

Renew us by your Holy Spirit,
unite us in the body of your Son,
and bring us with all your people
into the joy of your eternal kingdom;
through Jesus Christ our Lord,
with whom and in whom,
by the power of the Holy Spirit,
we worship you, Father almighty,
in songs of never-ending praise:
Blessing and honour and glory and power
are yours for ever and ever. Amen.

Continue on page 218 at The Lord's Prayer

The Lord is here.
His Spirit is with us.
or
The Lord be with you
and also with you.

Lift up your hearts.
We lift them to the Lord.

Let us give thanks to the Lord our God.
It is right to give our thanks and praise.

Father, Lord of all creation,
we praise you for your goodness and your love.
When we turned away you did not reject us.
You came to meet us in your Son,
welcomed us as your children
and prepared a table where we might feast with you.

In Christ you shared our life
that we might live in him and he in us.
He opened wide his arms upon the cross
and, with love stronger than death,
he made the perfect sacrifice for sin.

Lord Jesus Christ, our redeemer,
on the night before you died
you came to table with your friends.
Taking bread, you gave thanks, broke it
and gave it to them saying,
Take, eat: this is my body which is given for you;
do this in remembrance of me.
Lord Jesus, we bless you:
you are the bread of life.

At the end of supper
you took the cup of wine, gave thanks, and said,
Drink this, all of you; this is my blood of the new covenant,
which is shed for you and for many for the forgiveness of sins;
do this in remembrance of me.
Lord Jesus, we bless you:
you are the true vine.

Praise to you, Lord Jesus Christ:
dying, you destroyed our death,
rising, you restored our life;
Lord Jesus, come in glory.

Holy Spirit, giver of life,
come upon us now;
may this bread and wine be to us
the body and blood of our Saviour Jesus Christ.
As we eat and drink these holy gifts
make us, who know our need of grace,
one in Christ, our risen Lord.

Father, Son, and Holy Spirit, Blessed Trinity:
with your whole Church throughout the world
we offer you this sacrifice of thanks and praise
and lift our voice to join the song of heaven,
for ever praising you and saying:
Holy, Holy, Holy Lord,
God of power and might.
Heaven and earth are full of your glory.
Hosanna in the highest.

Thanks be to you, our God, for your gift beyond words.
Amen. Amen. Amen.

Continue on page 218 at The Lord's Prayer

The presiding minister says

As our Saviour Christ has taught us, so we pray

Our Father in heaven,
> **hallowed be your name,**
> **your kingdom come,**
> **your will be done,**
>> **on earth as in heaven.**

Give us today our daily bread.
> **Forgive us our sins**
> **as we forgive those who sin against us.**

Lead us not into temptation
> **but deliver us from evil.**

For the kingdom, the power, and the glory are yours
> **now and for ever. Amen.**

or

As our Saviour Christ has taught us, we are bold to say

Our Father, who art in heaven,
> **hallowed be thy name,**
> **thy kingdom come,**
> **thy will be done,**
>> **on earth as it is in heaven.**

Give us this day our daily bread.
> **And forgive us our trespasses**
> **as we forgive those who trespass against us.**

And lead us not into temptation,
> **but deliver us from evil.**

For thine is the kingdom, the power, and the glory
> **for ever and ever. Amen.**

THE BREAKING OF THE BREAD

The presiding minister (who may be assisted by the deacon) breaks the consecrated bread in preparation for the Communion.

The bread which we break
is a sharing in the body of Christ.
We being many are one body,
for we all share in the one bread.

The presiding minister says

Draw near with faith.
Receive the body of our Lord Jesus Christ which he gave for you,
and his blood which he shed for you.
Remember that he died for you,
and feed on him in your hearts by faith with thanksgiving.
or
The gifts of God for the people of God.
Jesus Christ is holy,
Jesus Christ is Lord,
to the glory of God the Father.
or
Jesus Christ is the Lamb of God,
who has taken away the sins of the world.
Happy are those who are called to his supper.
Lord, I am not worthy to receive you,
but only say the word and I shall be healed.

The presiding minister and people receive communion.

The minister who gives the bread and wine says

The body of our Lord Jesus Christ, which was given for you,
preserve your body and soul to eternal life. Take and eat this in
remembrance that Christ died for you, and feed on him in your
heart by faith with thanksgiving.

The blood of our Lord Jesus Christ, which was shed for you,
preserve your body and soul to eternal life. Drink this in
remembrance that Christ's blood was shed for you, and be thankful.
or
The body of Christ keep you in eternal life.
The blood of Christ keep you in eternal life.
or
The body of Christ given for you.
The blood of Christ shed for you.

and the communicant replies **Amen.**

The following anthem may be sung after the Breaking of the Bread or during the Communion:

Jesus, Lamb of God, have mercy on us.

Jesus, bearer of our sins, have mercy on us.

Jesus, Redeemer of the world, grant us peace.

or

Lamb of God, you take away the sin of the world, have mercy on us.

Lamb of God, you take away the sin of the world, have mercy on us.

Lamb of God, you take away the sin of the world, grant us peace.

Other hymns or anthems may be sung.

THE GREAT SILENCE

When all have received communion, the presiding minister, other ministers and people keep silence for reflection.

Going Out as God's People

A hymn may be sung here or before the Dismissal.

PRAYER AFTER COMMUNION

The appropriate Post Communion Prayer (pages 241-336), or the following may be said:

Father of all, we give you thanks and praise,
that when we were still far off
you met us in your Son and brought us home.
Dying and living, he declared your love,
gave us grace, and opened the gate of glory.
May we who share Christ's body live his risen life;
we who drink his cup bring life to others;
we whom the Spirit lights give light to the world.
Keep us firm in the hope you have set before us,
so we and all your children shall be free,
and the whole earth live to praise your name;
through Christ our Lord. **Amen.**

All say

Almighty God,
we thank you for feeding us
with the spiritual food
of the body and blood of your Son Jesus Christ.
Through him we offer you our souls and bodies
to be a living sacrifice.
Send us out in the power of your Spirit
to live and work to your praise and glory. Amen.

DISMISSAL

The presiding minister may say the seasonal blessing,
or another suitable blessing, or

The peace of God,
which passes all understanding,
keep your hearts and minds
in the knowledge and love of God,
and of his Son Jesus Christ our Lord;
ending:
and the blessing of God almighty,
the Father, the Son and the Holy Spirit,
be with you and remain with you always. **Amen.**

A minister says

Go in peace to love and serve the Lord
in the name of Christ. Amen.

From Easter Day to Pentecost:

Go in the peace of the Risen Christ. Alleluia! Alleluia!
Thanks be to God. Alleluia! Alleluia!

Appendix

A. Commandments and Beatitudes

Hear these commandments which God has given to his people, and take them to heart:

I AM THE LORD YOUR GOD: YOU SHALL HAVE NO OTHER GODS BUT ME.
You shall love the Lord your God with all your heart, with all your soul, and with all your mind and with all your strength. *Matthew 22: 37*

YOU SHALL NOT MAKE FOR YOURSELF ANY IDOL.
God is Spirit, and those who worship him must worship in spirit and in truth. *John 4: 24*

YOU SHALL NOT DISHONOUR THE NAME OF THE LORD YOUR GOD.
You shall worship him with reverence and awe. *Hebrews 12: 28*

REMEMBER THE LORD'S DAY, AND KEEP IT HOLY.
Christ is risen from the dead: set your mind on things that are above, not on things that are on the earth. *Colossians 3: 1, 2*

**Lord, have mercy on us,
and write these your laws in our hearts.**

HONOUR YOUR FATHER AND YOUR MOTHER.
Live as servants of God, honour all people, love your brothers and sisters in Christ. *1 Peter 2: 16*

YOU SHALL NOT COMMIT MURDER.
Be reconciled to your brother and sister: overcome evil with good.
Matthew 5: 24, Romans 13: 21

YOU SHALL NOT COMMIT ADULTERY.
Know that your body is a temple of the Holy Spirit. *1 Corinthians 6: 19*

YOU SHALL NOT STEAL.
Be honest in all that you do and care for those in need.   *Ephesians 4: 28*

YOU SHALL NOT BE A FALSE WITNESS.
Let everyone speak the truth.   *Ephesians 4: 25*

YOU SHALL NOT COVET ANYTHING WHICH BELONGS TO YOUR NEIGHBOUR.
Remember the words of the Lord Jesus: It is more blessed to give than to receive. Love your neighbour as yourself, for love is the fulfilling of the law.
Acts 20: 35, Romans 13: 9,10

Lord, have mercy on us,
and write all these your laws in our hearts.

2. THE BEATITUDES

Let us hear our Lord's blessing on those who follow him:
Blessed are the poor in spirit,
for theirs is the kingdom of heaven.
Jesus, remember me
when you come into your kingdom.

Blessed are the meek,
for they shall inherit the earth.
Jesus, remember me
when you come into your kingdom.

Blessed are those who weep,
for they shall be consoled.
Jesus, remember me
when you come into your kingdom.

Blessed are those who hunger and thirst after justice, for they shall be satisfied.
Jesus, remember me
when you come into your kingdom.

Blessed are the merciful,
for they shall obtain mercy.
Jesus, remember me
when you come into your kingdom.

Blessed are the pure in heart,
for they shall see God.
Jesus, remember me
when you come into your kingdom.

Blessed are the peacemakers,
for they shall be called the children of God.
Jesus, remember me
when you come into your kingdom.

Blessed are those who suffer persecution for the sake of justice,
for theirs is the kingdom of heaven.
Jesus, remember me
when you come into your kingdom.

B. Seasonal Variations

ADVENT

PENITENTIAL KYRIES

Turn to us again, O God our Saviour,
and let your anger cease from us.
> Lord, have mercy.
> **Lord, have mercy.**

Show us your mercy, O Lord,
and grant us your salvation.
> Christ, have mercy
> **Christ, have mercy.**

Your salvation is near for those that fear you,
that glory may dwell in our land.
> Lord, have mercy.
> **Lord, have mercy.**

In the tender mercy of our God,
the dayspring from on high shall break upon us,
to give light to those who dwell in darkness
and in the shadow of death,
and to guide our feet into the way of peace.   *Luke 1: 78,79*

Salvation is your gift
through the coming of your Son our Saviour Jesus Christ,
and by him you will make all things new
when he returns in glory to judge the world:

Christ the sun of righteousness shine upon you,
gladden your hearts
and scatter the darkness from before you:

CHRISTMAS

Lord God, mighty God,
you are the creator of the world.
>   Lord, have mercy.
>   **Lord, have mercy.**

Lord Jesus, Son of God and Son of Mary,
you are the Prince of Peace.
>   Christ, have mercy.
>   **Christ, have mercy.**

Holy Spirit,
by your power the Word was made flesh
and came to dwell among us.
>   Lord, have mercy.
>   **Lord, have mercy.**

Unto us a child is born, unto us a son is given,
and his name shall be called the Prince of Peace.   *Isaiah 9: 6*

You have given Jesus Christ your only Son
to be born of the Virgin Mary,
and through him you have given us power
to become the children of God:

Christ, who by his incarnation gathered into one
all things earthly and heavenly,
fill you with his joy and peace:

EPIPHANY

God be merciful to us and bless us,
and make his face to shine on us.
> Lord, have mercy.
> **Lord, have mercy.**

May your ways be known on earth,
your saving power to all nations.
> Christ, have mercy.
> **Christ, have mercy.**

You, Lord, have made known your salvation,
and reveal your justice in the sight of the nations.
> Lord, have mercy.
> **Lord, have mercy.**

Our Saviour Christ is the Prince of Peace.
Of the increase of his government and of peace
there shall be no end.   *Isaiah 9: 6,7*

For Jesus Christ our Lord
who in human likeness revealed your glory,
to bring us out of darkness
into the splendour of his light:

Christ the Son be manifest to you,
that your lives may be a light to the world:

LENT

In the wilderness we find your grace:
you love us with an everlasting love.
> Lord, have mercy.
> **Lord, have mercy.**

There is none but you to uphold our cause;
our sin cries out and our guilt is great.
> Christ, have mercy.
> **Christ, have mercy.**

Heal us, O Lord, and we shall be healed;
Restore us and we shall know your joy.
> Lord, have mercy.
> **Lord, have mercy.**

Being justified by faith,
we have peace with God through our Lord Jesus Christ. *Romans 5: 1,2*

Through Jesus Christ our Lord,
who was in every way tempted as we are, yet did not sin;
by whose grace we are able to overcome all our temptations:

Christ give you grace to grow in holiness,
to deny yourselves,
and to take up your cross and follow him:

Lord God,

you sent your Son to reconcile us to yourself and to one another.

Lord, have mercy.
Lord, have mercy.

Lord Jesus,

you heal the wounds of sin and division.

Christ, have mercy.
Christ, have mercy.

Holy Spirit,

through you we put to death the sins of the body – and live.

Lord, have mercy.
Lord, have mercy.

INTRODUCTION TO THE PEACE

Now in union with Christ Jesus you who were once far off have been brought near through the shedding of Christ's blood; for he is our peace.

Ephesians 2: 17

PREFACE

Through Jesus Christ our Saviour,
who, for the redemption of the world,
humbled himself to death on the cross;
that, being lifted up from the earth,
he might draw all people to himself:

BLESSING

Christ draw you to himself
and grant that you find in his cross
a sure ground for faith,
a firm support for hope,
and the assurance of sins forgiven:

EASTER

Lord God, you raised your Son from the dead.
> Lord, have mercy.
> **Lord, have mercy.**

Lord Jesus, through you we are more than conquerors.
> Christ, have mercy.
> **Christ, have mercy.**

Holy Spirit, you help us in our weakness.
> Lord, have mercy.
> **Lord, have mercy.**

INTRODUCTION TO THE PEACE

The risen Christ came and stood among his disciples and said, Peace be with you. Then were they glad when they saw the Lord.   *John 20: 19,20*

PREFACE

Above all we praise you
for the glorious resurrection of your Son
Jesus Christ our Lord,
the true paschal lamb who was sacrificed for us;
by dying he destroyed our death;
by rising he restored our life:

BLESSING

The God of peace,
who brought again from the dead our Lord Jesus,
that great shepherd of the sheep,
through the blood of the eternal covenant,
make you perfect in every good work to do his will,
working in you that which is well-pleasing in his sight:
or
God the Father,
by whose glory Christ was raised from the dead,
raise you up to walk with him in the newness of his risen life:

ASCENSION

God our Father,
you exalted your Son to sit at your right hand.

> Lord, have mercy.
> **Lord, have mercy.**

Lord Jesus, you are the way, the truth and the life.

> Christ, have mercy.
> **Christ, have mercy.**

Holy Spirit, Counsellor,
you are sent to be with us for ever.

> Lord, have mercy.
> **Lord, have mercy.**

INTRODUCTION TO THE PEACE

Jesus said, Peace I leave with you; my peace I give to you.
I do not give to you as the world gives.   *John 14: 27,28*

PREFACE

Through Jesus Christ our Lord,
who after he had risen from the dead
ascended into heaven,
where he is seated at your right hand to intercede for us
and to prepare a place for us in glory:

BLESSING

Christ our exalted King
pour on you his abundant gifts
make you faithful and strong to do his will
that you may reign with him in glory:

PENTECOST

PENITENTIAL KYRIES

Great and wonderful are your deeds,
Lord God the Almighty

> Lord, have mercy.
> **Lord, have mercy.**

You are the King of glory, O Christ.
Christ, have mercy.
Christ, have mercy.

Come Holy Ghost, our souls inspire.
Lord, have mercy.
Lord, have mercy.

INTRODUCTION TO THE PEACE

The fruit of the Spirit is love, joy, peace.
If we live in the Spirit, let us walk in the Spirit.   *Galatians 5: 22*

PREFACE

Through Jesus Christ our Lord,
according to whose promise
the Holy Spirit came to dwell in us,
making us your children,
and giving us power to proclaim the gospel throughout the world:

BLESSING

The Spirit of truth lead you into all truth,
give you grace to confess that Jesus Christ is Lord,
and to proclaim the words and works of God:

TRINITY SUNDAY

PENITENTIAL KYRIES

Father, you come to meet us when we return to you.
Lord, have mercy.
Lord, have mercy.

Jesus, you died on the cross for our sins.
Christ, have mercy.
Christ, have mercy.

Holy Spirit, you give us life and peace.
Lord, have mercy.
Lord, have mercy.

Peace to you from God our heavenly Father.
Peace from his Son Jesus Christ who is our peace.
Peace from the Holy Spirit the Life-giver.
The peace of the Triune God be always with you.
And also with you.

You have revealed your glory
as the glory of your Son and of the Holy Spirit:
three persons equal in majesty, undivided in splendour,
yet one Lord, one God,
ever to be worshipped and adored:

God the Holy Trinity
make you strong in faith and love,
defend you on every side,
and guide you in truth and peace:

TRANSFIGURATION

Your unfailing kindness, O Lord, is in the heavens,
and your faithfulness reaches to the clouds.

> Lord, have mercy.
> **Lord, have mercy.**

Your righteousness is like the strong mountains,
and your justice as the great deep.

> Christ, have mercy.
> **Christ, have mercy.**

For with you is the well of life:
and in your light shall we see light.

> Lord, have mercy.
> **Lord, have mercy.**

Christ will transfigure our human body
and give it a form like that of his own glorious body.
We are the Body of Christ. We share his peace.

Philippians 3: 21   1 Corinthians 11: 27   Romans 5: 1

Through Jesus Christ our Lord,
whose divine glory shone forth upon the holy mountain
before chosen witnesses of his majesty;
when your own voice from heaven
proclaimed him your beloved Son:

The God of all grace,
who called you to his eternal glory in Christ Jesus,
establish, strengthen and settle you in the faith:

These variations may be used on the Sunday before Lent if the Transfiguration option is taken.

THE PRESENTATION, THE ANNUNCIATION, THE VISITATION AND THE BIRTH OF THE BLESSED VIRGIN MARY

Lord God, mighty God,
you are the creator of the world.

Lord, have mercy.
Lord, have mercy.

Lord Jesus, Son of God and Son of Mary,
you are the Prince of Peace.

Christ, have mercy.
Christ, have mercy.

Holy Spirit,
by your power the Word was made flesh
and came to dwell among us.

Lord, have mercy.
Lord, have mercy.

Unto us a child is born, unto us a son is given:
and his name is called the Prince of Peace. *Isaiah 9: 7*

You chose the Blessed Virgin Mary
to be the mother of your Son
and so exalted the humble and meek;
your angel hailed her as most highly favoured,
and with all generations we call her blessed:

Christ the Son of God, born of Mary,
fill you with his grace
to trust his promises and obey his will:

SAINTS' DAYS

Lord, you are gracious and compassionate.
> Lord, have mercy.
> **Lord, have mercy.**

You are loving to all,
and your mercy is over all your creation.
> Christ, have mercy.
> **Christ, have mercy.**

Your faithful servants bless your name,
and speak of the glory of your kingdom.
> Lord, have mercy.
> **Lord, have mercy.**

We are fellow-citizens with the saints
and of the household of God,
through Christ our Lord,
who came and preached peace to those who were far off
and those who were near. *Ephesians 2: 19,17*

In the saints
you have given us an example of godly living,
that, rejoicing in their fellowship,
we may run with perseverance the race that is set before us,
and with them receive the unfading crown of glory:

God give you grace
to share the inheritance of .... and of his saints in glory:

IRISH SAINTS

O taste and see that the Lord is good;
happy are those who trust in him.
> Lord, have mercy.
> **Lord, have mercy.**

The Lord ransoms the lives of his servants
and none who trust in him will be destroyed.
> Christ, have mercy.
> **Christ, have mercy.**

Come my children, listen to me:
I will teach you the fear of the Lord.
> Lord, have mercy.
> **Lord, have mercy.**

Peace be to you, and peace to your house, and peace to all who are yours.

1 Samuel 25: 6

To this land you sent the glorious gospel
through the preaching of Patrick.
You caused it to grow and flourish in [the life of your servant .... and in]
the lives of men and women, filled with your Holy Spirit,
building up your Church to send forth the good news to other places:

God, who in days of old gave to this land the benediction of his holy Church,
fill you with his grace to walk faithfully in the steps of the saints
and to bring forth fruit to his glory:

MICHAELMAS

Holy, holy, holy is the Lord of hosts;
the whole earth is full of his glory.

> Lord, have mercy.
> **Lord, have mercy.**

Woe is me, for I am lost;
I am a person of unclean lips.

> Christ, have mercy.
> **Christ, have mercy.**

Your guilt is taken away,
and your sin forgiven.

> Lord, have mercy.
> **Lord, have mercy.**

Hear again the song of the angels:
Glory to God in the highest, and on earth peace.   *Luke 2: 14*

A Preface is not used on the festival of Saint Michael and all Angels.

The God of all creation
guard you by his angels,
and grant you the citizenship of heaven:

C. Forms of Intercession

ONE

Almighty and everliving God,
hear the prayers which we offer in faith and love:

For peace, and for your salvation to be known throughout the world ...

For the one, holy, catholic and apostolic Church
and for the unity of all Christian people ...

For all who serve and lead in your Church,
for bishops, priests and deacons ...

For all your people, growing in the faith of Christ,
and passing it on to generations yet to come ...

For all who live and work in this community ...

For families, and for those who live alone ...

For all who are sick in body or in mind,
and for those who care for them ...

For all in authority,
and especially for [*N.I. Elizabeth* our *Queen*] [*R.I.* our President] ...

For all who have been entrusted with the responsibility of government ...

For those who work for peace, justice and righteousness throughout the
world ...

Rejoicing in the fellowship of your holy apostles and martyrs, and of all
your servants departed this life in your faith and fear, we commend ourselves and one another and our whole life to you, Lord God; through
Jesus Christ our Lord. **Amen.**

TWO

Almighty God, our heavenly Father,
you promised through your Son Jesus Christ
to hear the prayers of those who ask in faith.

Lord of your people:
strengthen your Church in all the world ...
renew the life of this diocese ...
bless .... our bishop, and build us up in faith and love.

Lord of creation:
look with favour on the world you have made,
guide the nations in the ways of justice and of peace,
and bless [*N.I. Elizabeth* our *Queen* and all in authority]
[*R.I.* our President, ... and all in authority].

Lord of our relationships:
comfort and sustain the communities in which we live and work ...
help us to love our neighbours as ourselves,
Enable us to serve our families and friends
and to love one another as you love us.

Lord of all healing:
relieve and protect those who are sick or suffering,
be with those who have any special need ...
and deliver all who know danger, violence or oppression.

Lord of eternity:
bind us together by your Holy Spirit,
in communion with .... and all who, having confessed the Faith,
have died in the peace of Christ, that we may entrust ourselves,
and one another, and our whole life to you, Lord God,
and come with all your saints to the joys of your eternal kingdom.
Amen.

THREE

Father, we pray for your holy catholic Church
that we all may be one.

Grant that every member of your Church may truly and humbly serve you:
that your name may be glorified by all people.

We pray for all bishops, priests and deacons
that they may be faithful ministers of your word and sacraments.

We pray for all who govern and hold authority in the nations of the world
that there may be justice and peace on the earth.

Give us grace to do your will in all that we undertake
that your glory may be proclaimed through our lives.

Have compassion on those who suffer from any grief or trouble
that they may be delivered from their distress.

We praise you for your saints who have entered their eternal joy
may we also come to share in the fulness of your kingdom.

We pray for our own needs and for those of others:

Silence. The people may add their own petitions.

Gracious God, grant that the desires of your people's hearts
may find favour in your sight,
through the intercession of Jesus Christ our Lord. **Amen.**

D. When the Consecrated Elements are insufficient

If either of the consecrated elements is insufficient, the presiding minister adds further bread or wine, silently, or using the following words:

Father,
having given thanks over the bread and the cup
according to the institution of your Son Jesus Christ,
who said, Take, eat, this is my body.
and/or
Drink this, this is my blood.

We pray that this bread/wine also may be to us his body/blood,
to be received in remembrance of him.

THE COLLECTS

The Christian Year

THE SEASON OF ADVENT

The First Sunday of Advent

Almighty God, COLLECT ONE

Give us grace that we may cast away the works of darkness,
and put upon us the armour of light,
now in the time of this mortal life,
in which thy Son Jesus Christ
came to visit us in great humility;
that in the last day,
when he shall come again in his glorious Majesty
to judge both the quick and the dead,
we may rise to the life immortal;
through him who liveth and reigneth with thee
and the Holy Spirit, now and ever.

This collect is said after the Collect of the day until Christmas Eve.

Almighty God, COLLECT TWO

Give us grace to cast away the works of darkness
and to put on the armour of light
now in the time of this mortal life
in which your Son Jesus Christ came to us in great humility;
that on the last day
when he shall come again in his glorious majesty
to judge the living and the dead,
we may rise to the life immortal;
through him who is alive and reigns with you and the Holy Spirit,
one God, now and for ever. 1

God our deliverer,
Awaken our hearts
to prepare the way for the advent of your Son,
that, with minds purified by the grace of his coming,
we may serve you faithfully all our days;
through Jesus Christ our Lord. 4

The Second Sunday of Advent

O Lord, COLLECT ONE
Raise up (we pray thee) thy power, and come among us,
and with great might succour us;
that whereas, through our sins and wickedness,
we are sore let and hindered in running the race that is set before us,
thy bountiful grace and mercy
may speedily help and deliver us;
through the satisfaction of thy Son our Lord,
to whom with thee and the Holy Spirit,
be honour and glory, world without end.

Collect of 5th before Advent may be used.

Father in heaven, COLLECT TWO
who sent your Son to redeem the world
and will send him again to be our judge:
Give us grace so to imitate him
in the humility and purity of his first coming
that when he comes again,
we may be ready to greet him with joyful love and firm faith;
through Jesus Christ our Lord. 15

Lord, POST COMMUNION
here you have nourished us with the food of life.
Through our sharing in this holy sacrament
teach us to judge wisely earthly things
and to yearn for things heavenly.
We ask this through Jesus Christ our Lord. 20

The Third Sunday of Advent

O Lord Jesu Christ,   COLLECT ONE
who at thy first coming didst send thy messenger
to prepare thy way before thee;
Grant that the ministers and stewards of thy mysteries
may likewise so prepare and make ready thy way,
by turning the hearts of the disobedient to the wisdom of the just,
that at thy second coming to judge the world
we may be found an acceptable people in thy sight,
who livest and reignest with the Father and the Holy Spirit,
ever one God, world without end.

O Lord Jesus Christ,   COLLECT TWO
who at your first coming sent your messenger
to prepare your way before you:
Grant that the ministers and stewards of your mysteries
may likewise so prepare and make ready your way
by turning the hearts of the disobedient to the wisdom of the just,
that at your second coming to judge the world
we may be found an acceptable people in your sight;
for you are alive and reign with the Father and the Holy Spirit,
one God, world without end. 1

Father,   POST COMMUNION
we give you thanks for these heavenly gifts.
Kindle us with the fire of your Spirit
that when Christ comes again
we may shine as lights before his face;
who is alive and reigns with you and the Holy Spirit,
one God, now and for ever. 4

The Fourth Sunday of Advent

Lord,
we beseech thee, give ear to our prayers,
and by thy gracious visitation
lighten the darkness of our hearts
by our Lord Jesus Christ;
who liveth and reigneth with thee
and the Holy Spirit, one God, now and for ever. 25

God our redeemer,
who prepared the blessed Virgin Mary
to be the mother of your Son:
Grant that, as she looked for his coming as our saviour,
so we may be ready to greet him
when he comes again as our judge;
who is alive and reigns with you and the Holy Spirit,
one God, now and for ever. 8

Heavenly Father,
you have given us a pledge of eternal redemption.
Grant that we may always eagerly celebrate
the saving mystery of the incarnation of your Son.
We ask this through him whose coming is certain,
whose day draws near,
your Son Jesus Christ our Lord. 20

THE SEASON OF CHRISTMAS

Christmas Eve

O God, COLLECT ONE
who makest us glad with the yearly remembrance
of the birth of thy only Son Jesus Christ;
Grant that, as we joyfully receive him for our Redeemer,
so we may with sure confidence,
behold him when he shall come to be our Judge,
who liveth and reigneth with thee and the Holy Spirit,
one God, world without end.

Almighty God, COLLECT TWO
you make us glad with the yearly remembrance
of the birth of your Son Jesus Christ:
Grant that, as we joyfully receive him as our redeemer,
we may with sure confidence behold him
when he shall come to be our judge;
who is alive and reigns with you and the Holy Spirit,
one God, now and for ever. 1

God for whom we wait, POST COMMUNION
you feed us with the bread of eternal life:
Keep us ever watchful, that we may be ready
to stand before the Son of Man, Jesus Christ our Lord. 16

The Nativity of our Lord (Night)

O God, COLLECT ONE
who madest this most holy night
to shine with the brightness of his coming,
who is the light of the world;
Grant that we who on earth hail the brightness of his appearing
may rejoice hereafter in the light of his heavenly glory;
who with thee and the Holy Spirit,
liveth and reigneth, one God, now and for ever.

Eternal God,   COLLECT TWO
who made this most holy night
to shine with the brightness of your one true light:
Bring us, who have known the revelation
of that light on earth,
to see the radiance of your heavenly glory;
through Jesus Christ our Lord. 2

God our Father,   POST COMMUNION
in this night you have made known to us again
the power and coming of our Lord Jesus Christ:
Confirm our faith and fix our eyes on him
until the day dawns
and Christ the Morning Star rises in our hearts.
To him be glory both now and for ever. 8

The Nativity of our Lord (Day)

Almighty God,   COLLECT ONE
who hast given us thy only-begotten Son
to take our nature upon him,
and as at this time to be born of a pure virgin;
Grant that we being regenerate,
and made thy children by adoption and grace,
may daily be renewed by thy Holy Spirit;
through the same our Lord Jesus Christ,
who liveth and reigneth with thee and the same Spirit,
ever one God, world without end.

Almighty God,   COLLECT TWO
you have given us your only-begotten Son
to take our nature upon him
and as at this time to be born of a pure virgin:
Grant that we, who have been born again
and made your children by adoption and grace,
may daily be renewed by your Holy Spirit;
through Jesus Christ our Lord. 1

God our Father,　　　　　　　　　　　　　　
whose Word has come among us
in the Holy Child of Bethlehem:
May the light of faith illumine our hearts
and shine in our words and deeds;
through him who is Christ the Lord. 16

The First Sunday of Christmas

Almighty God,　　　　　　　　　　　　　　COLLECT ONE
who hast given us thy only-begotten Son
to take our nature upon him,
and as at this time to be born of a pure virgin;
Grant that we being regenerate,
and made thy children by adoption and grace,
may daily be renewed by thy Holy Spirit;
through the same our Lord Jesus Christ,
who liveth and reigneth with thee and the same Spirit,
ever one God, world without end.

Almighty God,　　　　　　　　　　　　　　COLLECT TWO
who wonderfully created us in your own image
and yet more wonderfully restored us
through your Son Jesus Christ:
Grant that, as he came to share in our humanity,
so we may share the life of his divinity;
who is alive and reigns with you and the Holy Spirit,
one God, now and for ever. 7

Heavenly Father,　　　　　　　　　　　　　POST COMMUNION
you have refreshed us with this heavenly sacrament.
As your Son came to live among us,
grant us grace to live our lives,
united in love and obedience,
as those who long to live with him in heaven;
through Jesus Christ our Lord. 24

The Second Sunday of Christmas

Almighty God, COLLECT ONE
who hast poured upon us the new light of thine incarnate Word;
Grant that the same light, enkindled in our hearts,
may shine forth in our lives;
through Jesus Christ our Lord.

Almighty God, COLLECT TWO
in the birth of your Son
you have poured on us the new light of your incarnate Word,
and shown us the fullness of your love:
Help us to walk in this light and dwell in his love
that we may know the fullness of his joy;
who is alive and reigns with you and the Holy Spirit,
one God, now and for ever. 2

Light eternal, POST COMMUNION
you have nourished us in the mystery
of the body and blood of your Son:
By your grace keep us ever faithful to your word,
in the name of Jesus Christ our Lord. 16

The Season of Epiphany

The Epiphany
6 January

O God,   Collect One
who by the leading of a star
didst manifest thy only-begotten Son to the Gentiles;
Mercifully grant, that we, which know thee now by faith,
may after this life have the fruition of thy glorious Godhead;
through Jesus Christ our Lord.

O God,   Collect Two
who by the leading of a star
manifested your only Son to the peoples of the earth:
Mercifully grant that we, who know you now by faith,
may at last behold your glory face to face;
through Jesus Christ our Lord. 1

Lord God,   Post Communion
the bright splendour whom the nations seek:
May we, who with the wise men
have been drawn by your light,
discern the glory of your presence in your incarnate Son;
who suffered, died, and was buried,
and who is alive and reigns with you and the Holy Spirit,
now and for ever. 8

The First Sunday after the Epiphany:
The Baptism of our Lord

O Lord,
COLLECT ONE
we beseech thee mercifully to receive
the prayers of thy people which call upon thee;
and grant that they may both perceive and know
what things they ought to do,
and also may have grace and power
faithfully to fulfil the same;
through Jesus Christ our Lord.

Eternal Father,
COLLECT TWO
who at the baptism of Jesus
revealed him to be your Son,
anointing him with the Holy Spirit:
Grant to us, who are born of water and the Spirit,
that we may be faithful to our calling as your adopted children;
through Jesus Christ our Lord. 7

Refreshed by these holy gifts, Lord God,
POST COMMUNION
we seek your mercy:
that by listening faithfully to your only Son,
and being obedient to the prompting of the Spirit,
we may be your children in name and in truth;
through Jesus Christ our Lord. 20

The Second Sunday after the Epiphany

Almighty and everlasting God,
COLLECT ONE
who dost govern all things in heaven and earth;
Mercifully hear the supplications of thy people,
and grant us thy peace all the days of our life;
through Jesus Christ our Lord.

Almighty God,
in Christ you make all things new:
Transform the poverty of our nature
by the riches of your grace,
and in the renewal of our lives
make known your heavenly glory;
through Jesus Christ our Lord. 7

God of glory,   POST COMMUNION
you nourish us with bread from heaven.
Fill us with your Holy Spirit
that through us the light of your glory
may shine in all the world.
We ask this in the name of Jesus Christ our Lord. 16

The Third Sunday after the Epiphany

Almighty and everlasting God,   COLLECT ONE
Mercifully look upon our infirmities,
and in all our dangers and necessities
stretch forth thy right hand to help and defend us;
through Jesus Christ our Lord.

Almighty God,   COLLECT TWO
whose Son revealed in signs and miracles
the wonder of your saving presence:
Renew your people with your heavenly grace,
and in all our weakness
sustain us by your mighty power;
through Jesus Christ our Lord. 7

Almighty Father,
your Son our Saviour Jesus Christ is the light of the world.
May your people,
illumined by your word and sacraments,
shine with the radiance of his glory,
that he may be known, worshipped,
and obeyed to the ends of the earth;
for he is alive and reigns with you and the Holy Spirit,
one God, now and for ever. 16

The Fourth Sunday after the Epiphany

O God, COLLECT ONE
who knowest us to be set
in the midst of so many and great dangers,
that by reason of the frailty of our nature
we cannot always stand upright;
Grant to us such strength and protection,
as may support us in all dangers,
and carry us through all temptations;
through Jesus Christ our Lord.

Creator God, COLLECT TWO
who in the beginning
commanded the light to shine out of darkness:
We pray that the light of the glorious gospel of Christ
may dispel the darkness of ignorance and unbelief,
shine into the hearts of all your people,
and reveal the knowledge of your glory
in the face of Jesus Christ our Lord. 8

Generous Lord, POST COMMUNION
in word and eucharist we have proclaimed
the mystery of your love.
Help us so to live out our days
that we may be signs of your wonders in the world;
through Jesus Christ our Saviour. 8

The Presentation of Christ in the Temple
2 February

May be observed on the Sunday between 28 January and 3 February.

Almighty and everliving God,   COLLECT ONE
we humbly beseech thy Majesty,
that, as thy only-begotten Son was this day
presented in the temple in substance of our flesh,
so we may be presented unto thee with pure and clean hearts,
by the same thy Son Jesus Christ our Lord.

Almighty and everliving God,   COLLECT TWO
clothed in majesty,
whose beloved Son was this day presented in the temple
in the substance of our mortal nature:
May we be presented to you with pure and clean hearts,
by your Son Jesus Christ our Lord. 1

God, for whom we wait,   POST COMMUNION
you fulfilled the hopes of Simeon and Anna,
who lived to welcome the Messiah.
Complete in us your perfect will,
that in Christ we may see your salvation,
for he is Lord for ever and ever. 16

BEFORE LENT

The Fifth Sunday before Lent
Occurrence depends on date of Easter.

O Lord,
we beseech thee to keep thy Church and household
continually in thy true religion;
that they who do lean only upon the hope of thy heavenly grace
may evermore be defended
by thy mighty power;
through Jesus Christ our Lord.

Almighty God,
by whose grace alone we are accepted
and called to your service:
Strengthen us by your Holy Spirit
and make us worthy of our calling;
through Jesus Christ our Lord. 2

Merciful God,
we thank you for inviting us to share
in the one bread and the one cup.
By your continuing grace
enable us to live as one family in Christ
and joyfully to seek to bring your salvation
to all who do not know you;
through Jesus Christ our Lord. 20

The Fourth Sunday before Lent
Occurrence depends on date of Easter.

O Lord, COLLECT ONE
we beseech thee favourably to hear the prayers of thy people;
that we, who are justly punished for our offences,
may be mercifully delivered by thy goodness,
for the glory of thy Name;
through Jesus Christ our Saviour,
who liveth and reigneth with thee and the Holy Spirit,
ever one God, world without end.

O God, COLLECT TWO
you know us to be set
in the midst of so many and great dangers,
that by reason of the frailty of our nature
we cannot always stand upright:
Grant to us such strength and protection
as may support us in all dangers
and carry us through all temptations;
through Jesus Christ our Lord. 1

God of tender care, POST COMMUNION
in this eucharist we celebrate your love for us and for all people.
May we show your love in our lives
and know its fulfilment in your presence.
We ask this in the name of Jesus Christ our Lord. 24

The Third Sunday before Lent
Occurrence depends on date of Easter.

Lord, COLLECT ONE
we beseech thee to keep thy household the Church
in continual godliness;
that through thy protection it may be free from all adversities,
and devoutly given to serve thee in good works,
to the glory of thy name;
through Jesus Christ our Lord.

Almighty God,
who alone can bring order
to the unruly wills and passions of sinful humanity:
Give your people grace
so to love what you command
and to desire what you promise;
that, among the many changes of the world,
our hearts may surely there be fixed
where true joys are to be found;
through Jesus Christ our Lord. 1

Merciful Father, POST COMMUNION
you gave Jesus Christ to be for us the bread of life,
that those who come to him should never hunger.
Draw us to our Lord in faith and love,
that we may eat and drink with him at his table in the kingdom,
where he is alive and reigns with you and the Holy Spirit,
now and for ever. 2

The Second Sunday before Lent
Occurrence depends on date of Easter.

O Lord God, COLLECT ONE
who seest that we put not our trust
in any thing that we do;
Mercifully grant that by thy power
we may be defended against all adversity;
through Jesus Christ our Lord.

Almighty God, COLLECT TWO
you have created the heavens and the earth
and made us in your own image:
Teach us to discern your hand in all your works
and your likeness in all your children;
through Jesus Christ our Lord,
who with you and the Holy Spirit
reigns supreme over all things, now and for ever. 2

God our creator,
by your gift the tree of life was set at the heart
of the earthly paradise,
and the Bread of life at the heart of your Church.
May we who have been nourished at your table on earth
be transformed by the glory of the Saviour's Cross
and enjoy the delights of eternity;
through Jesus Christ our Lord. II

The Sunday before Lent

O Lord,
who hast taught us that all our doings without charity
are nothing worth;
Send thy Holy Spirit,
and pour into our hearts that most excellent gift of charity,
the very bond of peace and of all virtues,
without which whosoever liveth is counted dead before thee;
Grant this for thine only Son Jesus Christ's sake.

Almighty Father,
whose Son was revealed in majesty
before he suffered death upon the cross:
Give us grace to perceive his glory,
that we may be strengthened to suffer with him
and be changed into his likeness, from glory to glory;
who is alive and reigns with you and the Holy Spirit,
one God, now and for ever. 7

or

O God, our teacher and our judge:
Enrich our hearts with the goodness of your wisdom
and renew us from within:
that all our actions, all our thoughts and all our words
may bear the fruit of your transforming grace;
through Jesus Christ our Lord. 20

Holy God
we see your glory in the face of Jesus Christ.
May we who are partakers at his table
reflect his life in word and deed,
that all the world may know
his power to change and save.
This we ask through Jesus Christ our Lord. 16

or

Lord,
in this sacrament you have nourished us
with the spiritual food of the body and blood of your dear Son.
Not only with our lips
but with our lives may we truly confess his name,
and so enter the kingdom of heaven.
We ask this through Christ our Lord. 24

THE SEASON OF LENT

Ash Wednesday

Almighty and everlasting God, COLLECT ONE
who hatest nothing that thou hast made,
and dost forgive the sins of all them that are penitent;
Create and make in us new and contrite hearts,
that we worthily lamenting our sins,
and acknowledging our wretchedness,
may obtain of thee, the God of all mercy,
perfect remission and forgiveness;
through Jesus Christ our Lord.

This collect may be said after the Collect of the day until Easter Eve.

Almighty and everlasting God, COLLECT TWO
you hate nothing that you have made
and forgive the sins of all those who are penitent:
Create and make in us new and contrite hearts
that we, worthily lamenting our sins
and acknowledging our wretchedness,
may receive from you, the God of all mercy,
perfect remission and forgiveness;
through Jesus Christ our Lord. 1

Almighty God, POST COMMUNION
you have given your only Son to be for us
both a sacrifice for sin and also an example of godly life:
Give us grace
that we may always most thankfully receive
these his inestimable gifts,
and also daily endeavour ourselves
to follow the blessed steps of his most holy life;
through Jesus Christ our Lord. 1

O Lord,
COLLECT ONE

who for our sake didst fast forty days and forty nights;
Give us grace to use such abstinence,
that, our flesh being subdued to the Spirit,
we may ever obey thy godly motions
in righteousness, and true holiness,
to thy honour and glory,
who livest and reignest with the Father and the Holy Spirit,
one God, world without end.

Almighty God,
COLLECT TWO

whose Son Jesus Christ fasted forty days in the wilderness,
and was tempted as we are, yet without sin:
Give us grace to discipline ourselves
in obedience to your Spirit;
and, as you know our weakness,
so may we know your power to save;
through Jesus Christ our Lord. 7

Lord God,
POST COMMUNION

you renew us with the living bread from heaven.
Nourish our faith,
increase our hope,
strengthen our love,
and enable us to live by every word
that proceeds from out of your mouth;
through Jesus Christ our Lord. 17

The Second Sunday in Lent

Almighty God, COLLECT ONE
who seest that we have no power of ourselves to help ourselves;
Keep us both outwardly in our bodies,
and inwardly in our souls;
that we may be defended from all adversities
which may happen to the body,
and from all evil thoughts
which may assault and hurt the soul;
through Jesus Christ our Lord.

Almighty God, COLLECT TWO
you show to those who are in error the light of your truth
that they may return to the way of righteousness:
Grant to all those who are admitted
into the fellowship of Christ's religion,
that they may reject those things
that are contrary to their profession,
and follow all such things
as are agreeable to the same;
through our Lord Jesus Christ. I

Creator of heaven and earth, POST COMMUNION
we thank you for these holy mysteries
given us by our Lord Jesus Christ,
by which we receive your grace
and are assured of your love,
which is through him now and for ever. 24

The Third Sunday in Lent

COLLECT ONE

We beseech thee, Almighty God,
mercifully to look upon thy people;
that by thy great goodness
they may be governed and preserved evermore, both in body and soul;
through Jesus Christ our Lord.

COLLECT TWO

Merciful Lord,
Grant your people grace to withstand the temptations
of the world, the flesh and the devil
and with pure hearts and minds to follow you, the only God;
through Jesus Christ our Lord. 1

POST COMMUNION

Lord our God,
you feed us in this life with bread from heaven,
the pledge and foreshadowing of future glory.
Grant that the working of this sacrament within us
may bear fruit in our daily lives;
through Jesus Christ our Lord. 20

The Fourth Sunday in Lent
Mothering Sunday

COLLECT ONE

Grant, we beseech thee, Almighty God,
that we, who for our evil deeds
do worthily deserve to be punished,
by the comfort of thy grace may mercifully be relieved;
through our Lord and Saviour Jesus Christ.

COLLECT TWO

Lord God
whose blessed Son our Saviour
gave his back to the smiters
and did not hide his face from shame:
Give us grace to endure the sufferings of this present time
with sure confidence in the glory that shall be revealed;
through Jesus Christ our Lord. 1

God of compassion,
whose Son Jesus Christ, the child of Mary,
shared the life of a home in Nazareth,
and on the cross drew the whole human family to himself:
Strengthen us in our daily living
that in joy and in sorrow
we may know the power of your presence
to bind together and to heal;
through Jesus Christ our Lord. 18

Father,   Post Communion
through your goodness
we are refreshed through your Son
in word and sacrament.
May our faith be so strengthened and guarded
that we may witness to your eternal love
by our words and in our lives.
Grant this for Jesus' sake, our Lord. 24

Or, for Mothering Sunday

Loving God,
as a mother feeds her children at the breast,
you feed us in this sacrament with spiritual food and drink.
Help us who have tasted your goodness
to grow in grace within the household of faith;
through Jesus Christ our Lord. 18

The Fifth Sunday in Lent

We beseech thee, Almighty God,   COLLECT ONE
look upon the hearty desires of thy humble servants,
and stretch forth the right hand of thy Majesty,
to be our defence against all our enemies;
through Jesus Christ our Lord.

Most merciful God,   COLLECT TWO
who by the death and resurrection of your Son Jesus Christ
delivered and saved the world:
Grant that by faith in him who suffered on the cross,
we may triumph in the power of his victory;
through Jesus Christ our Lord. 7

God of hope,   POST COMMUNION
in this eucharist we have tasted
the promise of your heavenly banquet
and the richness of eternal life.
May we who bear witness to the death of your Son,
also proclaim the glory of his resurrection,
for he is Lord for ever and ever. 16

The Sixth Sunday in Lent: Palm Sunday

Almighty and everlasting God,   COLLECT ONE
who, of thy tender love towards mankind,
hast sent thy Son, our Saviour Jesus Christ,
to take upon him our flesh,
and to suffer death upon the cross,
that all mankind should follow the example of his great humility;
Mercifully grant,
that we may both follow the example of his patience,
and also be made partakers of his resurrection;
through the same Jesus Christ our Lord.

Almighty and everlasting God,
who, in your tender love towards the human race,
sent your Son our Saviour Jesus Christ
to take upon him our flesh
and to suffer death upon the cross:
Grant that we may follow the example
of his patience and humility,
and also be made partakers of his resurrection;
through Jesus Christ our Lord. 1

Lord Jesus Christ,
you humbled yourself in taking the form of a servant
and in obedience died on the cross for our salvation.
Give us the mind to follow you
and to proclaim you as Lord and King,
to the glory of God the Father. 2

Monday in Holy Week

Almighty and everlasting God,
who, of thy tender love towards mankind,
hast sent thy Son, our Saviour Jesus Christ,
to take upon him our flesh,
and to suffer death upon the cross,
that all mankind should follow the example of his great humility;
Mercifully grant,
that we may both follow the example of his patience,
and also be made partakers of his resurrection;
through the same Jesus Christ our Lord.

Almighty God,
whose most dear Son went not up to joy,
but first he suffered pain,
and entered not into glory before he was crucified:
Mercifully grant that we, walking in the way of his cross,
may find it none other than the way of life and peace;
through Jesus Christ our Lord. 2

Lord Jesus Christ,
you humbled yourself in taking the form of a servant
and in obedience died on the cross for our salvation.
Give us the mind to follow you
and to proclaim you as Lord and King,
to the glory of God the Father. 2

Tuesday in Holy Week

Almighty and everlasting God, COLLECT ONE
who, of thy tender love towards mankind,
hast sent thy Son, our Saviour Jesus Christ,
to take upon him our flesh,
and to suffer death upon the cross,
that all mankind should follow the example of his great humility;
Mercifully grant,
that we may both follow the example of his patience,
and also be made partakers of his resurrection;
through the same Jesus Christ our Lord.

O God, COLLECT TWO
who by the passion of your blessed Son made
an instrument of shameful death
to be for us the means of life:
Grant us so to glory in the cross of Christ,
that we may gladly suffer pain and loss
for the sake of your Son our Saviour Jesus Christ;
who lives and reigns with you and the Holy Spirit,
one God, now and for ever. 2

Lord Jesus Christ, POST COMMUNION
you humbled yourself in taking the form of a servant
and in obedience died on the cross for our salvation.
Give us the mind to follow you
and to proclaim you as Lord and King,
to the glory of God the Father. 2

Almighty and everlasting God,   COLLECT ONE
who, of thy tender love towards mankind,
hast sent thy Son, our Saviour Jesus Christ,
to take upon him our flesh,
and to suffer death upon the cross,
that all mankind should follow the example of his great humility;
Mercifully grant,
that we may both follow the example of his patience,
and also be made partakers of his resurrection;
through the same Jesus Christ our Lord.

Lord God,   COLLECT TWO
whose blessed Son our Saviour
gave his back to the smiters,
and did not hide his face from shame:
Give us grace to endure the sufferings
of this present time,
with sure confidence in the glory that shall be revealed;
through Jesus Christ your Son our Lord. 2

Lord Jesus Christ,   POST COMMUNION
you humbled yourself in taking the form of a servant
and in obedience died on the cross for our salvation.
Give us the mind to follow you
and to proclaim you as Lord and King,
to the glory of God the Father. 2

Maundy Thursday

O Lord,

who in a wonderful sacrament hast left us a memorial of thy passion;
Grant us so to reverence the sacred mysteries of thy body and blood
that we may perceive within ourselves
the fruits of thy redemption;
who livest and reignest with the Father and the Holy Spirit,
one God, now and for ever. 26

or

Almighty and everlasting God,
who, of thy tender love towards mankind,
hast sent thy Son, our Saviour Jesus Christ,
to take upon him our flesh,
and to suffer death upon the cross,
that all mankind should follow the example of his great humility;
Mercifully grant,
that we may both follow the example of his patience,
and also be made partakers of his resurrection;
through the same Jesus Christ our Lord.

God our Father,

you have invited us to share in the supper
which your Son gave to his Church
to proclaim his death until he comes:
May he nourish us by his presence,
and unite us in his love;
who is alive and reigns with you and the Holy Spirit,
one God, now and for ever. 9

or

Almighty God,
at the Last Supper your Son Jesus Christ
washed the disciples' feet
and commanded them to love one another.
Give us humility and obedience to be servants of others
as he was the servant of all;
who gave up his life and died for us,
yet is alive and reigns with you and the Holy Spirit,
one God, now and for ever. 2

Lord Jesus Christ,
in this wonderful sacrament
you have given us a memorial of your passion.
Grant us so to reverence the sacred mysteries
of your body and blood
that we may know within ourselves
the fruits of your redemption,
for you are alive and reign with the Father and the Holy Spirit,
one God, now and for ever. 2

or

O God,
your Son Jesus Christ has left us this meal of bread and wine
in which we share his body and his blood.
May we who celebrate this sign of his great love
show in our lives the fruits of his redemption;
who is alive and reigns with you and the Holy Spirit,
one God, now and for ever. 16

Good Friday

Almighty God,
we beseech thee graciously to behold this thy family,
for which our Lord Jesus Christ was contented to be betrayed,
and given up into the hands of wicked men,
and to suffer death upon the cross,
who now liveth and reigneth with thee
and the Holy Spirit, ever one God, world without end.

Almighty and everlasting God,
by whose Spirit the whole body of the Church
is governed and sanctified;
Receive our supplications and prayers,
which we offer before thee for all estates of men
in thy holy Church,
that every member of the same,
in his vocation and ministry,
may truly and godly serve thee;
through our Lord and Saviour Jesus Christ.

Almighty Father,
Look with mercy on this your family
for which our Lord Jesus Christ
was content to be betrayed
and given up into the hands of sinners
and to suffer death upon the cross;
who is alive and glorified with you and the Holy Spirit,
one God, now and for ever. 1

No Post Communion is provided for Good Friday.

Easter Eve

COLLECT ONE

Grant, O Lord,
that as we are baptized into the death
of thy blessed Son our Saviour Jesus Christ,
so by continual mortifying our corrupt affections
we may be buried with him;
and that, through the grave, and gate of death,
we may pass to our joyful resurrection;
for his merits, who died, and was buried,
and rose again for us,
thy Son Jesus Christ our Lord.

COLLECT TWO

Grant, Lord,
that we who are baptized into the death
of your Son our Saviour Jesus Christ
may continually put to death our evil desires
and be buried with him;
and that through the grave and gate of death
we may pass to our joyful resurrection;
through his merits, who died and was buried
and rose again for us,
your Son Jesus Christ our Lord. I

No Post Communion is provided for Easter Eve.

The First Sunday of Easter: Easter Day

Almighty God,
who through thine only-begotten Son Jesus Christ
hast overcome death,
and opened unto us the gate of everlasting life;
We humbly beseech thee,
that, as by thy special grace preventing us
thou dost put into our minds good desires,
so by thy continual help we may bring the same to good effect;
through Jesus Christ our Lord,
who liveth and reigneth with thee and the Holy Spirit,
ever one God, world without end.

If there are two celebrations of the Holy Communion this collect may be used at the first.

O God,
who for our redemption didst give thine only-begotten Son
to the death of the cross,
and by his glorious resurrection
hast delivered us from the power of our enemy;
Grant us so to die daily from sin,
that we may evermore live with him in the joy of his resurrection;
through the same Christ our Lord.

Almighty God,
through your only-begotten Son Jesus Christ
you have overcome death
and opened to us the gate of everlasting life:
Grant that, as by your grace going before us
you put into our minds good desires,
so by your continual help we may bring them to good effect;
through Jesus Christ our risen Lord
who is alive and reigns with you and the Holy Spirit,
one God, now and for ever. ɪ

Living God,
for our redemption you gave your only-begotten Son
to the death of the cross,
and by his glorious resurrection
you have delivered us from the power of our enemy.
Grant us so to die daily unto sin,
that we may evermore live with him in the joy of his risen life;
through Jesus Christ our Lord. 4

The Second Sunday of Easter

Almighty Father,   COLLECT ONE
who hast given thine only Son to die for our sins,
and to rise again for our justification;
Grant us so to put away the leaven
of malice and wickedness,
that we may alway serve thee in pureness of living and truth;
through the merits of the same thy Son
Jesus Christ our Lord.

Almighty Father,   COLLECT TWO
you have given your only Son to die for our sins
and to rise again for our justification:
Grant us so to put away the leaven
of malice and wickedness
that we may always serve you in pureness of living and truth;
through the merits of your Son
Jesus Christ our Lord. 1

Lord God our Father,   POST COMMUNION
through our Saviour Jesus Christ
you have assured your children of eternal life
and in baptism have made us one with him.
Deliver us from the death of sin
and raise us to new life in your love,
in the fellowship of the Holy Spirit,
by the grace of our Lord Jesus Christ. 7

The Third Sunday of Easter

COLLECT ONE

Almighty God,
who hast given thine only Son
to be unto us both a sacrifice for sin,
and also an ensample of godly life;
Give us grace that we may always
most thankfully receive that his inestimable benefit,
and also daily endeavour ourselves
to follow the blessed steps of his most holy life;
through the same Jesus Christ our Lord.

COLLECT TWO

Almighty Father,
who in your great mercy gladdened the disciples
with the sight of the risen Lord:
Give us such knowledge of his presence with us,
that we may be strengthened
and sustained by his risen life
and serve you continually in righteousness and truth;
through Jesus Christ our Lord. 7

POST COMMUNION

Living God,
your Son made himself known to his disciples
in the breaking of bread.
Open the eyes of our faith,
that we may see him in all his redeeming work;
who is alive and reigns with you and the Holy Spirit,
one God, now and for ever. 16

The Fourth Sunday of Easter

Almighty God,

who showest to them that be in error
the light of thy truth,
to the intent that they may return
into the way of righteousness;
Grant unto all them that are admitted
into the fellowship of Christ's Religion,
that they may eschew those things
that are contrary to their profession,
and follow all such things as are agreeable to the same;
through our Lord Jesus Christ.

Almighty God,

whose Son Jesus Christ is the resurrection and the life:
Raise us, who trust in him,
from the death of sin to the life of righteousness,
that we may seek those things which are above,
where he reigns with you and the Holy Spirit,
one God, now and for ever. 7

Merciful Father,

POST COMMUNION

you gave your Son Jesus Christ to be the good shepherd,
and in his love for us to lay down his life and rise again.
Keep us always under his protection,
and give us grace to follow in his steps;
through Jesus Christ our Lord. 2

This may be used as Collect Two in year B.

The Fifth Sunday of Easter

O Almighty God, COLLECT ONE
who alone canst order the unruly wills and affections of sinful men;
Grant unto thy people,
that they may love the thing which thou commandest,
and desire that which thou dost promise;
that so, among the sundry and manifold changes of the world,
our hearts may surely there be fixed,
where true joys are to be found;
through Jesus Christ our Lord.

Lord of all life and power, COLLECT TWO
who through the mighty resurrection of your Son
overcame the old order of sin and death
to make all things new in him:
Grant that we, being dead to sin
and alive to you in Jesus Christ,
may reign with him in glory;
to whom with you and the Holy Spirit
be praise and honour, glory and might,
now and in all eternity. 7

Eternal God, POST COMMUNION
in word and sacrament
we proclaim your truth in Jesus Christ and share his life.
In his strength may we ever walk in his way,
who is alive and reigns with you and the Holy Spirit,
one God, now and for ever. 24

The Sixth Sunday of Easter: Rogation Sunday

O Lord, COLLECT ONE
from whom all good things do come;
Grant to us thy humble servants,
that by thy holy inspiration
we may think those things that be good,
and by thy merciful guiding may perform the same;
through our Lord Jesus Christ.

God our redeemer, COLLECT TWO
you have delivered us from the power of darkness
and brought us into the kingdom of your Son:
Grant, that as by his death he has recalled us to life,
so by his continual presence in us he may raise us to eternal joy;
through Jesus Christ our Lord. 9

God our Father, POST COMMUNION
whose Son Jesus Christ gives the water of eternal life:
May we also thirst for you,
the spring of life and source of goodness,
through him who is alive and reigns with you
and the Holy Spirit,
one God, now and for ever. 16

The Ascension Day

Grant, we beseech thee, Almighty God, COLLECT ONE
that like as we do believe thy only-begotten Son
our Lord Jesus Christ
to have ascended into the heavens;
So we may also in heart and mind thither ascend,
and with him continually dwell,
who liveth and reigneth with thee and the Holy Spirit,
one God, world without end.

Grant, we pray, Almighty God,   COLLECT TWO
that as we believe your only-begotten Son our Lord Jesus Christ
to have ascended into the heavens;
so we in heart and mind may also ascend
and with him continually dwell;
who is alive and reigns with you and the Holy Spirit,
one God, now and for ever. 1

God our Father,   POST COMMUNION
you have raised our humanity in Christ
and feed us with the bread of heaven.
Mercifully grant that, nourished with such spiritual blessings,
we may set our hearts in the heavenly places;
where he now lives and reigns for ever. 10

The Seventh Sunday of Easter:
Sunday after Ascension Day

O God the King of glory,   COLLECT ONE
who hast exalted thine only Son Jesus Christ
with great triumph unto thy kingdom in heaven;
We beseech thee, leave us not comfortless;
but send to us thine Holy Spirit to comfort us,
and exalt us unto the same place
whither our Saviour Christ is gone before,
who liveth and reigneth with thee and the Holy Spirit,
one God, world without end.

O God the King of Glory,   COLLECT TWO
you have exalted your only Son Jesus Christ
with great triumph to your kingdom in heaven:
Mercifully give us faith to know
that, as he promised,
he abides with us on earth to the end of time;
who is alive and reigns with you and the Holy Spirit,
one God, now and for ever. 16

Eternal Giver of love and power, Post Communion
your Son Jesus Christ has sent us into all the world
to preach the gospel of his kingdom.
Confirm us in this mission,
and help us to live the good news we proclaim;
through Jesus Christ our Lord. 16

Day of Pentecost: Whitsunday

God, Collect One
who as at this time didst teach the hearts of thy faithful people,
by the sending to them the light of thy Holy Spirit;
Grant us by the same Spirit
to have a right judgment in all things,
and evermore to rejoice in his holy comfort;
through the merits of Christ Jesus our Saviour,
who liveth and reigneth with thee,
in the unity of the same Spirit, one God, world without end.

Almighty God, Collect Two
who on the day of Pentecost
sent your Holy Spirit to the apostles
with the wind from heaven and in tongues of flame,
filling them with joy and boldness to preach the gospel:
By the power of the same Spirit
strengthen us to witness to your truth
and to draw everyone to the fire of your love;
through Jesus Christ our Lord. 2

Faithful God, Post Communion
who fulfilled the promises of Easter
by sending us your Holy Spirit
and opening to every race and nation the way of life eternal:
Open our lips by your Spirit,
that every tongue may tell of your glory;
through Jesus Christ our Lord. 16

Weekdays after the Day of Pentecost

O Lord,   COLLECT ONE
from whom all good things do come;
Grant to us thy humble servants,
that by thy holy inspiration
we may think those things that be good,
and by thy merciful guiding may perform the same;
through our Lord Jesus Christ.

O Lord, from whom all good things come: COLLECT TWO
Grant to us your humble servants,
that, by your holy inspiration
we may think those things that be good,
and by your merciful guiding may perform the same;
through our Lord Jesus Christ. 1

Gracious God, lover of all,   POST COMMUNION
in this sacrament
we are one family in Christ your Son,
one in the sharing of his body and blood,
and one in the communion of his Spirit.
Help us to grow in love for one another
and come to the full maturity of the Body of Christ.
We make our prayer through your Son our Saviour. 16

Trinity Sunday

Almighty and everlasting God,
who hast given unto us thy servants grace
by the confession of a true faith
to acknowledge the glory of the eternal Trinity,
and in the power of the Divine Majesty to worship the Unity;
We beseech thee,
that thou wouldest keep us steadfast in this faith,
and evermore defend us from all adversities,
who livest and reignest, one God, world without end.

Almighty and everlasting God,
you have given us your servants grace,
by the confession of a true faith,
to acknowledge the glory of the eternal Trinity
and in the power of the divine majesty to worship the Unity:
Keep us steadfast in this faith,
that we may evermore be defended from all adversities;
for you live and reign, one God, for ever and ever. 1

Almighty God,
may we who have received this holy communion,
worship you with lips and lives
proclaiming your majesty
and finally see you in your eternal glory:
Holy and Eternal Trinity,
one God, now and for ever. 24

The First Sunday after Trinity

O God, COLLECT ONE
the strength of all them that put their trust in thee;
Mercifully accept our prayers;
and because through the weakness of our mortal nature
we can do no good thing without thee, grant us the help of thy grace,
that in keeping of thy commandments
we may please thee both in will and deed;
through Jesus Christ our Lord.

God, COLLECT TWO
the strength of all those who put their trust in you:
Mercifully accept our prayers
and, because through the weakness of our mortal nature
we can do no good thing without you, grant us the help of your grace,
that in the keeping of your commandments
we may please you, both in will and deed;
through Jesus Christ our Lord. 1

Eternal Father, POST COMMUNION
we thank you for nourishing us
with these heavenly gifts.
May our communion strengthen us in faith,
build us up in hope,
and make us grow in love;
for the sake of Jesus Christ our Lord. 8

The Second Sunday after Trinity

O Lord, COLLECT ONE
who never failest to help and govern them
whom thou dost bring up in thy steadfast fear and love;
Keep us, we beseech thee,
under the protection of thy good providence,
and make us to have a perpetual fear and love of thy holy Name;
through Jesus Christ our Lord.

Lord, you have taught us COLLECT TWO
that all our doings without love are nothing worth:
Send your Holy Spirit
and pour into our hearts that most excellent gift of love,
the true bond of peace and of all virtues,
without which whoever lives is counted dead before you.
Grant this for your only Son Jesus Christ's sake. 1

Loving Father, POST COMMUNION
we thank you for feeding us at the supper of your Son.
Sustain us with your Spirit,
that we may serve you here on earth
until our joy is complete in heaven,
and we share in the eternal banquet
with Jesus Christ our Lord. 8

The Third Sunday after Trinity

O Lord, COLLECT ONE
we beseech thee mercifully to hear us;
and grant that we, to whom thou hast given
an hearty desire to pray,
may by thy mighty aid be defended and comforted
in all dangers and adversities;
through Jesus Christ our Lord.

Almighty God, COLLECT TWO
you have broken the tyranny of sin
and have sent the Spirit of your Son into our hearts
whereby we call you Father:
Give us grace to dedicate our freedom to your service,
that we and all creation may be brought
to the glorious liberty of the children of God;
through Jesus Christ our Lord. 7

O God,
whose beauty is beyond our imagining
and whose power we cannot comprehend:
Give us a glimpse of your glory on earth
but shield us from knowing more than we can bear
until we may look upon you without fear;
through Jesus Christ our Saviour. 3

The Fourth Sunday after Trinity

O God, the protector of all that trust in thee,
without whom nothing is strong, nothing is holy;
Increase and multiply upon us thy mercy;
that, thou being our ruler and guide,
we may so pass through things temporal,
that we finally lose not the things eternal:
Grant this, O heavenly Father,
for Jesus Christ's sake our Lord.

O God, the protector of all who trust in you,
without whom nothing is strong, nothing is holy:
Increase and multiply upon us your mercy;
that with you as our ruler and guide,
we may so pass through things temporal
that we finally lose not the things eternal:
Grant this, heavenly Father,
for Jesus Christ's sake, our Lord. 1

Eternal God,
comfort of the afflicted and healer of the broken,
you have fed us at the table of life and hope.
Teach us the ways of gentleness and peace,
that all the world may acknowledge
the kingdom of your Son Jesus Christ our Lord. 16

The Fifth Sunday after Trinity

Grant, O Lord, we beseech thee,
that the course of this world
may be so peaceably ordered by thy governance,
that thy Church may joyfully serve thee
in all godly quietness;
through Jesus Christ our Lord.

COLLECT ONE

Almighty and everlasting God,
by whose Spirit the whole body of the Church
is governed and sanctified:
Hear our prayer which we offer for all your faithful people,
that in their vocation and ministry
they may serve you in holiness and truth
to the glory of your name;
through our Lord and Saviour Jesus Christ. 1

COLLECT TWO

Holy and blessed God,
as you give us the body and blood of your Son,
guide us with your Holy Spirit,
that we may honour you not only with our lips
but also with our lives;
through Jesus Christ our Lord. 16

POST COMMUNION

The Sixth Sunday after Trinity

O God,
who hast prepared for them that love thee
such good things as pass man's understanding;
Pour into our hearts such love toward thee,
that we, loving thee above all things,
may obtain thy promises,
which exceed all that we can desire;
through Jesus Christ our Lord.

COLLECT ONE

Merciful God, COLLECT TWO
you have prepared for those who love you
such good things as pass our understanding:
Pour into our hearts such love toward you
that we, loving you above all things,
may obtain your promises,
which exceed all that we can desire;
through Jesus Christ our Lord. I

God of our pilgrimage, POST COMMUNION
you have led us to the living water.
Refresh and sustain us
as we go forward on our journey,
in the name of Jesus Christ our Lord. 16

The Seventh Sunday after Trinity

Lord of all power and might, COLLECT ONE
who art the author and giver of all good things;
Graft in our hearts the love of thy Name,
increase in us true religion,
nourish us with all goodness,
and of thy great mercy keep us in the same;
through Jesus Christ our Lord.

Lord of all power and might, COLLECT TWO
the author and giver of all good things:
Graft in our hearts the love of your name,
increase in us true religion,
nourish us with all goodness,
and of your great mercy keep us in the same;
through Jesus Christ our Lord. I

Lord God,
whose Son is the true vine and the source of life,
ever giving himself that the world may live:
May we so receive within ourselves
the power of his death and passion
that, in his saving cup,
we may share his glory and be made perfect in his love;
for he is alive and reigns with you and the Holy Spirit,
now and for ever. 8

The Eighth Sunday after Trinity

O God,
whose never-failing providence ordereth all things
both in heaven and earth;
We humbly beseech thee to put away from us
all hurtful things,
and to give us those things which be profitable for us;
through Jesus Christ our Lord.

Blessed are you, O Lord,
and blessed are those who observe and keep your law:
Help us to seek you with our whole heart,
to delight in your commandments
and to walk in the glorious liberty
given us by your Son, Jesus Christ. 15

Strengthen for service, Lord,
the hands that holy things have taken;
may the ears which have heard your word
be deaf to clamour and dispute;
may the tongues which have sung your praise be free from deceit;
may the eyes which have seen the tokens of your love
shine with the light of hope;
and may the bodies which have been fed with your body
be refreshed with the fulness of your life;
glory to you for ever. 18

The Ninth Sunday after Trinity

Grant to us, Lord, we beseech thee, COLLECT ONE
the spirit to think and do always
such things as be rightful;
that we, who cannot do any thing
that is good without thee,
may by thee be enabled to live according to thy will;
through Jesus Christ our Lord.

Almighty God, COLLECT TWO
who sent your Holy Spirit
to be the life and light of your Church:
Open our hearts to the riches of his grace,
that we may bring forth the fruit of the Spirit
in love and joy and peace;
through Jesus Christ our Lord. 2

Holy Father, POST COMMUNION
who gathered us here around the table of your Son
to share this meal with the whole household of God:
In that new world where you reveal the fulness of your peace,
gather people of every race and language
to share in the eternal banquet
of Jesus Christ our Lord. 19

The Tenth Sunday after Trinity

Let thy merciful ears, O Lord, COLLECT ONE
be open to the prayers of thy humble servants;
and that they may obtain their petitions,
make them to ask such things as shall please thee;
through Jesus Christ our Lord.

Let your merciful ears, O Lord,
be open to the prayers of your humble servants;
and that they may obtain their petitions,
make them to ask such things as shall please you;
through Jesus Christ our Lord. 1

COLLECT TWO

O God,
as we are strengthened by these holy mysteries,
so may our lives be a continual offering,
holy and acceptable in your sight;
through Jesus Christ our Lord. 16

POST COMMUNION

The Eleventh Sunday after Trinity

O God,
who declarest thy almighty power
most chiefly in shewing mercy and pity;
Mercifully grant unto us such a measure of thy grace,
that we, running the way of thy commandments,
may obtain thy gracious promises,
and be made partakers of thy heavenly treasure;
through Jesus Christ our Lord.

COLLECT ONE

O God,
you declare your almighty power
most chiefly in showing mercy and pity:
Mercifully grant to us such a measure of your grace,
that we, running the way of your commandments,
may receive your gracious promises,
and be made partakers of your heavenly treasure;
through Jesus Christ our Lord. 1

COLLECT TWO

Lord of all mercy,
we your faithful people have celebrated
the memorial of that single sacrifice
which takes away our sins and brings pardon and peace.
By our communion
keep us firm on the foundation of the gospel
and preserve us from all sin;
through Jesus Christ our Lord. 10

The Twelfth Sunday after Trinity

Almighty and everlasting God,
who art always more ready to hear than we to pray,
and art wont to give more than either we desire, or deserve;
Pour down upon us the abundance of thy mercy;
forgiving us those things whereof our conscience is afraid,
and giving us those good things
which we are not worthy to ask,
but through the merits and mediation
of Jesus Christ, thy Son, our Lord.

Almighty and everlasting God,
you are always more ready to hear than we to pray
and to give more than either we desire, or deserve:
Pour down upon us the abundance of your mercy,
forgiving us those things of which our conscience is afraid,
and giving us those good things
which we are not worthy to ask
save through the merits and mediation
of Jesus Christ your Son our Lord. 1

God of compassion,
in this eucharist we know again your forgiveness
and the healing power of your love.
Grant that we who are made whole in Christ
may bring that forgiveness and healing to this broken world,
in the name of Jesus Christ our Lord. 16

The Thirteenth Sunday after Trinity

Almighty and merciful God,
of whose only gift it cometh
that thy faithful people do unto thee true and laudable service;
Grant, we beseech thee,
that we may so faithfully serve thee in this life,
that we fail not finally to attain thy heavenly promises;
through the merits of Jesus Christ our Lord.

Almighty God,
who called your Church to bear witness
that you were in Christ reconciling the world to yourself:
Help us to proclaim the good news of your love,
that all who hear it may be drawn to you;
through him who was lifted up on the cross,
and reigns with you and the Holy Spirit,
one God, now and for ever. 7

God our creator,
you feed your children with the true manna,
the living bread from heaven.
Let this holy food sustain us through our earthly pilgrimage
until we come to that place
where hunger and thirst are no more;
through Jesus Christ our Lord. 12

The Fourteenth Sunday after Trinity

Almighty and everlasting God,
Give unto us the increase of faith, hope, and charity;
and, that we may obtain that which thou dost promise,
make us to love that which thou dost command;
through Jesus Christ our Lord.

Almighty God,
whose only Son has opened for us
a new and living way into your presence:
Give us pure hearts and steadfast wills
to worship you in spirit and in truth,
through Jesus Christ our Lord. 7

Lord God,
the source of truth and love:
Keep us faithful to the apostles' teaching and fellowship,
united in prayer and the breaking of bread,
and one in joy and simplicity of heart,
in Jesus Christ our Lord. 13

The Fifteenth Sunday after Trinity

Keep, we beseech thee,
O Lord, thy Church with thy perpetual mercy;
and, because the frailty of man without thee cannot but fall,
keep us ever by thy help from all things hurtful,
and lead us to all things profitable to our salvation;
through Jesus Christ our Lord.

God,
who in generous mercy sent the Holy Spirit
upon your Church in the burning fire of your love:
Grant that your people may be fervent
in the fellowship of the gospel;
that, always abiding in you,
they may be found steadfast in faith and active in service;
through Jesus Christ our Lord. 12

Eternal God,
we have received these tokens of your promise.
May we who have been nourished with holy things
live as faithful heirs of your promised kingdom.
We ask this in the name of Jesus Christ our Lord. 16

The Sixteenth Sunday after Trinity

O Lord, we beseech thee,   COLLECT ONE
let thy continual pity cleanse and defend thy Church;
and, because it cannot continue in safety without thy succour,
preserve it evermore by thy help and goodness;
through Jesus Christ our Lord.

O Lord,   COLLECT TWO
Hear the prayers of your people who call upon you;
and grant that they may both perceive and know
what things they ought to do,
and also may have grace and power faithfully to fulfil them;
through Jesus Christ our Lord. 1

God of mercy,   POST COMMUNION
through our sharing in this holy sacrament
you make us one body in Christ.
Fashion us in his likeness here on earth,
that we may share his glorious company in heaven,
where he lives and reigns now and for ever. 20

The Seventeenth Sunday after Trinity

Lord, we pray thee   COLLECT ONE
that thy grace may always prevent and follow us,
and make us continually to be given to all good works;
through Jesus Christ our Lord.

Almighty God,   COLLECT TWO
you have made us for yourself,
and our hearts are restless till they find their rest in you:
Teach us to offer ourselves to your service,
that here we may have your peace,
and in the world to come may see you face to face;
through Jesus Christ our Lord. 2

God our guide,
you feed us with bread from heaven
as you fed your people Israel.
May we who have been inwardly nourished
be ready to follow you
all the days of our pilgrimage on earth,
until we come to your kingdom in heaven.
This we ask in the name of Jesus Christ our Lord. 16

The Eighteenth Sunday after Trinity

Lord, we beseech thee,
Grant thy people grace to withstand the temptations
of the world, the flesh, and the devil,
and with pure hearts and minds to follow thee
the only God;
through Jesus Christ our Lord.

Almighty and everlasting God:
Increase in us your gift of faith
that, forsaking what lies behind,
we may run the way of your commandments
and win the crown of everlasting joy;
through Jesus Christ our Lord. 7

All praise and thanks, O Christ,
for this sacred banquet,
in which by faith we receive you,
the memory of your passion is renewed,
our lives are filled with grace,
and a pledge of future glory given,
to feast at that table where you reign
with all your saints for ever. 21

The Nineteenth Sunday after Trinity
The Fifth Sunday before Advent takes precedence.

O God, COLLECT ONE
forasmuch as without thee
we are not able to please thee;
Mercifully grant, that thy Holy Spirit
may in all things direct and rule our hearts;
through Jesus Christ our Lord.

O God, COLLECT TWO
without you we are not able to please you;
Mercifully grant that your Holy Spirit
may in all things direct and rule our hearts;
through Jesus Christ our Lord. 1

Holy and blessed God, POST COMMUNION
you feed us with the body and blood of your Son
and fill us with your Holy Spirit.
May we honour you,
not only with our lips but in lives dedicated
to the service of Jesus Christ our Lord. 19

The Twentieth Sunday after Trinity
The Fifth Sunday before Advent takes precedence.

O almighty and most merciful God, COLLECT ONE
of thy bountiful goodness keep us, we beseech thee,
from all things that may hurt us;
that we, being ready both in body and soul,
may cheerfully accomplish those things
that thou wouldest have done;
through Jesus Christ our Lord.

Almighty God, COLLECT TWO
whose Holy Spirit equips your Church with a rich variety of gifts:
Grant us so to use them that, living the gospel of Christ
and eager to do your will,
we may share with the whole creation in the joys of eternal life;
through Jesus Christ our Lord. 7

God our Father, POST COMMUNION
whose Son, the light unfailing,
has come from heaven to deliver the world
from the darkness of ignorance:
Let these holy mysteries open the eyes of our understanding
that we may know the way of life, and walk in it without stumbling;
through Jesus Christ our Lord. 12

The Twenty-first Sunday after Trinity
The Fifth Sunday before Advent takes precedence.

Grant, we beseech thee, merciful Lord, COLLECT ONE
to thy faithful people pardon and peace;
that they may be cleansed from all their sins,
and serve thee with a quiet mind;
through Jesus Christ our Lord.

Merciful Lord, COLLECT TWO
Grant to your faithful people pardon and peace,
that we may be cleansed from all our sins
and serve you with a quiet mind;
through Jesus Christ our Lord. 1

Father of light, POST COMMUNION
in whom is no change or shadow of turning,
you give us every good and perfect gift
and have brought us to birth by your word of truth.
May we be a living sign of that kingdom,
where your whole creation will be made perfect
in Jesus Christ our Lord. 14

The Fifth Sunday before Advent

Blessed Lord, COLLECT ONE
who hast caused all holy Scriptures to be written for our learning;
Grant that we may in such wise hear them,
read, mark, learn and inwardly digest them,
that by patience, and comfort of thy holy Word,
we may embrace, and ever hold fast
the blessed hope of everlasting life,
which thou hast given us in our Saviour Jesus Christ.

Blessed Lord, COLLECT TWO
who caused all holy Scriptures to be written for our learning:
Help us to hear them,
to read, mark, learn and inwardly digest them
that, through patience, and the comfort of your holy word,
we may embrace and for ever hold fast
the blessed hope of everlasting life,
which you have given us in our Saviour Jesus Christ. 1

God of all grace, POST COMMUNION
your Son Jesus Christ fed the hungry
with the bread of his life and the word of his kingdom.
Renew your people with your heavenly grace,
and in all our weakness
sustain us by your true and living bread,
who is alive and reigns with you and the Holy Spirit,
one God, now and for ever. 16

All Saints' Day

1 November
May be observed on the nearest Sunday.

O almighty God, COLLECT ONE
who hast knit together thine elect
in one communion and fellowship,
in the mystical body of thy Son Christ our Lord;
Grant us so to follow thy blessed saints
in all virtuous and godly living,
that we may come to those unspeakable joys,
which thou hast prepared for them that unfeignedly love thee;
through Jesus Christ our Lord.

Almighty God, COLLECT TWO
you have knit together your elect
in one communion and fellowship
in the mystical body of your Son Christ our Lord:
Grant us grace so to follow your blessed saints
in all virtuous and godly living
that we may come to those inexpressible joys
that you have prepared for those who truly love you;
through Jesus Christ our Lord. 1

God, the source of all holiness POST COMMUNION
and giver of all good things:
May we, who have shared at this table
as strangers and pilgrims here on earth,
be welcomed with all your saints
to the heavenly feast on the day of your kingdom;
through Jesus Christ our Lord. 8

The Fourth Sunday before Advent

O God, our refuge and strength, COLLECT ONE
who art the author of all godliness;
Be ready, we beseech thee, to hear
the devout prayers of thy Church;
and grant that those things which we ask faithfully
we may obtain effectually;
through Jesus Christ our Lord.

Almighty and eternal God, COLLECT TWO
you have kindled the flame of love in the hearts of the saints:
Grant to us the same faith and power of love,
that, as we rejoice in their triumphs,
we may be sustained by their example and fellowship;
through Jesus Christ our Lord. 8

Lord of heaven, POST COMMUNION
in this eucharist you have brought us near
to an innumerable company of angels
and to the spirits of the saints made perfect.
As in this food of our earthly pilgrimage
we have shared their fellowship,
so may we come to share their joy in heaven;
through Jesus Christ our Lord. 12

The Third Sunday before Advent

O Lord, we beseech thee, COLLECT ONE
absolve thy people from their offences;
that through thy bountiful goodness
we may all be delivered from the bonds of those sins,
which by our frailty we have committed;
Grant this, O heavenly Father, for Jesus Christ's sake,
our blessed Lord and Saviour.

Almighty Father, COLLECT TWO
whose will is to restore all things
in your beloved Son, the king of all:
Govern the hearts and minds of those in authority,
and bring the families of the nations,
divided and torn apart by the ravages of sin,
to be subject to his just and gentle rule;
who is alive and reigns with you and the Holy Spirit,
one God, now and for ever. 7

God of peace, POST COMMUNION
whose Son Jesus Christ proclaimed the kingdom
and restored the broken to wholeness of life:
Look with compassion on the anguish of the world,
and by your healing power
make whole both people and nations;
through our Lord and Saviour Jesus Christ. 7

The Second Sunday before Advent

O God, COLLECT ONE
whose blessed Son was manifested
that he might destroy the works of the devil,
and make us the sons of God, and heirs of eternal life;
Grant us, we beseech thee, that, having this hope,
we may purify ourselves, even as he is pure;
that when he shall appear again with power and great glory,
we may be made like unto him
in his eternal and glorious kingdom;
where with thee, O Father, and thee, O Holy Spirit,
he liveth and reigneth, ever one God, world without end.

Heavenly Father, COLLECT TWO
whose blessed Son was revealed to destroy the works of the devil
and to make us the children of God and heirs of eternal life:
Grant that we, having this hope,
may purify ourselves even as he is pure;
that when he shall appear in power and great glory,
we may be made like him
in his eternal and glorious kingdom;
where he is alive and reigns with you and the Holy Spirit,
one God, now and for ever. 1

Gracious Lord, POST COMMUNION
in this holy sacrament you give substance to our hope.
Bring us at the last to that pure life for which we long,
through Jesus Christ our Saviour. 8

The Sunday before Advent:
The Kingship of Christ

Stir up, we beseech thee, O Lord, COLLECT ONE
the wills of thy faithful people;
that they, plenteously bringing forth the fruit of good works,
may of thee be plenteously rewarded;
through Jesus Christ our Lord.

Eternal Father, COLLECT TWO
whose Son Jesus Christ ascended to the throne of heaven
that he might rule over all things as Lord and King:
Keep the Church in the unity of the Spirit
and in the bond of peace,
and bring the whole created order to worship at his feet,
who is alive and reigns with you and the Holy Spirit,
one God, now and for ever. 2

Stir up, O Lord,
the wills of your faithful people;
that plenteously bearing the fruit of good works
they may by you be plenteously rewarded;
through Jesus Christ our Lord. 1

Weekdays of the week before Advent

Stir up, we beseech thee, O Lord,   COLLECT ONE
the wills of thy faithful people;
that they, plenteously bringing forth the fruit of good works,
may of thee be plenteously rewarded;
through Jesus Christ our Lord.

Stir up, O Lord,   COLLECT TWO
the wills of your faithful people;
that plenteously bearing the fruit of good works
they may by you be plenteously rewarded;
through Jesus Christ our Lord. 1

All powerful God,   POST COMMUNION
by giving us a share in these divine mysteries
you gladden our hearts.
Remain with us now
and let us never be separated from you.
Grant this through Jesus Christ our Lord. 20

Festivals

The Naming and Circumcision of Jesus *1 January*

Almighty God, COLLECT ONE
who madest thy blessed Son to be circumcised,
and obedient to the law for man;
Grant us the true circumcision of the Spirit;
that, our hearts and all our members being mortified
from all worldly and carnal lusts,
we may in all things obey thy holy will;
through the same thy Son Jesus Christ our Lord.

Almighty God, COLLECT TWO
whose blessed Son was circumcised
in obedience to the law for our sake
and given the Name that declares your saving love:
Give us grace faithfully to bear his Name,
to worship him in the freedom of the Spirit,
and to proclaim him as the Saviour of the world;
who is alive and reigns with you and the Holy Spirit,
one God, now and for ever. ɪ

Eternal God, POST COMMUNION
whose incarnate Son was given the name of Saviour:
Grant that we who have shared in this sacrament of our salvation
may live out our years
in the power of the name of Jesus Christ our Lord. ɪ

O God, COLLECT ONE
who, through the preaching of the blessed apostle Saint Paul,
hast caused the light of the Gospel
to shine throughout the world;
Grant, we beseech thee,
that we, having his wonderful conversion in remembrance,
may shew forth our thankfulness unto thee for the same,
by following the holy doctrine which he taught;
through Jesus Christ our Lord.

Almighty God, COLLECT TWO
who caused the light of the gospel
to shine throughout the world
through the preaching of your servant Saint Paul:
Grant that we who celebrate his wonderful conversion
may follow him in bearing witness to your truth;
through Jesus Christ our Lord. 1

Gracious God, POST COMMUNION
you filled your apostle Paul with love for all the churches.
May this sacrament which we have received
foster love and unity among your people.
This we ask in the name of Jesus Christ our Lord. 16

Saint Brigid *1 February*

Father, COLLECT ONE
by the leadership of thy blessed servant Brigid
thou didst strengthen the Church in this land;
As we give thee thanks for her life of devoted service,
inspire us with new life and light,
and give us perseverance to serve thee all our days;
through Jesus Christ our Lord.

Father,
by the leadership of your blessed servant Brigid
you strengthened the Church in this land:
As we give you thanks for her life of devoted service,
inspire us with new life and light,
and give us perseverance to serve you all our days;
through Jesus Christ our Lord. 2

God of truth,
whose Wisdom set her table and invited us to eat
the bread and drink the wine of the kingdom.
Help us to lay aside all foolishness
and to live and walk in the way of insight,
that in fellowship with all your saints
we may come to the eternal feast of heaven;
through Jesus Christ our Lord. 13

Saint Patrick

17 March

O almighty God,
who in thy providence didst choose thy servant Patrick
to be the apostle of the Irish people,
that he might bring those
who were wandering in darkness and error
to the true light and knowledge of thee;
Grant us so to walk in that light,
that we may come at last to the light of everlasting life;
through the merits of Jesus Christ thy Son our Lord.

Almighty God,
in your providence you chose your servant Patrick
to be the apostle of the Irish people,
to bring those who were wandering in darkness and error
to the true light and knowledge of your Word:
Grant that walking in that light
we may come at last to the light of everlasting life;
through Jesus Christ our Lord. 1

Hear us, most merciful God,
for that part of the Church
which through your servant Patrick you planted in our land;
that it may hold fast the faith entrusted to the saints
and in the end bear much fruit to eternal life:
through Jesus Christ our Lord. 1

Saint Joseph of Nazareth

19 March

O God,
who from the family of thy servant David
didst raise up Joseph to be the guardian of thine incarnate Son
and spouse of his virgin mother;
Give us grace to imitate his uprightness of life
and his obedience to thy commands:
through the same thy Son Jesus Christ our Lord. 6

COLLECT ONE

God our Father,
who from the family of your servant David
raised up Joseph the carpenter
to be the guardian of your incarnate Son
and husband of the Blessed Virgin Mary:
Give us grace to follow his example
of faithful obedience to your commands;
through our Lord Jesus Christ,
who is alive and reigns with you and the Holy Spirit,
one God, now and for ever. 13

COLLECT TWO

Heavenly Father,
whose Son grew in wisdom and stature
in the home of Joseph the carpenter of Nazareth,
and on the wood of the cross perfected
the work of the world's salvation.
Help us, strengthened by this sacrament of his passion,
to count the wisdom of the world as foolishness,
and to walk with him in simplicity and trust;
through Jesus Christ our Lord. 13

POST COMMUNION

The Annunciation of our Lord Jesus Christ
to the Blessed Virgin Mary   *25 March*

We beseech thee, O Lord,
pour thy grace into our hearts;
that, as we have known the incarnation of thy Son Jesus Christ
by the message of an angel,
so by his cross and passion
we may be brought unto the glory of his resurrection;
through the same Jesus Christ our Lord.

Pour your grace into our hearts, Lord,   Collect Two
that as we have known the incarnation of your Son Jesus Christ
by the message of an angel,
so by his cross and passion
we may be brought to the glory of his resurrection;
through Jesus Christ our Lord. 2

God Most High,   Post Communion
whose handmaid bore the Word made flesh:
We thank you that in this sacrament of our redemption
you visit us with your Holy Spirit
and overshadow us by your power.
May we like Mary be joyful in our obedience,
and so bring forth the fruits of holiness;
through Jesus Christ our Lord. 8

Saint Mark   *25 April*

O almighty God,   Collect One
who hast instructed thy holy Church
with the heavenly doctrine of thy evangelist Saint Mark;
Give us grace, that, being not like children
carried away with every blast of vain doctrine,
we may be established in the truth of thy holy Gospel;
through Jesus Christ our Lord.

Almighty God,
who enlightened your holy Church
through the inspired witness of your evangelist Saint Mark:
Grant that we, being firmly grounded
in the truth of the gospel,
may be faithful to its teaching both in word and deed;
through Jesus Christ our Lord. 7

Blessed Lord,
you have fed us at this table with sacramental gifts.
May we always rejoice and find strength
in the gift of the gospel
announced to us by Saint Mark,
and come at last to the fullness of everlasting life;
through Jesus Christ our Lord. 24

Saint Philip and Saint James 1 *May*

O almighty God,
whom truly to know is everlasting life;
Grant us perfectly to know thy Son Jesus Christ
to be the way, the truth, and the life;
that, following in the steps of thy holy apostles,
Saint Philip and Saint James,
we may steadfastly walk in the way that leadeth to eternal life;
through the same thy Son Jesus Christ our Lord.

Almighty Father,
whom truly to know is eternal life:
Teach us to know your Son Jesus Christ
as the way, the truth, and the life;
that we may follow the steps of your holy apostles
Philip and James,
and walk steadfastly in the way that leads to your glory;
through Jesus Christ our Lord. 1

Holy God,
in Jesus Christ we find the way to you.
May we, who have met him in this banquet,
be kept in your unending love,
and see you at work in your world,
through your Son, who is Lord for ever and ever. 16

Saint Matthias

O almighty God,
who into the place of the traitor Judas didst choose
thy faithful servant Matthias
to be of the number of the twelve apostles;
Grant that thy Church,
being alway preserved from false apostles,
may be ordered and guided by faithful and true pastors;
through Jesus Christ our Lord.

Almighty God,
who in the place of the traitor Judas
chose your faithful servant Matthias
to be of the number of the Twelve:
Preserve your Church from false apostles
and, by the ministry of faithful pastors and teachers,
keep us steadfast in your truth;
through Jesus Christ our Lord. 1

Lord God,
the source of truth and love,
Keep us faithful to the apostles' teaching and fellowship,
united in prayer and the breaking of bread,
and one in joy and simplicity of heart,
in Jesus Christ our Lord. 13

Almighty God,   COLLECT ONE
by whose grace Elizabeth rejoiced with Mary
and greeted her as the mother of the Lord;
Look with favour on thy lowly servants
that, with Mary, we may magnify thy holy name
and rejoice to acclaim her Son our Saviour,
who liveth and reigneth with thee and the Holy Spirit,
one God, now and for ever.

Mighty God,   COLLECT TWO
by whose grace Elizabeth rejoiced with Mary
and greeted her as the mother of the Lord:
Look with favour on your lowly servants
that, with Mary, we may magnify your holy name
and rejoice to acclaim her Son our Saviour,
who is alive and reigns with you and the Holy Spirit,
one God, now and for ever. 7

Gracious God,   POST COMMUNION
who gave joy to Elizabeth and Mary
as they recognised the signs of redemption at work within them:
Help us, who have shared in the joy of this eucharist,
to know the Lord deep within us
and his love shining out in our lives,
that the world may rejoice in your salvation;
through Jesus Christ our Lord. 13

O God, who didst call thy servant Columba   COLLECT ONE
from among the princes of this land
to be a herald and evangelist of thy kingdom;
Grant that thy Church,
having his faith and courage in remembrance,
may so proclaim the splendour of thy grace,
that people everywhere will come to know thy Son
as their Saviour, and serve him as their King;
who liveth and reigneth with thee and the Holy Spirit,
one God, now and for ever.

O God, you called your servant Columba   COLLECT TWO
from among the princes of this land
to be a herald and evangelist of your kingdom:
Grant that your Church, remembering his faith and courage,
may so proclaim the splendour of your grace
that people everywhere will come to know your Son
as their Saviour, and serve him as their King;
who lives and reigns with you and the Holy Spirit,
one God, now and for ever. 2

Lord Jesus, King of Saints,   POST COMMUNION
you blessed Columba to find refuge in you
both at home and in exile.
May we, who have tasted your goodness at this table,
come with all your saints to the royal banquet
of your kingdom in heaven;
where with the Father and the Holy Spirit
you reign, for ever. 24

O Lord God almighty,   COLLECT ONE
who didst endue thy holy apostle Barnabas
with singular gifts of the Holy Spirit;
Leave us not, we beseech thee, destitute of thy manifold gifts,
nor yet of grace to use them alway to thy honour and glory;
through Jesus Christ our Lord.

Bountiful God, giver of all gifts,   COLLECT TWO
who poured your Spirit upon your servant Barnabas:
Help us, by his example, to be generous in all our judgments,
and unselfish in our service;
through Jesus Christ our Lord. 2

Just and merciful God,   POST COMMUNION
we have heard your word
and received new life at your table.
Kindle in us the flame of love
by which your apostle Barnabas bore witness to the gospel,
and send us out in Jesus' name
to encourage our brothers and sisters in faith.
We ask this for his sake. 24

The Birth of Saint John the Baptist   *24 June*

Almighty God,   COLLECT ONE
by whose providence thy servant John Baptist
was wonderfully born,
and sent to prepare the way of thy Son our Saviour,
by preaching of repentance;
Make us so to follow his doctrine and holy life,
that we may truly repent according to his preaching;
and after his example constantly speak the truth,
boldly rebuke vice, and patiently suffer for the truth's sake;
through Jesus Christ our Lord.

Almighty God, COLLECT TWO
by whose providence your servant John the Baptist was wonderfully born,
and sent to prepare the way of your Son our Saviour,
by the preaching of repentance:
Lead us to repent according to his preaching,
and, after his example, constantly to speak the truth,
boldly to rebuke vice, and patiently to suffer for the truth's sake;
through Jesus Christ our Lord. 1

Merciful Lord, POST COMMUNION
whose prophet John the Baptist
proclaimed your Son as the Lamb of God
who takes away the sin of the world:
Grant, that we who in this sacrament have known
your forgiveness and your life-giving love,
may ever tell of your mercy and your peace;
through Jesus Christ our Lord. 13

Saint Peter   *29 June*

O almighty God, COLLECT ONE
who by thy Son Jesus Christ didst give
to thy apostle Saint Peter many excellent gifts,
and commandedst him earnestly to feed thy flock;
Make, we beseech thee, all bishops and pastors
diligently to preach thy holy Word,
and the people obediently to follow the same,
that they may receive the crown of everlasting glory;
through Jesus Christ our Lord.

Almighty God, COLLECT TWO
who inspired your apostle Saint Peter
to confess Jesus as Christ and Son of the living God:
Build up your Church upon this rock,
that in unity and peace it may proclaim one truth
and follow one Lord, your Son our Saviour Christ,
who is alive and reigns with you and the Holy Spirit,
one God, now and for ever. 1

Heavenly Father,
ever renew the life of your Church
by the power of this sacrament.
Keep us united in your love
through the teaching of the apostles and the breaking of bread,
in the name of Jesus Christ the Lord. 16

Saint Thomas

3 July

Almighty and everliving God, COLLECT ONE
who, for the more confirmation of the faith
didst suffer thy holy apostle Thomas
to be doubtful of thy Son's resurrection;
Grant us so perfectly, and without all doubt,
to believe in thy Son Jesus Christ,
that our faith in thy sight may never be reproved.
Hear us, O Lord, through the same Jesus Christ,
to whom, with thee and the Holy Spirit,
be all honour and glory, now and for evermore.

Almighty and eternal God, COLLECT TWO
who, for the firmer foundation of our faith,
allowed your holy apostle Thomas
to doubt the resurrection of your Son
till word and sight convinced him:
Grant to us, who have not seen, that we also may believe
and so confess Christ as our Lord and our God;
who is alive and reigns with you and the Holy Spirit,
one God, now and for ever. 7

God of hope, POST COMMUNION
in this eucharist we have tasted
the promise of your heavenly banquet
and the richness of eternal life.
May we who bear witness to the death of your Son,
also proclaim the glory of his resurrection,
for he is Lord for ever and ever. 16

Almighty God,   COLLECT ONE
whose blessed Son restored Mary Magdalene
to health of body and mind,
and called her to be a witness to his resurrection;
Mercifully grant that by thy grace
we may be healed of our infirmities
and know thee in the power of his endless life;
who with thee and the Holy Spirit,
liveth and reigneth one God, now and for ever. 6

Almighty God,   COLLECT TWO
whose Son restored Mary Magdalene
to health of mind and body
and called her to be a witness to his resurrection:
Forgive our sins and heal us by your grace,
that we may serve you in the power of his risen life;
who is alive and reigns with you and the Holy Spirit,
one God, now and for ever. 7

God of life and love,   POST COMMUNION
whose risen Son called Mary Magdalene by name
and sent her to tell of his resurrection to his apostles:
In your mercy, help us,
who have been united with him in this eucharist,
to proclaim the good news
that he is alive and reigns with you and the Holy Spirit,
one God, now and for ever. 13

Grant, O merciful God, COLLECT ONE
that as thine holy apostle Saint James,
leaving his father and all that he had,
without delay was obedient unto the calling
of thy Son Jesus Christ, and followed him;
so we, forsaking all worldly and carnal affections,
may be evermore ready to follow thy holy commandments;
through Jesus Christ our Lord.

Merciful God, COLLECT TWO
whose holy apostle Saint James,
leaving his father and all that he had,
was obedient to the calling of your Son Jesus Christ
and followed him even to death:
Help us, forsaking the false attractions of the world,
to be ready at all times to answer your call without delay;
through Jesus Christ our Lord. 1

Father, POST COMMUNION
we have eaten at your table
and drunk from the cup of your kingdom.
Teach us the way of service
that in compassion and humility
we may reflect the glory of Jesus Christ,
Son of Man and Son of God, our Lord. 16

O almighty God,
whose only-begotten Son was transfigured
before chosen witnesses on the holy mount,
and amidst the exceeding glory spake of his decease
which he should accomplish at Jerusalem;
Grant to us thy servants
that, beholding the brightness of his countenance,
we may be strengthened to bear our cross;
through the same Jesus Christ our Lord.

Father in heaven,
whose Son Jesus Christ was wonderfully transfigured
before chosen witnesses upon the holy mountain,
and spoke of the exodus he would accomplish at Jerusalem:
Give us strength so to hear his voice and bear our cross in this world,
that in the world to come we may see him as he is;
where he is alive and reigns with you and the Holy Spirit,
one God, now and for ever. 2

Holy God,
we see your glory in the face of Jesus Christ.
May we who are partakers at his table
reflect his life in word and deed,
that all the world may know his power to change and save.
This we ask through Jesus Christ our Lord. 16

Saint Bartholomew   *24 August*

O almighty and everlasting God,
who didst give to thine apostle Bartholomew
grace truly to believe and to preach thy Word;
Grant, we beseech thee, unto thy Church,
to love that Word which he believed,
and both to preach and receive the same;
through Jesus Christ our Lord.

Almighty and everlasting God, COLLECT TWO
who gave to your apostle Bartholomew
grace truly to believe and to preach your word:
Grant that your Church may love that word which he believed
and may faithfully preach and receive the same;
through Jesus Christ our Lord. 1

God of our salvation, POST COMMUNION
you have fed us at the table of your Son Jesus Christ our Lord.
Lead us in his way of service,
that your kingdom may be known on earth,
your saving power among all nations.
Grant this for his name's sake. 16

The Birth of the Blessed Virgin Mary   *8 September*

Almighty God, COLLECT ONE
who didst look upon the lowliness of the blessed Virgin Mary
and didst choose her to be the mother of thine only Son;
Grant that we, who are redeemed by his blood,
may share with her in the glory of thine eternal kingdom;
through Jesus Christ our Lord.

Almighty God, COLLECT TWO
who looked upon the lowliness of the blessed Virgin Mary
and chose her to be the mother of your only Son:
Grant that we who are redeemed by his blood
may share with her in the glory of your eternal kingdom;
through Jesus Christ our Lord. 7

Almighty and everlasting God, POST COMMUNION
who stooped to raise fallen humanity
through the child-bearing of blessed Mary:
Grant that we who have seen your glory
revealed in our human nature,
and your love made perfect in our weakness,
may daily be renewed in your image,
and conformed to the pattern of your Son, Jesus Christ our Lord. 8

Saint Matthew

O almighty God,
who by thy blessed Son didst call Matthew
from the receipt of custom to be an apostle and evangelist;
Grant us grace to forsake all covetous desires,
and inordinate love of riches,
and to follow the same thy Son Jesus Christ,
who liveth and reigneth with thee and the Holy Spirit,
one God, now and for ever.

O almighty God,
whose blessed Son called Matthew the tax-collector
to be an apostle and evangelist:
Give us grace to forsake the selfish pursuit of gain
and the possessive love of riches;
that we may follow in the way of your Son Jesus Christ,
who is alive and reigns with you and the Holy Spirit,
one God, now and for ever. 1

God of mercy and compassion,
we have shared the joy of salvation
that Matthew knew when Jesus called him.
Renew our calling to proclaim the one
who came not to call the righteous but sinners to salvation,
your Son Jesus Christ our Lord. 16

Saint Michael and all Angels

O everlasting God,
who hast ordained and constituted
the services of angels and men in a wonderful order;
Mercifully grant, that as thy holy angels alway
do thee service in heaven,
so, by thy appointment, they may succour and defend us on earth;
through Jesus Christ our Lord.

Everlasting God,
you have ordained and constituted the ministries
of angels and mortals in a wonderful order:
Grant that as your holy angels always serve you in heaven,
so, at your command,
they may help and defend us on earth;
through Jesus Christ our Lord. 1

Lord of heaven,
in this eucharist you have brought us near
to an innumerable company of angels
and to the spirits of the saints made perfect.
As in this food of our earthly pilgrimage
we have shared their fellowship,
so may we come to share their joy in heaven;
through Jesus Christ our Lord. 8

Saint Philip the Deacon   *11 October*

Lord God,
whose Spirit guided Philip the deacon
to show how ancient prophecies are fulfilled in Jesus Christ;
Open our minds to understand the Scriptures,
and deepen our faith in him;
who liveth and reigneth with thee and the Holy Spirit,
one God, for ever and ever. 3

Lord God,
your Spirit guided Philip the deacon
to show how ancient prophecies are fulfilled in Jesus Christ:
Open our minds to understand the Scriptures,
and deepen our faith in him;
who is alive and reigns with you and the Holy Spirit,
one God, for ever and ever. 3

We thank you, Lord, for calling and using
people with different gifts to build your kingdom.
May we, who are strengthened by this sacrament,
like Philip and his family rejoice to serve you
by the witness of our lives and homes;
though Jesus Christ our Lord. 24

Saint Luke

18 October

Almighty God,
who calledst Luke the physician,
whose praise is in the gospel,
to be an evangelist, and physician of the soul;
May it please thee, that by the wholesome medicines
of the doctrine delivered by him,
all the diseases of our souls may be healed;
through the merits of thy Son Jesus Christ our Lord.

COLLECT ONE

Almighty God,
you called Luke the physician,
whose praise is in the gospel,
to be an evangelist and physician of the soul:
By the grace of the Spirit
and through the wholesome medicine of the gospel,
give your Church the same love and power to heal;
through Jesus Christ our Lord. 1

COLLECT TWO

Living God,
may we who have shared these holy mysteries
enjoy health of body and mind
and witness faithfully to your gospel,
in the name of Jesus Christ our Lord. 16

POST COMMUNION

Saint James, the Brother of our Lord

Grant, we beseech thee, O God,
that after the example of thy servant, James the Just,
brother of our Lord,
thy Church may give itself continually to prayer
and to the reconciliation of all who are at variance and enmity;
through Jesus Christ our Lord. 6

Lord, God of peace:
Grant that after the example of your servant,
James the brother of our Lord,
your Church may give itself continually to prayer
and to the reconciliation of all
who are caught up in hatred or enmity;
through Jesus Christ our Lord. 3

Lord Jesus Christ,
we thank you that after your resurrection you appeared to James,
and endowed him with gifts of leadership for your Church.
May we, who have known you now in the breaking of bread,
be people of prayer and reconciliation.
We ask it for your love's sake. 24

Saint Simon and Saint Jude

O almighty God,
who hast built thy Church upon the foundation
of the apostles and prophets,
Jesus Christ himself being the head corner-stone;
Grant us so to be joined together
in unity of spirit by their doctrine,
that we may be made an holy temple acceptable unto thee;
through Jesus Christ our Lord.

Almighty God,
who built your Church upon the foundation
of the apostles and prophets
with Jesus Christ himself as the chief corner-stone:
So join us together in unity of spirit by their doctrine
that we may be made a holy temple acceptable to you;
through Jesus Christ our Lord. 1

Lord God,
the source of truth and love:
Keep us faithful to the apostles' teaching and fellowship,
united in prayer and the breaking of bread,
and one in joy and simplicity of heart,
in Jesus Christ our Lord. 13

All Saints' Day

1 November

May be observed on the nearest Sunday.

O almighty God, COLLECT ONE
who hast knit together thine elect
in one communion and fellowship,
in the mystical body of thy Son Christ our Lord;
Grant us so to follow thy blessed saints
in all virtuous and godly living,
that we may come to those unspeakable joys,
which thou hast prepared for them that unfeignedly love thee;
through Jesus Christ our Lord.

Almighty God, COLLECT TWO
you have knit together your elect
in one communion and fellowship
in the mystical body of your Son Christ our Lord:
Grant us grace so to follow your blessed saints
in all virtuous and godly living
that we may come to those inexpressible joys
that you have prepared for those who truly love you;
through Jesus Christ our Lord. 1

God, the source of all holiness

and giver of all good things:
May we who have shared at this table
as strangers and pilgrims here on earth
be welcomed with all your saints
to the heavenly feast on the day of your kingdom;
through Jesus Christ our Lord. 8

Saint Andrew

Almighty God,

who didst give such grace unto thy holy apostle Saint Andrew,
that he readily obeyed the calling of thy Son Jesus Christ,
and followed him without delay;
Grant unto us all, that we being called by thy holy Word,
may forthwith give up ourselves obediently
to fulfil thy holy commandments;
through the same Jesus Christ our Lord.

Almighty God,

who gave such grace to your apostle Saint Andrew
that he readily obeyed the call of your Son Jesus Christ
and brought his brother with him:
Call us by your holy Word
and give us grace to follow without delay,
and to tell the good news of your kingdom;
through Jesus Christ our Lord. 2

Father,

may the gifts we have received at your table
keep us alert for your call
that we may always be ready to answer,
and, following the example of Saint Andrew,
always be ready to bear our witness
to our Saviour Jesus Christ. 24

Saint Stephen

Grant, O Lord,
that in all our sufferings here upon earth
for the testimony of thy truth,
we may steadfastly look up to heaven,
and by faith behold the glory that shall be revealed;
and, being filled with the Holy Spirit,
may learn to love and bless our persecutors
by the example of thy first martyr Saint Stephen,
who prayed for his murderers to thee,
O blessed Jesus, who standest at the right hand of God
to succour all those that suffer for thee,
our only Mediator and Advocate.

Gracious Father,
who gave the first martyr Stephen
grace to pray for those who stoned him:
Grant that in all our sufferings for the truth
we may learn to love even our enemies
and to seek forgiveness for those who desire our hurt,
looking up to heaven to him who was crucified for us,
Jesus Christ, our Mediator and Advocate,
who is alive and reigns with you and the Holy Spirit,
one God, now and for ever. 1

Merciful Lord,
we thank you for these signs of your mercy,
we praise you for feeding us at your table
and giving us joy in honouring Stephen,
first martyr of the new Israel;
through Jesus Christ our Lord. 14

Merciful Lord,
we beseech thee to cast thy bright beams of light
upon thy Church,
that it, being enlightened by the doctrine
of thy blessed apostle and evangelist Saint John,
may so walk in the light of thy truth,
that it may at length attain to the light of everlasting life;
through Jesus Christ our Lord.

COLLECT ONE

Merciful Lord,
cast your bright beams of light upon the Church;
that, being enlightened by the teaching
of your blessed apostle and evangelist Saint John,
we may so walk in the light of your truth
that we may at last attain to the light of everlasting life
through Jesus Christ your incarnate Son our Lord. 1

COLLECT TWO

Grant, O Lord, we pray,
that the Word made flesh proclaimed by your apostle John
may ever abide and live within us;
through Jesus Christ our Lord. 20

POST COMMUNION

O almighty God,
who out of the mouths of babes and sucklings
hast ordained strength,
and madest infants to glorify thee by their deaths:
Mortify and kill all vices in us,
and so strengthen us by thy grace,
that by the innocency of our lives,
and constancy of our faith even unto death,
we may glorify thy holy Name;
through Jesus Christ our Lord.

<small>COLLECT ONE</small>

Heavenly Father,
whose children suffered at the hands of Herod:
By your great might frustrate all evil designs,
and establish your reign of justice, love and peace;
through Jesus Christ our Lord. 16

<small>COLLECT TWO</small>

Eternal God,
comfort of the afflicted and healer of the broken,
you have fed us this day at the table of life and hope.
Teach us the ways of gentleness and peace,
that all the world may acknowledge
the kingdom of your Son Jesus Christ our Lord. 16

<small>POST COMMUNION</small>

Special Occasions

Dedication Festival

O almighty God,   COLLECT ONE
to whose glory we celebrate the dedication of this house of prayer;
We praise thee for the many blessings
thou hast given to those who worship here,
and we pray that all who seek thee in this place
may find thee, and, being filled with the Holy Spirit,
may become a living temple acceptable to thee;
through Jesus Christ our Lord.

Almighty God,   COLLECT TWO
to whose glory we celebrate the dedication of this house of prayer:
We praise you for the many blessings
you have given to those who worship here,
and we pray that all who seek you in this place
may find you, and, being filled with the Holy Spirit,
may become a living temple acceptable to you
through Jesus Christ our Lord. 2

Father in heaven,   POST COMMUNION
your church on earth is a sign of heavenly peace,
an image of the new and eternal Jerusalem.
Grant to us in the days of our pilgrimage
that, fed with the living bread of heaven,
and united in the body of your Son,
we may become the temple of your presence,
the place of your glory on earth,
and a sign of your peace in the world;
through Jesus Christ our Lord. 13

Harvest Thanksgiving

O almighty and everlasting God, COLLECT ONE
who hast graciously given unto us
the fruits of the earth in their season;
We yield thee humble and hearty thanks for this thy bounty;
beseeching thee to give us grace rightly
to use the same to thy glory,
and the relief of those that need;
through Jesus Christ our Lord,
who liveth and reigneth with thee and the Holy Spirit,
one God, world without end.

or

O almighty God and heavenly Father;
We glorify thee that thou hast fulfilled to us thy gracious promise,
that, while the earth remaineth,
seed-time and harvest shall not fail.
We bless thee for the kindly fruits of the earth,
which thou hast given to our use.
Teach us, we beseech thee, to remember
that it is not by bread alone that man doth live;
and grant us evermore to feed on him
who is the true bread from heaven,
Jesus Christ our Lord,
to whom with thee and the Holy Spirit,
be all honour and glory, world without end.

Eternal God, COLLECT TWO
you crown the year with your goodness
and give us the fruits of the earth in their season:
Grant that we may use them to your glory,
for the relief of those in need
and for our own well-being;
through Jesus Christ our Lord. I

Lord of the harvest,
with joy we have offered thanksgiving for your love in creation
and have shared in the bread and wine of the kingdom.
By your grace plant within us such reverence
for all that you give us
that will make us wise stewards of the good things we enjoy;
through Jesus Christ our Lord.   13

The Guidance of the Holy Spirit
For the Opening of a Synod

God,
who didst teach the hearts of thy faithful people,
by the sending to them the light of thy Holy Spirit;
Grant us by the same Spirit to have a right judgment in all things,
and evermore to rejoice in his holy comfort;
through the merits of Christ Jesus our Saviour,
who liveth and reigneth with thee,
in the unity of the same Spirit, one God, world without end.

God,
who from of old taught the hearts of your faithful people
by sending to them the light of your Holy Spirit:
Grant us by the same Spirit to have a right judgment in all things
and evermore to rejoice in his holy comfort;
through the merits of Christ Jesus our Saviour,
who is alive and reigns with you in the unity of the Spirit,
one God, now and for ever.   1

or

Almighty God,
you have given your Holy Spirit to the Church to lead us into all truth:
Bless with the Spirit's grace and presence
the members of this .... (*synod/vestry/etc*);
keep *us/them* steadfast in faith and united in love,
that *we/they* may manifest your glory and prepare the way of your kingdom;
through Jesus Christ our Lord.   7

God of power,
whose Holy Spirit renews your people
in the bread and wine we bless and share:
May the boldness of the Spirit transform us,
the gentleness of the Spirit lead us,
and the gifts of the Spirit equip us
to serve and worship you;
through Jesus Christ our Lord. 22

Ember Days: Ministry

For the ministry of all Christian people

Almighty and everlasting God,
by whose Spirit the whole body of the Church
is governed and sanctified:
Hear our prayer which we offer for all your faithful people,
that in their vocation and ministry
they may serve you in holiness and truth
to the glory of your name;
through our Lord and Saviour Jesus Christ. 1

For those to be ordained

Almighty God, the giver of all good gifts,
by your Holy Spirit you have appointed
various orders of ministry in the Church:
Look with mercy on your *servant(s)* now called to be
deacons / priests / a bishop;
maintain *them* in truth and renew *them* in holiness,
that by word and good example *they* may faithfully serve you
to the glory of your name
and the benefit of your Church;
through the merits of our Saviour Jesus Christ. 1

The words in italics are varied as required.

For vocations to Holy Orders

Almighty God,
you have entrusted to your Church
a share in the ministry of your Son our great High Priest:
Inspire by your Holy Spirit the hearts of many
to offer themselves for ordination in your Church,
that strengthened by his power,
they may work for the increase of your kingdom
and set forward the eternal praise of your name;
through Jesus Christ our Lord. 2

For the inauguration of a new ministry

God our Father, Lord of all the world,
through your Son you have called us into the fellowship
of your universal Church:
Hear our prayer for your faithful people
that in their vocation and ministry
each may be an instrument of your love,
and give to your servant ... now to be ... *installed,/ instituted, /* ....
the needful gifts of grace;
through our Lord and Saviour Jesus Christ.

Heavenly Father,
whose ascended Son gave gifts of leadership
and service to the Church:
Strengthen us who have received this holy food
to be good stewards of your manifold grace;
through him who came not to be served but to serve,
and give his life as a ransom for many,
Jesus Christ our Lord. 13

or

Lord of the harvest,
you have fed your people in this sacrament
with the fruits of creation made holy by your Spirit.
By your grace raise up among us faithful labourers
to sow your word and reap the harvest of souls;
through Jesus Christ our Lord. 10

Rogation Days

Almighty God, COLLECT
whose will it is that the earth and the sea
should bear fruit in due season:
Bless the labours of those who work on land and sea,
grant us a good harvest
and the grace always to rejoice in your fatherly care;
through Jesus Christ our Lord. 23

or

Almighty God and Father,
you have so ordered our life
that we are dependent on one another:
Prosper those engaged in commerce and industry
and direct their minds and hands
that they may rightly use your gifts in the service of others;
through Jesus Christ our Lord. 23

God our creator, POST COMMUNION
you give seed for us to sow and bread for us to eat.
As you have blessed the fruit of our labour in this eucharist,
so we ask you to give all your children their daily bread,
that the world may praise you for your goodness;
through Jesus Christ our Lord. 22

Mission

Almighty God, COLLECT
who called your Church to witness
that you were in Christ reconciling the world to yourself:
Help us to proclaim the good news of your love,
that all who hear it may be drawn to you;
through him who was lifted up on the cross,
and reigns with you and the Holy Spirit,
one God, now and for ever. 2

Eternal Giver of love and power, POST COMMUNION
your Son Jesus Christ has sent us into all the world
to preach the gospel of his kingdom.
Confirm us in this mission,
and help us to live the good news we proclaim;
through Jesus Christ our Lord. 16

Peace

Almighty God, COLLECT
from whom all thoughts of truth and peace proceed:
Kindle, we pray, in every heart the true love of peace;
and guide with your pure and peaceable wisdom
those who take counsel for the nations of the earth,
that in tranquillity your kingdom may go forward,
till the earth is filled with the knowledge of your love;
through Jesus Christ our Lord. 1

God our Father, POST COMMUNION
your Son is our peace
and his cross the sign of reconciliation.
Help us, who share the broken bread,
to bring together what is scattered and to bind up what is wounded,
that Christ may bring in the everlasting kingdom of his peace;
who is alive and reigns with you and the Holy Spirit,
one God, now and for ever. 13

Unity

Heavenly Father, COLLECT
you have called us in the body of your Son Jesus Christ
to continue his work of reconciliation
and reveal you to the world:
forgive us the sins which tear us apart;
give us the courage to overcome our fears
and to seek that unity which is your gift and your will;
through Jesus Christ our Lord. 7

or

Lord Jesus Christ,
who said to your apostles,
Peace I leave with you, my peace I give to you:
look not on our sins but on the faith of your Church,
and grant it the peace and unity of your kingdom;
where you are alive and reign with the Father
and the Holy Spirit, one God, now and for ever. 1

Eternal God and Father, <small>POST COMMUNION</small>
whose Son at supper prayed that his disciples might be one,
as he is one with you:
Draw us closer to him,
that in common love and obedience to you
we may be united to one another
in the fellowship of the one Spirit,
that the world may believe that he is Lord,
to your eternal glory;
through Jesus Christ our Lord. 8

Bible Sunday

Blessed Lord,
who caused all holy scriptures to be written for our learning:
help us to hear them,
to read, mark, learn and inwardly digest them
that, through patience, and the comfort of your holy word,
we may embrace and for ever hold fast
the hope of everlasting life,
which you have given us in our Saviour Jesus Christ. 1

God of all grace,
your Son Jesus Christ fed the hungry
with the bread of his life
and the word of his kingdom.
Renew your people with your heavenly grace,
and in all our weakness
sustain us by your true and living bread,
who is alive and reigns with you and the Holy Spirit,
one God, now and for ever. 16

The numbers after all the modern prayers, some of which have been adapted, indicate their sources as follows:

1   *Book of Common Prayer*, Church of Ireland 1926, 1933, 1962
2   *Alternative Prayer Book*, Church of Ireland 1984
3   *An Anglican Prayer Book*, Church of Southern Africa 1989
4   *Book of Common Prayer,* Church in Wales 1984
5   *A Prayer Book for Australia,* 1978
6   *Book of Common Prayer*, Episcopal Church of the USA 1979
7   *Alternative Service Book*, Church of England 1980
8   *Promise of His Glory*, Church of England 1990
9   *Lent, Holy Week and Easter*, Church of England 1988
10 *After Communion*, Charles MacDonnell, Mowbray 1985
11 Original prayer by Kenneth Stevenson
12 Original prayer by David Silk
13 *Common Worship*, Church of England 2000
14 Original prayer by members of the Inter-Provincial Consultation
15 *Celebrating Common Prayer*, Society of Saint Francis 1992
16 *Book of Alternative Services*, Anglican Church of Canada 1986
17 Prayer in use at Westcott House, Cambridge
18 *Enriching the Christian Year*, Alcuin Club / SPCK 1993
19 *Patterns for Worship*, Church of England 1995
20 Material prepared by the International Commission on English in the Liturgy (ICEL)
21 Prayer ascribed to Thomas Aquinas from *Missale Romanum*
22 Original prayer by Janet Morley
23 *A New Zealand Prayer Book,* 1988
24 Original prayer by Brian Mayne
25 *Book of Common Prayer* 1549-1662
26 *Scottish Prayer Book* 1929

See the acknowledgment of copyright permissions on page 790

SERVICE FOR ASH WEDNESDAY
THE BEGINNING OF LENT

The Gathering of God's People

The sacrifice of God is a broken spirit: a broken and contrite heart you
will not despise.   *Psalm 51: 17*
Lord, have mercy.

*In these or other suitable words, the presiding minister explains the meaning of
Lent and invites the people to observe it faithfully.*

Brothers and sisters in Christ: since early days Christians have observed with
great devotion the time of our Lord's passion and resurrection. It became the
custom of the Church to prepare for this by a season of penitence and
fasting.

At first this season of Lent was observed by those who were preparing for
baptism at Easter and by those who were to be restored to the Church's
fellowship from which they had been separated through sin. In course of
time the Church came to recognize that, by a careful keeping of these
days, all Christians might take to heart the call to repentance and the
assurance of forgiveness proclaimed in the gospel, and so grow in faith
and in devotion to our Lord.

I invite you, therefore, in the name of the Lord to observe a holy Lent, by
self-examination and repentance; by prayer, fasting, and self-denial; and
by reading and meditating on God's holy word.

THE COLLECT

Silence may be kept.
Then the priest says
Let us pray for grace to keep Lent faithfully.
Almighty and everlasting God
you hate nothing that you have made
and forgive the sins of all those who are penitent.
Create and make in us new and contrite hearts,

that we may be truly sorry for our sins
and obtain from you, the God of all mercy,
perfect remission and forgiveness;
through Jesus Christ our Lord. Amen.

Proclaiming and Receiving the Word

Either two or three readings from scripture follow. The First Reading and the
Gospel are always read, but the Second Reading may be omitted.

THE FIRST READING
Joel 2: 1-2, 12-17 or Isaiah 58: 1-12

At the end the reader may say
This is the word of the Lord.
Thanks be to God.

THE PSALM

Psalm 51: 1-18 may be said or sung and this refrain may be used:
Have mercy on us, O Lord, for we have sinned against you.

THE SECOND READING
2 Corinthians 5: 20b - 6: 10

At the end the reader may say
This is the word of the Lord.
Thanks be to God.

CANTICLE
Saviour of the World (page 130)
or a hymn may be sung.

Stand

THE GOSPEL
Matthew 6: 1-6 and 16-21

After it is introduced:
Glory to you, Lord Jesus Christ.

At the conclusion the minister says
This is the Gospel of the Lord.
Praise to you, Lord Jesus Christ.

THE SERMON

The Liturgy of Penitence

The presiding minister says
Let us now call to mind our sin and the infinite mercy of God.

Kneel

THE COMMANDMENTS
are read (page 222). There should be two readers if possible, one reading the Old Testament statement and the second the New Testament interpretation.

THE LITANY

Litany Two (page 175) follows.

Silence is kept for a time, after which is said
Make our hearts clean, O God,
and renew a right spirit within us.

Father eternal, giver of light and grace,
we have sinned against you and against our neighbour,
in what we have thought, in what we have said and done,
through ignorance, through weakness,
through our own deliberate fault.
We have wounded your love, and marred your image in us.
We are sorry and ashamed, and repent of all our sins.
For the sake of your Son Jesus Christ, who died for us,
forgive us all that is past;
and lead us out from darkness to walk as children of light. Amen.

God our Father,
the strength of all who put their trust in you,
mercifully accept our prayers;
and because, in our weakness,
we can do nothing good without you,
grant us the help of your grace,
that in keeping your commandments
we may please you, both in will and deed;
through Jesus Christ our Lord. **Amen.**

Or

The priest pronounces the Absolution:

Almighty God,
who forgives all who truly repent,
have mercy upon you,
pardon and deliver you from all your sins,
confirm and strengthen you in all goodness
and keep you in life eternal;
through Jesus Christ our Lord. **Amen.**

If the Holy Communion is not to follow, one of the forms of Intercession (pages 237-239) or the Weekday Intercession for Friday (page 143) is used.

The service concludes with the Lord's Prayer, and the following prayer:

Lord our God,
grant us grace to desire you with our whole heart;
that so desiring, we may seek and find you;
and so finding, may love you;
and so loving, may hate those sins
from which you have delivered us;
through Jesus Christ our Lord. **Amen.**

Celebrating at the Lord's Table

If Holy Communion One is to follow, it begins with
'Lift up your hearts...' *(page 186)*

If Holy Communion Two is to follow, it begins with the Prayer of Humble Access, (page 207) or the prayer below may be said in place of it:

Most merciful Lord,
your love compels us to come in.
Our hands were unclean, our hearts were unprepared;
we were not fit even to eat the crumbs from under your table.
But you, Lord, are the God of our salvation,
and share your bread with sinners.
So cleanse and feed us with the precious body and blood of your Son,
that he may live in us and we in him;
and that we, with the whole company of Christ,
may sit and eat in your kingdom. Amen.

In Holy Communion Two any of the three eucharistic prayers may be used with the appropriate seasonal variations for Lent (page 227).

Going Out as God's People

The following prayer is said after which the service may conclude in silence, the congregation leaving the church quietly.

Lord our God,
grant us grace to desire you with our whole heart;
that so desiring, we may seek and find you;
and so finding, may love you;
and so loving, may hate those sins
from which you have delivered us;
through Jesus Christ our Lord. **Amen.**

This prayer, Blessing and Dismissal may be used if desired:

Almighty God,
we thank you for feeding us
with the spiritual food
of the body and blood of your Son Jesus Christ.
Through him we offer you our souls and bodies
to be a living sacrifice.
Send us out in the power of your Spirit
to live and work to your praise and glory. Amen.

Christ give you grace to grow in holiness,
to deny yourselves,
and to take up your cross and follow him;
and the blessing of God Almighty,
the Father, the Son and the Holy Spirit,
be with you, and remain with you always. **Amen.**

Go in peace to love and serve the Lord.
In the name of Christ. Amen.

This service may be adapted to meet local custom.

Christian Initiation

THE MINISTRATION OF PUBLIC BAPTISM OF INFANTS

TO BE USED IN THE CHURCH

At the Font

Priest

Hath this Child been already baptized, or no?

If the answer is, No; *the priest proceeds*

Dearly beloved, forasmuch as all men are conceived and born in sin, and that our Saviour Christ saith, Except a man be born again, he cannot see the kingdom of God, and also saith, Except a man be born of water and of the Spirit, he cannot enter into the kingdom of God; I beseech you to call upon God the Father, through our Lord Jesus Christ, that of his bounteous mercy he will grant to *this Child* that thing which by nature *he* cannot have; that *he* may be baptized with water and the Holy Spirit, and received into Christ's holy Church, and be made a lively member of the same.

Almighty and immortal God, the aid of all that need, the helper of all that flee to thee for succour, the life of them that believe, and the resurrection of the dead; We call upon thee for *this Infant*, that *he*, coming to thy Holy Baptism, may receive remission of *his* sins by spiritual regeneration. Receive *him*, O Lord, as thou hast promised by thy well-beloved Son, saying, Ask, and ye shall have; seek, and ye shall find; knock, and it shall be opened unto you: So give now unto us that ask; let us that seek find; open the gate unto us that knock; that *this Infant* may enjoy the everlasting benediction of thy heavenly washing, and may come to the eternal kingdom which thou hast promised by Christ our Lord. **Amen.**

or

Almighty and everlasting God, who of thy mercy didst save Noah and his family in the ark from perishing by water; and also didst safely lead the children of Israel thy people through the Red Sea, figuring thereby thy Holy Baptism; and by the Baptism of thy well-beloved Son Jesus Christ, in the river Jordan, didst sanctify water to the mystical washing away of sin; We beseech thee, for thine infinite mercies, that thou wilt mercifully look upon *this Child*; wash *him* and sanctify *him* with the Holy Spirit; that *he*, being delivered from thy wrath, may be received into the ark of Christ's Church; and being steadfast in faith, joyful through hope, and rooted in charity, may so pass the waves of this troublesome world, that finally *he* may come to the land of everlasting life, there to reign with thee world without end; through Jesus Christ our Lord. **Amen.**

THE GOSPEL

Hear the words of the Gospel, written by Saint Mark, in the tenth chapter, at the thirteenth verse.

They brought young children to Christ, that he should touch them: and his disciples rebuked those that brought them. But when Jesus saw it, he was much displeased, and said unto them, Suffer the little children to come unto me, and forbid them not: for of such is the kingdom of God. Verily I say unto you, Whosoever shall not receive the kingdom of God as a little child, he shall not enter therein. And he took them up in his arms put his hands upon them, and blessed them.

THE EXHORTATION

Beloved, ye hear in this Gospel the words of our Saviour Christ, that he commanded the children to be brought unto him; how he blamed those that would have kept them from him; how he exhorteth all men to follow their innocency. Ye perceive how by his outward gesture and deed he declared his good will toward them; for he embraced them in his arms, he laid his hands upon them, and blessed them, Doubt ye not therefore, but earnestly believe, that he will likewise favourably receive *this* present *Infant*; that he will embrace *him* with the arms of his mercy; that he will give unto *him* the blessing of eternal life, and make *him* partaker of his everlasting kingdom.

Wherefore, we being thus persuaded of the good will of our heavenly Father towards *this Infant*, declared by his Son Jesus Christ; and nothing doubting but that he favourably alloweth this charitable work of ours, in bringing *this Infant* to his Holy Baptism; let us faithfully and devoutly give thanks unto him, and say,

Almighty and everlasting God, heavenly Father, We give thee humble thanks, For that thou hast vouchsafed to call us to the knowledge of thy grace, and faith in thee: Increase this knowledge, And confirm this faith in us evermore. Give thy Holy Spirit to this Infant, That *he* may be born again, And be made an heir of everlasting salvation; Through our Lord Jesus Christ, Who liveth and reigneth with thee and the Holy Spirit, Now and for ever. Amen.

THE PROMISES

The priest says to the godfathers and godmothers

Dearly beloved, ye have brought *this Child* here to be baptized; ye have prayed that our Lord Jesus Christ would vouchsafe to receive *him*, to release *him* of *his* sins, to sanctify *him* with the Holy Spirit, to give *him* the kingdom of heaven, and everlasting life. Ye have heard also that our Lord Jesus Christ hath promised in his Gospel to grant all these things that ye have prayed for; which promise he, for his part, will most surely keep and perform.

Wherefore, after this promise made by Christ, *this Infant* must also faithfully, for *his* part, promise by you that are *his* Sureties (until *he* come of age to take it upon *himself*), that *he* will renounce the devil and all his works, and constantly believe God's holy Word, and obediently keep his Commandments. I demand therefore,

Dost thou, in the name of this Child, renounce the devil and all his works, the vain pomp and glory of the world, with all covetous desires of the same, and the sinful desires of the flesh, so that thou wilt not follow nor be led by them?
I renounce them all.

Dost thou believe in God the Father Almighty, Maker of heaven and earth? And in Jesus Christ his only Son our Lord? And that he was conceived by the Holy Spirit, born of the Virgin Mary; that he suffered under Pontius Pilate, was crucified, dead, and buried; that he descended into hell, and the third day rose again from the dead; that he ascended into heaven, and sitteth at the right hand of God the Father Almighty; and from thence shall come to judge the quick and the dead? And dost thou believe in the

Holy Spirit; the holy Catholic Church; the Communion of Saints; the Forgiveness of sins; the Resurrection of the body; and the life everlasting? **All this I steadfastly believe.**

Wilt thou be baptized in this faith?
That is my desire.

Wilt thou then obediently keep God's holy will and Commandments, and walk in the same all the days of thy life?
I will, God being my helper.

Priest

O merciful God, grant that the old Adam in *this Child* may be so buried, that the new man may be raised up in *him*. **Amen.**

Grant that all carnal affections may die in *him*, and that all things belonging to the Spirit may live and grow in *him*. **Amen.**

Grant that *he* may have power and strength to have victory, and to triumph, against the devil, the world, and the flesh. **Amen.**

Grant that whosoever is here dedicated to thee by our office and ministry may also be endued with heavenly virtues, and everlastingly rewarded, through thy mercy, O blessed Lord God, who dost live, and govern all things, world without end. **Amen.**

The Baptism

Almighty, everliving God, whose most dearly beloved Son Jesus Christ, for the forgiveness of our sins, did shed out of his most precious side both water and blood; and gave commandment to his disciples, that they should go teach all nations, and baptize them in the Name of the Father, and of the Son, and of the Holy Spirit; Regard, we beseech thee, the supplications of thy Congregation; sanctify this water to the mystical washing away of sin; and grant that *this Child*, now to be baptized therein, may receive the fulness of thy grace, and ever remain in the number of thy faithful and elect children; through Jesus Christ our Lord. **Amen.**

Then the priest takes the child, and says to the godfathers and godmothers
Name this Child.

Naming the child, the priest dips it in the water, or pours water upon the child's head, saying
.... I baptize thee In the Name of the Father, and of the Son, and of the Holy Spirit. Amen.

Priest
We receive this Child into the Congregation of Christ's flock; and * do sign *him* with the sign of the Cross, in token that hereafter *he* shall not be ashamed to confess the faith of Christ crucified, and manfully to fight under his banner, against sin, the world, and the devil; and to continue Christ's faithful soldier and servant unto *his* life's end. **Amen.**

* *Here the priest makes the sign of the cross upon the child's forehead.*

Seeing now, dearly beloved brethren, that *this Child is* regenerate, and grafted into the body of Christ's Church, let us give thanks unto Almighty God for these benefits; and with one accord make our prayers unto him, that *this Child* may lead the rest of *his* life according to this beginning.

Prayers

All kneel

Our Father, who art in heaven, Hallowed be thy Name, Thy kingdom come, Thy will be done, On earth as it is in heaven. Give us this day our daily bread. And forgive us our trespasses, As we forgive those who trespass against us. And lead us not into temptation, But deliver us from evil. For thine is the kingdom, The power, And the glory, For ever and ever. Amen.

We yield thee hearty thanks, most merciful Father, that it hath pleased thee to regenerate *this Infant* with thy Holy Spirit, to receive *him* for thine own *Child* by adoption, and to incorporate *him* into thy holy Church. And humbly we beseech thee to grant, that *he,* being dead unto sin, may live unto righteousness, and being buried with Christ in his death, may also be partaker of his resurrection; so that finally, with the residue of thy holy Church, *he* may inherit thine everlasting kingdom; through Christ our Lord. **Amen.**

The Charge

All stand

Forasmuch as *this Child* hath promised by you *his* Sureties to renounce the devil and all his works, to believe in God, and to serve him; ye must remember, that it is your parts and duties to see that *this Infant* be taught, so soon as *he* shall be able to learn, what a solemn vow, promise, and profession *he hath* here made by you; and that *he* be virtuously brought up to lead a godly and a Christian life; remembering always, that Baptism doth represent unto us our profession; which is, to follow the example of our Saviour Christ, and to be made like unto him; that, as he died, and rose again for us, so should we, who are baptized, die to sin, and rise again unto righteousness; continually overcoming all our evil passions, and daily increasing in all virtue and godliness of living.

Ye are to take care that *this Child* be brought to the bishop to be confirmed by him, so soon as *he* can say the Creed, the Lord's Prayer, and the Ten Commandments, and be further instructed in the Church Catechism set forth for that purpose.

The grace of our Lord Jesus Christ, and the love of God, and the fellowship of the Holy Spirit, be with us all evermore. **Amen.** *2 Corinthians 13: 14*

It is certain by God's Word, that children which are baptized, dying before they commit actual sin, are undoubtedly saved.
Whereas the sign of the Cross is by this Office appointed to be used in Baptism according to the ancient and laudable custom of the Church, it is not thereby intended to add any new rite to the Sacrament as a part of it, or necessary to it; or that the using that sign is of any virtue or efficacy of itself; but only to remind all Christians of the Death and Cross of Christ, which is their hope and their glory; and to put them in mind of their obligation to bear the Cross in such manner as God shall think fit to lay it upon them, and to become conformable to Christ in his sufferings; as more largely is expressed in the thirtieth Canon of the Church of England (1604).

1 The Minister of every parish shall teach the people the meaning of Baptism and the responsibilities of those who bring children to be baptized.

2 When there are children to be baptized, the parents shall give due notice to the Minister of the Parish, who shall thereupon appoint the time for the Baptism.

3 Sponsors and godparents must be baptized Christians and persons of discreet age, and at least two shall be members of the Church of Ireland or of a Church in communion therewith (Canon 25.4). It is desirable that parents be sponsors for their own children.

4 It is desirable that members of the parish be present to support, by their faith and prayer, those who are to be baptized and received into the fellowship of the Church.

5 When this order of Baptism is used with one of the prescribed services in any church, the Minister may dispense with such parts of that service as the Ordinary shall permit.

6 The font should be so situated that Baptism may be administered in an orderly fashion.

CONFIRMATION

Or Laying on of Hands upon those that are Baptized and Come to Years of Discretion

The bishop (or some other minister appointed) says

To the end that Confirmation may be ministered to the more edifying of such as shall receive it, the Church hath thought good to order, That none hereafter shall be confirmed, but such as can say the Creed, the Lord's Prayer, and the Ten Commandments; and have been further instructed in the Church Catechism, set forth for that purpose: Which order is very fitting to be observed; to the end that children being now come to the years of discretion, and having learned what their Godfathers and Godmothers promised for them in Baptism, they may themselves, with their own mouth and consent, openly before the Church, ratify and confirm the same; and also promise, that by the grace of God they will evermore endeavour faithfully to observe such things, as they, by their own confession, have assented unto.

The bishop may address the candidates.

THE RENEWAL OF BAPTISMAL PROMISES

The bishop says

Do you here, in the presence of God, and of this Congregation, renew and confirm the solemn promise and vow of your Baptism?
I do.

Do you renounce the devil and all his works, the vain pomp and glory of the world, with all covetous desires of the same, and the sinful desires of the flesh, so that you will not follow nor be led by them?
I renounce them all.

Do you believe in God the Father Almighty, Maker of heaven and earth? And in Jesus Christ his only Son our Lord? And that he was conceived by the Holy Spirit, born of the Virgin Mary; that he suffered under Pontius Pilate, was crucified, dead, and buried; that he descended into hell, and the third day rose again from the dead; that he ascended into heaven, and sitteth at the right hand of God the Father Almighty; and from thence shall come to judge the quick and the dead?

And do you believe in the Holy Spirit; the holy Catholic Church; the Communion of Saints; the Forgiveness of sins; the Resurrection of the body; and the life everlasting?

All this I steadfastly believe.

Will you then obediently keep God's holy will and Commandments, and walk in the same all the days of your life?

I will, by God's help.

The congregation stands, and the bishop says
Our help is in the Name of the Lord:
who hath made heaven and earth.

Blessed be the Name of the Lord:
henceforth, world without end.

Lord, hear our prayer
and let our cry come unto thee.

Confirmation Prayer and the Laying on of Hands

All kneel. The bishop, still standing, says
Let us pray.
Almighty and everliving God, who hast vouchsafed to regenerate these thy servants by Water and the Holy Spirit, and hast given unto them forgiveness of all their sins; Strengthen them, we beseech thee, O Lord, with the Holy Spirit the Comforter, and daily increase in them thy manifold gifts of grace: the spirit of wisdom and understanding; the spirit of counsel and spiritual strength; the spirit of knowledge and true godliness; and fill them, O Lord, with the spirit of thy holy fear, now and for ever. **Amen.**

Those to be confirmed kneel before the bishop, who shall lay his hand upon the head of each one, saying

Defend, O Lord, this thy Child [*or* this thy servant] with thy heavenly grace, that *he* may continue thine for ever; and daily increase in thy Holy Spirit, more and more, until *he* come unto thy everlasting kingdom. **Amen.**

The bishop may address the newly confirmed.

PRAYERS

Then the bishop says
The Lord be with you
and with thy spirit.

All kneeling down, the bishop continues
Let us pray.
Our Father, who art in heaven,
    hallowed be thy name,
    thy kingdom come,
    thy will be done,
        on earth as it is in heaven.
Give us this day our daily bread.
    And forgive us our trespasses
    as we forgive those who trespass against us.
And lead us not into temptation,
    but deliver us from evil.
For thine is the kingdom, the power, and the glory,
    for ever and ever. Amen.

Almighty and everliving God, who makest us both to will and to do those things that be good and acceptable unto thy divine Majesty; We make our humble supplications unto thee for these thy servants, upon whom (after the example of thy holy Apostles) we have now laid our hands, to certify them (by this sign) of thy favour and gracious goodness towards them. Let thy fatherly hand, we beseech thee, ever be over them; let thy Holy Spirit ever be with them; and so lead them in the knowledge and obedience of thy Word, that in the end they may obtain everlasting life; through our Lord Jesus Christ, who with thee and the Holy Spirit liveth and reigneth, ever one God, world without end. **Amen.**

And also this, or some other collect

O God, whose blessed Son was manifested that he might destroy the works of the devil, and make us the sons of God, and heirs of eternal life; Grant us, we beseech thee, that, having this hope, we may purify ourselves, even as he is pure; that when he shall appear again with power and great glory, we may be made like unto him in his eternal and glorious kingdom; where with thee, O Father, and thee, O Holy Spirit, he liveth and reigneth, ever one God, world without end. **Amen.**

THE BLESSING

The bishop says

The blessing of God Almighty, the Father, the Son, and the Holy Spirit be upon you, and remain with you for ever. **Amen.**

When Confirmation is ministered only to those baptized in riper years, the Preface shall be omitted.

And there shall none be admitted to the Holy Communion, until such time as he be confirmed, or be ready and desirous to be confirmed.

HOLY BAPTISM

Baptism marks the beginning of a journey with God which continues for the rest of our lives, the first step in response to God's love. For all involved, particularly the candidates but also parents and sponsors, it is a joyful moment when we rejoice in what God has done for us in Christ, making serious promises and declaring the faith. The wider community of the local church and friends welcome the new Christian, promising support and prayer for the future. Hearing and doing these things provides an opportunity to remember our own baptism and reflect on the progress made on that journey, which is now to be shared with this new member of the Church.

The service paints many vivid pictures of what happens on the Christian way. There is the sign of the cross, the badge of faith in the Christian journey, which reminds us of Christ's death for us. Our 'drowning' in the water of baptism, where we believe we die to sin and are raised to new life, unites us to Christ's dying and rising, a picture that can be brought home vividly by the way the baptism is administered. Water is also a sign of new life; we are born again by water and the Spirit through faith in Jesus Christ. And as a sign of that new life, there may be a lighted candle, a picture of the light of Christ conquering the darkness of evil. All who are baptized walk in that light for the rest of their lives.

As you pray for the candidates, picture them with yourself and the whole Church throughout the ages, journeying into the fulness of God's love.

The Gathering of God's People

The presiding minister greets the people in these or other suitable words:
Grace, mercy and peace
from God our Father and the Lord Jesus Christ
be with you all
and also with you.

or
From Easter Day to Pentecost
Christ is risen.
The Lord is risen indeed. Alleluia! *Luke 24: 34*

The minister may use these or other words:
Our Lord Jesus Christ has told us
that to enter the kingdom of heaven
we must be born again of water and the Spirit,
and has given us baptism as the sign and seal of this new birth.
Here we are washed by the Holy Spirit and made clean.
Here we are clothed with Christ,
dying to sin that we may live his risen life.
As children of God, we have a new dignity
and God calls us to fulness of life.

PENITENCE

The minister says
Let us affirm our trust in God's mercy,
and confess that we need forgiveness.

A pause for reflection after which these or other suitable words or the seasonal Penitential Kyries (pages 224-236) are used:

Lord God, you created the world, and made us in your own image.
Forgive us when we turn away from you.
Lord, have mercy.
Lord, have mercy.

Lord God, through your Son you overcame evil and death.
Rescue us from slavery to sin.

> Christ, have mercy
> **Christ, have mercy.**

Lord God, by your Spirit you restore us to fellowship with you and with one another. Breathe your love and freedom into our lives.

> Lord, have mercy.
> **Lord, have mercy.**

This hymn of praise or some other may be said or sung.

Glory to God in the highest,
and peace to God's people on earth.
Lord God, heavenly king,
almighty God and Father,
we worship you, we give you thanks,
we praise you for your glory.
Lord Jesus Christ, only Son of the Father,
Lord God, Lamb of God,
you take away the sin of the world:
have mercy on us;
you are seated at the right hand of the Father:
receive our prayer.
For you alone are the Holy One:
you alone are the Lord:
you alone are the Most High,
Jesus Christ, with the Holy Spirit,
in the Glory of God the Father. Amen.

The presiding minister says
Let us pray.
The community may pray silently.

The Collect of the Day or a Collect from pages 392-395 is said.

Proclaiming and Receiving the Word

READINGS

from the Old Testament and/or the New Testament should normally be as appointed in the Table of Readings. Special baptismal readings can be found on page 396.

After each reading the reader may say
This is the word of the Lord.
Thanks be to God.
Silence may follow each reading.

A canticle, psalm, hymn or anthem may be sung between the readings.

All stand

THE GOSPEL

The reader says
Hear the Gospel of our Saviour Christ, according to ..., chapter ..., beginning at verse ...
Glory to you, Lord Jesus Christ.

After the Gospel, the reader says
This is the Gospel of the Lord.
Praise to you, Lord Jesus Christ.

THE SERMON

Silence may follow.

The Presentation

The presiding minister invites the candidates and their sponsors to stand in view of the congregation.
The presiding minister invites the sponsors of baptismal candidates to present the candidates.
We welcome *those* who *come* to be baptized. I invite *their* sponsors to present *them* now.

The sponsors answer
We present .... to be baptized.

The presiding minister says to the sponsors of those unable to answer for themselves
Parents and godparents, will you accept the responsibilities placed upon you in bringing .... for baptism and answer on *their* behalf?
By your own prayers and example, by your teaching and love, will you encourage *them* in the life and faith of the Christian Community?
With the help of God, we will.

In baptism *these children* begin *their* journey in faith.
You speak for *them* today.
Will you care for *them*, and help *them* to take *their* place within the life and worship of Christ's Church?
With the help of God, we will.

The Decision

At this point testimony may be given by one or more of the candidates.

The presiding minister says to the candidates able to answer for themselves, and to the sponsors of other candidates
In baptism, God calls us from darkness to his marvellous light.
To follow Christ means dying to sin and rising to new life with him.
Therefore I ask:
Do you reject the devil and all proud rebellion against God?
I reject them.
Do you renounce the deceit and corruption of evil?
I renounce them.
Do you repent of the sins that separate us from God and neighbour?
I repent of them.

Do you turn to Christ as Saviour?
I turn to Christ.
Do you submit to Christ as Lord?
I submit to Christ.
Do you come to Christ, the Way, the Truth and the Life?
I come to Christ.

The presiding minister says to the congregation
You have heard these our brothers and sisters respond to Christ.
Will you support them in this calling?

The congregation answers
We will support them.

The presiding minister makes the sign of the cross on the forehead of each candidate for baptism, either here or after the baptism with water, saying
Christ claims you for his own.
Receive the sign of the cross.

Live as a disciple of Christ,
fight the good fight,
finish the race, keep the faith.
Confess Christ crucified,
proclaim his resurrection,
look for his coming in glory.

May almighty God deliver you from the powers of darkness,
restore in you the image of his glory,
and lead you in the light and obedience of Christ. **Amen.**

A hymn may be sung.

The Baptism
The presiding minister and the candidates go to the place where the water for baptism is, and the presiding minister begins the thanksgiving prayer.

Water is poured into the font.

Praise God who made heaven and earth.
Who keeps his promise for ever.

Let us give thanks to the Lord our God.
It is right to give our thanks and praise.

We give you thanks that at the beginning of creation your Holy Spirit moved upon the waters to bring forth light and life.

With water you cleanse and replenish the earth; you nourish and sustain all living things.

Thanks be to God.

We give you thanks that through the waters of the Red Sea you led your people out of slavery into freedom, and brought them through the river Jordan to new life in the land of promise.

Thanks be to God.

We give you thanks for your Son Jesus Christ: for his baptism by John, for his anointing with the Holy Spirit.

Thanks be to God.

We give you thanks that through the deep waters of death Jesus delivered us from our sins and was raised to new life in triumph.

Thanks be to God.

We give you thanks for the grace of the Holy Spirit who forms us in the likeness of Christ and leads us to proclaim your Kingdom.

Thanks be to God.

And now we give you thanks that you have called *names/these your servants* to new birth in your Church through the waters of baptism.

Pour out your Holy Spirit in blessing and sanctify this water
so that *those* who *are* baptized in it may be made one with Christ in his death and resurrection.

May *they* die to sin, rise to newness of life, and continue for ever in Jesus Christ our Lord, through whom we give you praise and honour in the unity of the Spirit, now and for ever. Amen.

Or

We thank you, almighty God, for the gift of water to sustain, refresh and cleanse all life.
Over water the Holy Spirit moved in the beginning of creation.
Through water you led the children of Israel
from slavery in Egypt to freedom in the Promised Land.
In water your Son Jesus received the baptism of John
and was anointed by the Holy Spirit as the Messiah, the Christ,
to lead us from the death of sin to newness of life.

We thank you, Father, for the water of baptism.
In it we are buried with Christ in his death.
By it we share in his resurrection.
Through it we are reborn by the Holy Spirit.
Therefore, in joyful obedience to your Son,
we baptize into his fellowship those who come to him in faith.

Now sanctify this water that, by the power of your Holy Spirit,
they may be cleansed from sin and born again.
Renewed in your image, may *they* walk by the light of faith
and continue for ever in the risen life of Jesus Christ our Lord;
to whom with you and the Holy Spirit
be all honour and glory, now and for ever. **Amen.**

The presiding minister shall ask the following question of each candidate for baptism, or, in the case of those unable to answer for themselves, the sponsors of each candidate:
Do you believe and accept the Christian faith into which you are (.... is) to be baptized?
I do.

The presiding minister addresses the congregation.
Brothers and sisters, I ask you to profess, together with *these candidates* the faith of the Church.

Do you believe and trust in God the Father?
I believe in God, the Father almighty,
creator of heaven and earth.

Do you believe and trust in God the Son?
I believe in Jesus Christ, God's only Son, our Lord
who was conceived by the Holy Spirit,
born of the Virgin Mary,
suffered under Pontius Pilate,
was crucified, died, and was buried;
he descended to the dead.
On the third day he rose again;
he ascended into heaven,
he is seated at the right hand of the Father,
and he will come again to judge the living and the dead.

Do you believe and trust in God the Holy Spirit?
I believe in the Holy Spirit,
the holy catholic Church,
the communion of saints,
the forgiveness of sins,
the resurrection of the body,
and the life everlasting. Amen.

The presiding minister baptizes by dipping the candidates in the water, or by
pouring water over them, saying
...., I baptize you in the name of the Father, and of the Son, and of the
Holy Spirit. **Amen.**

The minister and those who have been baptized may return from the font.

If those who have been baptized were not signed with the cross immediately
after the Decision, they are signed now.

The minister continues
God has called you into his Church.

The congregation joins the minister, saying
We therefore receive and welcome you
as a member with us of the body of Christ,
as a child of the one heavenly Father,
and as an inheritor of the kingdom of God.

THE PEACE

All stand. The Peace is introduced with these or other suitable words:
We are the body of Christ.
By one spirit we were all baptized into one body.
Let us then pursue all that makes for peace
and builds up our common life together.

The presiding minister says
The peace of the Lord be always with you
and also with you.

All may exchange a sign of peace.
A hymn may be sung.

Holy Communion, when it follows, begins with Celebrating at the Lord's Table
(page 208).
If Holy Communion does not follow, the service continues with the Prayers of
the People, ending with the Lord's Prayer and the Dismissal.

At Holy Communion this Proper Preface may be used in Eucharistic Prayer 1:
Because by water and the Holy Spirit
you have made us a holy people in Jesus Christ our Lord,
raised us to new life in him
and renewed in us the image of your glory.

The appropriate seasonal Post Communion prayer (pages 392-395), or the
following may be said:
Gracious God,
in baptism you make us one family in Christ your Son,
one in the sharing of his body and his blood,
one in the communion of his Spirit.
Help us to grow in love for one another
and come to the full maturity of the body of Christ. **Amen.**

Holy Baptism Two

The presiding minister says
As our Saviour Christ has taught us, so we pray
Our Father in heaven ...

or
As Jesus has taught us we are bold to say
Our Father, who art in heaven ...

Going Out as God's People

A hymn may be sung here or before the Dismissal.

The presiding minister may say the seasonal blessing or another suitable blessing
or
The God of all grace,
who called you to his eternal glory in Christ Jesus,
establish, strengthen and settle you in the faith;
and the blessing of God almighty,
the Father, the Son and the Holy Spirit,
be upon you and remain with you always. **Amen.**

The newly baptized may be sent out with these words:
God has delivered us from the dominion of darkness
and has given us a place with the saints in light.

You have received the light of Christ;
walk in this light all the days of your life.
**Shine as a light in the world
to the glory of God the Father.**

Go in peace to love and serve the Lord:
In the name of Christ. Amen.

1 The presiding minister or another person may give each of the newly baptized a lighted candle. This may happen during THE DISMISSAL before the words 'God has delivered us...'

2 Where italicized plural pronouns are used in this service these should be altered if necessary to the appropriate single pronoun.

3 THE ADMINISTRATION OF BAPTISM. A threefold administration of water, whether by dipping or pouring, is a very ancient practice of the Church. A single administration is also lawful and valid.

4 CONDITIONAL BAPTISM. If it is not certain that a person was baptized with water in the name of the Father, and of the Son, and of the Holy Spirit, then the usual service of baptism is used, but the form of the words at the baptism shall be:

> .... if you have not already been baptized
> I baptize you in the name of the Father, and of the Son,
> and of the Holy Spirit. Amen.

5 EMERGENCY BAPTISM. In a case of urgent necessity it is sufficient to name the candidate and pour water on the person's head, saying

> .... I baptize you in the name of the Father, and of the Son,
> and of the Holy Spirit. Amen.

Suitable prayers and the Lord's Prayer should be said.

Prayers

that may be used at the Prayers of the People

Father, we thank you that .... *have* now been born again of water and the Holy Spirit, and *have* become your own *children* by adoption, and *members* of your Church.
Grant that *they* may grow in the faith in which *they* have been baptized;
(Grant that *they themselves* may profess it when *they* come to be confirmed;)
Grant that *they* may bear witness to it by a life of service to others;
and that at all things belonging to the Spirit may live and grow in *them*;
through Jesus Christ our Lord. **Amen.**

When children have been baptized this prayer may be added:
Almighty God,
bless the home of *these children*,
and give such grace and wisdom to all who have the care of *them*,
that by their word and good example
they may teach *them* to know and love you;
through Jesus Christ our Lord. **Amen.**

For all who are baptized into Christ
Gracious God,
we, who have been brought from death to life,
dedicate ourselves to you.
Produce in us the fruit of your Spirit;
equip us to serve your people and advance your Gospel in the world;
enable us to live in holiness and righteousness;
and to please you in all that we do;
in the name of Jesus our Saviour. **Amen.**

At the baptism of a child
Merciful God,
in your infinite love you have made a new covenant with us
in your Son our Saviour Jesus Christ,
promising to be our God and the God of our children.
Enable all who are baptized in your name to live as a covenant people.
Fulfil your promises for *these children*, we pray,
and grant that *they* may grow in your faith and service
until *their lives'* end;
through Jesus Christ our Lord. **Amen**

A prayer for parents
Heavenly Father,
we pray for the parents of *these children*;
give them the spirit of wisdom and love.
May their children grow up to love and reverence you
and their home share in the joy of your eternal kingdom. **Amen.**

For godparents
God of truth and love,
we pray for the godparents of ....
Enable them to share with their godchildren
what you have revealed to us in your holy gospel.
We ask this in the name of the Saviour Jesus Christ. **Amen.**

HOLY BAPTISM
IN THE CONTEXT OF MORNING OR EVENING PRAYER
OR A SERVICE OF THE WORD

The presiding minister may say
Our Lord Jesus Christ has told us
that to enter the kingdom of heaven
we must be born again of water and the Spirit,
and has given us baptism as the sign and seal of this new birth.
Here we are washed by the Holy Spirit and made clean.
Here we are clothed with Christ,
dying to sin that we may live his risen life.
As children of God, we have a new dignity
and God calls us to fulness of life.

At the baptism of an infant the following may be added:
Holy Baptism is administered to infants
on the understanding that they will be brought up in the fellowship of
Christ's Church;
that they will be taught the Christian faith;
and that, when they have publicly confessed this faith,
they will be confirmed by the bishop and admitted to the Holy Communion.

The Presentation

*The presiding minister invites the candidates and their sponsors to stand in
view of the congregation.*

*The presiding minister invites the sponsors of baptismal candidates to present
the candidates.*
We welcome *those* who *come* to be baptized. I invite *their* sponsors to present
them now.

The sponsors answer
We present .... to be baptized.

Parents and godparents, will you accept the responsibilities placed upon you in bringing .... for baptism and answer on *their* behalf. By your own prayers and example, by your teaching and love, will you encourage *them* in the life and faith of the Christian community?

With the help of God, we will.

In baptism *these children begin their* journey in faith.
You speak for *them* today.
Will you care for *them*,
and help *them* to take *their* place
within the life and worship of Christ's Church?
With the help of God, we will.

The Decision

At this point testimony may be given by one or more of the candidates.

The presiding minister says to the candidates able to answer for themselves, and to the sponsors of other candidates

In baptism, God calls us from darkness into his marvellous light.
To follow Christ means dying to sin and rising to new life with him.
Therefore I ask:
Do you reject the devil and all proud rebellion against God?
I reject them.
Do you renounce the deceit and corruption of evil?
I renounce them.
Do you repent of the sins that separate us from God and neighbour?
I repent of them.

Do you turn to Christ as Saviour?
I turn to Christ.
Do you submit to Christ as Lord?
I submit to Christ.
Do you come to Christ, the Way, the Truth and the Life?
I come to Christ.

The presiding minister says

Do you turn to Christ?
I do.

Do you then renounce the devil and all his works?
I do, by God's help.

Will you obey and serve Christ?
I will, by God's help.

The presiding minister says to the congregation

You have heard these our brothers and sisters respond to Christ.
Will you support them in this calling?

The congregation answers

We will support them.

The presiding minister makes the sign of the cross on the forehead of each candidate for baptism, either here or after the baptism with water.

A hymn may be sung.

The Baptism

The presiding minister and the candidates go to the place where the water for baptism is.
The presiding minister begins the thanksgiving prayer on page 362.
Water is poured into the font.

One of the prayers on pages 363-364 is said.

The presiding minister shall ask the following question of each candidate for baptism, or, in the case of those unable to answer for themselves, the sponsors of each candidate:

Do you believe and accept the Christian faith into which you are (.... is) to be baptized?
I do.

The presiding minister addresses the congregation
Brothers and sisters, I ask you to profess together with these candidates the faith of the Church.

Do you believe and trust in God the Father?
I believe in God, the Father almighty,
creator of heaven and earth.

Do you believe and trust in God the Son?
I believe in Jesus Christ, God's only Son, our Lord
who was conceived by the Holy Spirit,
born of the Virgin Mary,
suffered under Pontius Pilate,
was crucified, died, and was buried;
he descended to the dead.
On the third day he rose again;
he ascended into heaven,
he is seated at the right hand of the Father,
and he will come again to judge the living and the dead.

Do you believe and trust in God the Holy Spirit?
I believe in the Holy Spirit,
the holy catholic Church,
the communion of saints,
the forgiveness of sins,
the resurrection of the body,
and the life everlasting. Amen.

The presiding minister baptizes by dipping the candidates in the water, or by pouring water over them, saying
...., I baptize you in the name of the Father, and of the Son, and of the Holy Spirit. **Amen.**

The minister and those who have been baptized may return from the font.
Unless those who have been baptized were signed with the cross immediately after the Decision, they are signed now, with the following words:
Christ claims you for his own.
Receive the sign of the cross.

When all the candidates have been signed, the minister says
Live as disciples of Christ,
fight the good fight,
finish the race, keep the faith.
Confess Christ crucified,
proclaim his resurrection,
look for his coming in glory.

The minister continues
God has called you into his Church.

The congregation joins the minister, saying
We therefore receive and welcome you
as a member with us of the body of Christ,
as a child of the one heavenly Father,
and as an inheritor of the kingdom of God.

Prayers of the People

The following prayer or other suitable prayer(s) may be said:
Father, we thank you that .... *have* now been born again of water and the
Holy Spirit, and *have* become your own *children* by adoption, and *members*
of your Church.
Grant that *they* may grow in the faith in which *they* have been baptized;
Grant that *they themselves* may confess it when *they come* to be confirmed;
Grant that *they* may bear witness to it by a life of service to others;
And that all things belonging to the Spirit may live and grow in *them*;
through Jesus Christ our Lord. **Amen.**

At the baptism of infants this, or another prayer for the family, may be used:
Almighty God, bless the home(s) of *these children*,
and give such grace and wisdom to all who have the care of *them*,
that by their word and good example
they may teach *them* to know and love you,
through Jesus Christ our Lord. **Amen.**

*Other prayers for the community of the baptized and for God's mission in the
world may be said, concluding with the Collect of the day and the Lord's
Prayer.*

As our Saviour Christ has taught us, so we pray
Our Father in heaven ...

or

As Jesus has taught us, we are bold to say
Our Father, who art in heaven ...

Going Out as God's People

The presiding minister may say the seasonal blessing or another suitable blessing
or

The God of all grace,
who called you to his eternal glory in Christ Jesus,
establish, strengthen and settle you in the faith;
and the blessing of God almighty,
the Father, the Son and the Holy Spirit,
be upon you and remain with you always. **Amen.**

The newly baptized may be sent out with these words.
God has delivered us from the dominion of darkness
and has given us a place with the saints in light.

You have received the light of Christ;
walk in this light all the days of your life.
Shine as a light in the world
to the glory of God the Father.

Go in peace to love and serve the Lord:
In the name of Christ. Amen.

The presiding minister or another person may give each of the newly baptized a
lighted candle. This may happen during Going Out as God's People before the
words God has delivered us ...

When Holy Baptism takes place during Morning or Evening Prayer, the sermon
follows the Third Canticle, and the Baptismal Rite follows the sermon. The rest
of Morning or Evening Prayer is omitted.

RECEIVING INTO THE CONGREGATION

It is expedient that those baptized in emergency should be publicly received and welcomed into the congregation. Such emergency baptisms should always be registered in the parish register of baptisms, noting where and by whom the baptism was administered. The receiving into the congregation may be noted in the margin.

The Gathering of God's People and Proclaiming and Receiving the Word are as in Holy Baptism (pages 358-360).

The Presentation

The presiding minister invites those who have been baptized in emergency, together with their sponsors, to stand in view of the congregation.

The presiding minister asks the sponsors
Have you made certain that .... *was* baptized with water in the Name of the Father, and of the Son, and of the Holy Spirit?
We have.

The presiding minister says to the sponsors
Parents and godparents, do you accept the responsibilities placed upon you as sponsors?
We do.

By your own prayers and example, by your teaching and love, will you encourage .... in the life and faith of the Christian community?
With the help of God, we will.

In baptism *these children* began their journey in faith.
You speak for *them* today.
Will you care for *them*,
and help *them* to take *their* place
within the life and worship of Christ's Church?
With the help of God, we will.

The Decision

At this point testimony may be given by one or more of those being received.

The presiding minister says to those able to answer for themselves, and to the sponsors of others

In baptism, God calls us from darkness to his marvellous light.

To follow Christ means dying to sin and rising to new life with him.

Therefore I ask:

Do you reject the devil and all proud rebellion against God?

I reject them.

Do you renounce the deceit and corruption of evil?

I renounce them.

Do you repent of the sins that separate us from God and neighbour?

I repent of them.

Do you turn to Christ as Saviour?

I turn to Christ.

Do you submit to Christ as Lord?

I submit to Christ.

Do you come to Christ, the Way, the Truth and the Life?

I come to Christ.

The presiding minister says to the congregation

You have heard these our brothers and sisters respond to Christ.

Will you support them in this calling?

The congregation answers

We will support them.

The presiding minister makes the sign of the cross on the forehead of each one, either here or after the profession of faith, saying

Christ claims you for his own.

Receive the sign of the cross.

Live as a disciple of Christ,

fight the good fight,

finish the race, keep the faith.

Confess Christ crucified,
proclaim his resurrection,
look for his coming in glory.

May almighty God deliver you from the powers of darkness,
restore in you the image of his glory,
and lead you in the light and obedience of Christ. **Amen.**

A hymn may be sung.

The Thanksgiving

The presiding minister says
Praise God who made heaven and earth.
Who keeps his promise for ever.

Let us give thanks to the Lord our God.
It is right to give him thanks and praise.

We give you thanks that at the beginning of creation your Holy Spirit
moved upon the waters to bring forth light and life.
With water you cleanse and replenish the earth; you nourish and sustain
all living things.
Thanks be to God.

We give you thanks that through the waters of the Red Sea you led your
people out of slavery into freedom, and brought them through the river
Jordan to new life in the land of promise.
Thanks be to God.

We give you thanks for your Son Jesus Christ: for his baptism by John,
for his anointing with the Holy Spirit.
Thanks be to God.

We give you thanks that through the deep waters of death Jesus delivered
us from our sins and was raised to new life in triumph.
Thanks be to God.

We give you thanks for the grace of the Holy Spirit who forms us in the likeness of Christ and leads us to proclaim your Kingdom.
Thanks be to God.

And now we give you thanks that you called .... / *these your servants* to new birth in your Church through the waters of baptism. **Amen.**

May .... and all who are baptized be made one with Christ in his death and resurrection. Dying to sin and rising to newness of life, may they continue for ever in Jesus Christ our Lord, through whom we give you praise and honour in the unity of the Spirit, now and for ever. **Amen.**

The presiding minister shall ask the following question of each of those being received, or, in the case of those unable to answer for themselves, their sponsors:
Do you believe and accept the Christian faith into which *you have* (.... *has*) been baptized?
I do.

The presiding minister addresses the congregation
Brothers and sisters, I ask you to profess the faith of the Church, together with those being received.
Do you believe and trust in God the Father?
I believe in God, the Father almighty,
creator of heaven and earth.

Do you believe and trust in God the Son?
I believe in Jesus Christ, God's only Son, our Lord
who was conceived by the Holy Spirit,
born of the Virgin Mary,
suffered under Pontius Pilate,
was crucified, died, and was buried;
he descended to the dead.
On the third day he rose again;
he ascended into heaven,
he is seated at the right hand of the Father,
and he will come again to judge the living and the dead.

Do you believe and trust in God the Holy Spirit?
I believe in the Holy Spirit,
the holy catholic Church,
the communion of saints,
the forgiveness of sins,
the resurrection of the body,
and the life everlasting. Amen.

If those who have been baptized were not signed with the cross immediately
after the Decision, they are signed now.

The presiding minister says
God has called you into his Church.

The congregation joins the minister, saying
We therefore receive and welcome you
as a member with us of the body of Christ,
as a child of the one heavenly Father,
and as an inheritor of the kingdom of God.

The service continues as in the service for Holy Baptism on pages 375-376.

CONFIRMATION

The bishop greets the people in these or other suitable words:
Grace, mercy and peace
from God our Father and the Lord Jesus Christ be with you all
and also with you.

or

From Easter Day to Pentecost
Christ is risen.
The Lord is risen indeed. Alleluia! *Luke 24: 34*

The bishop may introduce the service with these or other suitable words:
Brothers and sisters, we meet today to support and to pray for those who have been baptized and instructed in the Christian faith and who now intend, in the presence of God and of this congregation, to make the promises of their baptism their own.

At the heart of this Confirmation service are two distinct, yet related, acts of confirming.

First the candidates will profess their faith in Christ, confirming their desire to serve God throughout their lives, to turn to Christ and to renounce all evil. Then, as bishop, I will lay my hand on them, praying that God's Spirit will confirm, strengthen and guide them as they strive, each day of their lives, to live up to the solemn commitment they will make today.

It is our privilege and joy as the people of God to hear the candidates' response to God's call and to renew our own baptismal commitment to our Lord Jesus Christ. It will be our responsibility to encourage the newly confirmed in their discipleship, so that the Christian family may be built up, recognizing the diverse gifts of all its members.

On this their Confirmation day, let us pray in silence for .... so that, increasing in the Holy Spirit more and more, they may experience God's wisdom and love for ever.

PENITENCE

Let us affirm our trust in God's mercy, and confess that we need forgiveness.

A pause for reflection after which these or other suitable words or the seasonal Penitential Kyries on pages 224-236 are used:

Lord God, you created the world, and made us in your own image.

Forgive us when we turn away from you.

Lord, have mercy.

Lord, have mercy.

Lord God, through your Son you overcame evil and death.

Rescue us from slavery to sin.

Christ, have mercy.

Christ, have mercy.

Lord God, by your Spirit you restore us to fellowship with you and with one another. Breathe your love and freedom into our lives.

Lord, have mercy.

Lord, have mercy.

The bishop says this absolution:

Almighty God have mercy on you,

forgive you your sins,

and keep you in eternal life. **Amen.**

GLORIA IN EXCELSIS

This hymn of praise or some other may be said or sung.

Glory to God in the highest,

and peace to God's people on earth.

Lord God, heavenly king,

almighty God and Father,

we worship you, we give you thanks,

we praise you for your glory.

Lord Jesus Christ, only Son of the Father,

Lord God, Lamb of God,

you take away the sin of the world:

have mercy on us;

you are seated at the right hand of the Father:

receive our prayer.

For you alone are the Holy One:

you alone are the Lord:

you alone are the Most High,

Jesus Christ, with the Holy Spirit,

in the glory of God the Father. Amen.

Let us pray.
The community may pray silently.

The Collect of the day, a collect from pages 392-394 or the following is said:
Heavenly Father,
by water and the Holy Spirit
you give your faithful people new life:
Guide and strengthen us by that same Spirit
that we who are born again
may serve you in faith and love,
and grow into the full stature of your Son Jesus Christ,
who lives and reigns with you and the Holy Spirit,
one God, now and for ever. **Amen.**

Proclaiming and Receiving the Word

from the Old Testament and/or the New Testament should normally be as appointed in the Table of Readings. Special initiation readings can be found on page 396.

After each reading the reader may say
This is the word of the Lord.
Thanks be to God.
Silence may follow each reading.
A canticle, psalm, hymn or anthem may be sung between the readings.

All stand.

The reader says
Hear the Gospel of our Saviour Christ, according to ..., chapter ...,
beginning at verse ...
Glory to you, Lord Jesus Christ.

After the Gospel, the reader says
This is the Gospel of the Lord.
Praise to you, Lord Jesus Christ.

Silence may follow.

The Presentation

The candidates are presented to the congregation.

Where appropriate, they are presented by their godparents or sponsors and the bishop may say

Who presents these persons for confirmation?

We do.

The bishop asks the candidates

Have you been baptized in the name of the Father, and of the Son, and of the Holy Spirit?

I have.

Are you ready with your own mouth and from your own heart to affirm your faith in Jesus Christ?

I am.

The bishop asks the clergy who have been responsible for pastoral care of the candidates

Have these persons been carefully prepared in their understanding of the Christian faith?

I believe they have.

Testimony by the candidates may follow.

The Decision

The bishop says to the candidates

In baptism, God calls us from darkness to his marvellous light. To follow Christ means dying to sin and rising to new life with him. Therefore I ask:

Do you reject the devil and all proud rebellion against God?

I reject them.

Do you renounce the deceit and corruption of evil?

I renounce them.

Do you repent of the sins that separate us from God and neighbour?
I repent of them.

Do you turn to Christ as Saviour?
I turn to Christ.
Do you submit to Christ as Lord?
I submit to Christ.
Do you come to Christ, the Way, the Truth and the Life?
I come to Christ.

The bishop says to the congregation
You have heard these our brothers and sisters respond to Christ.
Will you support them in this calling?

The congregation answers
We will support them.

The Profession of Faith
The bishop asks the candidates
Do you .... believe and accept the Christian faith into which you are
baptized?
I do.

The bishop addresses the congregation
Brothers and sisters, I ask you to profess together with *these candidates*
the faith of the Church.

Do you believe and trust in God the Father?
I believe in God, the Father almighty,
creator of heaven and earth.

Do you believe and trust in God the Son?
I believe in Jesus Christ, God's only Son, our Lord
who was conceived by the Holy Spirit,
born of the Virgin Mary,
suffered under Pontius Pilate,
was crucified, died, and was buried;

he descended to the dead.
On the third day he rose again;
he ascended into heaven,
he is seated at the right hand of the Father,
and he will come again to judge the living and the dead.

Do you believe and trust in God the Holy Spirit?
I believe in the Holy Spirit,
the holy catholic Church,
the communion of saints,
the forgiveness of sins,
the resurrection of the body,
and the life everlasting. Amen.

The bishop and the candidates gather at the place of confirmation. A hymn,
psalm, canticle or a litany may be used.

The Confirmation
The bishop says
Our help is in the name of the Lord
who made heaven and earth.

Blessed be the name of the Lord
now, and for ever. Amen.

Silence

The bishop prays the confirmation prayer
Almighty and everliving God,
whose Son Jesus Christ was crucified and rose again
to break the power of sin and death:
We give you thanks and praise for the gift of your Holy Spirit
by whom your servants have been born again
and made your children.
Grant that in the power of the same Holy Spirit
they may continue to grow
in the knowledge and likeness of Christ;
increase in them your gracious gifts,

the spirit of wisdom and understanding,
the spirit of right judgment and inward strength,
the spirit of knowledge and godly living;
and fill them, O Lord, with the spirit of reverence for you.

*Those who are to be confirmed kneel before the bishop, who lays a hand upon
each of them saying*
Confirm ...., O Lord, with your heavenly grace,
that *he/she* may continue to be yours for ever,
and daily increase in your Holy Spirit more and more
until *he/she* comes to your eternal kingdom.
And each one of them answers **Amen**.

*Those receiving the laying on of hands for reaffirmation kneel before the bishop,
who lays a hand upon each of them saying*
...., may the Holy Spirit
who has begun a good work in you
direct and uphold you
in the service of Christ and his kingdom.
God, the Father, the Son and the Holy Spirit,
bless, preserve and keep you.
And each one of them answers **Amen**.

The bishop continues
Heavenly Father,
we pray for your servants
upon whom we have now laid our hands,
after the example of the apostles,
to assure them by this sign
of your favour towards them.
May your fatherly hand ever be over them.
Let your Holy Spirit ever be with them.
Lead them to know and obey your word,
and keep them in eternal life;
through Jesus Christ our Lord.
The congregation responds **Amen**.

The Commission

The bishop may use this commission:

Those who are baptized are called to worship and serve God.
Will you continue in the apostles' teaching and fellowship,
in the breaking of the bread, and in the prayers?
With the help of God, I will.

Will you persevere in resisting evil,
and, whenever you fall into sin, repent and return to the Lord?
With the help of God, I will.

Will you proclaim by word and example
the good news of God in Christ?
With the help of God, I will.

Will you seek and serve Christ in all people,
loving your neighbour as yourself?
With the help of God, I will.

THE PEACE

All stand. The Peace is introduced with these or other suitable words:
God has made us one in Christ.
He has set his seal upon us
and, as a pledge of what is to come,
has given the Spirit to dwell in our hearts.

The bishop says
The peace of the Lord be always with you
and also with you.

All may exchange a sign of peace.
A hymn may be sung.

*Holy Communion, when it follows, begins with Celebrating at the Lord's Table
(page 208).*

If Holy Communion does not follow, the service continues with the Prayers of the People, ending with the Lord's Prayer and the Dismissal.

At Holy Communion this Proper Preface may be used in Eucharistic Prayer 1:
Because by water and the Holy Spirit
you have made us a holy people in Jesus Christ our Lord;
raised us to new life in him
and renewed in us the image of your glory.

The appropriate seasonal Post Communion prayer (pages 392-394) or the following may be said:
God of mercy,
by whose grace alone we are accepted
and equipped for your service:
stir up in us the gifts of your Holy Spirit
and make us worthy of our calling;
that we may bring forth the fruit of the Spirit
in love and joy and peace;
through Jesus Christ our Lord. **Amen.**

THE LORD'S PRAYER

The bishop says
As our Saviour Christ has taught us, so we pray
Our Father in heaven ...
or
As Jesus has taught us, we are bold to say
Our Father, who art in heaven ...

Going Out as God's People

The bishop may say the seasonal blessing or another suitable blessing or

The God of all grace,
who called you to his eternal glory in Christ Jesus,
establish, strengthen and settle you in the faith;
and the blessing of God almighty,
the Father, the Son and the Holy Spirit,
be upon you and remain with you always. **Amen.**

The deacon says

Go in peace to love and serve the Lord:
In the name of Christ. Amen.

Seasonal Variations and Readings

The three sets of variants for these principal baptismal seasons each contain: Introduction, a Collect, a Post Communion Prayer and a Blessing.

EPIPHANY :: THE BAPTISM OF OUR LORD :: TRINITY SUNDAY

After the Greeting instead of Our Lord Jesus Christ has told us ... *the minister may say*

At our Lord's baptism in the river Jordan,
God showed himself to all who have eyes to see and ears to hear.
The Father spoke from heaven, the Spirit descended as a dove
and Jesus was anointed with power from on high.
For us baptism is the door of faith,
through which we enter the Kingdom of Heaven.
As children of God, we are adopted as his sons and daughters,
and called to proclaim the wonders of him
who called us out of darkness into his marvellous light.

THE COLLECT

Lord of all time and eternity,
you opened heaven's gate and revealed yourself as Father
by the voice that called Jesus your beloved Son,
baptizing him, in the power of the spirit;
reveal yourself to us now, to claim us as your children,
and so complete the heavenly work of our rebirth
in the waters of the new creation;
through Jesus Christ our Lord. **Amen.**

POST COMMUNION

God of glory,
you inspired us with the breath of life
which brought to birth a new world in Christ.
May we who are reborn in him
be transformed by the renewal of our lives,
that the light of your new creation
may flood the world with your abundant grace;
through Christ our Lord. **Amen.**

God, who in his Christ gives us a spring of water
welling up to eternal life,
perfect in you the image of his glory;
and the blessing ...

EASTER DAY TO THE DAY OF PENTECOST

After the Greeting instead of Our Lord Jesus Christ has told us ... *the minister
may say*

God raised Jesus Christ from the dead
and sent the Holy Spirit to recall the whole world to himself.
In baptism we die to sin and rise to newness of life in Christ.
Here we find rebirth in the spirit,
and set our minds on his heavenly gifts.
As children of God, we are continually created anew,
as we walk the path of faith,
and feed on the forgiveness of his healing grace.

THE COLLECT

Heavenly Father,
by the power of your Holy Spirit
you give to your faithful people
new life in the water of baptism.
Guide and strengthen us by the same spirit,
that we who are born again
may serve you in faith and love,
and grow into the full stature of your Son, Jesus Christ,
who is alive and reigns with you and the Holy Spirit
now and for ever. **Amen.**

POST COMMUNION

Author of life divine,
in the resurrection of your Son,
you set before us the mystery of his triumph over sin and death;
may all who are washed in the waters of rebirth
rise to newness of life
and find the promised presence of your abundant grace;
through Jesus Christ our Lord. **Amen.**

God the Father,
by whose glory Christ was raised from the dead,
strengthen you by his life-giving Spirit
to walk with him in the paths of righteousness and peace;
and the blessing of God almighty,
the Father, the Son and the Holy Spirit,
be with you and remain with you always. **Amen.**

IN ALL SAINTS-TIDE

After the Greeting instead of Our Lord Jesus Christ has told us ... *the minister may say*
In baptism, God calls us to be his friends
and to make us holy in his Son Jesus Christ.
On this journey of faith we have no abiding city,
for we have promise of the heavenly Jerusalem,
where the whole creation is brought to a new birth in the Holy Spirit.
Here we are united in the company of all the faithful,
and we look for the coming of the eternal kingdom.
As children of God, we look through this passing age
for the signs of the dawn of everlasting glory.

THE COLLECT

Almighty Father,
you have made us heirs through hope of your everlasting kingdom
and in the waters of baptism you have promised
a measure of grace overflowing to all eternity.
Take our sins and guilt away,
and so inflame us with the life of your Spirit
that we may know your favour and goodness towards us
and walk in newness of life,
both now and for ever;
through Jesus Christ our Lord. **Amen.**

Lord, in the vision of your heavenly kingdom
you reveal among us the promise of your glory.
May that glory be ours
as we claim our citizenship in the kingdom
where you are alive and reign, one God, for ever and ever. **Amen.**

May God, who kindled the fire of his love in the hearts of the saints,
give you joy in their fellowship,
and strengthen you to follow them in the way of holiness;
and the blessing of God almighty,
the Father, the Son and the Holy Spirit,
be with you and remain with you always. **Amen.**

Readings and Psalms for Christian Initiation

Sets of readings follow below, those for Holy Baptism being grouped according to the four headings: 1 General, 2 Epiphany :: Baptism of our Lord :: Trinity, 3 Easter to Pentecost, 4 All Saints.

Psalm	Old Testament	New Testament	Gospel
1. General			
(a) Ps 66: 5-12	Isa 43: 1-7	Rom 5: 6-11	Mk 1: 1-11
(b) Ps 89: 21-22, 25-29	Gen 17: 1-8 (-11) (or 22: 15-18)	Gal 3: 27 - 4:7	Jn 15: 1-11
(c) Ps 51: 1-6	2 Kings 5: 1-15a	Titus 3: 3-7	Jn 3: 1-8
(d) Ps 46: 1-7	Gen 7: 1, 7-16	1 Pet 3: 18-22	Mt 28: 16-20
2. Epiphany :: Baptism of our Lord :: Trinity			
(a) Ps 67	Exodus 33: 12-20 or Isa 9: 2, 3, 6-7	2 Cor 3:12 - 4:6	Jn 1: 14-18
(b) Ps 146: 5-9 (-12)	Isa 42: 5-8	Acts 9: 10-20	Lk 3: 15-17, 21-22
(c) Ps 50: 1-6	Isa 63: 15, 16; 64: 1-4	1 Cor 10: 1-4	Mk 1: 1-11
3. Easter to Pentecost			
(a) Ps 118: 19-24	Ezek 37: 1-14	Rom 6: 3-11	Mt 28: 16-20
(b) Ps 51: 6-13	Ezek 36: 24-28	Titus 3: 3-7	Jn 20: 19-23
(c) Ps 46: 1-7	Ezek 47: 1-12	Rev 22: 1-5	Jn 7: 37-39
4. All Saints			
(a) Ps 98: 1-4	Exod 19: 3-8	Rev 5: 6-10	Mt 28: 16-20
(b) Ps 63: 1-6	Isa 44: 1-5	Heb 11:32 - 12:2	Mt 5: 1-12 (-16)
(c) Ps 92: 10-15	Hos 14: 4-8	1 Pet 2: 4-10	Jn 15: 1-11
Confirmation			
(a) Ps 84: 1-7	Ezek 37: 1-14	1 Pet 2: 4-10	Jn 7: 37-39
(b) Ps 96: 1-10	Isa 11: 1-10	Gal 5: 16-25	Jn 15: 12-17

HOLY BAPTISM, CONFIRMATION AND HOLY COMMUNION

THE STRUCTURE OF THE SERVICE

The Gathering of God's People
> The Greeting
> The Collect

Proclaiming and Receiving the Word
> Readings and Psalm
> The Gospel
> The Sermon

The Presentation
> The Decision

The Baptism
> Thanksgiving prayer over the water
> Profession of Faith
> The Baptism

Confirmation
> Confirmation
> Commission
> The Peace

Celebrating at the Lord's Table
> The Taking of the Bread and Wine
> The Great Thanksgiving
> The Lord's Prayer
> The Breaking of the Bread
> The Communion
> The Great Silence

Going Out as God's People
> Prayer after Communion
> Dismissal

This basic structure of Holy Baptism, Confirmation and Holy Communion may be adapted at the bishop's discretion to meet particular circumstances.

THE RENEWAL OF BAPTISMAL VOWS

A form which may be used at Easter, Pentecost, the Baptism of our Lord, on Ash Wednesday, at the close of a mission or on other suitable occasions.

The renewal of baptismal vows may be made at Morning or Evening Prayer, or at Holy Communion after the sermon, and the creed may be omitted. The prayers of intercession and of penitence may be omitted.

At Easter the minister says

As we celebrate again the death and resurrection of our Lord Jesus Christ we remember that through these saving acts we have died and been buried with him in baptism, so that we might rise with him to a new life within the family of his Church.

We now meet to renew the promises made at our baptism, to affirm our allegiance to Christ and our rejection of all that is evil.

On other occasions the minister says

In our baptism we died with Christ and were buried with him, so that we might rise with him to a new life within the family of his Church.

We now meet to renew the promises made at our baptism, to affirm our allegiance to Christ and our rejection of all that is evil.

Stand

THE FIRST FORM

The minister says

Do you renew and affirm the promises made at your baptism?
I do.
Do you reject the devil and all proud rebellion against God?
I reject them.

Do you renounce the deceit and corruption of evil?
I renounce them.
Do you repent of the sins that separate us from God and neighbour?
I repent of them.

Do you turn to Christ as Saviour?
I turn to Christ.
Do you submit to Christ as Lord?
I submit to Christ.
Do you come to Christ, the Way, the Truth and the Life?
I come to Christ.

Do you believe and trust in God the Father?
I believe in God, the Father almighty,
creator of heaven and earth.

Do you believe and trust in God the Son?
I believe in Jesus Christ, God's only Son, our Lord
who was conceived by the Holy Spirit,
born of the Virgin Mary,
suffered under Pontius Pilate,
was crucified, died, and was buried;
he descended to the dead.
On the third day he rose again;
he ascended into heaven,
he is seated at the right hand of the Father,
and he will come again to judge the living and the dead.

Do you believe and trust in God the Holy Spirit?
I believe in the Holy Spirit,
the holy catholic Church,
the communion of saints,
the forgiveness of sins,
the resurrection of the body,
and the life everlasting. Amen.

Or

THE SECOND FORM

The minister says
Do you renew and affirm the promises made when you were baptized?
I do.

Do you turn in faith to Christ?
I do.

Do you then renounce all evil?
I do, by God's help.

Will you obey and serve Christ?
I will, by God's help.

Do you believe and trust in God the Father,
creator of heaven and earth?
I believe and trust in him.

Do you believe and trust in his Son Jesus Christ,
who redeemed the world?
I believe and trust in him.

Do you believe and trust in the Holy Spirit
who gives life to the people of God?
I believe and trust in him.

This is the faith of the Church.
This is our faith.
We believe and trust in one God,
Father, Son, and Holy Spirit.

The minister continues
Those who are baptized are called to worship and serve God.

Will you continue in the apostles' teaching and fellowship,
in the breaking of bread, and in the prayers?
With the help of God, I will.

Will you persevere in resisting evil,
and, whenever you fall into sin, repent and return to the Lord?
With the help of God, I will.

Will you proclaim by word and example
the good news of God in Christ?
With the help of God, I will.

Will you seek and serve Christ in all people,
loving your neighbour as yourself?
With the help of God, I will.

Will you acknowledge Christ's authority over human society,
by prayer for the world and its leaders,
by defending the weak, and by seeking peace and justice?
With the help of God, I will.

The minister says
Let us pray.
Almighty God,
you have given us the will to do all these things:
Give us the courage and strength to achieve them
to the honour and glory of your name,
and the good of your Church and people;
through Jesus Christ our Lord,
who lives and reigns with you and the Holy Spirit,
one God, now and for ever. **Amen.**

May Christ dwell in your hearts through faith,
that you may be rooted and grounded in love
and bring forth the fruit of the Spirit. **Amen.**

THANKSGIVING AFTER THE BIRTH OF A CHILD

THANKSGIVING AFTER ADOPTION

Thanksgiving after the Birth of a Child is giving thanks for the safety of the mother in giving birth to the child and for the life of the new-born baby. It is most appropriate to have the service in the hospital or at home soon after the birth. It is not in any way a substitute for the sacrament of baptism.

Thanksgiving after Adoption may be used in the home. If the child was baptized before adoption the service provides an opportunity for receiving him or her into the life of the parish and may be used at Holy Communion or at Morning or Evening Prayer. This service should not be used before the official Adoption Order has been made.

Minister

Let us thank God that in his goodness he has given you this *son/ daughter.*

After the birth the parents say

God our Father,
maker of all that is living,
we praise you for the wonder and joy of creation.
We thank you for the life of this child,
for a safe delivery,
and for the privilege of parenthood.
Accept our thanks and praise
through Jesus Christ our Lord. Amen.

After adoption the adoptive parents say

God our Father,
maker of all that is living,
we praise you for the wonder and joy of creation.
We thank you for the life of this child,
for his/her adoption into our family,
and for the privilege of parenthood,
accept our thanks and praise
through Jesus Christ our Lord. Amen.

Father in heaven,
bless these parents
that they may cherish their child,
make them wise and understanding to help *him* as *he* grows,
and surround this family with the light of your truth
and the warmth of your love;
through Jesus Christ our Lord. **Amen.**

PSALM VERSES

I will give you thanks O Lord with my whole heart,
I will tell of all the wonders you have done.
I will rejoice and be glad in you,
I will make my songs to your name O Most High. *9: 1,2*

For you Lord are my hope,
you are my confidence, O Lord, from my youth upward.
On you have I leaned since my birth,
you are he that brought me out of my mother's womb
and my praise is of you continually. *71: 5,6*

or Psalm 127 or 128 or 145

SUGGESTED READINGS

Genesis 1: 26-28, 31a; 1 Samuel 1: 20-28; Romans 8: 28-30; 12: 1-10;
Ephesians 3: 14-21; Matthew 7: 24-27; Luke 2: 22-28a; John 16: 21

PRAYERS

Minister

Let us pray.
Heavenly Father,
your blessed Son shared the life of an earthly home at Nazareth.
Bless the home of this family,
and help all the members of it to live together in your love.
Teach them to serve you and each other,
and make them always ready to show your love to those in need;
for the sake of Jesus Christ our Lord. **Amen.**

and/or

God our Father,
we pray for all who have the care of this child.
Guide them by your Holy Spirit,
that they may bring *him* up in the ways of truth and love.
Through their care enable *him* to grow in grace
and become daily more like your Son,
our Saviour Jesus Christ. **Amen.**

This prayer may be used if the child has not been baptized:
God our Father,
we pray for this child
that in faith *he* may be received by baptism
into the family of your Church,
and become an inheritor of your kingdom;
through Jesus Christ our Lord. **Amen.**

Our Father in heaven ...
or
Our Father, who art in heaven ...

Minister
My soul proclaims the greatness of the Lord,
my spirit rejoices in God my saviour.

Glory and honour and power are yours by right, O Lord our God;
for you created all things and by your will they have their being.

BLESSING

Priest
The love of the Lord Jesus Christ draw you to himself,
the power of the Lord Jesus strengthen you in his service,
the joy of the Lord Jesus fill your hearts;
and the blessing of God almighty
the Father, the Son, and the Holy Spirit,
be with you and remain with you always. **Amen.**

Marriage Services

SOLEMNIZATION OF MATRIMONY

Introduction

The priest says to the congregation

Dearly beloved, we are gathered together here in the sight of God, and in the face of this congregation, to join together this man and this woman in holy matrimony; which is an honourable estate, instituted of God in the time of man's innocency, signifying unto us the mystical union that is betwixt Christ and his Church; which holy estate Christ adorned and beautified with his presence, and first miracle that he wrought, in Cana of Galilee; and is commended in Holy Scripture to be honourable among all men: and therefore is not by any to be enterprised, nor taken in hand, unadvisedly, lightly, or wantonly; but reverently, discreetly, advisedly, soberly, and in the fear of God; duly considering the causes for which matrimony was ordained:

First, for the increase of mankind, according to the will of God, and for the due ordering of families and households, that children might be brought up in the fear and nurture of the Lord, and to the praise of his holy Name;

Secondly, for the hallowing of the union betwixt man and woman, and for the avoidance of sin;

Thirdly, for the mutual society, help, and comfort, that the one ought to have of the other, both in prosperity and adversity.

Into which holy estate these two persons present come now to be joined. Therefore if any man can shew any just cause why they may not lawfully be joined together, let him now speak, or else hereafter for ever hold his peace.

The minister says to the couple

I require and charge you both, as ye will answer at the dreadful day of judgment when the secrets of all hearts shall be disclosed, that if either of you know any impediment, why ye may not be lawfully joined together in matrimony, ye do now confess it. For be ye well assured, that so many as are coupled together otherwise than God's Word doth allow are not joined together by God; neither is their matrimony lawful.

The Marriage

The minister says to the man

.... Wilt thou have this woman to thy wedded wife, to live together after God's ordinance in the holy estate of matrimony? Wilt thou love her, comfort her, honour, and keep her, in sickness and in health; and, forsaking all other, keep thee only unto her, so long as ye both shall live?
I will.

The minister says to the woman

.... Wilt thou have this man to thy wedded husband, to live together after God's ordinance in the holy estate of matrimony? Wilt thou love him, honour, and keep him, in sickness and in health; and forsaking all other, keep thee only unto him, so long as ye both shall live?
I will.

Or the minister may say to the woman

.... Wilt thou have this man to thy wedded husband, to live together after God's ordinance in the holy estate of matrimony? Wilt thou obey him and serve him, love, honour, and keep him, in sickness and in health; and forsaking all other, keep thee only unto him, so long as ye both shall live?
I will.

The minister asks

Who giveth this woman to be married to this man?

The minister receives the woman at her father's or friend's hands.

THE MARRIAGE VOWS

The man, with his right hand taking the woman by her right hand, says after the minister

I .... take thee .... to my wedded wife, to have and to hold from this day forward, for better for worse, for richer for poorer, in sickness and in health, to love and to cherish, till death us do part, according to God's holy ordinance; and thereto I plight thee my troth.

The woman, with her right hand taking the man by his right hand, says after the minister

I .... take thee .... to my wedded husband, to have and to hold from this day forward, for better for worse, for richer for poorer, in sickness and in health, to love and to cherish, till death us do part, according to God's holy ordinance; and thereto I give thee my troth.

Or the woman, with her right hand taking the man by his right hand, says after the minister

I .... take thee .... to my wedded husband, to have and to hold from this day forward, for better for worse, for richer for poorer, in sickness and in health, to love, cherish, and to obey, till death us do part, according to God's holy ordinance; and thereto I give thee my troth.

GIVING AND RECEIVING OF A RING

The man gives to the woman a ring, laying it on the book.

The man puts the ring on the fourth finger of the woman's left hand and, holding the ring there, says

With this ring I thee wed, with my body I thee worship, and with all my worldly goods I thee endow: In the Name of the Father, and of the Son, and of the Holy Spirit. Amen.

If the woman gives the man a ring, she puts the ring on the fourth finger of the man's left hand and, holding the ring there, says

With this ring I thee wed, with my body I thee worship, and with all my worldly goods I thee endow: In the Name of the Father, and of the Son, and of the Holy Spirit. Amen.

PRAYER

The man and the woman kneel. The priest says

Let us pray.

O eternal God, Creator and Preserver of all mankind, Giver of all spiritual grace, the Author of everlasting life; Send thy blessing upon these thy servants, this man and this woman, whom we bless in thy Name; that, as Isaac and Rebecca lived faithfully together, so these persons may surely perform and keep the vow and covenant betwixt them made (whereof this ring given and received is a token and pledge), and may ever remain in perfect love and peace together, and live according to thy laws; through Jesus Christ our Lord. **Amen.**

Joining their right hands together, the priest says
Those whom God hath joined together let no man put asunder.

DECLARATION

The minister speaks to the people
Forasmuch as .... and .... have consented together in holy wedlock, and have witnessed the same before God and this company, and thereto have given and pledged their troth either to other, and have declared the same by giving and receiving of a ring, and by joining of hands; I pronounce that they be man and wife together: In the Name of the Father, and of the Son, and of the Holy Spirit. **Amen.**

BLESSING

The minister adds this Blessing:
God the Father, God the Son, God the Holy Spirit, bless, preserve, and keep you; the Lord mercifully with his favour look upon you; and so fill you with all spiritual benediction and grace, that ye may so live together in this life, that in the world to come ye may have life everlasting. **Amen.**

PRAYERS AFTER THE MARRIAGE

The minister goes to the Lord's Table.
One of the following Psalms (or a Psalm from the list on page 418) is said or sung.

THE PSALM

Psalm 128 Beati omnes
1   Blessed are all they that fear the Lord, ▪
    and walk in his ways.
2   For thou shalt eat the labours of thine hands; ▪
    O well is thee, and happy shalt thou be.
3   Thy wife shall be as the fruitful vine ▪
    upon the walls of thine house.
4   Thy children like the olive-branches ▪
    round about thy table.

5   Lo, thus shall the man be blessed ■
     that feareth the Lord.

6   The Lord from out of Sion shall so bless thee ■
     that thou shalt see Jerusalem in prosperity all thy life long.

7   Yea, that thou shalt see thy children's children ■
     and peace upon Israel.

        Glory be to the Father, ■
        and to the Son, and to the Holy Spirit;
        as it was in the beginning, ■
        is now, and ever shall be, world without end. Amen.

or Psalm 67 Deus misereatur

1   God be merciful unto us, and bless us; ■
     and shew us the light of his countenance,
        and be merciful unto us:

2   That thy way may be known upon earth, ■
     thy saving health among all nations.

3   Let the people praise thee, O God; ■
     yea, let all the people praise thee.

4   O let the nations rejoice and be glad, ■
     for thou shalt judge the folk righteously,
        and govern the nations upon earth.

5   Let the people praise thee, O God; ■
     yea, let all the people praise thee.

6   Then shall the earth bring forth her increase, ■
     and God, even our own God, shall give us his blessing.

7   God shall bless us, ■
     and all the ends of the world shall fear him.

        Glory be to the Father, ■
        and to the Son, and to the Holy Spirit;
        as it was in the beginning, ■
        is now, and ever shall be, world without end. Amen.

The man and the woman kneel before the Lord's Table, the minister says
Let us pray.

Lord, have mercy upon us.
Christ, have mercy upon us.
Lord, have mercy upon us.

Our Father, who art in heaven,
   hallowed be thy Name,
   thy kingdom come,
   thy will be done,
      On earth as it is in heaven.
Give us this day our daily bread.
   And forgive us our trespasses
   as we forgive those who trespass against us.
And lead us not into temptation,
   but deliver us from evil. Amen.

O Lord, save thy servant, and thy handmaid,
who put their trust in thee.

O Lord, send them help from thy holy place;
and evermore defend them.

Be unto them a tower of strength;
from the face of their enemy.

O Lord, hear our prayer;
and let our cry come unto thee.

O God of Abraham, God of Isaac, God of Jacob, bless these thy servants, and sow the seed of eternal life in their hearts; that whatsoever in thy holy Word they shall profitably learn, they may in deed fulfil the same. Look, O Lord, mercifully upon them from heaven, and bless them. And as thou didst send thy blessing upon Abraham and Sarah, to their great comfort, so vouchsafe to send thy blessing upon these thy servants; that they obeying thy will, and alway being in safety under thy protection, may abide in thy love unto their lives' end; through Jesus Christ our Lord. **Amen.**

This prayer may follow:

O merciful Lord and heavenly Father, by whose gracious blessing mankind is increased; Bestow, we beseech thee, on these thy servants the heritage and gift of children, and grant that they may also live together so long in godly love and honesty, that they may see their children christianly and virtuously brought up, to thy praise and honour; through Jesus Christ our Lord. **Amen.**

O God, who by thy mighty power hast made all things of nothing; who also (after other things set in order) didst appoint, that out of man (created after thine own image and similitude) woman should take her beginning; and, knitting them together, didst teach that it should never be lawful to put asunder those whom thou by Matrimony hadst made one: O God, who hast so consecrated the state of Matrimony, that in it is signified and represented the spiritual marriage and unity betwixt Christ and his Church: Look mercifully upon these thy servants, that both this man may love his wife, according to thy Word (as Christ did love his spouse the Church, who gave himself for it, loving and cherishing it even as his own flesh), and also that this woman may be loving and amiable, faithful and obedient to her husband; and in all quietness, sobriety, and peace, be a follower of holy and godly matrons. O Lord, bless them both, and grant them to inherit thy everlasting kingdom; through Jesus Christ our Lord. **Amen.**

Prayers from those on pages 424-427 may be preferred.

The minister says

Almighty God, who at the beginning did create our first parents, Adam and Eve, and did sanctify and join them together in marriage; Pour upon you the riches of his grace, sanctify and bless you, that ye may please him both in body and soul, and live together in holy love unto your lives' end. **Amen.**

Unless there is to be a celebration of the Holy Communion a reading from Holy Scripture follows. If there is a sermon it is preached here.

Here may follow an anthem or hymn.

If there is no Communion, the minister says

Let us pray.

O eternal God, we humbly beseech thee favourably to behold these thy servants .... and .... now joined in wedlock according to thy holy ordinance; and grant that they, seeking first thy kingdom and righteousness, may obtain the manifold blessings of thy grace; through Jesus Christ our Lord. **Amen.**

O almighty Lord, and everlasting God, vouchsafe, we beseech thee, to direct, sanctify, and govern both our hearts and bodies, in the ways of thy laws, and in the works of thy commandments; that through thy most mighty protection, both here and ever, we may be preserved in body and soul; through our Lord and Saviour Jesus Christ. **Amen.**

The grace of our Lord Jesus Christ, and the love of God, and the fellowship of the Holy Spirit be with us all evermore. **Amen.**

It is appropriate that the newly married couple should receive the Holy Communion at the time of their Marriage, or at the first opportunity after their Marriage.

Holy Communion at the Time of a Marriage

O eternal God, we humbly beseech thee favourably to behold these thy servants now joined in wedlock according to thy holy ordinance; and grant that they, seeking first thy kingdom and righteousness, may obtain the manifold blessings of thy grace; through Jesus Christ our Lord. **Amen.**

THE EPISTLE

Ephesians 5: 20-33

Giving thanks always for all things unto God and the Father, in the Name of our Lord Jesus Christ; submitting yourselves one to another in the fear of God. Wives, submit yourselves unto your own husbands, as unto the Lord. For the husband is the head of the wife, even as Christ is the head of the church: and he is the saviour of the body. Therefore as the church is subject unto Christ; so let the wives be to their own husbands in every thing. Husbands, love your wives, even as Christ also loved the church, and gave himself for it; that he might sanctify and cleanse it with the washing of water by the Word, that he might present it to himself a glorious church, not having spot, or wrinkle, or any such thing; but that it should be holy and without blemish. So ought men to love their wives as their own bodies. He that loveth his wife loveth himself: for no man ever yet hated his own flesh; but nourisheth and cherisheth it, even as the Lord the church: for we are members of his body, of his flesh, and of his bones. For this cause shall a man leave his father and mother, and shall be joined unto his wife; and they two shall be one flesh. This is a great mystery: but I speak concerning Christ and the church. Nevertheless let every one of you in particular so love his wife even as himself; and the wife see that she reverence her husband.

THE GOSPEL

Matthew 19: 4-6

Jesus said, Have ye not read, that he which made them at the beginning made them male and female, and said, For this cause shall a man leave father and mother, and shall cleave to his wife; and they twain shall be one flesh? Wherefore they are no more twain, but one flesh. What therefore God hath joined together, let not man put asunder.

Or readings from the list on page 418 may be preferred.

On the day of the marriage if anyone alleges or declares any impediment why the man and woman may not lawfully marry, the person alleging or declaring the impediment is required to deposit, or by sureties guarantee, such sum as would cover the cost of the wedding and of all other expenses incurred in connection therewith. The wedding must then be deferred until such time as the truth is tried. Should the impediment not be upheld the amount deposited or guaranteed shall become the property of the man and woman, and the person alleging or declaring the impediment shall be liable for the legal costs incurred.

THE MARRIAGE SERVICE

The Entry

The people stand.

The minister may greet the bridal or marriage party with:
Blessed are they who come in the name of the Lord.
We bless you from the house of the Lord.
O give thanks to the Lord, for he is good,
For his steadfast love endures for ever. *Psalm 118: 26; 136: 1 (adapted)*

A hymn may be sung or instrumental music played during the entrance.

The Lord be with you
and also with you.

The minister may say
God is love, and those who live in love live in God,
and God lives in them.   *1 John 4: 16*

The Introduction

The minister says
We have come together in the presence of God
to witness the marriage of .... and ....,
to ask his blessing on them
and to share in their joy.
Our Lord Jesus Christ was himself a guest
at a wedding at Cana of Galilee,
and through his Spirit he is with us now.

The scriptures set before us marriage as part of God's creation
and a holy mystery
in which man and woman become one flesh.
It is God's purpose that, as husband and wife
give themselves to each other
in love throughout their lives,
they shall be united in that love
as Christ is united with his Church.

Marriage was ordained that husband and wife
may comfort and help each other,
living faithfully together in plenty and in need,
in sorrow and in joy.

It is intended that with delight and tenderness
they may know each other in love,
and through the joy of their bodily union
they may strengthen the union of their hearts and lives.

It is intended that they may be blessed
in the children they may have,
in caring for them and in bringing them up
in accordance with God's will
to his praise and glory.

In marriage husband and wife begin a new life together in the community.
It is a permanent commitment that all should honour.
It must not be undertaken carelessly, lightly or selfishly,
but by God's help, with reverence, responsibility,
respect and the promise to be faithful.

This is a way of life, created and hallowed by God,
that .... and .... are now about to begin.
They will each give their consent to the other;
they will join hands and exchange solemn vows,
and in token of this they will give and receive a ring.

Therefore on this their wedding day we pray with them,
that, strengthened and guided by God,
they may fulfil his purpose
for the whole of their earthly life together.

THE COLLECT

The minister says
Almighty God,
through your Son Jesus Christ you send the Holy Spirit
to be the life and light of all your people:
Open the hearts of these your servants
to the riches of his grace,
that they may bring forth the fruit of the Spirit
in love and joy and peace;
through Jesus Christ our Lord. **Amen.**

Proclaiming and Receiving the Word

One or more readings from the Holy Scriptures.

READINGS

Genesis 1: 26-28; Song of Solomon 2: 10-13; 8: 6, 7; Ecclesiastes 3: 1-8;
Ecclesiastes 4: 9-12; Jeremiah 31: 31-34

Psalm 67, 121, 127, 128

Romans 12: 5-7,13; 1 Corinthians 13; Ephesians 3: 14-21; Ephesians 4: 1-6;
Ephesians 5: 21-33; Philippians 4: 4-9; Colossians 3: 12-17; 1 John 3: 18-24;
1 John 4: 7-12

Matthew 5: 1-10; Matthew 7: 21, 24-27; Mark 10: 6-9,13-16; John 2: 1-11;
John 15: 1-8 or 15: 9-17

THE SERMON

The Marriage

The minister says to the congregation
I am required by law to ask anyone present who knows a reason why ....
and .... may not lawfully marry to declare it now.

The minister says to the couple
The vows you are about to take
are to be made in the name of God,
who is judge of all
and knows all the secrets of our hearts;
therefore if either of you knows any reason
why you may not lawfully marry
you must declare it now.

THE CONSENT

The minister says to the bridegroom
..... will you take .... to be your wife?
Will you love her, comfort her,
honour and care for her,
and, forsaking all others,
be faithful to her as long as you both shall live?

He answers
I will.

The minister says to the bride
.... will you take .... to be your husband?
Will you love him, comfort him,
honour and care for him,
and, forsaking all others,
be faithful to him as long as you both shall live?

She answers
I will.

The bride and bridegroom face each other. The bridegroom takes the bride's right hand in his and says

I .... take you .... to be my wife,

to have and to hold

from this day forward,

for better, for worse,

for richer, for poorer,

in sickness, and in health,

to love and to cherish

till death us do part,

according to God's holy law.

This is my solemn vow.

They loose hands. The bride takes the bridegroom's right hand in hers and says

I .... take you .... to be my husband,

to have and to hold

from this day forward,

for better, for worse,

for richer, for poorer,

in sickness and in health,

to love and to cherish

till death us do part,

according to God's holy law.

This is my solemn vow.

They loose hands.

GIVING AND RECEIVING OF A RING

The minister receives the ring(s) and may say

Heavenly Father,

may *this ring* be to .... and ....

a symbol of unending love and faithfulness

to remind them of the vow and covenant

which they have made this day.

*The bridegroom takes the ring and places it on the fourth finger of the bride's
left hand, and holding it there says*

I give you this ring
as a sign of our marriage.
With my body I honour you,
and all that I have I share with you
in the name of God,
Father, Son and Holy Spirit.

If this is the one ring used, before they loose hands the bride says

I receive this ring
as a sign of our marriage.
With my body I honour you,
and all that I have I share with you
in the name of God,
Father, Son and Holy Spirit.

*If the bride gives a ring, they loose hands and she places it on the fourth finger
of the bridegroom's left hand, and holding it there says*

I give you this ring
as a sign of our marriage.
With my body I honour you,
and all that I have I share with you
in the name of God,
Father, Son and Holy Spirit.

THE DECLARATION

The priest addresses the people

In the presence of God, and before this congregation
.... and .... have given their consent
and made their marriage vows to each other.
They have declared their marriage
by the joining of hands
and by the giving and receiving of a ring.
Therefore in the name of God
I pronounce that they are husband and wife.

The priest joins the right hands of the husband and wife together, and says
What God has joined together
let no one put asunder. *Mark 10: 9*

The congregation remains standing.
The husband and wife kneel, and the priest says
God the Father, God the Son, and God the Holy Spirit
bless, preserve and keep you:
the Lord mercifully grant you the riches of his grace
that you may live together in faith and love,
and receive the blessings of eternal life. **Amen.**

The newly married couple may say
O God our Father,
we thank you for uniting our lives
and for giving us to each other in the fulfilment of love.
Watch over us at all times,
guide and protect us,
and give us faith and patience,
that, as we hold each other's hand in yours,
we may draw strength from you
and from each other;
through Jesus Christ our Lord. Amen.

The priest says
Will you the family and friends of .... and .... support and encourage them
in their marriage?
We will.

Blessed are you, heavenly Father:
> **you give joy to the bridegroom and the bride.**

Blessed are you, Lord Jesus Christ:
> **you have brought new life to all your people.**

Blessed are you, Holy Spirit of God:
you bring us together in love.

Blessed be the Father, the Son, and the Holy Spirit:
one God, to be praised for ever. Amen.

The registration of the marriage may take place now in the church, or at the end of the service.

A psalm or hymn may be sung.

The Prayers

The couple kneel at the Lord's Table.

The prayers are led by the minister or by others appointed by the minister, using either of the following forms. Other prayers may be included.

Silence may be kept.

THE FIRST FORM

Now that .... and .... have given themselves to each other in marriage, let us pray that God will keep them and all other married couples faithful to their marriage vows.

May they live and grow together in love and peace all the days of their life,
Lord, in your mercy
hear our prayer.

May they truly and faithfully perform those vows which they have made together in your sight,
Lord, in your mercy
hear our prayer.

May their life together be a witness to your love in this troubled world; may unity overcome division, forgiveness heal injury, and joy triumph over sorrow,
Lord, in your mercy
hear our prayer.

May their home be a place of love, security and truth, (and may they be blessed with the gift of children),

> Lord, in your mercy
> **hear our prayer.**

We pray for their families and friends, and all who share with them in the happiness of this day,

> Lord, in your mercy
> **hear our prayer.**

We pray for your Church, united to Christ as a bride is to her husband, that it may be faithful to him in love and truthfulness,

> Lord, in your mercy
> **hear our prayer.**

We remember with thankfulness our relatives and friends departed this life in your faith and fear, especially ... and we pray that we may share with them the joys of your eternal kingdom,

> Lord, in your mercy
> **hear our prayer.**

Merciful Father,
accept these our thanksgivings and prayers
for the sake of your Son
our Saviour Jesus Christ. Amen.

Continue on page 427

THE SECOND FORM

One or more of these prayers is said.

For husband and wife
Lord God, faithful from generation to generation,
bless these your servants.
May your word be a lamp to their feet
and a light to their path;
that they may obey your will,
live in safety under your protection,
and abide in your love unto their lives' end;
through Jesus Christ our Lord. **Amen.**

Almighty God, giver of life and love:
Bless .... and .... whom you have now joined in marriage.
Grant them wisdom and devotion in their life together,
that each may be to the other a strength in need,
a comfort in sorrow, and a companion in joy.
So unite their wills in your will
and their spirits in your Spirit,
that they may live and grow together in love and peace
all the days of their life;
through Jesus Christ our Lord. **Amen.**

Almighty and merciful Father,
the strength of all who put their trust in you:
We pray that as you have brought .... and .... together,
you will so enrich them by your grace
that they may truly and faithfully keep those vows
which they have made to one another in your sight;
through Jesus Christ our Lord. **Amen.**

O God, you consecrated marriage
to be a sign of the spiritual unity between Christ and his Church:
Bless these your servants,
that they may love, honour and cherish each other
in faithfulness and patience,
in wisdom and true godliness;
that their home may be a place of blessing and peace;
through Jesus Christ our Lord,
who lives and reigns with you and the Holy Spirit,
one God, now and for ever. **Amen.**

God of all grace, friend and companion,
look in favour on .... and ....
and on all who are made one in marriage.
In your love deepen their love,
strengthen their wills
to keep the promises they have made this day,
that they may continue in life-long faithfulness to each other;
through Jesus Christ our Lord. **Amen.**

God our Creator,
we thank you for your gift of sexual love
by which husband and wife may delight in each other,
and share with you the joy of creating new life.
By your grace may the love of .... and .... remain strong
and may they rejoice in your goodness all their days;
through Jesus Christ our Lord. **Amen.**

For the gift of children
Heavenly Father, maker of all things,
you enable us to share in your work of creation:
Bless this couple with the gift of children,
and give them grace to make their home
a place of love, security and truth,
that their children may grow up to know and love you
in your Son Jesus Christ our Lord. **Amen.**

For Christian witness in marriage
Eternal God, true and loving Father,
in marriage you make your servants one.
May their life together witness to your love
in this troubled world,
may unity overcome division,
forgiveness heal injury,
and joy triumph over sorrow;
through Jesus Christ our Lord. **Amen.**

Almighty God, our heavenly Father,
you gave marriage to be a source of blessing:
We thank you for the joys of family life:
May we know your presence and peace in our homes,
fill them with your love,
and use them for your glory;
through Jesus Christ our Lord. **Amen.**

The couple may say

God of tenderness and strength,
you have brought our paths together
and led us to this day;
go with us now as we travel through good times,
through trouble or through change.
Bless our home, our partings and our meetings.
Make us worthy of each other's best,
and tender with each other's dreams,
trusting in your love in Jesus Christ. Amen.

THE PEACE

The minister says

Jesus said, A new commandment I give to you,
that you love one another:
even as I have loved you, that you also love one another. *John 13: 34*

The peace of the Lord be always with you
and also with you.

It is appropriate that the congregation share with one another a sign of peace.
This may be introduced by the words:

Let us offer one another a sign of peace.

A hymn may be sung.

The bride and bridegroom should receive Holy Communion at the time of their
marriage or at the first opportunity after their marriage.

When Holy Communion is celebrated at the time of the marriage the Holy
Communion begins at Celebrating at the Lord's Table on (page 208) or in
Holy Communion One at **Lift up your hearts ...** *(page 186).*

PROPER PREFACE

We give you thanks
because you have made the union
between Christ and his Church
a pattern for the marriage
between husband and wife:

The minister says

As our Saviour Christ has taught us, so we pray
Our Father in heaven ...

or

As our Saviour Christ has taught us, we are bold to say
Our Father, who art in heaven ...

The minister may say

The grace of our Lord Jesus Christ,
and the love of God,
and the fellowship of the Holy Spirit,
be with us all evermore. **Amen.**

or

God the Holy Trinity
make you strong in faith and love,
defend you on every side,
and guide you in truth and peace:
And the blessing of God Almighty,
the Father, the Son, and the Holy Spirit
be with you, and remain with you always. **Amen.**

NOTES

1 As much notice as possible should be given to the minister of the parish to allow sufficient time for adequate pastoral preparation before marriage.

2 All readings in Proclaiming and Receiving the Word must be from Holy Scripture. These may be used where printed in the service or after The Affirmation by the People. At Holy Communion there are at least two readings, of which the Gospel must be one.

3 Hymns or canticles may be sung at suitable points during the service.

4 The minister and the couple should together choose the readings, hymns, music and the prayers to be used in the service. If a Bible or New Testament is to be presented to the bride and bridegroom it is appropriate that this should be done before the readings.

5 If Holy Communion is celebrated at the marriage, its reception should not be restricted to the bridal party.

On the day of the marriage if anyone alleges or declares any impediment why the man and woman may not lawfully marry, the person alleging or declaring the impediment is required to deposit, or by sureties guarantee, such sum as would cover the cost of the wedding and of all other expenses incurred in connection therewith. The wedding must then be deferred until such time as the truth is tried. Should the impediment not be upheld the amount deposited or guaranteed shall become the property of the man and woman, and the person alleging or declaring the impediment shall be liable for the legal costs incurred.

BANNS OF MARRIAGE

The banns of all that are to be married together (save when a licence shall be issued for such marriage) must be published on three separate Sundays or Feast-Days in the time of Divine Service after the Nicene Creed or immediately after the final reading at Morning or Evening Prayer in either:

(a) the Church of the parish in which the persons to be married dwell provided that if Divine Service is not celebrated in that Church on any occasion when such publication should be made the banns may be published on any such occasion in another Church of the parochial union or group which the congregation is accustomed to attend instead of in that Church,

or (b) the Church of which the persons to be married are registered as vestrymen by reason of being accustomed members thereof.

The clergyman, or a person who has been admitted by the Bishop of the Diocese to the office of Reader in the Church, saying after the accustomed manner:

> I publish the Banns of Marriage between M. of .... and N. of ....
> If any of you know cause, or just impediment, why these two persons should not be joined together in holy Matrimony, ye are to declare it.
> This is the *first* (*second*, or *third*) time of asking.

Unless the two persons that are to be married to each other dwell in the same parish or are both registered as vestrymen by reason of being accustomed members of the same Church the banns must be published in manner aforesaid separately in respect of each of them in the appropriate Church as hereinbefore provided and matrimony shall not be solemnized betwixt them without certificates of the banns being thrice called in each such Church. (*Statute of the General Synod Chapter 1 of 1975.*)

Unless and until the necessary enabling legislation has been passed in Northern Ireland to give effect to the above provisions, the following rubrics still apply in Northern Ireland:

The Banns of all that are to married together (save when a licence shall be issued for such Marriage) must be published in the Church three several Sundays or Feast-Days, in the time of Divine Service, after the Nicene Creed, or immediately after the final reading at Morning or Evening Prayer; the Curate saying after the accustomed manner,

I publish the Banns of Marriage etc., as above

And if two persons that are to be married to each other dwell in divers Parishes, the Banns must be asked in both Parishes; and the Curate of the one Parish shall not solemnize Matrimony betwixt them, without a certificate of the Banns being thrice asked, from the Curate of the other Parish.

NOTICE OF INTENTION TO MARRY

Those intending to be married in the Republic of Ireland are advised that three months' notice is required to be given to the local Registrar of Marriages.

MARRIAGE BY LICENCE

The Bishop of each Diocese has Surrogates who may issue a Licence for a Marriage to take place without the publication of Banns. The Bishop, or in the Republic of Ireland, a Commissary officially authorized, may issue a Special Licence for a marriage. The appropriate Licence must be produced to the priest who officiates at the marriage.

Editor's Note:

Subsequent to General Synod 2003 changes have been made to the Marriage Laws in Northern Ireland. Information about the new procedures can be obtained from the Registrar General for Northern Ireland or from the local diocesan authorities.

It is anticipated that changes will also be made in the Marriage Law in the Republic of Ireland.

A FORM OF PRAYER AND DEDICATION
AFTER A CIVIL MARRIAGE

The married couple enter the church together.

The presiding minister says
Grace, mercy and peace
from God our Father and the Lord Jesus Christ
be with you all.
And also with you.

God is love and those who live in love live in God, and God lives in them.
1 John 4: 6

Unless the Lord builds the house, those who labour build in vain.
Psalm 127: 1

.... and .... you stand in the presence of God as husband and wife to dedicate to him your life together, that he may consecrate your marriage and empower you to keep the covenant and promise you have solemnly declared.

The scriptures set before us marriage as part of God's creation
and a holy mystery
in which man and woman become one flesh.
It is God's purpose that, as husband and wife
give themselves to each other
in love throughout their lives,
they shall be united in that love
as Christ is united with his Church.

[Marriage was ordained that husband and wife
may comfort and help each other,
living faithfully together in plenty and in need,

in sorrow and in joy.
It is intended that with delight and tenderness
they may know each other in love,
and through the joy of their bodily union
they may strengthen the union of their hearts and lives.

It is intended that they may be blessed
in the children they may have,
in caring for them and in bringing them up
in accordance with God's will
to his praise and glory.

In marriage husband and wife begin a new life together in the community.
It is a permanent commitment that all should honour.
It must not be undertaken carelessly, lightly or selfishly,
but by God's help, with reverence, responsibility,
respect and the promise to be faithful.]

You now wish to affirm your desire to live together as followers of Christ, and you have come to him, the fountain of grace, that strengthened by the prayers of the Church, you may be enabled to fulfil your marriage vows in love and faithfulness.

A hymn may be sung.

THE COLLECT

The minister says
God our Father,
you have taught us through your Son
that love is the fulfilling of the law.
Grant to your servants that, loving one another,
they may continue in your love until their lives' end:
through Jesus Christ our Lord. **Amen.**

Proclaiming and Receiving the Word

One or more readings from the Scriptures. When there is Holy Communion there are at least two readings, of which the final one is the Gospel.

THE SERMON

A hymn may be sung.

The Dedication

The husband and wife face the minister, who says
.... and .... you have committed yourselves to each other in marriage,
and your marriage is recognised by law.
The Church of Christ understands marriage to be,
in the will of God,
the union of a man and a woman,
for better, for worse,
for richer, for poorer,
in sickness and in health,
to love and to cherish,
till parted by death.
Is this your understanding of the covenant and vow
that you have made?

Husband and wife
It is.

The minister says to the husband
.... you have taken .... to be your wife. Will you continue to love her, comfort her, honour and protect her, and forsaking all others, be faithful to her as long as you both shall live?

He answers
I will.

The minister says to the wife
.... you have taken .... to be your husband. Will you continue to love him, comfort him, honour and protect him, and forsaking all others, be faithful to him as long as you both shall live?

She answers
I will.

The minister may say as the husband and wife join their wedding-ring hands
Heavenly Father, may *these rings* be to .... and .... a symbol of unending love and faithfulness, to remind them of the vow and covenant they have made; through Jesus Christ our Lord. Amen.

The minister says to the congregation
Will you the family and friends of .... and ...., who have gathered here today, continue to support them in their marriage?

The congregation answers
We will.

The husband and wife kneel and say together
Heavenly Father,
we offer you our souls and bodies,
our thoughts and words and deeds,
our love for one another.
Unite our wills in your will,
that we may grow together
in love and peace
all the days of our life;
through Jesus Christ our Lord. Amen.

The minister may say one or both of the following:
Almighty God give you grace to persevere,
that he may complete in you
the work he has already begun;
through Jesus Christ our Lord. **Amen.**

The Lord bless you and watch over you,
the Lord make his face shine upon you
and be gracious to you,
the Lord look kindly on you and give you peace
all the days of your life. **Amen**.

A hymn may be sung.

The couple kneel at the Lord's Table.
The prayers are led by the minister or by others appointed by the minister
using the following or other suitable prayers.

For husband and wife
Lord God,
bless these your servants.
May your word be a lamp to their feet
and a light to their path;
that they may obey your will,
live in safety under your protection,
and abide in your love unto their lives' end;
through Jesus Christ our Lord. **Amen.**

Almighty God, giver of life and love,
bless .... and ...., and all others whom you have joined in marriage.
Grant them wisdom and devotion in their life together,
that each may be to the other
a strength in need, a comfort in sorrow, and a companion in joy.
So unite their wills in your will,
and their spirits in your Spirit,
that they may live and grow together in love and peace
all the days of their life;
through Jesus Christ our Lord. **Amen.**

O God, you consecrated marriage
to be a sign of the spiritual unity
between Christ and his Church:

Bless these your servants,
that they may love, honour and cherish each other
in faithfulness and patience,
in wisdom and true godliness;
that their home may be a place of blessing and peace;
through Jesus Christ our Lord,
who lives and reigns with you and the Holy Spirit,
one God, now and for ever. **Amen.**

God our Creator,
we thank you for your gift of sexual love
by which husband and wife may delight in each other,
and share with you the joy of creating new life.
By your grace may the love of .... and .... remain strong
and may they rejoice in your goodness all their days,
through Jesus Christ our Lord. **Amen.**

For the gift of children
Heavenly Father, maker of all things,
you enable us to share in your work of creation:
Bless this couple with the gift of children,
and give them grace to make their home
a place of love, security and truth,
that their children may grow up to know and love you
in your Son Jesus Christ our Lord. **Amen.**

For Christian witness in marriage
Eternal God, true and loving Father,
in marriage you make your servants one:
May their life together witness to your love
in this troubled world,
may unity overcome division,
forgiveness heal injury,
and joy triumph over sorrow;
through Jesus Christ our Lord. **Amen.**

Almighty God, our heavenly Father,
you gave marriage to be a source of blessing.
We thank you for the joys of family life.
May we know your presence and peace in our homes:
fill them with your love,
and use them for your glory;
through Jesus Christ our Lord. **Amen.**

THE PEACE

The minister says
Jesus said, A new commandment I give to you,
that you love one another:
even as I have loved you, that you also love one another. *John 13: 34*

The peace of the Lord be always with you
and also with you.

*It is appropriate that the congregation share with one another a sign of peace.
This may be introduced by the words:*
Let us offer one another a sign of peace.

A hymn may be sung.

*When Holy Communion Two is celebrated the service continues at Celebrating
at the Lord's Table on (page 208), Holy Communion One at* Lift up your
hearts ... *(page 186).*

PROPER PREFACE

We give you thanks
because you have made the union between Christ and his Church
a pattern for the marriage between husband and wife:

THE LORD'S PRAYER

If there is no celebration of Holy Communion the minister says
As our Saviour Christ has taught us, so we pray
Our Father in heaven ...

or

As our Saviour Christ has taught us, we are bold to say
Our Father, who art in heaven ...

The minister may say
The grace of our Lord Jesus Christ,
and the love of God,
and the fellowship of the Holy Spirit,
be with us all evermore. **Amen.**
or
God the Holy Trinity
make you strong in faith and love,
defend you on every side,
and guide you in truth and peace;
and the blessing of God Almighty,
the Father, the Son, and the Holy Spirit
be with you, and remain with you always. **Amen.**

1 This service is used at the discretion of the minister. It is one in which the couple, already married, wish to dedicate to God their life together. Because it is not a marriage service, no entry may be made in the register of marriages.

2 Because the marriage has already taken place, no ring is to be given or received in the course of the service.

3 All readings in Proclaiming and Receiving the Word must be from Holy Scripture.

4 The minister and the couple should together choose the readings, hymns, music and the prayers to be used in the service.

5 If Holy Communion is celebrated at this service, all communicants should be free to receive.

Ministry to those who are sick

MINISTRY TO THOSE WHO ARE SICK
AND TO OTHERS REQUIRING PARTICULAR PASTORAL CARE

NOTES

1 MEANS OF GRACE. The Lord has provided means of grace by which he touches his people with his healing love and power. These include the Scriptures, prayer, Holy Communion, the laying on of hands and anointing with oil. In administering these means of grace, the church works alongside the medical profession in continuing Christ's healing ministry.

2 HOLY COMMUNION. Christians unable to receive Communion in their local church because of illness or disability are encouraged to ask for the sacrament.

In case of need Holy Communion may be celebrated in hospital or at home. The full forms of either Holy Communion One or Two may be used or the shorter form provided on pages 442-445.

Communion is normally received in both kinds separately, but may be by intinction or in either kind. (See Canon 13 (5))

PREPARATION. Careful devotional preparation before the service is recommended to every communicant. The form provided may be used.

SPIRITUAL COMMUNION. Those who are incapable of receiving the sacrament are to be assured that, although not receiving the elements in the mouth, they are by faith partakers of the body and blood of Christ and of the benefits he conveys to us by them.

When Holy Communion is administered at hospital or at home some Ministry of the Word should be included.

3 SPIRITUAL GUIDANCE AND COUNSEL. Those with a troubled conscience who may require spiritual guidance and counsel should consult the minister and seek the benefit of absolution through the ministry of God's holy Word.

4 The experience of illness can bring a fuller realization of dependence on God. The courage, endurance and comfort which God gives can lead to a more mature Christian life.

5 In these orders the minister may substitute such singular forms for the plural when ministering to an individual as may be appropriate in the circumstances.

Preparation for Communion

For private personal use before the Service.

Jesus says: Come to me all that labour and are heavy laden, and I will refresh you. *Matthew 11: 28*

God so loved the world, that he gave his only Son, that all who believe in him should not perish, but have eternal life. *John 3: 16*

I am the bread of life. Whoever comes to me shall never be hungry and whoever believes in me shall never be thirsty. *John 6: 35*

THANKSGIVING

Thank God for all the many blessings you have received, and for all that is at present being done for you; for all doctors and nurses; (for this hospital and all who work here).

REPENTANCE

Ask God's forgiveness for the ways in which you have failed him and others.

INTERCESSION AND PETITION

Pray for all those you love:
> *(for the other patients in your ward;)*
> *(for all who will be receiving communion with you;)*
> *for all who look after you;*
> *for all in need;*
> *for yourself, that you may come closer to God and his healing power.*

Lord Jesus Christ,
you came to the poor and powerless
and gave them hope.
Come to me in this wonderful sacrament
and raise me up in love to you, for I am helpless without you.

Be calm in the knowledge that you are under the protection of Almighty God.

Holy Communion One   (*page 180*)

Or

Holy Communion Two   (*page 201*)

The following variations may be used.

The following prayer may be used in place of the Collect for Purity:
God of peace,
you teach us that in returning to you we shall be saved:
By the power of your Spirit lift us to your presence,
where quietness and confidence shall be our strength;
and where we may be still and know that you are God;
through Jesus Christ our Lord. **Amen.**

THE COLLECT
of the day may be said.

The Ministry of the Word

READINGS

One or more readings from Scripture: a gospel reading should normally be included. Readings may be those of the day or from those suggested on page 453.

PENITENCE

The priest says
If we say we have no sin, we deceive ourselves, and the truth is not in us.
If we confess our sins, God is faithful and just, and will forgive our sins
and cleanse us from all unrighteousness.   *1 John 1: 8*

Let us confess our sins.

A short pause for self-examination.
Almighty God, our heavenly Father,
we have sinned in thought and word and deed,
and in what we have left undone.
We are truly sorry, and we humbly repent.
For the sake of your Son, Jesus Christ,
have mercy on us and forgive us,
that we may walk in newness of life
to the glory of your name. Amen.

The priest says
Almighty God,
who forgives all who truly repent,
have mercy on you,
pardon and deliver you from all your sins,
confirm and strengthen you in all goodness,
and keep you in eternal life;
through Jesus Christ our Lord. **Amen.**

PRAYER

Those present may mention personal needs and thanksgivings.
The laying on of hands and/or anointing with oil may take place here or after
receiving Holy Communion (page 447).

THE GREAT THANKSGIVING

The priest takes the bread and wine.

The Lord is here.
His Spirit is with us.

Lift up your hearts.
We lift them to the Lord.

Let us give thanks to the Lord our God.
It is right to give our thanks and praise.

We give you thanks, our God and Father,
for you have created us and you sustain us.
Through your only Son Jesus Christ
you have revealed your love and your care for all your people;
you are ready to forgive and to save in time of need;
so we proclaim your glory, saying
Holy, holy, holy Lord,
God of power and might,
Heaven and earth are full of your glory.
Hosanna in the highest.

Our Lord Jesus Christ,
on the night that he was betrayed, took bread;
and when he had given thanks to you, he broke it,
and gave it to his disciples, saying:
Take, eat, this is my body which is given for you.
Do this in remembrance of me.

In the same way, after supper he took the cup;
and when he had given thanks to you,
he gave it to them, saying:
Drink this, all of you, for this is my blood of the new covenant
which is shed for you and for many
for the forgiveness of sins.
Do this, as often as you drink it,
in remembrance of me.

Therefore, Father, with this bread and this cup
we do as Christ your Son commanded:
we remember his passion and death,
we celebrate his resurrection and ascension,
and we look for the coming of his kingdom.

Accept through him our great high priest
this our sacrifice of praise and thanksgiving;
and, as we eat and drink these holy gifts,
grant by the power of the life-giving Spirit,
that we may be made one in your holy Church
and partakers of the body and blood of your Son,
that he may dwell in us and we in him:

Through the same Jesus Christ our Lord,
by whom, and with whom, and in whom,
in the unity of the Holy Spirit,
all honour and glory are yours, Almighty Father,
for ever and ever.   Amen.

THE LORD'S PRAYER
is said

The priest breaks the bread, saying
The bread which we break
is a sharing in the body of Christ.
We, being many, are one body
for we all share in the one bread.

After all have received, silence is kept for a space and the priest says
Let us pray.
Almighty God,
we thank you for feeding us with the spiritual food
of the body and blood of your Son Jesus Christ.
Through him we offer you our souls and bodies
to be a living sacrifice.
Strengthen us by the power of your Spirit
to live and work to your praise and glory. Amen.

The peace of God, which passes all understanding,
keep your heart and mind
in the knowledge and love of God,
and of his Son Jesus Christ our Lord;
and the blessing of God Almighty,
the Father, the Son, and the Holy Spirit,
be with you and remain with you always. **Amen.**

Penitence and Reconciliation

Those who feel their conscience troubled in any way should be encouraged to open their heart on the matter.

The minister says
If we say we have no sin, we deceive ourselves and the truth is not in us. If we confess our sins, God is faithful and just, and will forgive us our sins and cleanse us from all unrighteousness. *1 John 1: 8*

In this faith make your humble confession to Almighty God.

The following prayer of confession may be used.
Almighty God, our heavenly Father,
I have sinned against you and against my neighbour
in thought and word and deed,
through my own deliberate fault, especially ...
I am truly sorry, and repent of all my sins.
For the sake of your Son our Lord Jesus Christ,
who died for me, have mercy on me
and forgive me all that is past,
that I may serve you in newness of life
to the glory of your Name. Amen.

A priest, if one is present, pronounces this absolution:
Almighty God, who forgives all who truly repent,
have mercy on you,
pardon and deliver you from all your sins,
confirm and strengthen you in all goodness,
and keep you in eternal life;
through Jesus Christ our Lord. **Amen.**

A deacon may use the Comfortable Words on page 185 and a suitable prayer.

The Laying on of Hands

At the laying on of hands for healing these or other suitable words are used:
In the name of our Lord Jesus Christ
who laid his hands on the sick
that they might be healed,
I lay my hands upon you ....

May almighty God,
Father, Son, and Holy Spirit
make you whole in body, mind and spirit,
give you light and peace,
and keep you in eternal life. **Amen.**

The laying on of hands may also take place during prayer, absolution or blessing.

Anointing with Oil

This form may be used or the provision in A Celebration of Wholeness and Healing on page 462.

If oil is to be consecrated the bishop or priest says
Heavenly Father, giver of life and salvation,
sanctify this oil for the healing of the sick.
Grant that those who in faith and repentance
receive this ministry
may, by the power of the Holy Spirit, be made whole;
through our Lord and Saviour Jesus Christ. **Amen.**

The minister says
Our Lord Jesus Christ went about preaching the Gospel and healing the sick. He commanded his disciples to lay hands on the sick that they might be healed, and Saint James writes, 'Is any among you sick? Let him call for the elders of the church, and let them pray over him, anointing him with oil in the Name of the Lord; and the prayer of faith will save the sick man, and the Lord will raise him up, and if he has committed any sins he will be forgiven.'

In continuing this ministry we will lay hands on ....
and anoint *him* with oil,
praying that the Lord will grant healing and restoration
and forgiveness according to his loving and gracious will.

After laying hands on the head of the sick person the priest, having dipped his thumb in the oil, anoints the person on the forehead, saying
In the faith of Jesus Christ,
we lay our hands upon you and anoint you,
in the name of the Father, and of the Son, and of the Holy Spirit. **Amen.**

Others present may lay on hands and anoint the sick person saying only
In the name of the Father, and of the Son, and of the Holy Spirit. **Amen.**

The minister says

As you are outwardly anointed with this oil
so may our heavenly Father grant you
the inward anointing of the Holy Spirit;
of his great mercy release you from suffering,
and restore you to wholeness and strength.
May he deliver you from all evil,
preserve you in all goodness,
and keep you in eternal life;
through Jesus Christ our Lord.   **Amen.**

Prayers

I believe and trust in God the Father
who made the world.
I believe and trust in his Son Jesus Christ
who redeemed mankind.
I believe and trust in the Holy Spirit
who gives life to the people of God.

SAINT PATRICK'S BREASTPLATE

Christ be with me, Christ within me,
Christ behind me, Christ before me,
Christ beside me, Christ to win me,
Christ to comfort and restore me,
Christ beneath me, Christ above me,
Christ in quiet, Christ in danger,
Christ in hearts of all that love me,
Christ in mouth of friend and stranger.

PRAYER OF SAINT RICHARD OF CHICHESTER

Lord Jesus Christ, we thank you
for all the benefits you have won for us,
for all the pains and insults you have borne for us.
Most merciful redeemer, friend and brother,
may we know you more clearly,
love you more dearly,
and follow you more nearly, day by day.

GOD BE IN MY HEAD

God be in my head, and in my understanding;
God be in my eyes, and in my looking;
God be in my mouth, and in my speaking;
God be in my heart, and in my thinking;
God be at my end, and at my departing.

Lord Jesus Christ, Son of God,
have mercy on me, a sinner.

Heavenly Father,
watch over those we love.
Remove all anxious fears from them.
Teach us to know that you are always near,
and that we are one in you for ever;
through Jesus Christ our Lord.

Almighty God,
you know our anxieties and fears.
Help me to cast all my cares on you,
and to know that you love me.
Give me peace of mind, and sure trust in you,
through Jesus Christ our Lord.

Lord Jesus Christ,
be near me in my time of weariness and pain
and sustain me by your grace.
Heal me according to your will,
and hold me in eternal life, my Lord and my God.

Lord Jesus Christ,
you took children in your arms and blessed them.
Hold .... in your love.
Fill .... with your peace.
Heal .... according to your will;
for your name's sake.

Lord Jesus,
by the loneliness of your suffering on the cross
be near to me in my need.
Banish my fears, increase my faith;
hold me in your love and fill me with your peace;
for your name's sake.

FOR DOCTORS, NURSES AND ALL WHO SHARE IN HEALING

Almighty God,
we pray you to continue Christ's healing work
in our hospitals and homes.
Give skill, understanding and sympathy
to all who minister to the sick,
and strengthen them in their work of mercy.

FOR THE CHURCH'S MINISTRY TO THOSE WHO ARE SICK

Bless, O Lord God, your Church in its ministry to those who are sick,
that it may fulfil your holy will and purpose,
and use all means of grace for the healing of your people;
and grant to those who desire your healing
true penitence, full pardon and perfect peace;
for your dear Son's sake, Jesus Christ our Lord.

THANKSGIVING AFTER TREATMENT OR SURGERY

Merciful Lord,
your compassion does not fail,
and your mercies are new every morning.
We thank you that you have given ....
relief from pain and hope of renewed health.
Continue your gracious work of healing
and restore .... to health, to serve you in gratitude and joy;
through Jesus Christ our Lord.

All praise and glory are yours, O Lord our God,
for you have called us to serve you in love.
Bless all who have grown old in your service.
Strengthen your servant .... with your Holy Spirit,
and keep *him* firm and serene in hope;
through Jesus Christ our Lord.

EVENING PRAYERS

Lighten our darkness, O Lord, we pray;
and in your great mercy defend us
from all perils and dangers of this night;
for the love of your only Son,
our Saviour Jesus Christ.

Be with us, merciful God, and protect us
through the silent hours of this night,
that we who are wearied
by the changes and chances of this fleeting world
may rest upon your eternal changelessness;
through Jesus Christ our Lord.

Save us, O Lord, while waking,
and guard us while sleeping,
that awake we may watch with Christ,
and asleep we may rest in peace.

Readings

PSALMS

Penitence	*86: 1-7 (page 691)*
Prayer	*130 (page 747)*
Thanksgiving	*103: 1-3 (page 709)*
Thanksgiving	*145: 14-16 (page 760)*

NEW TESTAMENT

God's Promises	*John 14: 18-21*
God's Love	*1 John 4: 7-12*
The Beatitudes	*Matthew 5: 1-10*
The Comforter	*John 15: 15-17*
The True Vine	*John 15: 1-5*

Preparation for Death

This commendation may be led by the priest or by any other Christian person, if possible with the family and friends of the dying person. All or part of the order may be used.

Who can separate us from the love of Christ? *Romans 8: 35*

We shall always be with the Lord. *1 Thessalonians 4: 17*

Come, you that are blessed by my Father,
inherit the kingdom prepared for you. *Matthew 25: 34*

Into your hands, O Lord, I commend my spirit. *Psalm 31: 5*

Lord Jesus, receive my spirit. *Acts 7: 59*

READING

Psalm 23 (page 616 or 468)
or
Psalm 121 (page 743)
or
John 14: 1-7,27
or
Romans 8: 31-35,37-39
Other readings may be chosen from those on page 453.

PRAYER OF COMMENDATION

The commendation may be accompanied by making the sign of the cross on the forehead of the dying person, recalling his or her baptism into Christ.
One of the following is used:

Almighty God,
with whom do live the spirits of those who depart in the Lord:
We humbly commend the soul of your servant ....
our dear *brother* into your hands
as into the hands of a faithful creator and most merciful Saviour.
Forgive *him* all *his* sins and receive *him* to yourself;
through Jesus Christ your only Son our Lord,
who lives and reigns with you and the Holy Spirit,
one God, now and for ever. **Amen.**
or

Lord Jesus Christ, Son of the living God,
remember your last hour
when on the cross you gave up your spirit to the Father.
Set your passion, cross and death
between your judgment and us
as we entrust .... to you.
We pray you to free us all from the pains of death
and from the wounds of sin;
that death may be the gate to life
and to unending fellowship with you;
for you are the resurrection and the life,
and to you be the glory for ever. **Amen.**

or

.... our companion in faith,
the Lord who gave you to us is taking you to himself.
He who died for you and rose again from death
is calling you to enjoy the peace of the heavenly city
in which there is neither sorrow nor pain,
and where weakness is transformed into strength.
He is calling you to see him face to face
that you may be made like him for ever.
He comes to welcome you with angels and archangels
and all his faithful people,
that you may know in its fulness the fellowship of the Holy Spirit.
Enter into the joy of your Lord and give glory to him,
Father, Son, and Holy Spirit. **Amen.**

or

Go forth upon your journey from this world, O Christian soul,
in the name of God the Father almighty who created you;
in the name of Jesus Christ who suffered death for you;
in the name of the Holy Spirit who sanctifies you;
in communion with the blessed saints,
and aided by angels and archangels
and all the armies of the heavenly host.
May your rest this day be in peace
and your dwelling place in the heavenly Jerusalem. **Amen.**

NUNC DIMITTIS *The Song of Simeon*

1 Lord, now you let your servant go in peace, ▪
  your word has been fulfilled.

2 My own eyes have seen the salvation ▪
  which you have prepared in the sight of every people.

3 A light to reveal you to the nations ▪
  and the glory of your people Israel.

  Glory to the Father, and to the Son, ▪
  and to the Holy Spirit;
  as it was in the beginning, is now, ▪
  and shall be for ever. Amen.

THE LORD'S PRAYER

THE BLESSING
when a priest is present

God give you grace
to share the inheritance of his saints in glory;
and the blessing of God almighty,
the Father, the Son, and the Holy Spirit,
be with you and remain with you always. **Amen.**

or

THE GRACE

The grace of our Lord Jesus Christ,
and the love of God,
and the fellowship of the Holy Spirit,
be with us all evermore. **Amen.**

A CELEBRATION OF WHOLENESS AND HEALING

The Gathering of God's People

In the name of Christ, we welcome you.
We have been called out of darkness into God's marvellous light.
Grace and peace be with you
and also with you.

The love of God has been poured into our hearts,
through the Holy Spirit who has been given to us:
we dwell in him and he lives in us.

Give thanks to the Lord and call upon his name;
make known his deeds among the peoples.

Sing to God, sing praises to his name;
and speak of all his marvellous works.

Holy, holy, holy is the Lord God almighty;
who was and is and is to come.

Heavenly Father,
you anointed your Son Jesus Christ
with the Holy Spirit and with power
to bring to us the blessings of your kingdom.
Anoint your Church with the same Holy Spirit,
that we who share in his suffering and victory
may bear witness to the gospel of salvation;
through Jesus Christ, your Son our Lord,
who is alive and reigns with you in the unity of the Holy Spirit,
one God, now and for ever. **Amen.**

Proclaiming and Receiving the Word

When the Gospel is announced the reader says
Hear the Gospel of our Saviour Christ according to ....
Glory to you, Lord Jesus Christ.

At the end
This is the Gospel of the Lord.
Praise to you, Lord Jesus Christ.

THE SERMON

Prayer and Penitence

PRAYERS OF INTERCESSION

God the Father, your will for all people is health and salvation.
We praise and bless you, Lord.

God the Son, you came that we might have life,
and might have it more abundantly.
We praise and bless you, Lord.

God the Holy Spirit, you make our bodies
the temple of your presence.
We praise and bless you, Lord.

Holy Trinity, one God, in you we live and move and have our being.
We praise and bless you, Lord.

Lord, grant your healing grace to all
who are sick, injured or disabled,
that they may be made whole.
Hear us, Lord of life.

Grant to all who are lonely, anxious or depressed
a knowledge of your will and an awareness of your presence.
Hear us, Lord of life.

Grant to all who minister to those who are suffering,
wisdom and skill, sympathy and patience.
Hear us, Lord of life.

Mend broken relationships, and restore to those in distress
soundness of mind and serenity of spirit.
Hear us, Lord of life.

Sustain and support those who seek your guidance
and lift up all who are brought low by the trials of this life.
Hear us, Lord of life.

Grant peace and a holy death to those who are dying,
and uphold by the grace and consolation of your Holy Spirit
those who are bereaved.
Hear us, Lord of life.

Restore to wholeness whatever is broken by human sin,
in our lives, in our nation, and in the world.
Hear us, Lord of life.

You are the Lord, you perform mighty wonders.
You have declared your power among the peoples.

With you, Lord, is the well of life
and in your light do we see light.

Hear us, Lord of life,
heal us, and make us whole.

Let us be silent before God.

A period of silence follows

O Lord our God, accept the fervent prayers of your people;
in the multitude of your mercies look with compassion
upon us and all who turn to you for help;
for you are gracious, O lover of souls,
and to you we give glory, Father, Son, and Holy Spirit,
now and for ever. **Amen.**

The gospel calls us to turn away from sin and be faithful to Christ.
As we offer ourselves to him in penitence and faith,
we renew our confidence and trust in his mercy.

Cast your burden upon the Lord and he will sustain you. *Psalm 55: 22*

In returning and rest you shall be saved.
In quietness and trust shall be your strength. *Isaiah 30: 15*

There follows a period of silent reflection and self-examination.

You raise the dead to life in the Spirit:
Lord, have mercy.
Lord, have mercy.

You bring pardon and peace to the sinner:
Christ, have mercy.
Christ, have mercy.

You bring light to those in darkness:
Lord, have mercy.
Lord, have mercy.

Or

CONFESSION

Almighty God, our heavenly Father,
we have sinned in thought and word and deed,
and in what we have left undone.
We are truly sorry and we humbly repent.
For the sake of your Son, Jesus Christ,
have mercy on us and forgive us,
that we may walk in newness of life
to the glory of your name. Amen

The priest says
God, the Father of mercies,
has reconciled the world to himself
through the death and resurrection of his Son, Jesus Christ,
not holding our sins against us,
but sending his Holy Spirit to shed abroad his love among us.
By the ministry of reconciliation entrusted by Christ to his Church,
receive his pardon and peace
to stand before him in his strength alone
this day and for evermore. **Amen.**

Laying on of Hands and Anointing

Oil for anointing may be brought to the priest.

Our help is in the name of the Lord
who has made heaven and earth.

Blessed be the name of the Lord:
now and for ever. Amen.

Blessed are you, sovereign God, gentle and merciful,
creator of heaven and earth.
Your Word brought light out of darkness,
and daily your Spirit renews the face of the earth.
When we turned away from you in sin,
your anointed Son took our nature and entered our suffering
to bring your healing to those in weakness and distress.
He broke the power of evil and set us free from sin and death
that we might become partakers of his glory.
His apostles anointed the sick in your name,
bringing wholeness and joy to a broken world.
By your grace renewed each day
you continue the gifts of healing in your Church
that your people may praise your name for ever.
If oil is to be consecrated these words are included:
[By the power of your Spirit may your blessing rest

on those who are anointed with this oil in your name;
may they be made whole in body, mind and spirit.]

Hear the prayer we offer for all your people.
Remember in your mercy those for whom we pray:
heal the sick, raise the fallen, strengthen the fainthearted
and enfold in your love the fearful and those who have no hope.
In the fulness of time complete your gracious work.
Reconcile all things in Christ and make them new.
Restore us in your image, renew us in your love,
that we may serve you as sons and daughters in your kingdom;
through your anointed Son, Jesus Christ, our Lord,
to whom with you and the Holy Spirit
we lift our voices of thanks and praise:
Blessed be God, our strength and our salvation,
now and for ever. Amen.

The laying on of hands is administered, using these or other suitable words:
In the name of God and trusting in his might alone,
receive Christ's healing touch to make you whole.

May Christ bring you wholeness of body, mind and spirit,
deliver you from every evil,
and give you his peace. **Amen.**

Anointing may be administered. The priest says
...., I anoint you in the name of God who gives you life.
Receive Christ's forgiveness, his healing and his love.

May the Father of our Lord Jesus Christ
grant you the riches of his grace, his wholeness and his peace. **Amen.**

After the laying on of hands and anointing, the presiding minister says
The almighty Lord,
who is a strong tower for all who put their trust in him,
whom all things in heaven, on earth and under the earth obey,
be now and evermore your defence.
May you believe and trust that the only name under heaven
given for health and salvation
is the name of our Lord Jesus Christ. **Amen.**

In confidence let us pray to the Father
for the coming of the kingdom among us:
Our Father in heaven, hallowed be your name ...

If there is to be Holy Communion see page 443.

Going Out as God's People

God who said: 'Let light shine out of darkness',
has caused his light to shine within us

to give the light of the knowledge of the glory of God
revealed in the face of Jesus Christ.

We have this treasure in earthen vessels
to show that the power belongs to God.

God has made us one in Christ.
He has set his seal upon us
and, as a pledge of what is to come,
has given the Spirit to dwell in our hearts.

The peace of the Lord be always with you
and also with you.

A minister says
Go in the joy and peace of Christ.
Thanks be to God.

A sign of peace may be exchanged.
The ministers and people depart.

Funeral Services

THE BURIAL OF THE DEAD

which may be used at the entrance to the churchyard, as the coffin is taken either into the church, or towards the grave.

The minister says

I am the resurrection and the life, saith the Lord: he that believeth in me, though he were dead, yet shall he live: and whosoever liveth and believeth in me shall never die. *John 11: 25,26*

I know that my Redeemer liveth, and that he shall stand at the latter day upon the earth: I myself shall see him with my own eyes. *Job 19: 25,27a*

We brought nothing into this world, and it is certain we can carry nothing out. The Lord gave, and the Lord hath taken away; blessed be the name of the Lord. *1 Timothy 6: 7; Job 1: 21*

Other sentences from page 490 may be used as required.

THE PSALM

Psalm 39 Dixi, custodiam

1   I said, I will take heed to my ways, ▪
     that I offend not in my tongue.
2   I will keep my mouth as it were with a bridle, ▪
     while the ungodly is in my sight.
3   I held my tongue, and spake nothing: ▪
     I kept silence, yea, even from good words;
          but it was pain and grief to me.
4   My heart was hot within me,
          and while I was thus musing the fire kindled ▪
     and at the last I spake with my tongue;
5   Lord, let me know mine end, and the number of my days, ▪
     that I may be certified how long I have to live.

6 Behold, thou hast made my days as it were a span long, ▪
and mine age is even as nothing in respect of thee;
    and verily every man living is altogether vanity.

7 For man walketh in a vain shadow, and disquieteth himself in vain; ▪
he heapeth up riches, and cannot tell who shall gather them.

8 And now, Lord, what is my hope? ▪
Truly my hope is even in thee.

9 Deliver me from all mine offences ▪
and make me not a rebuke unto the foolish.

10 I became dumb, and opened not my mouth, ▪
for it was thy doing.

11 Take thy plague away from me; ▪
I am even consumed by the means of thy heavy hand.

12 When thou with rebukes dost chasten man for sin,
    thou makest his beauty to consume away,
    like as it were a moth fretting a garment; ▪
every man therefore is but vanity.

13 Hear my prayer, O Lord, and with thine ears consider my calling; ▪
hold not thy peace at my tears.

14 For I am a stranger with thee, ▪
and a sojourner, as all my fathers were.

15 O spare me a little, that I may recover my strength, ▪
before I go hence, and be no more seen.
    Glory be to the Father, ▪
    and to the Son and to the Holy Spirit;
    as it was in the beginning, ▪
    is now, and ever shall be, world without end. Amen.

or

Psalm 90 *Domine, refugium*

1 Lord, thou hast been our refuge ▪
from one generation to another.

2 Before the mountains were brought forth,
    or ever the earth and the world were made, ▪
thou art God from everlasting, and world without end.

3 Thou turnest man to destruction; ▪
again thou sayest, Come again, ye children of men.

4   For a thousand years in thy sight are but as yesterday, ▪
    seeing that is past as a watch in the night.

5   As soon as thou scatterest them, they are even as a sleep, ▪
    and fade away suddenly like the grass.

6   In the morning it is green, and groweth up; ▪
    but in the evening it is cut down, dried up, and withered.

7   For we consume away in thy displeasure, ▪
    and are afraid at thy wrathful indignation.

8   Thou hast set our misdeeds before thee ▪
    and our secret sins in the light of thy countenance.

9   For when thou art angry all our days are gone; ▪
    we bring our years to an end, as it were a tale that is told.

10 The days of our age are threescore years and ten;
        and though men be so strong that they come to fourscore years, ▪
    yet is their strength then but labour and sorrow;
        so soon passeth it away, and we are gone.

11 But who regardeth the power of thy wrath; ▪
    for even thereafter as a man feareth, so is thy displeasure.

12 So teach us to number our days ▪
    that we may apply our hearts unto wisdom.

13 Turn thee again, O Lord, at the last, ▪
    and be gracious unto thy servants.

14 O satisfy us with thy mercy, and that soon, ▪
    so shall we rejoice and be glad all the days of our life.

15 Comfort us again now after the time that thou hast plagued us, ▪
    and for the years wherein we have suffered adversity.

16 Show thy servants thy work ▪
    and their children thy glory.

17 And the glorious majesty of the Lord our God be upon us; ▪
    prosper thou the work of our hands upon us,
        O prosper thou our handywork.
        Glory be to the Father ...

or

Psalm 23 Dominus regit me

1   The Lord is my shepherd; ▪
    therefore can I lack nothing.

2　He shall feed me in a green pasture ▪
　　and lead me forth beside the waters of comfort.

3　He shall convert my soul ▪
　　and bring me forth in the paths of righteousness,
　　　　for his Name's sake.

4　Yea, though I walk through the valley of the shadow of death,
　　　　I will fear no evil; ▪
　　for thou art with me; thy rod and thy staff comfort me.

5　Thou shalt prepare a table before me against them that trouble me; ▪
　　thou hast anointed my head with oil, and my cup shall be full.

6　But thy loving-kindness and mercy shall follow me
　　　　all the days of my life, ▪
　　and I will dwell in the house of the Lord for ever.
　　　　Glory be to the Father ...

or

Psalm 103 Benedic, anima mea

1　Praise the Lord, O my soul, ▪
　　and all that is within me praise his holy Name.

2　Praise the Lord, O my soul, ▪
　　and forget not all his benefits;

3　Who forgiveth all thy sin ▪
　　and healeth all thine infirmities;

4　Who saveth thy life from destruction ▪
　　and crowneth thee with mercy and loving-kindness;

5　Who satisfieth thy mouth with good things, ▪
　　making thee young and lusty as an eagle.

6　The Lord executeth righteousness and judgment ▪
　　for all them that are oppressed with wrong.

7　He showed his ways unto Moses, ▪
　　his works unto the children of Israel.

8　The Lord is full of compassion and mercy, ▪
　　long-suffering, and of great goodness.

9　He will not alway be chiding, ▪
　　neither keepeth he his anger for ever.

10　He hath not dealt with us after our sins, ▪
　　nor rewarded us according to our wickednesses.

11 For look how high the heaven is in comparison of the earth, ▪
    so great is his mercy also toward them that fear him.

12 Look how wide also the east is from the west, ▪
    so far hath he set our sins from us.

13 Yea, like as a father pitieth his own children, ▪
    even so is the Lord merciful unto them that fear him.

14 For he knoweth whereof we are made; ▪
    he remembereth that we are but dust.

15 The days of man are but as grass, ▪
    for he flourisheth as a flower of the field.

16 For as soon as the wind goeth over it, it is gone, ▪
    and the place thereof shall know it no more.

17 But the merciful goodness of the Lord endureth for ever and ever
        upon them that fear him, ▪
    and his righteousness upon children's children;

18 Even upon such as keep his covenant ▪
    and think upon his commandments to do them.

19 The Lord hath prepared his seat in heaven, ▪
    and his kingdom ruleth over all.

20 O praise the Lord, ye angels of his, ye that excel in strength, ▪
    ye that fulfil his commandment, and hearken unto the voice
        of his words.

21 O praise the Lord, all ye his hosts, ▪
    ye servants of his that do his pleasure.

22 O speak good of the Lord, all ye works of his,
        in all places of his dominion; ▪
    praise thou the Lord, O my soul.
        Glory be to the Father ...

Versions of the above psalms in the Church Hymnal may be used.

THE MINISTRY OF THE WORD

1 Corinthians 15: 20-58

Now is Christ risen from the dead, and become the first-fruits of them
that slept. For since by man came death, by man came also the resurrection of the dead. For as in Adam all die, even so in Christ shall all be
made alive. But every man in his own order: Christ the first-fruits; after-

ward they that are Christ's, at his coming. Then cometh the end, when he shall have delivered up the kingdom to God, even the Father; when he shall have put down all rule and all authority and power. For he must reign, till he hath put all enemies under his feet. The last enemy that shall be destroyed is death.

[For, He hath put all things under his feet. But when he saith, All things are put under him, it is manifest that he is excepted which did put all things under him. And when all things shall be subdued unto him, then shall the Son also himself be subject unto him that put all things under him, that God may be all in all. Else what shall they do which are baptized for the dead, if the dead rise not at all? Why are they then baptized for the dead? and why stand we in jeopardy every hour? I protest by your rejoicing which I have in Christ Jesus our Lord, I die daily. If after the manner of men I have fought with beasts at Ephesus, what advantageth it me, if the dead rise not? Let us eat and drink, for tomorrow we die. Be not deceived: Evil communications corrupt good manners. Awake to righteousness, and sin not; for some have not the knowledge of God: I speak this to your shame.]

But someone may say, How are the dead raised up? and with what body do they come? How foolish! That which thou sowest is not quickened, except it die: and that which thou sowest, thou sowest not that body that shall be, but bare grain, it may chance of wheat, or of some other grain; but God giveth it a body, as it hath pleased him, and to every seed his own body. [All flesh is not the same flesh: but there is one kind of flesh of men, another flesh of beasts, another of fishes, and another of birds. There are also celestial bodies, and bodies terrestrial: but the glory of the celestial is one, and the glory of the terrestrial is another. There is one glory of the sun, and another glory of the moon, and another glory of the stars; for one star differeth from another star in glory.]

So also is the resurrection of the dead. It is sown in corruption; it is raised in incorruption: it is sown in dishonour; it is raised in glory: it is sown in weakness; it is raised in power: it is sown a natural body; it is raised a spiritual body. There is a natural body, and there is a spiritual body. [And so it is written, The first man Adam was made a living soul; the last Adam was made a quickening spirit. Howbeit that was not first which is spiritual, but that which is natural; and afterward that which is spiritual. The first man is of the earth, earthy: the second man is the Lord from heaven. As is the earthy, such are they that are earthy: and as is the heavenly, such are they also that are heavenly. And as we have borne the image of the earthy, we shall also bear the image of the heavenly.

Now this I say, brethren, that flesh and blood cannot inherit the kingdom of God; neither doth corruption inherit incorruption.]

Behold, I show you a mystery: We shall not all sleep, but we shall all be changed, in a moment, in the twinkling of an eye, at the last trump: for the trumpet shall sound, and the dead shall be raised incorruptible, and we shall be changed. For this corruptible must put on incorruption, and this mortal must put on immortality. So when this corruptible shall have put on incorruption, and this mortal shall have put on immortality, then shall be brought to pass the saying that is written, Death is swallowed up in victory. O death, where is thy sting? O grave, where is thy victory? The sting of death is sin; and the strength of sin is the law: but thanks be to God, which giveth us the victory through our Lord Jesus Christ. Therefore, my beloved, be ye steadfast, unmoveable, always abounding in the work of the Lord, forasmuch as ye know that your labour is not in vain in the Lord.

Verses enclosed by square brackets [ ] may be omitted.

or

1 Thessalonians 4: 13-18

I would not have you to be ignorant, brethren, concerning them which are asleep, that ye sorrow not, even as others which have no hope. For if we believe that Jesus died and rose again, even so them also which sleep in Jesus will God bring with him. For this we say unto you by the word of the Lord, that we which are alive and remain unto the coming of the Lord shall not prevent them which are asleep. For the Lord himself shall descend from heaven with a shout, with the voice of the archangel, and with the trump of God: and the dead in Christ shall rise first: Then we which are alive and remain shall be caught up together with them in the clouds, to meet the Lord in the air: and so shall we ever be with the Lord. Wherefore comfort one another with these words.

Other readings from the list on page 484 may be preferred.
Other readings from the list on page 484 may be preferred.
If there is a Sermon it is preached here.

Grant, O Lord, that as we are baptized into the death of thy blessed Son our Saviour Jesus Christ, so by continual mortifying our corrupt affections we may be buried with him; and that through the grave, and gate of death, we may pass to our joyful resurrection; for his merits, who died, and was buried, and rose again for us, thy Son Jesus Christ our Lord. **Amen.**

Grant, O Lord, to all who are bereaved, the spirit of faith and courage, that they may have strength to meet the days to come with steadfastness and patience, not sorrowing as those without hope, but in thankful remembrance of thy great goodness in past years, and in the sure expectation of a joyful reunion in the heavenly places; and this we ask in the Name of Jesus Christ our Lord. **Amen.**

The minister goes before the coffin as it is carried to the grave.

THE COMMITTAL

Man that is born of a woman hath but a short time to live, and is full of misery. He cometh up, and is cut down, like a flower; he fleeth as it were a shadow, and never continueth in one stay.

In the midst of life we are in death: of whom may we seek for succour, but of thee, O Lord, who for our sins art justly displeased?

Yet, O Lord God most holy, O Lord most mighty, O holy and most merciful Saviour, deliver us not into the bitter pains of eternal death.

Thou knowest, Lord, the secrets of our hearts; shut not thy merciful ears to our prayers; but spare us, Lord most holy, O God most mighty, O holy and merciful Saviour, thou most worthy Judge eternal, suffer us not, at our last hour, for any pains of death, to fall from thee.

While the earth is cast upon the body by some standing by, the minister says,

Forasmuch as it hath pleased Almighty God to take unto himself the soul of our dear *brother* ...., here departed: we therefore commit *his* body to the ground; earth to earth, ashes to ashes, dust to dust; in sure and certain hope of the resurrection to eternal life, through our Lord Jesus Christ; who shall change our mortal body, that it may be like unto his glorious body, according to the mighty working, whereby he is able to subdue all things to himself.

Scripture says: I, John, heard a voice from heaven, saying unto me, Write this, From henceforth blessed are the dead which die in the Lord; even so, saith the Spirit, for they rest from their labours.   *Revelation 14: 13*

PRAYERS AFTER THE COMMITTAL

The minister says

Lord, have mercy upon us.

Christ, have mercy upon us.

Lord, have mercy upon us.

Our Father, who art in heaven,
   hallowed be thy name,
   thy kingdom come,
   thy will be done,
      on earth as it is in heaven.
Give us this day our daily bread.
   And forgive us our trespasses
   as we forgive those who trespass against us.
And lead us not into temptation,
   but deliver us from evil. Amen.

Almighty God, with whom do live the spirits of them that depart hence in the Lord, and with whom the souls of the faithful, after they are delivered from the burden of the flesh, are in joy and felicity; We bless thy holy Name for all thy servants departed this life in thy faith and fear; beseeching thee that it may please thee, of thy gracious goodness, shortly to accomplish the number of thine elect, and to hasten thy kingdom; that we, with all those that are departed in the true faith of thy holy Name, may have our perfect consummation and bliss, both in body and soul, in thy eternal and everlasting glory; through Jesus Christ our Lord. **Amen.**

O merciful God, the Father of our Lord Jesus Christ, who is the resurrection and the life; in whom whosoever believeth shall live, though he die; and whosoever liveth, and believeth in him, shall not die eternally; who also hath taught us, by his holy Apostle Saint Paul, not to be sorry, as men without hope, for them that sleep in him; We meekly beseech thee,

O Father, to raise us from the death of sin unto the life of righteousness; that, when we shall depart this life, we may rest in him, as our hope is this our *brother* doth; and that, at the general resurrection in the last day, we may be found acceptable in thy sight; and receive that blessing, which thy well-beloved Son shall then pronounce to all that love and fear thee: Grant this, we beseech thee, O merciful Father, through Jesus Christ our Mediator and Redeemer. **Amen.**

The Prayers after the Committal (above) may be said in the church before the coffin leaves.

The grace of our Lord Jesus Christ,
and the love of God,
and the fellowship of the Holy Spirit,
be with us all evermore. **Amen.**

When they come to the grave, if the burial ground is not consecrated, the minister shall say

O Lord Jesus Christ, who by thy burial didst sanctify an earthly sepulchre: Vouchsafe, we beseech thee, to bless and hallow this grave; that it may be a peaceful resting-place for the body of thy servant; through thy mercy, O Blessed Saviour, who livest and reignest with the Father and the Holy Spirit, one God, world without end. **Amen.**

Hymns may be sung at appropriate places in this order of service.

THE BURIAL OF CHILDREN

As pages 466.

Psalm 23 Dominus regit me

1 The Lord is my shepherd; ▪
   therefore can I lack nothing.

2 He shall feed me in a green pasture ▪
   and lead me forth beside the waters of comfort.

3 He shall convert my soul ▪
   and bring me forth in the paths of righteousness,
       for his Name's sake.

4 Yea, though I walk through the valley of the shadow of death,
       I will fear no evil; ▪
   for thou art with me; thy rod and thy staff comfort me.

5 Thou shalt prepare a table before me against them that trouble me; ▪
   thou hast anointed my head with oil, and my cup shall be full.

6 But thy loving-kindness and mercy shall follow me
       all the days of my life, ▪
   and I will dwell in the house of the Lord for ever.

       Glory be to the Father, ▪
       and to the Son and to the Holy Spirit;
       as it was in the beginning, ▪
       is now, and ever shall be, world without end. Amen.

THE MINISTRY OF THE WORD

1 Thessalonians 4: 13-18

I would not have you to be ignorant, brethren, concerning them which are asleep, that ye sorrow not, even as others which have no hope. For if we believe that Jesus died and rose again, even so them also which sleep in Jesus will God bring with him. For this we say unto you by the word of the Lord, that we which are alive and remain unto the coming of the Lord shall not prevent them which are asleep. For the Lord himself shall descend from heaven with a shout, with the voice of the archangel, and with the trump of God: and the dead in Christ shall rise first: Then we which are alive and remain shall be caught up together with them in the clouds, to meet the Lord in the air: and so shall we ever be with the Lord. Wherefore comfort one another with these words.

or   *Revelation 21: 3-7*

I heard a great voice out of heaven, saying, Behold, the tabernacle of God is with men, and he will dwell with them, and they shall be his people, and God himself shall be with them, and be their God. And God shall wipe away all tears from their eyes; and there shall be no more death, neither sorrow, nor crying, neither shall there be any more pain: for the former things are passed away. And he that sat upon the throne said, Behold, I make all things new. And he said unto me, Write: for these words are true and faithful.

Other readings from the list on page 506 may be preferred.
If there is a Sermon it is preached here.

PRAYERS

Grant, O Lord, to all who are bereaved, the spirit of faith and courage, that they may have strength to meet the days to come with steadfastness and patience, not sorrowing as those without hope, but in thankful remembrance of thy great goodness in past years, and in the sure expectation of a joyful reunion in the heavenly places; and this we ask in the Name of Jesus Christ our Lord. **Amen.**

Appropriate prayers adapted from those on pages 510-513 may be added.
The minister goes before the coffin as it is carried to the grave.

THE COMMITTAL

Man that is born of a woman hath but a short time to live, and is full of misery. He cometh up, and is cut down, like a flower; he fleeth as it were a shadow, and never continueth in one stay.
In the midst of life we are in death: of whom may we seek for succour, but of thee, O Lord, who for our sins art justly displeased?
Yet, O Lord God most holy, O Lord most mighty, O holy and most merciful Saviour, deliver us not into the bitter pains of eternal death.
Thou knowest, Lord, the secrets of our hearts; shut not thy merciful ears to our prayers; but spare us, Lord most holy, O God most mighty, O holy and merciful Saviour, thou most worthy Judge eternal, suffer us not, at our last hour, for any pains of death, to fall from thee.

While the earth is cast upon the body by some standing by, the minister says

Forasmuch as it hath pleased Almighty God to take unto himself the soul of this dear child .... here departed: we therefore commit *his* body to the ground; earth to earth, ashes to ashes, dust to dust; in sure and certain hope of the resurrection to eternal life, through our Lord Jesus Christ; who shall change our mortal body, that it may be like unto his glorious body, according to the mighty working, whereby he is able to subdue all things to himself.

Then shall be said or sung

Scripture says: These are they which follow the Lamb whithersoever he goeth. And in their mouth was found no guile: for they are without fault before the throne of God. *Revelation 14: 4,5*

PRAYERS AFTER THE COMMITTAL

The minister says

Lord, have mercy upon us.
Christ, have mercy upon us.
Lord, have mercy upon us.

Our Father, who art in heaven,
hallowed be thy name,
thy kingdom come,
thy will be done,
on earth as it is in heaven.
Give us this day our daily bread.
And forgive us our trespasses
as we forgive those who trespass against us.
And lead us not into temptation,
but deliver us from evil. Amen.

O Lord Jesus Christ, who didst take little children into thine arms and bless them; Open thou our eyes, we beseech thee, that we may perceive that thou hast taken this child into the arms of thy love, and blessed *him* with the blessings of thy gracious favour; who livest and reignest with the Father and the Holy Spirit, one God, world without end. **Amen.**

O God, the fountain of life, whose ways are hidden and whose work is wonderful; who makest nothing in vain, and lovest that which thou hast made; Comfort the souls of thy servants, who by the death of this child are sore stricken and bereaved; and grant that they may so love and serve thee in this present life, that they, with *him*, may in the end obtain the fulness of thy promises, and be clothed with the perfection of glory in thy eternal kingdom; through the merits of thy Son, our Saviour Jesus Christ. **Amen**.

The Prayers after the Committal (above) may be said in the church before the coffin leaves.

The grace of our Lord Jesus Christ,
and the love of God,
and the fellowship of the Holy Spirit,
be with us all evermore. **Amen.**

THE FUNERAL SERVICE

1 *Sentences*

Sentences of scripture may be used at the entry, after the Introduction, where they lead into prayer, or at other suitable points.

2 *Psalms and Readings*

Psalms and readings should normally be drawn from those set out on page 484. A psalm should normally be included, except that a scriptural song may take its place. There must always be one reading from scripture. At Holy Communion there should be two readings, one of which is a gospel reading.

3 *The Sermon*

There should be a relevant exposition of the Scriptures read. An appropriate place for any 'tribute' to the deceased is before the Penitential Kyries.

4 *Hymns*

Hymns may be sung at suitable places in the service.

5 *The Committal*

The Committal, though printed as the final section of the service, is used at the point at which it is needed: when the body is buried in a cemetery or churchyard, at the end of the service in church when cremation is not to follow immediately or at a crematorium when the interment of ashes is not to follow immediately.

The Funeral Service

Gathering in God's Name
Prayers of Penitence
The Collect
Proclaiming and Receiving The Word
The Prayers
The Farewell
The Committal
The Dismissal

The Funeral Service with Holy Communion

After the Prayers

The Peace
The Great Thanksgiving
The Breaking of the Bread
The Communion

The Farewell, the Committal and the Dismissal follow

Gathering in God's Name

The coffin may be received at the door of the church, and the minister may say

We receive the body of our *brother/sister* ....
with confidence in God, the giver of life,
who raised the Lord Jesus from the dead.

Grant, Lord, that we who are baptized into the death
of your Son our Saviour Jesus Christ
may continually put to death our evil desires
and be buried with him;
that through the grave and gate of death
we may pass to our joyful resurrection,
through his merits, who died and was buried,
and rose again for us, your Son Jesus Christ our Lord. **Amen.**

SENTENCES OF SCRIPTURE

The minister may add 'Alleluia!' to any of these sentences.

'I am the resurrection and the life,' says the Lord.
'Those who believe in me, even though they die, yet shall they live,
and everyone who lives and believes in me shall never die.' *John 11: 25,26*

I am persuaded that neither death, nor life,
nor angels, nor principalities,
nor powers, nor things present, nor things to come,
nor height, nor depth, nor anything else in all creation,
will be able to separate us from the love of God in Christ Jesus our Lord.
Romans 8: 38,39

We brought nothing into this world, and we can take nothing out.
The Lord gave, and the Lord has taken away,
blessed be the name of the Lord. *1 Timothy 6: 7; Job 1: 21*

A further selection of sentences of scripture is given on page 490.

GREETING

The minister says

We meet in the name of Christ
who died and was raised
by the glory of God the Father.

Grace and mercy be with you all
and also with you.

The minister introduces the service in these or other suitable words:
We have come here today to remember before God our dear *brother/sister*
....; to give thanks for *his/her* life, to leave *him/her* in the keeping of God
his/her creator, redeemer and judge, to commit *his/her* body to be *buried/
cremated*, and to comfort one another in our grief, in the hope that is ours
through the death and resurrection of Jesus Christ.
Therefore we pray that here today we may know the peace of Christ in
communion with all God's faithful servants.

Standing
God of all consolation,
whose Son Jesus Christ was moved to tears
at the grave of Lazarus his friend:
Look with compassion on us your children in our loss;
give to our troubled hearts the light of hope,
and strengthen in us the gift of faith,
in Jesus Christ our Lord. **Amen.**

A hymn may be sung.

PENITENTIAL KYRIES

The minister may say
As children of a loving heavenly Father,
let us seek the forgiveness of God,
for he is full of gentleness and compassion.

Call to remembrance, O Lord, your compassion,
and your loving kindness, for they have been from of old.

> Lord, have mercy.
> **Lord, have mercy.**

Remember not my sins nor my transgressions,
but according to your mercy think on me.

> Christ, have mercy.
> **Christ, have mercy.**

O keep my life, and deliver me, put me not to shame,
for I have put my trust in you.

> Lord, have mercy.
> **Lord, have mercy.**

The minister may say
May God our Father forgive us our sins
and bring us to the eternal joy of his kingdom
where dust and ashes have no dominion. **Amen.**

THE COLLECT

The minister invites the people to pray, silence is kept, and the minister says the Collect.
Merciful Father,
hear our prayers and comfort us,
renew our trust in your Son, whom you raised from the dead,
strengthen our faith
that all who have died in the love of Christ will share in his resurrection;
who is alive and reigns with you, in the unity of the Holy Spirit,
one God, now and for ever. **Amen.**

Proclaiming and Receiving the Word

A READING FROM THE OLD OR NEW TESTAMENT
may be read.

Romans 8: 18-21,31-35,37-39 or 1 Corinthians 15: 20-26,35-38,42-44a,53-58
Alternative readings: Isaiah 61: 1-3; Lamentations 3:22-26; Wisdom 3: 1-5,9 or 3: 1-9
1 Corinthians 15: 3-6; Philippians 3: 7-14; 2 Corinthians 4: 14-18; Revelation 21: 1-7

A PSALM

Psalms 23, 42: 1-7, 90, 116:1-9, 118: 14-21, 130 are suitable.

A READING FROM THE NEW TESTAMENT
is read.

At Holy Communion this is always a Gospel Reading.
John 5: 19-25 or John 6: 35-40 or John 14: 1-6,27 or Matthew 5: 1-10

THE SERMON

I believe in God, the Father almighty,
creator of heaven and earth.
I believe in Jesus Christ, God's only Son, our Lord
who was conceived by the Holy Spirit,
born of the Virgin Mary,
suffered under Pontius Pilate,
was crucified, died, and was buried;
he descended to the dead.
On the third day he rose again;
he ascended into heaven,
he is seated at the right hand of the Father,
and he will come again to judge the living and the dead.
I believe in the Holy Spirit,
the holy catholic Church,
the communion of saints,
the forgiveness of sins,
the resurrection of the body,
and the life everlasting. Amen.

or

Part 2 of the canticle TE DEUM

You, Christ, are the King of glory, ▪
the eternal Son of the Father.
When you took our flesh to set us free ▪
you humbly chose the virgin's womb.
You overcame the sting of death ▪
and opened the kingdom of heaven to all believers.
You are seated at God's right hand in glory. ▪
We believe that you will come to be our judge.
Come then, Lord, and help your people, ▪
bought with the price of your own blood,
and bring us with your saints ▪
to glory everlasting.

If the Holy Communion is celebrated, the Nicene Creed is used.

The prayers usually follow this sequence:

> *Thanksgiving for the life of the departed.*
>
> *Prayer for those who mourn.*
>
> *Prayer for readiness to live in the light of eternity.*

The prayers conclude with this prayer:

Heavenly Father,

in your Son Jesus Christ

you have given us a true faith and a sure hope.

Strengthen this faith and hope in us all our days,

that we may live as those who believe in the communion of saints,

the forgiveness of sins,

and the resurrection to eternal life;

through Jesus Christ our Lord. Amen.

If the Committal is not to follow as part of the same service in the same place, the Lord's Prayer is said now.

This prayer may be added:

O God,

the maker and redeemer of all:

We pray for the coming of your kingdom,

that in the last day,

when you bring together all things in Christ,

we, with all who have died in him,

may enjoy the fulfilment of your promises;

through Jesus Christ our Lord. **Amen.**

or

May God in his infinite love and mercy

bring the whole Church

living and departed in the Lord Jesus,

to a joyful resurrection

and the fulfilment of his eternal kingdom. **Amen.**

or

To God the Father who loved us,

and made us accepted in the Beloved.

To God the Son who loved us,

and loosed us from our sins by his own blood,

To God the Holy Spirit
who sheds the love of God abroad in our hearts,
To the one true God be all love and all glory
for time and for eternity. **Amen.**

The Farewell in Christ

The minister stands by the coffin and may invite others to gather around it.
The minister says
Our help is in the name of the Lord,
who has made heaven and earth.

A time of silence is kept.

THE EASTER ANTHEMS *1 Corinthians 15: 20-22*
    Christ has been raised from the dead, ▪
    the firstfruits of those who sleep.
    For as by man came death, ▪
    by man has come also the resurrection of the dead.
    For as in Adam all die, ▪
    even so in Christ shall all be made alive.
        Glory to the Father, and to the Son, ▪
        and to the Holy Spirit;
        as it was in the beginning is now, ▪
        and shall be for ever. **Amen.**

The minister says
God our creator and redeemer,
by your power Christ conquered death and entered into glory.
Confident of his victory
and claiming his promises,
we now leave your servant …. in your gracious keeping;
in the name of Jesus our Lord,
who died and is alive
and reigns with you and the Holy Spirit,
one God, now and for ever. **Amen.**

The Committal

Sentences of Scripture may be used.

The minister says

Praise be to the God and Father of our Lord Jesus Christ.
In his great mercy he has given us new birth into a living hope
through the resurrection of Jesus Christ from the dead. *1 Peter 1: 3*

Either

The Lord is full of compassion and mercy,
slow to anger and of great kindness.
As a father cares for his children,
so does the Lord care for those who fear him.
For he himself knows of what we are made;
he remembers that we are but dust.
Our days are like the grass;
we flourish like a flower of the field.
When the wind goes over it, it is gone,
and its place shall know it no more.
But the merciful goodness of the Lord endures for ever
on those who fear him,
and his righteousness on children's children.

or

Man that is born of a woman has but a short time to live
and is in need of mercy.
Like a flower we blossom and then wither,
like a shadow we flee and never stay.
In the midst of life we are in death;
to whom can we turn for help,
but to you, Lord, who are justly angered by our sins?

Lord God, holy and mighty, holy and immortal,
holy and most merciful Saviour,
Judge of the living and the dead,
deliver us not into the bitter pains of eternal death.
You know the secrets of our hearts;
in your mercy hear our prayer,
forgive us our sins, and in your love keep us in life everlasting.

When the body has been lowered into the grave, or at a cremation, the minister says
Almighty God, our heavenly Father,
you have given us a sure and certain hope
of the resurrection to eternal life.
In your keeping are all those who have departed in Christ.
We here commit the body of our *brother/sister* .... to the ground
(or to be cremated):
earth to earth, ashes to ashes, dust to dust;
in the name of our Lord Jesus Christ,
who died, and was buried, and rose again for us,
and who shall change our mortal body
that it may be like his glorious body,
according to the mighty working
by which he is able to subdue all things to himself.

Thanks be to God who gives us the victory
through Jesus Christ our Lord. **Amen.**

Blessed are the dead who die in the Lord.
They are blessed indeed, says the Spirit,
for they rest from their labours. *Revelation 14: 13*

THE LORD'S PRAYER
is said if it has not already been used in the service.
As our Saviour Christ has taught us, so we pray
Our Father in heaven ...
or
As our Saviour Christ has taught us, we are bold to say
Our Father, who art in heaven ...

THE DISMISSAL

The minister may say
God be in my head, and in my understanding.
God be in mine eyes, and in my looking.
God be in my mouth, and in my speaking.
God be in my heart, and in my thinking.
God be at mine end, and at my departing. **Amen.**

The minister may use one of the following endings:

Lord, you will show us the path of life:
in your presence is the fulness of joy
and from your right hand flow delights for evermore. *Psalm 16: 11*

or

May God give to you
and to all those whom you love
his comfort and his peace,
his light and his joy,
in this world and the next;
and the blessing of God almighty,
the Father, the Son and the Holy Spirit,
be upon you and remain with you always. **Amen.**

or

The grace of our Lord Jesus Christ,
and the love of God,
and the fellowship of the Holy Spirit,
be with us all evermore. **Amen.** *2 Corinthians 13: 14*

Other Sentences of Scripture

The eternal God is your refuge,
and underneath are the everlasting arms. *Deuteronomy 33: 27*

I know that my Redeemer lives,
and that in the end he will stand upon the earth.
I myself will see him with my own eyes. *Job 19: 25,27a*

Blessed are those who mourn,
for they shall be comforted. *Matthew 5: 4*

No eye has seen, no ear has heard,
nor has the heart of man conceived
what God has prepared for those who love him. *1 Corinthians 2: 9*

Holy, holy, holy is the Lord God almighty,
who was, and is, and is to come. *Revelation 4: 8b*

Christ has been raised from the dead:
the first fruits of those who sleep. *1 Corinthians 15: 20*

Other sentences from Holy Scripture may be used.

Prayers

This form may be used:

God of mercy, Lord of Life,
you have made us in your own image to reflect your truth and light:
we give you thanks for ....,
for the grace and mercy *he/she* received from you,
for all that was good and true in *his/her* life,
for the memories we treasure today.
[Especially we thank you ...]
Silence

Lord in your mercy,
hear our prayer.

Your mighty power brings good out of evil,
joy out of grief and life out of death.
Look in mercy on all who mourn (especially ....),
give them patient faith in times of darkness
and strengthen them with the knowledge of your love.
Silence

Lord in your mercy,
hear our prayer.

You are tender towards your children
and your mercy is over all your works.
Heal the memories of hurt and failure.
Give us the wisdom and grace to use aright
the time that is left to us on earth,
to turn to Christ and follow in his steps
in the way that leads to everlasting life.
Silence

Lord in your mercy,
hear our prayer.

Merciful Father,
entrusting into your hands all that you have made
and rejoicing in our communion with all your faithful people,
we make our prayers through Jesus Christ our Saviour. **Amen.**

Thanksgivings

Father of all, in whom we are one with your saints,
we remember with thanksgiving
those whom we love but see no longer.
Keep us in unbroken fellowship
with your whole Church,
and grant that at the last
we may all rejoice together in your heavenly home;
through Jesus Christ our Lord. **Amen.**

Heavenly Father,
we thank you for your servant .... ;
for the example *he/she* has left us,
and for the fellowship we have enjoyed with *him/her*.
We rejoice in your promise of eternal life
through Jesus Christ our Lord,
in whom the bond of love is never broken. **Amen.**

**Almighty God, we praise you for the blessings
brought to us through your church.
We bless you for the grace of the sacraments,
for our fellowship in Christ
with you and with each other,
for the teaching of the scriptures,
and for the preaching of your word.
We thank you for the holy example of your saints,
for your faithful servants departed this life,
and for the memory and example
of all that has been good and true in their lives.
Number us with them, we pray you,
in the company of the redeemed in heaven;
through Jesus Christ our Lord. Amen.**

Eternal God, we give thanks
for all those who have died in faith,
for the unceasing praise of the company of heaven,
for the promise to those who mourn
that all tears shall be wiped away,
for the pledge of death destroyed and victory won,
for our foretaste of eternal life
through baptism and eucharist,
for our hope in the Spirit,
for the communion of saints.
May we live by faith, walk in hope and be renewed in love,
until the world reflects your glory
and you are all in all.
Even so, come, Lord Jesus. Amen.

For those who mourn
Almighty God,
Father of all mercies, and giver of all comfort:
Deal graciously, we pray, with those who mourn,
that, casting all their care on you,
they may know the consolation of your love;
through Jesus Christ our Lord. **Amen.**

Give faith and comfort, O Lord,
to all who are bereaved (especially to ....).
Strengthen them to meet the days to come
with steadfastness and patience,
not sorrowing as those without hope,
but in thankful remembrance of your mercy in the past,
and waiting for a joyful reunion in heaven
in Jesus Christ our Lord. **Amen.**

Almighty God,
whose power can bring good out of evil:
Give us faith and light in times of darkness,
and help us to understand your ways;
through Jesus Christ our Lord. **Amen.**

Grant, Lord, that we who lay to rest
the body of our *brother/sister*,
in hope of resurrection to eternal life,
may firmly believe and continue
in the fellowship and communion of your saints;
through Jesus Christ our Lord. **Amen**.

Grant us, Lord, the wisdom and the grace
to use aright the time that is left to us here on earth.
Lead us to repent of our sins,
the evil we have done and the good we have not done;
and strengthen us to follow the steps of your Son,
in the way that leads to the fulness of eternal life;
through Jesus Christ our Lord. **Amen**.

The Communion of Saints

Eternal God, you hold all souls in life:
May the bright beams of your light and heavenly comfort
shine on your whole Church,
and grant that we, following the good example
of those who loved and served you here
and are now at rest,
may at last enter with them
into the fulness of your unending joy;
through Jesus Christ our Lord. **Amen**.

Almighty God,
grant that all those who believe in you
may be united in the full knowledge of your love,
and the unclouded vision of your glory;
through Jesus Christ our Lord. **Amen**.

O Lord,
support us all the day long
until the shades lengthen, and the evening comes,
and the busy world is hushed,
the fever of life is over,

and our work is done.
Then, Lord, in your mercy grant us safe lodging,
a holy rest, and peace at the last;
through Jesus Christ our Lord. **Amen**.

Resurrection

Merciful God, Father of our Lord Jesus Christ,
who is the resurrection and the life of all who believe in him,
and who, by his apostle Saint Paul,
has taught us not to grieve as people without hope
for those who sleep in him:
Raise us from the death of sin to the life of righteousness,
that when we depart this life we may rest in him,
as our hope is this our *brother/sister* .... does,
and that at the resurrection on the last day
we may be found acceptable to you,
and receive the kingdom prepared for all who love and fear you.
Grant this, merciful Father, through Jesus Christ,
our Mediator and Redeemer. **Amen**.

Bring us, Lord our God,
at our last awakening,
into the house and gate of heaven,
to enter into that gate,
and dwell in that house,
where there shall be
no darkness nor dazzling,
but one equal light;
no noise nor silence,
but one equal music;
no fears nor hopes,
but one equal possession;
no ends nor beginnings,
but one equal eternity;
in the habitation of your glory and dominion,
world without end. **Amen**.

Let us thank Almighty God for all his blessings.

For all your blessings in creation,
for the beauty of earth and sea and sky,
for all your works,
and for the wisdom with which you have ordered them.
>We thank you, Lord,
>**and bless your holy name.**

For the happiness of our earthly life,
for all our powers of mind and body,
for faithful friends,
and for the joy of loving and being loved.
>We thank you, Lord,
>**and bless your holy name.**

For all your servants departed this life in your faith and fear,
for the example they have left us,
and for the blessed hope of reunion with them hereafter.
>We thank you, Lord,
>**and bless your holy name.**

For the great salvation given to us in Jesus Christ,
for his suffering and his dying,
for his rising again
and his ascending into heaven.
>We thank you, Lord,
>**and bless your holy name.**

For the hope of a new heaven and a new earth,
for the place that Christ has gone to prepare for us,
and for the promised vision of your glory.
>We thank you, Lord,
>**and bless your holy name.**

Prayer for the hallowing of a grave

Almighty Father,
our Lord Jesus Christ sanctified the grave by his burial in a new tomb.
Bless and hallow this grave,
as a resting place for the body of ....,
whom we have left in your gracious keeping.
We look for the promised resurrection,
at the coming of our Lord Jesus Christ,
who is alive and reigns in glory,
with you and the Holy Spirit,
one God, now and for ever. **Amen.**

When the Body is brought to church on the eve of a funeral

This form may also be adapted for use in the home before the funeral service.

The coffin is received at the door of the church.

The minister says
We receive the body of our *brother/sister* ....
with confidence in God, the giver of life,
who raised the Lord Jesus from the dead.

Grant, Lord,
that we who are baptized into the death of your Son,
our Saviour Jesus Christ
may continually put to death our evil desires
and be buried with him;
that through the grave and gate of death
we may pass to our joyful resurrection;
through his merits, who died and was buried,
and rose again for us,
your Son, Jesus Christ our Lord. **Amen.**

*Preceding the coffin into the church, the minister says one or more of the sentences
of scripture on page 490.*

A hymn may be sung.

PSALM

Psalm 139: 1-11

1   O Lord, you have searched me out and known me; ▪
you know my sitting down and my rising up;
you discern my thoughts from afar.

2   You mark out my journeys and my resting place ▪
and are acquainted with all my ways.

3   For there is not a word on my tongue, ▪
but you, O Lord, know it altogether.

4   You encompass me behind and before ▪
and lay your hand upon me.

5   Such knowledge is too wonderful for me, ▪
    so high that I cannot attain it.

6   Where can I go then from your spirit? ▪
    Or where can I flee from your presence?

7   If I climb up to heaven, you are there; ▪
    if I make the grave my bed, you are there also.

8   If I take the wings of the morning ▪
    and dwell in the uttermost parts of the sea,

9   Even there your hand shall lead me, ▪
    your right hand hold me fast.

10   If I say, 'Surely the darkness will cover me ▪
    and the light around me turn to night,'

11   Even darkness is no darkness with you;
      the night is as clear as the day; ▪
  darkness and light to you are both alike.
      Glory to the Father, and to the Son, ▪
      and to the Holy Spirit;
      as it was in the beginning is now, ▪
      and shall be for ever. **Amen.**

A READING
from scripture

NUNC DIMITTIS

1   Now, Lord, you let your servant go in peace: ▪
    your word has been fulfilled.

2   My own eyes have seen the salvation ▪
    which you have prepared in the sight of every people.

3   A light to reveal you to the nations ▪
    and the glory of your people Israel.
      Glory to the Father, and to the Son, ▪
      and to the Holy Spirit;
      as it was in the beginning is now, ▪
      and shall be for ever. **Amen.**

PRAYERS

Eternal God, we come to you
because ...., whom we knew and loved, has died:
and our hearts are numb, our minds perplexed.

Whatever we may be thinking and feeling,
we know that you understand.
For you made us,
and in your Son Jesus you shared our life and experience.
Accept us as we are,
forgive us our lack of faith,
inspire in us a living hope;
through Jesus Christ our Lord. **Amen.**

Heavenly Father,
God of hope and giver of all comfort:
we thank you for all the gifts of your providence and grace.
We thank you for ....
and for all that *he/she* has meant to us all.
Comfort those who mourn with the assurance
of the life which is beyond this life,
and of a reunion with those we have loved
and who wait for us in your heavenly presence;
through Jesus Christ our Lord. **Amen.**

O Lord, support us all the day long,
until the shades lengthen, and the evening comes,
and the busy world is hushed,
the fever of life is over
and our work done.
Then, Lord, in your mercy, grant us safe lodging,
a holy rest, and peace at the last;
through Jesus Christ our Lord. **Amen.**

Lighten our darkness, O Lord, we pray,
and in your great mercy defend us
from all perils and dangers of this night;
for the love of your only Son, our Saviour Jesus Christ. **Amen.**

THE LORD'S PRAYER

Other prayers may be said.

A hymn may be sung.

A Form for use at the Burial of Ashes after Cremation

Some or all of these sentences may be read.

The eternal God is our refuge, and underneath are the everlasting arms.
Deuteronomy 33: 27

Trust in the Lord at all times,
pour out your hearts before him: God is a refuge for us. *Psalm 62: 8*

God so loved the world that he gave his only Son, so that everyone who believes in him may not perish but may have eternal life. *John 3: 16*

For I am convinced that neither death, nor life, nor angels, nor rulers, nor things present, nor things to come, nor powers, nor height, nor depth, nor anything else in all creation, will be able to separate us from the love of God in Christ Jesus our Lord. *Romans 8: 38,39*

Blessed be the God and Father of our Lord Jesus Christ! By his great mercy he has given us a new birth into a living hope through the resurrection of Jesus Christ from the dead, and into an inheritance that is imperishable, undefiled, and unfading, kept in heaven for you. *1 Peter 1: 3,4*

PRAYER

God, Lord of life and conqueror of death,
our help in every time of trouble:
We thank you for the assurance of the Gospel
that in your keeping the souls of the faithful find lasting peace and joy,
and that, though we see our loved ones no more, they are safe with you.
Comfort all who mourn.
May memories of .... be a consolation for the present
and a strength for the future.
By the glorious resurrection of your Son
confirm in us the hope of eternal life,
and enable us to put our whole trust in your goodness and mercy;
through Jesus Christ our Lord. **Amen.**

A READING
from the New Testament

1 Corinthians 15: 19-26 or 2 Corinthians 4:16 - 5:1 is suitable.

The Interment

The minister says

The Lord says: 'Do not be afraid. I am the first and the last, and I am the Living One. I was dead, and I am alive for ever and ever.' *Revelation 1: 17-18*

We have entrusted our *brother/sister* .... to God's gracious keeping.
We now commit *his/her* ashes to the ground
in sure and certain hope of the resurrection to eternal life,
in the name of our Lord Jesus Christ,
who died, and was buried, and rose again for us,
and who shall change our mortal body
that it may be like his glorious body,
according to the mighty working
by which he is able to subdue all things to himself.
Thanks be to God who gives us the victory
through Jesus Christ our Lord. **Amen.**

PRAYER

Eternal God,
by your Son's rising from the dead,
you have destroyed the power of death.
In you the dead find life for ever,
and the faithful who served you on earth
praise you for all eternity in heaven.
Comfort us in the hope of everlasting life
and support us with your sure love and your guiding hand.
Bring us at the last, with all the faithful,
to the full knowledge of your love
and the unclouded vision of your glory;
through Jesus Christ our Lord. **Amen.**

Our Father in heaven,
    hallowed be your name,
    your kingdom come,
    your will be done,
        on earth as in heaven.
Give us today our daily bread.
    Forgive us our sins
    as we forgive those who sin against us.
Lead us not into temptation
    but deliver us from evil.
For the kingdom, the power, and the glory are yours
    now and for ever. Amen.

The grace of our Lord Jesus Christ,
and the love of God,
and the fellowship of the Holy Spirit,
be with us all evermore. **Amen.**

In the case of the committal of ashes on land or at sea the Guidelines *of the*
House of Bishops currently in force should be followed.

THE FUNERAL SERVICE FOR A CHILD

Gathering in God's Name

The coffin may be received at the door of the church (page 482).

The coffin may be received at the door of the church (page 482).

SENTENCES OF SCRIPTURE

The minister may use any of the sentences on pages 466 and 490.

The following may be used:

The Lord tends his flock like a shepherd:
he gathers the lambs in his arms
and carries them close to his heart. *Isaiah 40: 11*

Blessed are the pure in heart
for they shall see God. *Matthew 5: 8*

Beloved, we are God's children now; what we will be has not yet been revealed. What we do know is this: when he is revealed, we will be like him, for we will see him as he is. *1 John 3: 2*

Let the little children come to me; do not stop them; for it is to such as these that the kingdom of God belongs. *Mark 10: 14*

I will comfort you, says the Lord, as a mother comforts her child,
and you shall be comforted. *Isaiah 66: 13*

GREETING

The minister says
We meet in the name of Christ
who died and was raised by the glory of God the Father.

Grace and mercy be with you all
and also with you.

The minister introduces the service in these or other suitable words:
We have come together to worship God,
to thank him for his love,
and to remember the [short] life on earth of ....;
to share our grief

and to leave *him/her* to the eternal care of God.
[We meet in the faith that death is not the end,
and may be faced without fear, bitterness or guilt.]

Standing
God of all mercies,
you make nothing in vain
and love all that you have made.
Comfort us in our grief,
and console us by the knowledge of your unfailing love;
through Jesus Christ our Lord. **Amen.**

A hymn may be sung.

THE COLLECT

The minister invites the people to pray, silence is kept, and the minister says the
Collect.
Merciful Father,
hear our prayers and comfort us,
renew our trust in your Son, whom you raised from the dead,
strengthen our faith
that all who have died in the love of Christ
will share in his resurrection;
who is alive and reigns with you, in the unity of the Holy Spirit,
one God, now and for ever. **Amen.**

Proclaiming and Receiving the Word

A READING FROM THE OLD OR NEW TESTAMENT
may be read.

Suitable readings are noted on page 484.

A PSALM

Psalm 23 or 84: 1-4 is suitable.

is read.

At Holy Communion this is always a Gospel Reading.

Romans 8: 18,28,35,37-39; 1 Corinthians 13: 1-13
Matthew 18: 1-5, 10; Mark 10: 13-16; John 6: 35-40 or John 14: 1-6,27

The Sermon

The Apostles' Creed or Part 2 of the canticle TE DEUM page 485 is said. If the Holy Communion is celebrated, the Nicene Creed is used.

The Prayers
as on pages 510-513

The prayers are concluded with this prayer:

Heavenly Father,
in your Son Jesus Christ
you have given us a true faith and a sure hope.
Strengthen this faith and hope in us all our days,
that we may live as those who believe in the communion of saints,
the forgiveness of sin,
and the resurrection to eternal life;
through Jesus Christ our Lord. Amen.

If the Committal is not to follow as part of the same service in the same place, the Lord's Prayer is said now.

The prayers on pages 511-513 may be added.

The Farewell in Christ

The minister stands by the coffin and may invite others to gather around it. The minister says

Our help is in the name of the Lord,
who has made heaven and earth.

A time of silence is kept.

The EASTER ANTHEMS (page 485) are said.

The minister says

God our creator and redeemer,
by your power Christ conquered death and entered into glory.
Confident of his victory
and claiming his promises,
we now leave your child .... in your gracious keeping;
in the name of Jesus our Lord,
who died and is alive
and reigns with you and the Holy Spirit,
one God, now and for ever. **Amen.**

or

Lord, faithful creator and most loving redeemer,
whose Son took little children in his arms and blessed them:
we now leave your child .... in your gracious keeping.
We believe *he/she* is yours in death as in life.
Comfort, we pray, all who have loved *him/her* on earth,
and bring us all to your everlasting kingdom;
through Jesus Christ our Lord. **Amen.**

The Committal

Sentences of scripture may be used.

The minister says

Praise be to the God and Father of our Lord Jesus Christ.
In his great mercy he has given us new birth into a living hope
through the resurrection of Jesus Christ from the dead. *1 Peter 1: 3*

The Lord is full of compassion and mercy,
slow to anger and of great kindness.
As a father cares for his children,
so does the Lord care for those who fear him.
For he himself knows of what we are made;
he remembers that we are but dust.
Our days are like the grass;
we flourish like a flower of the field.

When the wind goes over it, it is gone,
and its place shall know it no more.
But the merciful goodness of the Lord endures for ever
on those who fear him,
and his righteousness on children's children.

When the body has been lowered into the grave, or at a cremation, the minister says
Almighty God, our heavenly Father,
you have given us a sure and certain hope
of the resurrection to eternal life.
In your keeping are all those who have departed in Christ.
We here commit the body of .... to the ground
(or to be cremated):
earth to earth, ashes to ashes, dust to dust;
in the name of our Lord Jesus Christ,
who died, and was buried, and rose again for us,
and who shall change our mortal body
that it may be like his glorious body,
according to the mighty working
by which he is able to subdue all things to himself.

Thanks be to God who gives us the victory
through Jesus Christ our Lord. **Amen.**

The Lamb who is at the throne will be their shepherd, and will lead them to springs of living water, and God will wipe away all tears from their eyes. *Revelation 7: 17*

THE LORD'S PRAYER
is said if it has not already been used in the service.

As our Saviour Christ has taught us, so we pray
Our Father in heaven ...
or
As our Saviour Christ has taught us, we are bold to say
Our Father, who art in heaven ...

The minister may say

God be in my head, and in my understanding.

God be in mine eyes, and in my looking.

God be in my mouth, and in my speaking.

God be in my heart, and in my thinking.

God be at mine end, and at my departing. **Amen.**

The minister may use one of the endings on page 489.

Prayers at the Funeral of a Child

This form may be used:
The Lord Jesus is the lover of his people and our only sure hope.
Let us ask him to deepen our faith and sustain us in this dark hour.

You became a little child for our sake, sharing our human life.
>To you we pray:
>**bless us and keep us, O Lord.**

You grew in wisdom, age and grace
and learned obedience through suffering.
>To you we pray:
>**bless us and keep us, O Lord.**

You welcomed children, promising them your kingdom.
>To you we pray:
>**bless us and keep us, O Lord.**

You comforted those who mourned the loss of children and friends.
>To you we pray:
>**bless us and keep us, O Lord.**

You took upon yourself the suffering and death of us all.
>To you we pray:
>**bless us and keep us, O Lord.**

You promised to raise up those who believe in you,
just as you were raised up in glory by the Father.
>To you we pray:
>**bless us and keep us, O Lord.**

Merciful Father,
entrusting into your hands all that you have made
and rejoicing in our communion with all your faithful people,
we make our prayers through Jesus Christ our Saviour. **Amen.**

Thanksgiving

Almighty God,
we praise you for the blessings
brought to us through your church.
We bless you for the grace of the sacraments,
for our fellowship in Christ
with you and with each other,
for the teaching of the scriptures,
and for the preaching of your word.
We thank you for the holy example of your saints,
for your faithful servants departed this life,
and for the memory and example
of all that has been good and true in their lives.
Number us with them, we pray you,
in the company of the redeemed in heaven;
through Jesus Christ our Lord. Amen.

For those who mourn

Almighty God,
Father of all mercies, and giver of all comfort:
we pray, with those who mourn,
parents and children, family, friends and neighbours.
Be gentle with them in their grief.
Show them the depths of your love,
and a glimpse of the kingdom of heaven.
Spare them the torments of guilt and despair.
Be with them as they weep
and help them to know that there is a greater light
where all tears will be wiped away.
This we ask in the name of Jesus Christ, the Risen Lord. **Amen**.

Most merciful God,
whose wisdom is beyond our understanding,
surround the family of .... with your love,
that they may not be overwhelmed by their loss,
but have confidence in your love,
and strength to meet the days to come.
We ask this through Christ our Lord. **Amen**.

Almighty God,
whose power can bring good out of evil:
Give us faith and light in times of darkness,
and help us to understand your ways;
through Jesus Christ our Lord. **Amen.**

For grace to live in the light of eternity
God of all mystery,
whose ways are beyond understanding,
lead us, who grieve at this untimely death,
to a new and deeper faith in your love,
which brought your only Son Jesus
through death into resurrection life.
We make our prayer in Jesus' name. **Amen.**

Following a miscarriage or stillbirth
God of compassion,
you make nothing in vain
and love all you have created;
we commend to you .... and ....'s child, ...,
for whom they poured out such great love,
for whom they cherished so many hopes and dreams.
We had longed to welcome *him/her* amongst us;
grant us the assurance that *he/she* is now encircled in your arms of love,
and shares the resurrection life of your Son, Jesus Christ. **Amen.**

The Communion of Saints
Almighty God,
grant that all those who believe in you
may be united in the full knowledge of your love,
and the unclouded vision of your glory;
through Jesus Christ our Lord. **Amen.**

Resurrection

Merciful God, Father of our Lord Jesus Christ,
who is the resurrection and the life of all who believe in him,
and who, by his apostle Saint Paul,
has taught us not to grieve as people without hope
for those who sleep in him:
Raise us from the death of sin to the life of righteousness,
that when we depart this life we may rest in him,
as our hope is this child .... does,
and that at the resurrection on the last day
we may be found acceptable to you,
and receive the kingdom prepared for all who love and fear you.
Grant this, merciful Father, through Jesus Christ,
our Mediator and Redeemer. Amen.

An Act of Thanksgiving
The form on page 496 may be used.

If required, the prayer for the hallowing of a grave on page 497 is used.

A FORM FOR USE IN THE HOME, FUNERAL HOME OR MORTUARY
PRIOR TO THE SERVICE IN CHURCH

The minister greets those present with words of scripture such as the following:
Jesus said,
'I am the resurrection and the life. Those who believe in me, even though they die, yet shall they live, and everyone who lives and believes in me shall never die.' *John 11: 25, 26*

The minister may say
God is with us,
God's love unites us,
God's purpose steadies us,
God's spirit comforts us.
Blessed be God for ever.

Merciful and compassionate God,
we bring you our grief in the loss of ....
and ask for courage to bear it.
We bring you our thanks for all you give us in those we love;
and we bring you our prayers for peace of heart
in the knowledge of your mercy and love, in Christ Jesus. **Amen.**

This prayer or another suitable prayer may be used.
Heavenly Father,
your Son Jesus Christ wept at the grave of Lazarus his friend.
Look with compassion on those who are now in sorrow and affliction.
Comfort them with your gracious consolation;
make them know that all things work together for good
to those who love you;
and give them always sure confidence in your fatherly care;
through Jesus Christ our Lord. **Amen.**

Verses from one or both of the following may be read:
Psalm 27 *or* Psalm 23

This or some other appropriate reading may follow:
Romans 8: 31b-39

The minister may stand beside the body and say
We leave in God's gracious keeping ....
as *his/her* body is taken on its last earthly journey.
God of all consolation,
in your unending love and mercy you turn
the darkness of death into the dawn of new life.
Your Son, our Lord Jesus Christ,
by dying for us, conquered death,
and by rising again, restored life.

May we not be afraid of death but desire to be with Christ,
and after our life on earth,
to be with those we love,
where every tear is wiped away and all things are made new.
We ask this through Jesus Christ. **Amen.**

THE LORD'S PRAYER

As our Saviour Christ has taught us, so we pray

Our Father in heaven,
    hallowed be your name,
    your kingdom come,
    your will be done,
        on earth as in heaven.
Give us today our daily bread.
    Forgive us our sins
    as we forgive those who sin against us.
Lead us not into temptation
    but deliver us from evil.
For the kingdom, the power, and the glory are yours
    now and for ever. Amen.

or

As our Saviour Christ has taught us, we are bold to say

Our Father, who art in heaven,

hallowed be thy name,

thy kingdom come,

thy will be done,

on earth as it is in heaven.

Give us this day our daily bread.

And forgive us our trespasses

as we forgive those who trespass against us.

And lead us not into temptation,

but deliver us from evil. Amen.

Either or both of the following may be used:

Eternal God, our heavenly Father,

you love us with an everlasting love

and you can turn the shadow of death into the morning.

We bow before you now with longing and submissive hearts.

Speak to us afresh your gracious promises,

that through patience and the comfort of the scriptures we may have hope

and be lifted above our darkness and distress

into the light and peace of your presence;

through Jesus Christ our Lord. **Amen.**

Now to the one who can keep us from falling

and set us in the presence of the divine glory,

jubilant and above reproach,

to the only God our Saviour,

be glory and majesty, might and authority,

through Jesus Christ our Lord,

before all time, now and for evermore. **Amen.**

The minister may add

Let us proceed in peace and in the faith of Christ. **Amen.**

Ordination Services

THE FORM AND MANNER OF
MAKING, ORDAINING, AND CONSECRATING, OF
BISHOPS, PRIESTS, AND DEACONS
ACCORDING TO THE ORDER OF
THE CHURCH OF IRELAND

It is evident unto all persons diligently reading holy Scripture and ancient Authors, that from the Apostles' time there have been these Orders of Ministers in Christ's Church; Bishops, Priests, and Deacons. Which Offices were evermore had in such reverend estimation, that no persons might presume to execute any of them, except they were first called, tried, examined, and known to have such qualities as are requisite for the same; and also by publick Prayer, with Imposition of Hands, were approved and admitted thereunto by lawful authority. And therefore, to the intent that these Orders may be continued, and reverently used and esteemed, in the Church of Ireland; no persons shall be accounted or taken to be a lawful Bishop, Priest, or Deacon in the Church of Ireland, or suffered to execute any of the said functions, except they be called, tried, examined, and admitted thereunto, according to the Form hereafter following, or hath had formerly Episcopal Consecration or Ordination.

And none shall be admitted a Deacon, except *he* be Twenty-three years of age, unless *he* have a Faculty. And every person which is to be admitted a Priest shall be full Four-and-twenty years old, and shall have served in the Office of a Deacon the space of a whole year at the least (except for reasonable causes it shall otherwise seem good to the Bishop). And every person which is to be ordained or consecrated Bishop shall be fully Thirty years of age.

And the Bishop, knowing either by *himself*, or by sufficient testimony, any person to be of virtuous conversation, and without crime; and, after examination and trial, finding *him* learned in the Latin Tongue, and sufficiently instructed in holy Scripture, and otherwise competently learned, may, at the times appointed in the Canon, or else, on urgent occasion, upon some other Sunday or Holy-day, in the face of the Church, admit *him* a Deacon, in such manner and form as hereafter followeth.

THE FORM AND MANNER OF
MAKING OF DEACONS

When the day appointed by the bishop is come, there shall be a sermon or exhortation, declaring the duty and office of such as come to be admitted deacons; how necessary that order is in the Church of Christ; and also, how the people ought to esteem them in their office.

When the sermon is ended, the archdeacon, or in his absence, one appointed in his stead, shall present unto the bishop (sitting in his chair, near to the holy table) such as desire to be ordained deacons (each of them being decently habited), saying these words:

Bishop, I present unto you these persons present, to be admitted Deacons.

The bishop

Take heed that the persons, whom ye present unto us, be apt and meet, for their learning and godly conversation, to exercise their ministry duly, to the honour of God, and the edifying of his Church.

The archdeacon shall answer

I have enquired of them, and also examined them, and think them so to be.

Then the bishop shall say unto the people

Brethren, if there be any of you who knoweth any impediment, or notable crime in any of these persons presented to be ordered Deacons, for the which *he* ought not to be admitted to that office, let *him* come forth in the Name of God, and show what the crime or impediment is.

And if any great crime or impediment be objected, the bishop shall surcease from ordering that person, until such time as the party accused shall be found clear of that crime.

Then the bishop (commending such as shall be found meet to be ordered to the prayers of the congregation) shall, with the clergy and people present, sing or say the Litany, as followeth:

O God the Father, of heaven: have mercy upon us miserable sinners.
O God the Father, of heaven: have mercy upon us miserable sinners.

O God the Son, Redeemer of the world: have mercy upon us miserable sinners.
O God the Son, Redeemer of the world: have mercy upon us miserable sinners.

O God the Holy Ghost, proceeding from the Father and the Son: have mercy upon us miserable sinners.
O God the Holy Ghost, proceeding from the Father and the Son: have mercy upon us miserable sinners.

O holy, blessed, and glorious Trinity, three Persons and one God: have mercy upon us miserable sinners.
O holy, blessed, and glorious Trinity, three Persons and one God: have mercy upon us miserable sinners.

Remember not, Lord, our offences, nor the offences of our forefathers; neither take thou vengeance of our sins: spare us, good Lord, spare thy people, whom thou hast redeemed with thy most precious blood, and be not angry with us for ever.
Spare us, good Lord.

From all blindness of heart; from pride, vain-glory, and hypocrisy; from envy, hatred, and malice, and all uncharitableness,
Good Lord, deliver us.

From all sedition, privy conspiracy, and rebellion; from all false doctrine, heresy, and schism; from hardness of heart, and contempt of thy Word and Commandment,
Good Lord, deliver us.

By the mystery of thy holy Incarnation; by thy holy Nativity and Circumcision; by thy Baptism, Fasting and Temptation,

Good Lord, deliver us.

By thine Agony and bloody Sweat; by thy Cross and Passion; by thy precious Death and Burial; by thy glorious Resurrection and Ascension; and by the coming of the Holy Ghost,

Good Lord, deliver us.

We sinners do beseech thee to hear us, O Lord God: and that it may please thee to rule and govern thy holy Church universal in the right way;

We beseech thee to hear us, good Lord.

That it may please thee to illuminate all bishops, priests, and deacons, with true knowledge and understanding of thy Word; and that both by their preaching and living they may set it forth and show it accordingly;

We beseech thee to hear us, good Lord.

That it may please thee to bless these thy servants, now to be admitted to the order of deacons, and to pour thy grace upon them; that they may duly execute their office, to the edifying of thy Church, and the glory of thy holy Name;

We beseech thee to hear us, good Lord.

That it may please thee to further the work of the Church in all the world, and to send forth labourers into thy harvest;

We beseech thee to hear us, good Lord.

That it may please thee to give to all thy people increase of grace, to hear meekly thy Word, and to receive it with pure affection, and to bring forth the fruits of the Spirit;

We beseech thee to hear us, good Lord.

That it may please thee to bring into the way of truth all such as have erred, and are deceived;

We beseech thee to hear us, good Lord.

That it may please thee to strengthen such as do stand; and to comfort and help the weak-hearted; and to raise up them that fall; and finally to beat down Satan under our feet;

We beseech thee to hear us, good Lord.

That it may please thee to forgive our enemies, persecutors, and slanderers, and to turn their hearts;

We beseech thee to hear us, good Lord.

That it may please thee to give us true repentance; to forgive us all our sins, negligences, and ignorances; and to endue us with the grace of thy Holy Spirit, to amend our lives according to thy holy Word;

We beseech thee to hear us, good Lord.

Son of God: we beseech thee to hear us.

Son of God: we beseech thee to hear us.

O Lamb of God: that takest away the sins of the world;

Grant us thy peace.

O Lamb of God: that takest away the sins of the world;

Have mercy upon us.

O Christ, hear us.

O Christ, hear us.

Lord, have mercy upon us.

Lord, have mercy upon us.

Christ, have mercy upon us.

Christ, have mercy upon us.

Lord, have mercy upon us.

Lord, have mercy upon us.

Then shall be sung or said the Service for the Communion, with the Collect, Epistle, and Gospel, as followeth:

THE COLLECT

Almighty God, who by thy divine providence hast appointed divers orders of ministers in thy Church, and didst inspire thine apostles to choose into the order of deacons the first martyr Saint Stephen, with others; Mercifully behold these thy servants now called to the like office and administration; replenish them so with the truth of thy doctrine, and adorn them with innocency of life, that, both by word and good example, they may faithfully serve thee in this office, to the glory of thy Name, and the edification of thy Church; through the merits of our Saviour Jesus Christ, who liveth and reigneth with thee and the Holy Ghost, now and for ever. **Amen.**

THE EPISTLE

1 Timothy 3: 8-13

Likewise must the deacons be grave, not double-tongued, not given to much wine, not greedy of filthy lucre; holding the mystery of the faith in a pure conscience. And let these also first be proved; then let them use the office of a deacon, being found blameless. Even so must their wives be grave, not slanderers, sober, faithful in all things. Let the deacons be the husbands of one wife, ruling their children and their own houses well. For they that have used the office of a deacon well purchase to themselves a good degree, and great boldness in the faith which is in Christ Jesus.

Or else this, out of the sixth chapter of the Acts of the Apostles:

Acts 6: 2-7

Then the twelve called the multitude of the disciples unto them, and said, It is not reason that we should leave the word of God, and serve tables. Wherefore, brethren, look ye out among you seven men of honest report, full of the Holy Ghost and wisdom, whom we may appoint over this business. But we will give ourselves continually to prayer, and to the ministry of the word. And the saying pleased the whole multitude: and they chose Stephen, a man full of faith and of the Holy Ghost, and Philip, and Prochorus, and Nicanor, and Timon, and Parmenas, and Nicolas a proselyte of Antioch, whom they set before the apostles: and when they had prayed, they laid their hands on them. And the word of God increased; and the number of the disciples multiplied in Jerusalem greatly; and a great company of the priests were obedient to the faith.

And before the Gospel, the bishop, sitting in his chair, shall examine every one of them that are to be ordered, in the presence of the people, after this manner following:

Do you trust that you are inwardly moved by the Holy Ghost to take upon you this Office and Ministration, to serve God for the promoting of his glory, and the edifying of his people?

Answer **I trust so.**

The bishop

Do you think that you are truly called, to this Office and Ministration, according to the will of our Lord Jesus Christ, and the due order of this Church?

Answer **I think so.**

The bishop

Do you unfeignedly believe all the Canonical Scriptures of the Old and New Testament?

Answer **I do believe them.**

The bishop

Will you diligently read the same unto the people assembled in the church where you shall be appointed to serve?

Answer **I will.**

The bishop

It appertaineth to the office of a deacon, in the church where *he* shall be appointed to serve, to assist the priest in Divine Service, and specially when *he* ministereth the Holy Communion, and to help *him* in the distribution thereof, and to read holy scriptures and homilies in the church; and to instruct the youth in the Catechism; in the absence of the priest to baptize infants; and to preach, if *he* be admitted thereto by the bishop. And furthermore, it is *his* office, where provision is so made, to search for the sick, poor, and impotent people of the parish, to intimate their estates, names, and places where they dwell, unto the curate, that by *his* exhortation they may be relieved with the alms of the parishioners, or others. Will you do this gladly and willingly?

Answer **I will so do, by the help of God.**

The bishop

Will you apply all your diligence to frame and fashion your own lives, and the lives of your families, according to the doctrine of Christ; and to make both yourselves and them, as much as in you lieth, wholesome examples of the flock of Christ?

Answer **I will so do, the Lord being my helper.**

The bishop

Will you reverently obey your Ordinary, and other ministers of the Church, and them to whom the charge and government over you is committed, following with a glad mind and will their godly admonitions?

Answer **I will endeavour myself, the Lord being my helper.**

Then the bishop, laying his hands severally upon the head of every one of them, humbly kneeling before him, shall say

Take thou authority to execute the Office of a Deacon in the Church of God committed unto thee; In the Name of the Father, and of the Son, and of the Holy Ghost. Amen.

Then shall the bishop deliver to every one of them the New Testament, saying

Take thou authority to read the Gospel in the Church of God, and to preach the same, if thou be thereto licensed by the Bishop *himself.*

Then one of them, appointed by the bishop, shall read

THE GOSPEL

Luke 12: 35-38

Let your loins be girded about, and your lights burning; and ye yourselves like unto men that wait for their lord, when he will return from the wedding; that, when he cometh and knocketh, they may open unto him immediately. Blessed are those servants, whom the lord when he cometh shall find watching. Verily I say unto you, that he shall gird himself, and make them to sit down to meat, and will come forth and serve them. And if he shall come in the second watch, or come in the third watch, and find them so, blessed are those servants.

Then shall the bishop proceed in the Communion: and all that are ordered shall tarry, and receive the Holy Communion the same day with the bishop.

Immediately before the Benediction shall be said these collects following:

Almighty God, giver of all good things,
who of thy great goodness hast vouchsafed to accept
and take these thy servants unto the office of deacons in thy Church;
Make them, we beseech thee, O Lord, to be modest, humble,
and constant in their ministration;

to have a ready will to observe all spiritual discipline;
that they, having always the testimony of a good conscience,
may continue stable and strong in this ministry;
through thy Son our Saviour Jesus Christ,
to whom be glory and honour, world without end. **Amen.**

Prevent us, O Lord, in all our doings
with thy most gracious favour,
and further us with thy continual help;
that in all our works, begun, continued, and ended in thee,
we may glorify thy holy Name,
and finally by thy mercy obtain everlasting life;
through Jesus Christ our Lord. **Amen.**

The peace of God, which passeth all understanding,
keep your hearts and minds in the knowledge and love of God,
and of his Son Jesus Christ our Lord:
And the blessing of God almighty,
the Father, the Son, and the Holy Ghost,
be amongst you and remain with you always. **Amen.**

The Form and Manner of
ORDERING OF PRIESTS

When the day appointed by the bishop is come, there shall be a sermon or exhortation, declaring the duty and office of such as come to be admitted priests; how necessary that order is in the Church of Christ; and also, how the people ought to esteem them in their office.

When the sermon is ended, the archdeacon, or, in his absence, one appointed in his stead, shall present unto the bishop (sitting in his chair, near to the holy table) all them that shall receive the order of Priesthood that day (each of them being decently habited), and say.

Bishop, I present unto you these persons present, to be admitted to the order of Priesthood.

The bishop

Take heed that the persons, whom ye present unto us, be apt and meet, for their learning and godly conversation, to exercise their ministry duly, to the honour of God, and the edifying of his Church.

The archdeacon shall answer

I have enquired of them, and also examined them, and think them so to be.

Then the bishop shall say unto the people

Good people, these are they whom we purpose, God willing, to receive this day unto the holy office of Priesthood: For after due examination we find not to the contrary, but that they be lawfully called to their function and ministry, and that they be persons meet for the same. But yet if there be any of you who knoweth any impediment, or notable crime, in any of them, for the which *he* ought not to be received into this holy ministry, let *him* come forth in the Name of God, and show what the crime or impediment is.

And if any great crime or impediment be objected, the bishop shall surcease from ordering that person, until such time as the party accused shall be found clear of that crime.

Then the bishop (commending such as shall be found meet to be ordered to the prayers of the congregation) shall, with the clergy and people present, sing or say the Litany, as followeth:

O God the Father, of heaven: have mercy upon us miserable sinners.
O God the Father, of heaven: have mercy upon us miserable sinners.

O God the Son, Redeemer of the world: have mercy upon us miserable sinners.
O God the Son, Redeemer of the world: have mercy upon us miserable sinners.

O God the Holy Ghost, proceeding from the Father and the Son: have mercy upon us miserable sinners.
O God the Holy Ghost, proceeding from the Father and the Son: have mercy upon us miserable sinners.

O holy, blessed, and glorious Trinity, three Persons and one God: have mercy upon us miserable sinners.
O holy, blessed, and glorious Trinity, three Persons and one God: have mercy upon us miserable sinners.

Remember not, Lord, our offences, nor the offences of our forefathers; neither take thou vengeance of our sins: spare us, good Lord, spare thy people, whom thou hast redeemed with thy most precious blood, and be not angry with us for ever.
Spare us, good Lord.

From all blindness of heart; from pride, vain-glory, and hypocrisy; from envy, hatred, and malice, and all uncharitableness,
Good Lord, deliver us.

From all sedition, privy conspiracy, and rebellion; from all false doctrine, heresy, and schism; from hardness of heart, and contempt of thy Word and Commandment,
Good Lord, deliver us.

By the mystery of thy holy Incarnation; by thy holy Nativity and Circumcision; by thy Baptism, Fasting and Temptation,
Good Lord, deliver us.

By thine Agony and bloody Sweat; by thy Cross and Passion; by thy precious Death and Burial; by thy glorious Resurrection and Ascension; and by the coming of the Holy Ghost,
Good Lord, deliver us.

We sinners do beseech thee to hear us, O Lord God: and that it may please thee to rule and govern thy holy Church universal in the right way;
We beseech thee to hear us, good Lord.

That it may please thee to illuminate all bishops, priests, and deacons, with true knowledge and understanding of thy Word; and that both by their preaching and living they may set it forth and show it accordingly;
We beseech thee to hear us, good Lord.

That it may please thee to bless these thy servants, now to be admitted to the order of Priests, and to pour thy grace upon them; that they may duly execute their office, to the edifying of thy Church, and the glory of thy holy Name;
We beseech thee to hear us, good Lord.

That it may please thee to further the work of the Church in all the world, and to send forth labourers into thy harvest;
We beseech thee to hear us, good Lord.

That it may please thee to give to all thy people increase of grace, to hear meekly thy Word, and to receive it with pure affection, and to bring forth the fruits of the Spirit;
We beseech thee to hear us, good Lord.

That it may please thee to bring into the way of truth all such as have erred, and are deceived;
We beseech thee to hear us, good Lord.

That it may please thee to strengthen such as do stand; and to comfort and help the weak-hearted; and to raise up them that fall; and finally to beat down Satan under our feet;
We beseech thee to hear us, good Lord.

That it may please thee to forgive our enemies, persecutors, and slanderers, and to turn their hearts;
We beseech thee to hear us, good Lord.

That it may please thee to give us true repentance; to forgive us all our sins, negligences, and ignorances; and to endue us with the grace of thy Holy Spirit, to amend our lives according to thy holy Word;
We beseech thee to hear us, good Lord.

Son of God: we beseech thee to hear us.
Son of God: we beseech thee to hear us.

O Lamb of God: that takest away the sins of the world;
Grant us thy peace.

O Lamb of God: that takest away the sins of the world;
Have mercy upon us.

O Christ, hear us.
O Christ, hear us.

Lord, have mercy upon us.
Lord, have mercy upon us.
Christ, have mercy upon us.
Christ, have mercy upon us.
Lord, have mercy upon us.
Lord, have mercy upon us.

Then shall be sung or said the Service for the Communion, with the Collect, Epistle, and Gospel, as followeth:

THE COLLECT

Almighty God, giver of all good things, who by thy Holy Spirit hast appointed divers orders of ministers in thy Church: Mercifully behold these thy servants now called to the office of Priesthood; and replenish them so with the truth of thy doctrine, and adorn them with innocency of life, that, both by word and good example, they may faithfully serve thee in this office, to the glory of thy Name, and the edification of thy Church;

through the merits of our Saviour Jesus Christ, who liveth and reigneth with thee and the Holy Ghost, world without end. **Amen.**

THE EPISTLE

Ephesians 4: 7-13

Unto every one of us is given grace according to the measure of the gift of Christ. Wherefore he saith, When he ascended up on high, he led captivity captive, and gave gifts unto men. (Now that he ascended, what is it but that he also descended first into the lower parts of the earth? He that descended is the same also that ascended up far above all heavens, that he might fill all things.) And he gave some, apostles; and some, prophets; and some, evangelists; and some, pastors and teachers; for the perfecting of the saints, for the work of the ministry, for the edifying of the body of Christ: till we all come, in the unity of the faith and of the knowledge of the Son of God, unto a perfect man, unto the measure of the stature of the fulness of Christ.

After this shall be read the Gospel, part of the ninth chapter of Saint Matthew, as followeth.

THE GOSPEL

Matthew 9: 36-38

When Jesus saw the multitudes, he was moved with compassion on them, because they fainted, and were scattered abroad, as sheep having no shepherd. Then saith he unto his disciples, The harvest truly is plenteous, but the labourers are few; pray ye therefore the Lord of the harvest, that he will send forth labourers into his harvest.

Or else this that followeth, out of the tenth chapter of Saint John.

John 10: 1-16

Verily, verily, I say unto you, He that entereth not by the door into the sheep-fold, but climbeth up some other way, the same is a thief and a robber. But he that entereth in by the door is the shepherd of the sheep. To him the porter openeth; and the sheep hear his voice: and he calleth his own sheep by name, and leadeth them out. And when he putteth forth his own sheep, he goeth before them, and the sheep follow him: for they know his voice. And a stranger will they not follow, but will flee from him: for they know not the voice of strangers. This parable spake Jesus unto them, but they understood not what things they were which he spake unto them. Then said Jesus unto them again, Verily, verily, I say unto you, I am the door of the sheep. All that ever came before me are thieves and robbers: but the sheep did not hear them. I am the door: by me if any man enter in, he shall be saved, and shall go in and out, and find pasture. The thief cometh not but for to steal, and to kill, and to destroy: I am come that they might have life, and that they might have it more abundantly. I am the good shepherd: the good shepherd giveth his life for the sheep. But he that is an hireling, and not the shepherd, whose own the sheep are not, seeth the wolf coming, and leaveth the sheep, and fleeth: and the wolf catcheth them, and scattereth the sheep. The hireling fleeth because he is an hireling, and careth not for the sheep. I am the good shepherd; and I know mine own, and mine own know me, even as the Father knoweth me, and I know the Father; and I lay down my life for the sheep. And other sheep I have, which are not of this fold: them also I must bring, and they shall hear my voice; and there shall be one flock, and one shepherd.

Then the bishop, sitting in his chair, shall say unto them as hereafter followeth:

You have heard, *brethren*, as well in your private examination, as in the exhortation which was now made to you, and in the holy Lessons taken out of the Gospel and the writings of the apostles, of what dignity and of how great importance this office is, whereunto ye are called. And now again we exhort you, in the Name of our Lord Jesus Christ, that you have in remembrance, into how high a dignity, and to how weighty an office and charge ye are called: that is to say, to be messengers, watchmen, and stewards of the Lord; to teach and to premonish, to feed and provide for the Lord's family; to seek for Christ's sheep that are dispersed abroad, and for his children who are in the midst of this naughty world, that they may be saved through Christ for ever.

Have always therefore printed in your remembrance, how great a treasure is committed to your charge. For they are the sheep of Christ, which he bought with his death, and for whom he shed his blood. The Church and Congregation whom you must serve, is his spouse and his body. And if it shall happen the same Church, or any member thereof, to take any hurt or hindrance by reason of your negligence, ye know the greatness of the fault, and also the horrible punishment that will ensue. Wherefore consider with yourselves the end of your ministry towards the children of God, towards the spouse and body of Christ; and see that you never cease your labour, your care and diligence, until you have done all that lieth in you, according to your bounden duty, to bring all such as are or shall be committed to your charge, unto that agreement in the faith and knowledge of God, and to that ripeness and perfectness of age in Christ, that there be no place left among you, either for error in religion, or for viciousness in life.

Forasmuch then as your office is both of so great excellency and of so great difficulty, ye see with how great care and study ye ought to apply yourselves, as well that ye may shew yourselves dutiful and thankful unto that Lord, who hath placed you in so high a dignity; as also to beware that neither you yourselves offend, nor be occasion that others offend. Howbeit, ye cannot have a mind and will thereto of yourselves; for that will and ability is given of God alone: therefore ye ought, and have need, to pray earnestly for his Holy Spirit. And seeing that you cannot by any other means compass the doing of so weighty a work, pertaining to the salvation of man, but with doctrine and exhortation taken out of the holy Scriptures, and with a life agreeable to the same; consider how studious ye ought to be in reading and learning the Scriptures, and in framing the manners both of yourselves, and of them that specially pertain unto you, according to the rule of the same Scriptures: and for this self-same cause, how ye ought to forsake and set aside (as much as you may) all worldly cares and studies.

We have good hope that you have well weighed and pondered these things with yourselves long before this time; and that you have clearly deter-mined, by God's grace, to give yourselves wholly to this office, whereunto it hath pleased God to call you: so that, as much as lieth in you, you will apply yourselves wholly to this one thing, and draw all your cares and stud-ies this way; and that you will continually pray to God the Father, by the mediation of our only Saviour Jesus Christ, for the heavenly assistance of the Holy Ghost; that, by daily reading and weighing of the Scriptures, ye may wax riper and stronger in your ministry; and that ye may so endeav-our yourselves, from time to time, to sanctify the lives of you and yours, and to fashion them after the rule and doctrine of Christ, that ye may be wholesome and godly examples and patterns for the people to follow.

And now, that this present Congregation of Christ here assembled may also understand your minds and wills in these things, and that this your promise may the more move you to do your duties, ye shall answer plainly to these things, which we, in the Name of God, and of his Church, shall demand of you touching the same.

Do you think in your heart that you be truly called, according to the will of our Lord Jesus Christ, and the order of this Church of Ireland, to the order and ministry of Priesthood?

Answer **I think it.**

The bishop

Are you persuaded that the holy Scriptures contain sufficiently all doctrine required of necessity for eternal salvation through faith in Jesus Christ? And are you determined out of the said Scriptures to instruct the people committed to your charge, and to teach nothing as required of necessity to eternal salvation but that which you shall be persuaded may be concluded and proved by the Scripture?

Answer **I am so persuaded, and have so determined, by God's grace.**

The bishop

Will you then give your faithful diligence always so to minister the doctrine and sacraments, and the discipline of Christ, as the Lord hath commanded, and as this Church hath received the same, according to the commandments of God; so that you may teach the people committed to your cure and charge with all diligence to keep and observe the same?

Answer **I will so do, by the help of the Lord.**

The bishop

Will you be ready, with all faithful diligence, to banish and drive away all erroneous and strange doctrines contrary to God's Word; and to use both public and private monitions and exhortations, as well to the sick as to the whole, within your cures, as need shall require, and occasion shall be given?

Answer **I will, the Lord being my helper.**

The bishop

Will you be diligent in prayers, and in reading of the holy Scriptures, and in such studies as help to the knowledge of the same, laying aside the study of the world and the flesh?

Answer **I will endeavour myself so to do, the Lord being my helper.**

The bishop

Will you be diligent to frame and fashion your own selves, and your families, according to the doctrine of Christ; and to make both yourselves and them, as much as in you lieth, wholesome examples and patterns to the flock of Christ?

Answer **I will apply myself thereto, the Lord being my helper.**

The bishop

Will you maintain and set forwards, as much as lieth in you, quietness, peace, and love, among all Christian people, and especially among them that are or shall be committed to your charge?

Answer **I will so do, the Lord being my helper.**

The bishop

Will you reverently obey your Ordinary, and other chief ministers, unto whom is committed the charge and government over you, following with a glad mind and will their godly admonitions, and submitting yourselves to their godly judgments?

Answer **I will so do, the Lord being my helper.**

Then shall the bishop, standing up, say
Almighty God,
who hath given you this will to do all these things;
Grant also unto you strength and power to perform the same;
that he may accomplish his work which he hath begun in you;
through Jesus Christ our Lord. **Amen.**

After this, the congregation shall be desired, secretly in their prayers, to make their humble supplications to God for all these things: for the which prayers there shall be silence kept for a space.

After which shall be sung or said by the bishop (the persons to be ordained priests all kneeling) Veni, Creator Spiritus; the bishop beginning, and the priests, and others that are present, answering by verses, as followeth:

Come, Holy Ghost, our souls inspire,
And lighten with celestial fire.
Thou the anointing Spirit art,
Who dost thy seven-fold gifts impart.

Thy blessed unction from above
Is comfort, life, and fire of love.
Enable with perpetual light
The dulness of our blinded sight.

Anoint and cheer our soiled face
With the abundance of thy grace.
Keep far our foes, give peace at home;
Where thou art guide, no ill can come.

Teach us to know the Father, Son,
And thee, of both, to be but One;
That, through the ages all along,
This may be our endless song:

Praise to thy eternal merit,
Father, Son, and Holy Spirit.

That done, the bishop shall pray in this wise, and say

Let us pray.

Almighty God and heavenly Father, who, of thine infinite love and goodness towards us, hast given to us thy only and most dearly beloved Son Jesus Christ, to be our Redeemer, and the Author of everlasting life; who, after he had made perfect our redemption by his death, and was ascended into heaven, sent abroad into the world his apostles, prophets, evangelists, doctors, and pastors; by whose labour and ministry he gathered together a great flock in all the parts of the world, to set forth the eternal praise of thy holy Name:

For these so great benefits of thy eternal goodness, and for that thou hast vouchsafed to call these thy servants here present to the same office and ministry appointed for the salvation of mankind, we render unto thee most hearty thanks, we praise and worship thee; and we humbly beseech thee, by the same thy blessed Son, to grant unto all, which either here or elsewhere call upon thy holy Name, that we may continue to show ourselves thankful unto thee for these and all other thy benefits; and that we may daily increase and go forwards in the knowledge and faith of thee and thy Son, by the Holy Spirit. So that as well by these thy ministers, as by them over whom they shall be appointed thy ministers, thy holy Name may be for ever glorified, and thy blessed kingdom enlarged; through the same thy Son Jesus Christ our Lord, who liveth and reigneth with thee in the unity of the same Holy Spirit, world without end. **Amen**.

When this prayer is done, the bishop with the priests present shall lay their hands severally upon the head of every one that receiveth the order of Priesthood; the receivers humbly kneeling upon their knees, and the bishop saying

Receive the Holy Ghost for the office and work of a Priest in the Church of God, now committed unto thee by the imposition of our hands.
Whose sins thou dost forgive, they are forgiven;
and whose sins thou dost retain, they are retained.
And be thou a faithful dispenser of the Word of God, and of his holy Sacraments;
In the Name of the Father, and of the Son, and of the Holy Ghost. Amen.

Then the bishop shall deliver to every one of them kneeling the Bible into his hand, saying

Take thou authority to preach the Word of God, and to minister the holy Sacraments in the congregation, where thou shalt be lawfully appointed thereunto.

When this is done, the Nicene Creed shall be sung or said; and the bishop shall after that go on in the Service of the Communion, which all they that receive orders shall take together, and remain in the same place where hands were laid upon them, until such time as they have received the Communion.

Immediately before the Benediction shall be said these collects:

Most merciful Father,

we beseech thee to send upon these thy servants thy heavenly blessing;

that they may be clothed with righteousness,

and that thy Word spoken by their mouths may have such success,

that it may never be spoken in vain.

Grant also that we may have grace to hear and receive

what they shall deliver out of thy most holy Word,

or agreeable to the same, as the means of our salvation;

that in all our words and deeds we may seek thy glory,

and the increase of thy kingdom;

through Jesus Christ our Lord. **Amen.**

Prevent us, O Lord, in all our doings

with thy most gracious favour,

and further us with thy continual help;

that in all our works, begun, continued, and ended in thee,

we may glorify thy holy Name,

and finally by thy mercy obtain everlasting life;

through Jesus Christ our Lord. **Amen.**

The peace of God, which passeth all understanding,

keep your hearts and minds in the knowledge and love of God,

and of his Son Jesus Christ our Lord:

And the blessing of God almighty,

the Father, the Son, and the Holy Ghost,

be amongst you and remain with you always. **Amen.**

And if on the same day the order of Deacons be given to some, and the order of Priesthood to others; the deacons shall first be presented, and then the priests: and it shall suffice that the Litany be once said for both. The Collects shall both be used; first that for Deacons, then that for Priests. The Epistle shall be Ephesians 4: 7-13, as before in this Office. Immediately after which, they that are to be made deacons shall be examined and ordained, as is above prescribed. Then one of them having read the Gospel (which shall be either out of St Matthew 9: 36-38, as before in this Office; or else St Luke 12: 35-38, as before in the Form of the Ordering of Deacons,) they that are to be made priests shall likewise be examined and ordained, as is in this Office before appointed.

THE FORM OF
ORDAINING OR CONSECRATING
OF AN
ARCHBISHOP OR BISHOP
WHICH IS ALWAYS TO BE PERFORMED UPON SOME SUNDAY OR HOLY-DAY

When all things are duly prepared in the church, and set in order, the archbishop (or some other bishop appointed) shall begin the Communion Service; in which this shall be

THE COLLECT

Almighty God, who by thy Son Jesus Christ didst give to thy holy Apostles many excellent gifts, and didst charge them to feed thy flock; Give grace, we beseech thee, to all bishops, the pastors of thy Church, that they may diligently preach thy Word, and duly administer the godly discipline thereof; and grant to the people, that they may obediently follow the same; that all may receive the crown of everlasting glory; through Jesus Christ our Lord. **Amen.**

And another bishop shall read

THE EPISTLE

1 Timothy 3: 1-7

This is a true saying, If a man desire the office of a bishop, he desireth a good work. A bishop then must be blameless, the husband of one wife, vigilant, sober, of good behaviour, given to hospitality, apt to teach; not given to wine, no striker, not greedy of filthy lucre; but patient, not a brawler, not covetous; one that ruleth well his own house, having his children in subjection with all gravity; (for if a man know not how to rule his own house, how shall he take care of the Church of God?) not a novice, lest being lifted up with pride he fall into the condemnation of the devil. Moreover, he must have a good report of them which are without; lest he fall into reproach and the snare of the devil.

or this

Acts 20: 17-35

From Miletus Paul sent to Ephesus, and called the elders of the Church. And when they were come to him, he said unto them, Ye know, from the first day that I came into Asia, after what manner I have been with you at all seasons, serving the Lord with all humility of mind, and with many tears, and temptations which befell me by the lying in wait of the Jews: and how I kept back nothing that was profitable unto you, but have showed you, and have taught you publicly, and from house to house, testifying both to the Jews, and also to the Greeks, repentance toward God, and faith toward our Lord Jesus Christ. And now, behold, I go bound in the spirit unto Jerusalem, not knowing the things that shall befall me there: save that the Holy Ghost witnesseth in every city, saying, that bonds and afflictions abide me. But none of these things move me, neither count I my life dear unto myself, so that I might finish my course with joy, and the ministry which I have received of the Lord Jesus, to testify the Gospel of the grace of God. And now, behold, I know that ye all, among whom I have gone preaching the kingdom of God, shall see my face no more. Wherefore I take you to record this day, that I am pure from the blood of all men. For I have not shunned to declare unto you all the counsel of God. Take heed therefore unto yourselves, and to all the flock, over the which the Holy Ghost hath made you overseers, to feed the Church of God, which he hath purchased with his own blood. For I know this, that after my departing shall grievous wolves enter in among you, not sparing the flock. Also of your own selves shall men arise, speaking perverse things, to draw away disciples after them. Therefore watch, and remember that by the space of three years I ceased not to warn everyone night and day with tears. And now, brethren, I commend you to God, and to the word of his grace, which is able to build you up, and to give you an inheritance among all them which are sanctified. I have coveted no man's silver, or gold, or apparel. Yea, ye yourselves know, that these hands have ministered unto my necessities, and to them that were with me. I have showed you all things, how that so labouring ye ought to support the weak, and to remember the words of the Lord Jesus, how he said, It is more blessed to give than to receive.

Then another bishop shall read

John 21: 15-17

Jesus saith to Simon Peter, Simon, son of Jonas, lovest thou me more than these? He saith unto him, Yea, Lord, thou knowest that I love thee. He saith unto him, Feed my lambs. He saith to him again the second time, Simon, son of Jonas, lovest thou me? He saith unto him, Yea, Lord, thou knowest that I love thee. He saith unto him, Feed my sheep. He saith unto him the third time, Simon, son of Jonas, lovest thou me? Peter was grieved because he said unto him the third time, Lovest thou me? And he said unto him, Lord, thou knowest all things; thou knowest that I love thee. Jesus saith unto him, Feed my sheep.

Or else this

John 20: 19-23

The same day at evening, being the first day of the week, when the doors were shut where the disciples were assembled, for fear of the Jews, came Jesus and stood in the midst, and saith unto them, Peace be unto you. And when he had so said, he showed unto them his hands and his side. Then were the disciples glad, when they saw the Lord. Then said Jesus to them again, Peace be unto you: as my Father hath sent me, even so send I you. And when he had said this, he breathed on them, and saith unto them, Receive ye the Holy Ghost: whose soever sins ye remit, they are remitted unto them; and whose soever sins ye retain, they are retained.

Or this

Matthew 28: 18-20

Jesus came and spake unto them, saying, All power is given unto me in heaven and in earth. Go ye therefore and teach all nations, baptizing them in the Name of the Father, and of the Son, and of the Holy Ghost; teaching them to observe all things whatsoever I have commanded you: and lo, I am with you alway, even unto the end of the world.

After the Gospel, and the Nicene Creed, and the sermon are ended, the elected bishop (vested with a rochet) shall be presented by two bishops unto the archbishop of that province (or to some other bishop appointed by lawful commission), the archbishop sitting in his chair, near the holy table, and the bishops that present him saying

Archbishop, we present unto you this godly and well-learned *man* to be ordained and consecrated Bishop.

Then shall the archbishop demand the Certificate of the Bench of Bishops of the election and fitness of the person to be consecrated, and cause it to be read. And then shall such person make the Declaration of Obedience to the archbishop, as followeth:

THE DECLARATION OF DUE OBEDIENCE TO THE ARCHBISHOP

In the Name of God, Amen. I, ..., chosen Bishop of the Church and See of .... do solemnly profess and promise all due reverence and obedience to the Archbishop of ...., and to *his* successors.

This Declaration shall not be made at the Consecration of an archbishop.

Then the archbishop shall move the congregation present to pray, saying thus to them:

Brethren, it is written in the Gospel of Saint Luke, that our Saviour Christ continued the whole night in prayer, before he did choose and send forth his twelve Apostles. It is written also in the Acts of the Apostles, that the disciples who were at Antioch did fast and pray, before they laid hands on Paul and Barnabas, and sent them forth. Let us therefore, following the example of our Saviour Christ and his Apostles, first fall to prayer, before we admit and send forth this person presented unto us, to the work whereunto we trust the Holy Ghost hath called *him*.

And then shall be sung or said the Litany, as followeth:

THE LITANY

O God the Father, of heaven: have mercy upon us miserable sinners.

O God the Father, of heaven: have mercy upon us miserable sinners.

O God the Son, Redeemer of the world: have mercy upon us miserable sinners.

O God the Son, Redeemer of the world: have mercy upon us miserable sinners.

O God the Holy Ghost, proceeding from the Father and the Son: have mercy upon us miserable sinners.

O God the Holy Ghost, proceeding from the Father and the Son: have mercy upon us miserable sinners.

O holy, blessed, and glorious Trinity, three Persons and one God: have mercy upon us miserable sinners.

O holy, blessed, and glorious Trinity, three Persons and one God: have mercy upon us miserable sinners.

Remember not, Lord, our offences, nor the offences of our forefathers; neither take thou vengeance of our sins: spare us, good Lord, spare thy people, whom thou hast redeemed with thy most precious blood, and be not angry with us for ever.

Spare us, good Lord.

From all blindness of heart; from pride, vain-glory, and hypocrisy; from envy, hatred, and malice, and all uncharitableness,

Good Lord, deliver us.

From all sedition, privy conspiracy, and rebellion; from all false doctrine, heresy, and schism; from hardness of heart, and contempt of thy Word and Commandment,

Good Lord, deliver us.

By the mystery of thy holy Incarnation; by thy holy Nativity and Circumcision; by thy Baptism, Fasting and Temptation,

Good Lord, deliver us.

By thine Agony and bloody Sweat; by thy Cross and Passion; by thy precious Death and Burial; by thy glorious Resurrection and Ascension; and by the coming of the Holy Ghost,

Good Lord, deliver us.

We sinners do beseech thee to hear us, O Lord God: and that it may please thee to rule and govern thy holy Church universal in the right way;

We beseech thee to hear us, good Lord.

That it may please thee to illuminate all bishops, priests, and deacons, with true knowledge and understanding of thy Word; and that both by their preaching and living they may set it forth and show it accordingly;
We beseech thee to hear us, good Lord.

That it may please thee to bless this our *Brother* elected, and to send thy grace upon *him*; that *he* may duly execute the Office whereunto *he* is called, to the edifying of thy Church, and to the honour, praise and glory of thy Name;
We beseech thee to hear us, good Lord.

That it may please thee to further the work of the Church in all the world, and to send forth labourers into thy harvest;
We beseech thee to hear us, good Lord.

That it may please thee to give to all thy people increase of grace, to hear meekly thy Word, and to receive it with pure affection, and to bring forth the fruits of the Spirit;
We beseech thee to hear us, good Lord.

That it may please thee to bring into the way of truth all such as have erred, and are deceived;
We beseech thee to hear us, good Lord.

That it may please thee to strengthen such as do stand; and to comfort and help the weak-hearted; and to raise up them that fall; and finally to beat down Satan under our feet;
We beseech thee to hear us, good Lord.

That it may please thee to forgive our enemies, persecutors, and slanderers, and to turn their hearts;
We beseech thee to hear us, good Lord.

That it may please thee to give us true repentance; to forgive us all our sins, negligences, and ignorances; and to endue us with the grace of thy Holy Spirit, to amend our lives according to thy holy Word;
We beseech thee to hear us, good Lord.

Son of God: we beseech thee to hear us.
Son of God: we beseech thee to hear us.

O Lamb of God: that takest away the sins of the world;
Grant us thy peace.

O Lamb of God: that takest away the sins of the world;
Have mercy upon us.

O Christ, hear us.
O Christ, hear us.

Lord, have mercy upon us.
Lord, have mercy upon us.
Christ, have mercy upon us.
Christ, have mercy upon us.
Lord, have mercy upon us.
Lord, have mercy upon us.

Then shall be said this prayer following:

Almighty God, giver of all good things, who by thy Holy Spirit hast appointed divers orders of ministers in thy Church; Mercifully behold this thy servant now called to the work and ministry of a bishop; and replenish *him* so with the truth of thy doctrine, and adorn *him* with innocency of life, that, both by word and deed, *he* may faithfully serve thee in this office, to the glory of thy Name, and the edifying and well-governing of thy Church; through the merits of our Saviour Jesus Christ, who liveth and reigneth with thee and the Holy Ghost, world without end. **Amen.**

Then the archbishop, sitting in his *chair, shall say to* him *that is to be consecrated,*

Brother, forasmuch as the holy Scripture and the ancient Canons command that we should not be hasty in laying on hands, and admitting any person to government in the Church of Christ, which he hath purchased with no less price than the effusion of his own blood; before I admit you to this Administration, I will examine you in certain Articles, to the end that the congregation present may have a trial, and bear witness, how you be minded to behave yourself in the Church of God.

Are you persuaded that you be truly called to this ministration, according to the will of our Lord Jesus Christ, and the order of this Church?
Answer **I am so persuaded.**

The archbishop
Are you persuaded that the holy Scriptures contain sufficiently all doctrine required of necessity for eternal salvation through faith in Jesus Christ? And are you determined out of the same holy Scriptures to instruct the people committed to your charge; and to teach or maintain nothing as required of necessity to eternal salvation, but that which you shall be persuaded may be concluded and proved by the same?
Answer **I am so persuaded and determined, by God's grace.**

The archbishop
Will you then faithfully exercise yourself in the same holy Scriptures, and call upon God by prayer, for the true understanding of the same; so as you may be able by them to teach and exhort with wholesome doctrine, and to withstand and convince the gainsayers?
Answer **I will so do, by the help of God.**

The archbishop
Are you ready, with all faithful diligence, to banish and drive away all erroneous and strange doctrine contrary to God's Word; and both privately and openly to call upon and encourage others to the same?
Answer **I am ready, the Lord being my helper.**

The archbishop
Will you deny all ungodliness and worldly lusts, and live soberly, righteously and godly in this present world; that you may show yourself in all things an example of good works unto others, that the adversary may be ashamed, having nothing to say against you?
Answer **I will so do, the Lord being my helper.**

The archbishop

Will you maintain and set forward, as much as shall lie in you, quietness, love, and peace among all Christian people; and such as be unquiet, disobedient and criminous within your diocese, correct and punish, according to such authority as you have by God's Word, and as to you shall be committed by the ordinance of this Church?

Answer **I will so do, by the help of God.**

The archbishop

Will you be faithful in ordaining, sending, or laying hands upon others?

Answer **I will so be, by the help of God.**

The archbishop

Will you show yourself gentle, and be merciful for Christ's sake to poor and needy people, and to all strangers destitute of help?

Answer **I will so show myself, by God's help.**

Then the archbishop, standing up, shall say,

Almighty God, our heavenly Father,

who hath given you a good will to do all these things;

Grant also unto you strength and power to perform the same;

that, he accomplishing in you the good work which he hath begun,

you may be found perfect and irreprehensible at the latter day;

through Jesus Christ our Lord. **Amen.**

Then shall the bishop-elect put on the rest of the episcopal habit; and kneeling down, Veni, Creator Spiritus, *shall be sung or said over* him, *the archbishop beginning, and the bishops, with others that are present, answering by verses, as followeth:*

> Come, Holy Ghost, our souls inspire,
> And lighten with celestial fire.
> Thou the anointing Spirit art,
> Who dost thy seven-fold gifts impart.
>
> Thy blessed unction from above,
> Is comfort, life, and fire of love.
> Enable with perpetual light
> The dulness of our blinded sight.

Anoint and cheer our soiled face
With the abundance of thy grace.
Keep far our foes, give peace at home:
Where thou art guide, no ill can come.

Teach us to know the Father, Son,
And thee, of both, to be but One.
That, through the ages all along,
This may be our endless song:

Praise to thy eternal merit,
Father, Son, and Holy Spirit.

That ended, the archbishop shall say
Lord, hear our prayer;
Answer **And let our cry come unto thee.**

Let us pray.
Almighty God and most merciful Father, who of thine infinite goodness
hast given thine only and dearly beloved Son Jesus Christ, to be our
Redeemer and the Author of everlasting life; who, after that he had made
perfect our redemption by his death, and was ascended into heaven, poured
down his gifts abundantly upon men, making some apostles, some
prophets, some evangelists, some pastors and doctors, to the edifying and
making perfect his Church; Grant, we beseech thee, to this thy servant
such grace, that *he* may evermore be ready to spread abroad thy Gospel,
the glad tidings of reconciliation with thee; and use the authority given
him, not to destruction, but to salvation; not to hurt, but to help: so that as a
wise and faithful servant, giving to thy family their portion in due season,
he may at last be received into everlasting joy; through Jesus Christ our
Lord, who with thee and the Holy Ghost liveth and reigneth, one God,
world without end. **Amen.**

*Then the archbishop and bishops present shall lay their hands upon the head of
the elected bishop kneeling before them upon his knees, the archbishop saying*
Receive the Holy Ghost for the office and work of a Bishop in the Church
of God, now committed unto thee by the imposition of our hands;
In the Name of the Father, and of the Son, and of the Holy Ghost. Amen.

And remember that thou stir up the grace of God
which is given thee by this imposition of our hands:
for God hath not given us the spirit of fear,
but of power, and love, and soberness.

Then the archbishop shall deliver him the Bible, saying
Give heed unto reading, exhortation, and doctrine.
Think upon the things contained in this Book.
Be diligent in them, that the increase coming thereby may be manifest
unto all men.
Take heed unto thyself, and to doctrine, and be diligent in doing them:
for by so doing thou shalt both save thyself and them that hear thee.
Be to the flock of Christ a shepherd, not a wolf; feed them, devour them
not.
Hold up the weak, heal the sick, bind up the broken, bring again the out-
casts, seek the lost.
Be so merciful, that you be not too remiss; so minister discipline, that
you forget not mercy:
that when the chief Shepherd shall appear
you may receive the never-fading crown of glory;
through Jesus Christ our Lord. **Amen.**

*Then the archbishop shall proceed in the Communion Service; with whom the
new consecrated bishop (with others) shall also communicate.*

And immediately before the Benediction shall be said these prayers:
Most merciful Father,
we beseech thee to send down upon this thy servant thy heavenly blessing;
and so endue *him* with thy Holy Spirit, that *he*, preaching thy Word,
may not only be earnest to reprove, beseech, and rebuke
with all patience and doctrine;
but also may be to such as believe a wholesome example,
in word, in conversation, in love, in faith, in chastity, and in purity;
that, faithfully fulfilling *his* course,
at the latter day *he* may receive the crown of righteousness
laid up by the Lord, the righteous Judge,
who liveth and reigneth, one God
with the Father and the Holy Ghost, world without end. **Amen.**

Prevent us, O Lord, in all our doings
with thy most gracious favour,
and further us with thy continual help;
that in all our works, begun, continued, and ended in thee,
we may glorify thy holy Name,
and finally by thy mercy obtain everlasting life;
through Jesus Christ our Lord. **Amen.**

The peace of God, which passeth all understanding,
keep your hearts and minds in the knowledge and love of God,
and of his Son Jesus Christ our Lord:
And the blessing of God almighty,
the Father, the Son, and the Holy Ghost,
be amongst you and remain with you always. **Amen.**

THE ORDINAL

1 *The threefold Ministry*

The Church of Ireland maintains the historic threefold ministry of bishops, priests (also called presbyters), and deacons. Its ministers are ordained by bishops according to authorized forms of service, with prayer and the laying on of hands (see the Preamble and Declaration to the Constitution of the Church of Ireland, the Preface to the Ordinal (1662), and the Constitution itself).

2 *Consecration of Bishops*

Bishops must be consecrated by at least three other bishops, joining together in the act of laying on of hands, of whom one shall be the archbishop of the province or a bishop acting as deputy. Two assisting bishops should accompany the archbishop throughout.

Such consecrations should take place on a Sunday or Holy Day.

A consecration may appropriately take place in the metropolitan cathedral or in a cathedral of the vacant see. In the latter case it is appropriate that, once consecrated, the new bishop receives the pastoral staff, is placed in the episcopal seat and subsequently presides at the Eucharist.

3 *Ordination of Priests and Deacons*

Priests (or presbyters) share with the bishop in laying hands on the heads of those ordained to the order of priest. The bishop alone lays hands on the heads of those ordained to the order of deacon.

4 *The Declarations*

The declarations as required by the Constitution of the Church of Ireland are taken prior to the service of ordination of deacons and priests.

5 *Form of Service*

Questions concerning the form of service to be used, and other matters concerning the conduct of the service, are to be determined by the bishop who presides at it, in accordance with the rubrics of the service and having regard to tradition and local custom.

6 *Readings*

The Readings will normally be those indicated in the service. On occasion the readings of the day may be used or readings may be selected from those provided in the Table of Readings page 70.

7 *Vesture*

The ordinand may be vested in the vesture of the order before the service begins, or at the appropriate point after the laying on of hands. Deacons and priests are vested with a scarf or stole according to individual choice, and bishops in their episcopal habit (see Canon 12).

8 *The Presentation*

Before the service, the ordinand is appropriately seated with those who will present *him/her* to the bishop; while, after the presentation, it is appropriate that all those being ordained should be seated together.

9 In these services appropriate changes are made to nouns and pronouns when there is only one candidate for ordination.

THE ORDINATION OF DEACONS

The Gathering of God's People

At the entry of the ministers, a hymn, a canticle, or a psalm may be sung. Those to be ordained should be seated among the congregation with those who will present them for ordination.

The bishop says
The Lord be with you
and also with you.

We are the body of Christ.
By the one Spirit we were all baptized into one body.

There is one Lord, one faith, one baptism:
One God and Father of all.

Saint Paul wrote:
Just as in a single human body there are many limbs and organs, all with different functions, so we who are united with Christ, though many, form one body, and belong to one another as its limbs and organs. We have gifts allotted to each of us by God's grace. *Romans 12: 5,6 (REB)*

Today, giving thanks for the variety of gifts and ministries that God has bestowed on the Church, we have come together to admit to the order of deacons those whom we believe God has chosen for this particular ministry within the body, seeking by prayer with the laying on of hands the bestowal of the Holy Spirit for that office and work. In doing so we are maintaining the historic threefold ministry of bishops, priest or presbyters, and deacons in the Church which it has received.

Each candidate is presented by sponsors to the bishop, with the words
Bishop ...., we present .... to be ordained deacon.

Archdeacon, are those responsible for their selection and training satisfied that they are called and ready to be ordained deacon in the Church of God?

Answer **They are satisfied.**

The bishop says to each candidate

...., do you believe in your heart that God has called you to the office and work of a deacon in his Church?

Answer **I believe that God has called me.**

Bishop

Let us pray.

Silence

God our Father, Lord of all the world,
we thank you that through your Son
you have called us into the fellowship of your universal Church.
Hear our prayer for your faithful people
that in their vocation and ministry
they may be instruments of your love,
and give to *these* your *servants* now to be ordained
the needful gifts of grace;
through our Lord and Saviour Jesus Christ. **Amen.**

On a principal holy day or festival the Collect of the Day may be used.

Proclaiming and Receiving the Word

THE FIRST READING
Isaiah 6: 1-8

THE PSALM
Psalm 119: 33-38

THE SECOND READING
Romans 12: 1-12

A canticle, hymn or anthem may be sung.

The reading is introduced with the following words:
Hear the Gospel of our Saviour Christ according to Saint Mark, chapter ten beginning at verse thirty-five.
Glory to you, Lord Jesus Christ.

And concludes with
This is the Gospel of the Lord:
Praise to you, Lord Jesus Christ.

THE SERMON

THE NICENE CREED

Mindful of our baptism we proclaim the faith of the universal church:
We believe ... *(page 205)*

The Rite of Ordination

THE DECLARATIONS

The candidates stand before the bishop, and the people sit.
The bishop says

Deacons in the Church of God serve in the name of Christ, and so remind the whole Church that serving others is at the heart of all ministry.

Deacons have a special responsibility to ensure that those in need are cared for with compassion and humility. They are to strengthen the faithful, search out the careless and the indifferent, and minister to the sick, the needy, the poor and those in trouble.

When called upon to do so, they may baptize, preach and give instruction in the faith.

Deacons assist the bishop and priest under whom they serve. When the people are gathered for worship, deacons are authorized to read the Gospel, lead the people in intercession, and distribute the bread and wine of Holy Communion.

The bishop asks those to be ordained

Do you believe and accept the holy Scriptures as revealing all things necessary for eternal salvation through faith in Jesus Christ?

Answer **I do.**

Do you believe and accept the doctrine of the Christian faith as the Church of Ireland has received it?

Answer **I do.**

In your ministry will you expound the Scriptures and teach that doctrine?

Answer **By the help of God, I will.**

Will you accept the discipline of this Church and give due respect to those set over you in the Lord?

Answer **By the help of God, I will.**

Will you be diligent in prayer, in reading holy Scripture, and in all studies that will deepen your faith and fit you to uphold the truth of the Gospel?

Answer **By the help of God, I will.**

Will you strive to fashion your own life and your family relationships according to the way of Christ?

Answer **By the help of God, I will.**

Will you be faithful in visiting the sick, in caring for the poor and needy, and in helping the oppressed?

Answer **By the help of God, I will.**

Will you promote unity, peace, and love among all Christian people, and especially among those whom you serve?

Answer **By the help of God, I will.**

Will you then, in the strength of the Holy Spirit, continually stir up the gift of God that is in you, to make Christ known to all people?

Answer **By the help of God, I will.**

The bishop presents the candidates to the people, and says
You have heard the testimony of those who present these candidates for ordination, and also their own declarations made before you. Those whose duty it is to inquire about these persons and examine them have also found them to be of godly life and sound learning, and believe them to be duly called to serve God in this ministry.

If any of you knows sufficient cause why any of these persons should not be ordained deacon, come forward and make it known.

Is it therefore your will that they should be ordained?
Answer **It is.**

Will you uphold them in their ministry?
Answer **We will.**

PRAYERS

Bishop
Because none of us can bear the weight of this ministry in our own strength, but only by the grace and power of God, let us pray earnestly for the outpouring of the Holy Spirit on these persons.

Let us pray also that God will each day enlarge and enlighten their understanding of the Scriptures, so that they may grow stronger and more mature in their ministry, as they fashion their lives and the lives of the people they serve on the word of God.

The bishop or some other minister leads the prayers for the candidates and for the ministry of the whole Church.
An Ordination Litany (page 585) should be used.

Silence is kept.

An appropriate hymn of invocation to the Holy Spirit is sung, kneeling.

The bishop stands. The congregation stands.
The candidates kneel before the bishop, who says
Praise God who made heaven and earth,
who keeps his promise for ever.

Let us give thanks to the Lord our God.
It is right to give our thanks and praise.

We praise and glorify you, most merciful Father,
because in your great love for humankind
you sent your only Son Jesus Christ
to take the form of a servant.
He came to serve and not to be served;
and taught us that he who would be great among us
must be the servant of all.
He humbled himself for our sake,
and in obedience accepted death,
even death on a cross;
therefore you highly exalted him
and gave him the name which is above every name.

And now we give you thanks
that you have called *these your servants*,
whom we ordain in your name
to share this ministry entrusted to your Church.

Here the bishop lays hands on the head of each candidate, and says
Pour out your Holy Spirit upon your servant ....
for the office and work of a deacon in your Church.

The bishop having laid hands on all of them, continues
Give to *these your servants*
grace and power to fulfil *their* ministry.
Make *them* faithful to serve, ready to teach,
constant in advancing your gospel;

and grant that, always having full assurance of faith,
abounding in hope,
and being rooted and grounded in love,
they may continue strong and steadfast
in your Son Jesus Christ our Lord;
to whom, with you and your Holy Spirit,
belong glory and honour, worship and praise,
now and for ever. **Amen.**

Continue on page 561

Or

Praise God who made heaven and earth,
who keeps his promise for ever.

Let us give thanks to the Lord our God.
It is right to give our thanks and praise.

We praise and glorify you,
because you have given us your only Son Jesus Christ,
the image of your eternal and invisible glory,
the firstborn of creation, and the head of the Church.
Glory to you, Lord.

We praise and glorify you, most merciful Father,
because in your great love for all people,
you sent your only Son Jesus Christ
to take the form of a servant.
Glory to you, Lord.

He came to serve and not to be served,
and taught us that those who would be great among us
must be the servants of all.
Glory to you, Lord.

He humbled himself for our sake,
and in obedience accepted death, even death on a cross;
therefore you highly exalted him
and gave him the name which is above every name.
Glory to you, Lord.

We praise and glorify you that by his death he has overcome death,
and having ascended into heaven,
he has poured out his gifts abundantly,
to equip your people for the work of ministry and the building up of his body.
Glory to you, Lord.

And now we give you thanks that you have called *these your servants*
whom we ordain in your name,
to share the work of ministry entrusted to your Church.
Glory to you, Lord.

Therefore, Father, through Christ our Lord,

Here the bishop lays hands on the head of each candidate and says
pour out your Holy Spirit upon ....
for the office and work of a deacon in your Church.

The bishop having laid hands on all of them, continues
Fill *them* with grace and power that *they* may fulfil *their* ministry.
Pour out your Spirit, Lord.

Make *them* faithful to serve,
ready to teach,
constant in advancing your Gospel,
proclaiming by word and action the word of salvation
with full assurance of faith,
abounding in hope
and rooted and grounded in love.
Pour out your Spirit, Lord.

Grant *them* wisdom and discipline to work faithfully
with *their* fellow-servants in Christ,
continuing strong and steadfast in your Son Jesus Christ our Lord.
Pour out your Spirit, Lord.

Accept our prayers, most merciful Father,
through your Son Jesus Christ our Lord,
to whom with you and your Holy Spirit,
belong glory and honour, worship and praise,
now and for ever. **Amen.**

Each of the newly-ordained deacons is vested with a scarf or stole, if this has not already been done.

The bishop gives a bible to each deacon, saying
Receive this Book, as a sign of the authority
which God has given you this day to proclaim his word to his people.
Make it known in your words and in your deeds.

Bishop
Brothers and sisters in Christ, I present to you these persons
who have been ordained deacons in the Church of God.

The new deacons may be welcomed.

THE PEACE

The bishop introduces the Peace with these or other suitable words:
Jesus said, A new commandment I give to you,
that you love one another:
even as I have loved you, that you love one another.

The peace of the Lord be always with you
and also with you.

It is appropriate that the congregation share with one another a sign of peace. This may be introduced with the words:
Let us offer one another a sign of peace.

Celebrating at the Lord's Table

PROPER PREFACE

Your Son Jesus Christ took the form of a servant,
and by his example taught us to be servants of all:

Going Out as God's People

After the Great Silence a hymn may be sung.
The bishop says
Let us pray.
Almighty God,
you have chosen and ordained these your servants
to be deacons in your church,
and given them the will to undertake this task:
Give them also the strength to perform it,
that they may complete the work which you have begun in them;
through Jesus Christ our Lord. **Amen.**

All say
Almighty God,
we thank you for feeding us
with the spiritual food
of the body and blood of your Son Jesus Christ.
Through him we offer you our souls and bodies
to be a living sacrifice.
Send us out in the power of your Spirit
to live and work to your praise and glory. Amen.

THE BLESSING

The bishop says
Almighty God,
stir up in you the gifts of his grace,
sustain each one of you in your ministry;
and the blessing of God almighty,
the Father, the Son, and the Holy Spirit,
be with you and remain with you always. **Amen.**

DISMISSAL

Go in peace to love and serve the Lord.
In the Name of Christ. Amen.

The newly-ordained depart, each carrying the bible, accompanied by represent-
atives of the parish and diocese.

THE ORDINATION OF PRIESTS
ALSO CALLED PRESBYTERS

The Gathering of God's People

At the entry of the ministers, a hymn, a canticle, or a psalm may be sung. Those to be ordained should be seated among the congregation with those who will present them for ordination.

The bishop says
The Lord be with you
and also with you.

We are the body of Christ.
By the one Spirit we were all baptized into one body.

There is one Lord, one faith, one baptism:
One God and Father of all.

Saint Paul wrote:
Just as in a single human body there are many limbs and organs, all with different functions, so we who are united with Christ, though many, form one body, and belong to one another as its limbs and organs. We have gifts allotted to each of us by God's grace. *Romans 12: 5,6 (REB)*

Today, giving thanks for the variety of gifts and ministries that God has bestowed on the Church, we have come together to admit to the order of priests those whom we believe God has chosen for this particular ministry within the body, seeking by prayer with the laying on of hands the bestowal of the Holy Spirit for that office and work. In doing so we are maintaining the historic threefold ministry of bishops, priests or presbyters, and deacons which this Church has received.

Each candidate is presented by sponsors to the bishop, with the words:
Bishop ...., we present .... to be ordained priest.

Archdeacon, are those responsible for *their* selection and training satisfied that *they* are called and ready to be ordained priest in the Church of God?

Answer **They are satisfied.**

The bishop says to each candidate

.... , do you believe in your heart that God has called you to the office and work of a priest in his Church?

Answer **I believe that God has called me.**

Bishop

Let us pray.

Silence

God our Father, Lord of all the world,
we thank you that through your Son
you have called us into the fellowship of your universal Church.
Hear our prayer for your faithful people
that in their vocation and ministry
they may be instruments of your love,
and give to *these* your *servants* now to be ordained
the needful gifts of grace;
through our Lord and Saviour Jesus Christ. **Amen.**

Proclaiming and Receiving the Word

THE FIRST READING
Isaiah 61: 1-3a

THE PSALM
Psalm 145: 1-7,21

THE SECOND READING
2 Corinthians 5: 14-19

A canticle, hymn or anthem may be sung.

THE GOSPEL READING
John 20: 19-23

The reading is introduced with the following words:

Hear the Gospel of our Saviour Christ according to Saint John, chapter twenty beginning at verse nineteen.

Glory to you, Lord Jesus Christ.

And concludes with

This is the Gospel of the Lord.

Praise to you, Lord Jesus Christ.

THE SERMON

THE NICENE CREED

Mindful of our baptism we proclaim the faith of the universal church:

We believe ... *(page 205)*

The Rite of Ordination

THE DECLARATIONS

The candidates stand before the bishop, and the people sit.
The bishop says

Priests (or presbyters) in the Church of God are called to work with the bishop and with other priests as servants and shepherds among the people to whom they are sent.

They are to proclaim the Word of the Lord, to call those who hear to repentance, and in Christ's name to pronounce absolution and declare the forgiveness of sins.

They are to baptize, and to catechize.

They are to preside at the celebration of the Holy Communion.

They are to lead God's people in prayer and worship, to intercede for them, to bless them in the name of the Lord, and to teach and encourage them by word and example.

They are to minister to the sick and to prepare the dying for their death.

They must always set the Good Shepherd before them as the pattern of their calling, caring for the people committed to their charge, and joining with them in a common witness, that the world may come to know God's glory and love.

The bishop says to those who are to be ordained

In the name of our Lord we ask you to remember the greatness of the trust now to be committed to your charge. You are to be messengers, watchers and stewards of the Lord; you are to teach and to admonish, to feed and provide for the Lord's family, to search for God's children in the wilderness of the world's temptations and to guide them through its confusions, so that they may be saved through Christ for ever.

Your ministry will be one of joy as well as of responsibility, of happiness as well as of diligence. Yet remember in your heart that if it should come about that the Church, or any of its members, is hurt or hindered by reason of your neglect, your fault will be great and God's judgment will follow. So pray constantly for his mercy and for the grace you will need to fulfil your call.

We trust that, supported by the prayers and encouragement of the household of faith, you long ago began to weigh and ponder all these things, and that you are fully determined, by the grace of God, to give yourselves wholly to his service. We trust that you will devote to him your best powers of mind and spirit, so that, as you daily follow the rule and teaching of our Lord, with the heavenly assistance of his Holy Spirit, you may grow into his likeness, and lead into holiness the lives of all with whom you have to do.

In order that we may know your mind and purpose, and that you may be strengthened in your resolve to fulfil your ministry, you must make the declarations we now put to you.

Do you believe and accept the holy Scriptures as revealing all things necessary for eternal salvation through faith in Jesus Christ?
Answer **I do.**

Do you believe and accept the doctrine of the Christian faith as the Church of Ireland has received it?
Answer **I do.**

In your ministry will you expound the Scriptures and teach that doctrine?
Answer **By the help of God, I will.**

Will you accept the discipline of this Church and give due respect to those set over you in the Lord?
Answer **By the help of God, I will.**

Will you be diligent in prayer, in reading holy Scripture, and in all studies that will deepen your faith and fit you to uphold the truth of the Gospel?
Answer **By the help of God, I will.**

Will you strive to fashion your own life and family relationships according to the way of Christ?
Answer **By the help of God, I will.**

Will you be faithful in visiting the sick, in caring for the poor and needy, and in helping the oppressed?
Answer **By the help of God, I will.**

Will you encourage God's people to be good stewards of their gifts, that every member may be equipped for the work of ministering, and that the Body of Christ be built up in love?
Answer **By the help of God, I will.**

Will you promote unity, peace, and love among all Christian people, and especially among those whom you serve?
Answer **By the help of God, I will.**

Will you then, in the strength of the Holy Spirit, continually stir up the gift of God that is in you, to make Christ known to all people?
Answer **By the help of God, I will.**

The bishop presents the candidates to the people, and says
You have heard the testimony of those who present these candidates for ordination, and also their own declarations made before you. Those whose duty it is to inquire about these persons and examine them have also found them to be of godly life and sound learning, and believe them to be duly called to serve God in this ministry.
If any of you knows sufficient cause why any of these persons should not be ordained priest, come forward and make it known.

Is it therefore your will that they should be ordained?
Answer **It is.**

Will you uphold them in their ministry?
Answer **We will.**

Bishop

Because none of us can bear the weight of this ministry in our own strength, but only by the grace and power of God, let us pray earnestly for the outpouring of the Holy Spirit on these persons.

Let us pray also that God will each day enlarge and enlighten their understanding of the Scriptures, so that they may grow stronger and more mature in their ministry, as they fashion their lives and the lives of their people on the Word of God.

The bishop or some other minister leads the prayers for the candidates and for the ministry of the whole Church.
An Ordination Litany (page 585) should be used.

Silence is kept.

The Veni Creator Spiritus *is sung, kneeling. (page 536)*

THE ORDINATION PRAYER
WITH THE LAYING ON OF HANDS

The bishop stands with the assisting priests beside him; the congregation stands.
The candidates kneel before the bishop, who says
Praise God who made heaven and earth,
who keeps his promise for ever.

Let us give thanks to the Lord our God.
It is right to give our thanks and praise.

We praise and glorify you, almighty Father,
because, in your infinite love,
you have formed throughout the world
a holy people for your own possession,
a royal priesthood, a universal Church.
We praise and glorify you
because you have given us your only Son Jesus Christ,
the image of your eternal and invisible glory,
the firstborn of all creation, and head of the Church.

We praise and glorify you
that by his death he has overcome death;
and that, having ascended into heaven,
he has poured out gifts abundantly
to equip your people for the work of ministry
and the building up of his body.

And now we give you thanks
that you have called *these your servants,*
whom we ordain in your name
to share this ministry entrusted to your Church.

Here the bishop and priests lay their hands on the head of each candidate as the bishop says
Pour out your Holy Spirit upon your servant ....
for the office and work of a priest in your Church.

The bishop then continues
Give to *these your servants* grace and power
to fulfil the ministry to which *they are* called,
to proclaim the gospel of your salvation;
to minister the sacraments of the new covenant;
to watch over and care for your people;
to pronounce absolution; and to bless them in your name.
As you have called *them* to your service
make *them* worthy of *their* calling.
Give *them* wisdom and discipline to work faithfully
with all *their* fellow servants in Christ
that the world may come to know your glory and your love.
Accept our prayers, most merciful Father,
through your Son Jesus Christ our Lord,
to whom, with you and your Holy Spirit,
belong glory and honour, worship and praise,
now and for ever. **Amen.**

Continue on page 571

Or
Praise God who made heaven and earth,
who keeps his promise for ever.

Let us give thanks to the Lord our God.
It is right to give our thanks and praise.

We praise and glorify you, almighty Father,
because in your infinite love you have formed throughout the world
a holy people for your own possession,
a royal priesthood, a universal Church.
Glory to you, Lord.

We praise and glorify you
because you have given us your only Son Jesus Christ,
the image of your eternal and invisible glory,
the firstborn of all creation and head of the Church.
Glory to you, Lord.

We praise and glorify you
that by his death he has overcome death
and having ascended into heaven,
he has poured out his gifts abundantly,
to equip your people for the work of ministry
and the building up of his body.
Glory to you, Lord.

And now we give you thanks that you have called *these your servants*,
whom we ordain in your name,
to share in the sacred ministry of the Gospel of Christ,
the Apostle and High Priest of our faith and the Shepherd of our souls.
Glory to you, Lord.

*Here the bishop and priests lay their hands on the head of each candidate as
the bishop says*
Pour out your Holy Spirit upon ....
for the office and work of a priest in your Church.

The bishop then continues
Fill *them* with grace and power that *they* may fulfil your call
to be *messengers* and *stewards* of the Lord,
to watch over and care for those committed to *their* charge,
and to join with them in a common witness to the world.
Pour out your Spirit, Lord.

Set *them* among your people to proclaim boldly the word of salvation,
and to share in Christ's work of reconciliation.
Together with them may they offer spiritual sacrifices
acceptable in your sight,
and celebrate the sacraments of the new covenant.
Pour out your Spirit, Lord.

Grant *them* wisdom and discipline to work faithfully
with all their fellow-servants in Christ,
to search for God's children in the wilderness of this world's temptations,
and to guide them through its confusions,
so that they may be saved through Christ for ever.
Pour out your Spirit, Lord.

Accept our prayers, most merciful Father,
through your Son Jesus Christ our Lord,
to whom with you and your Holy Spirit,
belong glory and honour, worship and praise,
now and for ever. **Amen.**

Each newly-ordained priest is now vested in the customary manner, if this has not already been done.

The bishop gives a bible to each priest, saying
Receive this Book,
as a sign of the authority which God has given you this day
to preach the Word and to minister his holy sacraments.

Bishop
Brothers and sisters in Christ, I present to you these persons who have been ordained priests in the Church of God.

The congregation may greet the newly-ordained priests.

The bishop introduces the Peace with these or other suitable words:
Jesus said, A new commandment I give to you,
that you love one another:
even as I have loved you, that you love one another.

The peace of the Lord be always with you
and also with you.

It is appropriate that the congregation share with one another a sign of peace.
This may be introduced with the words
Let us offer one another a sign of peace.

Celebrating at the Lord's Table

PROPER PREFACE

Within the royal priesthood of your Church
you ordain ministers to proclaim your word,
to care for your people
and to celebrate the sacraments of the new covenant:

Going Out as God's People

After the Great Silence a hymn may be sung.
The bishop says
Let us pray.

Almighty God,
you have chosen and ordained these your servants
to be ministers and stewards of your word and sacraments
and given them the will to undertake these things:
Give them also the strength to perform them,
that they may complete that work which you have begun in them;
through Jesus Christ our Lord. **Amen.**

All say
Almighty God,
we thank you for feeding us
with the spiritual food
of the body and blood of your Son Jesus Christ.
Through him we offer you our souls and bodies
to be a living sacrifice.
Send us out in the power of your Spirit
to live and work to your praise and glory. Amen.

THE BLESSING

The bishop says
Almighty God,
stir up in you the gifts of his grace,
sustain each one of you in your ministry;
and the blessing of God almighty,
the Father, the Son and the Holy Spirit,
be with you and remain with you always. **Amen**.

The newly-ordained priests stand before the bishop.
The bishop says
Remember always with thanksgiving
that the treasure now entrusted to you is Christ's own flock,
bought through the shedding of his own blood on the cross.
The Church and the congregation among whom you will minister
are one with him; they are his body.
Go forth to serve them with joy,
build them up in faith,
and do all in your power to bring them to loving obedience to Christ.

DISMISSAL

Go in peace to love and serve the Lord.
In the name of Christ. Amen.

The newly-ordained priests depart, each carrying the bible, accompanied by
representatives of the parish and diocese.

THE ORDINATION OR CONSECRATION
OF A BISHOP

The Gathering of God's People

At the entry of the ministers a hymn, a canticle, or a psalm may be sung.

The archbishop says

The Lord be with you
and also with you.

We are the body of Christ.
By the one Spirit we were all baptized into one body.

There is one Lord, one faith, one baptism:
One God and Father of all.

Saint Paul wrote:
Just as in a single human body there are many limbs and organs, all with different functions, so we who are united with Christ, though many, form one body, and belong to one another as its limbs and organs. We have gifts allotted to each of us by God's grace.   *Romans 12: 5,6 (REB)*

Today, giving thanks for the variety of gifts and ministries that God has bestowed on the Church we have come together to admit to the order of bishops *one* whom we believe God has chosen for this particular ministry within the body, seeking by prayer with the laying on of hands the bestowal of the Holy Spirit for that office and work. In doing so we are maintaining the historic threefold ministry of bishops, priest or presbyters, and deacons which this Church has received.

The bishop-elect is presented by sponsors to the archbishop, with the words:
Archbishop .... , we present .... , and believe *him* to be called and ready to be ordained bishop in the Church of God.

The archbishop says to the bishop-elect

Do you believe, so far as you know your heart, that God has called you to the office and work of a bishop in his Church?

Answer **I believe that God has called me.**

Archbishop

Let us pray

Silence

God our Father, Lord of all the world,
we thank you that through your Son
you have called us into the fellowship of your universal Church.
Hear our prayer for your faithful people
that in their vocation and ministry
they may be instruments of your love,
and give to *this your servant* now to be ordained
the needful gifts of grace;
through Jesus Christ our Lord. **Amen.**

Proclaiming and Receiving the Word

THE FIRST READING
Numbers 27: 15-20,22,23

THE PSALM
Psalm 119: 165-174

THE SECOND READING
2 Corinthians 4: 1-10

A canticle, hymn or anthem may be sung.

THE GOSPEL READING
John 21: 15-17

The reading is introduced with the following words:

Hear the Gospel of our Saviour Christ according to Saint John, chapter twenty-one beginning at verse fifteen.
Glory to you, Lord Jesus Christ.

And concludes with

This is the Gospel of the Lord:
Praise to you, Lord Jesus Christ.

Mindful of our baptism we proclaim the faith of the universal church:
We believe ... *(page 205)*

The Rite of Ordination

The archbishop says
Let the authority for the ordination be read.

The Provincial Registrar reads the certificate of election and the certificate of the approval of the House of Bishops.

The bishop-elect makes the Declaration of Canonical Obedience:
In the name of God. Amen.

I, ... , chosen bishop of the Church and See of .... solemnly promise all due reverence and canonical obedience to the archbishop of .... and to *his* successors.

The bishop-elect stands before the archbishop, and the people sit.

The archbishop says
Bishops are called to lead in serving and caring for the people of God and to work with them in the oversight of the Church. As chief pastors they share with their fellow bishops a special responsibility to maintain and further the unity of the Church, to uphold its discipline, to guard its faith and to promote its mission throughout the world. It is their duty to watch over and pray for all those committed to their charge, and to teach and govern them after the example of the apostles, speaking in the name of God and interpreting the gospel of Christ. They are to know their people and be known by them. They are to ordain and to send new ministers, guiding those who serve with them and enabling them to fulfil their ministry.

They are to baptize and confirm, to preside at the Holy Communion, and to lead the offering of prayer and praise. They are to be merciful, but with firmness, and to minister discipline, but with mercy. They are to have special care for the sick and for the outcast and needy; and to those who turn to God they are to declare the forgiveness of sins.

In order that we may know your mind and purpose, and that you may be strengthened in your resolve to fulfil your ministry, you must make the declarations we now put to you.

Do you believe and accept the holy Scriptures as revealing all things necessary for eternal salvation through faith in Jesus Christ?
Answer **I do.**

Do you believe and accept the doctrine of the Christian faith as the Church of Ireland has received it?
Answer **I do.**

In your ministry will you expound the Scriptures and teach that doctrine?
Answer **By the help of God, I will.**

Will you guard the faith, unity and discipline of the Church?
Answer **By the help of God, I will.**

Will you be faithful in ordaining deacons and priests and in commissioning readers, and will you sustain them in their ministry?
Answer **By the help of God, I will.**

Will you encourage all baptized people in their gifts and ministries and support them by your prayers?
Answer **By the help of God, I will.**

Will you be faithful in visiting the sick, in caring for the poor and needy, and in helping the oppressed?
Answer **By the help of God, I will.**

Will you be diligent in prayer, in reading holy Scripture, and in such studies that will deepen your faith and fit you to uphold the truth of the Gospel against error?

Answer **By the help of God, I will.**

Will you strive to fashion your own life and your family relationships according to the way of Christ?

Answer **By the help of God, I will.**

Will you promote unity, peace, and love among all Christian people, and especially among those whom you serve?

Answer **By the help of God, I will.**

Will you then be a faithful witness to Christ to those among whom you live, and lead your people to obey our Saviour's command to make disciples of all nations?

Answer **By the help of God, I will.**

The archbishop presents the bishop-elect to the people, and says

You have heard the testimony of those who present .... to be consecrated bishop, and also *his* own declarations before you. Those who have authority to do so have chosen *him* as a person of godly life and sound learning. Is it therefore your will that *he* should be ordained?

Answer **It is.**

Will you uphold .... in *his* ministry?

Answer **We will.**

PRAYERS

Archbishop

Because none of us can bear the weight of this ministry in our own strength, but only by the grace and power of God, let us pray earnestly for the outpouring of the Holy Spirit on .....

Let us pray also that God will each day enlarge and enlighten *his* understanding of the Scriptures, so that *he* may grow stronger and more mature in *his* ministry, as *he* fashions *his* life and the lives of *his* people on the word of God.

The archbishop or some other person leads the prayers for the bishop-elect and for the ministry of the whole Church.

An Ordination Litany (page 585) should be used.

Silence is kept.

The Veni Creator Spiritus *(page 536) is sung, kneeling.*

THE ORDINATION PRAYER
WITH THE LAYING ON OF HANDS

The archbishop stands with the bishops who assist; the people stand.
The bishop-elect kneels before the archbishop, who says

Praise God who made heaven and earth,
Who keeps his promise for ever.

Let us give thanks to the Lord our God.
It is right to give our thanks and praise.

We praise and glorify you, almighty Father,
because, in your infinite love,
you have formed throughout the world
a holy people for your own possession,
a royal priesthood, a universal Church.
We praise and glorify you
because you have given us your only Son Jesus Christ,
the image of your eternal and invisible glory,
the firstborn of all creation,
to be the Apostle and High Priest of our faith;
and the Shepherd of our souls.
We praise and glorify you
that by his death he has overcome death;
and that, having ascended into heaven,
he has poured out gifts abundantly
to equip your people for the work of ministry
and the building up of his body.

And now we give you thanks
that you have called *this your servant*,
whom we ordain in your name
to share this ministry entrusted to your Church.

Here the archbishop and other bishops lay their hands on the head of the bishop-elect as the archbishop says

Pour out your Holy Spirit upon your servant ....
for the office and work of a bishop in your Church.

The archbishop then continues

Give to *this your servant* grace and power
which you gave to your apostles,
to lead those committed to *his* charge in proclaiming the gospel of salvation.
Through *him* increase your Church, renew its ministry,
and unite its members in a holy fellowship of truth and love.
Enable *him* as a true shepherd to feed and govern your flock,
to be wise as a teacher,
and steadfast as a guardian of the faith and sacraments of your Church.
Guide and direct *him* in presiding at the worship of your people.
Give *him* humility, to use *his* authority to heal, not to hurt;
to build up, not to destroy.
Defend *him* from all evil, that as *a ruler* over your household
and *an ambassador* for Christ *he* may stand before you blameless,
and finally, with all your servants, enter your eternal joy.
Accept our prayers, most merciful Father,
through your Son Jesus Christ our Lord,
to whom, with you and your Holy Spirit,
belong glory and honour, worship and praise,
now and for ever. **Amen.**

Continue on page 584

Or

Praise God who made heaven and earth,
who keeps his promise for ever.

Let us give thanks to the Lord our God.
It is right to give our thanks and praise.

We praise and glorify you, almighty Father,
because in your infinite love
you have formed throughout the world
a holy people for your own possession,
a royal priesthood, a universal Church.
Glory to you, Lord.

We praise and glorify you
because you have given us your only Son Jesus Christ,
the image of your eternal and invisible glory,
the firstborn of all creation,
to be the Apostle and High Priest of our faith,
and the Shepherd of our souls.
Glory to you, Lord.

We praise and glorify you
that by his death he has overcome death;
and that, having ascended into heaven,
he has poured out his gifts abundantly
to equip your people for the work of ministry
and the building up of his body.
Glory to you, Lord.

And now we give you thanks
that you have called *this your servant,*
whom we ordain in your name,
to share in this ministry entrusted to your Church.
Glory to you, Lord.

Here the archbishop and other bishops lay their hands on the head of the bishop-elect, as the archbishop says
Pour out your Holy Spirit upon your servant ....
for the office and work of a bishop in your Church.

The archbishop then continues
Give to *this your servant* grace and power
which you gave to your apostles,
to lead those committed to *his* charge in proclaiming the gospel of salvation.
Pour out your Spirit, Lord.

Through *him* increase your Church, renew its ministry,
and unite its members in a holy fellowship of truth and love.
Pour out your Spirit, Lord.

Enable *him* as a true shepherd to feed and govern your flock,
to be wise as a teacher,
and steadfast as a guardian of the faith and sacraments of your Church.
Pour out your Spirit, Lord.

Guide and direct *him* in presiding at the worship of your people.
Give *him* humility, to use *his* authority to heal, not to hurt;
to build up, not to destroy.
Pour out your Spirit, Lord.

Defend *him* from all evil, that as *a ruler* over your household
and *an ambassador* for Christ *he* may stand before you blameless,
and finally, with all your servants, enter your eternal joy.
Pour out your Spirit, Lord.

Accept our prayers, most merciful Father,
through your Son Jesus Christ our Lord,
to whom, with you and your Holy Spirit,
belong glory and honour, worship and praise,
now and for ever. **Amen.**

The newly-ordained bishop is vested with the episcopal habit if this has not already been done.

The archbishop gives the bible to the bishop, saying
Receive this Book; here are words of eternal life.
Take them for your guide, and declare them to the world.

Archbishop
Brothers and sisters in Christ, I present to you ...., Bishop in the Church of God.

The newly-consecrated bishop may be welcomed.

The archbishop introduces the Peace with these or other suitable words:

Jesus said, A new commandment I give to you,
that you love one another:
even as I have loved you, that you love one another.

The peace of the Lord be always with you
and also with you.

It is appropriate that the congregation share with one another a sign of peace.
This may be introduced with the words:

Let us offer one another a sign of peace.

Celebrating at the Lord's Table

Within the royal priesthood of your Church
you ordain ministers to proclaim your word,
to care for your people
and to celebrate the sacraments of the new covenant:

Going Out as God's People

After the Great Silence a hymn may be sung.

The archbishop says

Let us pray.

Almighty God,
you have chosen and consecrated ....
to be *a shepherd* and *guardian* of your flock,
and given *him* the will to undertake these things:
Give *him* also the strength to perform them,
that you may complete the work which you have begun in *him*;
through Jesus Christ our Lord. **Amen.**

Almighty God,
we thank you for feeding us
with the spiritual food
of the body and blood of your Son Jesus Christ.
Through him we offer you our souls and bodies
to be a living sacrifice.
Send us out in the power of your Spirit
to live and work to your praise and glory. Amen.

THE BLESSING

The archbishop says
Almighty God,
stir up in you the gifts of his grace,
sustain each one of you in your ministry;
and the blessing of God almighty,
the Father, the Son and the Holy Spirit,
be with you and remain with you always. **Amen.**

The newly-consecrated bishop stands before the archbishop.

The archbishop gives the pastoral staff to the new bishop, saying
Keep watch over the flock of which the Holy Spirit has appointed you
shepherd.
Encourage the faithful, restore the lost, build up the body of Christ;
that when the Chief Shepherd shall appear, you may receive the unfading
crown of glory.

DISMISSAL

Go in peace to love and serve the Lord.
In the name of Christ. Amen.

*The new bishop departs, carrying the bible and pastoral staff, accompanied by
the diocesan representatives.*

AN ORDINATION LITANY

Either of the following is used.

God the Father, Creator of heaven and earth,
have mercy on us.

God the Son, Redeemer of the world,
have mercy on us.

God the Holy Spirit, giver of life,
have mercy on us.

Holy, blessed and glorious Trinity,
three Persons in one God,
have mercy on us.

Save us, good Lord:
from all sin and wickedness,
from pride, hypocrisy and conceit,
from envy, hatred and malice, and all uncharitableness,
save us, good Lord.

From sins of thought, word and deed,
from the lusts of the flesh,
from the deceits of the world and the snares of the devil,
save us, good Lord.

From fire, storm and flood,
from disease, pestilence and want,
from war and murder, and from dying unprepared,
save us, good Lord.

From all false doctrine,
from hardness of heart,
and from contempt of your word and commandment,
save us, good Lord.

In times of sorrow and in times of joy,
in the hour of death,
and in the day of judgement,
save us, good Lord.

Save us, Lord Christ:
by the mystery of your holy incarnation,
by your birth, childhood and obedience,
by your baptism, fasting and temptation,
save us, Lord Christ.

By your ministry in word and work,
by your mighty acts of power,
and by your preaching of the kingdom,
save us, Lord Christ.

By your agony and trial,
by your cross and passion,
and by your precious death and burial,
save us, Lord Christ.

By your mighty resurrection,
by your glorious ascension,
and by your sending of the Holy Spirit,
save us, Lord Christ.

Hear us, good Lord:
govern and direct your holy Church,
fill it with love and truth,
and grant it that unity which is your will,
hear us, good Lord.

Give your Church courage to preach the gospel
and to make disciples of all the nations,
hear us, good Lord.

Give knowledge and understanding
to bishops, priests and deacons,
that by their life and teaching they may proclaim your word,
hear us, good Lord.

At the Ordination of Deacons
Bless your *servants* now to be made *deacons*
that *they* may faithfully serve your Church
and reveal your glory in the world,
hear us, good Lord.

At the Ordination of Priests
Bless your *servants* now to be made *priests*
that *they* may faithfully serve your Church
and reveal your glory in the world,
hear us, good Lord.

At the Ordination of Bishops
Bless your *servant* now to be made *bishop*
in faithfully serving your Church
and revealing your glory in the world,
hear us, good Lord.

Give all people grace to receive your word
and to bring forth the fruit of the Spirit,
hear us, good Lord.

Bring all who have erred and are deceived
into the way of truth,
hear us, good Lord.

Saviour of the world,
forgive our sins, known and unknown,
things done, and left undone;
grant us the grace of your Holy Spirit
that we may amend our lives according to your holy word,
and share with all your people the joys of your eternal kingdom.

Jesus, Lamb of God,
have mercy on us.

Jesus, bearer of our sins,
have mercy on us.

Jesus, Redeemer of the world,
give us your peace.

Bishop
Lord, you are merciful and forgive our sins.
You hear those who pray in the name of your Son.
Grant that what we have asked in faith
we may obtain according to your will;
through Jesus Christ our Lord. **Amen.**

Or

God the Father,
Have mercy on us.

God the Son,
Have mercy on us.

God the Holy Spirit,
Have mercy on us.

Holy Trinity, one God,
Have mercy on us.

We humbly pray that you will hear us, good Lord.
Grant to your people the forgiveness of sins,
growth in grace,
and the fruit of the Spirit.
Lord, hear our prayer.

Send your peace to the world
which you have reconciled to yourself
by the ministry of your Son, Jesus Christ.
Lord, hear our prayer.

Heal the divisions of your Church,
that all may be one,
so that the world may believe.
Lord, hear our prayer.

Lead the members of your Church in their vocation and ministry,
that they may serve you in true and godly living.
Lord, hear our prayer.

Raise up faithful and able ministers for your Church,
that the gospel may be known to all people.
Lord, hear our prayer.

Fill them with compassion,
clothe them with humility,
and move them to care for all your people.
Lord, hear our prayer.

Inspire all bishops, priests and deacons with your love,
that with all your people they may hunger for truth.
Lord, hear our prayer.

Bless your *servants* ....
who are to be admitted to the order of ....
pour your grace upon *them*,
that *they* may faithfully fulfil the duties of this ministry,
build up your Church and glorify your name.
Lord, hear our prayer.

Sustain by the indwelling of your Holy Spirit,
all who are called to the ordained ministries of your Church,
and encourage them to persevere to the end.
Lord, hear our prayer.

Gather us with all your saints into your eternal kingdom.
Lord, hear our prayer.

Bishop
Eternal God and Father,
you have promised to hear those who pray
in the name of your Son:
Grant that what we have asked in faith,
we may obtain according to your will;
through Jesus Christ our Lord. **Amen.**

The Psalter

About The Psalter

This version of the Psalter may be used in a number of different ways including the following:

1   **Reading the Psalms together.** Psalms may be said by a solo voice while everyone listens in silence; by everyone together; with the verses alternated between one half of the congregation and the other; with the verses alternated between the presiding minister and the others; by half-verse, the presiding minister saying the first half and the congregation responding with the second half.

2   **Chanting the Psalms.** To help congregations to join in the singing of the psalms to Anglican chant, red pointing marks have been inserted in the text (see the following page for details). It is possible to adapt the pointing to cover other forms of chant: for example, if a simple chant with four notes per verse is used, the words of each half-verse are sung to one note until the last bar line | is reached, the next note being used for the remaining syllable(s).

3   **Using Refrains.** Certain phrases or verses may be selected as a refrain for use in that psalm. The service leader draws attention to the verse or phrase chosen and invites the congregation to say or sing it after each paragraph of the psalm is said or sung by the presiding minister or a cantor. The end of a paragraphs is marked by a full-stop after the verse number or the † sign which also serves as a sign when the psalms are sung to Anglican chant.

The Gloria. Each psalm or group of psalms may end with

Glory | be · to the | Father, ▪
and to the Son, | and · to the | Holy | Spirit;
as it | was in · the be|ginning, ▪
is now and ever shall be, | world with·out | end. A|men.

Or

Glory to the Father, and | to the | Son, ▪
and | to the | Holy | Spirit;
as it was in the be|ginning · is | now, ▪
and shall be for | ever | A|men.

Blessed
This is read as 'bless-ed' in the Psalter.

Psalters. The Psalter contained in the Book of Common Prayer (1926) remains authorised for use in public worship as an alternative to this Psalter.

Pointing for singing

The pointing of psalms in this book is taken by permission from the pointed psalter of the Royal School of Church Music, © 2002. The following extracts from the Introduction help to explain the principles which underlie it:

'In pointing the psalms for Anglican chant we have to balance consistency of method with the individuality of each psalm. The pace of the texts varies from one psalm to another, as do word patterns – partly because of the original Hebrew text, and partly because of the preferences of different translators and text editors. There are some verses where only one pointing solution is possible, others where method dictates choice of pointing, others where it is a matter of personal preference, and some where there is no really satisfactory solution. All of the pointing observes the convention of the textual and musical caesura at the mid verse which is characteristic of recitation of the psalms. This is indicated by the square sign ■. However, there are times when the musical patterns (and especially the number of chords in the second part of the verse) has required either the caesura to be moved [from the original Common Worship Psalter text], or for two verses to be combined and treated musically as one verse, or for one verse to be subdivided and treated musically as two verses.

Pointing marks have been kept to a minimum. The upright dash | corresponds to the bar lines of the chant. Where there are two syllables between the bar lines, one chord is sung to each syllable. Where there are three or four syllables between the bar lines, the second chord is reserved for the last syllable – except where there is a dot · between two syllables. The dot indicates the mid point of the bar, and the chord changes after that dot for the remaining syllables of the bar. All psalms are pointed for use with double chants (i.e. chants whose music encompasses two verses of text), even in those psalms where a single chant (i.e. one whose music is repeated every verse) may be preferable. Where there are odd numbers of verses in a psalm, or section of a psalm, the second part of the chant has to be repeated to accommodate this. This is indicated by the sign †.'

Psalm 1

1. Blessed are they who have not walked in the | counsel · of the | wicked, ▪
nor lingered in the way of sinners,
 nor sat in the as|sembly | of the | scornful.

2 Their delight is in the | law of the | Lord ▪
and they meditate on his | law | day and | night.

3. Like a tree planted by streams of water
 bearing fruit in due season, with leaves that | do not | wither, ▪
whatever they | do, | it shall | prosper.

4 As for the wicked, it is not | so with | them; ▪
they are like chaff which the | wind | blows a|way.

5 Therefore the wicked shall not be able to | stand in the | judgment, ▪
nor the sinner in the congre|gation | of the | righteous.

6 For the Lord knows the | way of the | righteous, ▪
but the | way of the | wicked shall | perish.

Psalm 2

1 Why are the | nations in | tumult, ▪
and why do the peoples de|vise a | vain | plot?

2 The kings of the earth rise up,
 and the rulers take | counsel to|gether, ▪
against the Lord | and a|gainst his a|nointed:

3. 'Let us break their | bonds a|sunder ▪
and | cast a|way their | cords from us.'

4 He who dwells in heaven shall | laugh them to | scorn; ▪
the Lord shall | have them | in de|rision.

5 Then shall he speak to them | in his | wrath ▪
and | terrify them | in his | fury:

6. 'Yet have I | set my | king ▪
upon my | holy | hill of | Zion.'

7 I will proclaim the de|cree of the | Lord; ▪
he said to me: 'You are my Son; this | day have | I be|gotten you.

8   'Ask of me and I will give you the nations for | your in|heritance ▪
     and the ends of the | earth for | your pos|session.

9.   'You shall break them with a | rod of | iron ▪
     and dash them in pieces | like a | potter's | vessel.'

10   Now therefore be | wise, O | kings; ▪
     be prudent, you | judges | of the | earth.

11. Serve the Lord with fear, and with trembling | kiss his | feet, ▪
     lest he be angry and you perish from the way,
             for his | wrath is | quickly | kindled.

12   Happy | are all | they ▪
     who | take | refuge in | him.

Psalm 3

1   Lord, how many | are my | adversaries; ▪
     many are | they who rise | up a|gainst me.

2.   Many are they who | say to my | soul, ▪
     'There is no | help for you | in your | God.'

3   But you, Lord, are a | shield a|bout me; ▪
     you are my glory, and the | lifter | up of my | head.

4.   When I cry a|loud · to the | Lord, ▪
     he will answer me | from his | holy | hill;

5   I lie down and sleep and | rise a|gain, ▪
     be|cause the | Lord sus|tains me.

6.   I will not be afraid of | hordes · of the | peoples ▪
     that have set themselves a|gainst me | all a|round.

7   Rise up, O Lord, and deliver me, | O my | God, ▪
     for you strike all my enemies on the cheek
             and | break the | teeth of the | wicked.

8   Salvation be|longs to the | Lord: ▪
     may your blessing | be up|on your | people.

1. Answer me when I call, O | God of my | righteousness; ∎
   you set me at liberty when I was in trouble;
   > have mercy on | me and | hear my | prayer.

2. How long will you nobles dis|honour my | glory; ∎
   how long will you love vain | things and | seek · after | falsehood?

3. But know that the Lord has shown me his | marvellous | kindness; ∎
   when I call upon the | Lord, | he will | hear me.

4. Stand in | awe, and | sin not; ∎
   commune with your own heart upon your | bed, | and be | still.

5. Offer the | sacrifices of | righteousness ∎
   and | put your | trust · in the | Lord.

6. There are many that say, 'Who will show us | any | good?' ∎
   Lord, lift up the | light of your | countenance up|on us.

7. You have put gladness | in my | heart, ∎
   more than when their corn and | wine and | oil in|crease.

8. In peace I will lie | down and | sleep, ∎
   for it is you Lord, only, who | make me | dwell in | safety.

1. Give ear to my | words, O | Lord; ∎
   con|sider my | lamen|tation.

2. Hearken to the voice of my crying, my | King and my | God, ∎
   for to | you I | make my | prayer.

3. In the morning, Lord, you will | hear my | voice; ∎
   early in the morning I make my ap|peal to | you, and look | up.

4. For you are the God who takes no | pleasure in | wickedness; ∎
   no | evil can | dwell with | you.

5. The boastful cannot | stand in your | sight; ∎
   you | hate all | those that work | wickedness.

6. You destroy | those who speak | lies; ∎
   the bloodthirsty and de|ceitful the | Lord · will ab|hor.

7   But as for me, through the greatness of your mercy,
          I will come I into your I house; ▪
      I will bow down towards your holy I temple in I awe of I you.
8.   Lead me, Lord, in your righteousness, belcause of my I enemies; ▪
      make your way I straight belfore my I face.

9   For there is no truth in their mouth,
          in their I heart · is deslitruction, ▪
      their throat is an open sepulchre,
          and they I flatter I with their I tongue.
10   Punish I them, O I God; ▪
      let them I fall · through their I own delvices.
11.   Because of their many transgressions I cast them I out, ▪
      for I they have relbelled algainst you.

12   But let all who take refuge in I you be I glad; ▪
      let them I sing out their I joy for I ever.
13   You will I shelter I them, ▪
      so that those who love your I name · may exlult in I you.
14   For you, O Lord, will I bless the I righteous; ▪
      and with your favour you will delfend them I as with a I shield.

Psalm 6

1   O Lord, rebuke me I not in your I wrath; ▪
      neither chasten me I in your I fierce I anger.
2   Have mercy on me, Lord, for I I am I weak; ▪
      Lord, heal me, I for my I bones are I racked.
3.   My soul also I shakes with I terror; ▪
      how I long, O I Lord, how I long?

4   Turn again, O Lord, and delliver my I soul; ▪
      save me for your I loving I mercy's I sake.
5.   For in death I no one relmembers you; ▪
      and who can I give you I thanks · in the I grave?

6   I am weary I with my I groaning; ▪
      every night I drench my pillow
          and I flood my I bed with my I tears.

7. My eyes are | wasted with | grief ▪
and worn away be|cause of | all my | enemies.

8 Depart from me, all | you that do | evil, ▪
for the Lord has | heard the | voice of my | weeping.

9 The Lord has heard my | suppli|cation; ▪
the | Lord · will re|ceive my | prayer.

10 All my enemies shall be put to | shame and con|fusion; ▪
they shall | suddenly turn | back · in their | shame.

Psalm 7

1 O Lord my God, in | you I take | refuge; ▪
save me from all who pur|sue me, | and de|liver me,

2. Lest they rend me like a lion and | tear me in | pieces ▪
while | there is | no one to | help me.

3 O Lord my God, if I have | done these | things: ▪
if there is any | wickedness | in my | hands,

4 If I have repaid my | friend with | evil, ▪
or plundered my | enemy with|out a | cause,

5† Then let my enemy pursue me and | over|take me, ▪
trample my life to the ground,
    and lay my | honour | in the | dust.

6 Rise up, O Lord, in your wrath;
    lift yourself up against the | fury · of my | enemies. ▪
Awaken, my God, the judgment | that you | have com|manded.

7. Let the assembly of the peoples | gather | round you; ▪
be seated high above them: O | Lord, | judge the | nations.

8 Give judgment for me
    according to my | righteousness, O | Lord, ▪
and according to the | innocence | that is | in me.

9. Let the malice of the wicked come to an end,
    but es|tablish the | righteous; ▪
for you test the mind and | heart, O | righteous | God.

10   God is my | shield · that is | over me; ▪
     he | saves the | true of | heart.

11   God is a | righteous | judge; ▪
     he is pro|voked | all day | long.

12   If they will not repent, God will | whet his | sword; ▪
     he has bent his | bow and | made it | ready.

13.   He has prepared the | weapons of | death; ▪
     he makes his | arrows | shafts of | fire.

14   Behold those who are in | labour with | wickedness, ▪
     who conceive evil | and give | birth to | lies.

15   They dig a pit and | make it | deep ▪
     and fall into the hole that | they have | made for | others.

16   Their mischief rebounds on their | own | head; ▪
     their violence | falls on their | own | scalp.

17   I will give thanks to the Lord | for his | righteousness, ▪
     and I will make music to the | name of the | Lord Most | High.

Psalm 8   FIRST VERSION

1.   *O | Lord our | governor,* ▪
     how glorious is your | name in | all the | world!

2   Your majesty above the | heavens is | praised ▪
     out of the | mouths of | babes at the | breast.

3†   You have founded a stronghold a|gainst your | foes, ▪
     that you might still the | enemy | and · the a|venger.

4   When I consider your heavens, the | work of your | fingers, ▪
     the moon and the | stars that | you have or|dained,

5   What is man, that you should be | mindful | of him; ▪
     the son of man, that | you should | seek him | out?

6.   You have made him little | lower · than the | angels ▪
     and | crown him with | glory and | honour.

7   You have given him dominion over the | works of your | hands ▪
     and put | all things | under his | feet,

8,9   All sheep and oxen,
        even the wild | beasts of the | field, ▪
   the birds of the air, the fish of the sea
        and whatsoever | moves · in the | paths of the | sea.

10   *O | Lord our | governor,* ▪
    how glorious is your | name in | all the | world!

Psalm 8 SECOND VERSION

1.   *O | Lord our | governor,* ▪
    how glorious is your | name in | all the | world!

2   Your majesty above the | heavens is | praised ▪
    out of the | mouths of | babes at the | breast.

3†   You have founded a stronghold a|gainst your | foes, ▪
    that you might still the | enemy | and · the a|venger.

4   When I consider your heavens, the | work of your | fingers, ▪
    the moon and the | stars that | you have or|dained,

5   What are mortals, that you should be | mindful | of them; ▪
    mere human beings, that | you should | seek them | out?

6.   You have made them little | lower · than the | angels ▪
    and | crown them with | glory and | honour.

7   You have given them dominion over the | works of your | hands ▪
    and put | all things | under their | feet,

8,9   All sheep and oxen,
        even the wild | beasts of the | field, ▪
   the birds of the air, the fish of the sea
        and whatsoever | moves · in the | paths of the | sea.

10   *O | Lord our | governor,* ▪
    how glorious is your | name in | all the | world!

Psalm 9

1   I will give thanks to you, Lord, with my ⁝ whole ⁝ heart; ▪
       I will tell of ⁝ all your ⁝ marvellous ⁝ works.

2   I will be glad and re⁝joice in ⁝ you; ▪
       I will make music to your ⁝ name, ⁝ O Most ⁝ High.

3.   When my enemies are ⁝ driven ⁝ back, ▪
       they stumble and ⁝ perish ⁝ at your ⁝ presence.

4   For you have maintained my right ⁝ and my ⁝ cause; ▪
       you sat on your throne ⁝ giving ⁝ righteous ⁝ judgment.

5   You have rebuked the nations and des⁝troyed the ⁝ wicked; ▪
       you have blotted out their ⁝ name for ⁝ ever and ⁝ ever.

6.   The enemy was ⁝ utterly laid ⁝ waste. ▪
       You uprooted their cities;
           their ⁝ very ⁝ memory has ⁝ perished.

7   But the Lord shall en⁝dure for ⁝ ever; ▪
       he has made ⁝ fast his ⁝ throne for ⁝ judgment.

8   For he shall rule the ⁝ world with ⁝ righteousness ▪
       and ⁝ govern the ⁝ peoples with ⁝ equity.

9   Then will the Lord be a refuge ⁝ for the op⁝pressed, ▪
       a refuge ⁝ in the ⁝ time of ⁝ trouble.

10. And those who know your name will put their ⁝ trust in ⁝ you, ▪
       for you, Lord, have ⁝ never failed ⁝ those who ⁝ seek you.

11   Sing praises to the Lord who ⁝ dwells in ⁝ Zion; ▪
       declare among the ⁝ peoples the ⁝ things · he has ⁝ done.

12. The avenger of blood ⁝ has re⁝membered them; ▪
       he did not forget the ⁝ cry ⁝ of the op⁝pressed.

13   Have mercy upon ⁝ me, O ⁝ Lord; ▪
       consider the trouble I suffer from those who hate me,
           you that lift me ⁝ up · from the ⁝ gates of ⁝ death;

14. That I may tell all your praises in the gates of the ⁝ city of ⁝ Zion ▪
       and re⁝joice in ⁝ your sal⁝vation.

15   The nations shall sink into the ⁝ pit of their ⁝ making ▪
       and in the snare which they set will their ⁝ own ⁝ foot be ⁝ taken.

16 The Lord makes himself known by his | acts of | justice; ▪
  the wicked are snared in the | works of their | own | hands.

17. They shall return to the | land of | darkness, ▪
  all the | nations · that for|get | God.

18 For the needy shall not always | be for|gotten ▪
  and the hope of the poor | shall not | perish for | ever.

19 Arise, O Lord, and let not mortals have the | upper | hand; ▪
  let the nations be | judged be|fore your | face.

20 Put them in | fear, O | Lord, ▪
  that the nations may know them|selves to | be but | mortal.

Psalm 10

1 Why stand so far | off, O | Lord? ▪
  Why hide your|self in | time of | trouble?

2 The wicked in their pride | persecute the | poor; ▪
  let them be caught in the | schemes they | have de|vised.

3. The wicked boast of their | heart's de|sire; ▪
  the covetous | curse · and re|vile the | Lord.

4 The wicked in their arrogance say, 'God will | not a|venge it'; ▪
  in all their | scheming God | counts for | nothing.

5 They are stubborn in all their ways,
   for your judgments are far above | out of their | sight; ▪
  they | scoff at | all their | adversaries.

6 They say in their heart, 'I shall | not be | shaken; ▪
  no harm shall | ever | happen to | me.'

7. Their mouth is full of cursing, de|ceit and | fraud; ▪
  under their | tongue lie | mischief and | wrong.

8 They lurk in the outskirts
   and in dark alleys they | murder the | innocent; ▪
  their eyes are ever | watching | for the | helpless.

9† They lie in wait, like a lion in his den;
   they lie in wait to | seize the | poor; ▪
  they seize the poor when they | get them | into their | net.

10   The innocent are broken and | humbled be|fore them; ▪
       the helpless | fall be|fore their | power.

11. They say in their heart, | 'God has for|gotten; ▪
       he hides his face away; | he will | never | see it.'

12   Arise, O Lord God, and lift | up your | hand; ▪
       for|get | not the | poor.

13. Why should the wicked be | scornful of | God? ▪
       Why should they say in their hearts, | 'You will | not a|venge it'?

14   Surely, you behold | trouble and | misery; ▪
       you see it and take it | into your | own | hand.

15   The helpless commit them|selves to | you, ▪
       for you are the | helper | of the | orphan.

16. Break the power of the wicked | and ma|licious; ▪
       search out their wickedness un|til you | find | none.

17   The Lord shall reign for | ever and | ever; ▪
       the nations shall | perish | from his | land.

18   Lord, you will hear the de|sire of the | poor; ▪
       you will incline your ear to the | fullness | of their | heart,

19   To give justice to the orphan | and op|pressed, ▪
       so that people are no longer driven in | terror | from the | land.

Psalm 11

1   In the Lord have I | taken | refuge; ▪
       how then can you say to me,
           'Flee like a | bird | to the | hills,

2   'For see how the wicked bend the bow
           and fit their arrows | to the | string, ▪
       to shoot from the shadows | at the | true of | heart.

3.   'When the foundations | are des|troyed, ▪
       what | can the | righteous | do?

4   The Lord is in his | holy | temple; ▪
       the | Lord's throne | is in | heaven.

5   His | eyes be|hold, ▪
       his eyelids try | every | mortal | being.

6. The Lord tries the righteous as | well as the | wicked, ▪
    but those who delight in | violence his | soul ab|hors.

7   Upon the wicked he shall rain coals of fire and | burning | sulphur; ▪
    scorching wind shall | be their | portion to | drink.

8   For the Lord is righteous;
        he loves | righteous | deeds, ▪
    and those who are upright | shall be|hold his | face.

Psalm 12

1   Help me, Lord, for no one | godly is | left; ▪
    the faithful have vanished from the | whole | human | race.

2. They all speak falsely | with their | neighbour; ▪
    they flatter with their lips, but | speak · from a | double | heart.

3   O that the Lord would cut off all | flattering | lips ▪
    and the | tongue that | speaks proud | boasts!

4   Those who say, 'With our tongue will | we pre|vail; ▪
    our lips we will use; | who is | lord | over us?'

5. 'Because of the oppression of the needy,
        and the | groaning · of the | poor, ▪
    I will rise up now,' says the Lord,
        'and set them in the | safety | that they | long for.'

6   The words of the | Lord are | pure words, ▪
    like silver refined in the furnace
        and purified | seven times | in the | fire.

7   You, O Lord, | will watch | over us ▪
    and guard us from | this · gene|ration for | ever.

8   The wicked strut on | every | side, ▪
    when what is vile is exalted by the | whole | human | race.

Psalm 13

1   How long will you forget me, O | Lord; for | ever? ▪
    How long will you | hide your | face | from me?

2.   How long shall I have anguish in my soul
       and grief in my heart, | day after | day? ▪
    How long shall my | enemy | triumph | over me?

3   Look upon me and answer, O | Lord my | God; ▪
    lighten my eyes, | lest I | sleep in | death;

4.   Lest my enemy say, 'I have pre|vailed a|gainst him,' ▪
    and my foes re|joice that | I have | fallen.

5   But I put my trust in your | steadfast | love; ▪
    my heart will re|joice in | your sal|vation.

6   I will | sing to the | Lord, ▪
    for he has | dealt so | bounti·fully | with me.

Psalm 14

1   The fool has said in his heart, 'There | is no | God.' ▪
    Corrupt are they, and abominable in their wickedness;
       there is | no one | that does | good.

2   The Lord has looked down from heaven
       upon the | children of | earth, ▪
    to see if there is anyone who is wise and | seeks | after | God.

3†   But every one has turned back;
       all alike have be|come cor|rupt: ▪
    there is none that does | good; | no, not | one.

4   Have they no knowledge, those | evil|doers, ▪
    who eat up my people as if they ate bread
       and do not | call up|on the | Lord?

5   There shall they be in | great | fear; ▪
    for God is in the | company | of the | righteous.

6   Though they would confound the | counsel · of the | poor, ▪
    yet the | Lord shall | be their | refuge.

7   O that Israel's salvation would | come · out of | Zion! ▪
    When the Lord restores the fortunes of his people,
       then will Jacob re|joice and | Israel be | glad.

1 Lord, who may | dwell in your | tabernacle? ▪
 Who may rest up|on your | holy | hill?

2. Whoever leads an | uncorrupt | life ▪
 and | does the | thing that is | right;

3 Who speaks the | truth · from the | heart ▪
 and | bears no de|ceit · on the | tongue;

4 Who does no | evil · to a | friend ▪
 and | pours no | scorn · on a | neighbour;

5† In whose sight the wicked are | not es|teemed, ▪
 but who honours | those who | fear the | Lord.

6 Whoever has | sworn · to a | neighbour ▪
 and | never goes | back · on that | word;

7,8 Who does not lend money in hope of gain,
  nor takes a bribe a|gainst the | innocent; ▪
 Whoever does these | things shall | never | fall.

1 Preserve me, O God, for in you have I | taken | refuge; ▪
 I have said to the Lord| 'You are my lord,
  all my | good de|pends on | you.'

2 All my delight is upon the godly that are | in the | land, ▪
 upon | those · who are | noble in | heart.

3† Though the idols are legion that | many run | after, ▪
 their drink offerings of blood I will not offer,
  neither make mention of their | names up|on my | lips.

4 The Lord himself is my portion | and my | cup; ▪
 in your hands a|lone | is my | fortune.

5 My share has fallen in a | fair | land; ▪
 indeed, I | have a | goodly | heritage.

6. I will bless the Lord who has | given me | counsel, ▪
 and in the night watches | he in|structs my | heart.

7 I have set the Lord | always be|fore me; ▪
 he is at my right | hand; I | shall not | fall.

8   Wherefore my heart is glad and my | spirit re|joices; ▪
      my flesh | also shall | rest se|cure.

9   For you will not abandon my | soul to | Death, ▪
      nor suffer your | faithful one to | see the | Pit.

10†   You will show me the path of life;
         in your presence is the | fullness of | joy ▪
      and in your right hand are | pleasures for | ever|more.

Psalm 17

1   Hear my just cause, O Lord; consider | my com|plaint; ▪
      listen to my prayer, which comes | not from | lying | lips.

2   Let my vindication come | forth from your | presence; ▪
      let your eyes be|hold | what is | right.

3.   Weigh my heart, ex|amine me by | night, ▪
      refine me, and you will find | no im|purity | in me.

4   My mouth does not trespass for | earthly re|wards; ▪
      I have | heeded the | words · of your | lips.

5.   My footsteps hold fast in the ways of | your com|mandments; ▪
      my feet have not | stumbled | in your | paths.

6   I call upon you, O God, for | you will | answer me; ▪
      incline your ear to me, and | listen | to my | words.

7   Show me your marvellous | loving|kindness, ▪
      O Saviour of those who take refuge at your right hand
         from | those who | rise up a|gainst them.

8   Keep me as the | apple · of your | eye; ▪
      hide me under the | shadow | of your | wings,

9.   From the wicked | who as|sault me, ▪
      from my enemies who surround me to | take a|way my | life.

10   They have closed their | heart to | pity ▪
      and their | mouth speaks | proud | things.

11   They press me hard, they surround me on | every | side, ▪
      watching how they may | cast me | to the | ground,

12   Like a lion that is greedy | for its | prey, ▪
      like a young lion | lurking in | secret | places.

13.   Arise, Lord; confront them and | cast them | down; ▪
      deliver me from the | wicked | by your | sword.

14 Deliver me, O Lord, | by your | hand ▪
from those whose | portion in | life · is un|lending,

15 Whose bellies you | fill with your | treasure, ▪
who are well supplied with children
and | leave their | wealth · to their | little ones.

16 As for me, I shall see your | face in | righteousness; ▪
when I awake and behold your | likeness, | I shall be | satisfied.

Psalm 18

1 I love you, O | Lord my | strength. ▪
The Lord is my crag, my | fortress and | my de|liverer,

2 My God, my rock in | whom I take | refuge, ▪
my shield, the horn of my sal|vation | and my | stronghold.

3† I cried to the Lord | in my | anguish ▪
and I was | saved | from my | enemies.

4 The cords of | death en|twined me ▪
and the torrents of des|truction | over|whelmed me.

5 The cords of the Pit | fastened a|bout me ▪
and the | snares of | death en|tangled me.

6 In my distress I | called upon the | Lord ▪
and cried | out to my | God for | help.

7. He heard my voice | in his | temple ▪
and my | cry | came to his | ears.

8 The earth | trembled and | quaked; ▪
the foundations of the mountains shook;
they | reeled be|cause he was | angry.

9 Smoke rose from his nostrils
and a consuming fire went | out of his | mouth; ▪
burning | coals | blazed forth | from him.

10 He parted the heavens | and came | down ▪
and thick | darkness was | under his | feet.

11. He rode upon the | cherubim and | flew; ▪
he came | flying · on the | wings of the | wind.

12 He made darkness his covering | round a|bout him, ▪
dark waters and thick | clouds | his pa|vilion.

13 From the brightness of his presence, | through the | clouds ∎
burst | hailstones and | coals of | fire.

14 The Lord also thundered | out of | heaven; ∎
the Most High uttered his voice
with | hailstones and | coals of | fire.

15. He sent out his | arrows and | scattered them; ∎
he hurled down | lightnings and | put them to | flight.

16 The springs of the | ocean were | seen, ∎
and the foun|dations · of the | world un|covered

16a at your re|buke, O | Lord, ∎
at the blast of the | breath of | your dis|pleasure.

17. He reached down from on | high and | took me; ∎
he drew me | out of the | mighty | waters.

18 He delivered me from my | strong | enemy, ∎
from foes that | were too | mighty | for me.

19 They came upon me in the | day of my | trouble; ∎
but the | Lord was | my up|holder.

20 He brought me out into a | place of | liberty; ∎
he rescued me be|cause he de|lighted | in me.

21. The Lord rewarded me after my | righteous | dealing; ∎
according to the cleanness of my | hands he | recom|pensed me,

22 Because I had kept the | ways of the | Lord ∎
and had not gone | wickedly a|way from my | God,

23 For I had an eye to | all his | laws, ∎
and did not cast | out his com|mandments | from me.

24 I was also whole|hearted be|fore him ∎
and I | kept myself | from in|iquity;

25. Therefore the Lord rewarded me after my | righteous | dealing, ∎
and according to the cleanness of my | hands | in his | sight.

26 With the faithful you | show yourself | faithful; ∎
with the | true you | show yourself | true;

27 With the pure you | show yourself | pure, ∎
but with the crooked you | show your|self per|verse.

28 For you will save a | lowly | people ∎
and bring down the | high | looks · of the | proud.

29   You also shall | light my | candle; ▪
      the Lord my God shall make my | darkness | to be | bright.

30   By your help I shall run at an | enemy | host; ▪
      with the help of my God | I can leap | over a | wall.

31.   As for God, his way is perfect;
        the word of the Lord is | tried · in the | fire; ▪
      he is a shield to | all who | trust in | him.

32   For who is God | but the | Lord, ▪
      and who is the | rock ex|cept our | God?

33   It is God who girds me a|bout with | strength ▪
      and | makes my | way | perfect.

34   He makes my | feet like | hinds' feet ▪
      so that I tread | surely | on the | heights.

35   He teaches my | hands to | fight ▪
      and my arms to | bend a | bow of | bronze.

36.   You have given me the shield of | your sal|vation; ▪
      your right hand upholds me
        and your | grace has | made me | great.

37   You enlarge my | strides be|neath me, ▪
      yet my | feet | do not | slide.

38   I will pursue my enemies and | over|take them, ▪
      nor turn again un|til I | have des|troyed them.

39.   I will smite them down so they | cannot | rise; ▪
      they shall | fall be|neath my | feet.

40   You have girded me with | strength · for the | battle; ▪
      you will cast | down my | enemies | under me;

41   You will make my foes turn their | backs up|on me ▪
      and I shall des|troy | them that | hate me.

42   They will cry out, but there shall be | none to | help them; ▪
      they will cry to the Lord, | but he | will not | answer.

43   I shall beat them as small as the | dust · on the | wind; ▪
      I will cast them out as the | mire | in the | streets.

44   You will deliver me from the | strife · of the | peoples; ▪
      you will | make me the | head · of the | nations.

45   A people I have not known shall serve me;
          as soon as they hear me, they ǀ shall oǀbey me; ▪
    strangers will ǀ humble themǀselves beǀfore me.

46.   The foreign peoples will ǀ lose ǀ heart ▪
    and come ǀ trembling ǀ out of their ǀ strongholds.

47   The Lord lives, and blessed ǀ be my ǀ rock! ▪
    Praised be the ǀ God of ǀ my salǀvation,

48   Even the ǀ God who ǀ vindicates me ▪
    and subǀdues the ǀ peoples ǀ under me!

49   You that deliver me from my enemies,
          you will set me up aǀbove my ǀ foes; ▪
    from the ǀ violent you ǀ will deǀliver me;

50   Therefore will I give you thanks, O Lord, aǀmong the ǀ nations ▪
    and sing ǀ praises ǀ to your ǀ name,

51† To the one who gives great victory ǀ to his ǀ king ▪
    and shows faithful love to his anointed,
          to David ǀ and his ǀ seed for ǀ ever.

Psalm 19

1   The heavens are telling the ǀ glory of ǀ God ▪
    and the ǀ firmament proǀclaims his ǀ handiwork.

2.   One day pours out its ǀ song · to anǀother ▪
    and one night unfolds ǀ knowledge ǀ to anǀother.

3   They have neither ǀ speech nor ǀ language ▪
    and their ǀ voices ǀ are not ǀ heard,

4.   Yet their sound has gone out into ǀ all ǀ lands ▪
    and their ǀ words · to the ǀ ends of the ǀ world.

5   In them has he set a tabernacle ǀ for the ǀ sun, ▪
    that comes forth as a bridegroom out of his chamber
          and rejoices as a ǀ champion to ǀ run his ǀ course.

6.   It goes forth from the end of the heavens
          and runs to the very ǀ end aǀgain, ▪
    and there is nothing ǀ hidden ǀ from its ǀ heat.

7   The law of the Lord is perfect, re|viving the | soul; ▪
the testimony of the Lord is sure
      and gives | wisdom | to the | simple.

8.   The statutes of the Lord are right and re|joice the | heart; ▪
the commandment of the Lord is pure
      and gives | light | to the | eyes.

9   The fear of the Lord is clean and en|dures for | ever; ▪
the judgments of the Lord are true and | righteous | alto|gether.

10   More to be desired are they than gold,
      more than | much fine | gold, ▪
sweeter also than honey, | dripping | from the | honeycomb.

11†   By them also is your | servant | taught ▪
and in keeping them | there is | great re|ward.

12   Who can tell how often | they of|fend? ▪
O cleanse me | from my | secret | faults!

13   Keep your servant also from presumptuous sins
      lest they get do|minion | over me; ▪
so shall I be undefiled, and | innocent of | great of|fence.

14   Let the words of my mouth and the meditation of my heart
      be acceptable | in your | sight, ▪
O Lord, my | strength and | my re|deemer.

Psalm 20

1   May the Lord hear you in the | day of | trouble, ▪
the name of the | God of | Jacob de|fend you;

2.   Send you | help from his | sanctuary ▪
and | strengthen you | out of | Zion;

3   Remember | all your | offerings ▪
and ac|cept your | burnt | sacrifice;

4   Grant you your | heart's de|sire ▪
and ful|fil | all your | mind.

5†   May we rejoice in your salvation
      and triumph in the | name of our | God; ▪
may the Lord per|form all | your pe|titions.

6   Now I know that the Lord will | save his a|nointed; ∎
      he will answer him from his holy heaven,
          with the mighty | strength of | his right | hand.

7.   Some put their trust in chariots and | some in | horses, ∎
      but we will call only on the | name of the | Lord our | God.

8   They are brought | down and | fallen, ∎
      but we are | risen | and stand | upright.

9   O Lord, | save the | king ∎
      and answer us | when we | call up|on you.

Psalm 21

1   The king shall rejoice in your | strength, O | Lord; ∎
      how greatly shall he re|joice in | your sal|vation!

2   You have given him his | heart's de|sire ∎
      and have not de|nied · the re|quest of his | lips.

3   For you come to meet him with | blessings of | goodness ∎
      and set a crown of pure | gold up|on his | head.

4.   He asked of you life | and you | gave it him, ∎
      length of | days, for | ever and | ever.

5   His honour is great because of | your sal|vation; ∎
      glory and majesty | have you | laid up|on him.

6   You have granted him ever|lasting fe|licity ∎
      and will make him | glad with | joy · in your | presence.

7†   For the king puts his | trust in the | Lord; ∎
      because of the loving-kindness of the Most High,
          he shall | not be | over|thrown.

8   Your hand shall mark down | all your | enemies; ∎
      your right hand will | find out | those who | hate you.

9   You will make them like a fiery oven in the | time of your | wrath; ∎
      the Lord will swallow them up in his anger |
          and the | fire will con|sume them.

10.   Their fruit you will root | out of the | land ∎
      and their | seed · from a|mong its in|habitants.

11   Because they intend ǀ evil aǀgainst you ▪
      and devise wicked schemes ǀ which they ǀ cannot perǀform,

12   You will ǀ put them to ǀ flight ▪
      when you ǀ aim your ǀ bow at their ǀ faces.

13   Be exalted, O Lord, in ǀ your own ǀ might; ▪
      we will make ǀ music and ǀ sing of your ǀ power.

Psalm 22

1   My God, my God, why have ǀ you forǀsaken me, ▪
     and are so far from my salvation,
         from the ǀ words of ǀ my disǀtress?

2   O my God, I cry in the daytime, but you ǀ do not ǀ answer; ▪
     and by night also, ǀ but I ǀ find no ǀ rest.

3   Yet you ǀ are the ǀ Holy One, ▪
     enthroned upǀon the ǀ praises of ǀ Israel.

4   Our forebears ǀ trusted in ǀ you; ▪
     they ǀ trusted, and ǀ you deǀlivered them.

5.   They cried out to you and ǀ were deǀlivered; ▪
     they put their trust in you ǀ and were ǀ not conǀfounded.

6   But as for me, I am a worm and ǀ no ǀ man, ▪
     scorned by all ǀ and desǀpised · by the ǀ people.

7   All who see me ǀ laugh me to ǀ scorn; ▪
     they curl their lips and ǀ wag their ǀ heads, ǀ saying,

8   'He trusted in the Lord; ǀ let him deǀliver him; ▪
     let him deǀliver him, if ǀ he deǀlights in him.'

9   But it is you that took me ǀ out of the ǀ womb ▪
     and laid me safe upǀon my ǀ mother's ǀ breast.

10   On you was I cast ever since ǀ I was ǀ born; ▪
     you are my God even ǀ from my ǀ mother's ǀ womb.

11†   Be not far from me, for trouble is ǀ near at ǀ hand ▪
     and ǀ there is ǀ none to ǀ help.

12   Mighty oxen ǀ come aǀround me; ▪
     fat bulls of Bashan close me ǀ in on ǀ every ǀ side.

13   They gape upon me ǀ with their ǀ mouths, ▪
     as it were a ǀ ramping · and a ǀ roaring ǀ lion.

14 I am poured out like water;
    all my bones are | out of | joint; ▪
 my heart has become like wax
    | melting · in the | depths of my | body.

15 My mouth is dried up like a potsherd;
    my tongue | cleaves to my | gums; ▪
 you have | laid me · in the | dust of | death.

16. For the hounds are all about me,
    the pack of evildoers close | in on | me; ▪
 they | pierce my | hands and my | feet.

17 I can count | all my | bones; ▪
 they stand | staring and | looking up|on me.

18 They divide my | garments a|mong them; ▪
 they cast | lots | for my | clothing.

19 Be not far from | me, O | Lord; ▪
 you are my | strength; | hasten to | help me.

20 Deliver my | soul · from the | sword, ▪
 my poor | life · from the | power of the | dog.

21. Save me from the | lion's | mouth, ▪
 from the horns of wild oxen. |
    You have | answered | me!

22 I will tell of your | name to my | people; ▪
 in the midst of the congre|gation | will I | praise you.

23 Praise the Lord, | you that | fear him; ▪
 O seed of Jacob, glorify him;
    stand in awe of | him, O | seed of | Israel.

24. For he has not despised nor abhorred the suffering of the poor;
    neither has he hidden his | face | from them; ▪
 but when they | cried to | him he | heard them.

25 From you comes my praise in the great | congre|gation; ▪
 I will perform my vows in the | presence of | those that | fear you.

26† The poor shall | eat · and be | satisfied; ▪
 those who seek the Lord shall praise him;
    their | hearts shall | live for | ever.

27 All the ends of the earth shall remember and ǀ turn to the ǀ Lord, ▪
and all the families of the ǀ nations shall ǀ bow beǀfore him.

28. For the kingdom ǀ is the ǀ Lord's ▪
and he ǀ rules ǀ over the ǀ nations.

29 How can those who sleep in the earth bow ǀ down in ǀ worship, ▪
or those who go down to the ǀ dust ǀ kneel beǀfore him?

30 He has saved my life for himself;
my desǀcendants shall ǀ serve him; ▪
this shall be told of the Lord for ǀ geneǀrations to ǀ come.

31† They shall come and make known his salvation,
to a people ǀ yet unǀborn, ▪
declaring that ǀ he, the ǀ Lord, has ǀ done it.

Psalm 23

1 The Lord ǀ is my ǀ shepherd; ▪
therefore ǀ can I ǀ lack ǀ nothing.

2. He makes me lie down in ǀ green ǀ pastures ▪
and leads me beǀside ǀ still ǀ waters.

3 He shall reǀfresh my ǀ soul ▪
and guide me in the paths of righteousness ǀ for his ǀ name's ǀ sake.

4. Though I walk through the valley of the shadow of death,
I will ǀ fear no ǀ evil; ▪
for you are with me;
your ǀ rod and your ǀ staff, they ǀ comfort me.

5 You spread a table before me
in the presence of ǀ those who ǀ trouble me; ▪
you have anointed my head with oil ǀ and my ǀ cup shall be ǀ full.

6 Surely goodness and loving mercy shall follow me
all the ǀ days of my ǀ life, ▪
and I will dwell in the ǀ house of the ǀ Lord for ǀ ever.

Psalm 24

1 The earth is the Lord's and ǀ all that ǀ fills it, ▪
the compass of the world and ǀ all who ǀ dwell thereǀin.

2. For he has founded it upǀon the ǀ seas ▪
and set it firm upon the ǀ rivers ǀ of the ǀ deep.

3   'Who shall ascend the | hill of the | Lord, ▪
    or who can rise | up · in his | holy | place?'

4   'Those who have clean hands and a | pure | heart, ▪
    who have not lifted up their soul to an idol,
        nor | sworn an | oath · to a | lie;

5   'They shall receive a | blessing · from the | Lord, ▪
    a just reward from the | God of | their sal|vation.'

6. Such is the company of | those who | seek him, ▪
    of those who seek your | face, O | God of | Jacob.

7   Lift up your heads, O gates;
        be lifted up, you ever|lasting | doors; ▪
    and the King of | glory | shall come | in.

8   'Who is the | King of | glory?' ▪
    'The Lord, strong and mighty,
        the | Lord · who is | mighty in | battle.'

9   Lift up your heads, O gates;
        be lifted up, you ever|lasting | doors; ▪
    and the King of | glory | shall come | in.

10 'Who is this | King of | glory?' ▪
    'The Lord of hosts, |
        he · is the | King of | glory.'

Psalm 25

1. To you, O Lord, I lift up my soul;
        O my God, in | you I | trust; ▪
    let me not be put to shame;
        let not my | enemies | triumph | over me.

2   Let none who look to you be | put to | shame, ▪
    but let the treacherous be | shamed | and frus|trated.

3   Make me to know your | ways, O | Lord, ▪
    and | teach me | your | paths.

4   Lead me in your | truth and | teach me, ▪
    for you are the God of my salvation;
        for you have I | hoped | all the day | long.

5. Remember, Lord, your com|passion and | love, ▪
    for they | are from | ever|lasting.

6   Remember not the sins of my youth or | my trans|gressions, ▪
       but think on me in your goodness, O Lord,
           ac|cording · to your | steadfast | love.

7   Gracious and upright | is the | Lord; ▪
       therefore shall he teach | sinners | in the | way.

8   He will guide the humble in | doing | right ▪
       and | teach his | way to the | lowly.

9.   All the paths of the Lord are | mercy and | truth ▪
       to those who keep his | covenant | and his | testimonies.

10   For your name's | sake, O | Lord, ▪
       be merciful to my | sin, for | it is | great.

11   Who are those who | fear the | Lord? ▪
       Them will he teach in the | way that | they should | choose.

12   Their soul shall | dwell at | ease ▪
       and their offspring | shall in|herit the | land.

13.   The hidden purpose of the Lord is for | those who | fear him ▪
       and | he will | show them his | covenant.

14   My eyes are ever | looking · to the | Lord, ▪
       for he shall pluck my | feet | out of the | net.

15   Turn to me and be | gracious | to me, ▪
       for I am alone | and brought | very | low.

16   The sorrows of my heart | have in|creased; ▪
       O bring me | out of | my dis|tress.

17.   Look upon my ad|versity and | misery ▪
       and for|give me | all my | sin.

18   Look upon my enemies, for | they are | many ▪
       and they bear a | violent | hatred a|gainst me.

19   O keep my soul | and de|liver me; ▪
       let me not be put to shame, for I have | put my | trust in | you.

20   Let integrity and | uprightness pre|serve me, ▪
       for my | hope has | been in | you.

21†   Deliver | Israel, O | God, ▪
       out of | all | his | troubles.

1   Give judgment for me, O Lord,
       for I have I walked with inItegrity; ■
     I have trusted in the I Lord and I have not I faltered.

2   Test me, O I Lord, and I try me; ■
     examine my I heart I and my I mind.

3   For your love is beIfore my I eyes; ■
     I have I walked I in your I truth.

4. I have not joined the company I of the I false, ■
     nor conIsorted I with the deIceitful.

5   I hate the gathering of I evilIdoers ■
     and I I will not sit I down · with the I wicked.

6   I will wash my hands in I innocence, O I Lord, ■
     that I may I go aIbout your I altar,

7   To make heard the I voice of I thanksgiving ■
     and tell of I all your I wonderful I deeds.

8. Lord, I love the house of your I habiItation ■
     and the I place · where your I glory aIbides.

9   Sweep me not aIway with I sinners, ■
     nor my I life I with the I bloodthirsty,

10 Whose hands are full of I wicked I schemes ■
     and their I right hand I full of I bribes.

11 As for me, I will I walk with inItegrity; ■
     redeem me, Lord, I and be I merciful I to me.

12 My I foot stands I firm; ■
     in the great congregation I I will I bless the I Lord.

1   The Lord is my light and my salvation;
       whom then I shall I I fear? ■
     The Lord is the strength of my life;
       of whom then I shall I I be aIfraid?

2   When the wicked, even my enemies and my foes,
       came upon me to I eat up my I flesh, ■
     they I stumbled I and I fell.

3.   Though a host encamp against me,
        my heart shall | not be a|fraid, ▪
    and though there rise up war against me,
        yet will I | put my | trust in | him.

4   One thing have I asked of the Lord
        and that a|lone I | seek: ▪
    that I may dwell in the house of the Lord |
        all the | days of my | life,

5.   To behold the fair |beauty · of the |Lord ▪
    and to | seek his | will · in his | temple.

6   For in the day of trouble
        he shall hide me | in his | shelter; ▪
    in the secret place of his dwelling shall he hide me
        and set me | high up|on a | rock.

7   And now shall he | lift up my | head ▪
    above my | enemies | round a|bout me;

8.   Therefore will I offer in his dwelling an oblation
        with | great | gladness; ▪
    I will sing and make | music | to the | Lord.

9   Hear my voice, O Lord, | when I | call; ▪
    have | mercy up|on me and | answer me.

10   My heart tells of your word, | 'Seek my | face.' ▪
    Your | face, Lord, | will I | seek.

11.   Hide | not your | face from me, ▪
    nor cast your | servant a|way · in dis|pleasure.

12   You have | been my | helper; ▪
    leave me not, neither forsake me, O | God of | my sal|vation.

13†   Though my father and my | mother for|sake me, ▪
    the | Lord will | take me | up.

14   Teach me your | way, O | Lord; ▪
    lead me on a level path,
        because of | those who | lie in | wait for me.

15   Deliver me not into the | will of my | adversaries, ▪
    for false witnesses have risen up against me,
        and | those who | breathe out | violence.

16   I believe that I shall see the | goodness · of the | Lord ▪
in the | land | of the | living.

17   Wait for the Lord;
        be strong and he shall | comfort your | heart; ▪
wait | patiently | for the | Lord.

Psalm 28

1   To you I call, O Lord my rock;
        be not | deaf · to my | cry, ▪
lest, if you do not hear me,
        I become like | those who go | down · to the | Pit.

2   Hear the voice of my prayer when I cry | out to | you, ▪
when I lift up my | hands · to your | holy of | holies.

3.   Do not snatch me away with the wicked,
        with the | evil|doers, ▪
who speak peaceably with their neighbours,
        while | malice is | in their | hearts.

4   Repay them ac|cording · to their | deeds ▪
and according to the | wickedness of | their de|vices.

5   Reward them according to the | work of their | hands ▪
and | pay them their | just de|serts.

6.   They take no heed of the Lord's doings,
        nor of the | works of his | hands; ▪
therefore shall he break them down |
        and not | build them | up.

7   Blessed | be the | Lord, ▪
for he has | heard the | voice of my | prayer.

8   The Lord is my strength | and my | shield; ▪
my heart has trusted in | him and | I am | helped;

9†   Therefore my heart | dances for | joy ▪
and in my | song | will I | praise him.

10   The Lord is the | strength of his | people, ▪
a safe | refuge for | his a|nointed.

11   Save your people and | bless your in|heritance; ▪
shepherd them and | carry | them for | ever.

Psalm 29

1 Ascribe to the Lord, you | powers of | heaven, ▪
    ascribe to the | Lord | glory and | strength.

2 Ascribe to the Lord the honour | due · to his | name; ▪
    worship the | Lord · in the | beauty of | holiness.

3. The voice of the Lord is upon the waters;
         the God of | glory | thunders; ▪
    the Lord is up|on the | mighty | waters.

4 The voice of the Lord is mighty in | oper|ation; ▪
    the voice of the Lord | is a | glorious | voice.

5 The voice of the Lord | breaks the | cedar trees; ▪
    the Lord | breaks the | cedars of | Lebanon;

6. He makes Lebanon | skip · like a | calf ▪
    and Sirion | like a | young wild | ox.

7 The voice of the Lord splits the flash of lightning;
         the voice of the Lord | shakes the | wilderness; ▪
    the Lord | shakes the | wilderness of | Kadesh.

8. The voice of the Lord makes the oak trees writhe
         and strips the | forests | bare; ▪
    in his | temple | all cry | 'Glory!'

9 The Lord sits enthroned a|bove the | water flood; ▪
    the Lord sits enthroned as | king for | ever|more.

10 The Lord shall give | strength to his | people; ▪
     the Lord shall give his | people the | blessing of | peace.

Psalm 30

1 I will exalt you, O Lord,
         because you have | raised me | up ▪
    and have not let my | foes | triumph | over me.

2 O | Lord my | God, ▪
    I cried out to | you and | you have | healed me.

3. You brought me up, O Lord, | from the | dead; ▪
    you restored me to life from among | those that go | down · to the | Pit.

4   Sing to the Lord, you | servants of | his; ▪
     give | thanks to his | holy | name.

5.   For his wrath endures but the twinkling of an eye,
          his favour | for a | lifetime. ▪
     Heaviness may endure for a night,
          but | joy comes | in the | morning.

6   In my prosperity I said,
          'I shall | never be | moved. ▪
     You, Lord, of your goodness,
          have | made my | hill so | strong.'

7   Then you | hid your | face from me ▪
     and | I was | utterly dis|mayed.

8.   To you, O | Lord, I | cried; ▪
     to the Lord I | made my | suppli|cation:

9   'What profit is there in my blood,
          if I go | down · to the | Pit? ▪
     Will the dust praise you | or de|clare your | faithfulness?

10. 'Hear, O Lord, and have | mercy up|on me; ▪
     O | Lord, | be my | helper.'

11   You have turned my mourning | into | dancing; ▪
     you have put off my sackcloth and | girded | me with | gladness;

12   Therefore my heart sings to | you without | ceasing; ▪
     O Lord my God, I will | give you | thanks for | ever.

Psalm 31

1   In you, O Lord, have I taken refuge;
          let me never be | put to | shame; ▪
     de|liver me | in your | righteousness.

2.   Incline your | ear to | me; ▪
     make | haste | to de|liver me.

3   Be my strong rock, a fortress to save me,
          for you are my | rock · and my | stronghold; ▪
     guide me, and | lead me | for your | name's sake.

4   Take me out of the net that they have laid | secretly | for me, ▪
       for | you | are my | strength.

5.   Into your hands I com|mend my | spirit, ▪
       for you have redeemed me | O | Lord | God of | truth.

6   I hate those who cling to | worthless | idols; ▪
       I | put my | trust · in the | Lord.

7   I will be glad and re|joice in your | mercy, ▪
       for you have seen my affliction
              and known my | soul | in ad|versity.

8.   You have not shut me up in the | hand of the | enemy; ▪
       you have set my | feet · in an | open | place.

9   Have mercy on me, Lord, for | I am in | trouble; ▪
       my eye is consumed with sorrow |
              my | soul · and my | body | also.

10   For my life is wasted with grief, and my | years with | sighing; ▪
       my strength fails me because of my affliction |
              and my | bones | are con|sumed.

11   I have become a reproach to all my enemies
              and even to my neighbours |
              an object of dread to | my ac|quaintances; ▪
       when they | see me · in the | street they | flee from me.

12. I am forgotten like one that is dead, | out of | mind; ▪
       I have be|come · like a | broken | vessel.

13   For I have heard the whispering of the crowd;
              fear is on | every | side; ▪
       they scheme together against me, and I | plot to | take my | life.

14   But my trust is in | you, O | Lord. ▪
       I have | said | 'You | are my | God.

15   'My times are | in your | hand; ▪
       deliver me from the hand of my enemies,
              and from | those who | persecute | me.

16. 'Make your face to | shine up·on your | servant, ▪
       and save me | for your | mercy's | sake.'

17   Lord, let me not be confounded
              for I have | called up|on you; ▪

but let the wicked be put to shame;
   let them be | silent | in the | grave.

18. Let the lying lips be | put to | silence ▪
  that speak against the righteous
   with | arrogance, dis|dain · and con|tempt.

19 How abundant is your goodness, O Lord,
   which you have laid up for | those who | fear you; ▪
  which you have prepared in the sight of all
   for those who | put their | trust in | you.

20. You hide them in the shelter of your presence
   from | those who | slander them; ▪
  you keep them safe in your refuge | from the | strife of | tongues.

21 Blessed | be the | Lord! ▪
  For he has shown me his steadfast love
   when I was | as a | city be|sieged.

22. I had said in my alarm,
   'I have been cut off from the | sight of your | eyes.' ▪
  Nevertheless, you heard the voice of my prayer |
   when I | cried | out to you.

23 Love the Lord, all | you his | servants; ▪
  for the Lord protects the faithful,
   but re|pays · to the | full the | proud.

24 Be strong and let your | heart take | courage, ▪
  all you who wait in | hope | for the | Lord.

Psalm 32

1 Happy the one whose transgression | is for|given, ▪
  and | whose | sin is | covered.

2. Happy the one to whom the Lord im|putes no | guilt, ▪
  and in whose | spirit there | is no | guile.

3 For I | held my | tongue; ▪
  my bones wasted away
   through my | groaning | all the day | long.

4   Your hand was heavy upon me ˈ day and ˈ night; ▪
       my moisture was dried up ˈ like the ˈ drought in ˈ summer.

5   Then I acknowledged my ˈ sin to ˈ you ▪
       and my inˈiquity I ˈ did not ˈ hide.

6.   I said, 'I will confess my transgressions ˈ to the ˈ Lord,' ▪
       and you forˈgave the ˈ guilt of my ˈ sin.

7   Therefore let all the faithful make their prayers to you
         in ˈ time of ˈ trouble; ▪
       in the great ˈ water flood, it ˈ shall not ˈ reach them.

8.   You are a place for me to hide in;
         you preˈserve me from ˈ trouble; ▪
       you surˈround me with ˈ songs · of deˈliverance.

9   'I will instruct you and teach you
         in the way that ˈ you should ˈ go; ▪
       I will ˈ guide you ˈ with my ˈ eye.

10.   'Be not like horse and mule which have ˈ no · underˈstanding; ▪
       whose mouths must be held with bit and bridle,
         or ˈ else · they will ˈ not stay ˈ near you.'

11   Great tribulations reˈmain for the ˈ wicked, ▪
       but mercy embraces ˈ those who ˈ trust in the ˈ Lord.

12   Be glad, you righteous, and reˈjoice in the ˈ Lord; ▪
       shout for joy, ˈ all who are ˈ true of ˈ heart.

Psalm 33

1   Rejoice in the Lord, ˈ O you ˈ righteous, ▪
       for it is good for the ˈ just to ˈ sing ˈ praises.

2   Praise the Lord ˈ with the ˈ lyre; ▪
       on the ten-stringed ˈ harp ˈ sing his ˈ praise.

3.   Sing for him a ˈ new ˈ song; ▪
       play ˈ skilfully, with ˈ shouts of ˈ praise.

4   For the word of the ˈ Lord is ˈ true ▪
       and ˈ all his ˈ works are ˈ sure.

5†   He loves ˈ righteousness and ˈ justice; ▪
       the earth is full of the lovingˈkindness ˈ of the ˈ Lord.

6   By the word of the Lord were the | heavens | made ▪
        and all their | host · by the | breath of his | mouth.

7   He gathers up the waters of the sea as | in a | waterskin ▪
        and lays up the | deep | in his | treasury.

8   Let all the earth | fear the | Lord; ▪
        stand in awe of him, | all who | dwell in the | world.

9.   For he spoke, and | it was | done; ▪
        he com|manded, and | it stood | fast.

10   The Lord brings the counsel of the | nations to | naught; ▪
        he frus|trates · the de|signs of the | peoples.

11   But the counsel of the Lord shall en|dure for | ever ▪
        and the designs of his heart from gene|ration to | gene|ration.

12.   Happy the nation whose | God · is the | Lord ▪
        and the people he has | chosen | for his | own.

13   The Lord looks | down from | heaven ▪
        and beholds | all the | children of | earth.

14   From where he sits enthroned he | turns his | gaze ▪
        on | all who | dwell on the | earth.

15.   He fashions | all the | hearts of them ▪
        and under|stands | all their | works.

16   No king is saved by the | might of his | host; ▪
        no warrior delivered | by his | great | strength.

17.   A horse is a vain hope | for de|liverance; ▪
        for all its | strength it | cannot | save.

18   Behold, the eye of the Lord is upon | those who | fear him, ▪
        on those who wait in | hope · for his | steadfast | love,

19.   To deliver their | soul from | death ▪
        and to | feed them in | time of | famine.

20   Our soul waits longingly | for the | Lord; ▪
        he is our | help | and our | shield.

21   Indeed, our heart re|joices | in him; ▪
        in his holy name | have we | put our | trust.

22†   Let your loving-kindness, O Lord, | be up|on us, ▪
        as we have | set our | hope on | you.

1   I will bless the | Lord at | all times; ▪
     his praise shall | ever be | in my | mouth.

2   My soul shall glory | in the | Lord; ▪
     let the | humble | hear and be | glad.

3.   O magnify the | Lord with | me; ▪
     let us ex|alt his | name to|gether.

4   I sought the Lord | and he | answered me ▪
     and de|livered me from | all my | fears.

5   Look upon him | and be | radiant ▪
     and your faces | shall not | be a|shamed.

6.   This poor soul cried, and the | Lord | heard me ▪
     and | saved me from | all my | troubles.

7   The angel | of the | Lord ▪
     encamps around those who | fear him | and de|livers them.

8.   O taste and see that the | Lord is | gracious; ▪
     blessed is the | one who | trusts in | him.

9   Fear the Lord, all | you his | holy ones, ▪
     for those who | fear him | lack | nothing.

10   Lions may lack and | suffer | hunger, ▪
     but those who seek the Lord lack | nothing | that is | good.

11.   Come, my children, and | listen to | me; ▪
     I will | teach · you the | fear · of the | Lord.

12   Who is there who de|lights in | life ▪
     and longs for | days · to en|joy good | things?

13   Keep your | tongue from | evil ▪
     and your | lips from | lying | words.

14.   Turn from evil | and do | good; ▪
     seek | peace | and pur|sue it.

15   The eyes of the Lord are up|on the | righteous ▪
     and his ears are | open | to their | cry.

16   The face of the Lord is against | those who do | evil, ▪
     to root out the re|membrance · of them | from the | earth.

17 The righteous cry and the | Lord | hears them ▪
and delivers them | out of | all their | troubles.

18. The Lord is near to the | broken|hearted ▪
and will save | those • who are | crushed in | spirit.

19 Many are the | troubles • of the | righteous; ▪
from them | all • will the | Lord de|liver them.

20 He keeps | all their | bones, ▪
so that not | one of | them is | broken.

21 But evil shall | slay the | wicked ▪
and those who hate the | righteous will | be con|demned.

22 The Lord ransoms the | life of his | servants ▪
and will condemn | none • who seek | refuge | in him.

Psalm 35

1 Contend, O Lord, with those that con|tend with | me; ▪
fight against | those that | fight a|gainst me.

2 Take up | shield and | buckler ▪
and | rise | up to | help me.

3. Draw the spear and bar the way against those | who pur|sue me; ▪
say to my soul, | 'I am | your sal|vation.'

4 Let those who seek after my life be shamed | and dis|graced; ▪
let those who plot my ruin fall back | and be | put to con|fusion.

5 Let them be as chaff be|fore the | wind, ▪
with the angel of the | Lord | thrusting them | down.

6. Let their way be | dark and | slippery, ▪
with the | angel • of the | Lord pur|suing them.

7 For they have secretly spread a net for me with|out a | cause; ▪
without any cause they have | dug a | pit for my | soul.

8. Let ruin come upon them | una|wares; ▪
let them be caught in the net they laid;
let them | fall in it to | their des|truction.

9 Then will my soul be joyful | in the | Lord ▪
and | glory in | his sal|vation.

10. My very bones will say, 'Lord, | who is | like you? ▪
   You deliver the poor from those that are too strong for them,
      the poor and needy from | those who | would de|spoil them.'

11 False witnesses rose | up a|gainst me; ▪
   they | charged me with | things I | knew not.

12 They rewarded me | evil for | good, ▪
   to the deso|lation | of my | soul.

13. But as for me, when they were sick I | put on | sackcloth ▪
   and | humbled my|self with | fasting;

14 When my prayer returned empty | to my | bosom, ▪
   it was as though I | grieved · for my | friend or | brother;

15 I behaved as one who | mourns for his | mother, ▪
   bowed down | and brought | very | low.

16. But when I stumbled, they gathered in delight;
      they gathered to|gether a|gainst me; ▪
   as if they were strangers I did not know
      they | tore at | me without | ceasing.

17 When I | fell they | mocked me; ▪
   they | gnashed at me | with their | teeth.

18 O Lord, how long will | you look | on? ▪
   Rescue my soul from their ravages,
      and my poor | life · from the | young | lions.

19. I will give you thanks in the great | congre|gation; ▪
   I will praise you | in the | mighty | throng.

20 Do not let my treacherous foes re|joice | over me, ▪
   or those who hate me without a cause |
      mock me | with their | glances.

21 For they do not | speak of | peace, ▪
   but invent deceitful schemes
      against those that are | quiet | in the | land.

22 They opened wide their mouths and de|rided me, | saying ▪
   'We have seen it | with our | very | eyes.'

23† This you have seen, O Lord; do | not keep | silent; ▪
   go not | far from | me, O | Lord.

24   Awake, arise, | to my | cause, ▪
     to my defence, my | God | and my | Lord!

25   Give me justice, O Lord my God,
         according | to your | righteousness; ▪
     let | them not | triumph | over me.

26.   Let them not say to themselves, 'Our | heart's de|sire!' ▪
     Let them not say, | 'We have | swallowed him | up.'

27   Let all who rejoice at my trouble be put to | shame and con|fusion; ▪
     let those who boast against me
         be | clothed with | shame · and dis|honour.

28.   Let those who favour my cause re|joice and be | glad; ▪
     let them say always,
         'Great is the Lord, who de|lights · in his | servant's | well-being.'

29   So shall my tongue be | talking of your | righteousness ▪
     and of your | praise | all the day | long.

Psalm 36

1   Sin whispers to the wicked, in the | depths of their | heart; ▪
     there is no fear of | God be|fore their | eyes.

2   They flatter themselves in their | own | eyes ▪
     that their abominable sin will | not be | found | out.

3   The words of their mouth are unrighteous and | full of de|ceit; ▪
     they have ceased to act wisely | and to | do | good.

4.   They think out mischief upon their beds
         and have set themselves in | no good | way; ▪
     nor do they ab|hor | that which is | evil.

5   Your love, O Lord, reaches | to the | heavens ▪
     and your | faithfulness | to the | clouds.

6   Your righteousness stands like the strong mountains,
         your justice like the | great | deep; ▪
     you, Lord, shall | save both | man and | beast.

7.   How precious is your loving | mercy, O | God! ▪
     All mortal flesh shall take refuge
         under the | shadow | of your | wings.

8　They shall be satisfied with the abundance | of your | house; ▪
　　they shall drink from the | river of | your de|lights.

9　For with you is the | well of | life ▪
　　and in your | light shall | we see | light.

10.　O continue your loving-kindness to | those who | know you ▪
　　and your righteousness to | those who are | true of | heart.

11　Let not the foot of pride | come a|gainst me, ▪
　　nor the hand of the un|godly | thrust me a|way.

12　There are they fallen, | all who work | wickedness. ▪
　　They are cast down and shall | not be | able to | stand.

Psalm 37

1　Fret not because of | evil|doers; ▪
　　be not | jealous of | those · who do | wrong.

2　For they shall soon | wither like | grass ▪
　　and like the green | herb | fade a|way.

3　Trust in the Lord and be | doing | good; ▪
　　dwell in the land | and be | nourished with | truth.

4.　Let your delight be | in the | Lord ▪
　　and he will | give you your | heart's de|sire.

5　Commit your way to the Lord and | put your | trust in him, ▪
　　and | he will | bring it to | pass.

6.　He will make your righteousness as | clear as the | light ▪
　　and your just | dealing | as the | noonday.

7　Be still before the | Lord and | wait for him; ▪
　　do not fret over those that prosper
　　　　as they | follow their | evil | schemes.

8.　Refrain from anger and a|bandon | wrath; ▪
　　do not fret, | lest · you be | moved to do | evil.

9　For evildoers | shall be cut | off, ▪
　　but those who wait upon the Lord | shall pos|sess the | land.

10　Yet a little while and the wicked shall | be no | more; ▪
　　you will search for their | place and | find them | gone.

11.   But the lowly shall pos|sess the | land ▪
and shall de|light · in a|bundance of | peace.

12   The wicked plot a|gainst the | righteous ▪
and | gnash at them | with their | teeth.

13   The Lord shall | laugh at the | wicked, ▪
for he | sees that their | day is | coming.

14   The wicked draw their sword and bend their bow
        to strike down the | poor and | needy, ▪
to slaughter | those who | walk in | truth.

15.   Their sword shall go through their | own | heart ▪
and their | bows | shall be | broken.

16   The little that the | righteous | have ▪
is better than great | riches | of the | wicked.

17   For the arms of the wicked | shall be | broken, ▪
but the | Lord up|holds the | righteous.

18   The Lord knows the | days of the | godly, ▪
and their in|heritance shall | stand for | ever.

19   They shall not be put to shame in the | perilous | time, ▪
and in days of famine | they shall | have e|nough.

20   But the | wicked shall | perish; ▪
like the glory of the meadows
        the enemies of the Lord shall vanish; |
        they shall | vanish like | smoke.

21.   The wicked borrow and | do not re|pay, ▪
but the | righteous are | generous in | giving.

22   For those who are blest by God shall pos|sess the | land, ▪
but those who are cursed by him | shall be | rooted | out.

23   When your steps are guided | by the | Lord ▪
and you de|light | in his | way,

24.   Though you stumble, you shall | not fall | headlong, ▪
for the Lord | holds you | fast · by the | hand.

25   I have been young and | now am | old, ▪
yet never have I seen the righteous forsaken,
        or their | children | begging their | bread.

26   All the day long they are | generous in | lending, ▪
     and their children | also | shall be | blest.

27.   Depart from evil | and do | good ▪
     and you | shall a|bide for | ever.

28   For the Lord loves the | thing · that is | right ▪
     and will | not for|sake his | faithful ones.

29   The unjust shall be des|troyed for | ever, ▪
     and the offspring of the wicked | shall be | rooted | out.

30.   The righteous shall pos|sess the | land ▪
     and | dwell in | it for | ever.

31   The mouth of the righteous | utters | wisdom, ▪
     and their tongue | speaks the | thing · that is | right.

32   The law of their God is | in their | heart ▪
     and their | footsteps | shall not | slide.

33.   The wicked | spy on the | righteous ▪
     and | seek oc|casion to | slay them.

34   The Lord will not leave them | in their | hand, ▪
     nor let them be con|demned when | they are | judged.

35   Wait upon the Lord and | keep his | way; ▪
     he will raise you up to possess the land,
        and when the wicked are up|rooted, | you shall | see it.

36   I myself have seen the wicked in | great | power ▪
     and flourishing like a | tree in | full | leaf.

37†   I went by and lo, | they were | gone; ▪
     I sought them, but | they could | nowhere be | found.

38   Keep innocence and heed the | thing · that is | right, ▪
     for that will | bring you | peace · at the | last.

39.   But the sinners shall | perish to|gether, ▪
     and the posterity of the wicked | shall be | rooted | out.

40   The salvation of the righteous | comes from the | Lord; ▪
     he is their stronghold | in the | time of | trouble.

41   The Lord shall stand by them | and de|liver them; ▪
     he shall deliver them from the wicked and shall save them,
        because they have | put their | trust in | him.

1   Rebuke me not, O Lord, | in your | anger, ▪
    neither chasten me | in your | heavy dis|pleasure.

2   For your arrows | have stuck | fast in me ▪
    and your hand | presses | hard up|on me.

3   There is no health in my flesh
        because of your | indig|nation; ▪
    there is no peace in my | bones be|cause of my | sin.

4. For my iniquities have gone | over my | head; ▪
    their weight is a | burden too | heavy to | bear.

5   My wounds | stink and | fester ▪
    be|cause of | my | foolishness.

6   I am utterly bowed down and brought | very | low; ▪
    I go about | mourning | all the day | long.

7   My loins are filled with | searing | pain; ▪
    there | is no | health in my | flesh.

8. I am feeble and | utterly | crushed; ▪
    I roar aloud because of the dis|quiet | of my | heart.

9   O Lord, you know all | my de|sires ▪
    and my sighing | is not | hidden | from you.

10 My heart is pounding, my | strength has | failed me; ▪
    the light of my | eyes is | gone | from me.

11 My friends and companions stand apart from | my af|fliction; ▪
    my | neighbours | stand afar | off.

12. Those who seek after my | life lay | snares for me; ▪
    and those who would harm me whisper evil
        and mutter | slander | all the day | long.

13 But I am like one who is | deaf and | hears not, ▪
    like one that is dumb, who | does not | open his | mouth.

14 I have become like one who | does not | hear ▪
    and from whose | mouth comes | no re|tort.

15 For in you, Lord, have I | put my | trust; ▪
    you will | answer me, O | Lord my | God.

16. For I said, 'Let them not | triumph | over me, ▪
    those who exult over me | when my | foot | slips.'

17   Truly, I am on the | verge of | falling ▪
         and my | pain is | ever | with me.

18   I will con|fess · my in|iquity ▪
         and be | sorry | for my | sin.

19   Those that are my enemies without any | cause are | mighty, ▪
         and those who hate me | wrongfully are | many in | number.

20.   Those who repay evil for good | are a|gainst me, ▪
         because the | good is | what I | seek.

21   Forsake me | not, O | Lord; ▪
         be not | far from me, | O my | God.

22   Make | haste to | help me, ▪
         O | Lord of | my sal|vation.

Psalm 39

1   I said, 'I will keep watch | over my | ways, ▪
         so that I of|fend not | with my | tongue.

2   'I will guard my | mouth · with a | muzzle, ▪
         while the | wicked are | in my | sight.'

3.   So I held my tongue | and said | nothing; ▪
         I kept silent | but to | no a|vail.

4   My distress increased, my heart grew | hot with|in me; ▪
         while I mused, the fire was kindled
             and I | spoke out | with my | tongue:

5   'Lord, let me know my end and the | number · of my | days, ▪
         that I may | know how | short my | time is.

6   'You have made my days but a handsbreadth,
             and my lifetime is as nothing | in your | sight; ▪
         truly, even those who stand | upright are | but a | breath.

7†   'We walk about like a shadow
             and in vain we | are in | turmoil; ▪
         we heap up riches and | cannot tell | who will | gather them.

8   'And now, | what is my | hope? ▪
         Truly my | hope is | even in | you.

9   'Deliver me from | all my trans|gressions ▪
         and do not | make me the | taunt · of the | fool.'

10   I fell silent and did not | open my | mouth, ▪
      for surely | it was | your | doing.

11   Take a|way your | plague from me; ▪
      I am con|sumed · by the | blows of your | hand.

12   With rebukes for sin you punish us;
        like a moth you con|sume our | beauty; ▪
      truly, | everyone is | but a | breath.

13.   Hear my prayer, O Lord, and give | ear to my | cry; ▪
      hold | not your | peace · at my | tears.

14   For I am but a | stranger with | you, ▪
      a wayfarer, as | all my | forebears | were.

15   Turn your gaze from me, that I may be | glad a|gain, ▪
      before I go my | way and | am no | more.

Psalm 40

1   I waited patiently | for the | Lord; ▪
      he inclined to | me and | heard my | cry.

2.   He brought me out of the roaring pit,
        out of the | mire and | clay; ▪
      he set my feet upon a rock and | made my | footing | sure.

3   He has put a new song in my mouth,
        a song of | praise · to our | God; ▪
      many shall see and fear
        and | put their | trust in the | Lord.

4.   Blessed is the one who | trusts in the | Lord, ▪
      who does not turn to the | proud that | follow a | lie.

5   Great are the wonders you have done, O Lord my God.
        How great | your de|signs for us! ▪
      There is none that | can be com|pared with | you.

6.   If I were to pro|claim them and | tell of them ▪
      they would be more than I am | able | to ex|press.

7   Sacrifice and offering you do | not de|sire ▪
      but my | ears | you have | opened;

8   Burnt offering and sacrifice for sin you have | not re|quired; ▪
        then | said I: | 'Lo, I | come.

9.   'In the scroll of the book it is written of me
        that I should do your will, | O my | God; ▪
        I delight to do it: your | law · is with|in my | heart.'

10   I have declared your righteousness in the great | congre|gation; ▪
        behold, I did not restrain my lips,
        and | that, O | Lord, you | know.

11   Your righteousness I have not hidden | in my | heart; ▪
        I have spoken of your | faithfulness and | your sal|vation;

11a.   I have not concealed your loving|kindness and | truth ▪
        from the | great | congre|gation.

12   Do not withhold your compassion from | me, O | Lord; ▪
        let your love and your | faithfulness | always pre|serve me,

13.   For innumerable troubles have come about me;
        my sins have overtaken me so that I | cannot look | up; ▪
        they are more in number than the hairs of my head, |
        and my | heart | fails me.

14   Be pleased, O Lord, | to de|liver me; ▪
        O | Lord, make | haste to | help me.

15   Let them be ashamed and altogether dismayed
        who seek after my life | to des|troy it; ▪
        let them be driven back and put to | shame who | wish me | evil.

16   Let those who heap | insults up|on me ▪
        be | desolate be|cause of their | shame.

17.   Let all who seek you rejoice in you | and be | glad; ▪
        let those who love your salvation say | always, 'The | Lord is | great.'

18   Though I am | poor and | needy, ▪
        the | Lord | cares for | me.

19   You are my helper and | my de|liverer; ▪
        O my | God, make | no de|lay.

1   Blessed are those who consider the | poor and | needy; ▪
     the Lord will deliver them | in the | time of | trouble.

2   The Lord preserves them and restores their life,
         that they may be happy | in the | land; ▪
     he will not hand them | over · to the | will of their | enemies.

3.   The Lord sustains them | on their | sickbed; ▪
     their sickness, | Lord, you | will re|move.

4   And so I said / 'Lord, be | merciful | to me; ▪
     heal me, for | I have | sinned a|gainst you.'

5   My enemies speak | evil a|bout me, ▪
     asking when I shall | die and my | name | perish.

6.   If they come to see me, they utter | empty | words; ▪
     their heart gathers mischief;
         when they go | out, they | tell it a|broad.

7   All my enemies whisper to|gether a|gainst me, ▪
     against me | they de|vise | evil,

8   Saying that a deadly thing | has laid | hold on me, ▪
     and that I will not rise a|gain from | where I | lie.

9†   Even my bosom friend, whom I trusted,
         who | ate of my | bread, ▪
     has lifted | up his | heel a|gainst me.

10   But you, O Lord, be | merciful | to me ▪
     and raise me up, | that I | may re|ward them.

11   By this I | know that you | favour me, ▪
     that my enemy | does not | triumph | over me.

12.   Because of my integrity | you up|hold me ▪
     and will set me be|fore your | face for | ever.

13   Blessed be the | Lord · God of | Israel, ▪
     from everlasting to everlasting. A|men and | A|men.

Psalm 42

1   As the deer | longs for the | water brooks, ▪
     so longs my | soul for | you, O | God.

2   My soul is athirst for God, even for the | living | God; ▪
     when shall I come be|fore the | presence of | God?

3.   My tears have been my bread | day and | night, ▪
     while all day long they say to me, | 'Where is | now your | God?'

4   Now when I think on these things, I pour | out my | soul: ▪
     how I went with the multitude
        and led the procession | to the | house of | God,

5† With the voice of | praise and | thanksgiving, ▪
     among | those who | kept | holy day.

6   *Why are you so full of heaviness,* | *O my* | *soul,* ▪
     and why are you | *so dis|quieted with|in me?*

7.   *O put your* | *trust in* | *God;* ▪
     for I will yet give him thanks,
        who is the help of my | *countenance,* | *and my* | *God.*

8   My soul is | heavy with|in me; ▪
     therefore I will remember you from the land of Jordan,
        and from Hermon | and the | hill of | Mizar.

9   Deep calls to deep in the | thunder · of your | waterfalls; ▪
     all your breakers and | waves | have gone | over me.

10   The Lord will grant his loving-kindness | in the | daytime; ▪
     through the night his song will be with me,
        a | prayer · to the | God of my | life.

11   I say to God my rock,
     'Why have | you for|gotten me, ▪
     and why go I so heavily, | while the | enemy op|presses me?'

12† As they crush my bones, my | enemies | mock me; ▪
     while all day long they say to me, | 'Where is | now your | God?'

13 *Why are you so full of heaviness,* | *O my* | *soul,* ▪
     and why are you | *so dis|quieted with|in me?*

14 *O put your* | *trust in* | *God;* ▪
     for I will yet give him thanks,
        who is the help of my | *countenance,* | *and my* | *God.*

Psalm 43

1 Give judgment for me, O God,
     and defend my cause against an un|godly | people; ▪
deliver me from the de|ceitful | and the | wicked.

2. For you are the God of my refuge;
     why have you | cast me | from you, ▪
and why go I so heavily, | while the | enemy op|presses me?

3 O send out your light and your truth, that | they may | lead me, ▪
and bring me to your holy | hill and | to your | dwelling,

4. That I may go to the altar of God,
     to the God of my | joy and | gladness; ▪
and on the lyre I will give thanks to | you, O | God my | God.

5 *Why are you so full of heaviness, | O my | soul, ▪*
and why are you | so dis|quieted with|in me?

6 *O put your | trust in | God; ▪*
for I will yet give him thanks,
     who is the help of my | countenance, | and my | God.

Psalm 44

1 We have heard with our ears, O God, our | forebears have | told us, ▪
all that you did in their | days, in | time of | old;

2. How with your hand you drove out nations and | planted us | in, ▪
and broke the power of | peoples and | set us | free.

3 For not by their own sword did our ancestors | take the | land ▪
nor | did their | own arm | save them,

4. But your right hand, your arm, and the | light of your | countenance, ▪
because | you were | gracious | to them.

5 You are my King | and my | God, ▪
who com|manded sal|vation for | Jacob.

6. Through you we drove | back our | adversaries; ▪
through your name | we trod | down our | foes.

7 For I did not | trust in my | bow; ▪
it was not my | own | sword that | saved me;

8   It was you that saved us | from our | enemies ▪
     and | put our | adversaries to | shame.

9†   We gloried in God | all the day | long, ▪
     and were | ever | praising your | name.

10   But now you have rejected us and | brought us to | shame, ▪
     and | go not | out · with our | armies.

11   You have made us turn our | backs · on our | enemies, ▪
     and our | enemies | have de|spoiled us.

12   You have made us like | sheep · to be | slaughtered, ▪
     and have | scattered us a|mong the | nations.

13. You have sold your people | for a | pittance ▪
     and made no | profit | on their | sale.

14   You have made us the | taunt of our | neighbours, ▪
     the scorn and derision of | those · that are | round a|bout us.

15   You have made us a byword a|mong the | nations; ▪
     among the | peoples they | wag their | heads.

16   My confusion is | daily be|fore me, ▪
     and | shame has | covered my | face,

17. At the taunts of the slanderer | and re|viler, ▪
     at the sight of the | enemy | and a|venger.

18   All this has come upon us,
          though we have | not for|gotten you ▪
     and have | not played | false · to your | covenant.

19   Our hearts have | not turned | back, ▪
     nor our | steps gone | out of your | way,

20. Yet you have crushed us in the | haunt of | jackals, ▪
     and covered us | with the | shadow of | death.

21   If we have forgotten the | name of our | God, ▪
     or stretched out our hands to | any | strange | god,

22   Will not God | search it | out? ▪
     For he knows the | secrets | of the | heart.

23. But for your sake are we killed | all the day | long, ▪
     and are counted as | sheep | for the | slaughter.

24　Rise up! Why I sleep, O I Lord? ▪
　　Awake, and do I not re|ject us for I ever.

25　Why do you I hide your I face ▪
　　and forget our I grief I and op|pression?

26　Our soul is bowed I down · to the I dust; ▪
　　our I belly I cleaves · to the I earth.

27　Rise up, O I Lord, to I help us ▪
　　and redeem us for the I sake of your I steadfast I love.

Psalm 45

1.　My heart is astir with I gracious I words; ▪
　　as I make my song for the king,
　　　　my tongue is the I pen · of a I ready I writer.

2　You are the I fairest of I men; ▪
　　full of grace are your lips,
　　　　for I God has I blest you for I ever.

3　Gird your sword upon your I thigh, O I mighty one; ▪
　　gird on your I majes|ty and I glory.

4.　Ride on and prosper in the I cause of I truth ▪
　　and for the sake of hu|mili|ty and I righteousness.

5　Your right hand will teach you I terrible I things; ▪
　　your arrows will be sharp in the heart of the king's enemies,
　　　　so that I peoples I fall be|neath you.

6　Your throne is I God's throne, for I ever; ▪
　　the sceptre of your I kingdom · is the I sceptre of I righteousness.

7.　You love righteousness and I hate in|iquity; ▪
　　therefore God, your God, has anointed you
　　　　with the oil of I gladness a|bove your I fellows.

8　All your garments are fragrant with myrrh, I aloes and I cassia; ▪
　　from ivory palaces the music of I strings I makes you I glad.

9†　Kings' daughters are among your I honourable I women; ▪
　　at your right hand stands the I queen in I gold of I Ophir.

10　Hear, O daughter; consider and in|cline your I ear; ▪
　　forget your own people I and your I father's I house.

11 So shall the king have | pleasure · in your | beauty; ▪
   he is your | lord, so | do him | honour.

12. The people of Tyre shall | bring you | gifts; ▪
   the richest of the | people shall | seek your | favour.

13 The king's daughter is all | glorious with|in; ▪
   her clothing is em|broidered | cloth of | gold.

14 She shall be brought to the king in | raiment of | needlework; ▪
   after her the | virgins · that are | her com|panions.

15. With joy and gladness shall | they be | brought ▪
   and enter into the | palace | of the | king.

16 'Instead of your fathers | you shall have | sons, ▪
   whom you shall make princes | over | all the | land.

17 'I will make your name to be remembered
        through | all · gene|rations; ▪
   therefore shall the peoples | praise you for | ever and | ever.'

Psalm 46

1 God is our | refuge and | strength, ▪
   a very | present | help in | trouble;

2 Therefore we will not fear, though the | earth be | moved, ▪
   and though the mountains | tremble · in the | heart of the | sea;

3† Though the waters | rage and | swell, ▪
   and though the mountains | quake · at the | towering | seas.

4 There is a river whose streams make glad the | city of | God, ▪
   the holy place of the | dwelling · of the | Most | High.

5 God is in the midst of her;
        therefore shall she | not be re|moved; ▪
   God shall | help her · at the | break of | day.

6 The nations are in uproar and the | kingdoms are | shaken, ▪
   but God utters his voice and the | earth shall | melt a|way.

7. *The Lord of | hosts is | with us; ▪*
   the God of | Jacob | is our | stronghold.

8 Come and behold the | works · of the | Lord, ▪
   what destruction he has | wrought up|on the | earth.

9. He makes wars to cease in | all the | world; ■
    he shatters the bow and snaps the spear
        and burns the | chariots | in the | fire.

10 'Be still, and know that | I am | God; ■
    I will be exalted among the nations;
        I will be ex|alted | in the | earth.'

11 *The Lord of| hosts is | with us; ■*
    the God of| Jacob | is our | stronghold.

Psalm 47

1   Clap your hands together, | all you | peoples; ■
    O sing to | God with | shouts of | joy.

2   For the Lord Most High | is to be | feared; ■
    he is the great | King · over | all the | earth.

3   He subdued the | peoples | under us ■
    and the | nations | under our | feet.

4. He has chosen our | heritage | for us, ■
    the pride of| Jacob, | whom he | loves.

5   God has gone up with a | merry | noise, ■
    the | Lord · with the | sound of the | trumpet.

6   O sing praises to | God, sing | praises; ■
    sing | praises · to our | King, sing | praises.

7. For God is the King of| all the | earth; ■
    sing | praises with | all your | skill.

8   God reigns | over the | nations; ■
    God has taken his seat up|on his | holy | throne.

9   The nobles of the peoples are | gathered to|gether ■
    with the | people · of the | God of| Abraham.

10 For the powers of the earth be|long to | God ■
    and he is | very | highly ex|alted.

1   Great is the Lord and | highly · to be | praised, ▪
      in the | city | of our | God.

2   His holy mountain is fair and | lifted | high, ▪
      the | joy of | all the | earth.

3   On Mount Zion, the di|vine | dwelling place, ▪
      stands the | city · of the | great | king.

4.   In her palaces God has | shown him|self ▪‿
      to | be a | sure | refuge.

5   For behold, the kings of the | earth as|sembled ▪
      and | swept | forward to|gether.

6   They saw, and | were dumb|founded; ▪
      dis|mayed, they | fled in | terror.

7.   Trembling seized them there;
          they writhed like a | woman in | labour, ▪
      as when the east wind | shatters the | ships of | Tarshish.

8   As we had heard, so have we seen
          in the city of the Lord of hosts, the | city · of our | God: ▪
      God has es|tablished | her for | ever.

9.   We have waited on your loving|kindness, O | God, ▪
      in the | midst | of your | temple.

10   As with your name, O God,
          so your praise reaches to the | ends of the | earth; ▪
      your right | hand is | full of | justice.

11.   Let Mount Zion rejoice and the daughters of | Judah be | glad, ▪
      be|cause of your | judgments, O | Lord.

12   Walk about Zion and go round about her;
          count | all her | towers; ▪
      consider well her | bulwarks; pass | through her | citadels,

13†   That you may tell those who come after
          that such is our God for | ever and | ever. ▪
      It is he that shall be our | guide for | ever|more.

1   Hear this, ǀ all you ǀ peoples; ▪
    listen, all ǀ you that ǀ dwell · in the ǀ world,

2   You of low or ǀ high deǀgree, ▪
    both ǀ rich and ǀ poor toǀgether.

3   My mouth shall ǀ speak of ǀ wisdom ▪
    and my heart shall ǀ meditate on ǀ underǀstanding.

4. I will incline my ǀ ear · to a ǀ parable; ▪
    I will unfold my ǀ riddle ǀ with the ǀ lyre.

5   Why should I fear in ǀ evil ǀ days, ▪
    when the ǀ malice · of my ǀ foes surǀrounds me,

6   Such as ǀ trust · in their ǀ goods ▪
    and glory in the aǀbundance ǀ of their ǀ riches?

7   For no one can indeed ǀ ransom anǀother ▪
    or pay to ǀ God the ǀ price of deǀliverance.

8   To ransom a soul ǀ is too ǀ costly; ▪
    there is ǀ no price ǀ one could ǀ pay for it,

9† So that they might ǀ live for ǀ ever, ▪
    and ǀ never ǀ see the ǀ grave.

10 For we see that the wise die also;
        with the foolish and ǀ ignorant they ǀ perish ▪
    and ǀ leave their ǀ riches to ǀ others.

11 Their tomb is their home for ever,
        their dwelling through ǀ all · geneǀrations, ▪
    though they call their lands ǀ after their ǀ own ǀ names.

12 Those who have honour, but lack ǀ underǀstanding, ▪
    are ǀ like the ǀ beasts that ǀ perish.

13. Such is the way of those who ǀ boast in themǀselves, ▪
    the end of those who deǀlight in their ǀ own ǀ words.

14 Like a flock of sheep they are destined to die; ǀ
        death is their ǀ shepherd; ▪
    they go ǀ down ǀ straight · to the ǀ Pit.

15 Their beauty shall ǀ waste aǀway, ▪
    and the land of the ǀ dead shall ǀ be their ǀ dwelling.

16. But God shall | ransom my | soul; ▪
    from the grasp of | death | will he | take me.

17 Be not afraid if | some grow | rich ▪
    and the | glory · of their | house in|creases,

18 For they will carry nothing away | when they | die, ▪
    nor will their | glory | follow | after them.

19 Though they count themselves happy | while they | live ▪
    and | praise you for | your suc|cess,

20 They shall enter the company | of their | ancestors ▪
    who will | nevermore | see the | light.

21 Those who have honour, but lack | under|standing, ▪
    are | like the | beasts that | perish.

Psalm 50

1   The Lord, the most mighty | God, has | spoken ▪
    and called the world from the rising of the | sun | to its | setting.

2   Out of Zion, perfect in beauty, | God shines | forth; ▪
    our God comes | and will | not keep | silence.

3   Consuming fire goes | out be|fore him ▪
    and a mighty | tempest | stirs a|bout him.

4   He calls the | heaven a|bove, ▪
    and the earth, that | he may | judge his | people:

5   'Gather to | me my | faithful, ▪
    who have | sealed my | covenant with | sacrifice.'

6. Let the heavens de|clare his | righteousness, ▪
    for | God him|self is | judge.

7   Hear, O my people, and | I will | speak: ▪
    'I will testify against you, O Israel;
        for | I am | God, your | God.

8   'I will not reprove you | for your | sacrifices, ▪
    for your burnt | offerings are | always be|fore me.

9. 'I will take no bull | out of your | house, ▪
    nor | he-goat | out of your | folds,

10 'For all the beasts of the | forest are | mine, ▪
    the cattle up|on a | thousand | hills.

11 'I know every | bird of the | mountains ∎
    and the | insect · of the | field is | mine.

12 'If I were hungry, I | would not | tell you, ∎
    for the whole world is | mine and | all that | fills it.

13. 'Do you think I eat the | flesh of | bulls, ∎
    or | drink the | blood of | goats?

14 'Offer to God a | sacrifice of | thanksgiving ∎
    and fulfil your | vows to | God Most | High.

15† 'Call upon me in the | day of | trouble; ∎
    I will deliver | you and | you shall | honour me.'

16 But to the | wicked, says | God: ∎
    'Why do you recite my statutes
        and take my | covenant up|on your | lips,

17 'Since you re|fuse to be | disciplined ∎
    and have | cast my | words be|hind you?

18 'When you saw a thief, | you made | friends with him ∎
    and you | threw in your | lot · with ad|ulterers.

19 'You have loosed your | lips for | evil ∎
    and | harnessed your | tongue · to de|ceit.

20† 'You sit and speak evil | of your | brother; ∎
    you slander your | own | mother's | son.

21 'These things have you done, and should | I keep | silence? ∎
    Did you think that I am even | such a | one as your|self?

22 'But no, I | must re|prove you, ∎
    and set before your eyes the | things that | you have | done.

23. 'You that forget God, con|sider this | well, ∎
    lest I tear you apart and | there is | none · to de|liver you.

24 'Whoever offers me the sacrifice of thanksgiving | honours | me ∎
    and to those who keep my way
        will I | show · the sal|vation of | God.'

1   Have mercy on me, O God, in ˈ your great ˈ goodness; ▪
     according to the abundance of your compassion ˈ
          blot out ˈ my ofˈfences.

2.   Wash me thoroughly ˈ from my ˈ wickedness ▪
     and ˈ cleanse me ˈ from my ˈ sin.

3   For I acˈknowledge my ˈ faults ▪
     and my ˈ sin is ˈ ever beˈfore me.

4   Against you only ˈ have I ˈ sinned ▪
     and done what is ˈ evil ˈ in your ˈ sight,

5†   So that you are justified ˈ in your ˈ sentence ▪
     and ˈ righteous ˈ in your ˈ judgment.

6   I have been wicked even ˈ from my ˈ birth, ▪
     a sinner ˈ when my ˈ mother conˈceived me.

7.   Behold, you desire truth ˈ deep withˈin me ▪
     and shall make me understand wisdom
          ˈ in the ˈ depths of my ˈ heart.

8   Purge me with hyssop and I ˈ shall be ˈ clean; ▪
     wash me and I ˈ shall be ˈ whiter than ˈ snow.

9   Make me hear of ˈ joy and ˈ gladness, ▪
     that the bones you have ˈ broken ˈ may reˈjoice.

10. Turn your ˈ face from my ˈ sins ▪
     and ˈ blot out ˈ all my misˈdeeds.

11   Make me a clean ˈ heart, O ˈ God, ▪
     and reˈnew a right ˈ spirit withˈin me.

12. Cast me not aˈway from your ˈ presence ▪
     and take not your ˈ holy ˈ spirit ˈ from me.

13   Give me again the joy of ˈ your salˈvation ▪
     and sustain me ˈ with your ˈ gracious ˈ spirit;

14† Then shall I teach your ˈ ways · to the ˈ wicked ▪
     and sinners ˈ shall reˈturn to ˈ you.

15   Deliver me from my guilt, O God,
         the God of | my sal|vation, ▪
     and my | tongue shall | sing of your | righteousness.

16.   O Lord, | open my | lips ▪
     and my | mouth shall pro|claim your | praise.

17   For you desire no sacrifice, | else · I would | give it; ▪
     you take no de|light in | burnt | offerings.

18.   The sacrifice of God is a | broken | spirit; ▪
     a broken and contrite heart, O God, | you will | not des|pise.

19   O be favourable and | gracious to | Zion; ▪
     build | up the | walls of Je|rusalem.

20   Then you will accept sacrifices offered in righteousness,
         the burnt offerings | and ob|lations; ▪
     then shall they offer up | bulls | on your | altar.

Psalm 52

1   Why do you glory in | evil, you | tyrant, ▪
     while the goodness of | God en|dures con|tinually?

2   You plot destruction, | you de|ceiver; ▪
     your tongue is | like a | sharpened | razor.

3   You love evil | rather than | good, ▪
     falsehood | rather · than the | word of | truth.

4   You love all | words that | hurt, ▪
     O | you de|ceitful | tongue.

5†   Therefore God shall utterly | bring you | down; ▪
     he shall take you and pluck you out of your tent
         and root you | out of the | land · of the | living.

6   The righteous shall | see this and | tremble; ▪
     they shall | laugh you to | scorn, and I | say:

7.   'This is the one who did not take | God · for a | refuge, ▪
     but trusted in great riches | and re|lied upon | wickedness.'

8   But I am like a spreading olive tree in the | house of | God; ▪
     I trust in the goodness of | God for | ever and | ever.

9   I will always give thanks to you for | what you have | done; ▪
     I will hope in your name, for your | faithful | ones de|light in it.

1   The fool has said in his heart, 'There | is no | God.' ▪
     Corrupt are they, and abominable in their wickedness;
        there is | no one | that does | good.

2   God has looked down from heaven upon the | children of | earth, ▪
     to see if there is anyone who is | wise and | seeks after | God.

3†   They are all gone out of the way;
        all alike have be|come cor|rupt; ▪
     there is no one that does | good, | no not | one.

4   Have they no knowledge, those | evil|doers, ▪
     who eat up my people as if they ate bread,
        and | do not | call upon | God?

5   There shall they be in great fear, such fear as | never | was; ▪
     for God will scatter the | bones of | the un|godly.

6   They will be | put to | shame, ▪
     because | God | has re|jected them.

7   O that Israel's salvation would | come · out of | Zion! ▪
     When God restores the fortunes of his people
        then will Jacob re|joice and | Israel be | glad.

1   Save me, O God, | by your | name ▪
     and | vindi·cate me | by your | power.

2   Hear my | prayer, O | God; ▪
     give | heed · to the | words of my | mouth.

3†   For strangers have risen up against me,
        and the ruthless seek | after my | life; ▪
     they have | not set | God be|fore them.

4   Behold, | God is my | helper; ▪
     it is the | Lord · who up|holds my | life.

5   May evil rebound on those who | lie in | wait for me; ▪
     des|troy them | in your | faithfulness.

6   An offering of a free heart | will I | give you ▪
     and praise your name, O | Lord, for | it is | gracious.

7   For he has delivered me out of | all my | trouble, ▪
     and my eye has seen the | downfall | of my | enemies.

1   Hear my | prayer, O | God; ▪
    hide not your|self from | my pe|tition.

2   Give heed to | me and | answer me; ▪
    I am | restless in | my com|plaining.

3   I am alarmed at the | voice of the | enemy ▪
    and at the | clamour | of the | wicked;

4. For they would bring down | evil up|on me ▪
    and are | set a|gainst me in | fury.

5   My heart is dis|quieted with|in me, ▪
    and the terrors of | death have | fallen up|on me.

6. Fearfulness and trembling are | come up|on me, ▪
    and a horrible | dread has | over|whelmed me.

7   And I said: 'O that I had | wings · like a | dove, ▪
    for then would I fly a|way and | be at | rest.

8   'Then would I flee | far a|way ▪
    and make my | lodging | in the | wilderness.

9. 'I would make | haste to es|cape ▪
    from the | stormy | wind and | tempest.'

10 Confuse their tongues, O Lord, | and di|vide them, ▪
    for I have seen violence and | strife | in the | city.

11 Day and night they go a|bout · on her | walls; ▪
    mischief and | trouble are | in her | midst.

12. Wickedness | walks in her | streets; ▪
    oppression and guile | never | leave her | squares.

13 For it was not an open enemy | that re|viled me, ▪
    for | then I | could have | borne it;

14 Nor was it my adversary that puffed himself | up a|gainst me, ▪
    for then I | would have | hid myself | from him.

15 But it was even you, one | like my|self, ▪
    my companion and my | own fa|miliar | friend.

16 We took sweet | counsel to|gether ▪
    and walked with the multitude | in the | house of | God.

17†   Let death come suddenly upon them;
        let them go down a׀live · to the ׀ Pit; ▪
    for wickedness inhabits their ׀ dwellings, their ׀ very ׀ hearts.

18   As for me, I will ׀ call upon ׀ God ▪
    and the ׀ Lord ׀ will de׀liver me.

19   In the evening and morning and at noonday
        I will pray and make my ׀ suppli׀cation, ▪
    and ׀ he shall ׀ hear my ׀ voice.

20.   He shall redeem my soul in peace
        from the battle ׀ waged a׀gainst me, ▪
    for ׀ many have ׀ come up׀on me.

21   God, who is enthroned of old, will hear and ׀ bring them ׀ down; ▪
    they will not repent, for they ׀ have no ׀ fear of ׀ God.

22   My companion stretched out his hands a׀gainst his ׀ friend ▪
    and has ׀ broken ׀ his ׀ covenant;

23.   His speech was softer than butter, though war was ׀ in his ׀ heart; ▪
    his words were smoother than oil, yet ׀ are they ׀ naked ׀ swords.

24   Cast your burden upon the Lord and he ׀ will sus׀tain you, ▪
    and will not let the ׀ righteous ׀ fall for ׀ ever.

25   But those that are bloodthirsty and de׀ceitful, O ׀ God, ▪
    you will bring ׀ down · to the ׀ pit of des׀truction.

26†   They shall not live out ׀ half their ׀ days, ▪
    but my trust shall ׀ be in ׀ you, O ׀ Lord.

Psalm 56

1   Have mercy on me, O God, for they ׀ trample ׀ over me; ▪
    all day long ׀ they as׀sault · and op׀press me.

2   My adversaries trample over me ׀ all the day ׀ long; ▪
    many are they that ׀ make proud ׀ war a׀gainst me.

3   In the day of my fear I put my ׀ trust in ׀ you, ▪
    in ׀ God whose ׀ word I ׀ praise.

4.   In God I trust, and ׀ will not ׀ fear, ▪
    for ׀ what can ׀ flesh ׀ do to me?

5   All day long they | wound me with | words; ▪
       their every | thought · is to | do me | evil.

6   They stir up trouble; they | lie in | wait; ▪
       marking my | steps, they | seek my | life.

7.   Shall they escape for | all their | wickedness? ▪
       In anger, O God, | cast the | peoples | down.

8   You have counted up my groaning;
          put my tears | into your | bottle; ▪
       are they not | written | in your | book?

9   Then shall my enemies turn back
          on the day when I | call up|on you; ▪
       this I know, for | God is | on my | side.

10. In God whose word I praise,
          in the Lord whose | word I | praise,▪
       in God I trust and will not fear: |
          what can | flesh | do to me?

11   To you, O God, will I ful|fil my | vows; ▪
       to you will I pre|sent my | offerings of | thanks,

12. For you will deliver my soul from death
          and my | feet from | falling, ▪
       that I may walk before | God · in the | light of the | living.

Psalm 57

1   Be merciful to me, O God, be | merciful to | me, ▪
       for my | soul takes | refuge in | you;

2.   In the shadow of your wings will | I take | refuge ▪
       until the storm of des|truction | has passed | by.

3   I will call upon the | Most High | God, ▪
       the God who ful|fils his | purpose | for me.

4.   He will send from heaven and save me
          and rebuke those that would | trample up|on me; ▪
       God will send forth his | love | and his | faithfulness.

5   I lie in the | midst of | lions, ▪
       people whose teeth are spears and arrows,
          and their | tongue a | sharp | sword.

6. *Be exalted, O God, a*|*bove the* | *heavens,* ▪
   and your glory | *over* | *all the* | *earth.*

7 They have laid a net for my feet;
       my soul is | pressed | down; ▪
   they have dug a pit before me
       and will | fall · into | it them|selves.

8. My heart is ready, O God, my | heart is | ready; ▪
   I will | sing and | give you | praise.

9 Awake, my soul; awake, | harp and | lyre, ▪
   that | I · may a|waken the | dawn.

10. I will give you thanks, O Lord, a|mong the | peoples; ▪
    I will sing praise to | you a|mong the | nations.

11 For your loving-kindness is as | high as the | heavens, ▪
   and your faithfulness | reaches | to the | clouds.

12 *Be exalted, O God, a*|*bove the* | *heavens,* ▪
   and your glory | *over* | *all the* | *earth.*

Psalm 58

1 Do you indeed speak | justly, you | mighty? ▪
   Do you | rule the | peoples with | equity?

2 With unjust heart you act through|out the | land; ▪
   your | hands | mete out | violence.

3 The wicked are estranged, even | from the | womb; ▪
   those who speak falsehood go a|stray | from their | birth.

4 They are as venomous | as a | serpent; ▪
   they are like the deaf | adder which | stops its | ears,

5† Which does not heed the | voice of the | charmers, ▪
   and is deaf to the | skilful | weaver of | spells.

6 Break, O God, their | teeth in their | mouths; ▪
   smash the | fangs of these | lions, O | Lord.

7 Let them vanish like water that | runs a|way; ▪
   let them | wither like | trodden | grass.

8 Let them be as the slimy | track of the | snail, ▪
   like the untimely birth that | never | sees the | sun.

9.   Before ever their pots feel the | heat of the | thorns, ■
     green or blazing, | let them be | swept a|way.

10   The righteous will be glad when they | see God's | vengeance; ■
     they will bathe their | feet · in the | blood of the | wicked.

11   So that people will say,
         'Truly, there is a harvest | for the | righteous; ■
     truly, there is a God who | judges | in the | earth.'

Psalm 59

1   Rescue me from my enemies, | O my | God; ■
     set me high above | those that rise | up a|gainst me.

2.   Save me from the | evil|doers ■
     and from | murderous | foes de|liver me.

3   For see how they lie in | wait · for my | soul ■
     and the mighty | stir up | trouble a|gainst me.

4.   Not for any fault or sin of | mine, O | Lord; ■
     for no offence, they run and pre|pare them|selves for | war.

5   Rouse yourself, come to my | aid and | see; ■
     for you are the Lord of | hosts, the | God of | Israel.

6.   Awake, and judge | all the | nations; ■
     show no mercy | to the | evil | traitors.

7   They return at nightfall and | snarl like | dogs ■
     and | prowl a|bout the | city.

8   They pour out evil words with their mouths;
         swords are | on their | lips; ■
     'For | who', they | say, 'can | hear us?'

9.   But you | laugh at them, O | Lord; ■
     you hold all the | nations | in de|rision.

10   For you, O my strength, | will I | watch; ■
     you, O God, | are my | strong | tower.

11   My God in his steadfast | love will | come to me; ■
     he will let me behold the | downfall | of my | enemies.

12. Slay them not, lest my | people for|get; ■
     send them reeling by your might
         and bring them | down, O | Lord our | shield.

13   For the sins of their mouth, for the | words of their | lips, ▪
let them be | taken | in their | pride.

14   For the cursing and falsehood | they have | uttered, ▪
consume them in wrath, consume them | till they | are no | more.

15.   And they shall know that God | rules in | Jacob, ▪
and | to the | ends of the | earth.

16   And still they return at nightfall and | snarl like | dogs ▪
and | prowl a|bout the | city.

17   Though they forage for | something · to de|vour, ▪
and | howl · if they | are not | filled,

18   Yet will I | sing your | strength ▪
and every morning | praise your | steadfast | love;

19   For you have | been my | stronghold, ▪
my refuge | in the | day of my | trouble.

20   To you, O my strength, | will I | sing; ▪
for you, O God, are my refuge,
        my | God of | steadfast | love.

Psalm 60

1   O God, you have cast us | off and | broken us; ▪
you have been angry; re|store us · to your|self a|gain.

2.   You have shaken the earth and | torn it a|part; ▪
heal its | wounds, | for it | trembles.

3   You have made your people drink | bitter | things; ▪
we reel from the | deadly | wine · you have | given us.

4   You have made those who | fear you to | flee, ▪
to es|cape · from the | range of the | bow.

5†   That your beloved may | be de|livered, ▪
save us by | your right | hand and | answer us.

6   God has spoken | in his | holiness: ▪
'I will triumph and divide Shechem,
        and share | out the | valley of | Succoth.

7   'Gilead is mine and Ma|nasseh is | mine; ▪
Ephraim is my | helmet and | Judah my | sceptre.

8†   'Moab shall be my washpot;
      over Edom will I ǀ cast my ǀ sandal; ▪
    across Philistia ǀ will I ǀ shout in ǀ triumph.'

9   Who will lead me into the ǀ strong ǀ city? ▪
    Who will ǀ bring me ǀ into ǀ Edom?

10   Have you not cast us ǀ off, O ǀ God? ▪
    Will you no longer ǀ go forth ǀ with our ǀ troops?

11   Grant us your help aǀgainst the ǀ enemy, ▪
    for ǀ earthly ǀ help · is in ǀ vain.

12   Through God will we ǀ do great ǀ acts, ▪
    for it is he that ǀ shall tread ǀ down our ǀ enemies.

Psalm 61

1   Hear my ǀ crying, O ǀ God, ▪
    and ǀ listen ǀ to my ǀ prayer.

2.   From the end of the earth I call to you with ǀ fainting ǀ heart; ▪
    O set me on the ǀ rock · that is ǀ higher than ǀ I.

3   For ǀ you are my ǀ refuge, ▪
    a strong ǀ tower aǀgainst the ǀ enemy.

4   Let me dwell in your ǀ tent for ǀ ever ▪
    and take refuge under the ǀ cover ǀ of your ǀ wings.

5.   For you, O God, will ǀ hear my ǀ vows; ▪
    you will grant the request of ǀ those who ǀ fear your ǀ name.

6   You will add length of days to the ǀ life of the ǀ king, ▪
    that his years may endure throughǀout all ǀ geneǀrations.

7   May he sit enthroned before ǀ God for ǀ ever; ▪
    may steadfast ǀ love and ǀ truth watch ǀ over him.

8   So will I always sing ǀ praise to your ǀ name, ▪
    and day by ǀ day fulǀfil my ǀ vows.

1   On God alone my soul in | stillness | waits; ■
from | him comes | my sal|vation.

2.   He alone is my rock and | my sal|vation, ■
my stronghold, so that | I shall | never be | shaken.

3   How long will all of you assail me | to des|troy me, ■
as you would a tottering wall | or a | leaning | fence?

4.   They plot only to thrust me down from my place of honour;
       lies are their | chief de|light; ■
they bless with their mouth, but | in their | heart they | curse.

5   Wait on God alone in stillness, | O my | soul; ■
for in | him | is my | hope.

6   He alone is my rock and | my sal|vation, ■
my stronghold, so that | I shall | not be | shaken.

7   In God is my strength | and my | glory; ■
God is my strong rock; in | him | is my | refuge.

8.   Put your trust in him | always, my | people; ■
pour out your hearts before him, for | God | is our | refuge.

9   The peoples are but a breath,
       the whole human | race · a de|ceit; ■
on the scales they are alto|gether | lighter than | air.

10   Put no trust in oppression; in robbery take no | empty | pride; ■
though wealth increase, | set not your | heart up|on it.

11   God spoke once, and twice have I | heard the | same, ■
that | power be|longs to | God.

12   Steadfast love belongs to | you, O | Lord, ■
for you repay everyone ac|cording | to their | deeds.

1   O God, you are my God; | eagerly I | seek you; ■
my | soul · is a|thirst for | you.

2   My flesh | also | faints for you, ■
as in a dry and thirsty | land · where there | is no | water.

3.   So would I gaze upon you in your | holy | place, ■
that I might behold your | power | and your | glory.

4   Your loving-kindness is better than | life it|self ▪
     and | so my | lips shall | praise you.

5   I will bless you as | long as I | live ▪
     and lift up my | hands | in your | name.

6.   My soul shall be satisfied, as with | marrow and | fatness, ▪
     and my mouth shall | praise you with | joyful | lips,

7   When I remember you up|on my | bed ▪
     and meditate on you in the | watches | of the | night.

8   For you have | been my | helper ▪
     and under the shadow of your | wings will | I re|joice.

9.   My | soul | clings to you; ▪
     your | right hand shall | hold me | fast.

10   But those who seek my soul | to des|troy it ▪
     shall go | down · to the | depths of the | earth;

11   Let them fall by the | edge of the | sword ▪
     and be|come a | portion for | jackals.

12   But the king shall rejoice in God;
       all those who swear by him | shall be | glad, ▪
     for the mouth of those who speak | lies | shall be | stopped.

Psalm 64

1   Hear my voice, O God, in | my com|plaint; ▪
     preserve my | life from | fear of the | enemy.

2   Hide me from the conspiracy | of the | wicked, ▪
     from the | gathering of | evil|doers.

3   They sharpen their | tongue · like a | sword ▪
     and aim their | bitter | words like | arrows,

4.   That they may shoot at the | blameless from | hiding places; ▪
     suddenly they | shoot, and | are not | seen.

5   They hold fast to their | evil | course; ▪
     they talk of laying snares, | saying, | 'Who will | see us?'

6.   They search out wickedness and lay a | cunning | trap, ▪
     for deep are the | inward | thoughts of the | heart.

7   But God will shoot at them with his | swift | arrow, ▪
     and | suddenly | they shall be | wounded.

8.   Their own tongues shall | make them | fall, ▪
     and all who see them shall | wag their | heads in | scorn.

9   All peoples shall fear and tell what | God has | done, ▪
     and they will | ponder | all his | works.

10   The righteous shall rejoice in the Lord
        and put their | trust in | him, ▪
     and all that are true of | heart | shall ex|ult.

Psalm 65

1   Praise is due to you, O | God, in | Zion; ▪
     to you that answer | prayer shall | vows be | paid.

2.   To you shall all flesh come to con|fess their | sins; ▪
     when our misdeeds prevail against us, |
        you will | purge them a|way.

3   Happy are they whom you choose
        and draw to your | courts to | dwell there. ▪
     We shall be satisfied with the blessings of your house,
        | even · of your | holy | temple.

4.   With wonders you will answer us in your righteousness,
        O God of | our sal|vation, ▪
     O hope of all the ends of the earth
        and | of the | farthest | seas.

5   In your strength you set | fast the | mountains ▪
     and are | girded a|bout with | might.

6   You still the | raging · of the | seas, ▪
     the roaring of their waves and the | clamour | of the | peoples.

7†   Those who dwell at the ends of the earth
        tremble | at your | marvels; ▪
     the gates of the morning and | evening | sing your | praise.

8   You visit the | earth and | water it; ▪
     you | make it | very | plenteous.

9   The river of God is | full of | water; ▪
     you prepare grain for your people,
        for | so you pro|vide · for the | earth.

10   You drench the furrows and | smooth out the | ridges; ▪
        you soften the ground with | showers and | bless its | increase.

11.   You crown the | year with your | goodness, ▪
        and your | paths · over|flow with | plenty.

12   May the pastures of the wilderness | flow with | goodness ▪
        and the | hills be | girded with | joy.

13   May the meadows be clothed with | flocks of | sheep ▪
        and the valleys stand so thick with corn
            that | they shall | laugh and | sing.

Psalm 66

1   Be joyful in God, | all the | earth; ▪
        sing the glory of his name;
            sing the | glory | of his | praise.

2   Say to God, 'How awesome | are your | deeds! ▪
        Because of your great strength
            your | enemies shall | bow be|fore you.

3† 'All the | earth shall | worship you, ▪
        sing to you, sing | praise | to your | name.'

4   Come now and behold the | works of | God, ▪
        how wonderful he is in his | dealings with | human|kind.

5   He turned the sea into dry land;
            the river they passed | through on | foot; ▪
        there | we re|joiced in | him.

6† In his might he rules for ever;
            his eyes keep watch | over the | nations; ▪
        let no | rebel rise | up a|gainst him.

7   Bless our God, | O you | peoples; ▪
        make the voice of his | praise | to be | heard,

8.   Who holds our | souls in | life ▪
        and suffers | not our | feet to | slip.

9   For you, O | God, have | proved us; ▪
        you have | tried us as | silver is | tried.

10   You brought us | into the | snare; ▪
      you laid heavy | burdens up|on our | backs.

11†   You let enemies ride over our heads;
           we went through | fire and | water; ▪
      but you brought us out | into a | place of | liberty.

12   I will come into your house with burnt offerings
           and will | pay you my | vows, ▪
      which my lips uttered
           and my mouth promised | when I | was in | trouble.

13.   I will offer you fat burnt sacrifices with the | smoke of | rams; ▪
      I will | sacrifice | oxen and | goats.

14   Come and listen⁄all | you who fear | God, ▪
      and I will tell you what | he has | done for my | soul.

15   I called out to him | with my | mouth ▪
      and his | praise was | on my | tongue.

16   If I had nursed evil | in my | heart, ▪
      the | Lord would | not have | heard me,

17   But in truth | God has | heard me; ▪
      he has | heeded the | voice of my | prayer.

18†   Blessed be God⁄who has not re|jected my | prayer, ▪
      nor withheld his | loving | mercy | from me.

Psalm 67

1   God be gracious to | us and | bless us ▪
      and make his | face to | shine up|on us,

2   That your way may be | known upon | earth, ▪
      your saving | power a|mong all | nations.

3†   *Let the peoples | praise you, O | God; ▪*
      let | all the | peoples | praise you.

4   O let the nations re|joice and be | glad, ▪
      for you will judge the peoples righteously
           and I | govern the | nations · upon | earth.

5.   *Let the peoples | praise you, O | God; ▪*
      let | all the | peoples | praise you.

6   Then shall the earth bring | forth her | increase, ▪
and God⁄our | own | God, will | bless us.

7   God | will | bless us, ▪
and all the | ends of the | earth shall | fear him.

Psalm 68

1   Let God arise and let his | enemies be | scattered; ▪
let those that | hate him | flee be|fore him.

2   As the smoke vanishes, so may they | vanish a|way; ▪
as wax melts at the fire,
        so let the wicked | perish · at the | presence of | God.

3.   But let the righteous be glad and re|joice before | God; ▪
let | them make | merry with | gladness.

4   Sing to God, sing praises to his name;
        exalt him who | rides · on the | clouds. ▪
The Lord is his | name; re|joice be|fore him.

5   Father of the fatherless, de|fender of | widows, ▪
God in his | holy | habi|tation!

6.   God gives the solitary a home
        and brings forth prisoners to | songs of | welcome, ▪
but the rebellious in|habit a | burning | desert.

7   O God, when you went forth be|fore your | people, ▪
when you | marched | through the | wilderness,

8   The earth shook and the heavens dropped down rain,
        at the presence of God, the | Lord of | Sinai, ▪
at the presence of | God, the | God of | Israel.

9.   You sent down a gracious | rain, O | God; ▪
you refreshed your in|heritance when | it was | weary.

10   Your people | came to | dwell there; ▪
in your goodness, O God, | you pro|vide · for the | poor.

11   The Lord | gave the | word; ▪
great was the company of | women who | bore the | tidings:

11a   'Kings and their armies they | flee, they | flee!' ▪
and women at home | are di|viding the | spoil.

12   Though you stayed a|mong the | sheepfolds, ▪
see now a dove's wings covered with silver
    and its | feathers with | green | gold.

13.   When the Almighty | scattered the | kings, ▪
it was like | snowflakes | falling on | Zalmon.

14   You mighty mountain, great | mountain of | Bashan! ▪
You towering | mountain, great | mountain of | Bashan!

15.   Why look with envy, you towering mountains,
    at the mount which God has de|sired · for his | dwelling, ▪
the place where the | Lord will | dwell for | ever?

16   The chariots of God are twice ten thousand,
    even | thousands · upon | thousands; ▪
the Lord is among them, the Lord of | Sinai in | holy | power.

17.   You have gone up on high and led cap|tivity | captive; ▪
you have received tribute,
    even from those who rebelled,
    that you may | reign as | Lord and | God.

18   Blessed be the Lord who bears our burdens | day by | day, ▪
for | God is | our sal|vation.

19   God is for us the God of | our sal|vation; ▪
God is the Lord who | can de|liver from | death.

20†   God will smite the | head of his | enemies, ▪
the hairy scalp of | those who | walk in | wickedness.

21   The Lord has said, 'From the | heights of | Bashan, ▪
from the depths of the | sea · will I | bring them | back,

22   'Till you dip your | foot in | blood ▪
and the tongue of your | dogs · has a | taste of your | enemies.'

23   We see your solemn pro|cessions, O | God, ▪
your processions into the sanctuary, my | God | and my | King.

24.   The singers go before, the musicians | follow | after, ▪
in the midst of | maidens | playing on | timbrels.

25   In your companies, | bless your | God; ▪
bless the Lord, you that | are · of the | fount of | Israel.

26   At the head there is Benjamin, least of the tribes,
        the princes of Judah in | joyful | company, ▪
    the princes of | Zebu|lun and | Naphtali.

27   Send forth your | strength, O | God; ▪
    establish, O God, what | you have | wrought in | us.

28.   For your temple's sake | in Je|rusalem ▪
    kings shall | bring their | gifts to | you.

29   Drive back with your word the wild | beast of the | reeds, ▪
    the herd of the | bull-like, the | brutish | hordes.

30   Trample down those who | lust · after | silver; ▪
    scatter the | peoples · that de|light in | war.

31†   Vessels of bronze shall be | brought from | Egypt; ▪
    Ethiopia will stretch | out her | hands to | God.

32   Sing to God, you | kingdoms · of the | earth; ▪
    make music in | praise | of the | Lord;

33.   He rides on the ancient | heaven of | heavens ▪
    and sends forth his | voice, a | mighty | voice.

34   Ascribe power to God, whose splendour is | over | Israel, ▪
    whose | power · is a|bove the | clouds.

35   How terrible is God in his | holy | sanctuary, ▪
    the God of Israel, who gives power and strength to his | people! |
        Blessed be | God.

Psalm 69

1   Save me, | O | God, ▪
    for the waters have come up, | even | to my | neck.

2   I sink in deep mire where there | is no | foothold; ▪
    I have come into deep waters | and the | flood sweeps | over me.

3.   I have grown weary with crying| my | throat is | raw; ▪
    my eyes have failed from | looking so | long · for my | God.

4   Those who hate me with|out · any | cause ▪
    are more than the | hairs | of my | head;

5   Those who would des|troy me are | mighty; ▪
    my enemies accuse me falsely:
        must I now give | back · what I | never | stole?

6. O God, you ǀ know my ǀ foolishness, ▪
   and my ǀ faults · are not ǀ hidden ǀ from you.

7 Let not those who hope in you
       be put to shame through me, Lord ǀ God of ǀ hosts; ▪
   let not those who seek you be disgraced because of ǀ me,
       O ǀ God of ǀ Israel.

8,9. For your sake have I suffered reproach;
       shame has ǀ covered my ǀ face. ▪
   I have become a stranger to my kindred,
       an alien ǀ to my ǀ mother's ǀ children.

10 Zeal for your house has ǀ eaten me ǀ up; ▪
    the scorn of those who ǀ scorn you has ǀ fallen upǀon me.

11 I humbled myǀself with ǀ fasting, ▪
    but that was ǀ turned to ǀ my reǀproach.

12 I put on ǀ sackcloth ǀ also ▪
    and beǀcame a ǀ byword aǀmong them.

13 Those who sit at the gate ǀ murmur aǀgainst me, ▪
    and the ǀ drunkards make ǀ songs aǀbout me.

14. But as for me, I make my prayer to ǀ you, O ǀ Lord; ▪
    at an acǀceptable ǀ time, O ǀ God.

15 Answer me, O God, in the abundance ǀ of your ǀ mercy ▪
    and ǀ with your ǀ sure salǀvation.

16 Draw me out of the mire, ǀ that I ǀ sink not; ▪
    let me be rescued from those who hate me
        and ǀ out of the ǀ deep ǀ waters.

17. Let not the water flood drown me,
        neither the deep ǀ swallow me ǀ up; ▪
    let not the Pit ǀ shut its ǀ mouth upǀon me.

18 Answer me, Lord, for your lovingǀkindness is ǀ good; ▪
    turn to me in the ǀ multitude ǀ of your ǀ mercies.

19 Hide not your ǀ face · from your ǀ servant; ▪
    be swift to answer me, ǀ for I ǀ am in ǀ trouble.

20. Draw near to my ǀ soul · and reǀdeem me; ▪
    deǀliver me beǀcause of my ǀ enemies.

21 You know my reproach, my shame and | my dis|honour; ▪
    my adversaries are | all | in your | sight.

22 Reproach has broken my heart; I am | full of | heaviness. ▪
    I looked for some to have pity, but there was no one,
        neither | found I | any to | comfort me.

23. They gave me | gall to | eat, ▪
    and when I was thirsty, they | gave me | vinegar to | drink.

24 Let the table before them | be a | trap ▪
    and their | sacred | feasts a | snare.

25 Let their eyes be darkened, that they | cannot | see, ▪
    and give them continual | trembling | in their | loins.

26 Pour out your indig|nation up|on them, ▪
    and let the heat of your | anger | over|take them.

27 Let their | camp be | desolate, ▪
    and let there be | no one to | dwell · in their | tents.

28† For they persecute the one whom | you have | stricken, ▪
    and increase the sorrows of | him whom | you have | pierced.

29 Lay to their charge | guilt upon | guilt, ▪
    and let them not re|ceive your | vindi|cation.

30. Let them be wiped out of the | book of the | living ▪
    and not be | written a|mong the | righteous.

31 As for me, I am | poor · and in | misery; ▪
    your saving help, O | God, will | lift me | up.

32. I will praise the name of | God · with a | song; ▪
    I will pro|claim his | greatness with | thanksgiving.

33 This will please the Lord more than an | offering of | oxen, ▪
    more than | bulls with | horns and | hooves.

34 The humble shall | see · and be | glad; ▪
    you who seek | God, your | heart shall | live.

35 For the Lord | listens · to the | needy, ▪
    and his own who are imprisoned | he does | not des|pise.

36 Let the heavens and the | earth | praise him, ▪
    the seas and | all that | moves | in them;

37   For God will save Zion and rebuild the | cities of | Judah; ▪
      they shall live there and | have it | in pos|session.

38   The children of his servants | shall in|herit it, ▪
      and they that love his | name shall | dwell there|in.

Psalm 70

1   O God, make | speed to | save me; ▪
      O | Lord, make | haste to | help me.

2.   Let those who seek my life‿
         be put to | shame and con|fusion; ▪
      let them be turned back and dis|graced‿
         who | wish me | evil.

3   Let those who | mock and de|ride me ▪
      turn | back be|cause of their | shame.

4.   But let all who seek you rejoice and be | glad in | you; ▪
      let those who love your salvation say | always, | 'Great is the | Lord!'

5   As for me, I am | poor and | needy; ▪
      come to me | quickly, | O | God.

6   You are my help and | my de|liverer; ▪
      O | Lord, do | not de|lay.

Psalm 71

1   In you, O Lord, do | I seek | refuge; ▪
      let me | never be | put to | shame.

2   In your righteousness, deliver me and | set me | free; ▪
      incline your | ear to | me and | save me.

3   Be for me a stronghold to which I may | ever re|sort; ▪
      send out to save me, for | you are my | rock · and my | fortress.

4.   Deliver me, my God, from the | hand of the | wicked, ▪
      from the grasp of the evil|doer | and the op|pressor.

5   For you are my hope, | O Lord | God, ▪
      my confidence, | even | from my | youth.

6   Upon you have I leaned from my birth,
         when you drew me from my | mother's | womb; ▪
      my praise | shall be | always of | you.

7   I have become a | portent to | many, ▪
      but you are my | refuge | and my | strength.

8   Let my mouth be | full of your | praise ▪
      and your | glory | all the day | long.

9.   Do not cast me away in the time of | old | age; ▪
      forsake me | not · when my | strength | fails.

10   For my enemies are | talking a|gainst me, ▪
      and those who lie in wait for my | life take | counsel to|gether.

11   They say, 'God has forsaken him;
         pur|sue him and | take him, ▪
      be|cause · there is | none · to de|liver him.'

12   O God, | be not | far from me; ▪
      come quickly to | help me, | O my | God.

13†   Let those who are against me‿
         be put to | shame and dis|grace; ▪
      let those who seek to do me evil
         be | covered with | scorn · and re|proach.

14   But as for me I will | hope con|tinually ▪
      and will | praise you | more and | more.

15   My mouth shall tell of your righteousness
         and salvation | all the day | long, ▪
      for I | know no | end of the | telling.

16   I will begin with the mighty works of the | Lord | God; ▪
      I will recall your | righteousness, | yours a|lone.

17.   O God, you have taught me since | I was | young, ▪
      and to this day I | tell · of your | wonderful | works.

18   Forsake me not, O God,
         when I am | old and grey-|headed, ▪
      till I make known your deeds to the next generation
         and your power to | all that | are to | come.

19   Your righteousness, O God, | reaches · to the | heavens; ▪
      in the great things you have done, | who is like | you, O | God?

20   What troubles and adversities | you have | shown me, ▪
      and yet you will turn and refresh me
         and bring me from the | deep of the | earth a|gain.

21. In|crease my | honour; ▪
    turn a|gain and | comfort | me.

22 Therefore will I praise you upon the harp
        for your faithfulness, | O my | God; ▪
    I will sing to you with the lyre, O | Holy | One of | Israel.

23 My lips will sing | out · as I | play to you, ▪
    and so will my | soul, which | you have re|deemed.

24† My tongue also will tell of your righteousness | all the day | long, ▪
    for they shall be shamed and disgraced
        who | sought to | do me | evil.

Psalm 72

1 Give the king your | judgments, O | God, ▪
    and your righteousness | to the | son of a | king.

2. Then shall he judge your | people | righteously ▪
    and your | poor | with | justice.

3 May the mountains | bring forth | peace, ▪
    and the little hills | righteousness | for the | people.

4. May he defend the poor a|mong the | people, ▪
    deliver the children of the | needy and | crush · the op|pressor.

5 May he live as long as the sun and | moon en|dure, ▪
    from one gene|ration | to an|other.

6 May he come down like rain upon the | mown | grass, ▪
    like the | showers that | water the | earth.

7† In his time shall | righteousness | flourish, ▪
    and abundance of peace
        till the | moon shall | be no | more.

8 May his dominion extend from | sea to | sea ▪
    and from the River | to the | ends of the | earth.

9. May his foes | kneel be|fore him ▪
    and his | enemies | lick the | dust.

10 The kings of Tarshish and of the isles | shall pay | tribute; ▪
    the kings of Sheba and | Seba | shall bring | gifts.

11. All kings shall fall | down be|fore him; ▪
    all | nations shall | do him | service.

12 For he shall deliver the | poor that cry | out, ▪
the needy and | those who | have no | helper.

13 He shall have pity on the | weak and | poor; ▪
he shall pre|serve the | lives of the | needy.

14. He shall redeem their lives from op|pression and | violence, ▪
and dear shall their | blood be | in his | sight.

15 Long may he live;
      unto him may be given | gold from | Sheba; ▪
may prayer be made for him continually
      and may they | bless him | all the day | long.

16 May there be abundance of grain on the earth,
      standing thick up|on the | hilltops; ▪
may its fruit flourish like Lebanon
      and its grain | grow · like the | grass of the | field.

17. May his name remain for ever
      and be established as long as the | sun en|dures; ▪
may all nations be blest in | him and | call him | blessed.

18 Blessed be the Lord, the | God of | Israel, ▪
who a|lone does | wonderful | things.

19 And blessed be his glorious | name for | ever. ▪
May all the earth be filled with his | glory.
      A|men. A|men.

Psalm 73

1 Truly, God is | loving to | Israel, ▪
to those | who are | pure in | heart.

2. Nevertheless, my feet were | almost | gone; ▪
my | steps had | well-nigh | slipped.

3 For I was | envious · of the | proud; ▪
I saw the | wicked in | such pros|perity;

4 For they | suffer no | pains ▪
and their | bodies are | sleek and | sound;

5 They come to no mis|fortune like | other folk; ▪
nor are they | plagued as | others | are;

6. Therefore pride | is their | necklace ∎
   and violence | wraps them | like a | cloak.

7 Their iniquity | comes from with|in; ∎
   the conceits of their | hearts | over|flow.

8 They scoff, and speak | only of | evil; ∎
   they talk of op|pression | from on | high.

9 They set their mouth a|gainst the | heavens, ∎
   and their tongue | ranges | round the | earth;

10. And so the | people | turn to them ∎
    and | find in | them no | fault.

11 They say, | 'How should | God know? ∎
   Is there knowledge | in the | Most | High?'

12 Behold, | these are the | wicked; ∎
   ever at ease, | they in|crease their | wealth.

13 Is it in vain that I | cleansed my | heart ∎
   and | washed my | hands in | innocence?

14 All day long have | I been | stricken ∎
   and | chastened | every | morning.

15 If I had said, 'I will | speak as | they do,' ∎
   I should have betrayed the gene|ration | of your | children.

16. Then thought I to | under|stand this, ∎
    but it | was too | hard for | me,

17 Until I entered the | sanctuary of | God ∎
   and under|stood the | end of the | wicked:

18 How you set them in | slippery | places; ∎
   you | cast them | down · to des|truction.

19 How suddenly do they | come to des|truction, ∎
   perish and | come to a | fearful | end!

20. As with a dream | when one a|wakes, ∎
    so, Lord, when you arise you | will des|pise their | image.

21 When my heart be|came em|bittered ∎
   and | I was | pierced · to the | quick,

22 I was but | foolish and | ignorant; ∎
   I was like a brute | beast in | your | presence.

23   Yet I am | always | with you; ▪
      you hold me | by my | right | hand.

24.   You will guide me | with your | counsel ▪
      and | afterwards re|ceive me with | glory.

25   Whom have I in | heaven but | you? ▪
      And there is nothing upon earth that I de|sire ·⏜
         in com|parison with | you.

26.   Though my flesh and my | heart | fail me, ▪
      God is the strength of my heart | and my | portion for | ever.

27   Truly, those who for|sake you will | perish; ▪
      you will put to silence the | faithless | who be|tray you.

28   But it is good for me to draw | near to | God; ▪
      in the Lord God have I made my refuge,
         that I may | tell of | all your | works.

Psalm 74

1   O God, why have you | utterly dis|owned us? ▪
      Why does your anger burn
         a|gainst the | sheep of your | pasture?

2   Remember your congregation that you | purchased of | old, ▪
      the tribe you redeemed for your own possession,
         and Mount | Zion | where you | dwelt.

3   Hasten your steps towards the | endless | ruins, ▪
      where the enemy has laid | waste | all your | sanctuary.

4.   Your adversaries roared in the | place · of your | worship; ▪
      they set up their | banners as | tokens of | victory.

5   Like men brandishing axes on high in a | thicket of | trees, ▪
      all her carved work they smashed | down
         with | hatchet and | hammer.

6   They set fire to your | holy | place; ▪
      they defiled the dwelling place of your name
         and | razed it | to the | ground.

7   They said in their heart, 'Let us make havoc of them | alto|gether,' ▪
      and they burned down all the sanctuaries of | God | in the | land.

8.   There are no signs to see, not one | prophet | left, ▪
      not one a|mong us who | knows how | long.

9   How long, O God, will the | adver·sary | scoff? ▪
     Shall the enemy blas|pheme your | name for | ever?

10   Why have you with|held your | hand ▪
     and hidden your | right hand | in your | bosom?

11. Yet God is my | king · from of | old, ▪
     who did deeds of sal|vation · in the | midst of the | earth.

12   It was you that divided the | sea · by your | might ▪
     and shattered the heads of the | dragons | on the | waters;

13   You alone crushed the | heads of Le|viathan ▪
     and gave him to the | beasts · of the | desert for | food.

14. You cleft the rock for | fountain and | flood; ▪
     you dried up | ever|flowing | rivers.

15   Yours is the day, yours | also the | night; ▪
     you es|tablished the | moon · and the | sun.

16. You set all the | bounds of the | earth; ▪
     you | fashioned both | summer and | winter.

17   Remember now, Lord, how the | enemy | scoffed, ▪
     how a foolish | people des|pised your | name.

18   Do not give to wild beasts the | soul of your | turtle dove; ▪
     forget not the | lives of your | poor for | ever.

19   Look upon | your cre|ation, ▪
     for the earth is full of darkness, | full of the | haunts of | violence.

20. Let not the oppressed turn a|way a|shamed, ▪
     but let the poor and | needy | praise your | name.

21   Arise, O God, maintain your | own | cause; ▪
     remember how fools re|vile you | all the day | long.

22   Forget not the | clamour · of your | adversaries, ▪
     the tumult of your enemies | that as|cends con|tinually.

Psalm 75

1   We give you thanks, O God, we | give you | thanks, ▪
     for your name is near, as your | wonderful | deeds de|clare.

2   'I will seize the ap|pointed | time; ▪
     I, the | Lord, will | judge with | equity.

3. 'Though the earth reels and | all that | dwell in her, ▪
    it is I that | hold her | pillars | steady.

4   'To the boasters I say, | "Boast no | longer," ▪
    and to the wicked, | "Do not | lift up your | horn.

5   ' "Do not lift up your | horn on | high; ▪
    do not | speak · with a | stiff | neck." '

6. For neither from the east | nor from the | west, ▪
    nor yet from the | wilderness comes | exal|tation.

7   But God a|lone is | judge; ▪
    he puts down one and | raises | up an|other.

8   For in the hand of the Lord there | is a | cup, ▪
    well mixed and | full of | foaming | wine.

9† He pours it out for all the | wicked · of the | earth; ▪
    they shall | drink it, and | drain the | dregs.

10 But I will re|joice for | ever ▪
    and make | music · to the | God of | Jacob.

11 All the horns of the wicked | will I | break, ▪
    but the horns of the | righteous shall | be ex|alted.

Psalm 76

1   In Judah | God is | known; ▪
    his | name is | great in | Israel.

2. At Salem | is his | tabernacle, ▪
    and his | dwelling | place in | Zion.

3   There broke he the flashing | arrows · of the | bow, ▪
    the shield, the | sword · and the | weapons of | war.

4   In the light of splendour | you ap|peared, ▪
    glorious | from the e|ternal | mountains.

5   The boastful were plundered; they have | slept their | sleep; ▪
    none of the | warriors can | lift their | hand.

6. At your rebuke, O | God of | Jacob, ▪
    both | horse and | chariot fell | stunned.

7   Terrible are | you in | majesty: ▪
    who can stand before your | face when | you are | angry?

8   You caused your judgment to be | heard from | heaven; ▪
      the earth | trembled | and was | still,

9   When God a|rose to | judgment, ▪
      to | save · all the | meek upon | earth.

10.   You crushed the | wrath of the | peoples ▪
      and | bridled the | wrathful | remnant.

11   Make a vow to the Lord your | God and | keep it; ▪
      let all who are round about him bring gifts
          to him that is | worthy | to be | feared.

12   He breaks down the | spirit of | princes ▪
      and strikes | terror · in the | kings of the | earth.

Psalm 77

1   I cry a|loud to | God; ▪
      I cry aloud to | God and | he will | hear me.

2   In the day of my trouble I have | sought the | Lord; ▪
      by night my hand is stretched out and does not tire;
          my | soul re|fuses | comfort.

3.   I think upon God | and I | groan; ▪
      I ponder, | and my | spirit | faints.

4   You will not let my | eyelids | close; ▪
      I am so troubled | that I | cannot | speak.

5   I consider the | days of | old; ▪
      I re|member the | years long | past;

6.   I commune with my | heart · in the | night; ▪
      my spirit | searches for | under|standing.

7   Will the Lord cast us | off for | ever? ▪
      Will he | no more | show us his | favour?

8   Has his loving mercy clean | gone for | ever? ▪
      Has his promise come to an | end for | ever|more?

9.   Has God for|gotten · to be | gracious? ▪
      Has he shut up his com|passion | in dis|pleasure?

10   And I said, 'My | grief is | this: ▪
      that the right hand of the Most | High has | lost its | strength.'

11   I will remember the | works of the | Lord ▪
      and call to mind your | wonders of | old | time.

12.   I will meditate on | all your | works ▪
      and | ponder your | mighty | deeds.

13   Your way, O | God, is | holy; ▪
      who is so | great a | god as | our God?

14   You are the | God who worked | wonders ▪
      and declared your | power a|mong the | peoples.

15.   With a mighty arm you re|deemed your | people, ▪
      the | children of | Jacob and | Joseph.

16   The waters saw you, O God;
         the waters saw you and | were a|fraid; ▪
      the | depths | also were | troubled.

17   The clouds poured out water; the | skies | thundered; ▪
      your arrows | flashed on | every | side;

18.   The voice of your thunder was in the whirlwind;
         your lightnings | lit up the | ground; ▪
      the | earth | trembled and | shook.

19   Your way was in the sea, and your paths in the | great | waters, ▪
      but your | footsteps | were not | known.

20   You led your | people like | sheep ▪
      by the | hand of | Moses and | Aaron.

Psalm 78

1   Hear my teaching, | O my | people; ▪
      incline your | ears · to the | words of my | mouth.

2   I will open my | mouth · in a | parable; ▪
      I will pour forth | mysteries | from of | old,

3.   Such as we have | heard and | known, ▪
      which our | forebears | have | told us.

4   We will not hide from their children,
         but will recount to gene|rations to | come, ▪
      the praises of the Lord and his power
         and the | wonderful | works · he has | done.

5 He laid a solemn charge on Jacob
   and made it a | law in | Israel, ∎
   which he com|manded them to | teach their | children,

6 That the generations to come might know,
   and the children | yet un|born, ∎
   that they in turn might | tell it | to their | children;

7 So that they might put their | trust in | God ∎
   and not forget the deeds of | God, but | keep · his com|mandments,

8. And not be like their forebears,
   a stubborn and rebellious | gene|ration, ∎
   a generation whose heart was not steadfast,
   and whose spirit | was not | faithful to | God.

9 The people of Ephraim, | armed · with the | bow, ∎
   turned | back · in the | day of | battle;

10 They did not keep the | covenant of | God ∎
   and re|fused to | walk in his | law;

11. They forgot what | he had | done ∎
   and the | wonders | he had | shown them.

12 For he did marvellous things in the | sight of their | forebears, ∎
   in the land of Egypt, | in the | field of | Zoan.

13 He divided the sea and | let them pass | through; ∎
   he made the | waters stand | still · in a | heap.

14 He led them with a | cloud by | day ∎
   and all the night | through · with a | blaze of | fire.

15 He split the hard | rocks · in the | wilderness ∎
   and gave them drink as | from the | great | deep.

16. He brought streams | out of the | rock ∎
   and made | water gush | out like | rivers.

17 Yet for all this they sinned | more a|gainst him ∎
   and defied the Most | High | in the | wilderness.

18 They tested | God · in their | hearts ∎
   and de|manded | food · for their | craving.

19 They spoke against | God and | said, ∎
   'Can God prepare a | table | in the | wilderness?

20. 'He struck the rock indeed, so that the waters gushed out
      and the streams | over|flowed, ▪
    but can he give bread or provide | meat | for his | people?'

21   When the Lord heard this, he was | full of | wrath; ▪
    a fire was kindled against Jacob
      and his | anger went | out against | Israel,

22   For they had no | faith in | God ▪
    and put no | trust in his | saving | help.

23   So he commanded the | clouds a|bove ▪
    and | opened the | doors of | heaven.

24   He rained down upon them | manna to | eat ▪
    and | gave them the | grain of | heaven.

25   So mortals ate the | bread of | angels; ▪
    he | sent them | food in | plenty.

26   He caused the east wind to | blow · in the | heavens ▪
    and led out the | south wind | by his | might.

27   He rained flesh upon them as | thick as | dust ▪
    and winged fowl | like the | sand of the | sea.

28   He let it fall in the | midst of their | camp ▪
    and | round a|bout their | tents.

29† So they ate and | were well | filled, ▪
    for he | gave them what | they de|sired.

30   But they did not | stop their | craving; ▪
    their | food was | still in their | mouths,

31   When the anger of God | rose a|gainst them, ▪
    and slew their strongest men
      and | felled the | flower of | Israel.

32   But for all this, they | sinned yet | more ▪
    and put no | faith in his | wonderful | works.

33.   So he brought their days to an end | like a | breath ▪
    and their | years in | sudden | terror.

34   Whenever he slew them, | they would | seek him; ▪
    they would repent and | earnestly | search for | God.

35   They remembered that | God · was their | rock ▪
    and the | Most High | God · their re|deemer.

36 Yet they did but flatter him ˈ with their ˈ mouth ▪
and disˈsembled ˈ with their ˈ tongue.

37 Their heart was not ˈ steadfast toˈwards him, ▪
neither were they ˈ faithful ˈ to his ˈ covenant.

38 But he was so merciful that he forgave their misdeeds
and did ˈ not desˈtroy them; ▪
many a time he turned back his wrath
and did not suffer his whole disˈpleasure ˈ to be ˈ roused.

39. For he remembered that they ˈ were but ˈ flesh, ▪
a wind that passes ˈ by and ˈ does not reˈturn.

40 How often they rebelled against him ˈ in the ˈ wilderness ▪
and ˈ grieved him ˈ in the ˈ desert!

41. Again and again they ˈ tempted ˈ God ▪
and provoked the ˈ Holy ˈ One of ˈ Israel.

42 They did not reˈmember his ˈ power ▪
in the day when he reˈdeemed them ˈ from the ˈ enemy;

43 How he had wrought his ˈ signs in ˈ Egypt ▪
and his ˈ wonders · in the ˈ field of ˈ Zoan.

44 He turned their ˈ rivers · into ˈ blood, ▪
so that they ˈ could not ˈ drink of their ˈ streams.

45 He sent swarms of flies among them, ˈ which deˈvoured them, ▪
and ˈ frogs which ˈ brought them ˈ ruin.

46 He gave their ˈ produce · to the ˈ caterpillar, ▪
the ˈ fruit of their ˈ toil · to the ˈ locust.

47 He destroyed their ˈ vines with ˈ hailstones ▪
and their ˈ sycamore ˈ trees · with the ˈ frost.

48 He delivered their ˈ cattle to ˈ hailstones ▪
and their ˈ flocks ˈ – to ˈ thunderbolts.

49 He set loose on them his ˈ blazing ˈ anger: ▪
fury, displeasure and trouble,
a ˈ troop of desˈtroying ˈ angels.

50 He made a way for his anger
and spared not their ˈ souls from ˈ death, ▪
but gave their life ˈ over ˈ to the ˈ pestilence.

51. He smote the ˈ firstborn of ˈ Egypt, ▪
the first fruits of their ˈ strength · in the ˈ tents of ˈ Ham.

52 But he led out his | people like | sheep ▪
and guided them in the | wilderness | like a | flock.

53 He led them to safety and they were | not a|fraid, ▪
but the | sea · over|whelmed their | enemies.

54 He brought them to his | holy | place, ▪
the mountain which his | right hand | took · in pos|session.

55. He drove out the nations before them
and shared out to them | their in|heritance; ▪
he settled the tribes of | Israel | in their | tents.

56 Yet still they tested God Most High
and re|belled a|gainst him, ▪
and | would not | keep his com|mandments.

57 They turned back and fell away | like their | forebears, ▪
starting aside | like an | unstrung | bow.

58† They grieved him | with their | hill altars ▪
and provoked him to dis|pleasure | with their | idols.

59 God heard and was | greatly | angered, ▪
and | utterly re|jected | Israel.

60 He forsook the | tabernacle at | Shiloh, ▪
the | tent · of his | presence on | earth.

61 He gave the ark of his strength | into cap|tivity, ▪
his splendour | into the | adver·sary's | hand.

62 He delivered his | people · to the | sword ▪
and | raged a|gainst his in|heritance.

63 The fire con|sumed their young | men; ▪
there was | no one · to la|ment their | maidens.

64. Their priests | fell · by the | sword, ▪
and their | widows made | no · lamen|tation.

65 Then the Lord woke as | out of | sleep, ▪
like a warrior who had been | over|come with | wine.

66 He struck his enemies | from be|hind ▪
and put them | to per|petual | shame.

67 He rejected the | tent of | Joseph ▪
and chose | not the | tribe of | Ephraim,

68   But he chose the | tribe of | Judah ▪
and the hill of | Zion, | which he | loved.

69.   And there he built his sanctuary like the | heights of | heaven, ▪
like the | earth · which he | founded for | ever.

70   He chose David | also, his | servant, ▪
and | took him a|way · from the | sheepfolds.

71   From following the ewes with their | lambs he | took him, ▪
that he might shepherd Jacob his people
        and | Israel | his in|heritance.

72   So he shepherded them with a de|voted | heart ▪
and with | skilful | hands he | guided them.

Psalm 79

1   O God, the heathen have come | into your | heritage; ▪
your holy temple have they defiled
        and made Je|rusalem a | heap of | stones.

2   The dead bodies of your servants they have given
        to be food for the | birds of the | air, ▪
and the flesh of your | faithful · to the | beasts of the | field.

3.   Their blood have they shed like water
        on every | side of Je|rusalem, ▪
and | there was | no one to | bury them.

4   We have become the | taunt of our | neighbours, ▪
the scorn and derision of | those that are | round a|bout us.

5   Lord, how long will you be | angry, for | ever? ▪
How long will your jealous | fury | blaze like | fire?

6.   Pour out your wrath upon the nations that | have not | known you, ▪
and upon the kingdoms that have not | called up|on your | name.

7   For they have de|voured | Jacob ▪
and | laid | waste his | dwelling place.

8   Remember not against us our | former | sins; ▪
let your compassion make haste to meet us,
        for | we are brought | very | low.

9.   Help us, O God of our salvation, for the | glory · of your | name; ▪
deliver us, and wipe away our sins | for your | name's | sake.

10 Why should the | heathen | say, ▪
    'Where is | now | their | God?'
11 Let vengeance for your servants' | blood · that is | shed ▪
    be known among the | nations | in our | sight.
12. Let the sorrowful sighing of the prisoners | come be|fore you, ▪
    and by your mighty arm
        preserve those | who are con|demned to | die.

13 May the taunts with which our neighbours | taunted you, | Lord, ▪
    return | sevenfold | into their | bosom.
14 But we that are your people and the sheep of your pasture
        will give you | thanks for | ever, ▪
    and tell of your praise from gene|ration to | gene|ration.

Psalm 80

1   Hear, O | Shepherd of | Israel, ▪
    you that led | Joseph | like a | flock;
2. Shine forth, you that are enthroned up|on the | cherubim, ▪
    before Ephraim, | Benjamin | and Ma|nasseh.

3   Stir up your | mighty | strength ▪
    and | come to | our sal|vation.
4. *Turn us a|gain, O | God; ▪*
    show the light of your countenance, | and we | shall be | saved.

5   O Lord | God of | hosts, ▪
    how long will you be | angry · at your | people's | prayer?
6. You feed them with the | bread of | tears; ▪
    you give them a|bundance of | tears to | drink.

7   You have made us the de|rision · of our | neighbours, ▪
    and our | enemies | laugh us to | scorn.
8. *Turn us again, O | God of | hosts; ▪*
    show the light of your countenance, | and we | shall be | saved.

9   You brought a | vine · out of | Egypt; ▪
    you drove | out the | nations and | planted it.
10. You made | room a|round it, ▪
    and when it had taken | root, it | filled the | land.

11   The hills were | covered · with its | shadow ▪
and the cedars of | God | by its | boughs.

12. It stretched out its | branches · to the | Sea ▪
and its | tendrils | to the | River.

13   Why then have you broken | down its | wall, ▪
so that all who pass | by pluck | off its | grapes?

14. The wild boar out of the wood | tears it | off, ▪
and all the | insects · of the | field de|vour it.

15   Turn again, O | God of | hosts, ▪
look down from | heaven | and be|hold;

16. Cherish this vine which your | right hand has | planted, ▪
and the branch that you | made so | strong for your|self.

17   Let those who burnt it with fire, who | cut it | down, ▪
perish | at the re|buke · of your | countenance.

18. Let your hand be upon the | man · at your | right hand, ▪
the son of man you | made so | strong · for your|self.

19   And so will we | not go | back from you; ▪
give us life, and we shall | call up|on your | name.

20   *Turn us again, O Lord | God of | hosts; ▪*
show the light of your countenance, | and we | shall be | saved.

Psalm 81

1   Sing merrily to | God our | strength, ▪
shout for | joy · to the | God of | Jacob.

2   Take up the song and | sound the | timbrel, ▪
the tuneful | lyre | with the | harp.

3. Blow the trumpet at the | new | moon, ▪
as at the full moon, up|on our | solemn | feast day.

4   For this is a | statute for | Israel, ▪
a | law · of the | God of | Jacob,

5† The charge he laid on the | people of | Joseph, ▪
when they came | out of the | land of | Egypt.

6   I heard a voice I did not I know, that I said: ∎
      'I eased their shoulder from the burden;
          their hands were set I free from I bearing the I load.

7   'You called upon me in trouble and I I deǀlivered you; ∎
      I answered you from the secret place of thunder
          and proved you I at the I waters of I Meribah.

8   'Hear, O my people, and I I will adǀmonish you: ∎
      O Israel, if you I would but I listen to I me!

9   'There shall be no strange I god aǀmong you; ∎
      you shall not I worship a I foreign I god.

10† 'I am the Lord your God,
          who brought you up from the I land of I Egypt; ∎
      open your mouth I wide and I I shall I fill it.'

11   But my people would not I hear my I voice ∎
      and I Israel would I not oǀbey me.

12. So I sent them away in the stubbornness I of their I hearts, ∎
      and let them walk I after their I own I counsels.

13   O that my people would I listen to I me, ∎
      that I Israel would I walk · in my I ways!

14   Then I should soon put I down their I enemies ∎
      and turn my I hand aǀgainst their I adversaries.

15   Those who hate the Lord would be I humbled beǀfore him, ∎
      and their I punishment would I last for I ever.

16   But Israel would I feed with the I finest I wheat ∎
      and with honey I from the I rock · would I I I satisfy them.

Psalm 82

1   God has taken his stand in the I council of I heaven; ∎
      in the midst of the I gods I he gives I judgment:

2.   'How long will you I judge unǀjustly ∎
      and show such I favour I to the I wicked?

3   'You were to judge the I weak · and the I orphan; ∎
      defend the I right · of the I humble and I needy;

4.   'Rescue the I weak · and the I poor; ∎
      deliver them I from the I hand of the I wicked.

5   'They have no knowledge or wisdom;
            they walk on | still in | darkness: ▪
        all the foun|dations · of the | earth are | shaken.

6.   'Therefore I say that though | you are | gods ▪
        and all of you | children · of the | Most | High,

7   'Nevertheless, you shall | die like | mortals ▪
        and | fall like | one of their | princes.'

8   Arise, O God and | judge the | earth, ▪
        for it is you that shall take all | nations | for your pos|session.

Psalm 83

1   Hold not your peace, O God, do | not keep | silent; ▪
        be | not un|moved, O | God;

2   For your enemies | are in | tumult ▪
        and those who | hate you | lift up their | heads.

3   They take secret counsel a|gainst your | people ▪
        and plot against | those | whom you | treasure.

4.   They say, 'Come, let us destroy them | as a | nation, ▪
        that the name of Israel | be re|membered no | more.'

5   They have conspired together | with one | mind; ▪
        they | are in | league a|gainst you:

6,7   The tents of Edom and the Ishmaelites, |
            Moab · and the | Hagarenes, ▪
        Gebal and Ammon and Amalek,
            the Philistines and | those who | dwell in | Tyre.

8†   Ashur | also has | joined them ▪
        and has lent a strong | arm · to the | children of | Lot.

9   Do to them as you | did to | Midian, ▪
        to Sisera and to Jabin | at the | river of | Kishon,

10.   Who | perished at | Endor ▪
        and be|came as | dung · for the | earth.

11   Make their commanders like | Oreb and | Zeëb, ▪
        and all their princes like | Zebah | and Zal|munna,

12   Who said, 'Let us | take · for our|selves ▪
        the pastures of | God as | our pos|session.'

13 O my God, | make them like | thistledown, ▪
    like | chaff be|fore the | wind.

14. Like fire that con|sumes a | forest, ▪
    like the | flame · that sets | mountains a|blaze,

15 So drive them | with your | tempest ▪
    and dis|may them | with your | storm.

16 Cover their faces with | shame, O | Lord, ▪
    that | they may | seek your | name.

17 Let them be disgraced and dis|mayed for | ever; ▪
    let them be | put to con|fusion and | perish;

18 And they shall know that you, whose | name is the | Lord, ▪
    are alone the Most High | over | all the | earth.

Psalm 84

1   How lovely is your dwelling place, O | Lord of | hosts! ▪
    My soul has a desire and longing to enter the courts of the Lord;
        my heart and my flesh re|joice · in the | living | God.

2   The sparrow has found her a house
        and the swallow a nest where she may | lay her | young: ▪
    at your altars, O Lord of | hosts, my | King · and my | God.

3. Blessed are they who | dwell in your | house: ▪
    they will | always be | praising | you.

4   Blessed are those whose | strength is in | you, ▪
    in whose | heart · are the | highways to | Zion,

5   Who going through the barren valley find | there a | spring, ▪
    and the early | rains will | clothe it with | blessing.

6. They will go from | strength to | strength ▪
    and ap|pear before | God in | Zion.

7   O Lord God of hosts, | hear my | prayer; ▪
    listen, O | God | of | Jacob.

8   Behold our de|fender, O | God, ▪
    and look upon the | face of | your a|nointed.

9. For one day | in your | courts ▪
    is | better | than a | thousand.

10   I would rather be a doorkeeper in the | house of my | God ■
      than | dwell · in the | tents of un|godliness.

11   For the Lord God is both sun and shield;
           he will give | grace and | glory; ■
      no good thing shall the Lord withhold
           from | those who | walk · with in|tegrity.

12   O Lord | God of | hosts, ■
      blessed are those who | put their | trust in | you.

Psalm 85

1   Lord, you were gracious | to your | land; ■
      you re|stored the | fortunes of | Jacob.

2   You forgave the of|fence of your | people ■
      and | covered | all their | sins.

3†   You laid a|side · all your | fury ■
      and turned from your | wrathful | indig|nation.

4   Restore us again, O | God our | Saviour, ■
      and | let your | anger | cease from us.

5   Will you be displeased with | us for | ever? ■
      Will you stretch out your wrath from one gene|ration | to an|other?

6.   Will you not give us | life a|gain, ■
      that your people | may re|joice in | you?

7   Show us your | mercy, O | Lord, ■
      and | grant us | your sal|vation.

8   I will listen to what the Lord | God will | say, ■
      for he shall speak peace to his people|and to the faithful,
           that they | turn not a|gain to | folly.

9.   Truly| his salvation is near to | those who | fear him, ■
      that his | glory may | dwell · in our | land.

10   Mercy and truth are | met to|gether, ■
      righteousness and | peace have | kissed each | other;

11.   Truth shall spring | up · from the | earth ■
      and | righteousness look | down from | heaven.

12   The Lord will indeed give ǀ all that is ǀ good, ∎
and our ǀ land will ǀ yield its ǀ increase.

13   Righteousness shall ǀ go beǀfore him ∎
and diǀrect his ǀ steps · in the ǀ way.

Psalm 86

1   Incline your ear, O ǀ Lord, and ǀ answer me, ∎
for I am ǀ poor ǀ and in ǀ misery.

2.   Preserve my soul, for ǀ I am ǀ faithful; ∎
save your servant, for I ǀ put my ǀ trust in ǀ you.

3   Be merciful to me, O Lord, for ǀ you are my ǀ God; ∎
I call upǀon you ǀ all the day ǀ long.

4   Gladden the ǀ soul of your ǀ servant, ∎
for to you, O ǀ Lord, I ǀ lift up my ǀ soul.

5†   For you, Lord, are ǀ good and forǀgiving, ∎
abounding in steadfast love to ǀ all who ǀ call upǀon you.

6   Give ear, O ǀ Lord, · to my ǀ prayer ∎
and listen to the ǀ voice of my ǀ suppliǀcation.

7.   In the day of my distress I will ǀ call upǀon you, ∎
for ǀ you will ǀ answer ǀ me.

8   Among the gods there is none like ǀ you, O ǀ Lord, ∎
nor ǀ any ǀ works like ǀ yours.

9   All nations you have made shall come and ǀ worship · you, O ǀ Lord, ∎
and shall ǀ gloriǀfy your ǀ name.

10.   For you are great and do ǀ wonderful ǀ things; ∎
you aǀlone ǀ are ǀ God.

11   Teach me your way, O Lord, and I will ǀ walk in your ǀ truth; ∎
knit my heart to you, that ǀ I may ǀ fear your ǀ name.

12   I will thank you, O Lord my God, with ǀ all my ǀ heart, ∎
and glorify your ǀ name for ǀ everǀmore;

13.   For great is your steadfast ǀ love toǀwards me, ∎
for you have delivered my ǀ soul · from the ǀ depths of the ǀ grave.

14   O God, the proud rise up against me
and a ruthless horde seek ǀ after my ǀ life; ∎
they have not ǀ set you beǀfore their ǀ eyes.

15.　But you, Lord, are gracious and | full of com|passion, ▪
　　slow to anger and | full of | kindness and | truth.

16　Turn to me and have | mercy up|on me; ▪
　　give your strength to your servant
　　　　and | save the | child · of your | handmaid.

17　Show me a token of your favour,
　　　　that those who hate me may see it and | be a|shamed; ▪
　　because you, O | Lord, have | helped and | comforted me.

Psalm 87

1　His foundation is on the | holy | mountains. ▪
　　The Lord loves the gates of Zion
　　　　more than | all the | dwellings of | Jacob.

2.　Glorious things are | spoken of | you, ▪
　　Zion, | city | of our | God.

3　I record Egypt and Babylon as | those who | know me; ▪
　　behold Philistia, Tyre and Ethiopia:
　　　　in | Zion | were they | born.

4　And of Zion it shall be said, | 'Each one was | born in her, ▪
　　and the Most | High him|self · has established | her.'

5　The Lord will record as he | writes up the | peoples, ▪
　　'This one | also was | born | there.'

6　And as they dance | they shall | sing, ▪
　　'All my | fresh | springs are | in you.'

Psalm 88

1　O Lord, God of | my sal|vation, ▪
　　I have cried | day and | night be|fore you.

2.　Let my prayer come | into your | presence; ▪
　　in|cline your | ear · to my | cry.

3　For my soul is | full of | troubles; ▪
　　my life draws | near · to the | land of | death.

4.　I am counted as one gone | down to the | Pit; ▪
　　I am like | one that | has no | strength,

5 Lost a|mong the | dead, ▪

  like the | slain who | lie in the | grave,

6. Whom you re|member no | more, ▪

  for | they are cut | off · from your | hand.

7 You have laid me in the | lowest | pit, ▪

  in a place of | darkness | in the a|byss.

8 Your anger lies | heavy up|on me, ▪

  and you have af|flicted me with | all your | waves.

9. You have put my | friends | far from me ▪

  and made me to | be ab|horred | by them.

10 I am so fast in prison that I | cannot get | free; ▪

  my eyes | fail from | all my | trouble.

11. Lord, I have called | daily up|on you; ▪

  I have stretched | out my | hands | to you.

12 Do you work wonders | for the | dead? ▪

  Will the | shades stand | up and | praise you?

13 Shall your loving-kindness be de|clared · in the | grave, ▪

  ʹyour faithfulness | in the | land · of des|truction?

14. Shall your wonders be | known · in the | dark ▪

  or your righteous deeds in the | land where | all is for|gotten?

15 But as for me, O Lord, | I will | cry to you; ▪

  early in the morning my | prayer shall | come be|fore you.

16. Lord, why have you re|jected my | soul? ▪

  Why have you | hidden your | face | from me?

17. I have been wretched and at the point of death | from my | youth; ▪

  I suffer your terrors | and am | no more | seen.

18 Your | wrath sweeps | over me; ▪

  your | horrors are | come · to des|troy me;

19 All day long they come a|bout me like | water; ▪

  they close me | in on | every | side.

20 Lover and friend have | you put | far from me ▪

  and hid my com|panions | out of my | sight.

1   My song shall be always of the loving-kindness ǀ of the ǀ Lord: ▪
     with my mouth will I proclaim your faithfulness
         throughǀout all ǀ geneǀrations.

2   I will declare that your love is esǀtablished for ǀ ever; ▪
     you have set your faithfulness as ǀ firm ǀ as the ǀ heavens.

3   For you said: 'I have made a covenant ǀ with my ǀ chosen one; ▪
     I have sworn an ǀ oath to ǀ David my ǀ servant:

4.   ' "Your seed will I esǀtablish for ǀ ever ▪
     and build up your throne for ǀ all ǀ geneǀrations." '

5   The heavens praise your ǀ wonders, O ǀ Lord, ▪
     and your faithfulness in the asǀsembly ǀ of the ǀ holy ones;

6   For who among the clouds can be comǀpared to the ǀ Lord? ▪
     Who is like the Lord aǀmong the ǀ host of ǀ heaven?

7   A God feared in the ǀ council · of the ǀ holy ones, ▪
     great and terrible above ǀ all those ǀ round aǀbout him.

8.   Who is like you, Lord ǀ God of ǀ hosts? ▪
     Mighty Lord, your ǀ faithfulness is ǀ all aǀround you.

9   You rule the ǀ raging · of the ǀ sea; ▪
     you still its ǀ waves when ǀ they aǀrise.

10   You crushed Rahab with a ǀ deadly ǀ wound ▪
     and scattered your enemies ǀ with your ǀ mighty ǀ arm.

11   Yours are the heavens; the earth ǀ also is ǀ yours; ▪
     you established the ǀ world and ǀ all that ǀ fills it.

12.   You created the ǀ north · and the ǀ south; ▪
     Tabor and Hermon reǀjoice ǀ in your ǀ name.

13   You have a ǀ mighty ǀ arm; ▪
     strong is your hand and ǀ high is ǀ your right ǀ hand.

14   Righteousness and justice are the founǀdation of your ǀ throne; ▪
     steadfast love and faithfulness ǀ go beǀfore your ǀ face.

15   Happy are the people who know the ǀ shout of ǀ triumph: ▪
     they walk, O ǀ Lord, · in the ǀ light of your ǀ countenance.

16   In your name they rejoice ǀ all the day ǀ long ▪
     and are exǀalted ǀ in your ǀ righteousness.

17   For you are the | glory of their | strength, ▪
      and in your favour | you lift | up our | heads.

18.   Truly the | Lord · is our | shield; ▪
      the Holy One of | Israel | is our | king.

19   You spoke once in a vision and said to your | faithful | people: ▪
      'I have set a youth above the mighty;
          I have raised a | young man | over the | people.

20.   'I have found | David my | servant; ▪
      with my holy | oil have | I a|nointed him.

21   'My hand shall | hold him | fast ▪
      and my | arm shall | strengthen | him.

22   'No enemy | shall de|ceive him, ▪
      nor any | wicked | person af|flict him.

23   'I will strike down his foes be|fore his | face ▪
      and | beat down | those that | hate him.

24.   'My truth also and my steadfast love | shall be | with him, ▪
      and in my | name · shall his | head be ex|alted.

25   'I will set his dominion up|on the | sea ▪
      and his | right hand up|on the | rivers.

26   'He shall call to me, | "You are my | Father, ▪
      my God, and the | rock of | my sal|vation; "

27† 'And I will make | him my | firstborn, ▪
      the most high a|bove the | kings · of the | earth.

28   'The love I have pledged to him will I | keep for | ever, ▪
      and my covenant | will stand | fast with | him.

29   'His seed also will I make to en|dure for | ever ▪
      and his | throne · as the | days of | heaven.

30   'But if his children for|sake my | law ▪
      and | cease to | walk in my | judgments,

31,32 'If they break my statutes and do not | keep my com|mandments, ▪
      I will punish their offences with a rod |
          and their | sin with | scourges.

33   'But I will not take from him my | steadfast | love ▪
      nor | suffer my | truth to | fail.

34 'My covenant will I not I break ▪
nor alter I what has gone I out of my I lips.

35 'Once for all have I I sworn · by my I holiness ▪
that I will I not prove I false to I David.

36 'His seed shall en|dure for I ever ▪
and his I throne · as the I sun be|fore me;

37† 'It shall stand fast for ever I as the I moon, ▪
the enduring I witness I in the I heavens.'

38 But you have cast off and rejected I your a|nointed; ▪
you have I shown fierce I anger a|gainst him.

39 You have broken the covenant I with your I servant, ▪
and have I cast his I crown · to the I dust.

40 You have broken down I all his I walls ▪
and I laid his I strongholds in I ruins.

41. All who pass I by de|spoil him, ▪
and he has be|come the I scorn · of his I neighbours.

42 You have exalted the right hand I of his I foes ▪
and made I all his I enemies re|joice.

43 You have turned back the I edge of his I sword ▪
and have I not up|held him in I battle.

44 You have made an I end of his I radiance ▪
and I cast his I throne · to the I ground.

45. You have cut short the I days of his I youth ▪
and have I covered I him with I shame.

46 How long will you hide yourself so I utterly, O I Lord? ▪
How long shall your I anger I burn like I fire?

47 Remember how I short my I time is, ▪
how frail you have I made all I mortal I flesh.

48 Which of the living shall I not see I death, ▪
and shall deliver their I soul · from the I power of I darkness?

49. Where, O Lord, is your steadfast I love of I old, ▪
which you swore to I David I in your I faithfulness?

50 Remember, O Lord, how your I servant is I scorned, ▪
how I bear in my bosom the I taunts of I many I peoples,

51 While your enemies ǀ mock, O ǀ Lord, ▪
    while they mock the ǀ footsteps of ǀ your aǀnointed.
52† Blessed be the Lord for ǀ everǀmore. ▪
    Aǀmen and ǀ Aǀmen.

Psalm 90

1   Lord, you have ǀ been our ǀ refuge ▪
    from one geneǀration ǀ to aǀnother.
2. Before the mountains were brought forth,
        or the earth and the ǀ world were ǀ formed, ▪
    from everlasting to everǀlasting ǀ you are ǀ God.

3   You turn us back to ǀ dust and ǀ say: ▪
    'Turn ǀ back, O ǀ children of ǀ earth.'
4   For a thousand years in your sight are ǀ but as ǀ yesterday, ▪
    which passes ǀ like a ǀ watch · in the ǀ night.
5   You sweep them away ǀ like a ǀ dream; ▪
    they fade away ǀ suddenly ǀ like the ǀ grass.
6   In the morning it is ǀ green and ǀ flourishes; ▪
    in the evening it is ǀ dried ǀ up and ǀ withered.
7. For we consume away in ǀ your disǀpleasure; ▪
    we are afraid at your ǀ wrathful ǀ indigǀnation.

8   You have set our misǀdeeds beǀfore you ▪
    and our secret ǀ sins · in the ǀ light of your ǀ countenance.
9   When you are angry, all our ǀ days are ǀ gone; ▪
    our years come to an ǀ end ǀ like a ǀ sigh.
10. The days of our life are three score years and ten,
        or if our strength endures, ǀ even ǀ four score; ▪
    yet the sum of them is but labour and sorrow,
        for they soon pass aǀway and ǀ we are ǀ gone.

11 Who regards the ǀ power of your ǀ wrath ▪
    and your indigǀnation like ǀ those who ǀ fear you?
12. So teach us to ǀ number our ǀ days ▪
    that we may apǀply our ǀ hearts to ǀ wisdom.

13   Turn again, O Lord; how long will ǀ you deǀlay? ▪
      Have comǀpassion ǀ on your ǀ servants.

14.   Satisfy us with your loving-kindness ǀ in the ǀ morning, ▪
      that we may rejoice and be ǀ glad ǀ all our ǀ days.

15   Give us gladness for the days ǀ you have afǀflicted us, ▪
      and for the years in which ǀ we have ǀ seen adǀversity.

16   Show your ǀ servants your ǀ works, ▪
      and let your ǀ glory be ǀ over their ǀ children.

17†   May the gracious favour of the Lord our God ǀ be upǀon us; ▪
      prosper our handiwork; O ǀ prosper the ǀ work · of our ǀ hands.

Psalm 91

1   Whoever dwells in the shelter of the ǀ Most ǀ High ▪
      and abides under the ǀ shadow ǀ of the Alǀmighty,

2.   Shall say to the Lord, 'My refuge ǀ and my ǀ stronghold, ▪
      my God, in ǀ whom I ǀ put my ǀ trust.'

3   For he shall deliver you from the ǀ snare of the ǀ fowler ▪
      and ǀ from the ǀ deadly ǀ pestilence.

4.   He shall cover you with his wings
          and you shall be safe ǀ under his ǀ feathers; ▪
      his faithfulness shall ǀ be your ǀ shield and ǀ buckler.

5   You shall not be afraid of any ǀ terror by ǀ night, ▪
      nor of the ǀ arrow that ǀ flies by ǀ day;

6   Of the pestilence that ǀ stalks in ǀ darkness, ▪
      nor of the ǀ sickness · that desǀtroys at ǀ noonday.

7   Though a thousand fall at your side
          and ten thousand at ǀ your right ǀ hand, ▪
      yet ǀ it shall ǀ not come ǀ near you.

8   Your eyes have ǀ only · to beǀhold ▪
      to ǀ see the reǀward · of the ǀ wicked.

9   Because you have made the ǀ Lord your ǀ refuge ▪
      and the ǀ Most ǀ High your ǀ stronghold,

10   There shall no evil ǀ happen to ǀ you, ▪
      neither shall any ǀ plague come ǀ near your ǀ tent.

11　For he shall give his angels ǀ charge ǀ over you, ▪
　　　to ǀ keep you in ǀ all your ǀ ways.

12　They shall bear you ǀ in their ǀ hands, ▪
　　　lest you dash your ǀ foot aǀgainst a ǀ stone.

13†　You shall tread upon the ǀ lion and ǀ adder; ▪
　　　the young lion and the serpent you shall ǀ trample ǀ underǀfoot.

14　Because they have set their love upon me,
　　　　therefore will ǀ I deǀliver them; ▪
　　　I will lift them up, beǀcause they ǀ know my ǀ name.

15　They will call upon me and ǀ I will ǀ answer them; ▪
　　　I am with them in trouble,
　　　　I will deǀliver them and ǀ bring them to ǀ honour.

16†　With long life ǀ will I ǀ satisfy them ▪
　　　and ǀ show them ǀ my salǀvation.

Psalm 92

1　It is a good thing to give ǀ thanks · to the ǀ Lord ▪
　　　and to sing praises to your ǀ name, ǀ O Most ǀ High;

2　To tell of your love ǀ early · in the ǀ morning ▪
　　　and of your ǀ faithfulness ǀ in the ǀ night-time,

3.　Upon the ten-stringed instrument, upǀon the ǀ harp, ▪
　　　and to the ǀ melody ǀ of the ǀ lyre.

4　For you, Lord, have made me ǀ glad · by your ǀ acts, ▪
　　　and I sing aǀloud · at the ǀ works of your ǀ hands.

5†　O Lord, how glorious ǀ are your ǀ works! ▪
　　　Your ǀ thoughts are ǀ very ǀ deep.

6　The senseless ǀ do not ǀ know, ▪
　　　nor do ǀ fools ǀ underǀstand,

7　That though the wicked ǀ sprout like ǀ grass ▪
　　　and all the ǀ workers · of inǀiquity ǀ flourish,

8.　It is only to be desǀtroyed for ǀ ever; ▪
　　　but you, O Lord, shall be exǀalted for ǀ everǀmore.

9　For lo, your enemies, O Lord,
　　　lo, your ǀ enemies shall ǀ perish, ▪
　　　and all the workers of inǀiquity ǀ shall be ǀ scattered.

10   But my horn you have exalted
　　　　like the horns of | wild | oxen; ▪
　　　　I am a|nointed with | fresh | oil.

11.   My eyes will look | down on my | foes; ▪
　　　　my ears shall hear the ruin of the evildoers |
　　　　　　who rise | up a|gainst me.

12   The righteous shall | flourish · like a | palm tree, ▪
　　　　and shall spread a|broad · like a | cedar of | Lebanon.

13   Such as are planted in the | house of the | Lord ▪
　　　　shall | flourish · in the | courts of our | God.

14   They shall still bear fruit in | old | age; ▪
　　　　they shall be vigorous | and in | full | leaf;

15   That they may show that the | Lord is | true; ▪
　　　　he is my rock,
　　　　　　and there is | no un|righteousness | in him.

Psalm 93

1   The Lord is king and has put on | glorious ap|parel; ▪
　　　　the Lord has put on his glory
　　　　　　and | girded him|self with | strength.

2.   He has made the whole | world so | sure ▪
　　　　that | it can|not be | moved.

3   Your throne has been es|tablished · from of | old; ▪
　　　　you | are from | ever|lasting.

4.   The floods have lifted up, O Lord,
　　　　　　the floods have lifted | up their | voice; ▪
　　　　the floods lift | up their | pounding | waves.

5   Mightier than the thunder of many waters,
　　　　　　mightier than the | breakers · of the | sea, ▪
　　　　the | Lord on | high is | mightier.

6   Your testimonies are | very | sure; ▪
　　　　holiness adorns your | house, O | Lord, for | ever.

1   Lord God to whom ˈ vengeance beˈlongs, ▪
O God to whom vengeance beˈlongs, shine ˈ out in ˈ majesty.

2   Rise up, O ˈ Judge · of the ˈ earth; ▪
give the ˈ arrogant their ˈ just deˈserts.

3   Lord, how ˈ long · shall the ˈ wicked, ▪
how ˈ long · shall the ˈ wicked ˈ triumph?

4.   How long shall the evilˈdoers ˈ boast ▪
and pour ˈ out such ˈ impudent ˈ words?

5,6   They crush your people, O Lord, and afˈflict your ˈ heritage. ▪
They murder the widow and the stranger;
      the ˈ orphans they ˈ put to ˈ death.

7.   And yet they say, 'The ˈ Lord · will not ˈ see, ▪
neither shall the ˈ God of ˈ Jacob reˈgard it.'

8   Consider, most ˈ stupid of ˈ people; ▪
you fools, ˈ when will you ˈ underˈstand?

9   He that planted the ear, shall ˈ he not ˈ hear? ▪
He that formed the ˈ eye, shall ˈ he not ˈ see?

10   He who corrects the nations, shall ˈ he not ˈ punish? ▪
He who teaches the ˈ peoples, does ˈ he lack ˈ knowledge?

11.   The Lord knows every ˈ human ˈ thought, ▪
that ˈ they are ˈ but a ˈ breath.

12   Blessed are those whom you ˈ chasten, O ˈ Lord, ▪
whom ˈ you inˈstruct · from your ˈ law;

13   That you may give them rest in ˈ days of adˈversity, ▪
until a ˈ pit is ˈ dug · for the ˈ wicked.

14   For the Lord will not ˈ fail his ˈ people, ▪
neither will ˈ he forˈsake · his inˈheritance.

15.   For justice shall reˈturn · to the ˈ righteous, ▪
and all that are ˈ true of ˈ heart shall ˈ follow it.

16   Who will rise up for me aˈgainst the ˈ wicked? ▪
Who will take my part aˈgainst the ˈ evilˈdoers?

17   If the Lord ˈ had not ˈ helped me, ▪
my soul would ˈ soon · have been ˈ put to ˈ silence.

18   And when I said, 'My | foot has | slipped', ▪
      your loving | mercy, O | Lord, up|held me.

19.   In the multitude of cares that | troubled my | heart, ▪
      your comforts | have re|freshed my | soul.

20   Will you have anything to do with the | throne of | wickedness, ▪
      which fashions | evil | through its | law?

21.   They gather together against the | life · of the | righteous ▪
      and con|demn the | innocent to | death.

22   But the Lord has be|come my | stronghold ▪
      and my | God the | rock of my | trust.

23   He will turn against them their own wickedness
         and silence them through their | own | malice; ▪
      the Lord our | God will | put them to | silence.

Psalm 95

1   O come, let us | sing · to the | Lord; ▪
      let us heartily rejoice in the | rock of | our sal|vation.

2.   Let us come into his | presence with | thanksgiving ▪
      and be | glad in | him with | psalms.

3   For the Lord is a | great | God ▪
      and a great | king a|bove all | gods.

4   In his hand are the | depths · of the | earth ▪
      and the heights of the | mountains are | his | also.

5†   The sea is his, | for he | made it, ▪
      and his hands have | moulded the | dry | land.

6   Come, let us worship and | bow | down ▪
      and kneel be|fore the | Lord our | Maker.

7.   For | he is our | God; ▪
      we are the people of his | pasture · and the | sheep of his | hand.

8   O that today you would | listen · to his | voice: ▪
      'Harden not your hearts as at Meribah,
         on that day at | Massah | in the | wilderness,

9.   'When your forebears tested me, and | put me · to the | proof, ▪
      though | they had | seen my | works.

10   'Forty years long I detested that gene|ration and | said, ∎
     "This people are wayward in their hearts;
       they | do not | know my | ways."

11   'So I | swore · in my | wrath, ∎
     "They shall not | enter | into my | rest."'

Psalm 96

1   Sing to the Lord a | new | song; ∎
     sing to the | Lord, | all the | earth.

2   Sing to the Lord and | bless his | name; ∎
     tell out his sal|vation from | day to | day.

3.   Declare his glory a|mong the | nations ∎
     and his | wonders a|mong all | peoples.

4   For great is the Lord and | greatly · to be | praised; ∎
     he is more to be | feared than | all | gods.

5   For all the gods of the nations | are but | idols; ∎
     it is the | Lord who | made the | heavens.

6.   Honour and majesty | are be|fore him; ∎
     power and | splendour are | in his | sanctuary.

7   Ascribe to the Lord, you families | of the | peoples; ∎
     ascribe to the | Lord | honour and | strength.

8   Ascribe to the Lord the honour | due to his | name; ∎
     bring offerings and | come in|to his | courts.

9.   O worship the Lord in the | beauty of | holiness; ∎
     let the | whole earth | tremble be|fore him.

10   Tell it out among the nations that the | Lord is | king. ∎
     He has made the world so firm that it cannot be moved;
       he will | judge the | peoples with | equity.

11   Let the heavens rejoice and let the | earth be | glad; ∎
     let the sea | thunder and | all · that is | in it;

12   Let the fields be joyful and | all · that is | in them; ∎
     let all the trees of the wood shout for | joy be|fore the | Lord.

13† For he comes, he comes to | judge the | earth; ∎
     with righteousness he will judge the world
       and the | peoples | with his | truth.

1   The Lord is king: let the | earth re|joice; ▪
     let the multitude | of the | isles be | glad.

2   Clouds and darkness are | round a|bout him; ▪
     righteousness and justice are the foun|dation | of his | throne.

3.   Fire | goes be|fore him ▪
     and burns up his | enemies on | every | side.

4   His lightnings | lit up the | world; ▪
     the | earth | saw it and | trembled.

5   The mountains melted like wax at the | presence · of the | Lord, ▪
     at the presence of the | Lord · of the | whole | earth.

6.   The heavens de|clared his | righteousness, ▪
     and all the | peoples have | seen his | glory.

7   Confounded be all who worship carved images
        and delight in | mere | idols. ▪
     Bow down be|fore him, | all you | gods.

8   Zion heard and was glad, and the daughters of | Judah re|joiced, ▪
     be|cause of your | judgments, O | Lord.

9.   For you, Lord, are most high over | all the | earth; ▪
     you are exalted | far a|bove all | gods.

10   The Lord loves | those who hate | evil; ▪
     he preserves the lives of his faithful
        and delivers them | from the | hand · of the | wicked.

11   Light has sprung | up · for the | righteous ▪
     and | joy · for the | true of | heart.

12   Rejoice in the | Lord, you | righteous, ▪
     and give | thanks · to his | holy | name.

1   Sing to the Lord a | new | song, ▪
     for | he · has done | marvellous | things.

2.   His own right hand and his | holy | arm ▪
     have | won for | him the | victory.

3   The Lord has made | known his sal|vation; ■
his deliverance has he openly | shown · in the | sight of the | nations.

4.   He has remembered his mercy and faithfulness
        towards the | house of | Israel, ■
and all the ends of the earth have seen the sal|vation | of our | God.

5   Sound praises to the Lord, | all the | earth; ■
break into | singing | and make | music.

6   Make music to the | Lord · with the | lyre, ■
with the | lyre · and the | voice of | melody.

7.   With trumpets and the | sound of the | horn ■
sound praises be|fore the | Lord, the | King.

8   Let the sea thunder and | all that | fills it, ■
the world and | all that | dwell up|on it.

9   Let the rivers | clap their | hands ■
and let the hills ring out together before the Lord,
        for he | comes to | judge the | earth.

10   In righteousness shall he | judge the | world ■
and the | peoples | with | equity.

Psalm 99

1   The Lord is king: let the | peoples | tremble; ■
he is enthroned above the cherubim: | let the | earth | shake.

2.   The Lord is | great in | Zion ■
and | high a|bove all | peoples.

3   Let them praise your name, which is | great and | awesome; ■
the | Lord our | God is | holy.

4   Mighty king, who loves justice, you have es|tablished | equity; ■
you have executed | justice and | righteousness in | Jacob.

5†   *Exalt the | Lord our | God; ■*
bow down before his | footstool, for | he is | holy.

6   Moses and Aaron among his priests
        and Samuel among those who | call upon his | name; ■
they called upon the | Lord | and he | answered them.

7   He spoke to them out of the | pillar of | cloud; ▪
     they kept his testimonies | and the | law · that he | gave them.

8   You answered them, O | Lord our | God; ▪
     you were a God who forgave them
          and | pardoned · them for | their of|fences.

9   *Exalt the Lord our God*
          and worship him upon his | holy | hill, ▪
     for the | Lord our | God is | holy.

1   O be joyful in the Lord, | all the | earth; ▪
     serve the Lord with gladness
          and come before his | presence | with a | song.

2. Know that the | Lord is | God; ▪
     it is he that has made us and we are his;
          we are his | people · and the | sheep of his | pasture.

3   Enter his gates with thanksgiving
          and his | courts with | praise; ▪
     give thanks to | him and | bless his | name.

4   For the Lord is gracious;
          his steadfast love is | ever|lasting, ▪
     and his faithfulness endures from gene|ration to | gene|ration.

1   I will sing of | faithfulness and | justice; ▪
     to you, O | Lord, | will I | sing.

2. Let me be wise in the | way that is | perfect: ▪
     when | will you | come to | me?

3   I will walk with | purity of | heart ▪‿
     with|in the | walls · of my | house.

4   I will not set be|fore my | eyes ▪‿
     a | counsel | that is | evil.

5. I abhor the | deeds · of un|faithfulness; ▪
     they | shall not | cling to | me.

6   A crooked heart | shall de|part from me; ▪
      I will not | know a | wicked | person.

7   One who slanders a | neighbour in | secret ▪
      I will | quickly | put to | silence.

8.   Haughty eyes and an | arrogant | heart ▪
      I | will | not en|dure.

9   My eyes are upon the | faithful · in the | land, ▪
      that | they may | dwell with | me.

10   One who walks in the | way · that is | pure ▪
      shall | be | my | servant.

11   There shall not | dwell in my | house ▪‿
      one that | practis|es de|ceit.

12   One who | utters | falsehood ▪‿
      shall not con|tinue | in my | sight.

13   Morning by morning will I | put to | silence ▪‿
      all the | wicked | in the | land,

14   To cut off from the | city · of the | Lord ▪‿
      all | those who | practise | evil.

Psalm 102

1   O Lord, | hear my | prayer ▪
      and let my | crying | come be|fore you.

2   Hide not your | face | from me ▪
      in the | day of | my dis|tress.

3.   Incline your | ear to | me; ▪
      when I | call, make | haste to | answer me,

4   For my days are con|sumed in | smoke ▪
      and my bones burn a|way as | in a | furnace.

5   My heart is smitten down and | withered like | grass, ▪
      so that I for|get to | eat my | bread.

6.   From the | sound of my | groaning ▪
      my | bones cleave | fast to my | skin.

7   I am become like a | vulture · in the | wilderness, ▪
      like an | owl that | haunts the | ruins.

8   I ǀ keep ǀ watch ▪
    and am become like a sparrow ǀ
        solitary upǀon the ǀ housetop.

9. My enemies revile me ǀ all the day ǀ long, ▪
    and those who rage at me have ǀ sworn toǀgether aǀgainst me.

10 I have eaten ǀ ashes for ǀ bread ▪
    and ǀ mingled my ǀ drink with ǀ weeping,

11 Because of your indigǀnation and ǀ wrath, ▪
    for you have taken me ǀ up and ǀ cast me ǀ down.

12. My days fade aǀway · like a ǀ shadow, ▪
    and ǀ I am ǀ withered like ǀ grass.

13 But you, O Lord, shall enǀdure for ǀ ever ▪
    and your ǀ name through ǀ all · geneǀrations.

14 You will arise and have ǀ pity on ǀ Zion; ▪
    it is time to have mercy upon her; ǀ
        surely the ǀ time has ǀ come.

15† For your servants love her ǀ very ǀ stones ▪
    and feel comǀpassion ǀ for her ǀ dust.

16 Then shall the nations fear your ǀ name, O ǀ Lord, ▪
    and all the ǀ kings · of the ǀ earth your ǀ glory,

17 When the Lord has ǀ built up ǀ Zion ▪
    and ǀ shown himǀself in ǀ glory;

18. When he has turned to the ǀ prayer · of the ǀ destitute ▪
    and has ǀ not desǀpised their ǀ plea.

19 This shall be written for ǀ those · that come ǀ after, ▪
    and a people yet unǀborn shall ǀ praise the ǀ Lord.

20 For he has looked down from his ǀ holy ǀ height; ▪
    from the heavens ǀ he beǀheld the ǀ earth,

21. That he might hear the ǀ sighings · of the ǀ prisoner ▪
    and set free ǀ those conǀdemned to ǀ die;

22 That the name of the Lord may be proǀclaimed in ǀ Zion ▪
    and his ǀ praises ǀ in Jeǀrusalem,

23. When peoples are ǀ gathered toǀgether ▪
    and kingdoms ǀ also, to ǀ serve the ǀ Lord.

24 He has brought down my | strength · in my | journey ▪
and has | shortened | my | days.

25. I pray, 'O my God, do not take me in the | midst of my | days; ▪
your years endure through|out all | gene|rations.

26 'In the beginning you laid the foun|dations · of the | earth, ▪
and the | heavens · are the | work of your | hands;

27 'They shall perish, but | you · will en|dure; ▪
they all shall | wear out | like a | garment.

28 'You change them like clothing, and | they · shall be | changed; ▪
but you are the same, | and your | years · will not | fail.

29 'The children of your servants | shall con|tinue, ▪
and their descendants shall be es|tablished | in your | sight.'

Psalm 103

1 Bless the Lord, | O my | soul, ▪
and all that is within me | bless his | holy | name.

2. Bless the Lord, | O my | soul, ▪
and for|get not | all his | benefits;

3 Who forgives | all your | sins ▪
and | heals all | your in|firmities;

4 Who redeems your | life · from the | Pit ▪
and crowns you with | faithful | love · and com|passion;

5† Who satisfies | you with | good things, ▪
so that your | youth is re|newed · like an | eagle's.

6 The Lord | executes | righteousness ▪
and judgment for | all who | are op|pressed.

7 He made his ways | known to | Moses ▪
and his | works · to the | children of | Israel.

8. The Lord is full of com|passion and | mercy, ▪
slow to anger | and of | great | kindness.

9 He will not | always ac|cuse us, ▪
neither will he | keep his | anger for | ever.

10† He has not dealt with us ac|cording · to our | sins, ▪
nor rewarded us ac|cording | to our | wickedness.

11 For as the heavens are high a|bove the | earth, ▪
so great is his | mercy · upon | those who | fear him.

12. As far as the east is | from the | west, ▪
so far has he | set our | sins | from us.

13 As a father has com|passion · on his | children, ▪
so is the Lord merciful to|wards | those who | fear him.

14. For he knows of what | we are | made; ▪
he re|members · that we | are but | dust.

15 Our days are | but as | grass; ▪
we | flourish · as a | flower of the | field;

16 For as soon as the wind goes over it, | it is | gone, ▪
and its | place shall | know it no | more.

17 But the merciful goodness of the Lord is from of old
  and endures for ever on | those who | fear him, ▪
and his | righteousness on | children's | children;

18. On those who | keep his | covenant ▪
and re|member · his com|mandments to | do them.

19 The Lord has established his | throne in | heaven, ▪
and his kingdom has do|minion | over | all.

20 Bless the Lord, you | angels of | his, ▪
you mighty ones who do his bidding
  and | hearken · to the | voice of his | word.

21 Bless the Lord, all | you his | hosts, ▪
you ministers of | his who | do his | will.

22 Bless the Lord, all you works of his,
  in all places of | his do|minion; ▪
bless the | Lord, | O my | soul.

Psalm 104

1 Bless the Lord, | O my | soul. ▪
O Lord my God, how | excellent | is your | greatness!

2. You are clothed with | majesty and | honour, ▪
wrapped in | light as | in a | garment.

3   You spread out the heavens ǀ like a ǀ curtain ∎
     and lay the beams of your dwelling place ǀ in the ǀ waters aǀbove.

4   You make the ǀ clouds your ǀ chariot ∎
     and ǀ ride on the ǀ wings · of the ǀ wind.

5.   You make the ǀ winds your ǀ messengers ∎
     and ǀ flames of ǀ fire your ǀ servants.

6   You laid the founǀdations · of the ǀ earth, ∎
     that it never should ǀ move at ǀ any ǀ time.

7.   You covered it with the ǀ deep · like a ǀ garment; ∎
     the waters stood ǀ high aǀbove the ǀ hills.

8   At your reǀbuke they ǀ fled; ∎
     at the voice of your ǀ thunder they ǀ hastened aǀway.

9   They rose up to the hills and flowed down to the ǀ valleys beǀneath, ∎
     to the place which ǀ you · had apǀpointed ǀ for them.

10. You have set them their bounds that they ǀ should not ǀ pass, ∎
     nor turn aǀgain to ǀ cover the ǀ earth.

11   You send the springs ǀ into the ǀ brooks, ∎
     which ǀ run aǀmong the ǀ hills.

12   They give drink to every ǀ beast · of the ǀ field, ∎
     and the wild ǀ asses ǀ quench their ǀ thirst.

13. Beside them the birds of the air ǀ make their ǀ nests ∎
     and ǀ sing aǀmong the ǀ branches.

14   You water the hills from your ǀ dwelling on ǀ high; ∎
     the earth is ǀ filled · with the ǀ fruit of your ǀ works.

15   You make grass to ǀ grow · for the ǀ cattle ∎
     and ǀ plants to ǀ meet our ǀ needs,

16   Bringing forth ǀ food · from the ǀ earth ∎
     and ǀ wine to ǀ gladden our ǀ hearts,

17† Oil to give us a ǀ cheerful ǀ countenance ∎
     and ǀ bread to ǀ strengthen our ǀ hearts.

18   The trees of the Lord are ǀ full of ǀ sap, ∎
     the cedars of ǀ Lebanon ǀ which he ǀ planted,

19   In which the birds ǀ build their ǀ nests, ∎
     while the fir trees are a ǀ dwelling ǀ for the ǀ stork.

20† The mountains are a refuge for the | wild | goats ▪
and the | stony | cliffs · for the | conies.

21 You appointed the moon to | mark the | seasons, ▪
and the sun | knows the | time · for its | setting.

22 You make darkness that it | may be | night, ▪
in which all the beasts of the | forest | creep | forth.

23 The lions | roar · for their | prey ▪
and | seek their | food from | God.

24 The sun rises and | they are | gone ▪
to lay themselves | down | in their | dens.

25† People go | forth · to their | work ▪
and to their | labour un|til the | evening.

26 O Lord, how manifold | are your | works! ▪
In wisdom you have made them all;
the | earth is | full · of your | creatures.

27 There is the sea, spread | far and | wide, ▪
and there move creatures beyond | number, both | small and | great.

28. There go the ships, and there is | that Le|viathan ▪
which you have | made to | play · in the | deep.

29 All of these | look to | you ▪
to give them their | food in | due | season.

30 When you give it | them, they | gather it; ▪
you open your hand and | they are | filled with | good.

31 When you hide your face | they are | troubled; ▪
when you take away their breath,
they die and re|turn a|gain · to the | dust.

32† When you send forth your spirit, they | are cre|ated, ▪
and you re|new the | face · of the | earth.

33 May the glory of the Lord en|dure for | ever; ▪
may the | Lord re|joice · in his | works;

34. He looks on the | earth · and it | trembles; ▪
he touches the | mountains | and they | smoke.

35 I will sing to the Lord as | long as I | live; ▪
I will make music to my God | while I | have my | being.

36   So shall my | song | please him ▪
       while I re|joice | in the | Lord.

37   Let sinners be consumed | out of the | earth ▪
       and the | wicked | be no | more.

37a   Bless the Lord, | O my | soul. ▪
       Alle|luia, | Alle|luia.

Psalm 105

1   O give thanks to the Lord and | call up·on his | name; ▪
       make known his | deeds a|mong the | peoples.

2.   Sing to | him, sing | praises, ▪
       and tell of | all his | marvellous | works.

3   Rejoice in the praise of his | holy | name; ▪
       let the hearts of them re|joice who | seek the | Lord.

4,5. Seek the Lord and his strength;
         seek his | face con|tinually. ▪
       Remember the marvels he has done,
         his wonders and the | judgments | of his | mouth,

6   O seed of | Abraham his | servant, ▪
       O | children of | Jacob his | chosen.

7   He is the | Lord our | God; ▪
       his | judgments · are in | all the | earth.

8   He has always been | mindful · of his | covenant, ▪
       the promise that he made for a | thousand | gene|rations:

9   The covenant he | made with | Abraham, ▪
       the | oath · that he | swore to | Isaac,

10   Which he established as a | statute for | Jacob, ▪
       an everlasting | coven|ant for | Israel,

11.   Saying, 'To you will I give the | land of | Canaan ▪
       to be the | portion of | your in|heritance.'

12   When they were but | few in | number, ▪
       of little account, and | sojourners | in the | land,

13   Wandering from | nation to | nation, ▪
       from one | kingdom · to an|other | people,

14   He suffered no one to | do them | wrong ▪
       and rebuked even | kings | for their | sake,

15. Saying, 'Touch not | my a|nointed ∎
and | do my | prophets no | harm.'

16 Then he called down famine | over the | land ∎
and broke | every | staff of | bread.

17 But he had sent a | man be|fore them, ∎
Joseph, | who was | sold · as a | slave.

18 They shackled his | feet with | fetters; ∎
his | neck was | ringed with | iron.

19. Until all he foretold | came to | pass, ∎
the | word · of the | Lord | tested him.

20 The king sent | and re|leased him; ∎
the ruler of | peoples | set him | free.

21 He appointed him | lord · of his | household ∎
and | ruler of | all · he pos|sessed,

22† To instruct his princes | as he | willed ∎
and to | teach his | counsellors | wisdom.

23 Then Israel | came · into | Egypt; ∎
Jacob | sojourned · in the | land of | Ham.

24 And the Lord made his people ex|ceedingly | fruitful; ∎
he made them too | many | for their | adversaries,

25† Whose heart he turned, so that they | hated his | people ∎
and dealt | craftily | with his | servants.

26 Then sent he | Moses his | servant ∎
and | Aaron whom | he had | chosen.

27 He showed his signs | through their | word ∎
and his wonders | in the | land of | Ham.

28. He sent darkness and | it grew | dark; ∎
yet they | did not | heed his | words.

29 He turned their waters | into | blood ∎
and | slew | all their | fish.

30 Their land | swarmed with | frogs, ∎
even | in their | kings' | chambers.

31 He spoke the word, and there came | clouds of | flies, ∎
swarms of | gnats within | all their | borders.

32. He gave them | hailstones for | rain ▪
    and flames of | lightning | in their | land.

33 He blasted their vines | and their | fig trees ▪
    and shattered | trees a|cross their | country.

34 He spoke the word, and the | grasshoppers | came ▪
    and young | locusts | without | number;

35 They ate every | plant in their | land ▪
    and de|voured the | fruit of their | soil.

36† He smote all the firstborn | in their | land, ▪
    the | first fruits of | all their | strength.

37 Then he brought them out with | silver and | gold; ▪
    there was not one a|mong their | tribes that | stumbled.

38 Egypt was glad at | their de|parting, ▪
    for a | dread of them had | fallen up|on them.

39. He spread out a | cloud · for a | covering ▪
    and a | fire to | light up the | night.

40 They asked and he | brought them | quails; ▪
    he satisfied them | with the | bread of | heaven.

41 He opened the rock, and the waters | gushed | out ▪
    and ran in the dry | places | like a | river.

42 For he remembered his | holy | word ▪
    and | Abra|ham, his | servant.

43. So he brought forth his | people with | joy, ▪
    his | chosen | ones with | singing.

44 He gave them the | lands · of the | nations ▪
    and they took pos|session · of the | fruit of their | toil,

45† That they might | keep his | statutes ▪
    and faithfully observe his | laws. | Alle|luia.

Psalm 106

1   Alleluia.
        Give thanks to the Lord, for | he is | gracious, ▪
    for his | faithfulness en|dures for | ever.

2   Who can express the mighty | acts · of the | Lord ▪
    or | show forth | all his | praise?

3.   Blessed are those who ob|serve · what is | right ▪
     and | always | do · what is | just.

4   Remember me, O Lord, in the favour you | bear · for your | people; ▪
     visit me in the | day of | your sal|vation;

5†   That I may see the prosperity of your chosen
       and rejoice in the | gladness · of your | people, ▪
     and ex|ult with | your in|heritance.

6   We have | sinned · like our | forebears; ▪
     we have done | wrong and | dealt | wickedly.

7   In Egypt they did not consider your wonders,
       nor remember the abundance of your | faithful | love; ▪
     they rebelled against the Most | High · at the | Red | Sea.

8.   But he saved them for his | name's | sake, ▪
     that he might | make his | power · to be | known.

9   He rebuked the Red Sea and it was | dried | up; ▪
     so he led them through the | deep as | through the | wilderness.

10   He saved them from the | adversary's | hand ▪
     and redeemed them | from the | hand · of the | enemy.

11   As for those that troubled them, the waters | over|whelmed them; ▪
     there | was not | one of them | left.

12†   Then they be|lieved his | words ▪
     and | sang a|loud his | praise.

13   But soon they for|got his | deeds ▪
     and | would not | wait · for his | counsel.

14   A craving | seized them · in the | wilderness, ▪
     and they put | God · to the | test · in the | desert.

15   He gave them | their de|sire, ▪
     but sent a | wasting | sickness a|mong them.

16.   They grew jealous of | Moses · in the | camp ▪
     and of Aaron, the | holy one | of the | Lord.

17   So the earth opened and | swallowed up | Dathan ▪
     and covered the | company | of A|biram.

18   A fire was | kindled · in their | company; ▪
     the | flame burnt | up the | wicked.

19   They made a ˅ calf at ˅ Horeb ▪
      and ˅ worshipped the ˅ molten ˅ image;

20.   Thus they ex˙changed their ˅ glory ▪
      for the image of an ˅ ox that ˅ feeds on ˅ hay.

21   They forgot ˅ God their ˅ saviour, ▪
      who had done such ˅ great ˅ things in ˅ Egypt,

22   Wonderful deeds in the ˅ land of ˅ Ham ▪
      and fearful things ˅ at the ˅ Red ˅ Sea.

23†   So he would have destroyed them,
         had not Moses his chosen stood before him ˅ in the ˅ breach, ▪
      to turn a˙way his ˅ wrath · from con˙suming them.

24   Then they scorned the ˅ Promised ˅ Land ▪
      and ˅ would not be˙lieve his ˅ word,

25   But ˅ murmured · in their ˅ tents ▪
      and would not ˅ heed the ˅ voice · of the ˅ Lord.

26   So he lifted his ˅ hand a˙gainst them ▪
      and swore to over˙throw them ˅ in the ˅ wilderness,

27.   To disperse their descendants a˙mong the ˅ nations, ▪
      and to ˅ scatter them through˙out the ˅ lands.

28   They joined themselves to the ˅ Baal of ˅ Peor ▪
      and ate sacrifices ˅ offered ˅ to the ˅ dead.

29   They provoked him to anger with their ˅ evil ˅ deeds ▪
      and a ˅ plague broke ˅ out a˙mong them.

30   Then Phinehas stood up and ˅ inter˙ceded ▪
      and ˅ so the ˅ plague was ˅ stayed.

31.   This was counted to ˅ him for ˅ righteousness ▪
      throughout all ˅ gene˙rations for ˅ ever.

32   They angered him also at the ˅ waters of ˅ Meribah, ▪
      so that Moses ˅ suffered ˅ for their ˅ sake;

33.   For they so em˙bittered his ˅ spirit ▪
      that he spoke ˅ rash words ˅ with his ˅ lips.

34   They did not des˙troy the ˅ peoples ▪
      as the ˅ Lord ˅ had com˙manded them.

35   They ˅ mingled · with the ˅ nations ▪
      and ˅ learned to ˅ follow their ˅ ways,

36 So that they | worshipped their | idols, ▪
   which be|came to | them a | snare.

37 Their own | sons and | daughters ▪
   they | sacrificed to | evil | spirits.

38 They shed | innocent | blood, ▪
   the | blood · of their | sons and | daughters,

39. Which they offered to the | idols of | Canaan, ▪
   and the | land · was de|filed with | blood.

40 Thus were they pol|luted · by their | actions, ▪
   and in their wanton deeds went | whoring · after | other | gods.

41 Therefore was the wrath of the Lord kindled a|gainst his | people, ▪
   and he ab|horred | his in|heritance.

42 He gave them over to the | hand · of the | nations, ▪
   and those who | hated | them ruled | over them.

43. So their | enemies op|pressed them ▪
   and put them in sub|jection | under their | hand.

44 Many a time did he deliver them,
      but they rebelled through their | own de|vices ▪
   and were | brought down | through their | wickedness.

45. Nevertheless, he | saw · their ad|versity, ▪
   when he | heard their | lamen|tation.

46 He remembered his | covenant | with them ▪
   and relented according to the | greatness · of his | faithful | love.

47. He made them | also · to be | pitied ▪
   by | all · who had | taken them | captive.

48 Save us, O | Lord our | God, ▪
   and gather us | from a|mong the | nations,

48a that we may give thanks to your | holy | name ▪
   and | glory | in your | praise.

49 Blessed be the Lord, the | God of | Israel, ▪
   from everlasting | and to | ever|lasting;

49a And let all the | people | say, ▪
   A|men. | Alle|luia.

1   O give thanks to the Lord, for | he is | gracious, ▪
for his steadfast | love en|dures for | ever.

2   Let the redeemed of the | Lord | say this, ▪
those he re|deemed · from the | hand of the | enemy,

3† And gathered out of the lands
       from the east and | from the | west, ▪
from the | north and | from the | south.

4   Some went astray in | desert | wastes ▪
and found no | path · to a | city to | dwell in.

5   Hungry | and | thirsty, ▪
their | soul was | fainting with|in them.

6   So they cried to the | Lord · in their | trouble ▪
and he de|livered them from | their dis|tress.

7.   He set their feet on the | right | way ▪
till they | came · to a | city to | dwell in.

8   *Let them give thanks to the | Lord · for his | goodness ▪*
and the | wonders he | does · for his | children.

9.   *For he satisfies the | longing | soul ▪*
and fills the | hungry | soul with | good.

10   Some sat in darkness and in the | shadow of | death, ▪
bound | fast in | misery and | iron,

11   For they had rebelled against the | words of | God ▪
and despised the | counsel · of the | Most | High.

12   So he bowed down their | heart with | heaviness; ▪
they stumbled and | there was | none to | help them.

13   Then they cried to the | Lord · in their | trouble, ▪
and he de|livered them from | their dis|tress.

14† He brought them out of darkness and out of the | shadow of | death, ▪
and | broke their | bonds a|sunder.

15   *Let them give thanks to the | Lord · for his | goodness ▪*
and the | wonders he | does · for his | children.

16   *For he has broken the | doors of | bronze ▪*
      and breaks the | bars of | iron in | pieces.

17   Some were foolish and took a re|bellious | way, ▪
      and were | plagued be|cause of | their wrongdoing.

18   Their soul abhorred all | manner of | food ▪
      and drew | near · to the | gates of | death.

19   Then they cried to the | Lord · in their | trouble, ▪
      and he de|livered them from | their dis|tress.

20.   He sent forth his | word and | healed them, ▪
      and | saved them | from des|truction.

21   *Let them give thanks to the | Lord · for his | goodness ▪*
      and the | wonders he | does · for his | children.

22.   *Let them offer him | sacrifices of | thanksgiving ▪*
      and tell of his | acts with | shouts of | joy.

23   Those who go down to the | sea in | ships ▪
      and ply their | trade in | great | waters,

24.   These have seen the | works · of the | Lord ▪
      and his | wonders | in the | deep.

25   For at his word the stormy | wind a|rose ▪
      and lifted | up the | waves of the | sea.

26   They were carried up to the heavens
          and down a|gain · to the | deep; ▪
      their soul | melted a|way · in their | peril.

27.   They reeled and | staggered · like a | drunkard ▪
      and were | at their | wits' | end.

28   Then they cried to the | Lord · in their | trouble, ▪
      and he brought them | out of | their dis|tress.

29   He made the | storm be | still ▪
      and the | waves of the | sea were | calmed.

30   Then were they glad because they | were at | rest, ▪
      and he brought them to the | haven | they de|sired.

31   *Let them give thanks to the | Lord · for his | goodness ▪*
      and the | wonders he | does · for his | children.

32. *Let them exalt him in the congre|gation · of the | people ▪*
    and praise him in the | council | of the | elders.

33. The Lord turns rivers | into | wilderness ▪
    and water springs | into | thirsty | ground;

34. A fruitful land he makes a | salty | waste, ▪
    because of the | wickedness of | those who | dwell there.

35. He makes the wilderness a | pool of | water ▪
    and water springs | out · of a | thirsty | land.

36. There he | settles the | hungry ▪
    and they | build a | city to | dwell in.

37. They sow fields and | plant | vineyards ▪
    and bring | in a | fruitful | harvest.

38. He blesses them, so that they | multiply | greatly; ▪
    he does not let their | herds of | cattle de|crease.

39. He pours con|tempt on | princes ▪
    and makes them | wander in | trackless | wastes.

40. They are diminished and | brought | low, ▪
    through | stress · of mis|fortune and | sorrow,

41† But he raises the | poor · from their | misery ▪
    and multiplies their | families like | flocks of | sheep.

42. The upright will see this | and re|joice, ▪
    but all | wickedness will | shut its | mouth.

43. Whoever is wise will | ponder these | things ▪
    and consider the loving|kindness | of the | Lord.

Psalm 108

1   My heart is ready, O God, my | heart is | ready; ▪
    I will | sing and | give you | praise.

2. Awake, my soul; awake, | harp and | lyre, ▪
    that I | may a|waken the | dawn.

3   I will give you thanks, O Lord, a|mong the | peoples; ▪
    I will sing praise to | you a|mong the | nations.

4. For your loving-kindness is as | high as the | heavens ▪
    and your faithfulness | reaches | to the | clouds.

5   Be exalted, O God, a|bove the | heavens ▪
      and your glory | over | all the | earth.

6.   That your beloved may | be de|livered, ▪
      save us by | your right | hand and | answer me.

7   God has spoken | in his | holiness: ▪
      'I will triumph and divide Shechem
          and share | out the | valley of | Succoth.

8   'Gilead is mine and Ma|nasseh is | mine; ▪
      Ephraim is my | helmet and | Judah my | sceptre.

9†   'Moab shall be my wash pot,
          over Edom will I | cast my | sandal, ▪
      across Philistia | will I | shout in | triumph.'

10   Who will lead me into the | strong | city? ▪
      Who will | bring me | into | Edom?

11. Have you not cast us | off, O | God? ▪
      Will you no longer go | forth | with our | troops?

12   O grant us your help a|gainst the | enemy, ▪
      for | earthly | help · is in | vain.

13   Through God will we | do great | acts, ▪
      for it is he that | shall tread | down our | enemies.

Psalm 109

1.   Keep silent no longer, O | God of my | praise, ▪
      for the mouth of wickedness and | treachery is | opened a|gainst me.

2   They have spoken against me with a | lying | tongue; ▪
      they encompassed me with words of hatred
          and fought a|gainst me with|out a | cause.

3   In return for my love, they set them|selves a|gainst me, ▪
      even though | I had | prayed for | them.

4.   Thus have they repaid me with | evil for | good, ▪
      and | hatred for | my good | will.

5   They say, 'Appoint a | wicked man | over him, ▪
      and let an accuser | stand at his | right | hand.

6. 'When he is judged, let | him be found | guilty, ▪
    and let his | prayer be | counted as | sin.

7   'Let his | days be | few ▪
    and let an|other | take his | office.

8   'Let his | children be | fatherless ▪
    and his | wife be|come a | widow.

9   'Let his children wander to | beg their | bread; ▪
    let them | seek it in | desolate | places.

10 'Let the creditor seize | all · that he | has; ▪
    let strangers | plunder the | fruit · of his | toil.

11 'Let there be no one to keep | faith | with him, ▪
    or have compassion | on his | fatherless | children.

12 'Let his line soon | come · to an | end ▪
    and his name be blotted | out · in the | next · gene|ration.

13 'Let the wickedness of his fathers be remembered be|fore the | Lord, ▪
    and no sin of his | mother be | blotted | out;

14 'Let their sin be always be|fore the | Lord, ▪
    that he may | root out their | name · from the | earth;

15 'Because he was not minded to | keep | faith, ▪
    but persecuted the poor and needy
        and sought to | kill the | broken|hearted.

16 'He loved cursing | and it | came to him; ▪
    he took no delight in | blessing | and it was | far from him.

17 'He clothed himself with cursing | as · with a | garment: ▪
    it seeped into his body like water
        and | into his | bones like | oil;

18 'Let it be to him like the cloak which he | wraps a|round him ▪
    and like the | belt · that he | wears con|tinually.'

19† Thus may the Lord re|pay · my ac|cusers ▪
    and | those · who speak | evil a|gainst me.

20 But deal with me, O Lord my God, ac|cording · to your | name; ▪
    O de|liver me, for | sweet · is your | faithfulness.

21 For I am | helpless and | poor ▪
    and my | heart · is dis|quieted with|in me.

22   I fade like a | shadow that | lengthens; ▪
        I am | shaken | off · like a | locust.

23   My knees are | weak through | fasting ▪
        and my | flesh is dried | up and | wasted.

24†   I have become a re|proach to | them; ▪
        those who see me | shake their | heads in | scorn.

25   Help me, O | Lord my | God; ▪
        save me for your | loving | mercy's | sake,

26   And they shall know that | this is your | hand, ▪
        that | you, O | Lord, have | done it.

27.   Though they curse, | may you | bless; ▪
        let those who rise up against me be confounded,
            but | let your | servant re|joice.

28   Let my accusers be | clothed · with dis|grace ▪
        and wrap themselves in their | shame as | in a | cloak.

29   I will give great thanks to the | Lord · with my | mouth; ▪
        in the midst of the | multitude | will I | praise him;

30   Because he has stood at the right hand | of the | needy, ▪
        to save them from | those who | would con|demn them.

Psalm 110

1   The Lord said to my lord, | 'Sit at my | right hand, ▪
        until I | make your | enemies your | footstool.'

2.   May the Lord stretch forth the | sceptre · of your | power; ▪
        rule from Zion | in the | midst · of your | enemies.

3   'Noble are you on this | day of your | birth; ▪
        on the holy mountain, from the womb of the dawn
            the dew of your | new birth | is up|on you.'

4.   The Lord has sworn and | will not re|tract: ▪
        'You are a priest for ever after the | order | of Mel|chizedek.'

5   The king at your | right hand, O | Lord, ▪
        shall smite down | kings · in the | day of his | wrath.

6   In all his majesty, he shall judge a|mong the | nations, ▪
        smiting heads over | all the | wide | earth.

7†   He shall drink from the brook be|side the | way; ▪
        therefore | shall he lift | high his | head.

1   Alleluia.

       I will give thanks to the Lord with my | whole | heart, ▪
in the company of the faithful and | in the | congre|gation.

2   The works of the | Lord are | great, ▪
sought | out by | all · who de|light in them.

3.   His work is full of | majesty and | honour ▪
and his | righteousness en|dures for | ever.

4   He appointed a memorial for his | marvellous | deeds; ▪
the Lord is | gracious and | full of com|passion.

5   He gave food to | those who | feared him; ▪
he is ever | mindful | of his | covenant.

6.   He showed his people the | power · of his | works ▪
in giving them the | heritage | of the | nations.

7   The works of his hands are | truth and | justice; ▪
all | his com|mandments are | sure.

8   They stand fast for | ever and | ever; ▪
they are | done in | truth and | equity.

9.   He sent redemption to his people;
       he commanded his | covenant for | ever; ▪
holy and | awesome | is his | name.

10   The fear of the Lord is the beginning of wisdom;
       a good understanding have | those who | live by it; ▪
his | praise en|dures for | ever.

1   Alleluia.

       Blessed are those who | fear the | Lord ▪
and have great de|light in | his com|mandments.

2   Their descendants will be | mighty · in the | land, ▪
a generation of the | faithful that | will be | blest.

3.   Wealth and riches will be | in their | house, ▪
and their | righteousness en|dures for | ever.

4   Light shines in the darkness | for the | upright; ▪
gracious and full of com|passion | are the | righteous.

5   It goes well with those who are | generous in | lending ▪
     and order | their af|fairs with | justice,

6.   For they will | never be | shaken; ▪
     the righteous will be held in | ever|lasting re|membrance.

7   They will not be afraid of any | evil | tidings; ▪
     their heart is steadfast, | trusting | in the | Lord.

8   Their heart is sustained and | will not | fear, ▪
     until they see the | downfall | of their | foes.

9.   They have given freely to the poor;
         their righteousness stands | fast for | ever; ▪
     their head will | be ex|alted with | honour.

10   The wicked shall see it and be angry;
         they shall gnash their | teeth · in des|pair; ▪
     the de|sire · of the | wicked shall | perish.

Psalm 113

1.   Alleluia.
         Give praise, you | servants · of the | Lord, ▪
     O | praise the | name · of the | Lord.

2   Blessed be the | name · of the | Lord, ▪
     from this time | forth · and for | ever|more.

3.   From the rising of the | sun · to its | setting ▪
     let the | name · of the | Lord be | praised.

4   The Lord is high a|bove all | nations ▪
     and his | glory a|bove the | heavens.

5   Who is like the | Lord our | God, ▪
     that | has his | throne so | high,

5a. Yet humbles him|self · to be|hold ▪
     the | things of | heaven and | earth?

6   He raises the | poor · from the | dust ▪
     and lifts the | needy | from the | ashes,

7   To | set them with | princes, ▪
     with the | princes | of his | people.

8   He gives the barren woman a | place in the | house ▪
     and makes her a joyful mother of | children. | Alle|luia.

1,2   When Israel came out of Egypt,
       the house of Jacob from a people of a | strange | tongue, ▪
   Judah became his sanctuary,
       | Israel | his do|minion.

3,4.   The sea saw that, and fled;
       Jordan was | driven | back. ▪
   The mountains skipped like rams,
       the little | hills like | young | sheep.

5   What ailed you, O | sea, · that you | fled? ▪
   O Jordan, that | you were | driven | back?

6   You mountains, that you | skipped like | rams, ▪
   you little | hills like | young | sheep?

7   Tremble, O earth, at the | presence · of the | Lord, ▪
   at the | presence · of the | God of | Jacob,

8   Who turns the hard rock into a | pool of | water, ▪
   the flint-stone | into a | springing | well.

Psalm 115

1   Not to us, Lord, not to us,
       but to your name | give the | glory, ▪
   for the sake of your | loving | mercy and | truth.

2.   Why should the | nations | say, ▪
   'Where is | now | their | God?'

3   As for our God, | he is in | heaven; ▪
   he | does what|ever he | pleases.

4   Their idols are | silver and | gold, ▪
   the | work of | human | hands.

5   They have mouths, but | cannot | speak; ▪
   eyes have | they, but | cannot | see;

6   They have ears, but | cannot | hear; ▪
   noses have | they, but | cannot | smell;

7   They have hands, but cannot feel;
       feet have they, but | cannot | walk; ▪
   not a whisper | do they | make · from their | throats.

8.   Those who make them I shall be¦come like them ∎
     and so will I all who I put their I trust in them.

9   But you, Israel, put your I trust · in the I Lord; ∎
     he is their I help I and their I shield.

10   House of Aaron, I trust · in the I Lord; ∎
     he is their I help I and their I shield.

11.   You that fear the Lord, I trust · in the I Lord; ∎
     he is their I help I and their I shield.

12   The Lord has been mindful of us and I he will I bless us; ∎
     may he bless the house of Israel;
        may he I bless the I house of I Aaron;

13   May he bless those who I fear the I Lord, ∎
     both I small and I great to¦gether.

14   May the Lord increase you I more and I more, ∎
     you I and your I children I after you.

15.   May you be I blest · by the I Lord, ∎
     the I maker of I heaven and I earth.

16   The heavens are the I heavens · of the I Lord, ∎
     but the earth he has en¦trusted I to his I children.

17   The dead do not I praise the I Lord, ∎
     nor I those gone I down into I silence;

18   But we will I bless the I Lord, ∎
     from this time forth for ever¦more. I Alle¦luia.

Psalm 116

1.   I love the Lord, for he has heard the voice of my I suppli¦cation; ∎
     because he inclined his ear to me
        on the I day I I called to I him.

2   The snares of death encompassed me;
        the pains of I hell took I hold of me; ∎
     by grief and I sorrow I was I I held.

3.   Then I called upon the I name · of the I Lord: ∎
     'O Lord, I I beg you, de¦liver my I soul.'

4   Gracious is the | Lord and | righteous; ▪
     our | God is | full of com|passion.

5   The Lord watches | over the | simple; ▪
     I was brought very | low | and he | saved me.

6   Turn again to your rest, | O my | soul, ▪
     for the | Lord · has been | gracious to | you.

7   For you have delivered my | soul from | death, ▪
     my eyes from | tears · and my | feet from | falling.

8.   I will walk be|fore the | Lord ▪
     in the | land | of the | living.

9   I believed that I should perish
       for I was | sorely | troubled; ▪
     and I said in my alarm, | 'Everyone | is a | liar.'

10.   How shall I re|pay the | Lord ▪
     for all the benefits | he has | given to | me?

11   I will lift up the | cup of sal|vation ▪
     and | call upon the | name · of the | Lord.

12   I will fulfil my | vows · to the | Lord ▪
     in the | presence of | all his | people.

13.   Precious in the | sight · of the | Lord ▪
     is the | death · of his | faithful | servants.

14   O Lord, | I am your | servant, ▪
     your servant, the child of your handmaid;
       you have | freed me | from my | bonds.

15   I will offer to you a | sacrifice of | thanksgiving ▪
     and | call upon the | name · of the | Lord.

16   I will fulfil my | vows · to the | Lord ▪
     in the | presence of | all his | people,

17†   In the courts of the | house · of the | Lord, ▪
     in the midst of you, O Je|rusalem. | Alle|luia.

Psalm 117

1   O praise the Lord, | all you | nations; ▪
     praise | him, | all you | peoples.

2   For great is his steadfast | love to|wards us, ▪
     and the faithfulness of the Lord endures for | ever. | Alle|luia.

1   O give thanks to the Lord, for ǀ he is ǀ good; ▪
his ǀ mercy enǀdures for ǀ ever.

2   Let Israel ǀ now proǀclaim, ▪
'His ǀ mercy enǀdures for ǀ ever.'

3   Let the house of Aaron ǀ now proǀclaim, ▪
'His ǀ mercy enǀdures for ǀ ever.'

4.   Let those who fear the ǀ Lord proǀclaim, ▪
'His ǀ mercy enǀdures for ǀ ever.'

5   In my constraint I ǀ called · to the ǀ Lord; ▪
the Lord ǀ answered and ǀ set me ǀ free.

6   The Lord is at my side; I ǀ will not ǀ fear; ▪
what can ǀ flesh ǀ do to ǀ me?

7.   With the Lord at my ǀ side · as my ǀ saviour, ▪
I shall see the ǀ downfall ǀ of my ǀ enemies.

8   It is better to take ǀ refuge · in the ǀ Lord ▪
than to put ǀ any ǀ confidence in ǀ flesh.

9.   It is better to take ǀ refuge · in the ǀ Lord ▪
than to put ǀ any ǀ confidence in ǀ princes.

10   All the ǀ nations enǀcompassed me, ▪
but by the name of the ǀ Lord I ǀ drove them ǀ back.

11   They hemmed me in, they hemmed me in on ǀ every ǀ side, ▪
but by the name of the ǀ Lord I ǀ drove them ǀ back.

12   They swarmed about me like bees;
they blazed like ǀ fire among ǀ thorns, ▪
but by the name of the ǀ Lord I ǀ drove them ǀ back.

13† Surely, I was ǀ thrust · to the ǀ brink, ▪
but the ǀ Lord ǀ came · to my ǀ help.

14   The Lord is my ǀ strength · and my ǀ song, ▪
and he has beǀcome ǀ my salǀvation.

15   Joyful ǀ shouts · of salǀvation ▪
sound ǀ from the ǀ tents · of the ǀ righteous:

16† 'The right hand of the Lord does mighty deeds;
the right hand of the Lord ǀ raises ǀ up; ▪
the right hand of the ǀ Lord does ǀ mighty ǀ deeds.'

17   I shall not | die, but | live ▪
      and de|clare the | works · of the | Lord.

18   The Lord has | punished me | sorely, ▪
      but he has not | given me | over to | death.

19   Open to me the | gates of | righteousness, ▪
      that I may | enter · and give | thanks · to the | Lord.

20.   This is the | gate · of the | Lord; ▪
      the | righteous shall | enter | through it.

21   I will give thanks to you, for | you have | answered me ▪
      and have be|come | my sal|vation.

22   The stone which the | builders re|jected ▪
      has be|come the | chief | cornerstone.

23†   This is the | Lord's | doing, ▪
      and it is | marvellous | in our | eyes.

24   This is the day that the | Lord has | made; ▪
      we will re|joice | and be | glad in it.

25.   Come, O Lord, and | save us we | pray. ▪
      Come, Lord, | send us | now pros|perity.

26   Blessed is he who comes in the | name · of the | Lord; ▪
      we | bless you · from the | house · of the | Lord.

27.   The Lord is God; he has | given us | light; ▪
      link the pilgrims with cords |
         right · to the | horns · of the | altar.

28   You are my God and | I will | thank you; ▪
      you are my | God and | I · will ex|alt you.

29   O give thanks to the Lord, for | he is | good; ▪
      his | mercy en|dures for | ever.

Psalm 119

    1 *Aleph*

1   Blessed are those whose | way is | pure, ▪
      who | walk · in the | law of the | Lord.

2   Blessed are those who | keep his | testimonies ▪
      and | seek him · with their | whole | heart,

3   Those who | do no | wickedness, ▪
     but | walk in | his | ways.

4   You, O | Lord, have | charged ▪
     that we should | diligently | keep · your com|mandments.

5   O that my ways were made | so di|rect ▪
     that | I might | keep your | statutes.

6   Then should I not be | put to | shame, ▪
     because I have re|gard for | all · your com|mandments.

7   I will thank you with an | unfeigned | heart, ▪
     when I have | learned your | righteous | judgments.

8   I will | keep your | statutes; ▪
     O for|sake me | not | utterly.

2 Beth

9   How shall young people | cleanse their | way ▪
     to keep themselves ac|cording | to your | word?

10   With my whole heart | have I | sought you; ▪
     O let me not go a|stray from | your com|mandments.

11   Your words have I hidden with|in my | heart, ▪
     that I | should not | sin a|gainst you.

12   Blessed are | you, O | Lord; ▪
     O | teach | me your | statutes.

13   With my lips have | I been | telling ▪
     of all the | judgments | of your | mouth.

14   I have taken greater delight in the | way of your | testimonies ▪
     than | in all | manner of | riches.

15   I will meditate on | your com|mandments ▪
     and | contem|plate your | ways.

16   My delight shall be | in your | statutes ▪
     and I will | not for|get your | word.

3 Gimel

17   O do good to your servant that | I may | live, ▪
     and | so · shall I | keep your | word.

18   Open my eyes, that | I may | see ▪
     the | wonders | of your | law.

19   I am a | stranger · upon | earth; ▪
     hide not | your com|mandments | from me.

20 My soul is con|sumed at | all times ▪
    with fervent | longing | for your | judgments.

21 You have re|buked the | arrogant; ▪
    cursed are those who | stray from | your com|mandments.

22 Turn from me | shame · and re|buke, ▪
    for | I have | kept your | testimonies.

23 Rulers also sit and | speak a|gainst me, ▪
    but your servant | meditates | on your | statutes.

24 For your testimonies are | my de|light; ▪
    they | are my | faithful | counsellors.

4 Daleth

25 My soul | cleaves · to the | dust; ▪
    O give me life ac|cording | to your | word.

26 I have acknowledged my ways and | you have | answered me; ▪
    O | teach | me your | statutes.

27 Make me understand the way of | your com|mandments, ▪
    and so shall I meditate | on your | wondrous | works.

28 My soul melts away in | tears of | sorrow; ▪
    raise me up ac|cording | to your | word.

29 Take from me the | way of | falsehood; ▪
    be | gracious to | me · through your | law.

30 I have chosen the | way of | truth ▪
    and your judgments | have I | laid be|fore me.

31 I hold | fast · to your | testimonies; ▪
    O Lord, let me | not be | put to | shame.

32 I will run the way of | your com|mandments, ▪
    when you have | set my | heart at | liberty.

5 He

33 Teach me, O Lord, the | way of your | statutes ▪
    and I shall | keep it | to the | end.

34 Give me understanding and I shall | keep your | law; ▪
    I shall | keep it · with my | whole | heart.

35 Lead me in the path of | your com|mandments, ▪
    for there|in is | my de|light.

36 Incline my | heart · to your | testimonies ▪
    and | not to | unjust | gain.

37 Turn away my eyes lest they | gaze on | vanities; ▪
    O | give me | life · in your | ways.

38 Confirm to your | servant your | promise, ▪
    which | stands for | all who | fear you.

39 Turn away the reproach | which I | dread, ▪
    be|cause your | judgments are | good.

40 Behold, I long for | your com|mandments; ▪
    in your | righteousness | give me | life.

6 *Waw*

41 Let your faithful love come unto | me, O | Lord, ▪
    even your salvation, ac|cording | to your | promise.

42   Then shall I answer | those who | taunt me, ▪
    for my | trust is | in your | word.

43 O take not the word of truth utterly | out of my | mouth, ▪
    for my | hope is | in your | judgments.

44 So shall I always | keep your | law; ▪
    I shall | keep it for | ever and | ever.

45 I will | walk at | liberty, ▪
    because I | study | your com|mandments.

46 I will tell of your testimonies, | even before | kings, ▪
    and I | will not | be a|shamed.

47 My delight shall | be in · your com|mandments, ▪
    which I | have | greatly | loved.

48 My hands will I lift up to your commandments, | which I | love, ▪
    and I will | meditate | on your | statutes.

7 *Zayin*

49 Remember your | word · to your | servant, ▪
    on which | you have | built my | hope.

50 This is my comfort | in my | trouble, ▪
    that your | promise | gives me | life.

51 The proud have de|rided me | cruelly, ▪
    but I have not | turned a|side from your | law.

52 I have remembered your everlasting | judgments, O | Lord, ▪
    and I | have | been | comforted.

53 I am seized with indig|nation · at the | wicked, ▪
    for | they · have for|saken your | law.

54 Your statutes have I been like I songs to me ▪
in the I house I of my I pilgrimage.

55 I have thought on your name in the I night, O I Lord, ▪
and I so · have I I kept your I law.

56 These blessings I have been I mine, ▪
for I I have I kept · your com|mandments.

8 Heth

57 You only are my I portion, O I Lord; ▪
I have I promised to I keep your I words.

58 I entreat you with I all my I heart, ▪
be merciful to me ac|cording I to your I promise.

59 I have con|sidered my I ways ▪
and turned my I feet I back · to your I testimonies.

60 I made haste and I did not de|lay ▪
to I keep I your com|mandments.

61 Though the cords of the I wicked en|tangle me, ▪
I do I not for|get your I law.

62 At midnight I will rise to I give you I thanks, ▪
be|cause of your I righteous I judgments.

63 I am a companion of all I those who I fear you, ▪
those who I keep I your com|mandments.

64 The earth, O Lord, is full of your I faithful I love; ▪
in|struct me I in your I statutes.

9 Teth

65 You have dealt graciously I with your I servant, ▪
ac|cording · to your I word, O I Lord.

66 O teach me true under|standing and I knowledge, ▪
for I have I trusted in I your com|mandments.

67 Before I was afflicted I I went a|stray, ▪
but I now I I keep your I word.

68 You are gracious I and do I good; ▪
O I Lord, I teach me your I statutes.

69 The proud have I smeared me with I lies, ▪
but I will keep your com| mandments · with my I whole I heart.

70 Their heart has become | gross with | fat, ▪
but my de|light is | in your | law.

71 It is good for me that I have | been af|flicted, ▪
that | I may | learn your | statutes.

72 The law of your mouth is | dearer to | me ▪
than a | hoard of | gold and | silver.

10 *Yodh*

73 Your hands have | made me and | fashioned me; ▪
give me understanding, that | I may | learn · your com|mandments.

74 Those who fear you will be glad | when they | see me, ▪
because | I have | hoped · in your | word.

75 I know, O Lord, that your | judgments are | right, ▪
and that in very faithfulness you | caused me | to be | troubled.

76 Let your faithful love | be my | comfort, ▪
according to your | promise | to your | servant.

77 Let your tender mercies come to me, that | I may | live, ▪
for your | law is | my de|light.

78 Let the proud be put to shame, for they | wrong me with | lies; ▪
but I will | meditate on | your com|mandments.

79 Let those who fear you | turn to | me, ▪
even | those who | know your | testimonies.

80 Let my heart be | sound · in your | statutes, ▪
that I may | not be | put to | shame.

11 *Kaph*

81 My soul is pining for | your sal|vation; ▪
I have | hoped | in your | word.

82 My eyes fail with | watching · for your | word, ▪
while I | say, 'O | when will you | comfort me?'

83 I have become like a wineskin | in the | smoke, ▪
yet I do | not for|get your | statutes.

84 How many are the | days of your | servant? ▪
When will you bring | judgment on | those who | persecute me?

85 The proud | have dug | pits for me ▪
in de|fiance | of your | law.

86 All your com|mandments are | true; ▪
help me, for they | persecute | me with | falsehood.

87 They had almost made an | end of me on | earth, ▪
but I have not for|saken | your com|mandments.

88 Give me life according to your | loving|kindness; ▪
so shall I keep the | testi·monies | of your | mouth.

12 *Lamedh*

89 O Lord, your word is | ever|lasting; ▪
it ever stands | firm | in the | heavens.

90 Your faithfulness also remains from one gene|ration · to an|other; ▪
you have established the | earth and | it a|bides.

91 So also your judgments stand | firm this | day, ▪
for | all things | are your | servants.

92 If your law had not been | my de|light, ▪
I should have | perished | in my | trouble.

93 I will never for|get · your com|mandments, ▪
for by | them · you have | given me | life.

94 I am | yours, O | save me! ▪
For | I have | sought · your com|mandments.

95 The wicked have waited for me | to des|troy me, ▪
but I will | meditate | on your | testimonies.

96 I have seen an end of | all per|fection, ▪
but your com|mandment | knows no | bounds.

13 *Mem*

97 Lord, how I | love your | law! ▪
All the day | long it | is my | study.

98 Your commandments have made me | wiser · than my | enemies, ▪
for | they are | ever | with me.

99 I have more understanding than | all my | teachers, ▪
for your testimonies | are my | medi|tation.

100 I am | wiser · than the | aged, ▪
be|cause I | keep · your com|mandments.

101 I restrain my feet from every | evil | way, ▪
that | I may | keep your | word.

102 I have not turned a|side · from your | judgments, ▪
for | you have | been my | teacher.

103 How sweet are your | words · on my | tongue! ▪
They are sweeter than | honey | to my | mouth.

104 Through your commandments I get | under|standing; ▪
therefore I | hate all | lying | ways.

14 *Nun*

105 Your word is a | lantern · to my | feet ▪
and a | light up|on my | path.

106 I have sworn and | will ful|fil it, ▪
to | keep your | righteous | judgments.

107 I am | troubled · above | measure; ▪
give me life, O Lord, ac|cording | to your | word.

108 Accept the freewill offering of my | mouth, O | Lord, ▪
and | teach | me your | judgments.

109 My soul is | ever · in my | hand, ▪
yet I do | not for|get your | law.

110 The wicked have | laid a | snare for me, ▪
but I have not | strayed from | your com|mandments.

111 Your testimonies have I claimed as my | heritage for | ever; ▪
for they are the | very | joy · of my | heart.

112 I have applied my heart to ful|fil your | statutes: ▪
always, | even | to the | end.

15 *Samekh*

113 I hate those who are | double|minded, ▪
but your | law | do I | love.

114 You are my hiding place | and my | shield ▪
and my | hope is | in your | word.

115 Away from | me, you | wicked! ▪
I will keep the com|mandments | of my | God.

116 Sustain me according to your promise, that | I may | live, ▪
and let me not be disap|pointed | in my | hope.

117 Hold me up and | I shall be | saved, ▪
and my delight shall be | ever | in your | statutes.

118   You set at nought those who de| part · from your | statutes, ▪
        for their de|ceiving | is in | vain.

119   You consider all the | wicked as | dross; ▪
        there|fore I | love your | testimonies.

120   My flesh | trembles for | fear of you ▪
        and | I am a|fraid · of your | judgments.

16 *Ayin*

121   I have done what is | just and | right; ▪
        O give me not | over to | my op|pressors.

122   Stand surety for your | servant's | good; ▪
        let | not the | proud op|press me.

123   My eyes fail with watching for | your sal|vation ▪
        and | for your | righteous | promise.

124   O deal with your servant according to your | faithful | love ▪
        and | teach | me your | statutes.

125   I am your servant; O grant me | under|standing, ▪
        that | I may | know your | testimonies.

126   It is time for you to | act, O | Lord, ▪
        for | they frus|trate your | law.

127   Therefore I | love · your com|mandments ▪
        above gold, | even | much fine | gold.

128   Therefore I direct my steps by | all your | precepts, ▪
        and all false | ways I | utterly ab|hor.

17 *Pe*

129   Your | testimonies are | wonderful; ▪
        there|fore my | soul | keeps them.

130   The opening of your | word gives | light; ▪
        it gives under|standing | to the | simple.

131   I open my mouth and | draw in my | breath, ▪
        as I | long for | your com|mandments.

132   Turn to me and be | gracious | to me, ▪
        as is your way with | those who | love your | name.

133   Order my | steps · by your | word, ▪
        and let no wickedness | have do|minion | over me.

134   Redeem me from | earthly op|pressors ▪
so that | I may | keep · your com|mandments.

135   Show the light of your countenance up|on your | servant ▪
and | teach | me your | statutes.

136   My eyes run down with | streams of | water, ▪
because the wicked | do not | keep your | law.

     18 *Tsadhe*

137   Righteous are | you, O | Lord, ▪
and | true | are your | judgments.

138   You have | ordered · your de|crees ▪
in | righteousness and | in great | faithfulness.

139   My indig|nation des|troys me, ▪
because my | adversaries for|get your | word.

140   Your word has been | tried · to the | uttermost ▪
and | so your | servant | loves it.

141   I am small and of | no · repu|tation, ▪
yet do I | not for|get · your com|mandments.

142   Your righteousness is an ever|lasting | righteousness ▪
and your | law | is the | truth.

143   Trouble and heaviness have taken | hold up|on me, ▪
yet my de|light · is in | your com|mandments.

144   The righteousness of your testimonies is | ever|lasting; ▪
O grant me under|standing and | I shall | live.

     19 *Qoph*

145   I call with my | whole | heart; ▪
answer me, O Lord, that | I may | keep your | statutes.

146   To you I | call, O | save me! ▪
And | I shall | keep your | testimonies.

147   Early in the morning I | cry to | you, ▪
for | in your | word · is my | trust.

148   My eyes are open before the | night | watches, ▪
that I may | meditate | on your | word.

149   Hear my voice, O Lord, according to your | faithful | love; ▪
according to your | judgment, | give me | life.

150   They draw near that in | malice | persecute me, ▪
who are | far | from your | law.

151   You, O Lord, are | near at | hand, ▪
     and | all · your com|mandments are | true.

152   Long have I | known · of your | testimonies, ▪
     that you have | founded | them for | ever.

20 Resh

153   O consider my af|fliction · and de|liver me, ▪
     for I do | not for|get your | law.

154   Plead my | cause · and re|deem me; ▪
     according to your | promise, | give me | life.

155   Salvation is | far · from the | wicked, ▪
     for they | do not | seek your | statutes.

156   Great is your com|passion, O | Lord; ▪
     give me life, ac|cording | to your | judgments.

157   Many there are that persecute | and op|press me, ▪
     yet do I not | swerve | from your | testimonies.

158   It grieves me when I | see the | treacherous, ▪
     for they | do not | keep your | word.

159   Consider, O Lord, how I | love · your com|mandments; ▪
     give me life ac|cording · to your | loving|kindness.

160   The sum of your | word is | truth, ▪
     and all your righteous judgments en|dure for | ever|more.

21 Shin

161   Princes have persecuted me with|out a | cause, ▪
     but my heart | stands in | awe of your | word.

162   I am as | glad of your | word ▪
     as | one who | finds great | spoils.

163   As for lies, I | hate · and ab|hor them, ▪
     but your | law | do I | love.

164   Seven times a day | do I | praise you, ▪
     be|cause of your | righteous | judgments.

165   Great peace have they who | love your | law; ▪
     nothing | shall | make them | stumble.

166   Lord, I have looked for | your sal|vation ▪
     and | I have ful|filled · your com|mandments.

167   My soul has | kept your | testimonies ▪
     and | greatly | have I | loved them.

168   I have kept your com|mandments and | testimonies, ▪
     for | all my | ways · are be|fore you.

    22 *Taw*

169   Let my cry come be|fore you, O | Lord; ▪
     give me understanding, ac|cording | to your | word.

170   Let my supplication | come be|fore you; ▪
     deliver me, ac|cording | to your | promise.

171   My lips shall pour | forth your | praise, ▪
     when | you have | taught me your | statutes.

172   My tongue shall | sing of your | word, ▪
     for | all · your com|mandments are | righteous.

173   Let your hand reach | out to | help me, ▪
     for I have | chosen | your com|mandments.

174   I have longed for your sal|vation, O | Lord, ▪
     and your | law is | my de|light.

175   Let my soul live and | it shall | praise you, ▪
     and let your | judgments | be my | help.

176   I have gone astray like a | sheep · that is | lost; ▪
     O seek your servant, for I do | not for|get · your com|mandments.

Psalm 120

1   When I was in trouble I | called · to the | Lord; ▪
    I | called · to the | Lord · and he | answered me.

2   Deliver me, O Lord, from | lying | lips ▪
    and | from a de|ceitful | tongue.

3   What shall be | given | to you? ▪
    What more shall be done to | you, de|ceitful | tongue?

4.   The | sharp | arrows ▪⌣
    of a warrior, | tempered in | burning | coals!

5   Woe is me, that I must | lodge in | Meshech ▪
    and | dwell a·mong the | tents of | Kedar.

6,7   My soul has dwelt too long with | enemies of | peace. ▪
    I am for making peace,
       but when I speak of it, | they make | ready for | war.

1   I lift up my | eyes · to the | hills; ▪
from | where is · my | help to | come?

2.   My help | comes · from the | Lord, ▪
the | maker of | heaven and | earth.

3   He will not suffer your | foot to | stumble; ▪
he who watches | over you | will not | sleep.

4.   Behold, he who keeps | watch · over | Israel ▪
shall | neither | slumber nor | sleep.

5   The Lord himself | watches | over you; ▪
the Lord is your | shade at | your right | hand,

6.   So that the sun shall not | strike you by | day, ▪
nei|ther the | moon by | night.

7   The Lord shall keep you | from all | evil; ▪
it is | he · who shall | keep your | soul.

8   The Lord shall keep watch over your going out
and your | coming | in, ▪
from this time | forth for | ever|more.

1   I was glad when they | said to | me, ▪
'Let us | go · to the | house of the | Lord.'

2.   And now our | feet are | standing ▪
within your | gates, | O Je|rusalem;

3   Jerusalem, | built · as a | city ▪
that is at | unity | in it|self.

4   Thither the tribes go up, the | tribes · of the | Lord, ▪
as is decreed for Israel,
to give | thanks · to the | name of the | Lord.

5†   For there are set the | thrones of | judgment, ▪
the | thrones · of the | house of | David.

6   O pray for the | peace · of Je|rusalem: ▪
'May they | prosper who | love | you.

7. 'Peace be with|in your | walls ▪
   and tran|quillity with|in your | palaces.'

8 For my kindred and com|panions' | sake, ▪
   I will | pray that | peace be | with you.

9 For the sake of the house of the | Lord our | God, ▪
   I will | seek to | do you | good.

Psalm 123

1 To you I lift | up my | eyes, ▪
   to you that | are en|throned · in the | heavens.

2. As the eyes of servants look to the | hand of their | master, ▪
   or the eyes of a | maid · to the | hand of her | mistress,

3 So our eyes wait upon the | Lord our | God, ▪
   until | he have | mercy up|on us.

4 Have mercy upon us, O Lord, have | mercy up|on us, ▪
   for we have had | more than e|nough · of con|tempt.

5† Our soul has had more than enough of the | scorn · of the | arrogant, ▪
   and | of the con|tempt · of the | proud.

Psalm 124

1,2 If the Lord himself had not been on our side,
       now may | Israel | say; ▪
    if the Lord had not been on our side,
       when | enemies rose | up a|gainst us;

3 Then would they have | swallowed · us a|live ▪
   when their | anger | burned a|gainst us;

4. Then would the waters have overwhelmed us
       and the torrent gone | over our | soul; ▪
   over our soul would have | swept the | raging | waters.

5 But blessed | be the | Lord ▪
   who has not given us over to | be a | prey · for their | teeth.

6 Our soul has escaped
       as a bird from the | snare · of the | fowler; ▪
   the snare is | broken and | we are de|livered.

7 Our help is in the | name · of the | Lord, ▪
   who | has made | heaven and | earth.

1 Those who trust in the Lord are | like Mount | Zion, ▪
 which cannot be moved, | but stands | fast for | ever.

2 As the hills stand a|bout Je|rusalem, ▪
 so the Lord stands round about his people,
  from this time | forth for | ever|more.

3. The sceptre of wickedness shall not hold sway
  over the land al|lotted · to the | righteous, ▪
 lest the righteous | turn their | hands to | evil.

4 Do good, O Lord, to | those · who are | good, ▪
 and to | those · who are | true of | heart.

5† Those who turn aside to crooked ways
  the Lord shall take away with the | evil|doers; ▪
 but let there be | peace | upon | Israel.

1 When the Lord restored the | fortunes of | Zion, ▪
 then were | we like | those who | dream.

2. Then was our mouth | filled with | laughter ▪
 and our | tongue with | songs of | joy.

3 Then said they a|mong the | nations, ▪
 'The | Lord · has done | great things | for them.'

4. The Lord has indeed done | great things | for us, ▪
 and | therefore | we re|joiced.

5 Restore again our | fortunes, O | Lord, ▪
 as the | river beds | of the | desert.

6 Those who | sow in | tears ▪
 shall | reap with | songs of | joy.

7† Those who go out weeping, | bearing the | seed, ▪
 will come back with shouts of joy, |
  bearing their | sheaves | with them.

Psalm 127

1   Unless the Lord | builds the | house, ▪
     those who | build it | labour in | vain.

2   Unless the Lord | keeps the | city, ▪
     the | guard keeps | watch in | vain.

3.   It is in vain that you hasten to rise up early
         and go so late to rest, eating the | bread of | toil, ▪
     for he | gives · his beloved | sleep.

4   Children are a heritage | from the | Lord ▪
     and the fruit of the | womb | is his | gift.

5   Like arrows in the | hand · of a | warrior, ▪
     so are the | children | of one's | youth.

6   Happy are those who have their | quiver | full of them: ▪
     they shall not be put to shame
         when they dispute with their | enemies | in the | gate.

Psalm 128

1   Blessed are all those who | fear the | Lord, ▪
     and | walk | in his | ways.

2   You shall eat the fruit of the | toil · of your | hands; ▪
     it shall go well with you, and | happy | shall you | be.

3.   Your wife within your house shall be like a | fruitful | vine; ▪
     your children round your table, like | fresh | olive | branches.

4   Thus shall the | one be | blest ▪
     who | fears | – the | Lord.

5   The Lord from out of | Zion | bless you, ▪
     that you may see Jerusalem in prosperity | all the | days of your | life.

6   May you see your | children's | children, ▪
     and may there be | peace | upon | Israel.

Psalm 129

1 'Many a time have they fought against me ǀ from my ǀ youth,' ▪
   may ǀ Israel ǀ now ǀ say;

2. 'Many a time have they fought against me ǀ from my ǀ youth, ▪
   but they have ǀ not preǀvailed aǀgainst me.'

3 The ploughers ǀ ploughed upon my ǀ back ▪
   and ǀ made their ǀ furrows ǀ long.

4. But the ǀ righteous ǀ Lord ▪
   has cut the ǀ cords · of the ǀ wicked in ǀ pieces.

5 Let them be put to shame and ǀ turned ǀ backwards, ▪
   as many ǀ as are ǀ enemies of ǀ Zion.

6. Let them be like grass upǀon the ǀ housetops, ▪
   which ǀ withers beǀfore it can ǀ grow,

7 So that no reaper can ǀ fill his ǀ hand, ▪
   nor a ǀ binder of ǀ sheaves his ǀ bosom;

8 And none who go by may say,
        'The blessing of the Lord ǀ be upǀon you. ▪
   We ǀ bless you · in the ǀ name of the ǀ Lord.'

Psalm 130

1 Out of the depths have I cried to you, O Lord;
        Lord, ǀ hear my ǀ voice; ▪
   let your ears consider well the ǀ voice · of my ǀ suppliǀcation.

2 If you, Lord, were to mark what is ǀ done aǀmiss, ▪
   O ǀ Lord, ǀ who could ǀ stand?

3† But there is forǀgiveness with ǀ you, ▪
   so ǀ that you ǀ shall be ǀ feared.

4 I wait for the Lord; my ǀ soul ǀ waits for him; ▪
   in his ǀ word ǀ is my ǀ hope.

5 My soul waits for the Lord,
        more than the night watch ǀ for the ǀ morning, ▪
   more than the ǀ night watch ǀ for the ǀ morning.

6 O Israel, ǀ wait · for the ǀ Lord, ▪
   for with the ǀ Lord ǀ there is ǀ mercy;

7   With him is | plenteous re|demption ▪
    and he shall redeem | Israel from | all their | sins.

Psalm 131

1   O Lord, my | heart · is not | proud; ▪
    my eyes are not | raised in | haughty | looks.
2   I do not occupy myself with | great | matters, ▪
    with | things that | are too | high for me.
3   But I have quieted and stilled my soul,
        like a weaned child on its | mother's | breast; ▪
    so my | soul is | quieted with|in me.
4   O Israel, | trust · in the | Lord, ▪
    from this time | forth for | ever|more.

Psalm 132

1   Lord, re|member for | David ▪
    all the | hardships | he en|dured;
2   How he swore an | oath · to the | Lord ▪
    and vowed a vow to the | Mighty | One of | Jacob:
3   'I will not come within the | shelter · of my | house, ▪
    nor | climb up | into my | bed;
4   'I will not allow my | eyes to | sleep, ▪
    nor | let my | eyelids | slumber,
5† 'Until I find a | place · for the | Lord, ▪
    a dwelling for the | Mighty | One of | Jacob.'

6   Now, we heard of the | ark in | Ephrathah ▪
    and found it | in the | fields of | Ja-ar.
7. Let us | enter his | dwelling place ▪
    and fall | low be|fore his | footstool.

8   Arise, O Lord, | into your | resting place, ▪
    you | and the | ark · of your | strength.
9   Let your priests be | clothed with | righteousness ▪
    and your | faithful ones | sing with | joy.
10† For your servant | David's | sake, ▪
    turn not away the | face of | your a|nointed.

11   The Lord has sworn an | oath to | David, ▪
     a promise from | which he | will not | shrink:

12   'Of the | fruit · of your | body ▪
     shall I | set up|on your | throne.

13.   'If your children keep my covenant
         and my testimonies that | I shall | teach them, ▪
     their children also shall sit upon your | throne for | ever|more.'

14   For the Lord has chosen | Zion · for him|self; ▪
     he has desired her | for his | habi|tation:

15   'This shall be my | resting place for | ever; ▪
     here will I dwell, for | I have | longed | for her.

16   'I will abundantly | bless · her pro|vision; ▪
     her | poor · will I | satisfy with | bread.

17   'I will clothe her | priests · with sal|vation, ▪
     and her faithful ones | shall re|joice and | sing.

18   'There will I make a horn to spring | up for | David; ▪
     I will keep a lantern | burning for | my a|nointed.

19†   'As for his enemies, I will | clothe them with | shame; ▪
     but on | him · shall his | crown be | bright.'

Psalm 133

1   Behold how good and | pleasant it | is ▪
     to | dwell to|gether in | unity.

2   It is like the precious oil up|on the | head, ▪
     running | down up|on the | beard,

3†   Even on | Aaron's | beard, ▪
     running down upon the | collar | of his | clothing.

4   It is like the | dew of | Hermon ▪
     running | down up·on the | hills of | Zion.

5   For there the Lord has | promised his | blessing: ▪
     even | life for | ever|more.

1   Come, bless the Lord, all you | servants · of the | Lord, ▪
      you that by night | stand · in the | house of the | Lord.

2,3   Lift up your hands towards the sanctuary
          and | bless the | Lord. ▪
      The Lord who made heaven and earth
          give you | blessing | out of | Zion.

Psalm 135

1   Alleluia.
        Praise the | name of the | Lord; ▪
      give praise, you | servants | of the | Lord,

2.   You that stand in the | house of the | Lord, ▪
      in the | courts · of the | house of our | God.

3   Praise the Lord, for the | Lord is | good; ▪
      make music to his | name, for | it is | lovely.

4   For the Lord has chosen Jacob | for him|self ▪
      and Israel | for his | own pos|session.

5.   For I know that the | Lord is | great ▪
      and that our Lord | is a|bove all | gods.

6   The Lord does whatever he pleases in heaven | and on | earth, ▪
      in the seas | and in | all the | deeps.

7.   He brings up the clouds from the | ends of the | earth; ▪
      he makes lightning with the rain
          and brings the | winds | out of his | treasuries.

8   He smote the | firstborn of | Egypt, ▪
      the | firstborn of | man and | beast.

9   He sent signs and wonders into your | midst, O | Egypt, ▪
      upon | Pharaoh and | all his | servants.

10   He smote | many | nations ▪
      and | slew | mighty | kings:

11   Sihon, king of the Amorites, and Og, the | king of | Bashan, ▪
      and | all the | kingdoms of | Canaan.

12.   He gave their land | as a | heritage, ▪
       a | heritage for | Israel his | people.

13   Your name, O Lord, en|dures for | ever ▪
       and shall be remembered through | all | gene|rations.

14.   For the Lord will | vindicate his | people ▪
       and have com|passion | on his | servants.

15   The idols of the nations are but | silver and | gold, ▪
       the | work of | human | hands.

16   They have mouths, but | cannot | speak; ▪
       eyes | have they, but | cannot | see;

17   They have ears, but | cannot | hear; ▪
       neither is there | any | breath · in their | mouths.

18.   Those who make them | shall become | like them, ▪
       and so will | all who | put their | trust in them.

19   Bless the Lord, O | house of | Israel; ▪
       O house of | Aaron, | bless the | Lord.

20   Bless the Lord, O | house of | Levi; ▪
       you who fear the | Lord, | bless the | Lord.

21†   Blessed be the | Lord from | Zion, ▪
       who dwells in Je|rusalem. | Alle|luia.

Psalm 136

1   Give thanks to the Lord, for | he is | gracious, ▪
       for his | mercy en|dures for | ever.

2   Give thanks to the | God of | gods, ▪
       for his | mercy en|dures for | ever.

3   Give thanks to the | Lord of | lords, ▪
       for his | mercy en|dures for | ever;

4   Who alone | does great | wonders, ▪
       for his | mercy en|dures for | ever;

5   Who by wisdom | made the | heavens, ▪
       for his | mercy en|dures for | ever;

6   Who laid out the earth up|on the | waters, ▪
       for his | mercy en|dures for | ever;

7   Who made the | great | lights, ▪
for his | mercy en|dures for | ever;

8   The sun to | rule the | day, ▪
for his | mercy en|dures for | ever;

9† The moon and the stars to | govern the | night, ▪
for his | mercy en|dures for | ever;

10 Who smote the | firstborn of | Egypt, ▪
for his | mercy en|dures for | ever;

11 And brought out Israel | from a|mong them, ▪
for his | mercy en|dures for | ever;

12 With a mighty hand and | outstretched | arm, ▪
for his | mercy en|dures for | ever;

13 Who divided the Red | Sea in | two, ▪
for his | mercy en|dures for | ever;

14 And made Israel to | pass · through the | midst of it, ▪
for his | mercy en|dures for | ever;

15 But Pharaoh and his host he overthrew in the | Red | Sea, ▪
for his | mercy en|dures for | ever;

16 Who led his people | through the | wilderness, ▪
for his | mercy en|dures for | ever;

17 Who | smote great | kings, ▪
for his | mercy en|dures for | ever;

18 And slew | mighty | kings, ▪
for his | mercy en|dures for | ever;

19 Sihon, | king of the | Amorites, ▪
for his | mercy en|dures for | ever;

20 And Og, the | king of | Bashan, ▪
for his | mercy en|dures for | ever;

21 And gave away their land | for a | heritage, ▪
for his | mercy en|dures for | ever;

22† A heritage for | Israel his | servant, ▪
for his | mercy en|dures for | ever;

23 Who remembered us when we | were in | trouble, ▪
for his | mercy en|dures for | ever;

24 And delivered us | from our | enemies, ▪
for his | mercy en|dures for | ever;

25 Who gives food to | all | creatures, ▪
for his | mercy en|dures for | ever.
26 Give thanks to the | God of | heaven, ▪
for his | mercy en|dures for | ever.

Psalm 137

1 By the waters of Babylon we sat | down and | wept, ▪
when | we re|membered | Zion.
2 As for our lyres, we | hung them | up ▪
on the | willows that | grow · in that | land.
3. For there our captors asked for a song,
our tormentors | called for | mirth: ▪
'Sing us | one of the | songs of | Zion.'

4 How shall we sing the | Lord's | song ▪
in a | strange | – | land?
5 If I forget you, | O Je|rusalem, ▪
let my right | hand for|get its | skill.
6. Let my tongue cleave to the roof of my mouth
if I do | not re|member you, ▪
If I set not Jerusalem a|bove my | highest | joy.

7 Remember, O Lord, against the people of Edom
the | day of Je|rusalem, ▪
how they said, 'Down with it, down with it, | even | to the | ground.'
8 O daughter of Babylon, | doomed · to des|truction, ▪
happy the one who repays you
for | all · you have | done to | us;
9† Who | takes your | little ones, ▪
and | dashes them a|gainst the | rock.

Psalm 138

1 I will give thanks to you, O Lord, with my | whole | heart; ▪
before the gods will | I sing | praise to | you.
2 I will bow down towards your holy temple and praise your name,
because of your | love and | faithfulness; ▪

for you have glorified your name
> | and your | word above | all things.

3.   In the day that I called to you, you | answered | me; ■
you | put new | strength in my | soul.

4   All the kings of the earth shall | praise you, O | Lord, ■
for they have | heard the | words of your | mouth.

5   They shall sing of the | ways of the | Lord, ■
that great is the | glory | of the | Lord.

6.   Though the Lord be high, he watches | over the | lowly; ■
as for the proud, he regards them | from a|far.

7   Though I walk in the midst of trouble, | you · will pre|serve me; ■
you will stretch forth your hand against the fury of my enemies; |
>   your right | hand will | save me.

8   The Lord shall make good his | purpose | for me; ■
your loving-kindness, O Lord, endures for ever;
>   for|sake · not the | work of your | hands.

Psalm 139

1   O Lord, you have searched me | out and | known me; ■
you know my sitting down and my rising up;
>   you dis|cern my | thoughts · from a|far.

2.   You mark out my journeys | and my | resting place ■
and are ac|quainted with | all my | ways.

3   For there is not a word | on my | tongue, ■
but you, O Lord, | know it | alto|gether.

4   You encompass me behind | and be|fore ■
and | lay your | hand up|on me.

5†   Such knowledge is too | wonderful | for me, ■
so high | that I | cannot at|tain it.

6   Where can I go then | from your | spirit? ■
Or where can I | flee | from your | presence?

7   If I climb up to heaven, | you are | there; ■
if I make the grave my bed, | you are | there | also.

8   If I take the | wings of the | morning ▪
     and dwell in the | uttermost | parts · of the | sea,

9.   Even there your | hand shall | lead me, ▪
     your | right hand | hold me | fast.

10   If I say, 'Surely the | darkness will | cover me ▪
     and the light a|round me | turn to | night,'

11. Even darkness is no darkness with you;
        the night is as | clear as the | day; ▪
     darkness and light to | you are | both a|like.

12   For you yourself created my | inmost | parts; ▪
     you knit me together | in my | mother's | womb.

13   I thank you, for I am fearfully and | wonderfully | made; ▪
     marvellous are your | works, my | soul knows | well.

14   My frame was not | hidden | from you, ▪
     when I was made in secret
        and woven in the | depths | of the | earth.

15   Your eyes beheld my form, as | yet un|finished; ▪
     already in your book were | all my | members | written,

16† As day by day | they were | fashioned ▪
     when as | yet | there was | none of them.

17   How deep are your counsels to | me, O | God! ▪
     How | great | is the | sum of them!

18. If I count them, they are more in number | than the | sand, ▪
     and at the end, I am | still | in your | presence.

19   O that you would slay the | wicked, O | God, ▪
     that the | bloodthirsty | might de|part from me!

20   They speak against you with | wicked in|tent; ▪
     your enemies take | up your | name for | evil.

21   Do I not oppose those, O Lord, | who op|pose you? ▪
     Do I not abhor | those who rise | up a|gainst you?

22. I hate them with a | perfect | hatred; ▪
     they have become my | own | enemies | also.

23   Search me out, O God, and | know my | heart; ▪
     try me | and ex|amine my | thoughts.

24   See if there is any way of | wickedness | in me ▪
and lead me in the | way | ever|lasting.

1   Deliver me, O Lord, from | evil|doers ▪
and pro|tect me | from the | violent,

2   Who devise evil | in their | hearts ▪
and stir up | strife | all the day | long.

3†   They have sharpened their tongues | like a | serpent; ▪
adder's | poison is | under their | lips.

4   Keep me, O Lord, from the | hands of the | wicked; ▪
protect me from the violent who | seek to | make me | stumble.

5   The proud have laid a snare for me
       and spread out a | net of | cords; ▪
they have set | traps a|long my | path.

6.   I have said to the Lord, | 'You are my | God; ▪
listen, O Lord, to the | voice of my | suppli|cation.

7   'O Lord God, the strength of | my sal|vation, ▪
you have covered my | head · in the | day of | battle.

8   'Do not grant the desires of the | wicked, O | Lord, ▪
do not | prosper their | wicked | plans.

9   'Let not those who surround me lift | up their | heads; ▪
let the evil of their own | lips | fall up|on them.

10.   'Let hot burning coals | rain up|on them; ▪
let them be cast into the depths, | that they | rise not a|gain.'

11   No slanderer shall prosper | on the | earth, ▪
and evil shall hunt down the | violent to | over|throw them.

12   I know that the Lord will bring justice | for the op|pressed ▪
and main|tain the | cause of the | needy.

13   Surely, the righteous will give | thanks · to your | name, ▪
and the upright shall | dwell | in your | presence.

1   O Lord, I call to you; | come to me | quickly; ▪
       hear my voice | when I | cry to | you.

2.   Let my prayer rise be|fore you as | incense, ▪
       the lifting up of my hands | as the | evening | sacrifice.

3   Set a watch before my | mouth, O | Lord, ▪
       and | guard the | door of my | lips;

4   Let not my heart incline to any | evil | thing; ▪
       let me not be occupied in wickedness with evildoers,
           nor taste the | pleasures | of their | table.

5.   Let the righteous smite me in friendly rebuke;
           but let not the oil of the unrighteous a|noint my | head; ▪
       for my prayer is continually a|gainst their | wicked | deeds.

6   Let their rulers be overthrown in | stony | places; ▪
       then they may | know · that my | words are | sweet.

7   As when a plough turns over the | earth in | furrows, ▪
       let their bones be | scattered · at the | mouth of the | Pit.

8.   But my eyes are turned to | you, Lord | God; ▪
       in you I take refuge; | do not | leave me de|fenceless.

9   Protect me from the snare which | they have | laid for me ▪
       and from the | traps of the | evil|doers.

10   Let the wicked fall into their | own | nets, ▪
       while | I pass | by in | safety.

1   I cry a|loud · to the | Lord; ▪
       to the Lord I | make my | suppli|cation.

2.   I pour out my com|plaint be|fore him ▪
       and | tell him | of my | trouble.

3   When my spirit faints within me, you | know my | path; ▪
       in the way wherein I walk | have they | laid a | snare for me.

4   I look to my right hand, and find | no one who | knows me; ▪
       I have no place to flee to, and | no one | cares for my | soul.

5.   I cry out to you, O | Lord, and | say: ▪
      'You are my refuge, my | portion · in the | land of the | living.

6   'Listen to my cry, for I am brought | very | low; ▪
      save me from my persecutors, for they | are too | strong | for me.

7   'Bring my | soul · out of | prison, ▪
      that I may give | thanks | to your | name;

7a   When you have dealt | bountifully | with me, ▪
      then shall the | righteous | gather a|round me.'

Psalm 143

1   Hear my | prayer, O | Lord, ▪
      and in your faithfulness give ear to my supplications;
         | answer me | in your | righteousness.

2   Enter not into judgment | with your | servant, ▪
      for in your sight shall | no one | living be | justified.

3.   For the enemy has pursued me,
         crushing my | life · to the | ground, ▪
      making me sit in | darkness like | those long | dead.

4   My spirit | faints with|in me; ▪
      my | heart with|in me is | desolate.

5   I remember the time past; I muse upon | all your | deeds; ▪
      I con|sider the | works of your | hands.

6.   I stretch | out my | hands to you; ▪
      my soul gasps for you | like a | thirsty | land.

7   O Lord, make haste to answer me; my | spirit | fails me; ▪
      hide not your face from me
         lest I be like | those who go | down · to the | Pit.

8   Let me hear of your loving-kindness in the morning,
         for in you I | put my | trust; ▪
      show me the way I should walk in,
         for I | lift up my | soul to | you.

9.   Deliver me, O Lord, | from my | enemies, ▪
      for I | flee to | you for | refuge.

10   Teach me to do what pleases you, for I you are my I God; ∎
        let your kindly spirit lead me I on a I level I path.

11   Revive me, O Lord, I for your I name's sake; ∎
        for your righteousness' sake, I bring me I out of I trouble.

12   In your faithfulness, slay my enemies,
            and destroy all the adversaries I of my I soul, ∎
        for I truly I I am your I servant.

Psalm 144

1   Blessed be the I Lord my I rock, ∎
        who teaches my hands for war I and my I fingers for I battle;

2.   My steadfast help and my fortress, my stronghold and my deliverer,
            my shield in I whom I I trust, ∎
        who sub|dues the I peoples I under me.

3   O Lord, what are mortals that I you should con|sider them; ∎
        mere human beings, that I you should take I thought for I them?

4.   They are like a I breath of I wind; ∎
        their days pass a|way I like a I shadow.

5   Bow your heavens, O Lord, I and come I down; ∎
        touch the I mountains and I they shall I smoke.

6.   Cast down your I lightnings and I scatter them; ∎
        shoot out your arrows I and let I thunder I roar.

7   Reach down your I hand from on I high; ∎
        deliver me and take me out of the great waters,
            from the I hand of I foreign I enemies,

8.   Whose I mouth speaks I wickedness ∎
        and their right hand I is the I hand of I falsehood.

9   O God, I will sing to you a I new I song; ∎
        I will play to you I on a I ten-stringed I harp,

10.   You that give sal|vation to I kings ∎
        and have de|livered I David your I servant.

11   Save me from the I peril · of the I sword ∎
        and deliver me from the I hand of I foreign I enemies,

12. Whose | mouth speaks | wickedness ▪
and whose right hand | is the | hand of | falsehood;

13 So that our sons in their youth may be like well|nurtured | plants, ▪
and our daughters like pillars carved for the | corners | of the | temple;

14 Our barns be filled with all | manner of | store; ▪
our flocks bearing thousands, and ten | thousands | in our | fields;

15 Our cattle be | heavy with | young: ▪
may there be no miscarriage or untimely birth,
no | cry of dis|tress · in our | streets.

16 Happy are the people whose | blessing this | is. ▪
Happy are the people who have the | Lord | for their | God.

Psalm 145

1 I will exalt you, O | God my | King, ▪
and bless your | name for | ever and | ever.

2. Every day | will I | bless you ▪
and praise your | name for | ever and | ever.

3 Great is the Lord and | highly · to be | praised; ▪
his greatness is be|yond all | searching | out.

4 One generation shall praise your | works · to an|other ▪
and de|clare your | mighty | acts.

5. They shall speak of the majesty | of your | glory, ▪
and I will tell of | all your | wonderful | deeds.

6 They shall speak of the might of your | marvellous | acts, ▪
and I will | also | tell of your | greatness.

7† They shall pour forth the story of your a|bundant | kindness ▪
and | joyfully | sing · of your | righteousness.

8 The Lord is | gracious and | merciful, ▪
long-suffering | and of | great | goodness.

9. The Lord is | loving to | everyone ▪
and his mercy is | over | all his | creatures.

10 All your works | praise you, O | Lord, ▪
and your | faithful | servants | bless you.

11 They tell of the | glory · of your | kingdom ■
    and | speak of your | mighty | power,

12† To make known to all peoples your | mighty | acts ■
    and the glorious | splendour | of your | kingdom.

13 Your kingdom is an ever|lasting | kingdom; ■
    your dominion en|dures through|out all | ages.

14 The Lord is sure in | all his | words ■
    and | faithful in | all his | deeds.

15. The Lord upholds all | those who | fall ■
    and lifts up all | those who are | bowed | down.

16 The eyes of all wait upon | you, O | Lord, ■
    and you give them their | food in | due | season.

17. You open | wide your | hand ■
    and fill | all things | living with | plenty.

18 The Lord is righteous in | all his | ways ■
    and | loving in | all his | works.

19 The Lord is near to those who | call up|on him, ■
    to all who | call up|on him | faithfully.

20. He fulfils the desire of | those who | fear him; ■
    he | hears their | cry and | saves them.

21 The Lord watches over | those who | love him, ■
    but all the | wicked shall | he des|troy.

22 My mouth shall speak the | praise of the | Lord, ■
    and let all flesh bless his holy | name for | ever and | ever.

Psalm 146

1   Alleluia.
        Praise the Lord, | O my | soul: ■
    while I | live · will I | praise the | Lord;

1a. As long as I | have any | being, ■
    I will sing | praises | to my | God.

2   Put not your trust in princes,
        nor in any | human | power, ■
    for there | is no | help in | them.

3   When their breath goes forth, they re|turn to the | earth; ▪
on that day | all their | thoughts | perish.

4   Happy are those who have the God of Jacob | for their | help, ▪
whose hope is | in the | Lord their | God;

5   Who made heaven and earth,
the sea and | all that is | in them; ▪
who | keeps his | promise for | ever;

6†   Who gives justice to those that | suffer | wrong ▪
and | bread to | those who | hunger.

7   The Lord looses | those that are | bound; ▪
the Lord opens the | eyes | of the | blind;

8.   The Lord lifts up those who are | bowed | down; ▪
the | Lord | loves the | righteous;

9   The Lord watches over the stranger in the land;
he upholds the | orphan and | widow; ▪
but the way of the wicked | he turns | upside | down.

10   The Lord shall | reign for | ever, ▪
your God, O Zion, throughout all gene|rations. | Alle|luia.

Psalm 147

1   Alleluia.
How good it is to make music | for our | God, ▪
how joyful to | honour | him with | praise.

2.   The Lord builds | up Je|rusalem ▪
and gathers to|gether the | outcasts of | Israel.

3.   He heals the | broken|hearted ▪
and | binds up | all their | wounds.

4.   He counts the | number · of the | stars ▪
and | calls them | all · by their | names.

5   Great is our Lord and | mighty in | power; ▪
his wisdom | is be|yond all | telling.

6   The Lord lifts | up the | poor, ▪
but casts down the | wicked | to the | ground.

7   Sing to the | Lord with | thanksgiving; ▪
make music to our | God up|on the | lyre;

8   Who covers the | heavens with | clouds ▪
and prepares | rain | for the | earth;

9.   Who makes grass to | grow upon the | mountains ▪
and green | plants to | serve our | needs.

10   He gives the | beasts their | food ▪
and the young | ravens | when they | cry.

11   He takes no pleasure in the | power of a | horse, ▪
no de|light in | human | strength;

12. But the Lord delights in | those who | fear him, ▪
who put their | trust · in his | steadfast | love.

13   Sing praise to the Lord, | O Je|rusalem; ▪
praise your | God, | O | Zion;

14   For he has strengthened the | bars of your | gates ▪
and has | blest your | children with|in you.

15. He has established | peace in your | borders ▪
and satisfies you | with the | finest | wheat.

16   He sends forth his command | to the | earth ▪
and his | word runs | very | swiftly.

17   He gives | snow like | wool ▪
and | scatters the | hoarfrost like | ashes.

18. He casts down his hailstones like | morsels of | bread; ▪
who | can en|dure his | frost?

19   He sends forth his | word and | melts them; ▪
he blows with his wind | and the | waters | flow.

20   He declares his | word to | Jacob, ▪
his | statutes and | judgments to | Israel.

21† He has not dealt so with any | other | nation; ▪
they do not know his | laws. | Alle|luia.

1 Alleluia.
  Praise the Lord ǀ from the ǀ heavens; ▪
 praise ǀ – him ǀ in the ǀ heights.

2. Praise him, all ǀ you his ǀ angels; ▪
 praise ǀ – him, ǀ all his ǀ host.

3 Praise him, ǀ sun and ǀ moon; ▪
 praise him, ǀ all you ǀ stars of ǀ light.

4 Praise him, ǀ heaven of ǀ heavens, ▪
 and you ǀ waters aǀbove the ǀ heavens.

5 Let them praise the ǀ name of the ǀ Lord, ▪
 for he commanded ǀ and they ǀ were creǀated.

6. He made them fast for ǀ ever and ǀ ever; ▪
 he gave them a law which ǀ shall not ǀ pass aǀway.

7 Praise the Lord ǀ from the ǀ earth, ▪
 you sea ǀ monsters and ǀ all ǀ deeps;

8 Fire and hail, ǀ snow and ǀ mist, ▪
 tempestuous ǀ wind, fulǀfilling his ǀ word;

9 Mountains and ǀ all ǀ hills, ▪
 fruit ǀ trees and ǀ all ǀ cedars;

10. Wild beasts and ǀ all ǀ cattle, ▪
 creeping ǀ things and ǀ birds · on the ǀ wing;

11 Kings of the earth and ǀ all ǀ peoples, ▪
 princes and all ǀ rulers ǀ of the ǀ world;

12. Young men and women, old and ǀ young toǀgether; ▪
 let them ǀ praise the ǀ name of the ǀ Lord.

13 For his name only ǀ is exǀalted, ▪
 his splendour aǀbove ǀ earth and ǀ heaven.

14 He has raised up the horn of his people
  and praise for all his ǀ faithful ǀ servants, ▪
 the children of Israel, a people who are ǀ near him. ǀ Alleǀluia.

1   Alleluia.

       O sing to the Lord a ǀ new ǀ song; ▪

    sing his praise in the congreǀgation ǀ of the ǀ faithful.

2   Let Israel rejoice ǀ in their ǀ maker; ▪

    let the children of Zion be ǀ joyful ǀ in their ǀ king.

3.   Let them praise his ǀ name · in the ǀ dance; ▪

    let them sing praise to ǀ him with ǀ timbrel and ǀ lyre.

4   For the Lord has pleasure ǀ in his ǀ people ▪

    and adorns the ǀ poor ǀ with salǀvation.

5   Let the faithful be ǀ joyful in ǀ glory; ▪

    let them reǀjoice ǀ in their ǀ ranks,

6.   With the praises of God ǀ in their ǀ mouths ▪

    and a ǀ two-edged ǀ sword · in their ǀ hands;

7   To execute vengeance ǀ on the ǀ nations ▪

    and ǀ punishment ǀ on the ǀ peoples;

8   To bind their ǀ kings in ǀ chains ▪

    and their ǀ nobles with ǀ fetters of ǀ iron;

9†   To execute on them the ǀ judgment deǀcreed: ▪

    such honour have all his faithful ǀ servants. ǀ Alleǀluia.

Psalm 150

1   Alleluia.

       O praise God ǀ in his ǀ holiness; ▪

    praise him in the ǀ firmament ǀ of his ǀ power.

2.   Praise him for his ǀ mighty ǀ acts; ▪

    praise him acǀcording · to his ǀ excellent ǀ greatness.

3   Praise him with the ǀ blast of the ǀ trumpet; ▪

    praise him upǀon the ǀ harp and ǀ lyre.

4.   Praise him with ǀ timbrel and ǀ dances; ▪

    praise him upǀon the ǀ strings and ǀ pipe.

5   Praise him with ǀ ringing ǀ cymbals; ▪

    praise him upǀon the ǀ clashing ǀ cymbals.

6   Let everything ǀ that has ǀ breath ▪

    praise the ǀ Lord. ǀ Alleǀluia.

A CATECHISM

The Church Catechism (1878)

THAT IS TO SAY

AN INSTRUCTION TO BE LEARNED OF EVERY PERSON

BEFORE HE BE BROUGHT TO BE CONFIRMED BY THE BISHOP

Question. What is your Name?

Answer. Christian Name or Names.

Question. Who gave you this Name?

Answer. My Godfathers and Godmothers in my Baptism; wherein I was made a member of Christ, the child of God, and an inheritor of the kingdom of heaven.

Question. What did your Godfathers and Godmothers then for you?

Answer. They did promise and vow three things in my name. First, that I should renounce the devil and all his works, the pomps and vanity of this wicked world, and all the sinful lusts of the flesh; Secondly, that I should believe all the Articles of the Christian faith; And thirdly, that I should keep God's holy will and commandments, and walk in the same all the days of my life.

Question. Dost thou not think that thou art bound to believe, and to do, as they have promised for thee?

Answer. Yes verily; and by God's help so I will. And I heartily thank our heavenly Father, that he hath called me to this state of salvation, through Jesus Christ our Saviour. And I pray unto God to give me his grace, that I may continue in the same unto my life's end.

Catechist.

Rehearse the Articles of thy Belief.

Answer.

I believe in God the Father Almighty, Maker of heaven and earth:
And in Jesus Christ his only Son our Lord, Who was conceived by the Holy Spirit, Born of the Virgin Mary, Suffered under Pontius Pilate, Was crucified, dead, and buried, He descended into hell; The third day he rose again from the dead, He ascended into heaven, And sitteth at the right hand of God the Father Almighty; From thence he shall come to judge the quick and the dead.

I believe in the Holy Spirit; The holy Catholic Church; The Communion of Saints; The Forgiveness of sins; The Resurrection of the body, And the life everlasting. Amen.

Question. What dost thou chiefly learn in these Articles of thy Belief?
Answer. First, I learn to believe in God the Father, who hath made me, and all the world;
Secondly, in God the Son, who hath redeemed me, and all mankind;
Thirdly, in God the Holy Spirit, who sanctifieth me, and all the elect people of God.

Question. You said that your Godfathers and Godmothers did promise for you, that you should keep God's Commandments. Tell me how many there be?
Answer. Ten.

Question. Which be they?
Answer. The same which God spake in the twentieth Chapter of Exodus, saying, I am the Lord thy God, who brought thee out of the land of Egypt, out of the house of bondage.

1. Thou shalt have none other gods but me.
2. Thou shalt not make to thyself any graven image, nor the likeness of any thing that is in heaven above, or in the earth beneath, or in the water under the earth; Thou shalt not bow down to them, nor worship them: for I the Lord thy God am a jealous God, and visit the sins of the fathers upon the children unto the third and fourth generation of them that hate me, and show mercy unto thousands in them that love me and keep my commandments.
3. Thou shalt not take the Name of the Lord thy God in vain; for the Lord will not hold him guiltless, that taketh his Name in vain.
4. Remember that thou keep holy the Sabbath day. Six days shalt thou labour, and do all that thou hast to do; but the seventh day is the Sabbath of the Lord thy God. In it thou shalt do no manner of work, thou, and thy son, and thy daughter, thy man-servant, and thy maid-servant, thy cattle, and the stranger that is within thy gates. For in six days the Lord made heaven and earth, the sea, and all that in them is, and resteth the seventh day: wherefore the Lord blessed the seventh day, and hallowed it.

5. Honour thy father and thy mother: that thy days may be long in the land which the Lord thy God giveth thee.

6. Thou shalt do no murder.

7. Thou shalt not commit adultery.

8. Thou shalt not steal.

9. Thou shalt not bear false witness against thy neighbour.

10. Thou shalt not covet thy neighbour's house, thou shalt not cover thy neighbour's wife, nor his servant, nor his maid, nor his ox, nor his ass, nor any thing that is his.

Question. What dost thou chiefly learn by these Commandments?

Answer. I learn two things: my duty towards God, and my duty towards my Neighbour.

Question. What is thy duty towards God?

Answer. My duty towards God is to believe in him, to fear him, and to love him, with all my heart, with all my mind, with all my soul, and with all my strength; to worship him, to give him thanks, to put my whole trust in him, to call upon him, to honour his holy Name and his Word, and to serve him truly all the days of my life.

Question. What is thy duty towards thy Neighbour?

Answer. My duty towards my Neighbour is to love him as myself, and to do to all men as I would they should do unto me: To love, honour, and succour my father and mother: To honour and obey N.I.[the *Queen*, and all that are put in authority under *her*:] R.I.[all that are put in authority over me:] To submit myself to all my governors, teachers, spiritual pastors and masters: To order myself lowly and reverently to all who are set over me: To hurt nobody by word or deed: To be true and just in all my dealing: To bear no malice nor hatred in my heart: To keep my hands from picking and stealing, and my tongue from evil-speaking, lying, and slandering: To keep my body in temperance, soberness, and chastity: Not to covet nor desire other men's goods; but to learn and labour truly to get mine own living, and to do my duty in that state of life, unto which it shall please God to call me.

Catechist.

My good Child, know this, that thou art not able to do these things of thyself, nor to walk in the commandments of God, and to serve him without his special grace; which thou must learn at all times to call for by diligent prayer. Let me hear therefore, if thou canst say the Lord's Prayer.

Answer.

Our Father, who art in heaven, Hallowed be thy name, Thy kingdom come, Thy will be done, on earth as it is in heaven. Give us this day our daily bread. And forgive us our trespasses, As we forgive those who trespass against us. And lead us not into temptation, But deliver us from evil. Amen.

Question. What desirest thou of God in this Prayer?

Answer. I desire my Lord God our heavenly Father, who is the giver of all goodness, to send his grace unto me, and to all people; that we may worship him, serve him, and obey him, as we ought to do. And I pray unto God, that he will send us all things that be needful both for our souls and bodies; and that he will be merciful unto us, and forgive us our sins; and that it will please him to save and defend us in all dangers spiritual and bodily; and that he will keep us from all sin and wickedness, and from our spiritual enemy, and from everlasting death. And this I trust he will do of his mercy and goodness, through our Lord Jesus Christ. And therefore I say, Amen, So be it.

Question. How many Sacraments hath Christ ordained in his Church?

Answer. Two only, as generally necessary to salvation; that is to say, Baptism, and the Supper of the Lord.

Question. What meanest thou by this word Sacrament?

Answer. I mean an outward and visible sign of an inward and spiritual grace given unto us, ordained by Christ himself, as a means whereby we receive the same, and a pledge to assure us thereof.

Question. How many parts are there in a Sacrament?

Answer. Two; the outward visible sign, and the inward spiritual grace.

Question. What is the outward visible sign or form in Baptism?

Answer. Water; wherein the person is baptized, In the Name of the Father, and of the Son, and of the Holy Spirit.

Question. What is the inward and spiritual grace?

Answer. A death unto sin, and a new birth unto righteousness: for being by nature born in sin, and the children of wrath, we are hereby made the children of grace.

Question. What is required of persons to be baptized?

Answer. Repentance, whereby they forsake sin; and Faith, whereby they steadfastly believe the promises of God, made to them in that Sacrament.

Question. Why then are Infants baptized, when by reason of their tender age they cannot perform them?

Answer. Because they promise them both, by their Sureties; which promise, when they come to age, themselves are bound to perform.

Question. Why was the Sacrament of the Lord's Supper ordained?

Answer. For the continual remembrance of the sacrifice of the death of Christ, and of the benefits which we receive thereby.

Question. What is the outward part or sign of the Lord's Supper?

Answer. Bread and Wine, which the Lord hath commanded to be received.

Question. What is the inward part, or thing signified?

Answer. The Body and Blood of Christ, which are verily and indeed taken and received by the faithful in the Lord's Supper.

Question. After what manner are the Body and Blood of Christ taken and received in the Lord's Supper?

Answer. Only after a heavenly and spiritual manner; and the mean whereby they are taken and received is Faith.

Question. What are the benefits whereof we are partakers thereby?

Answer. The strengthening and refreshing of our souls by the Body and Blood of Christ, as our bodies are by the Bread and Wine.

Question. What is required of them who come to the Lord's Supper?

Answer. To examine themselves, whether they repent them truly of their former sins, steadfastly purposing to lead a new life; have a lively faith in God's mercy through Christ, with a thankful remembrance of his death; and be in charity with all men.

THE CREED (COMMONLY CALLED) OF
SAINT ATHANASIUS

Quicunque Vult

Whosoever will be saved:
before all things it is necessary that he hold the Catholic Faith.
Which Faith except every one do keep whole and undefiled:
without doubt he shall perish everlastingly.

And the Catholic Faith is this:
That we worship one God in Trinity, and Trinity in Unity;
Neither confounding the Persons: nor dividing the Substance.
For there is one Person of the Father, another of the Son:
and another of the Holy Ghost.
But the Godhead of the Father, of the Son, and of the Holy Ghost, is all one:
the Glory equal, the Majesty co-eternal.
Such as the Father is, such is the Son: and such is the Holy Ghost.
The Father uncreate, the Son uncreate: and the Holy Ghost uncreate.
The Father incomprehensible, the Son incomprehensible:
and the Holy Ghost incomprehensible.
The Father eternal, the Son eternal: and the Holy Ghost eternal.
And yet they are not three eternals: but one eternal.
As also there are not three incomprehensibles, nor three uncreated:
but one uncreated, and one incomprehensible.
So likewise the Father is Almighty, the Son Almighty:
and the Holy Ghost Almighty.
And yet they are not three Almighties: but one Almighty.
So the Father is God, the Son is God: and the Holy Ghost is God.
And yet they are not three Gods: but one God.
So likewise the Father is Lord, the Son Lord: and the Holy Ghost Lord.
And yet not three Lords: but one Lord.
For like as we are compelled by the Christian verity:
to acknowledge every Person by himself to be God and Lord;
So are we forbidden by the Catholic Religion:
to say, there be three Gods, or three Lords.
The Father is made of none: neither created, nor begotten.
The Son is of the Father alone: not made, nor created, but begotten.

The Holy Ghost is of the Father and of the Son:
neither made, nor created, nor begotten, but proceeding.
So there is one Father, not three Fathers; one Son, not three Sons:
one Holy Ghost, not three Holy Ghosts.
And in this Trinity none is afore, or after other:
none is greater, or less than another;
But the whole three Persons are co-eternal together: and co-equal.
So that in all things, as is aforesaid:
the Unity in Trinity, and the Trinity in Unity is to be worshipped.
He therefore that will be saved: must thus think of the Trinity.

Furthermore it is necessary to everlasting salvation:
that he also believe rightly the Incarnation of our Lord Jesus Christ.
For the right Faith is that we believe and confess:
that our Lord Jesus Christ, the Son of God, is God and Man;
God, of the Substance of the Father, begotten before the worlds:
and Man, of the Substance of his Mother, born in the world;
Perfect God, and perfect Man:
of a reasonable soul and human flesh subsisting;
Equal to the Father, as touching his Godhead:
and inferior to the Father, as touching his Manhood.
Who although he be God and Man: yet he is not two, but one Christ;
One, not by conversion of the Godhead into flesh:
but by taking of the Manhood into God;
One altogether, not by confusion of Substance: but by unity of Person.
For as the reasonable soul and flesh is one man:
so God and Man is one Christ:
Who suffered for our salvation:
descended into hell, rose again the third day from the dead.
He ascended into heaven, he sitteth on the right hand of the Father, God
Almighty: from whence he shall come to judge the quick and the dead.
At whose coming all men shall rise again with their bodies:
and shall give account for their own works.
And they that have done good shall go into life everlasting:
and they that have done evil into everlasting fire.

This is the Catholic Faith:
which except a man believe faithfully, he cannot be saved.

Glory be to the Father, and to the Son: and to the Holy Ghost;
as is was in the beginning, is now, and ever shall be: world without end.
Amen.

Preamble to the Constitution (1870)

Articles of Religion

THE PREAMBLE AND DECLARATION

ADOPTED BY THE GENERAL CONVENTION IN THE YEAR 1870

In the Name of the Father, and of the Son, and of the Holy Ghost. Amen:
Whereas it hath been determined by the Legislature that on and after the
1st day of January, 1871, the Church of Ireland shall cease to be established by law; and that the ecclesiastical law of Ireland shall cease to exist
as law save as provided in the *Irish Church Act, 1869,* and it hath thus
become necessary that the Church of Ireland should provide for its own
regulation:

We, the archbishops and bishops of this the Ancient Catholic and
Apostolic Church of Ireland, together with the representatives of the clergy and laity of the same, in General Convention assembled in Dublin in
the year of our Lord God one thousand eight hundred and seventy, before
entering on this work, do solemnly declare as follows:

I.

1. The Church of Ireland doth, as heretofore, accept and unfeignedly
believe all the Canonical Scriptures of the Old and New Testament, as
given by inspiration of God, and containing all things necessary to salvation; and doth continue to profess the faith of Christ as professed by the
Primitive Church.

2. The Church of Ireland will continue to minister the doctrine, and
sacraments, and the discipline of Christ, as the Lord hath commanded; and
will maintain inviolate the three orders of bishops, priests or presbyters,
and deacons in the sacred ministry.

3. The Church of Ireland, as a reformed and Protestant Church, doth
hereby reaffirm its constant witness against all those innovations in doctrine and worship, whereby the Primitive Faith hath been from time to
time defaced or overlaid, and which at the Reformation this Church did
disown and reject.

The Church of Ireland doth receive and approve The Book of the Articles of Religion, commonly called the Thirty-nine Articles, received and approved by the archbishops and bishops and the rest of the clergy of Ireland in the synod holden in Dublin, A.D. 1634; also, The Book of Common Prayer and Administration of the Sacraments, and other Rites and Ceremonies of the Church, according to the use of the Church of Ireland; and the Form and Manner of Making, Ordaining and Consecrating of Bishops, Priests and Deacons, as approved and adopted by the synod holden in Dublin, A.D. 1662, and hitherto in use in this Church. And this Church will continue to use the same, subject to such alterations only as may be made therein from time to time by the lawful authority of the Church.

III.

The Church of Ireland will maintain communion with the sister Church of England, and with all other Christian Churches agreeing in the principles of this Declaration; and will set forward, so far as in it lieth, quietness, peace, and love, among all Christian people.

IV.

The Church of Ireland, deriving its authority from Christ, Who is the Head over all things to the Church, doth declare that a General Synod of the Church of Ireland, consisting of the archbishops and bishops, and of representatives of the clergy and laity, shall have chief legislative power therein, and such administrative power as may be necessary for the Church, and consistent with its episcopal constitution.

ARTICLES OF RELIGION

AGREED UPON BY THE ARCHBISHOPS AND BISHOPS OF BOTH PROVINCES AND
THE WHOLE CLERGY, IN THE CONVOCATION HOLDEN AT LONDON IN THE YEAR
1562 FOR THE AVOIDING OF THE DIVERSITIES OF OPINIONS, AND FOR THE
ESTABLISHMENT OF CONSENT TOUCHING TRUE RELIGION.

Received and approved by the Archbishops and Bishops, and the rest of the Clergy of Ireland, in the Synod holden in Dublin, A.D. 1634.

Received and approved by the Archbishops and Bishops, and the Clergy and the laity of the Church of Ireland, in the Convention holden in Dublin, A.D. 1870.

1. Of Faith in the Holy Trinity.

There is but one living and true God, everlasting, without body, parts, or passions; of infinite power, wisdom, and goodness; the Maker, and Preserver of all things both visible and invisible. And in the unity of this Godhead there be three Persons, of one substance, power, and eternity; the Father, the Son, and the Holy Ghost.

2. Of the Word or Son of God, which was made very Man.

The Son, which is the Word of the Father, begotten from everlasting of the Father, the very and eternal God, of one substance with the Father, took Man's nature in the womb of the blessed Virgin, of her substance: so that two whole and perfect Natures, that is to say, the Godhead and Manhood, were joined together in one Person, never to be divided, whereof is one Christ, very God, and very Man; who truly suffered, was crucified, dead, and buried, to reconcile his Father to us, and to be a sacrifice, not only for original guilt, but also for actual sins of men.

3. Of the going down of Christ into Hell.

As Christ died for us, and was buried; so also it is to be believed that he went down into Hell.

4. Of the Resurrection of Christ.

Christ did truly rise again from death, and took again his body, with flesh, bones, and all things appertaining to the perfection of Man's nature; wherewith he ascended into Heaven, and there sitteth, until he return to judge all men at the last day.

5. Of the Holy Ghost.

The Holy Ghost, proceeding from the Father and the Son, is of one substance, majesty, and glory, with the Father and the Son, very and eternal God.

6. Of the Sufficiency of the holy Scriptures for Salvation.

Holy Scripture containeth all things necessary to salvation: so that whatsoever is not read therein, nor may be proved thereby, is not to be required of any man, that it should be believed as an article of the Faith, or be thought requisite or necessary to salvation. In the name of the holy Scripture we do understand those canonical Books of the Old and New Testament, of whose authority was never any doubt in the Church.

Of the Names and Number of the Canonical Books

Genesis, Exodus, Leviticus, Numbers, Deuteronomy, Joshua, Judges, Ruth, The First Book of Samuel, The Second Book of Samuel, The First Book of Kings, The Second Book of Kings, The First Book of Chronicles, The Second Book of Chronicles, The First Book of Esdras, The Second Book of Esdras, The Book of Esther, The Book of Job, The Psalms, The Proverbs, Ecclesiastes or Preacher, Cantica, or Songs of Solomon, Four Prophets the greater, Twelve Prophets the less.

And the other Books (as Hierome saith) the Church doth read for example of life and instruction of manners; but yet doth it not apply them to establish any doctrine; such are these following:

The Third Book of Esdras, The Fourth Book of Esdras, The Book of Tobias, The Book of Judith, The rest of the Book of Esther, The Book of Wisdom, Jesus the Son of Sirach, Baruch the Prophet, The Song of the Three Children, The Story of Susanna, Of Bel and the Dragon, The Prayer of Manasses, The First Book of Maccabees, The Second Book of Maccabees.

All the Books of the New Testament, as they are commonly received, we do receive, and account them for Canonical.

7. Of the Old Testament.

The Old Testament is not contrary to the New: for both in the Old and New Testament everlasting life is offered to Mankind by Christ, who is the only Mediator between God and Man, being both God and Man. Wherefore they are not to be heard which feign that the old Fathers did look only for transitory promises. Although the Law given from God by Moses, as touching Ceremonies and Rites, do not bind Christian men, nor the Civil precepts thereof ought of necessity to be received in any commonwealth; yet notwithstanding, no Christian man whatsoever is free from the obedience of the Commandments which are called Moral.

8. Of the Three Creeds.

The Three Creeds, Nicene Creed, Athanasius' Creed, and that which is commonly called the Apostles' Creed, ought thoroughly to be received and believed: for they may be proved by most certain warrants of holy Scripture.

9. Of Original or Birth-Sin.

Original sin standeth not in the following of Adam (as the Pelagians do vainly talk), but it is the fault and corruption of the Nature of every man, that naturally is engendered of the offspring of Adam; whereby man is very far gone from original righteousness, and is of his own nature inclined to evil, so that the flesh lusteth always contrary to the spirit; and therefore in every person born into this world, it deserveth God's wrath and damnation. And this infection of nature doth remain, yea in them that are regenerated; whereby the lust of the flesh, called in the Greek, *phrónema sarkós*, which some do expound the wisdom, some sensuality, some the affection, some the desire, of the flesh, is not subject to the Law of God. And although there is no condemnation for them that believe and are baptized, yet the Apostle doth confess, that concupiscence and lust hath of itself the nature of sin.

10. Of Free-Will.

The condition of Man after the fall of Adam is such, that he cannot turn and prepare himself, by his own natural strength and good works, to faith and calling upon God: Wherefore we have no power to do good works pleasant and acceptable to God, without the grace of God by Christ preventing us, that we may have a good will, and working with us, when we have that good will.

11. Of the Justification of Man.

We are accounted righteous before God, only for the merit of our Lord and Saviour Jesus Christ, by Faith, and not for our own works or deservings: Wherefore, that we are justified by Faith only is a most wholesome Doctrine, and very full of comfort, as more largely expressed in the Homily of Justification.

12. Of Good Works.

Albeit that Good Works, which are the fruits of Faith, and follow after Justification, cannot put away our sins, and endure the severity of God's judgment; yet are they pleasing and acceptable to God in Christ, and do spring out necessarily of a true and lively Faith; insomuch that by them a lively Faith may be as evidently known as a tree discerned by the fruit.

13. Of Works before Justification.

Works done before the grace of Christ, and the Inspiration of his Spirit, are not pleasant to God, forasmuch as they spring not of faith in Jesus Christ, neither do they make men meet to receive grace, or (as the School-authors say) deserve grace of congruity: yea rather, for that they are not done as God hath willed and commanded them to be done, we doubt not but they have the nature of sin.

14. Of Works of Supererogation.

Voluntary Works besides, over and above, God's Commandments, which they call Works of Supererogation, cannot be taught without arrogancy and impiety: for by them men do declare, that they do not only render unto God as much as they are bound to do, but that they do more for his sake than of bounden duty is required: whereas Christ saith plainly, When ye have done all that are commanded to you, say, We are unprofitable servants.

15. Of Christ alone without Sin.

Christ in the truth of our nature was made like unto us in all things, sin only except, from which he was clearly void, both in his flesh, and in his spirit. He came to be the Lamb without spot, who, by sacrifice of himself once made, should take away the sins of the world, and sin (as Saint John saith) was not in him. But all we the rest (although baptized, and born again in Christ) yet offend in many things; and if we say we have no sin, we deceive ourselves, and the truth is not in us.

16. Of Sin after Baptism.

Not every deadly sin willingly committed after Baptism is sin against the Holy Ghost, and unpardonable. Wherefore the grant of repentance is not to be denied to such as fall into sin after Baptism. After we have received the Holy Ghost, we may depart from grace given, and fall into sin, and by the grace of God we may arise again, and amend our lives. And therefore they are to be condemned, which say, they can no more sin as long as they live here, or deny the place of forgiveness to such as truly repent.

17. Of Predestination and Election.

Predestination to Life is the everlasting purpose of God, whereby (before the foundations of the world were laid) he hath constantly decreed by his counsel secret to us, to deliver from curse and damnation those whom he hath chosen in Christ out of mankind, and to bring them by Christ to everlasting salvation, as vessels made to honour. Wherefore, they which be endued with so excellent a benefit of God be called according to God's purpose by his Spirit working in due season: they through Grace obey the calling: they be justified freely: they be made sons of God by adoption: they be made like the image of his only-begotten Son Jesus Christ: they walk religiously in good works, and at length, by God's mercy, they attain to everlasting felicity.

As the godly consideration of Predestination, and our Election in Christ, is full of sweet, pleasant, and unspeakable comfort to godly persons, and such as feel in themselves the working of the Spirit of Christ, mortifying the works of the flesh, and their earthly members, and drawing up their mind to high and heavenly things, as well because it doth greatly establish and confirm their faith of eternal Salvation to be enjoyed through Christ, as because it doth fervently kindle their love towards God: So, for curious and carnal persons, lacking the Spirit of Christ, to have continually before their eyes the sentence of God's Predestination, is a most dangerous downfall, whereby the devil doth thrust them either into desperation, or into wretchlessness of most unclean living, no less perilous than desperation.

Furthermore, we must receive God's promises in such wise, as they be generally set forth to us in Holy Scripture: and, in our doings, that Will of God is to be followed,which we have expressly declared unto us in the Word of God.

18. Of obtaining eternal Salvation only by the Name of Christ.

They also are to be had accursed that presume to say, That every man shall be saved by the Law or Sect which he professeth, so that he be diligent to frame his life according to that Law, and the light of Nature. For holy Scripture doth set out unto us only the Name of Jesus Christ, whereby men must be saved.

19. Of the Church.

The visible Church of Christ is a congregation of faithful men, in which the pure Word of God is preached, and the Sacraments be duly ministered according to Christ's ordinance in all those things that of necessity are requisite to the same.

As the Church of Jerusalem, Alexandria, and Antioch, have erred; so also the Church of Rome hath erred, not only in their living and manner of Ceremonies, but also in matters of Faith.

20. Of the Authority of the Church.

The Church hath power to decree Rites or Ceremonies, and authority in Controversies of Faith: and yet it is not lawful for the Church to ordain anything that is contrary to God's Word written, neither may it so expound one place of Scripture, that it be repugnant to another. Wherefore, although the Church be a witness and a keeper of holy Writ, yet, as it ought not to decree any thing against the same, so besides the same ought not to enforce any thing to be believed for necessity of salvation.

21. Of the Authority of General Councils.

General Councils may not be gathered together without the commandment and will of Princes. And when they be gathered together (forasmuch as they be an assembly of men, whereof all be not governed with the Spirit and Word of God), they may err, and sometimes have erred, even in things pertaining unto God. Wherefore things ordained by them as necessary to salvation have neither strength nor authority, unless it may be declared that they be taken out of holy Scripture.

22. Of Purgatory.

The Romish Doctrine concerning Purgatory, Pardons, Worshipping and Adoration, as well of Images as of Relics, and also Invocation of Saints, is a fond thing, vainly invented, and grounded upon no warranty of Scripture, but rather repugnant to the Word of God.

23. Of Ministering in the Congregation.

It is not lawful for any man to take upon him the office of public preaching, or ministering the Sacraments in the Congregation, before he be lawfully called and sent to execute the same. And those we ought to judge lawfully called and sent, which be chosen and called to this work by men who have public authority given unto them in the Congregation, to call and send Ministers into the Lord's vineyard.

24. Of Speaking in the Congregation in such a Tongue as the people under-standeth.

It is a thing plainly repugnant to the Word of God, and the custom of the Primitive Church, to have public Prayer in the Church, or to minister the Sacraments, in a tongue not understanded of the people.

25. Of the Sacraments.

Sacraments ordained of Christ be not only badges or tokens of Christian men's profession, but rather they be certain sure witnesses, and effectual signs of grace and God's good will towards us, by the which he doth work invisibly in us, and doth not only quicken, but also strengthen and confirm our Faith in him.

There are two Sacraments ordained of Christ our Lord in the Gospel, that is to say, Baptism, and the Supper of the Lord.

Those five commonly called Sacraments, that is to say, Confirmation, Penance, Orders, Matrimony, and extreme Unction, are not to be counted for Sacraments of the Gospel, being such as have grown partly of the corrupt following of the Apostles; partly are states of life allowed in the Scriptures; but yet have not like nature of Sacraments with Baptism, and the Lord's Supper, for that they have not any visible sign or ceremony ordained of God.

The Sacraments were not ordained of Christ to be gazed upon, or to be carried about, but that we should duly use them. And in such only as worthily receive the same they have a wholesome effect or operation: but they that receive them unworthily, purchase to themselves damnation, as Saint Paul saith.

26. Of the Unworthiness of the Ministers, which hinders not the effect of the Sacraments.

Although in the visible Church the evil be ever mingled with the good, and sometime the evil have chief authority in the ministration of the Word and Sacraments, yet forasmuch as they do not the same in their own name, but in Christ's, and do minister by his commission and authority, we may use their Ministry, both in hearing the Word of God, and in the receiving of the Sacraments. Neither is the effect of Christ's ordinance taken away by their wickedness, nor the grace of God's gifts diminished from such as by faith and rightly do receive the Sacraments ministered unto them; which be effectual, because of Christ's institution and promise, although they be ministered by evil men.

Nevertheless, it appertaineth to the discipline of the Church, that enquiry be made of evil Ministers, and that they be accused by those that have knowledge of their offences; and finally, being found guilty, by just judgment be deposed.

27. Of Baptism.

Baptism is not only a sign of profession, and mark of difference, whereby Christian men are discerned from other that be not christened, but it is also a sign of Regeneration or new Birth, whereby, as by an instrument, they that receive Baptism rightly are grafted into the Church; the promises of forgiveness of sin, and of our adoption to be the sons of God by the Holy Ghost, are visibly signed and sealed; Faith is confirmed, and Grace increased by virtue of prayer unto God. The Baptism of young Children is in any wise to be retained in the Church, as most agreeable with the institution of Christ.

28. Of the Lord's Supper.

The Supper of the Lord is not only a sign of the love that Christians ought to have among themselves one to another; but rather it is a Sacrament of our Redemption by Christ's death: insomuch that to such as rightly, worthily, and with faith, receive the same, the Bread which we break is a partaking of the Body of Christ; and likewise the Cup of Blessing is a partaking of the Blood of Christ.

Transubstantiation (or the change of the substance of Bread and Wine) in the Supper of the Lord, cannot be proved by holy Writ, but is repugnant to the plain words of Scripture, overthroweth the nature of a Sacrament, and hath given occasion to many superstitions.

The Body of Christ is given, taken, and eaten, in the Supper, only after an heavenly and spiritual manner. And the mean whereby the Body of Christ is received and eaten in the Supper, is Faith.

The Sacrament of the Lord's Supper was not by Christ's ordinance reserved, carried about, lifted up, or worshipped.

29. Of the Wicked which do not eat the Body of Christ in the use of the Lord's Supper.

The Wicked, and such as be void of a lively faith, although they do carnally and visibly press with their teeth (as Saint Augustine saith) the Sacrament of the Body and Blood of Christ, yet in no wise are they partakers of Christ: but rather, to their condemnation, do eat and drink the sign or Sacrament of so great a thing.

30. Of both kinds.
The Cup of the Lord is not to be denied to the Lay-people: for both the parts of the Lord's Sacrament, by Christ's ordinance and commandment, ought to be ministered to all Christian men alike.

31. Of the one Oblation of Christ finished upon the Cross.
The offering of Christ once made is that perfect redemption, propitiation, and satisfaction, for all the sins of the whole world, both original and actual; and there is none other satisfaction for sin, but that alone. Wherefore the sacrifices of Masses, in the which it was commonly said, that the Priest did offer Christ for the quick and the dead, to have remission of pain or guilt, were blasphemous fables, and dangerous deceits.

32. Of the Marriage of Priests.
Bishops, Priests, and Deacons, are not commanded by God's Law, either to vow the estate of single life, or to abstain from marriage: therefore it is lawful also for them, as for all other Christian men, to marry at their own discretion, as they shall judge the same to serve better to godliness.

33. Of Excommunicate Persons, how they are to be avoided.
That person which by open denunciation of the Church is rightly cut off from the unity of the Church, and excommunicated, ought to be taken of the whole multitude of the faithful, as an Heathen and Publican, until he be openly reconciled by penance, and received into the Church by a Judge that hath the authority thereunto.

34. Of the Traditions of the Church.
It is not necessary that the traditions and ceremonies be in all places one, or utterly like; for at all times they have been divers, and may be changed according to the diversity of countries, times, and men's manners, so that nothing be ordained against God's Word. Whosoever, through his private judgment, willingly and purposely, doth openly break the traditions and ceremonies of the Church, which be not repugnant to the Word of God, and be ordained and approved by common authority, ought to be

rebuked openly (that other may fear to do the like), as he that offendeth against the common order of the Church, and hurteth the authority of the Magistrate, and woundeth the consciences of the weak brethren.

Every particular or national Church hath authority to ordain, change, and abolish, ceremonies or rites of the Church ordained only by man's authority, so that all things be done to edifying.

35. Of Homilies.

The Second Book of Homilies, the several titles whereof we have joined under this Article, doth contain a godly and wholesome Doctrine, and necessary for these times, as doth the former Book of Homilies, which were set forth in the time of Edward the Sixth; and therefore we judge them to be read in Churches by the Ministers, diligently and distinctly, that they may be understanded of the people.

Of the Names of the Homilies

1 Of the right Use of the Church.

2 Against Peril of Idolatry.

3 Of repairing and keeping clean of Churches.

4 Of good Works: first of Fasting.

5 Against Gluttony and Drunkenness.

6 Against Excess of Apparel.

7 Of Prayer.

8 Of the Place and Time of Prayer.

9 That Common Prayers and Sacraments ought to be ministered in a known tongue.

10 Of the reverent Estimation of God's Word.

11 Of Alms-doing.

12 Of the Nativity of Christ.

13 Of the Passion of Christ.

14 Of the Resurrection of Christ.

15 Of the worthy receiving of the Sacrament of the Body and Blood of Christ.

16 Of the Gifts of the Holy Ghost.

17 For the Rogation days.

18 Of the State of Matrimony.

19 Of Repentance.

20 Against Idleness.

21 Against Rebellion.

36. Of Consecration of Bishops and Ministers.

The Book of Consecration of Archbishops and Bishops, and Ordering of Priests and Deacons, lately set forth in the time of Edward the Sixth, and confirmed at the same time by authority of Parliament, doth contain all things necessary to such Consecration and Ordering: neither hath it any thing, that of itself is superstitious and ungodly. And therefore, whosoever are consecrate or ordered according to the Rites of that Book, since the second year of the aforenamed King Edward unto this time, or hereafter shall be consecrated or ordered according to the same Rites; we decree all such to be rightly, orderly, and lawfully consecrated and ordered.

37. Of the Power of the Civil Magistrates.

The King's Majesty hath the chief power in this Realm of England, and other his Dominions, unto whom the chief Government of all Estates of this Realm, whether they be Ecclesiastical or Civil, in all causes doth appertain, and is not, nor ought to be, subject to any foreign Jurisdiction.

Where we attribute to the King's Majesty the chief government, by which Titles we understand the minds of some slanderous folks to be offended; we give not to our Princes the ministering either of God's Word, or of the Sacraments, the which thing the Injunctions also lately set forth by Elizabeth our Queen do most plainly testify; but that only prerogative, which we see to have been given always to all godly Princes in holy Scriptures by God himself; that is, that they should rule all estates and degrees committed to their charge by God, whether they be Ecclesiastical or Temporal, and restrain with the civil sword the stubborn and evil-doers.

The Bishop of Rome hath no jurisdiction in this Realm of England.

The Laws of the Realm may punish Christian men with death, for heinous and grievous offences.

It is lawful for Christian men, at the commandment of the Magistrate, to wear weapons, and serve in the wars.

38. Of Christian men's Goods, which are not common.

The Riches and Goods of Christians are not common, as touching the right, title, and possession of the same; as certain Anabaptists do falsely boast. Notwithstanding, every man ought, of such things as he possesseth, liberally to give alms to the poor, according to his ability.

39. Of a Christian man's Oath.

As we confess that vain and rash swearing is forbidden Christian men by our Lord Jesus Christ, and James his Apostle, so we judge, that Christian Religion doth not prohibit, but that a man may swear when the Magistrate requireth, in a cause of faith and charity, so it be done according to the Prophet's teaching in justice, judgment, and truth.

ACKNOWLEDGMENTS

In recent years sharing between Liturgical Commissions in the Anglican Communion of material, often at draft stage, has meant that it is not always possible to identify in the final product the original source of a prayer or part of a service order. Material is discussed, changes are made even during the synodical process. Where the authorship has been overlooked and permission not sought or acknowledged here the publisher, if made aware of the fact, will endeavour to rectify such omissions in subsequent printings.

The Representative Body of the Church of Ireland and the publisher are grateful to the following holders of copyright for granting permission to use their material:

The Archbishops' Council of the Church of England for material excerpted or adapted from *Common Worship* © 2000; *Common Worship: Pastoral Services* © 2000; *Common Worship: Initiation Services* © 1998; *Promise of His Glory* © 1991; *Lent, Holy Week and Easter* © 1986; *Alternative Service Book* © 1980. Used by permission.

The Division of Christian Education of the National Council of Christian Churches of the United States of America for scripture quotations from the *New Revised Standard Version* of the Bible © 1989 and from *Revised Standard Version* © 1973. Used by permission. All rights reserved.

The Oxford and Cambridge University Presses for scripture quotations identified as (REB) from the *Revised English Bible* © 1989.

The English Language Liturgical Consultation (ELLC) for texts excerpted or adapted from *Praying Together* © 1988.

The General Synod of the Anglican Church of Canada for prayers noted above on page 337. Excerpted from the *Book of Alternative Services* © 1985. Used by permission.

The Publication Committee of the Church of the Province of Southern Africa for prayers noted above on page 337 from *An Anglican Prayer Book* © 1989, The Provincial Trustees of CPSA.

The Trustees of the General Synod of the Anglican Church of Australia for Eucharistic Prayer 2 excerpted from *An Australian Prayer Book* © 1978, for *An Ordination Litany* and for material in Holy Baptism Two excerpted or adapted from *A Prayer Book for Australia* © 1995.

The Trustees of the Church of Aotearoa New Zealand and Polynesia for a prayer noted above on page 337 from *A New Zealand Prayer Book – He Karakia Mihinare o Aotearoa* © 1989. Used by permission.

The Representative Body of the Church in Wales for a prayer noted above on page 337 from *The Book of Common Prayer of the Church in Wales* © 1984.

The European Province of the Society of Saint Francis for prayers noted above on page 337 from *Celebrating Common Prayer* © 1992, 1996.

The Consultation on Common Texts for the *Revised Common Lectionary* © 1992 adapted for use in the Church of Ireland with permission.

The Trustees of Westcott House, Cambridge for a prayer noted above on page 337.

The Right Reverend Dr David Stancliffe for the Proper Preface at Holy Baptism Two.

The Panel of Worship of the Church of Scotland for prayers in Funeral Services Two excerpted or adapted from the *Book of Common Order of the Church of Scotland* © 1994.

The Continuum International Press for prayers by C. L. MacDonnell and David Silk noted above on page 337. Used by permission.

SPCK and the Joint Liturgical Group for weekday intercessions and thanksgivings adapted from *The Daily Office* © 1968. SPCK for prayers noted above on page 337 by Janet Morley, Michael Perham and Kenneth Stevenson. Used by permission of the publisher.

The Reverend Paul Gibson and Barbara Liotscos of the Anglican Church of Canada for their translation of the canticle, *Song of Wisdom*.

David L. Frost, John A. Emerton and A. A. Macintosh, for *Venite, Jubilate* and *Ecce Nunc* in Canticles from *The Psalms: A New Translation for Worship*, © 1976, 1977. Used by permission.

Subject Index of Prayers and Collects

Key: 1: or 11: indicate traditional language or modern. Next number is the page number. The number in brackets indicates the number of the prayer/collect on that page.

– consolation of memories of: II: 501 (last)
– hope of reunion with: II: 485 (I), 492 (2, 3), 494 (3, 4), 500 (2)
– hope of the resurrection for: II: 482 (I), 485 (2), 494 (I), 502 (last)
– Prayer for Complete Happiness: I: 474 (3)
– remembrance of: II: 492 (2)
– thanksgiving for life of: II: 491 (I), 492 (2, 3, 4), 493 (I), 500 (2)
– thanksgiving for peace and joy of the souls of: II: 501 (last)
– See also Funeral Home, prayers for use in
Faithfulness: I: 152 (3)
Family, the: II: 263 (I), 403 (last), 451 (2)
– family life: II: 263 (I)
– family and friends: II: 451 (2)
– of the nations: II: 300 (I, 2)
– thanksgiving for the joys of family life: II: 426 (last)
Farmers: II: 333 (I)
Fear, for courage to overcome: II: 335 (I). See also Trouble
Fellowship, Christian: II: 292 (2, 4)
Forgiveness: I: 259 (I), 290 (2), 296 (3), 299 (4); II 102 (last), 259 (2), 290 (3)
Friends: II: 451 (2). See also Absent Friends
Funeral Home, prayers for use in: 514-516
Funerals: I: 473-475, II: 491-496
– of a child: I: 477-479, II: 510-513
– after cremation: II: 502
– eve of: II: 498-500
– prior to (at funeral home or mortuary): II: 514-515
– the Burial Collect: I: 474 (last), II: 482 (last)

General Synod: See Synod
Gifts of the Spirit: See Holy Spirit
Glory of God: II: 284 (I)
God be in my head: II: 450 (last), 489, 509
Godparents: See Baptism
[Good Friday: 270]

Gospel, spread of: II: 252 (3), 279 (3), 334 (I)
– living the Gospel: I: 297 (I), II: 279 (I), 297 (2)
– preaching the Gospel: I: 195 (3); II: 279 (I, 3)
– witness to: II: 458 (last)
– to dispel ignorance and unbelief: II: 252 (3).
– See also Bible
Government: I: 98 (2) [NI only]; I: 98 (3), II: 98 (4) [RI only]
Grace: I: 289 (3), 293 (4), 307 (I). II: 251 (I), 256 (I), 289 (4), 307 (2)
– for a married couple: II: 418 (last)
– to live in the light of eternity, prayers for: II: 494 (I, 2)
– Collect for: I: 96 (last)
– and Protection, Collect for: I: 97 (3)
Guidance: I: 250 (I), 277 (I), 284 (2), 295 (I). II: 114 (3, 4), 280 (2), 284 (3), 295 (2).

Happiness, Prayer for Complete: I: 474 (3). See also Faithful Departed
Harvest: I: 147 (5), 329 (I, 2). II: 329 (3)
– thanksgiving for: I: 329 (I, 2), II: 329 (3)
Healing: I: 146 (3, 4). II: 146 (5), 300 (2), 463 (I)
– of memories: II: 491 (3)
– wholeness of life: II: 300 (2)
– See also Suffering
Health, thanks for hope of renewed: II: 452 (4)
Help: I: 194 (I), 195 (2), 251 (3). II: 460 (last)
High Court of Parliament, Collect for: I: 98 (2). [NI only]
Holy Communion:
– preparation for: I: 180 (2), II: 201 (last), 441 (last)
– at preparation of the Table: II: 208 (I-4)
– before receiving: I: 187 (last). II: 207 (I), 441 (last)
– after receiving: II: 220 (last), 221 (I)
– thanksgiving for institution of: I: 268 (I). II: 269 (3)

Holy Orders: See Ordination
Holy Scriptures: See Bible
Holy Spirit: I: 257 (2). II: 283 (I), 458
   (last)
– comfort of: I: 278 (3)
– fruit of: II: 288 (2)
– gifts of: II: 296 (I), 390
– guidance of : I: 295 (I), 330 (2). II:
   114 (4), 295 (2), 330 (3), 384 (I)
– light of: I: 330 (2). II: 330 (3)
– strength of: II: 254 (2), 384 (I)
[Holy Week: 265-271]
Hope, to strengthen: II: 484 (last)
Hospitals: I: 146 (5). See also Healing
Humanity: I: 99 (2). II: 263 (I), 318 (5)
Humble Access, Prayer of: I: 187 (last).
   II: 207 (I)
Humility: I: 264 (4), II: 265 (I)

Illness, in time of: II: 451 (4). See also
   Suffering
Industry: II: 333 (2)
Infirmaries: I: 146 (5). See also
   Healing
Ignorance, to dispel: II: 252 (3)
Inauguration of a new ministry: II: 332
   (2)
Institution of a new ministry: II:
   332 (2)
Ireland: I: 145 (4)
– the church in: I: 149 (5)
– See also Saints, Irish

Jesus Prayer: 451 (I)
Journey, Christian: II: 286 (2)
Joy, everlasting: II: 294 (3)
Judgement:
– a right: I: 330 (2). II: 330 (3)
– preparation for Day of: I: 241 (I), 243
   (I). II: 241 (2), 242 (3), 243 (2)
Justice: II: 327 (2)

Kingdom of God: II: 394 (last), 485 (I)
– to be a living sign of: II: 296 (5)
Kingship of Christ: II: 301 (4)
[Kyries, Penitential: 224-236]

Land, those who work on: II: 333 (I)
Law of God, observance of: I: 194
   (last). II: 287 (3)
[Lent: 259-265]

Lenten fast: I: 260 (I). II: 260 (2)
Life, daily: I: 152 (I). II: 114 (4), 263 (I)
– hope of eternal: I: 300 (3). II: 301 (I),
   502 (last)
– new life in Christ: II: 273 (4)
Light of Christ: I: 248 (I). II: 248 (2)
Litany, The: I: 170. II: 175
– the Ordination Litanies: II: 585-590
Lord's Day, Prayer for Right Use of: I:
   151 (last)
Lord's Prayer: I: 86. II: 112.
Love, for the gift of: I: 285 (4). II: 283
   (I), 286 (I)
– of God, for: II: 341 (last)
– of God's name: I: 286 (3). II: 286 (4)
– the command to love: II: 269 (I)

Mankind: See Humanity
Marriage: II: 424-427
– after a civil marriage: II: 433 (last),
   436-438
– for Christian witness in: II: 426 (3)
– for the gift of children: I: 412 (2). II:
   426 (2)
– for the married couple: II: 422 (2),
   424 (last), 425 (I-4), 426 (I). 427 (I)
– the Marriage Collect: II: 418
– Prayer for Blessing: I: 408 (last)
– Prayer for Divine Blessing: I: 412 (I)
– Prayer for Fruitfulness: I: 412 (2)
– Prayer for Holy Married Life: I: 412 (3)
Mary: See St Mary
Meeting, church: II: 330 (4)
Mercy: I: 262 (I), 284 (2), 290 (2). II:
   284 (3), 290 (3)
Ministry, general: I: 196 (I). II: 270 (2),
   285 (2)
– ordained; I: 195 (3), 243 (I). II: 243 (2)
– Ministry of all Christian People,
   Collect for: II: 331 (2)
– inauguration of a new ministry: II:
   332 (2)
– increase of the ministry: I: 148 (3)
– to the sick: II: 452 (3)
– for vocations to Holy Orders: II: 332 (I)
– See also Ordination
Miscarriage, in the event of: II: 512
Mission: II: 334 (I, 2)
– abroad: I: 150 (3)

– parochial: 1: 151 (1)
Monarch [NI only]
– the Royal Family: 1: 98
– the Queen: 1: 146 (1)
– Prayer for the Queen's Majesty: 1: 97
Money: See Wealth
Morning Prayer, Collects for: 1: 96. 11:
    114
[Mothering Sunday: 263]
Mourn, those who: See Bereaved

[Naming of Jesus: 303]
Nations of the World: 1: 195 (4). 11:
    279 (4), 300 (1, 2), 334 (3)
– mission to: 11: 279 (1)
Need, those in: 1: 151 (2). 11: 144, 329 (3)
New Year: 1: 147 (4)
Night: See Evening, Compline
Nominators, Parochial: 1: 149 (1)
Nurses: 1: 146 (3). 11: 452 (2). See also
    Healing

Oireachtas, Houses of: 1: 98 (4). [RI
only]
Ordination: 1: 195 (5). 11: 331 (3), 332 (1)
– on day of: 1: 148 (2). 11: 331 (3)
– for those to be admitted to Holy
    Orders: 1: 148 (1)
– for those to be ordained: 11: 331 (3)

Pain, in time of: 11: 451 (4). See also
    Suffering
[Palm Sunday: 264-265]
Pardon: 1: 152 (2), 296 (3). 11: 102 (3)
    See also Forgiveness
Parents: 11: 370 (2), 403 (1)
Parish: 1: 150 (2)
– during a vacancy: 1: 149 (1)
Parish organisations: 11: 330 (4)
Parliament: 1: 98 (2). [NI only]
[Passiontide: 264-271]
Pastoral Care: 1: 151 (2)
Patience: 1: 264 (4). 11: 265 (1)
Patronal Festival: See Dedication
Peace: 1: 97 (1), 296 (3), 250 (4). 11:
    102 (3), 115 (1), 334 (3), 335 (2)
– bond of: 11: 283 (1), 301 (4)
– inner: 11: 293 (5)
– of mind: 11: 451 (3)

– of the world: 1: 145 (2), 195 (4), 285
    (1). 11: 300 (1, 2), 334 (3)
– Collect for, at Morning Prayer: 1: 96
    (1). 11: 114 (1)
– Collect for, at Evening Prayer: 1: 97
    (1). 11: 115 (1)
Penitence: See Confession
[Pentecost: 279]
Perils, Collect for Aid against all: 1: 97 (2)
Persecution, in time of: 1: 266 (2), 325 (1).
    11: 266 (3), 267 (2), 325 (2)
Persecutors: See Enemies
Personal Relationships: 11: 141
Physicians: 1: 146 (3)
Politicians: 1: 98 (2) [NI only]. 1: 98 (4)
    [RI only]. See also Government
Prayers, answering of: 1: 288 (4), 299
    (1). 11: 152 (6), 153 (1), 289 (1).
– for acceptance of: 11: 341 (1), 460 (last)
Preaching the Gospel: See Gospel
Preparation for Holy Communion,
    Prayer of: 11: 201 (last)
Presbyters: See Ministry, and
    Ordination
Presence of Christ: 11: 277 (2), 278 (4)
Presence of God: 11: 293 (5), 442 (1)
– Prayer for Recollection of: 1: 114 (4),
    152 (1)
[Presentation of Christ: 253]
President, the: 1: 98. [RI only] See also
    Government
Priesthood. See Ministry, and
    Ordination
Protection: 1: 152 (4), 194 (last), 284 (2).
    11: 284 (3).
– from adversity: 1: 256 (3), 261 (1). 11:
    114 (1)
– from danger: 1: 251 (3), 252 (2). 11:
    114 (2), 255 (2)
– from enemies: 1: 96 (1), 264 (1).
    11: 114 (1)
– from harm: 1: 292 (3), 295 (4)
– of Christ: 11: 275 (3)
– of God's providence: 1: 282 (4)
– for grace and protection: 1: 97 (3)
Providence of God: 1: 287 (2)
– for protection of: 282 (4)
Purity: 1: 300 (3). 11: 301 (1)
– Collect for: 1: 180 (2). 11: 201 (last)

Queen [NI only]: See Monarch

Readiness to live in the light of eternity.
  See Grace
Recollection of Presence of God,
  Prayer for: I: 152 (I)
Reconciliation: II: 335 (I, 3)
– work of the church: II: 291 (2), 462 (I)
Religion: See True Religion
Renewal, spiritual: II: 251 (I), 257 (4),
  392 (last)
Repentance: I: 259 (I). II: 259 (2)
Resurrection, hope of: I: 271 (I). II: 271
  (2), 495 (last)
– for a child who has died: II: 513 (2)
Riches: See Wealth
Righteousness: II: 275 (2)
[Rogation Days: I: 147 (last). II: 333
– Rogation Sunday: 277]
Royal Family [NI only]: See Monarch

Sabbath: See Lord's Day
Sacraments, thanksgiving for: II: 492
  (last). See also Baptism, and Holy
  Communion
Sadness, in time of: II: 263 (I). See
  also Bereaved
Saints:
– communion of: II: 484 (last), 485 (I,
  2), 494 (3, 4), 513 (I)
– example of: I: 298 (I). II: 298 (2),
  299 (2), 492 (last)
– fellowship with: II: 299 (2), 492 (2)
– thanksgiving for: II: 493 (I)
[All Saints: 298]
Irish Saints:
– [St Brigid: 304-305]
– [St Columba: 311]
– [St Patrick: 305-306]
St Chrysostom, Prayer of: I: 100(I)
St Mary, See Blessed Virgin Mary
St Patrick's Breastplate: II: 450 (2)
St Richard of Chichester, Prayer of: II:
  450 (3)
Schools, parish: I: 150 (2)
Scripture: See Bible
Seafarers: I: 147 (3). II: 333 (I)
Seanad: I: 98 (4). [RI only]
Second Coming, preparation for: I: 241
  (I), 243 (I). II: 241 (2), 242 (3), 243 (2)

Service, Christian: I: 274 (I), 291 (I).
  II: 269 (I), 283 (4), 285 (2), 293 (5),
  369 (3)
Sick: See Suffering
Sin, to die to: I: 272 (2). II: 273 (I). See
  also Confession
Sorrow: See Sadness
Spirit: See Holy Spirit, and Renewal,
  spiritual
St: See Saints
Stewardship: I: 329 (I). II: 329 (3)
Stillbirth, in the event of: II: 512. See
  also Bereavement
Stillness: II: 442 (I)
Strength: I: 252 (2)
Suffering: I: 151 (2). II: 143, 146 (5), 451
  (4), 452 (I)
– for strength in: II: 257 (3), 262 (5)
– ministry to the sick: II: 452 (2, 3)
– of a sick child: II: 451 (5)
Surgeons: I: 146 (3)
Surgery, before: II: 452 (I)
– thanksgiving after: II: 452 (4)
– See also Suffering
Synod: II: 330 (4)
– General Synod: I: 150 (I)
– Collect for the Opening of: I: 330 (2)

Temptation, in time of: I: 252 (2), 288
  (I), 294 (2). II: 255 (2), 256 (I), 260
  (2), 262 (2)
Thanksgiving:
– an Act of: II: 496
– a General (at Morning and Evening
  Prayer): I: 99 (3)
– for the Holy Scriptures: I: 153 (4)
Treatment, before: II: 452 (I)
– thanksgiving after: II: 452 (4)
– See also Suffering
[Trinity: 281]
Trouble, in time of: I: 261 (I), 281 (I).
  II: 281 (2)
True religion: I: 254 (I), 275 (I), 286 (3).
  II: 261 (2), 286 (4)

Unbelief, to dispel: II: 252 (3)
Unity, Christian: I: 149 (2, 3). II: 301 (4),
  335 (I, 2, 3)

Vacancy of a Parish: I: 149 (I)